Psychological Treatment of Older Adults

Lee Hyer, PhD, ABPP, is professor of psychiatry and health behavior at the Mercer School of Medicine and the Georgia Neurosurgical Institute. He is board certified in psychology through the American Board of Professional Psychology (ABPP). He is a fellow of several divisions of the American Psychological Association (APA), a member of the International Society of Traumatic Stress, and the Gerontological Society of America. He has been a professor of psychiatry for many years at the Medical College of Georgia; at the Veterans Administration (VA); and at the University of Medicine and Dentistry of New Jersey, Robert Wood Johnson Medical School. He is the recipient of several awards given by the VA, the Distinguished Researcher Award from Psychologists in Long-Term Care (2005); and was honored as Mentor of the Year, APA Division of Clinical Psychology (2007). His professional contributions include more than 200 articles and book chapters, and he has written three books. Dr. Hyer has been the clinical editor of several journals, as well as a reviewer. He currently is the recipient of several grants on topics ranging from pain, cognitive training, cognitive assessment, and depression/anxiety, all of which are related to older adults.

Psychological Treatment of Older Adults

A Holistic Model

Lee Hyer, PhD, ABPP

SPRINGER PUBLISHING COMPANY

NEW YORK

Springer Publishing Company, LLC
11 West 42nd Street
New York, NY 10036
www.springerpub.com

Acquisitions Editor: Sheri W. Sussman
Composition: Exeter Premedia Services Private Ltd.

ISBN: 978-0-8261-9591-3
e-book ISBN: 978-0-8261-9592-0

13 14 15 16 17 / 5 4 3 2 1

The author and the publisher of this Work have made every effort to use sources believed to be reliable to provide information that is accurate and compatible with the standards generally accepted at the time of publication. The author and publisher shall not be liable for any special, consequential, or exemplary damages resulting, in whole or in part, from the readers' use of, or reliance on, the information contained in this book. The publisher has no responsibility for the persistence or accuracy of URLs for external or third-party Internet websites referred to in this publication and does not guarantee that any content on such websites is, or will remain, accurate or appropriate.

Library of Congress Cataloging-in-Publication Data
Hyer, Lee, 1944– author.
Psychological treatment of older adults : A holistic model/Lee Hyer
    p. ; cm.
  Includes bibliographical references and index.
  ISBN 978-0-8261-9591-3—ISBN 978-0-8261-9592-0 (e-book)
  I. Title.
  [DNLM: 1. Aged—psychology. 2. Psychotherapy—methods. 3. Geriatric Psychiatry—methods. 4. Holistic Health. 5. Mental Disorders—psychology. 6. Mental Disorders—therapy. WT 150]
  RC451.4.M54
  618.97'8914—dc23

                        2013020124

Printed in the United States of America by Gasch Printing.

Contents

Foreword   Peter A. Lichtenberg, PhD   *xi*

Preface   *xv*

1. **Introduction**   *1*
   Process of Care   *6*
   Backdrop   *8*
   Best Predictors   *11*
   Conclusion   *28*

2. **Model of Care**   *31*
   Model   *33*
   Case Formulation and the Five Domains of Treatment   *38*
   Watch and Wait Ingredients   *41*
   Perspective   *45*
   Conclusion   *49*

3. **Psychotherapy**   *51*
   Lee Hyer and Maria Anastasiades

   Problems of Science   *52*
   General Reviews: Data Related to Older Adults   *54*
   Late-Life Psychotherapy Overview   *57*
   Medications   *60*
   Our Position   *62*
   Necessary Psychotherapy Features   *65*
   Core Treatment Factor: Psychoeducation   *65*
   Core Treatment Factor: Alliance   *67*
   Core Treatment Factor: Monitoring   *69*
   Core Treatment Factor: Case-Based Approach   *70*
   Recommended Treatment Factor: Motivational Interviewing   *71*
   Recommended Treatment Factor: Behavioral Activation   *74*

Recommended Treatment Factor: IPT   *74*
Recommended Treatment Factor: PST   *76*
Recommended Treatment Factor: Transdiagnostic Model   *76*
Recommended Treatment Factor: Prevention   *78*
Recommended Treatment Factor: Case Manager   *80*
Recommended Treatment Factor: Exercise   *81*
Recommended Treatment Factor: Modules   *81*
Recommended Treatment Factor: Cognitive Training   *82*
Recommended Treatment Factor: Psychotherapist
    as Neuroscientist   *84*
Recommended Treatment Factor: Booster Sessions   *85*
Conclusion   *87*

4. **Depression**   *89*
Prevalence and Biology   *90*
Phenomenology of Depression   *91*
Correlative Symptoms   *98*
Treatment Studies   *104*
Predictors of Depression at Late Life and When to Change   *110*
Recommended Treatment   *111*
Special Case of Home Care   *121*
Conclusion   *122*

5. **Anxiety at Later Life**   *123*
Prevalence   *124*
Phenomena of Anxiety   *125*
Anxiety and Cognition   *129*
Anxiety and the Brain   *130*
Treatment Studies   *131*
Medication   *133*
Modules and Venues and Other Therapies   *134*
Exercise   *136*
Treatment Summary   *137*
Formal Treatment Package   *139*
Special Case: PTSD   *143*
Conclusion   *146*

6. **Cognition**   *147*
Normal Aging: What Is Up With Cognition?   *150*
Continuum of Cognitive Decline   *154*
MCI   *156*
Dementia Criteria and Confusion   *159*
Memory   *164*
EF Problems (and Depression)   *166*
Medical Treatment for Dementia   *169*
Conclusion   *174*

7. **Cognitive Training**   *175*
   Cognition Training   *176*
   Overview   *178*
   Holistic Programs   *180*
   Working Memory and Older Adults   *181*
   Cognitive Compromise: MCI or Mild Dementia   *182*
   Conclusion   *196*

8. **Health Issues**   *197*
   Integrated Care   *199*
   Too Many Best Care Practices   *199*
   Mental Health   *202*
   Core Problems   *205*
   Conclusion   *230*

9. **Medical Problems**   *231*
   Richard Ackermann

   Principles of Geriatric Health Care   *231*
   Conclusion   *247*

10. **Behavioral Health Treatment of Older Adults
    in Primary Care**   *249*
    Catherine Yeager

    The Development of the Patient-Centered Medical Home   *251*
    Role and Expertise of the Primary Care Psychologist   *254*
    Common Behavioral Health Interventions in Primary Care   *265*
    Common Presenting Problems in Primary Care   *272*
    Conclusion   *281*
    Notes   *282*

11. **Life Issues**   *283*
    Lee Hyer, Maria Anastasiades, and Sanna Catherine Tillitski

    Old-Age Perspective   *285*
    Evaluation: Point of Care and Long View   *287*
    Different Prisms of Treatment   *288*
    Practical Issues for Community Care   *293*
    Long-Term Care   *307*
    Conclusion   *310*

12. **Assessment**   *313*
    Lee Hyer and Sanna Catherine Tillitski

    The Whole Person   *316*
    Cognition   *318*
    Function: Think Outside the Box   *324*
    Depression   *328*
    Anxiety   *330*

Psychotherapy Measures   *331*
Personality Assessment   *332*
Caregivers   *335*
General Adjustment   *338*
Testing in Different Settings   *340*
Other Relevant Variables   *341*
Conclusion   *342*

13. **Summary**   *343*
Summary of Watch and Wait Model   *344*
Postscript   *351*

Appendix A – Memory Clinic and Cogmed Tasks   *353*
Appendix B – CBT and Related Interventions   *361*
Appendix C – Insomnia Manual   *385*
References   *395*
Index   *445*

Foreword

Forty years ago, in their groundbreaking book *Aging and Mental Health,* Robert Butler and Myrna Lewis (1973) foreshadowed some of the emerging themes of integrated mental and physical health care in the 21st century. They identified three directions to move toward in mental health treatment: (1) restitution capacity, (2) opportunity for growth and renewal, and (3) the need for perspective. Butler and Lewis believed that older adults were flexible and could heal from losses, that older adults would benefit from psychological treatments and improve their functioning, and that older adults had a need to integrate meaning from their life histories. Butler and Lewis practiced geriatric psychiatry and mental health treatment at a time when "the understanding of the total problem" (p. 146) was paramount—emotional and psychological strengths and weaknesses, physical capabilities, and family and social life. Modern geriatric psychiatry, as documented by Lee Hyer in his book *Psychological Treatment of Older Adults: A Holistic Model,* has adopted an almost entirely biological model for treating mental health problems such as depression and anxiety. This trend is increasing despite the evidence that medications have not produced particularly strong results. In *Psychological Treatment of Older Adults,* Hyer has given us a road map for more fully executing a more effective, less intensive model of care to address the problems of older adults. Presented in a clear, powerful, and comprehensive fashion, Hyer provides a rationale and road map for best practices with older adults.

In 2008, the Institute of Medicine (IOM) published *Retooling for an Aging America: Building the Health Care Workforce,* which decried the lack of trained professionals to work with older adults. More recently the IOM published a follow-up study that demonstrated that a workforce trained to care for mental health problems of older adults is especially lacking. Hyer could not have picked a better time to share his research and expertise in practical, integrated approaches to mental health care. Although there have been several excellent models of integrated care (e.g., IMPACT, PEARLS), these models have been single-disease focused (e.g., late-life depression). Although this is a wonderful way to do careful research on a single disorder, it leaves the clinician in practice settings wondering what to do about comorbid mental health problems and how their treatment should relate to an evidence-based protocol that was based on treatment of a single disorder. What should clinicians do about mild cognitive problems, serious chronic illness such as diabetes, or accompanying anxiety or sleep problems? Hyer offers a new model called Watch and Wait that arms the clinician with an approach that, when used, captures the needs of the "whole person."

Psychological Treatment of Older Adults: A Holistic Model provides a road map that reaches for the ideals set by Butler and Lewis. The approach presented focuses on relationship building, prevention, education, multipronged interventions for common comorbid problems, and communication. It does so in the context of a team—including professionals from different disciplines, and including patients and their families. One of Watch and Wait's major principles is guided by modern cognitive neuroscience. The authors deftly bring together three major findings on the brain and cognition: First, that aging includes normal age-related cognitive decline. Second, that excess cognitive disability often exists. Research has demonstrated that older adults can improve their memory, problem solving, and psychomotor speed, for instance, through cognitive training. Third, that the issues of cognitive decline, particularly executive function, are heightened in those older adults suffering from depression caused by heightened white matter brain deterioration—a neuroradiological finding in many who suffer late-life depression.

One of the gems contained in this book is the reminder to do no harm. Hyer advocates for a good dose of relationship building and psychoeducation before proceeding to treatment. When treatment is necessary, he advocates for psychological treatment as the best first-line treatment, because medications do not produce better results than psychological treatment, and can, and often do, produce harmful side effects in older adults. Psychoeducation has been underemphasized in mental health care with older adults. Age-related brain and body changes, and their resulting functional and behavioral impacts, are not widely known to the lay public. The use of psychoeducation is also a cornerstone of behavior change. Motivational interviewing, discussed in the book, begins with psychoeducation. The importance of a good rapport and therapeutic relationship is also emphasized.

When intervention is indicated, Hyer offers a sound and convincing rationale as to why attention to elements of mental health, cognitive neuroscience, and health psychology are important. First, the literature he reviews illustrates convincingly that depression, anxiety, executive dysfunction, pain, and sleep problems are very often present in the older adult. Therefore, it is important to assess and treat each of these areas. This is the first time a step-by-step approach to geriatric mental health care has been so complete and yet so easily implemented by clinicians, and digested by the older person in treatment. Hyer is clearly skilled in a variety of standard psychotherapies for older adults, behavioral interventions for health conditions, and brief cognitive assessment and training.

Although *Psychological Treatment of Older Adults: A Holistic Model* provides clinicians with straightforward recommendations, the Watch and Wait approach was developed by a thorough knowledge of the research literature. One of the phenomenal aspects of this book is the research reviews it provides, which are extensive and broad in their scope. It is clear that Lee Hyer is an exceptional scholar–clinician and geropsychologist. His understanding of research methods and measurements and his ability to digest and translate the literature come through very clearly.

Finally, throughout the book the author echoes Butler and Lewis's "perspective theme." Hyer writes, "[T]herapy is ultimately an exercise in self-improvement, in perspective and in toleration of the throes of living." Hyer understands that the issues of legacy and meaning are present in his older adult clients, and that attention to these issues is important. The manner in which these issues are addressed can be dramatically affected by the presence of cognitive dysfunction and dementia. Personhood is a theme that Hyer extends and brings into his assessment and treatment approach.

This is one of the best mental health and aging books I have ever read. I have long known and admired Lee Hyer, and after hearing him present on these themes for several years during annual American Psychological Association workshops: "What Do Psychologists Need to Know About Working With Older Adults," I am delighted to see a complete account of his assessment and treatment approaches in writing. This book is one that I will turn to often in my teaching of doctoral students, and in my work with older adults.

Peter A. Lichtenberg, PhD
Director
Institute of Gerontology and
the Merrill Palmer Skillman Institute
Wayne State University

Preface

This book is a labor of love. It is formulated on the belief that psychiatric care of older adults is wanting and that their psychological treatment needs updating and change. This care needs direction and a scaffold of assessment and treatment that makes sense in the 21st century. It needs a balance of our science and the realities of later life.

In this book we address psychiatric and psychological components of older adults: What is the best way to understand modal psychosocial problems of late life, taking into account what science has to offer, what seems commonsensical, and what can be done? What are the reasonable concepts and teachings regarding care of older adults? To benefit depressed or anxious elderly patients in the community, we believe that we must employ comprehensive-care algorithms targeting both modifiable predictors of poor outcomes and organizational barriers to care. One does not need an advanced degree to know that, if there is a bacterial infection, an antibiotic is in order. But, we need skills and the knowledge "to close the deal" for a depressed, anxious, demented, medically frail, or adjustment-impaired older adult. We need reasonable ways to handle the all-too-frequent confusion and challenge of living with problems at later life.

In the past 10 years, results and trends have been enlightening but disappointing. The importance of medical care, use of selective serotonin reuptake inhibitors (SSRIs) and their medication brethren, issues related to suicide, subsyndromal states, and validation of variants of talk psychotherapies (e.g., cognitive behavioral therapy [CBT]) have been in play. As we indicate in the book, treatments work at best only 50% of the time and most often not permanently; people continue on as both system and self-change fail; patients often wax and wane in progress in therapy but do not fully remit; long-term treatment is still largely an anomaly; the specific therapies do not seem to register as effective; dismantling studies have been few and uninformative regarding particular, validated findings; and it seems that the general effects of our care strategies are more beneficial than are specific effects. Again, we require better models. Even the extant models lack reasonable evidence for efficacy.

For older adults with the usual problems of depression, anxiety, and cognitive decline, as well as an admixture of somatic ills and life problems, a focus on integrated care seems not only reasonable but now required. Treating "depressive symptoms" in isolation, especially with modal comorbid anxious, cognitive, and physical symptoms, risks a slower or less-effective reduction in depressive symptoms. Targeting an organized patchwork of psychological problems—in this case depression, anxiety, cognitive impairment, adjustment, and some disability—requires better strategies and care algorithms; a concerted effort to help the patient adapt and better cope with his or her problems. Evidence for such multifaceted approaches to treatment is nascent, and so we must borrow from the depths of literature for each problem and look at the efficacy for older adults, as well as what works for younger adults. This book argues for a case-based model with differences in the approach and in the interventions.

We need an all-encompassing model for change. Accordingly, the model of geriatric depression, for example, needs to integrate the current biological concepts of depression with patients' unique reactions to adverse experiences and with their unmet social and health care needs. The care algorithms based on this model should, of course, target clinical/biological predictors of adverse outcomes of depression, but also should address unmet needs through linkage to appropriate social services; enhance the competencies of elderly persons so that they make use of their resources; and attend to patient psychotherapy issues of needed psychoeducation, apathetic behaviors, rigid thoughts, and agitated or dysphoric emotions.

We provide a model of care that encompasses more than a diagnosis. Clinical and psychosocial predictors for a single intervention, an antidepressant, or an isolated psychosocial intervention have been tried; they are less than impactful. Areas in which they have been found wanting include anxiety, hopelessness, executive dysfunction, limitations in physical and emotional functions, chronicity of the current episode, medical comorbidities, and low income.

Such predictors can help in personalizing the first step of treatment for a given patient. A patient with one or more predictors of poor outcome may receive interventions targeting each modifiable predictor. But there is more to the equation: There is a need for a broader scope of care and follow-up. Low-income depressed elderly patients whose symptoms did not respond to an adequate trial of an antidepressant and who experience social problems along with hopelessness would, we believe, benefit from a holistic trial of coordinated care focusing on core targets as well as secondary problems. This can be done deliberatively and professionally through a tried-and-true model of case management in the Watch and Wait model we espouse.

PROBLEM

Over the past 30 years, there has been a dramatic change in the treatment of older adults where mental health is concerned. Before, this treatment was seen as providing care to debilitated elders who needed to be coddled; now, a cottage industry is developing of semiempirically supported issues in a context of primary care. In the past year, there has emerged a view that there is no such thing as aging. Aging, rather, is not a causal variable; it is a marker on the temporal axis along which various exposures and disease processes operate. Aging is not a meaningful explanation by itself as to why one might experience a problem like cognitive decline or impairment. It is rather one variable in the room with a patient.

In this context too, the grand fear at later life, dementia, is also a non-event. It is the end stage of a "brain at risk," a poor accumulation of health behaviors and genetics. We need to look at the whole person who is older and has accumulated stuff. What is the "stuff" of most concern?

As neuroscientists and careful reviewers are seeing, aging is taking on a different form. Longitudinal studies in coronary heart disease mortality show that the relative risk of either genetic or environmental factors is less important at older age than at midlife. The importance of a life span perspective argues for including the aggregated experiences of the person and the complexity of assessing the whole person; more to the point, treating the whole person. This is not easily done in a psychotherapy room with two people.

There is, we believe, a taxonomy crisis that is occurring in psychiatry. At the core, this taxonomy crisis involves cognitive decline and depression. In the past year, there was considerable debate as to what dementia is, what are the better biomarkers for this disease process, whether it is a component of normal aging, and how to treat this disease. Similarly, anxiety and depression as constructs are confusing when these are applied to late-life patients. Better thinking models now know that depression and anxiety, like dementia, exist both at the threshold level and at the subclinical level. Perhaps the focus should be not on identifying markers or items that place the person on a continuum, not on whether that person is in a specific group, but on looking at the person who has a profile of symptoms and problems, often mixed in origin. There is, then, an additive process where risk factors in genes and the environment accumulate and the person is treated not as one with a Major Depressive Disorder, but as one with a profile of problems.

Similarly, there is a revolution occurring in psychotherapy. Long gone are adherence and allegiance to psychotherapy schools. Increasingly it is apparent that the models of the *DSM* (*Diagnostic and Statistical Manual of Mental Disorders*) are faulty. The new *DSM-5* is just a model of constructs; some say it is a mess. At the very least, there is some consensus that the new manual is excessive (more than 900 pages), makes suspect claims that its decisions are science-based, and acknowledges that mental disorders are medical disorders (American Psychiatric Association, 2013). In this book, we attempt to address the core features of the target disorders as they represent older adults and the science of the past decade. Depression and anxiety, for example, are not so much comorbid as they are co-occurring events coming from the same place with similar expression. Mixed anxiety and depression, therefore, are the mode at late life. The variations in the amalgam of symptoms and their expression are as many as there are people. The permutations can be quite large.

Similarly, over the past three decades the differential effectiveness of competing therapeutic approaches in psychology only marginally exists. The superiority, for example, of psychopharmacologic interventions or of psychological approaches is simply not provable. In fact, the use of the psychiatric classification at late life is not a good one. This suggests not only that psychiatric and psychological issues are more complex than medical ones, but that one system is very much grounded in the other.

The figures can be discouraging, especially for the common problems seen in later life; cognitive problems, problem behaviors, depression, and anxiety. As we elaborate in the text, the National Comorbidity Survey Replication found an adequate treatment rate of only about 42%. However, two large-scale studies, IMPACT and PROSPECT, using collaborative care management in primary care, found that fewer than half of older patients with major depression who underwent interventions experienced as much as a 50% reduction in depressive symptoms. In the IMPACT study, only about a quarter of patients became completely free of depressive symptoms. Over the iterations of levels of STAR*D (Sequenced Treatment Alternatives to Relieve Depression; Fava, 2009), remission rates decreased from 28% to single digits. Relapse rates were over 50% and dropout rates were almost 25%. If these are our best data, what does the real world look like?

During this time, we have become a medically focused society. Antidepressant use has doubled. Roughly 10% of the population takes an antidepressant. Among those who take psychotropic medications, roughly 50% take two medications and 33% take three. As we look at these data for older adults, roughly 44% are noncompliant. The placebo effect with older adults is also quite high, approximating that of the efficacy of intervention effects or medications. We have legions of psychiatric disorders, some of which recur, so relapse is a natural part of the phenomenon.

PROPOSAL

Given these concerns, what is a health care provider to do? This book constitutes an effort to simplify the mental health problems at later life around five core areas with some flexibility regarding assessment and treatment. The five areas are depression; anxiety; cognition; medical concerns, especially pain and sleep; and adjustment. Adjustment, the last variable, involves all of the day-to-day reality-based concerns that unfold for older adults. Based on this model, it is also believed that better psychological and psychiatric care can be attained in the context of primary care.

Several rubrics drive the thinking where treatment is concerned. We believe in a Watch and Wait model; that is, people are assessed and careful monitoring is instituted in which the patient is given hope, psychoeducation, support, and a belief that change will occur with careful preparation. This is clear case-based, person-centered care that leads to the application of best evidence. This is another way of looking at a stepped-care model. In this effort, teams are used and monitoring and special efforts are made to address all of the five areas, not just the one that is of most concern. In this effort, too, booster sessions and "steps" of model issues can be applied. These involve community-based interventions from lectures to support to caregiver therapies and environmental interventions. In effect, the psychotherapist becomes a psychosocial care manager.

In addition to this, the new model advocates the health care provider's use of solid psychosocial factors. These involve care modules and the application of psychotherapy principles based on a therapeutic alliance. As we are dealing with older adults, there is an emphasis on the usage of other components that are now more important in the 21st century. These involve the brain as metaphor, such that the re-regulation of neuronal networks parallels symptomatic changes in the psychotherapy itself. Cognitive retraining, too, becomes a core part of many of the treatment efforts. CBT and problem-solving therapy (PST), as well as interpersonal therapy (IPT), set the stage for these to occur. Life habits, such as exercise, diet, leisure, and general health care, become part of the "psychotherapy." Other issues are involved, such as usage of home care, bibliotherapy, telephone therapy, pretherapy, and booster sessions.

This now becomes the new normal and, as care unfolds, it takes a village to care for the older patient. This can be done in several ways in which you are targeting one person but also can involve many others. Community-based programs are now requisite for change. We need to expand on current models, respecting the personal needs of a person who is older but also introducing steps that make a difference, a process that is prudent and deliberate, and perhaps a community that takes the role of helper.

The belief, then, is that the basic approaches for the care for older adults require change. This is, no doubt, already going on, but imperfectly. There is a need to rethink traditional case formulations, proceeding from the real world, targeting issues, and entering mental health treatment. This is best done slowly and with flexibility. There is no desire here to usurp the scientist–practitioner model, as we need to do formal assessments and attend to the input of science. We do need, however, to apply the better-known canons of our sciences to the person and formulate real plans that are titrated to tangible outcomes.

This is a book for the psychosocial and medical practitioners who wish to address the new care of older adults. It is intended to simplify and to address a "just sufficient" level of data and extant research, to be integrative, to be practical, and to challenge professionals to assess and treat this population inside and outside the box. Most importantly, it stresses the need for teams, interdisciplinary activity, and primary care involvement.

ROAD MAP OF THE BOOK

Chapter 1 provides a backdrop to the field of gerontology and geriatrics. It addresses the changes of the past decade, the current clinical field, and the need for a change. Although global, it makes the case that old age is distinct where psychiatric care is at issue: this is a place where effective clinicians can think and make a difference in the care of older adults. It provides needed background information for the care of older adults.

In Chapter 2, we explicate our model and present important axioms of care. We have been discussing the need for this. There is some intended redundancy as we seek to expand our ideas. The Watch and Wait model is explained. It is based on the five ingredients described here in the Preface.

Chapter 3 is the province of psychotherapy. Psychological problems at late life are best dealt with by the therapeutic response based on modular interventions. Because the modal problems at late life—anxiety, depression, somatization (pain), and cognitive decline, as well as adjustment—are interconnected, this model is appropriate. We also believe that the components of CBT, as well as PST and IPT, have empirically supported modules that are best to consider for effective therapy. There is, therefore, a unified approach to treating problems at late life.

Chapter 4 tackles the first of the core problems of later life: depression. Most patients fail in treatment because their problems exceed the ability or the effectiveness of our science, or they or we expect too much from our therapies. We need to know this and apply what we can do with—and know the difference between what we can and cannot do. We address the problems of construct depression, its diagnosis, problems with extant treatment, problems with aging and this disorder, problems with executive function as applies to aging, and problems with the overlap of the other issues in this book. We highlight treatment and seek integration with the other factors.

In Chapter 5, we consider a frequent side effect of depression: anxiety. This chapter follows the pattern of depression: phenomenology prevalence, existing studies, problems with remission, and new ideas about treatment. We emphasize the transdiagnostic model as it applies to both depression and anxiety and discuss the importance of the interface with the other modules.

In Chapter 6, we address cognition, cognitive decline to be exact. We discuss the continuum of cognition, the importance of executive function and working memory, and the new ideas about cognitive training. We show, again, the overlap with the other variables. Cognition has become the symbol of aging and THE marker of progress and regress; we contextualize but respect this position.

Chapter 7 provides data on two memory training programs. We strongly advocate for the application of such programs in the normative care of older adults. These programs are critical to care, especially when depression and anxiety are also present.

The first of three chapters on health/medical issues begins with Chapter 8. Here, we consider health issues for the care of older adults. These are many and easily affect function and psychological adjustment. We target core heath issues of general health, pain, stress, and sleep. We devote ample time to lifestyle components that now subserve healthy aging in ways only recently validated.

Chapter 9 considers core medical components. Richard Ackermann, MD, Professor of Family Medicine, Chief of Geriatrics, Mercer School of Medicine, outlines what mental health care providers need to know about medical problems at late life. He addresses the usual problems of older adults in primary care. The emphasis is on geriatric medical assessment, common problems, typical out-of-range labs, usual patterns in the reduction of medications, and how best to interface with mental health.

Catherine Yeager, PhD, author of Chapter 10, discusses how the psychosocial model can be applied in primary care. This is now the new normal, but more importantly it is a necessity for treatment-as-usual of psychiatric problems. Psychosocial approaches are now commonly—and often poorly—applied across the country. The integration of medical and psychological care, the use of teams, and the practice of assessment and follow-up are critical to this discussion.

In Chapter 11, we consider life issues. We provide the needed perspective on the importance of life problems at later life, and highlight adjustment and caregiving as special issues. Long-term care is also addressed. Life can become complicated at late life; aspects of frailty can be imposing; social support can be bankrupt. We discuss the vagaries of adjustment and the importance of this issue, and how it interacts with the psychiatric problems and better models of care.

Assessment is a key component of our model and we discuss its value in Chapter 12. We address the core measures of dementia (cognition), anxiety, depression, and function. Testing and sharing test results with patients has been found to increase hope and motivation to change, increase self-awareness, decrease the sense of aloneness and isolation with one's condition, confirm one's self-efficacy, and enhance the therapeutic alliance. We highlight the role of caregivers and family members who participate in the assessment process. They too benefit from testing feedback, often experiencing a healthier appreciation of their loved one's strengths and weaknesses, and feeling empowered to meet their loved one's needs in a more compassionate, competent, and realistic way.

Throughout, we provide cases and address the need for a dynamic formulation with all the components noted previously. We provide appendices that address memory retraining, CBT, and sleep.

CONCLUSION

This book highlights a "whole person" model of care rather than assessing and treating symptoms or syndromes in isolation. The emphasis is both research-based and clinically practical, emphasizing five core factors of psychosocial impairment in older adults: depression, anxiety, cognitive deficits, adjustment or life problems, and health issues. These provide, we believe, an adequate understanding likely to result in successful outcomes for common syndromes or problems at later life.

The key involves a deliberative Watch and Wait model in which treatment is based on careful case-based assessment and a considered monitoring for empirically supported interventions. This model trumps the usual shoot-from-the-hip interventions that seek quick cures. Each factor is addressed from its empirically supported influence as applied to older adults, as well as its interaction with the other factors. Distinct treatment modules are isolated for each factor and reasonable pathways to clinical problems are provided. The text addresses the unique difficulties of diagnosing the aging population, the pitfalls of existing treatments, and the need for brain-based and practical models for care. Also covered are the importance of primary medicine, issues of daily life adjustment, use of selective serotonin reuptake inhibitors (SSRIs) and other medications, suicide, subsyndromal states, the use of CBT, and promising models of caregiving and long-term care, as well as the psychological treatment of older adults from an economic perspective. Plentiful case examples and call-outs enhance information.

Again, this book has been a labor of passion for many years in the VA, and at three medical schools. In addition to Rich Ackermann and Catherine Yeager, I have been enriched by the help of the PhD clinical psychology students at Mercer School of Medicine, Maria Anastasiades and Sanna Catherine Tillitski. It is also the product of several grants and the efforts of many students and colleagues, all contributing to its formulation and thinking. I celebrate them. There is no better age group to assess and to treat than older adults, no better efficacy or reward to be found, and no better area for intellectual curiosity mixing science and art to good ends.

CHAPTER 1

Introduction

All models are wrong; some are useful.

—*John Box*

In the past few years demographers have been predicting that someone was recently born who will live 1,000 years. Others cite that for 160 years we have gained 3 months per year in our average life span; that, if people reach the age of 65, they will live on average 18.5 years more; and that the median age has skyrocketed in the past few decades in all developed countries. We also know from the myth of Eos and Tithonus that living a long life is noble and desired, but that debility and maladies co-occur with age. Aging can be for the good or can create problems.

As we sort through the constructs of bioage and how to optimize the compression of morbidity so all of us live vibrantly until the very end, we present a book on the realities of aging in the early 21st century. We have identified five factors that we believe are "sufficient" for the care of older adults. We present chapters identifying and arguing for each and their inter-actions in the mental health and help required for older adults.

A typical case for late life patients follows. This particular female is best seen as one with multiple problems and needs. She has depression, anxiety, and somatic/sleep problems, and presents with cognitive complaints. She needs a coordinator who can assist her with her psychological, social, health, and practical problems and needs. This entails a holistic view of her situation and a considered approach to her plight. The answer, then, lies not in a *Diagnostic and Statistical Manual* (*DSM*) diagnosis, not just in a medica-tion for psychiatric care, and not in a private therapy session. It lies in holis-tic care and in case-based and empirically supported therapies and social realities, as well as general health. This is not easily done.

Case: Mrs. R: Cognitive decline, emotional problems, health issues

BACKGROUND: The patient is a 69-year-old female who is a resident of a small town in Georgia. She lives by herself and over the past few years has begun to experience problems with her memory and "thinking." She indicated that she was getting lost and she was forgetting conversations and having difficulty remembering things that she should have recalled. This was on the heels of problems over the past decade that involved breast cancer, heart problems with replacement of a pacemaker, methicillin-resistant *Staphylococcus aureus* (MRSA), as well as considerable back pain with a back operation. She is also on a considerable number of medications. On a subsequent meeting, her cousin corroborated this.

She is a native of Georgia. She was adopted by older parents who raised her with no evident problems. She graduated from high school and went to vocational school. She worked for a department store in North Carolina, and then for an electronics corporation in Georgia. About 7 years ago, she developed a disability and was awarded Social Security disability. She was married at age 20, and remained in this union for 18 years. She has two children, both girls, who are supportive. She currently lives by herself and receives Social Security.

Medically, Mrs. R has a psychiatrist as well as a primary care provider (PCP). She is on a considerable number of medications, including Lyrica, digoxin, diovan, Xopenex, bumetanide, lamotrigine, lansoprazole, carvedilol, hydrocodone, diclofenac, and metformin. She is also on Paxil, Aricept, diazepam, and trazodone for psychiatric issues. She has a psychiatric history that dates back to her late 50s. She has had surgeries throughout the years, including knee surgery and back surgery. She also has a history of migraines and diabetes. Currently, she is in considerable pain owing to her back. She indicates that she has sleep problems and is taking trazodone and risperidone. She is a survivor of breast cancer in 1993. A pacemaker was implanted 1 to 2 years after her breast cancer. She can perform all of her activities of daily living (ADL) and instrumental activities of daily living (IADL), and indicates that day to day, she does light housework, puzzles, paints, and remains in her home most of the day.

She drove to this appointment on her own. She was perky, relevant, answered questions well, and was engaging. She was pleasant to talk with, smiled, and interchanged well. There was no evidence of memory or word-finding problems on interview. That said, she did indicate that she has had depression and anxiety for many years. As seen, she is on several medications for both pain and psychiatric problems. She denied being very anxious at present. She appears to have good insight into her condition and shows good judgment. There is no evidence of perceptual anomalies or delusionary thinking.

TEST RESULTS: Mrs. R has a premorbid intelligence score placing her in the low-average area intellectually based on the WAIS-III (Wechsler Adult Intelligence Scale) Vocabulary score. Her cognitive battery total was normal (MoCA [Montreal Cognitive Assessment] and RBANS [Repeatable Battery for Neuropsychological Status]). She was average in attention, visuospatial skills, language, new learning, and memory. She also was average on executive function. There were mild deficits on an adjustment scale. She was not impaired functionally.

EMOTIONAL ASSESSMENT: On the MINI (Mini-International Neuropsychiatric Interview) she scored positive for depression (MDD [Major Depressive Disorder]) and anxiety (GAD [Generalized Anxiety Disorder]). Emotional self-report scales indicated also that she had depression and anxiety. She rated as depressed (BDI-II [Beck Depression Inventory = 30; GDS-SF [Short Form] = 11) and anxious (GAD-7 = 11 and SAST [Short Anxiety Screening Test] = 27, both anxiety ranges).

The MBMD (Millon Behavioral Medicine Diagnostic) indicated that she has a cooperative, dejected, inhibited, and denigrated personality profile. This is quite complex but suggests that she prefers to be more detached, is depressive in her general outlook, and self-defeating when stressed. She has stress moderators that cause problems—illness apprehension, functional deficits, pain sensitivity, and pessimism, as well as social isolation. She showed problems with treatment prognostics also—utilization excess and interventional fragility. Her concerns about her pain sensitivity are especially noteworthy. She is also inactive and has problems with eating.

Stress Moderators: Intrapersonal and extrapersonal characteristics that affect medical problems. They target cognitive appraisals, resources, and context factors.

Moderator			Weakness	Strength
Illness Apprehension	vs.	Illness Acceptance	×	
Functional Deficits	vs.	Functional Competence	×	
Pain Sensitivity	vs.	Pain Tolerance	×	
Social Isolation	vs.	Social Support	×	
Future Pessimism	vs.	Future Optimism	×	
Spiritual Absence	vs.	Spiritual Faith		×

Treatment Prognostics: Behaviors and attitudinal aspects that may complicate or enhance treatment efficacy.

Treatment Prognostic			Weakness	Strength
Interventional Fragility	vs.	Interventional Resilience	×	
Medication Abuse	vs.	Medication Conscientiousness		×
Information Discomfort	vs.	Information Receipt		×
Utilization Excess	vs.	Appropriate Utilization	×	
Problematic Compliance	vs.	Optimal Compliance		×

PAIN and SLEEP: She has high pain sensitivity on the MBMD. She rated her pain at present as 4/10; average 8/10. She has problems with activity (6/10), mood (5/10), walking (6/10), work (7/10), relations with people (5/10), sleep (7/10), and enjoyment of life (7/10). Sleep currently is a problem as she sleeps excessively, is often groggy in the morning, and has an ESS (Epworth Sleepiness Scale) = 10 (insomnia). She takes several meds for sleep, both standard and PRN (pro re nata [as needed]).

PROFILE: She is responding well cognitively but has health issues as well as depression and anxiety. She does have some problems in executive function as well as some isolated tests in the other domains. She even reads well. She is not responding as one with either dementia or even mild cognitive impairment (MCI). She is in pain and sleep is a concern. She is living by herself and doing reasonably well. Her psychiatric problems with depression and anxiety are longstanding. She is inactive. She is passive and isolated and can be very depressive as well as self-defeating in her personality pattern.

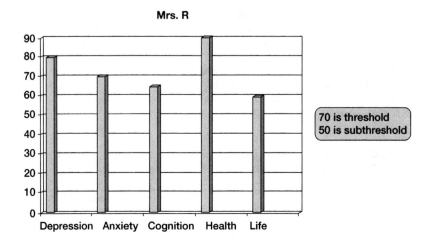

Mrs. R

70 is threshold
50 is subthreshold

Mrs. R—WATCH AND WAIT

Sessions 1 to 3:
She was assessed and given feedback. A problem list was formulated involving her core issues and a priority of goals. These included a close liaison with her physicians, including her PCP and psychiatrist. She was presented with tasks of monitoring her sleep, pain, and health problems. She was to consider, as possible interventions, exercise and a reduction in medications over time. She was also to think about structuring her day, as she was passive and somewhat depressive in outlook. She was to identify what she enjoyed. Her stress moderators were outlined, as were her treatment prognostics, especially interventional fragility. She was committed to the plan and was challenged to see a new perspective on her problems. In addition, issues that are strengths were noted. This included cognition. She may benefit, however, from cognitive stimulation and structure.

Watch and Wait Category	Check
Validate Problem	×
Psychoeducation of Model	×
Assessment	×
Monitoring	×
Case Formulation	×
Check Alliance	×

Sessions 4 to 12:
Issues addressed included a depression focus in the form of behavioral activation and mood ratings, and self-rewards and self-control techniques. She also became more social and involved with her church. Pain was lessened with a close connection with the pain clinic, a spinal cord stimulator implanted, and relaxation. Her health was monitored and she had no outstanding problems during the treatment period. She also joined a Memory Training program that she flourished in. Sleep continued to be a problem but she now had at least 6 hours per night. Relapse issues were discussed and she is seen every 3 months.

This is a case-based model and it addresses the profile of problems for a particular patient. Each will have a profile that best features his or her issues. The task is to establish a plan that works. We believe that a Watch and Wait approach is optimal. Remember that the target is to get the patient on board, to provide a plan and a direction via psychoeducation and monitoring. A delay in treatment is treatment, not a postponement of care. Then the patient is on board and necessary personnel can be accessed and committed. Watch and Wait sets the expectancy that a therapeutic accelerant will eventually unfold either from the perspective of the total situation or from an epiphany of the patient. We also may be in this case for the long haul.

This chapter addresses the psychiatric and psychological components of older adults. What is the best way to address the modal psychosocial problems of late life, taking into account what science has to offer, what seems commonsensical, and what can be done? What are the reasonable concepts and learning required for care of older adults? Like Blaise Pascal, we must place our bets. With older adults we witness a decline in being, a (likely) medically impacted person, a psychologically complex entity who is most often bothered by anxiety and depression, as well as somatic issues, and who has (probably) less cognitive power and in some cases considerably less. Older adults are also living longer and experience the vagaries of various adjustment concerns (Suthers et al., 2010). The need to transition from simple care to more intensive, multimodal care for the late-life patient with multiple needs is upon us.

In the long run, to benefit depressed or anxious elderly patients in the community, personalization of care must employ comprehensive common-sense care algorithms targeting both modifiable predictors of poor outcomes and organizational barriers to care. Whether this care can be done on a grand societal level ("it takes a village") is unknown. We believe, however, that psychosocial care can evolve and move from intuitive to precision care. The latter has well-defined boundaries that a diagnosis assists in setting and that treatments match, but there is more. One does not need an advanced degree to know that if there is a bacterial infection, then an antibiotic is in order. But we need skills to deal with closing the deal, follow-ups, side effects, messy socialization, personal reactions, iatrogenic nuances, and, yes, life. Older adults are messy and develop side effects to what appears to be best-practice care.

In the past 10 years, there remains a vacuum in hard evidence, as results and trends have been enlightening but disappointing. Some of the notable areas have been the importance of medical care, use of selective serotonin reuptake inhibitors (SSRIs) and their medication brethren, issues related to suicide, subsyndromal states, and validation of variants of cognitive behavioral therapy (CBT). But treatments work at best only 50% of the time, and most often not permanently; people continue on as both systems and self-change fail; patients often wax and wane, getting a little better before they come to see a therapist and at different times during the treatment; and long-term treatment is still largely an anomaly. There is little in the way of proof of specific effects in therapies: dismantling studies have not provided robust findings, and it seems that general effects of care are greater than specific effects. We need better models, especially with older adults.

Our position is simple: Treating "depressive symptoms" in isolation, while disregarding the patient's whole person, especially cognitive and physical limitations, risks slower or less-effective reduction in depressive symptoms. Targeting an organized patchwork of psychological problems—in our example—case, depression, anxiety, cognitive impairment, adjustment, and some disability—allows a concerted focus to help the patient adapt and cope with her or his problems, promoting successful outcomes for the prime target, depression. Evidence for such multifaceted approaches to treatment is nascent, and so we must borrow from data regarding each problem and look at the efficacy for older adults, as well as what works for younger adults. Although the best care is case based, with older adults there is more to consider. Reality and psychological problems conspire to create greater problems in treatment.

Applied science is not practical; we require a "reparticularization" of scientific knowledge to individual patients (Cassell, 1991). This allows the practice of care for older adults not to go from science to practice but from science through patients and expertise, as well as clinical and real-life conditions, back to actual clinical practice. For older adults, experimental science is not a sufficient knowledge base for psychological practice.

PROCESS OF CARE

Algorithms are perhaps brittle and often don't work well in the shadows; skilled decision makers are more sensitive to the context of problems at later life. We need informed and adaptive decision makers. The STAR*D (Sequenced Treatment Alternatives to Relieve Depression) study (Fava, 2009) showed us that only 33% of more difficult depressives respond to four alterations in treatment with meds and that there were high rates of relapse. We need skilled therapeutic flexibility as a response to this finding. As with schizophrenia, in which the treatment of early responders is often found to be more cost-effective than the treatment of early nonresponders, we need to know where and to whom we can best devote energies. And for those who are not responsive, we need commonsense care and reasonable treatment rubrics. In the cost-effectiveness vernacular, the early responder is considered a dominant choice over the early nonresponder, but, beyond clinical acumen for matching patients with treatments, a clinician cannot choose which individuals will be early responders to a specific antipsychotic medication. We need clinical acumen for older adults so that these parameters can be available and known and the clinician can respond accordingly.

We do not need or require a crystal ball for what works with whom for older adults. Andreescu et al. (2010) identified predictors of full response both at baseline and on change in depressive symptoms after treatment is under way. The authors used signal detection theory on pooled data from three acute treatment trials of either nortriptyline or paroxetine. They found that response by the fourth week of treatment was a critical factor in determining the probability of response by 12 weeks. Of course, a strong treatment response by the fourth week suggests that the treatment should continue. However, if only a moderate response has occurred by that time, the clinician has to choose whether to continue the same treatment or do something different—switch to another treatment, for example, or augment the first treatment with another drug or a nonbiological intervention. Interestingly, in this study patients who had low levels of anxiety at baseline had a 61% chance of full response, whereas those with moderate or severe anxiety at baseline had a 39% chance of response. The probability of full response was even lower (33%) in patients who had experienced depressive episodes earlier in life. Using the probability of full response in treatment, then, decisions can spare patients from long exposure to treatments that have a low likelihood of success, as well as from premature discontinuation of treatments that would likely be helpful. One can see how such information is helpful in treatment.

Of course, there is more. Psychotherapy groups have been applying these ideas for many years (e.g., Lambert et al., 1996). The score on the OQ-45 (Outcome Questionnaire-45) over three sessions affects outcomes. The American Association of Geriatric Psychiatry (AAGP) also has advocated for clinical prudence when there is no or a partial response early in the treatment. So far, however, the empirical basis for personalizing treatment principally consists of post hoc analyses of unitary treatments (e.g., a course of an antidepressant or psychotherapy). Although this knowledge is necessary, it is insufficient for two reasons. First, a one-disorder patient, like a depressed elder, faces a bewildering constellation of other health threats and social constraints, and thus has many different contributors to poor treatment outcomes. Second, the skills available in various treatment settings and sectors can promote or inhibit treatment success.

We need an all-encompassing model to effect change. Accordingly, the model of geriatric depression has to integrate the current biological concepts of depression with patients' unique reactions to adverse experiences and with their unmet social and health care needs. The care algorithms based on this model should target clinical/biological predictors of adverse outcomes of depression, but also address unmet needs through linkage to appropriate social services; enhance the competencies of elderly persons so that they make use of their resources; and attend to patient psychotherapy issues of psychoeducation, behaviors, thoughts, and emotions.

We need models of care, then, that encompass more than one diagnosis. Clinical and psychosocial predictors of response to single antidepressants or comprehensive interventions have been identified. These include anxiety, hopelessness, executive dysfunction, limitations in physical and emotional functions, chronicity of the current episode, and low income. There are of course more predictors to consider. But such predictors can help in personalizing the first step of treatment for a given patient. Accordingly, a patient with one or more predictors of poor outcome may receive interventions targeting each modifiable predictor, as well as more vigilant follow-up. For example, a low-income depressed elderly patient whose symptoms did not respond to an adequate trial of an antidepressant and who is experiencing hopelessness may benefit from a trial of psychotherapy focusing on hopelessness, as well as case management connecting him or her with social services.

BACKDROP

We are in the midst of a revolution in science, especially neuroscience, which is replacing usual care for all. This really applies to older adults. We of course do not yet know what causes aging and how can we prevent the harmful aspects of old age (Le Couteur & Sinclair, 2010). We also have the limitations of our sciences; there is a 33% upper limit for years of problems averted for any psychiatric therapy. In psychiatry, it is reasonable to expect that only 38% to 46% get better (show a response) and that one half to two thirds will not remit (Nelson, 2010) when depression is at issue. In fact, about 25% remit with no treatment. We also know from the National Institutes of Health (NIH) Conference on Alzheimer's Disease (AD) and Cognitive Decline in 2010 that very little is firm. Several "obvious" predictors are now wavering: adequate folic acid, low-fat diet, alcohol, vitamins, statins, cognitive rehabilitation, education, leisure, physical activity, metabolic syndrome, low social support, never married, homocysteine, obesity, and nonsteroidal anti-inflammatory drugs (NSAIDs) use, to name those most represented. Maybe Apo-E (apolipoprotein E), diabetes, smoking, and depression will prove helpful in understanding AD. But even these "sure fire" predictors possess noise. There are no firm biomarkers for AD; really, even the diagnosis is suspect (Mungus, 2010).

In fact, we are in a taxonomy crisis where dementia, anxiety, and depression are concerned, especially at late life. The focus should be on identifying items that place a person on the continuum, not whether he or she is or is not in the group. The additive effect, in which many risk factors of genes and environment accumulate, represents a better model of care. It is an aggregate effect. We have a poor recent history of efficacy in psychiatry and psychology.

Over 50 years of research have suggested that the following are more true than not:

1. The differential effectiveness of competing therapeutic approaches does not exist
2. The superiority of psychopharmacological over psychological approaches is untrue
3. The utility of psychiatric classification as determining the course of Rx (prescription) is poor
4. The short and effective treatments for older adults have weak effect sizes and large NNT (number needed to treat)
5. Good lifestyle habits make a difference
6. At later life, a focus on caregiving is most beneficial

We do have some reasonable facts, however. Prevention works (Smits et al., 2008). Public health models suggest that we do best if we target "indicated or high risk subjects." We know that even small changes in core capacities of older adults can lead to large changes in complex behavior (Salthouse, 2001). With time, things can get better. Psychiatry clinics as they have been designed (set apart and medication driven) are becoming increasingly anachronistic as far as older adults are concerned. The "placebo effect" is strong in most treatments, certainly those relevant to psychiatry. In fact, a better focus for the efficacy of psychotherapy is a "substantive effect," which equals the real effect–placebo effect. This is likely to be in the single digits. Depression itself, except for the very impaired, is probably a placebo-treated disease. Specific treatments are probably placebo-engineered events. The NNT necessary for remission is quite high for most psychiatric disorders at late life. Most often when change occurs, there is a response but no remission. Although "omics" (genomics) is not yet ready for prime time, there is now a firm belief that a careful look at the brain and body are necessary. Medically unexplained symptoms (MUPS) are now the norm.

Old-old age (older than 84) is not friendly for psychiatric care. This group represents a distinct problem, in that treatment may well be less effective. As clinicians, we are constantly in the battle for a "best fit" for adaptation—the assimilation and accommodation dance in which older adults can be provided a model, a perspective for change to occur. In the recent past, we (Hyer & Intrieri, 2006) argued that the SOC model (selective optimization and compensation) was optimal for this. Regardless, how this is done in the context of general mental health problems takes time and prudence.

What can health care providers do? As a general rule, we believe that we should pay less attention to the nuanced differences in treatment (one antidepressant vs. another, one psychotherapy vs. another, meds vs. psychotherapy). Although we should be aware of these, these differences help providers of care for older adults less than those providing care to other age groups. Published reports suggest that attending to novel "significantly better" or "evidence-based" interventions will result in better patient outcomes, but doing so with older adults often diverts attention from the real-world issues, and has only marginal evidence of benefit. In effect, we will argue that knowledge and actuarial foundation are necessary but not sufficient for treating older adults. Attention to the basics of living and general health are equally important (Thielke, Vannoy, & Unützer, 2007).

The belief here is that the basics of care for older adults require some change. There is a need to march carefully over the case, proceeding from the real world, targeting issues, and entering mental health treatment. This requires assessment and monitoring as well as flexibility. There is no desire here to usurp the scientist–practitioner model, as we need to do formal assessments and attend to the input of science. But, as noted before, we need more. Mast (2012) argues for a "whole person" approach in which the value of "the person" of the diagnostic category becomes as important as the process of the diagnosis and treatment plan. We agree, but add that we need to apply the better-known canons of our sciences to the person and formulate real plans that are titrated to tangible outcomes.

When dealing with older adults, we are often doing some application of translational research because few psychotherapy interventions have been designed expressly for elders. The translational component involves focusing on the time span of the problem, the nature and scope of the hypothesis, dose adjustments, and patient population characteristics. Early on in therapy with older individuals, treatment is titrated (individually adapted). This includes a time frame that is short, hypotheses that are narrow in scope, small doses of the intervention, close monitoring of coping/potential, and choices of narrow treatment targets. In later phases of treatment, there is the requisite alteration in goals, which are simplified for reality's sake. Psychotherapies are never just pure techniques to be used directly off the shelf. As this process has unfolded over the years, however, efforts to document the applicability of all-purpose psychotherapy research data show that such psychotherapies appear to be relevant to older adults only if practiced in an aging-informed manner (Hinrichsen & Clougherty, 2006). Both context and outcomes matter. With older adults, both are complex. For outcomes, the issue is never just symptom abatement. Rather, therapy should aim at symptom relief *and* improving overall quality of life (QoL).

Some Good News

The good news is that most psychotherapies developed for younger patients appear useful for older adults when applied in an age-informed and age-sensitive manner.

Hinrichsen and Clougherty (2006)

In no particular order, we have fashioned a series of components that are at the core of this book. The critical issue in the Watch and Wait model (last point below) is what to do (what to think) before the total plan is activated. The application of this model hinges on the challenge of when to shift from the wait point to the activate point: When does the therapist pull the trigger for more active care? We will dialogue about this throughout the book.

General Issues

Older age involves chronic conditions.

Mental and physical illness are conjoined.

Current psychological treatment is inadequate.

Current assessments address dichotomous problems, but a focus on continuous and individual symptoms is required.

Primary care is the new psychiatric care.

Professional silos are a problem: teams are complex and necessary.

Current models of care (e.g., IMPACT, PEARLS) are helpful.

Step care works: specialty clinics are applied last.

Patient-centered care is underperformed and critical.

Public health models work well.

The clinician's attitude and skills are critical.

Psychoeducation is chief among the curative agents.

The Watch and Wait model is understudied.

BEST PREDICTORS

We identify and briefly discuss the best predictors of our science for our modal psychosocial problems at late life: cognition, depression, anxiety, medical/somatic problems, and adjustment. We start with age. We address 10 issues, the core five we espouse and necessary other features of the care model.

Age

Aging is complex and variable. The phenomenon of aging is itself a problem from most perspectives. We do not know well what cell senescence is or what causes the allostatic load to assert a negative influence (on age). We do not know the true savings in number of years lived for most of our treatment efforts. Just the idea of an 85-year-old who is optimally healthy coming for care can be problematic. Within 5 years, 80% will develop considerable medical problems (Beekman et al., 2006). Variability itself is not an optimal sign at older ages. Although this can be a nonevent for younger age groups and inherent within and between all biological systems, this is often a problem at late life. Intraindividual variability (IIV) is associated with problems in cognition, especially working memory (WM), volumetric decline, demyelination, blood flow, vascular injury, and many neurological conditions.

Where age is concerned, we have had a culture change. In 1959, older people had the highest poverty rate (35%), followed by children (27%); by 2007, the proportion of older adults in poverty was 10%. In fact, in 2007 older people in the middle-income group made up the largest share of older people by category (33%), with those in the high-income group up to 31% (Federal Interagency Forum on Aging-Related Statistics, 2010). Health ratings also were up. In 2008, 75% of people 65 or older rated their health as good, very good, or excellent; for 85 and older, these rates were still somewhat respectable at 66%. Life expectancy (the average number of years lived by a group of people born in the same year) along with a growing burden of chronic diseases also keeps rising (Peck, Hurwicz, Ory, Yuma, & Cook, 2010).

Percentages of lifestyle problems are also noteworthy. For starters, if you are a male in the United States and 65, you can expect to live an average 18.5 more years; if you are 85, you can expect 6.8 more years. Life expectancy has increased by a year in the past decade, the time spent seriously sick is up by 1.5 years, and time disabled has accrued by 2 years (Suthers, 2008). For people 65 or older, diseases of the heart, followed by malignant neoplasms, and then stroke, lead for cause of death. Older men and women have hypertension and arthritis at rates over 50%. In 2008, 32% of people 65 or older are considered obese; 11% smoke; 25% spend time in leisure; and watching TV occupied the most leisure time (> 50%) (Federal Interagency Forum on Aging-Related Statistics, 2010).

A related factor: We have a special problem with the old-old group, those older than 84. Interestingly, it is only at about age 80 that the vagaries of living become more apparent—percentage with disability rises, percentage going into long-term care facilities increases, and the percentage married is lower. Older adults seek mental health at 3% to 6% levels (of all actual visits), as they see little connection between symptoms and mental problems. They most assuredly do not go to psychiatric clinics. Problematically, cognitive decline or depressive symptoms are actually more frequent in the old-old but this is generally due to aging-specific variables. Not surprisingly, older adults seek mental health care through presentation of somatic problems (Karlin & Duffy, 2004). It is also true that the number of medications/person, number of medical visits, and number of falls, to name a few, are highest in this old-old group.

Although professional, policy, and other recent developments portend an increase in service use, there has been scant empirical attention devoted to the current use of mental health treatment by the elderly, and almost nothing is known about the correlates of mental health need and service use among older adults. Karlin, Duffy, and Gleaves (2008) examined patterns of serious mental illness, specific mental health syndromes, and service use among older (65+) and younger (18 to 64) adults throughout the United States, and the extent to which various factors predict mental health need and the use and magnitude of mental health treatment. In addition, the study examined factors related to unmet needs, as well as age group differences in perceived benefit from treatment. The findings reveal that older adults were three times less likely than their younger counterparts to receive any outpatient mental health treatment. Only 2.5% of older individuals used any outpatient mental health service in the past year, versus 7.0% of younger adults. These results indicate that the low rate of usage by older adults may be partly a function of limited subjective perception of need for mental health care. It is important to consider that though mental health problems appear to be significantly undertreated in older and younger age groups, Karlin et al. (2008) also noted that those older adults who make it into services typically benefit considerably from treatment.

Common problems run the gamut from basic risk and safety issues to reasonable prevention. Major areas of focus would include polypharmacy, adverse drug events, medication compliance, fall prevention, continence care, and caregiver management of problem behaviors. These areas are problematic and can significantly impact the quality of everyday life.

Special Older Adult Concerns

Common conditions go undiagnosed and untreated: Too much of the time, common and treatable conditions, such as cognitive impairment, nutrition problems, sleep disorders, fall risk, overactive bladder and incontinence, mobility disorders, and depression are undiagnosed.

Health and care needs of the oldest old: Included in this frail population are many minority and rural elders. The population 85+ is the fastest growing population and places the most demands on the health care system.

Minority/disadvantaged: African American and Hispanic elders especially are at greater risk of health problems and often receive less treatment for their conditions.

Health literacy: The Institute of Medicine has stated that "90 million people have difficulty understanding and acting upon health information." The prevalence of limited health literacy is highest among older adults, minority populations, those who are poor, and medically underserved people.

Older adults face many challenges, as society's view of their role transforms once they enter their sixth and seventh decades of life. The attitudes, values, and norms that have previously been constructed by society regarding aging are constantly evolving to accommodate the growing older adult population. However, a large segment of our culture adheres to negative stereotypes and prejudices associated with the process of aging. The practice of expressing prejudice and holding undesirable views toward a person due to his or her age—particularly older adults—is known as *ageism*. Ageism may have an effect on the perceived physical functioning, cognition, and emotional health of an older adult who is faced with this form of social prejudice. Coudin and Alexopoulos (2010) determined that older adults who were presented with a narrative-focused cognitive task after having read materials imbued with negative stereotyping toward older adults reported lower levels of subjective health and extraversion, higher feelings of loneliness, and more frequent help-seeking behavior. These findings can be extrapolated to the notion that older adults who internalize negative messages that they receive from society regarding aging may experience problems in maintaining a positive self-image and developing suitable coping skills to adjust to biopsychosocial changes they encounter as they age.

Let's not kid ourselves: Aging is replete with disease and impairment, often unrecognized or inadequately treated. But there may be better ways of accounting for these problems than just age. Health confounds the results of age all the time. Health is based on self-reports and many studies simply overestimate the effect of age because they do not know about health. Ignorance of health in the study of morbidity does aging no favor. We have come to know that aging is a factor in people at risk across the life span, but in reality, it is only a marker for other more important issues like health or cognition (brain at risk) in the identification process of persons at high risk for end-stage problems like AD. Once a MCI or dementia diagnosis is given, much is lost in the long-term preventative sense. Age is not just a simple causal factor and cannot be viewed usefully as a basis for understanding cognitive changes.

Brain Issues

We have passed the decade of the brain (1990s) and are now firmly entrenched in the neuroscience era. At late life, this emphasis is welcome. Older adults lose brainpower and eventually lose functioning. Most often these losses are correlated (Royall et al., 2007). Park and Reuter-Lorenz (2010) noted that the older brain presents with a symphony of degenerative expressions and develops scaffolding to address these, sometimes done well and sometimes not. Speed of processing and handling of intellectually fluid tasks decompensate initially, while the person tries to adapt and assimilate/accommodate with skill training and coping. In this brain and decline context, we are also seeing that cognitive training and exercise, to name two, make a difference. For cognitively healthy people we can be confident of several issues: (1) that mnemonic strategies work; (2) that older adults improve, but less so than do younger groups; (3) that they can maintain skilled memory performance for 6 months; (4) that they show little transfer; and (5) that affect, attitude, and effort, as well as stress, matter. For cognitively less healthy subjects, we are now seeing that several studies are showing some promise (e.g., Loewenstein, Acevedo, Czaja, & Duara, 2004) that caregivers really can help with compensation strategies (Hyer & Ragan, 2003), and that multimethod packages with caregivers help (Hyer et al., in press).

It is now more than two decades since there was reasonable documentation that depression is a function of frontal–striatal problems (Coffey et al., 1992). Other early studies through the years documented that over 50% of patients with late-onset MDD had such problems (Fujikawa, Yamawaki, & Touhouda, 1993). The influence of white and gray matter hyperintensities, as well as subcortical infarcts or hyperintensities, have been shown to be associated with more severe symptoms, more hospital admissions for depression, longer hospitalizations for depression, resistance to medications, and executive-function problems.

Late-life depression has been a special problem as far as brain issues are concerned. Knowledge of brain problems in the context of depression is informative in two ways. First, identifying persisting abnormalities during remission (of depression) may indicate a high risk for relapse or persistent cognitive impairment. Second, finding brain abnormalities predictive of poor outcomes of depression may initiate a search for their clinical correlates, which then can be used to personalize treatment. Sheline, Wang, Gado, Csernansky, and Vannier (1996) long ago peered into the soul of the person, the brain, using functional MRI (or PET) to compare activation and deactivation of brain regions in currently depressed elderly patients, elderly patients in remission from depression, and healthy elderly comparison subjects. Depressed patients show attenuated activation of the right middle frontal gyrus and greater deactivation of the posterior part of the posterior cingulate relative to remitted patients and comparison subjects. We have been and are now increasingly accountable, even wedded, to the rumblings of our brains, so much so that we now can apply behavior or cognitive markers, like executive function, as proxies for brain work (supramarginal gyrus bilaterally, the left anterior cingulate, and the anterior part of the posterior cingulate), and these also mimic depression.

In the list below, we outline how the brain is important in therapy with older adults. We start from the position that re-regulation of neuronal networks parallels symptomatic changes in psychotherapy. Older brains confess their problems with symptoms, both cognitive and affective. Adjustment also suffers. The therapist is the manager of the therapy and, as such, he or she uses the brain as the explanatory mechanism for the dialogue. The mind and brain are indivisible; problems in life are reflected in or caused by brain input; and the use of the brain model can assist in the understanding of this. The therapist as neuroscientist can use and foster these issues.

Psychotherapist as Neuroscientist

- Mind and brain are indivisible.
- Re-regulation of neuronal networks parallels symptomatic changes in psychotherapy.
- Narratives resculpture neuronal networks throughout life.
- Activation of the left hemisphere assists in top-down or placebo effect.
- Strategies of cognitive retraining assist in the treatment of depression and anxiety.
- Lower amygdala-related anxiety and hypometabolism in temporal lobes allow for reduced anxiety and increased problem solving.
- Activate placebo: it uses the prefrontal lobes in a top-down cortical modulation of mood, emotion, and immune activity. Placebo effect is one of the core conditions of treatment—necessary and, at times, sufficient for change.
- Appreciate the centrality of stress: early stress impairs!

Cozolino (2010)

When it comes to the worst aspect of cognition at late life, dementia, the focus may be poorly targeted. The focus should be on a continuum of cognitive impairment connected to health risk factors, lifestyle habits, and reasonable preventative targets. We need to see a "brain at risk" stance in which we recognize that disease occurs long before symptoms are present. The vascular hypothesis and information from preventative cardiology make this point clear and convincing. It should be clear now that research on a variety of disciplines shows that cognition and mental health are intertwined across the life course.

We can add one more feature of age and brain: The idea of considering dementia without age is a nonstarter, as the type of symptoms, the number of neuritic plaques, and the phenomenology of problems are different for differing older ages. There is then variability in the whole older group that is best reflected in the category of young-old and old-old. Cognition as it marks the brain is a harbinger of problems of all sorts, both physical and mental, across the later years of life, but brains are not "universals." In addition, as we shall argue later, the (latent) structure of dementia is better seen as dimensional rather than categorical: There is no objective or taxonic boundary separating those who do and do not meet the criteria for dementia of the Alzheimer's type (Walters, 2010).

The concept of dementia is obsolete.

Hachinski (2008)

Make no mistake: The new, more dynamic picture of the brain makes psychology even more crucial. Researchers can only explain the very complex pattern of brain activity by relating it to what they know about categorization and attention. Knowing the activity of a specific wire in the computer does not tell us much about the overall processing and functioning of the computer. Neuroscience may be sexier than psychology but it will be psychology that will unfold the nuances and science of human activity.

People often assume that knowing the brain is all that you need to explain how the mind works, so that neuroscience will replace psychology. That may account for the curious popular enthusiasm for the phrenological "lighting up" studies. It is as if the very thought that something psychological is "in the brain" gives us a little explanatory frisson, even though we have known for at least a century that everything psychological is "in the brain" in some sense. But it would be just as accurate to say that knowing about the mind explains how the brain works.

Gopnik (2013)

Anxiety

A forgotten problem in the psychological care of older adults is the phenomenology of anxiety and what to do about it. Anxiety disorders are the most common psychiatric illnesses in the United States, with approximately 30%

of the population experiencing anxiety-related symptoms in their lifetime (Kessler et al., 2005). Current rates of anxiety extend to 10%, with its symptoms actually doubling that number.

Most anxiety problems occur in early life (50% to 97%). In general, the fact that anxiety may attack in early or late life is unremarkable except for medical problems: Late onset actually shows more medical symptoms. In general, early onset was most characterized by obsessive-compulsive disorder, panic disorder, and specific phobias; late onset is most characteristic of posttraumatic stress disorder (PTSD), agoraphobia, and adjustment with anxiety.

Although GAD levels (e.g., Montorio, Nuevo, Márquez, Izal, & Losada, 2003), as well as depression and anxiety in general, are lower in older age than in other ages (e.g., George, Blazer, Winfield-Laird, Leaf, & Fischback, 1988), only 33% of older GAD patients reported using mental health resources (Blazer, 1997). Older adults with GAD are more disabled, have worse QoL, and demand greater health care utilization than nonanxious groups (Porensky et al., 2009). Also, 90% of older adults with GAD report dissatisfaction with sleep and the majority report depression. However, problems with anxiety show first at the primary care clinic (PCC); both medication use and numbers are up. Younger ages also do better in terms of assessment and treatment where anxiety is concerned.

Anxiety is both brain based and unique at late life. It is common at late life and GAD is the most frequent diagnosis. This type of worry is really connected to depression and often to medical problems. Worry and nervous tension (as opposed to specific anxiety syndromes, such as panic disorder) are common presentations of depression in older people. Unfortunately, many physicians tend to focus on the symptoms of depression or anxiety alone, thus failing to consider the possibility of comorbidity. Often patients who have both anxiety and depressive symptoms are more likely to be given a benzodiazepine rather than treatment for depression. Older adults with depression too often may worry about memory loss without showing objective evidence of memory impairment in simple tests of memory. These patients should be evaluated for symptoms of depression or anxiety, with careful follow-up to watch for the development of dementia.

Anxiety Facts

GAD levels (e.g., Montorio et al., 2003) and anxiety in general are lower at older age (e.g., George et al., 1988).

Research on subthreshold problems with anxiety in nonclinical older samples indicates that mental health is not better in older age.

Literature on the dimensional approach suggests that this is a better model of psychopathology.

Older individuals respond differently than younger adults, potentially requiring special attention in psychiatric care.

Depression

The construct depression has changed the face of confidence regarding the canons of established psychiatry. Yes, it exists and is prevalent, but its phenomenology is complex and varied. Older persons with significant depression may have fewer symptoms than the number required by the *Diagnostic and Statistical Manual of Mental Disorders* (DSM-5; American Psychiatric Association, 2013). Clinicians have come to know that older adults who express feelings of hopelessness or worthlessness, admit to thoughts of death or suicide, and have at least two other symptoms of depression, can be at increased risk for functional disability, cognitive impairment, psychological distress, and death, even if they do not display symptoms, such as sadness or loss of interest or pleasure in activities that were formerly enjoyed (nondysphoric depression). Depressive symptoms, especially at later life, are also associated with development of functional impairment as measured by performance tests (avoiding reliance on self-report of function).

Depression Issues at Late Life

- *At the least, "It is apparent that the 'oldest old' (> 75) present different from the 'young old.'" (p. 379)*

  Lu and Ahmed (2010)

- *"The heterogeneity in symptom presentation among older adults diagnosed with MDD can potentially inform the development of the DSM-5." (p. 387)*

  Hybels, Blazer, Pieper, Landerman, and Steffens (2009)

Older patients with depression may present with somatic complaints for which a medical etiology cannot be found or that are disproportionate to the extent of medical illness. Patients who express somatic symptoms as a manifestation of depression seem to be less willing to mention psychological symptoms to their physician. Certainly, illnesses such as pancreatic carcinoma or hypothyroidism might cause symptoms that mimic depression. Therefore, addressing the patient's psychological distress, while appropriately evaluating the possible diagnoses, is important. Clinical experience suggests too that physicians are less likely to move from recognition to treatment of the illness in older patients than in younger patients. Physicians, like patients and their families, are usually able to find a "reason" for depression in the older person. That said, treatment is often delayed or not pursued at all. Physicians may believe that a medical illness is a contraindication to treatment with antidepressants, but older patients with physical illness seem just as likely to respond to SSRIs as older patients without physical illness. Now, in this book, we are searching for the right admixture of soma and psych treatments for better care.

At late life, several varieties of depression can exist. As intimated earlier, there are varieties of the phenomenology of depression. The brain typology of a serotonin depression (guilt, suicidal ideation), a norepinephrine and dopamine depression (executive function problems, fatigue), and holistic depression (all neurotransmitters showing sleep, agitation, or retardation) still may apply but is not point to point. There are shades of gray. Major, minor, and mixed depression exist at late life. Annoyingly subsyndromal depression (often defined as > 16 on Center for Epidemiologic Studies Depression Scale [CES-D] but full MDD criteria are not met) is also a pervasive problem. All of these states are prevalent; all assert an influence on QoL; and all segue to MDD at some point, if not handled when the symptoms are first noted. These states are highly prevalent and have a propensity to convert to MDD, especially when there is a history of MDD (Chopra et al., 2005). Most patients do not solicit treatment.

Of interest too is that there are no clear biomarkers of depression. This is said despite the fact that (a) there are MRI changes in late-life depression, (b) based on twin studies, at least 16% of the variance for depression is heritable, (c) 5HT2A and 5HT1A receptor binding decreases with an increased incidence of homozygous "short" alleles in the promoter region of the 5-HT transporter, (d) CRF (corticotrophin-releasing factor) hypersecretes (in LLD [late-life depression]), and (5) the Hamilton Depression Rating Scale (HAM-D) factors correlate with distinct brain regions. In addition, there is comorbid weight loss, cardiovascular disease, increased platelet activation, lower T-cell response, poor blastogenic response to mitogens, and high level of cytokine interleukin 6, as well as elevated homocysteine levels. Despite this, depression is generally not measured by biomarkers. This state is best viewed as an epigenetic disease in which nature and nurture dance for dominance.

Depression, then, is often the driving force in the panoply of symptom domains. In fact, anxiety often may lead the pack to a diagnosis, but depression is part of the problem. Depression is comorbid with everything bad. On the one side of the coin, depression can be punishing. William Styron (1989) described depression as "the gray drizzle of horrors." On the other side, depression may be overrated. It is a natural phenomenon and is intended to provoke more internality and self-reflection and self-analysis. It is a common sign and symptom. But its true prevalence may be considerably less than 12%, perhaps closer to 2%. If we mark depression as a true disorder that is debilitating, not episodic and marginal in intensity, it may be a less serious disorder and more a universal annoyance that peaks on occasion to cause some problems.

Medical/Somatic Issues

Older adults have historically used health services at higher rates than anyone and mental health services at substantially low rates. If they do seek help for mental problems, it is in a PCC. We also know that medical care is directly related to mental health. It is estimated that over 70% of medical problems, especially unexplained ones, are attributed to mental health issues (see Chapter 10). Modal problems for older adults include cognitive decline, depressive symptoms, anxiety issues, or unexplained somatic concerns. Patients with depression and significant comorbidities are especially costly to the health care system. Depressed patients with diabetes, for example, have more trouble adhering to their diets and checking blood glucose levels, and they exercise less, smoke more, and die at about twice the rate as those without depression. It is costly not to treat these people, not to develop preventative programs for them, and not to have educative targets around diabetic problems.

The pathways leading to comorbidity of mental and medical disorders are complex or bidirectional. Medical disorders may lead to mental disorders, mental conditions may place a person at risk for medical disorders, and mental and medical disorders may share common risk factors. Comorbidity between medical and mental conditions is the rule rather than the exception. In the 2001–2003 National Comorbidity Survey Replication (NCS-R), a nationally representative epidemiological survey, more than 68% of adults with a mental disorder (diagnosed with a structured clinical interview) reported having at least one general medical disorder, and 29% of those with a medical disorder had a comorbid mental health condition (Kessler et al., 2005). In addition to the high prevalence of these conditions, there is also evidence that having each type of disorder is a risk factor for developing the other.

Worse, medical conditions are most often grouped into "triads" (i.e., common co-occurrences of three diseases together). Psychiatric disorders were among seven of the top 10 most frequently diagnosed comorbidity triads in the most expensive 5% of Medicaid beneficiaries with disabilities. The most common triad was comorbid psychiatric conditions, cardiovascular disease, and central nervous system disorders, which affected 9.5% of all beneficiaries and 24% of the most expensive group of beneficiaries. The 2001–2003 NCS-R found that approximately 25% of American adults meet criteria for at least one diagnosable mental disorder in any given year, and more than half report one or more chronic general medical conditions (Kessler et al., 2005).

When mental and medical conditions co-occur, the combination is associated with elevated symptom burden, functional impairment, decreased length and quality of life, and increased costs. The impact of having comorbid conditions is at least additive but at times may be synergistic, with the cumulative burden greater than the sum of the individual conditions. Comorbid mental and medical conditions are associated with substantial individual and societal costs. Melek and Norris (2008) analyzed the expenditures for comorbid medical conditions and mental disorders using the 2005 Medstat MarketScan national claims database. They looked at the medical expenditures, mental health expenditures, and total expenditures of individuals with one of 10 common chronic conditions with and without comorbid depression or anxiety. They found that the presence of comorbid depression or anxiety significantly increased medical and mental health care expenditures, with over 80% of the increase occurring in medical expenditures.

We note too that other medical/somatic issues affect the QoL for older adults. Two that are prevalent are sleep and pain. Sleep problems become more common with age, affect QoL for individuals and their families, and can increase health care costs. Older people are often prescribed a range of drugs for their health problems (including those for sleep), many of which have side effects. Total sleep duration appears to show a modest improvement after treatment, but this effect declines with time. Pain also is prevalent and asserts an influence over care programs. In fact, the more the person suffers from pain, the more likely he or she will have depression/anxiety, and the more likely each will be resistant to treatment for any psychiatric disorder.

There is no easy summary here. Chances are that, if you are older and have a mental problem, you seek help from a PCC and have attributed your problems to physical symptoms. Depression care invariably means antidepressant medication treatment (40%). You are also treated by PCPs who are accurate in diagnosis from only 30% to 50% (Berardi et al., 2005) of the time. If you are treated, you are most often prescribed medication. In fact, you are also taking several medications and, in general, are adjusting worse. Often you are misdiagnosed as either a false positive or a negative. If older, you are, in part, at fault as you do not resonate to mental problems, especially when they can be attributed to general health concerns. If, as an older adult, you say that your problem is somatic, your PCP misses psychiatric diagnosis (85%) (Wittchen, Kessler, Beesdo, Krause, & Hoyer, 2002). If accurately diagnosed, you are not followed up well or the medications do not prove effective. If you have anxiety, medication use increases with the number of anxiety diagnoses (Kroenke, Spitzer, Williams, Monahan, & Löwe, 2007). We hope to correct this.

Adjustment

The evidence is that adjustment suffers as the above issues percolate. Adjustment problems are always salient but become a big issue if one of the following components is present. First, adjustment suffers just by getting older; at age 80, 60% of adults start having problems with IADL. As noted above, this increases as spousal loss occurs and presence in long-term care facilities (LTC) expands. Second, adjustment is at issue when there are ADL or IADL functional problems. A 75-year-old male with one ADL problem has the roughly the life expectancy of an 85-year-old without one.

Third, cognition and function cohabit; approximately 40% of common variance is shared (Royall et al., 2007). Adjustment has an equal chance of predicting dementia and related problems as do neuropsychological or medical predictions. This is especially the case when IADL are assessed. But, adjustment is often the forgotten component in care, as the focus is on medical and psychiatric/psychological problems. Once one is in a LTC facility, adjustment becomes even more important when morbidity and mortality are at issue.

Fourth, QoL is critical for reasonable living; QoL is adjustment. How the person lives, with whom, with what supports, money, options, and with ability to act as she or he would like become central to well-being. What is involved in happiness is complex, but clearly involves the desire to be ambulatory, to have reasonable resources, to be social, to feel some self-efficacy, and to live where the person desires. Some decades ago Rowe and Kahn (1997) set the bar for successful aging very high. Only about 8% of older adults have this as a designation because most have medical maladies and limits on function. Guided by Rowe and Kahn's conceptualization of successful aging and other attempts to evaluate this phenomenon, successful aging has been defined as having: (a) no major disease; (b) no disability in ADL; (c) no more than one difficulty in seven measures of physical functioning; (d) obtaining a median or better cognitive score for functioning; and (e) being actively engaged (McLaughlin, Connell, Heeringa, Li, & Roberts, 2010). McLaughlin et al. found that only 11.9% met these criteria. Yaffe and colleagues (2007) evaluated determinants of successful cognitive aging in men and women: 30% were maintainers, 53% were decliners, and 16% were major decliners.

Factors that distinguished maintainers from decliners were:

White race

More education/literacy

Working or volunteering

Living with someone

Self-rated health as good to excellent

Consuming more than one alcohol drink daily

Moderate to vigorous exercise

Nonsmoker

Lower BMI (body mass index)

Lack of high blood pressure, diabetes, or stroke

Lacking an ApoE4

Lower levels of C-reactive protein, interleukin-6, fasting glucose, and triglycerides

---

For our purposes, the presence of anxiety, depression, cognition problems, or medical concerns affects adjustment and vice versa. Measuring and targeting common living/adjustment accounts for as much of the variance of change as any of the variables by themselves. In this book, we include adjustment under life issues.

Psychotherapy Works, Even at Late Life

In the main, psychotherapy does work; at least in part. Although most patients do not remit, most will show some response to change. As noted, we start from the position that psychological problems at late life are best dealt with by therapy involving watching and waiting. This means getting commitment; providing direction; targeting early relief; and basing interventions on to-be-determined modules for anxiety, depression, somatization (pain), and cognitive decline. The components of core therapies, like CBT, problem-solving therapy (PST), and interpersonal therapy (IPT), incorporate the best modules for change. This represents a unified approach to treating problems at late life. At base, the common approach involves more than the core psychotherapeutic responses of experiencing the emotion, changing the cognition, and behaviorally acting. Again, the core rules of care expressed by these approaches involving goals, agendas, and structures, as well as techniques, communicate the basics of change. In fact, psychotherapy in the 21st century is a modality in which there is a melding of theories and borrowing of techniques that make pure models of care (e.g., CBT) difficult to find.

The intervention of change for an older adult in turmoil is a beginning. The careful therapist will know that the chances of recurrence are high. The antidotes to this are awareness of the existence of the problem, a focus on relapse, an educational gathering of social resources, a team approach, and a loose monitoring over time. Good science can inform practice and good practice is good policy. That said, there are many variables in the throughput of therapy; the health care provider must act on clinical common sense before best practice can be implemented, or the two might collide.

Both context and outcomes interact and matter. For outcomes, the issue is never just symptom abatement. Rather, therapy should aim at symptom relief *and* improving overall QoL. Residual symptoms portend relapse or a lower QoL. But a careful and caring focus for the long term will assist the therapist in the consideration of both.

Reality constraints on outcome cannot be easily captured by research. These include: the client's readiness to change; acceptability of the treatment and preferences of the client; caregiver acceptance; availability of desired or needed services; probability of third-party-payer approval; tolerance of incongruous recommendations; prior treatment failures or successes; and side effects. Hence, with older adults, the core targets of therapy (depression, anxiety, and somatic issues) must be approached with the additional considerations of these generic background and life markers for adequate outcome coverage.

Although evaluation questions necessarily focus on the reasons why an elder is seeking treatment, such a narrow focus is not helpful for understanding process changes over time or other longer-term and broader concerns. In translating empirically supported treatments (ESTs) to older adults, and in targeting this translation to the most researched psychotherapy, CBT, we must concentrate on more general outcomes (not just diagnosis), as well as specific markers associated with the identified problem. For the treatment of depression, for example, CBT will involve the alteration of cognitions to reduce depressive symptomatology, as well as alterations within the context. With older adults, therapy demands a scientific attitude; a skillful and flexible delivery of services; quantitative monitoring of the client's progress; and an awareness of the personologic, interpersonal, and cultural characteristics of the client as well as QoL themes.

The efficacy of change also resides in the common-factor details that are the context of therapy. Psychotherapy does not work like medicine; nonspecific factors are integral to both, but prepotent for mental health care. This allows the patient to generate change in many ways: spontaneous recovery, self-generated change, placebo effects, resilience, posttraumatic growth, corrective effects of disclosure, and feedback. Always there is a need to take into account the context of practice; evidence-based practice may not be practical. In addition, the therapist effects are at least equal to the treatment effects. Furthermore, at late life, the realities of practice that science cannot address well, such as socioeconomic status (SES), medical comorbidities, and patient attitudes, are prevalent. In general, clinical experience and science do butt heads with later-life issues. At late life, psychotherapy is both an art and a science.

Social Reality/Cost

There is the Jurassic Park problem: Just because you can do something does not mean that you should.

                                                                              Unknown

---

We do not do a good job of health care in this country. We spend twice the amount of other countries and end up in the middle of the pack on just about every outcome marker of health. Only 25% of people with a *DSM* diagnosis actually get treatment; only 10% of people with lifestyle problems (smoking, poor diets) ever seek professional help. Mental health is costly—adding substantial costs to most medical problems. We have already established that unmet mental health needs lead to problems downstream. The pharmaceuticals have not changed this. We need a better model of care.

The issue for providers, health care administrators, and policy makers is to balance good care and cost. This is not easy, as it requires a thoughtful program of preventative self-care and reasoned medical service use based on patient-centered input by the older adult and his or her caregiver/family. In the Institute of Medicine report, *Retooling for an Aging America* (2008), a vision of health in America is laid out. First, the health care needs of the older population will be best served by a patient-centered, preference-sensitive approach. Patient-centeredness includes taking into account the increasing sociodemographic and cultural diversity of older Americans. Second, services will need to be efficient so that wasteful and ineffective care is reduced. Third, interdisciplinary teams will provide comprehensive, seamless care across various delivery sites and be supported by easily accessible health information systems fitted to emerging care needs and delivery modalities. Last, older adults will be active partners in their own care until they no longer have the capacity for competent decision making. Ideally, there will be a partnership between provider and patient that includes: (a) clear information, (b) adoption of healthy lifestyles, (c) informed self-management of chronic conditions, and (d) increased participation in one's own care.

Social reality is also a problem. SES has long been viewed as a strong marker of QoL. Recent studies have illustrated the fact that socioeconomic status and our living environment begin to play an even more significant role in our QoL as we age, particularly with respect to the development of chronic diseases. Freedman, Grafova, Schoeni, and Rogowski (2008) used subject data from the 2002 Health and Retirement Study to postulate that a correlation exists between the characteristics of the neighborhood that an older adult inhabits and his or her late-life morbidity. It was found that women aged 55 and older living in an economically disadvantaged neighborhood predicted the onset of critical heart problems. In addition, Freedman et al. demonstrated that older adults—both men and women—living in more highly segregated, higher-crime areas were at greater risk of developing cancer. SES predicts QoL and general health better than perhaps any other researched factor. Lack of monetary resources, restricted access to quality health care, and environmental stressors add to the deterioration of older adults living in low-income environments. The practice of negative habits such as lack of physical activity, poor diet, and smoking also influences the onset of other chronic disorders such as hypertension and diabetes.

Gender and race should also be examined with regard to the aging process and the use of health care services to promote overall well-being. Income and wealth certainly influence health care resources available to older adults, especially considering the availability and costs of health maintenance organization (HMO) enrollment plans, Medicare, Medicaid, private insurance, and government assistance. Per Cameron and colleagues (2010), women report more health needs and disability in terms of functional limitations and report fewer economic resources in terms of income. Davitt and Kaye (1996) also investigated differences that exist concerning quality of home health care offered to minority groups and other vulnerable populations due to current national health care policies. Gender and racial disparities may exist as older adults seek preventative care, physician visits, hospital admissions, and home health care.

Also we have this: A new Agency for Healthcare Research and Quality (AHRQ)-funded study finds that about one in seven elderly patients (14%) admitted to the hospital for an injury will be readmitted within 30 days. The study examined 2006 data from hospitals in 11 states for admissions with a principal diagnosis of injury using AHRQ's Healthcare Cost and Utilization Project State inpatient databases. The most common reasons for readmission were surgery of the upper or lower extremities, pneumonia, heart failure, septicemia, and urinary tract infection. Three-quarters of injury patients were discharged to nursing homes or home health care. Patients who had severe injuries, received transfusions, experienced a patient-safety indicator event, had an infection, and were discharged to a nursing home or home health care had higher readmission rates. The study's authors suggest that strategies to reduce readmission rates among elderly injury patients should focus on preventing complications and infections during the hospital stay and also address nursing home and home health care (Spector, Mutter, Owens, & Limcangco, 2012).

Caregiving

It has been estimated that 65.7 million Americans served as caregivers in the past year. This is 28% of the population. Nearly one third of American households reported at least one person serving in an unpaid caregiving role. The typical caregiver is a female, 48 years old, taking care of one person on an unpaid basis. But more than one third (34%) report taking care of two or more people. Most are providing care for a relative (86%). On average, caregivers have been on the job for 4.6 years and 31% have been doing this for 5 or more years. The typical person receiving the unpaid care is a female (62%) who is 61 years old and gets about 20.4 hours per week of active care. Burden was rated as medium-high by 51% of respondents, with 35% relying on paid caregiving and 66% on other unpaid caregiving. Stress of caregiving is notable.

Throughout the life span, levels of caregiver burden increase as the physical health and mental capacity of the care recipient deteriorate. Caregivers are often confronted with issues of frailty, cognitive deficits, and behavior problems at the hands of their ailing spouses. Lack of adequate coping skills and a positive support system can lead to caregivers experiencing depressive symptoms, problems with anxiety, and other emotional disorders. In addition, older adult caregivers who expend all of their time and energy on taking care of their loved ones often neglect their own personal health, resulting in a myriad of physical ailments.

The responsibility of caring for a spouse inherently holds an overall increase in burden. Pinquart and Sörensen (2005) ascertained that spouse caregivers report high levels of physical burden, financial burden, and relationship strain between themselves and the care recipient. As a result, physicians, social workers, and mental health professionals who encounter older adults living in a caregiver dyad should extend resources that help improve the overall well-being of the spouse caregiver. Resources should include psychoeducational and support groups for couples living with a particular disorder (i.e., Parkinson disease, Alzheimer's disease, stroke, etc.); skill-training programs focused on behavior management, depression, and anger management; and psychotherapy of the cognitive-behavioral orientation (Gallagher-Thompson & Coon, 2007). The physical and emotional well-being of the caregiver directly impacts those reciprocal aspects of the care recipient; therefore, health care professionals should promote increased self-awareness and self-care for the caregiver.

Not enough emphasis can be placed on how greatly impacted a spouse caregiver may be from exposure to the psychological, physical, and spiritual distress that their care recipient endures in their presence. According to Monin and Schulz (2009), the nature of caregiving exposes caregivers to increased cognitive empathy, prolonged bereavement, and extended observations of physical pain in the care recipients. The emotional toll resulting from witnessing the decline of a spouse can also manifest itself as physiological distress such as fatigue and somatic symptoms. In addition, taking on the caregiver role causes some spouses to experience existential crises of their own regarding their legacy, personal values, and meaning in life.

The Domain Dance

We have advocated for a holistic approach to the assessment and treatment of older adults. This is anything but linear and clean. The older adult is waiting to be parsed apart and validated. The most-assessed targets are cognition and depression. Cognitive compromise associated with late-life depression can present anywhere along a continuum from MCI to a frank dementia. A mood disturbance in an older adult can initially present as a subjective cognitive complaint. Likewise, the existence of depression can exacerbate previously existing cognitive difficulties. In community-dwelling residents, the combination of impaired cognition and depressive symptoms doubles in frequency at 5-year intervals beyond age 70; combined depression and cognitive dysfunction are present in 25% of individuals aged 85 years or older. There is ample evidence that the presence of comorbid cognitive deficits is associated with reduced treatment responsiveness in late-life depression.

This interactive effect applies to the other problem domains of anxiety, somatic/pain/sleep, and adjustment. Most psychosocial interventions for the acute treatment of geriatric major depression focus on "young-old" (average age of 65 to 70 years), cognitively intact, ambulatory older adults who can follow outpatient treatment. Clearly, this is only a subsample of the population who are in need. Additionally, homebound, rural, and low-income older adults may not have the same access to effective interventions for depression as those living in situations more conducive to receiving traditional psychotherapeutic treatment (Kiosses, Arean, Teri, & Alexopoulos, 2010). Furthermore, interventions may not be available or appropriate for ethnically and culturally diverse populations.

We have also noted above that factors such as comorbid illness can serve as a barrier to treatment. Evidence suggests, for example, that depressed older adults with comorbid physical illness and cognitive impairment have a reduced intervention effectiveness (see Chapter 4), a fact that argues for evidence-based psychosocial interventions to help depressed older adults with cognitive impairment and disability. Studies have not indicated significant treatment remission differences between early-onset and late-onset depression, although older adults who had an early-onset depression may be slower to remit (Chapter 4). This is because they have more "other" problems, principally involving cognition, anxiety, and pain/sleep.

What can providers do? We believe that the appropriate core treatment involves nonpharmacological interventions in a careful application of modules. It is not that this form of treatment is so much better than medication or the combination of psychotherapy and medication, but that this form of treatment almost never causes harm and always leads to better results in some cases. As indicated, we believe that the Watch and Wait strategy is most important here. The judicious application of monitoring and waiting for success or failure to be expressed is suggested, so that an observation period is a part of the treatment plan.

The recent studies in primary care regarding depression (e.g., IMPACT) made one important contribution: the idea of a step-care model with a Watch and Wait background. Mistakes are made in the care of mental health problems when decisions are made too quickly, empirical science is suspect, or commitment (of the patient) is not certain. Step care establishes a slow pattern of treatment in which the problem is assessed and monitored, and problem-solving interventions are slowly but deliberatively introduced. Problems confess themselves. Recall that the social reality of the patient is of equal concern to the psychiatric problems and requires intervention. Frequently, the monitoring of patients' symptoms and the reconsideration of treatments may produce as much benefit for patients as a medication or psychotherapy, and may fit better with the patient's desires.

CONCLUSION

Psychological problems in late life are best dealt with by addressing several targets noted here. This overview of problems warrants a Watch and Wait strategy. Eventually, the therapeutic response can be based on modular interventions. The modal problems at late life—anxiety, depression, somatization (pain), and cognitive decline, as well as adjustment—are interactive. Dealing with these issues requires much of the health care provider. It is fortunate that emotional disorders have a similar underlying structure and that the components of CBT, including PST and IPT, have modules that can be effective in care.

Something more than standard care is required. In a review of long-term care and the value of psychiatric medication, Reichman and Conn (2010) noted the evidence in support of various models of psychogeriatric services in nursing homes reported on nine controlled trials and concluded that liaison-style services that employed educational approaches, treatment guidelines, and ongoing involvement of mental health staff are more effective than a purely case-based consultation model. This latter model almost exclusively involved medication.

- The narrow emphasis of [traditional psychiatric care] is not serving the nursing home population adequately. We continue to rely nearly exclusively on medication management in our clinical nursing home practices, even though our confidence in the efficacy and safety of the historically most treasured psychotropic agents has been seriously eroded…. We must acknowledge that the newer generation medication therapies have not delivered substantial enough gains over their predecessors.
- What are the specific contributors to the display of mental illness in the nursing home? In this milieu, they are the physical environment, the processes of care, and the behavior of people (care providers and other residents).
- [I]t is time to shed our overreliance on biological determinants and the disease models of mental illness. It is time for a reappraisal.

Reichman and Conn (2010, pp. 1050–1052)

We agree and believe that these statements apply to the overall care of older adults.

CHAPTER 2

Model of Care

Treatment of older adults accounts for less than 10% of the total mental health costs, which have been flat for over a decade. When dealing with older adults, we are often doing some application of translational research, because few psychotherapy interventions have been designed expressly for older adults. The translational component involves focusing on the time span of the problem, the nature and scope of the hypothesis, dose adjustments, and patient population characteristics. Early on in therapy with older individuals, treatment is almost always titrated and adjusted. Adjustments include a time frame that is malleable, hypotheses that are narrow in scope, small doses of intervention, close monitoring of coping/ potential, and choices of narrow treatment targets. In later phases of treatment, there is a requisite alteration in goals, which are simplified for reality's sake. However, as this process has unfolded over the years, efforts to document the applicability of all-purpose psychotherapy research data appear to show that these data are relevant to older adults, if the psychotherapy is practiced in an aging-informed manner (Hinrichsen, 2008).

To complicate matters, we are learning that aging itself is not a causal variable (Spiro & Sherif, 2011). Rather, it is a marker on a temporal axis along which various exposures and disease processes operate. Aging is thus not a meaningful explanation for why one might experience cognitive decline or impairment. Health and biological aging are better markers or predictors. Dementia in this context is an end stage of a process of a "brain at risk," a poor accumulation of health, behaviors, and genetics. Our interest is in what is causing the person to age or, in the case of psychological problems, what are the relevant mediators and/or moderators in play for a particular person. When looked at this way, age matters in only a limited sense.

To benefit depressed elderly patients in the community, personalization of care must employ comprehensive care algorithms targeting both modifiable predictors of poor outcomes and organizational barriers to care. Accordingly, the model of geriatric depression needs to integrate the current biological concepts of depression with patients' unique reactions to adverse experiences and with their unmet social and health care needs. The care algorithms based on this model should:

1. Target clinical/biological predictors of adverse outcomes of depression;
2. Address unmet needs through linkage to appropriate social services;
3. Enhance the competencies of elderly persons so that they make use of their resources; and
4. Attend to patient psychoeducation needs.

Alexopoulos (2008)

There are, of course, other problems here, as older adults have baggage: somatic and health baggage. There are no or few formal studies on somatization in older adults. But this issue is considerable: How does one integrate the care of older adults with complex somatic presentations? To label as "psychiatric" a patient who has undefined symptoms, or to see patients as "psychogenic" are both unhelpful. The typical process regarding the formation of a somatic problem and its transformation to a medical symptom is interesting. The experience of the somatic symptom is followed by a pathological or psychological attribution that leads to the formation of a symptom. At some point, mediators influence this translation. These mediators can be anything from reduced cognition to background variables. In fact, a somatic attribution style seems to be a stable phenomenon ("I got dizzy all of a sudden because I was under lots of stress [psychological] or there must be something wrong with my heart [somatic]"). We need to have a way to encapsulate this issue into holistic care, into biopsychosocial care.

The best way to treat people is to create a plan of care that supports the kind of life they want to live, not the kind of disease treatment we think best for them.

Brad Stuart, MD, Chief Medical Officer, Sutter Care at Home

In this chapter, we outline the Watch and Wait model, which we believe represents an improvement in psychosocial care. We explain its strengths and outline its components. We address the necessity of case formulation and the five factors that best represent this. We then articulate the ingredients of the Watch and Wait model and what is involved in applying them. At the end, we provide perspective for older adults and discuss optimal aging. A sense about the big picture of life for older adults is then provided.

MODEL

The reality and the translation of controlled efficacy data for older adults are lacking: One cannot find adequate data for many common psychiatric problems related to older adults. The amount of practical and immediately translatable data is quite small. The tension between remaining true to the empirically supported data and dealing with the realities of the older patient is palpable. A reasonable default axiom is to try techniques that are empirically supported and make changes when and as needed. Another reasonable default axiom is to stand on the skill of the therapist: This part of the therapy equation always trumps the efficacy of the technique.

We espouse a newer model of psychotherapy for older adults. The biopsychosocial model has more than 40 years of history under its belt. It nicely espouses the idea that the person of the patient is complex but understandable. For care to be effective, there is a need for a comprehensive approach. The variables for clarity include the biological, the psychological, and the social. This means that care is all-encompassing and alterable. In a sense, we need to broaden our scope to get a reasonable understanding of the person and a reasonable problem list for interventions. Each case is unique, and there are many idiosyncratic features and complexities. We believe, however, that five variables are sufficient for provision of good care. Again, these variables are selected to represent domains of care that address necessary life problems so that later life can be better handled or altered. A response to the panorama of the five variables leads to change and better quality of life.

There are two core features of the model. First, older adults have a profile of problems. The five components include depression, anxiety, cognition, medical/somatic status, and practical life issues. They apply to both outpatients and inpatients. In Figure 2.1, Patient A has more depression and somatization; Patient B has more anxiety and cognition problems; Patient C has many problems but fewer life adjustment issues; Patient D has cognition and life issues; and Patient E has somatic issues and life issues. Even though

FIGURE 2.1 Model for Therapies for Older Adults

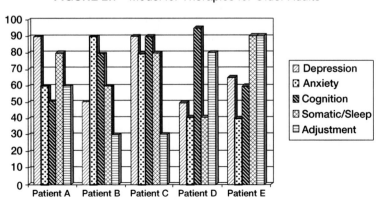

the target issues for each of these patients differ, all components are relevant all the time.

Given the complexity of patients, the normal application of empirically supported treatments (ESTs), the nuances of the research, and use of predictor variables in care, though helpful, are not robust enough to warrant allegiance beyond just some respect. The reality constraints of living into later life make outcomes worse for older adults; these constraints include the client's readiness to change, acceptability of the treatment and preferences of the patient, caregiver acceptance, availability of desired or needed services, tolerance of incongruous recommendations, prior treatment failures or successes, side effects, and so forth. In a sense, the three core components of therapy—research, clinical experience, and client characteristics—still apply but take on different meanings at late life.

Second, the Watch and Wait strategy also seems most reasonable. The belief is that a careful and slow process of care—assessment, psychoeducation, watching and waiting, building trust, weighing options, using teams, and then using modules—is most appropriate. The therapist does not pick one best treatment at the outset. Rather, the therapist recognizes how individuals present with and experience depression or other problems, carefully selects treatment options, and applies objective measures to treatment response. Changes are made with careful deliberation where monitoring and an exposé of the issues dictate change. After all, one does not get better if one does not experience the intervention. We also know that in the complex treatment of older adults, the choice of treatment plan is critical and necessary for change.

This is, in effect, a step-care approach. A step-care approach to treatment delivery systems represents a reasonable attempt to maximize efficiency of resource allocation of ESTs. This is a kind of pyramid. Less intensive treatments are used to treat greater numbers of patients at the bottom of the pyramid, whereas fewer patients are treated with the progressively more intense treatments at the top of the pyramid. The entry level is simple, cost-efficient, and least intrusive. Succeeding levels become more intrusive and expensive. The "stepped-up" care is progressive and programmatic. This stepped-up care can mean a change to more treatment or addition of another mode of care.

This is best done with several of the following "axioms" (see list on p. 35). Related to a case-based profile, we start the process with a watch and wait strategy. This involves a case formulation, careful monitoring, considerable psychoeducation, and a deliberate process of determining the best intervention. Problems actually confess themselves best over time. We know that ESTs are mildly efficacious, but generally there is a lack of clinically significant differences between treatment and placebo that applies to mildly depressed and anxious patients. So, this careful waiting process, with education and support as well as a focus on the direction of care, is important. The frequent monitoring of patients' symptoms and the frequent reconsideration of treatments may produce as much benefit for patients as medication or psychotherapy and may fit better with the patient's desires. A health care team, too, needs to be in place; one in which there is genuine dialogue and shared responsibility, not the tried but often routine physician-led grouping of professionals.

Make no mistake: The patient needs to feel some relief, but the need to have this relief grounded in a context is paramount. Depression needs perspective, as it tends to be recurrent and calls for a response that reflects this. The older adult is also given to other maladies that can be persuasive. These contribute to the construction of a reality that can be oppressive. What we need is for the patient to be entered into a "Truman Show" where everything can go his or her way for a certain period before reality can be reasserted. This is the start of the "corrective emotional experience." Again, this is done by the second or third session in which the patient and the therapist are in alliance. This is connected inseparably to outcomes. Perhaps in the end, good therapy is about real perspective taking and remaining engaged. This is very different from the "treatment ritual" of medication administration in which the patient is absolved of responsibility and care often unfolds without a relationship.

This applies also to the combined use of medication and psychotherapy. There is good reason to believe that combined therapy will lead to a more lasting recovery, but this choice is complex can take many forms. Regardless, a watch and wait approach is recommended.

Treatment Axioms

Watch and Wait—Step-Care Process

- Establishing rapport—an alliance—is critical
- Psychoeducation
- Validate position and concerns (as if the position is the correct one, one that is psychologically appropriate and the choice is the only one that could be made).
- Establish some relief or hope of relief.
- Be believable/likeable as a therapist: placebo rocks!!!!
- Monitor outcome targets for many problems, both practical and psychological.
- DO NOT pick one best treatment at the outset. Rather, recognize how patients present with and experience depression, apply and reapply objective measures of treatment response, and make changes until the patient improves.
- Track outcomes. Use these as lab values. Do not accept "Fine" as an outcome or marker of depression. If you are not measuring something, it has not occurred. Patients get better who just receive monitoring.
- Use therapy modules after initial watching and waiting.
- Establish a steady state where there is some degree of relief over time. Wait for a steady state when symptoms remain as a response.
- Change the treatment to suit the person.
- Use brain as a metaphor and for actual change markers.
- Feedback on patient change also works for the therapist.
- Use a team: patient, family, provider, mental health consultant, care manager.
- Problems recur and recur . . .
- Therapy is a long-term commitment; you are in it for the long haul.

Importantly, what is done at the starting gate is crucial. Problems ensue because the treatment was the wrong type, not well set up, and in many cases programmatic. The list below notes problems related to such unreflective care. In general, the problems for most older adults are not at the moderate or severe level. They are mostly mild. This includes extended problems with dementia issues. Thus, the interventions generally need to be tailored to one who has mild problems, who has multiple problems, and who is suspect about the process. One therapeutic ideal, then, is the application of a form of reasonable, deliberative "psycho" therapy that is closely monitored.

Watch and Wait → Reflect and Prepare

FIVE FAILURE POINTS:
1. Deciding too quickly to initiate care
2. Underdosing
3. Inadequate trial duration (6 weeks is necessary)
4. Insufficient frequency of follow-up
5. Lack of monitoring

We start from the position that success in treatment with older adults is attainable but requires changes in the practice, scope, and longevity of the care. Psychological problems at late life are best dealt with by a therapeutic response based on modular interventions. These are critical and they are done across time. If, as indicated earlier, the modal problems at late life—anxiety, depression, somatization (pain and sleep as well as good health management), and cognitive decline—are intertwined, each can differently influence quality of life, as each can be an equal-opportunity offender to any older person.

In this regard, we believe that emotional disorders have an approximately similar underlying structure. The form of the symptoms develops as a function of learning and experiences. Fortunately, the components of cognitive behavioral therapy (CBT), including problem-solving therapy (PST) and interpersonal therapy (IPT), represent modules that are similar and also have a modicum of efficacy. There is, therefore, a soft consensus on a unified approach to treating problems at late life.

But of course there is more. We need to assure that social reality is in place (home, no excessive alcohol, social care, etc.) for any particular elder. This is often a big issue. We need to titrate our own dosage. Paradoxically, many patients do not seek change in treatment if they are faltering. As noted earlier, only about 10% of older adults do actually seek treatment for depression. For severe mental illness, this number is worse. The gateway is primary care, and the gatekeeper is the primary care doctor. In the context of real change, efficacy helps, but it is not the only factor. We should always consider nonpharmacological treatment first. Efficacious treatment always involves some aspect of nonpharmaceutical therapy. As remission rates are poor, improvement will be best when a long-term focus is in play. Treatments need to be altered if patients do not remit in a reasonable period of time. With that being said, even partial changes in context and a vision to allow the older adult to appreciate small changes and continue on the same path are curative.

Medication problems: the optimal duration of acute psychopharmocology at late life is unknown; type and timing of switches of therapies is unclear; the best augmentation strategies of any treatment remains a mystery; predictors of treatment response are not settled; indications for and duration of maintenance therapies are also in doubt; and what constitutes the best mediators and moderators of therapy are cloudy.

Reynolds et al. (2006)

Remember that the differences among the core depression problems (Major Depressive Disorder [MDD], mixed depression and anxiety, subsyndromal depression) are subtle and of less importance than most clinicians think. Treatment for any of them involves respect, monitoring, and a clinical watch. Risk factors account for only a small portion of the variance in the cause and persistence of depression in older adults, and attempting to uncover exactly why someone has become depressed has little advantage for clinicians. In fact, dementia changes little in the way of care, if the therapist can allow himself or herself to deal with the whole person and psychiatric/real/medical issues as if dementia is only a part of the entire picture. The clinician is then dealing with a problem list in the same way he or she would if no degenerative disease were present, with the person(ality) dictating the process of the therapy. When there is a depression or anxiety, there is also a probable brain disorder, and behavior and cognition are the last to change. More in the way of an intervention is required. Recall too that patients at late life come with baggage, the accumulations of the life already lived.

Additional Watch and Wait Musings

Assuring that social reality is in place (home, no alcohol, social care, etc.)

1. Nonpharmaceutical treatment should be considered first. Period. It is true that these forms of Rx are not so much better than medications or the combo, BUT they are the least noxious and always some form of treatment involves nonpharmaceutical treatments.
2. If meds are used, assure that the dosage is appropriate. Many patients receive inappropriate doses because a slow process of deliberation and titration is not in place.
3. Compliance is an issue. More than 30% of older adults do not comply and this is associated with poorer outcomes. Most patients do not seek a change in Rx if they are faltering.

4. Make sure a mental health professional is involved at some point.
5. A lack of clinically significant differences between treatment and placebo applies to mildly depressed patients. As a result, there may be many options.
6. Monitoring of patients' symptoms and the frequent reconsideration of treatments may produce as much benefit for patients as a medication or psychotherapy and may fit better with the patient's desires. Track outcomes of various sorts. Use these as you would lab values. If you are not measuring something, it has not occurred. Patients get better who just receive monitoring.
7. Do not accept "fine" as an outcome or marker of depression.
8. Remission rates are only about 20%. Change treatments if patients do not remit for 6 to 8 weeks. Tinkering is the key.
9. Depression may impact issues downstream. That is, the use of other interventions/meds later in the course of treatment may be discussed.

CASE FORMULATION AND THE FIVE DOMAINS OF TREATMENT

Truth needs to be confronted with the question: "Can it be lived?"

Nietzsche

Case formulation is critical. At later life, any symptom can be generated by multiple permutations of multiple causal factors amid multiple causal paths. The case manager formulates cases based on confirming and disconfirming data to determine whether selected empirically supported causal variables (e.g., cognitive distortions, medically related problems, poor self-control, ineffective problem solving, low rate of positive reinforcement) are relevant, operative, and meaningful to this particular patient. Of course there can be different ways to implement a given clinical technique. Cognitive restructuring, for example, can be tested by decreasing self-defeating thinking, using behavioral experiments to test the validity of a belief, bibliotherapy, modeling, mild refutation, didactic explanations, homework assignments, visualization, and use of caregivers, to name a few.

The case formulation can be rather stock. The model provided by Barlow is most helpful: The patient is assessed, monitored, and followed over time. Nomothetic treatment is identified and applied. Problems are noted and, when prophecy fails, the person-based characteristics are entered. Should change not be seen, then the therapy is altered, perhaps in the service of a functional analysis.

Psychotherapy itself has several new gifts. One of these is an understanding of the brain. A re-regulation of neuronal networks parallels symptomatic changes in psychotherapy. In fact, changes as a result of CBT and IPT at least cause commensurate changes in the brain, as is the case with medications. The therapist can inform the patient that he or she is not at fault, that his or her brain has been co-opted, and that change will occur as the therapist assists the patient in the differential registration and rerouting of CBT properties and processes; the amygdala, for example, has usurped the brain's evaluative skills and needs to be quieted.

Another is that psychological problems at late life are best dealt with by modular interventions. This is so because the modal problems at late life—anxiety, depression, somatization (pain), and cognitive decline—interact such that emotional disorders have a similar underlying structure. The components of CBT, including PST and IPT, represent modules that allow for an intermeshing of their components. The search is for the right mix of modules for change. This mixture will change with each person.

General Treatment Ideas for Older Adults

- Depressed/anxious patients do not get adequate Rx
- Treatment works BUT … mediators reign
- Treatment in general is less effective than in younger groups
- Pretreatment interventions → role induction, vicarious therapy pretraining, experiential pretraining (for example, TIPS [Treatment Initiation Program] for meds)
- Diabetes → needs of the patient and patient role
- Motivational interviewing works
- Older patient may be different from other patients of other ages
- Older adults want a "say" in prescription but want doctor to be the authority. Patient decision-making models work. Patient values, shared decision making, lifestyles, mutually agreed-on goals assist in change (Heisler et al., 2009).
- Cognition: MMSE (Mini Mental State Examination) of 18 is best for a cognitive focus

---

There are others and we address those here. From a larger perspective, however, there is a soft consensus on a unified approach to treating problems at late life. At base, this involves core psychotherapeutic responses of experiencing the emotion, changing the cognition, and behaviorally acting. We are asking for something more. Older adults demand more: Medication and psychotherapy have limits. The nature of change is grounded in the ESTs but also equally in the practical concerns of the person, both medical and psychosocial. For medications, we know that there is little relationship between dosage and plasma levels of an antidepressant and outcome; for psychotherapy, there is even less. Successful doctors who have plans and who implement a watch and wait attitude get better results. This is true regardless of whether treatment is with selective serotonin reuptake inhibitors (SSRIs)/serotonin–norepinephrine reuptake inhibitors (SNRIs)/tricyclic antidepressants (TCAs)/anxiolitics/placebo/psychotherapy or whatever. The key is a careful therapist connection and accepting therapist belief system. The whole here (Watch and Wait, open therapist, selected modules) is greater than the sum of its parts.

Both context and outcomes do, of course, matter. With older adults both are complex. "Truth" is elusive where best-practice psychotherapy is at issue.

For outcomes, the issue is never just symptom abatement. Rather, therapy should aim at both symptom relief *and* improvement of the patient's overall quality of life (QoL). Moreover, although evaluation questions necessarily focus on the reasons why an elder is seeking treatment, such a narrow focus is only helpful for limited targets; for understanding process changes over time or other longer-term and broader concerns, more is demanded. In translating ESTs to older adults, and in targeting this translation to the most researched psychotherapy, CBT, we must concentrate on more general outcomes (not just diagnosis), as well as specific markers associated with the identified problem. With older adults, effective therapy also demands a scientific attitude; a skillful and flexible delivery of services; quantitative monitoring of the client's progress; and an awareness of the personal, interpersonal, and cultural characteristics of the client as well as QoL themes.

We present a case of a man with problems. We present these data prior to the Watch and Wait model because we want to be assured that we have adequate data to identify the five factors.

Case: Mr. C

BACKGROUND: Mr. C is a 79-year-old male who is a resident of a middle-sized southeastern town. He lives by himself and over the past few years has begun to experience problems with feeling alone and getting nervous. He is, however, social and has friends. He also notes that his thinking is now making him feel worse. That said, he believed that his memory was about the same as always. This was on the heels of problems over the past decade that involved heart problems with replacement of a pacemaker, as well as back pain. He is also on seven medications for heart, blood pressure (BP), cholesterol, and sleep.

He was adopted by older parents who raised him in a very positive fashion. He graduated from high school and went to a "lab school" at a Veterans Administration center. He worked at this job all his life and retired 9 years ago. He was married at age 20, and remained in this union for 48 years. He has two children who live in other states but he has an active social group. He has been a widower for 11 years. He lives on a pension and on Social Security. He has no psychiatric history but has had surgeries—knee surgery and back surgery. He is currently not in pain, but pain can be a problem. He indicates that sleep has been a problem but now he takes medications for this. He also indicates that he can do all of the activities of daily living (ADL) and instrumental activities of daily living (IADL), and, day to day, he does light housework, puzzles, and paints, and is residing in his home.

TEST RESULTS: Cognitive scores were largely normal. He had 29/30 on MoCA, 30/30 on MMSE, and had a Repeatable Battery for the Assessment of Neuropsychological Score (RBANS) Index of 98. Memory was especially good. These were all normal and suggested no further treatment in this area.

On the MINI (Mini-International Neuropsychiatric Interview) he scored positive for MDD and subclinical for anxiety (GAD [Generalized Anxiety Disorder]). He also has had a few panic attacks. Emotional self-report scales indicated depression and some anxiety. He rated as depressed (BDI [Beck Depression Inventory] = 30; GDS-SF [Geriatric Depression Scale-Short Form] = 8) and anxious on the GAD-9 (11) but not the SAST (Short Anxiety Screening Test) (17). He is also motivated for treatment. There was little pain and sleep was acceptable with meds. There were no other psychiatric symptoms.

His MBMD (Millon Behavioral Medicine Diagnostic) indicated that he has a cooperative, dejected, and inhibited personality profile. This pattern suggests that he prefers to be more detached, is depressive in outlook, and seems to be open to suggestions and has no issues with compliance. He is also inactive and has problems with eating.

Mr. C's profile indicates that depression and anxiety are prepotent and require initial responses. He is also taking several meds, lives alone, relates excessive eating, and indicates little activity. A problem list focusing on depression and fear-based issues as well as activity and some minor adjustment issues is in order.

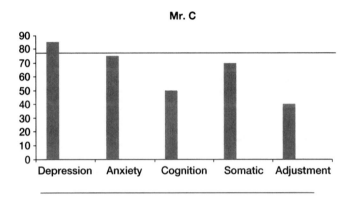

WATCH AND WAIT INGREDIENTS

The Watch and Wait model needs clarification. It is the most important part of the therapy. The first few sessions are critical and set the stage for ensuing interventions. The following elements portray necessary features of this part of the therapy, which lasts for the first two to three sessions. Validation, listening, planning, checking out, monitoring, educating, accepting, directing, pacing, leading, and being humble are necessary features.

1. Validate the problem: "What you are doing is okay, even normal, if one sees things from your perspective. If I think as you do and have the issues you have, I would react the same. Now let's see if we can make some changes."
2. Psychoeducation: "This is what seems to be going on. Again, it is common and we can make a difference. Depression is…"
3. Get on the same page: Let patients know about the Watch and Wait model. Small changes are important; being in the present is critical; homework and monitoring are necessary.
4. Offer direction and leadership empathically: "I can help. You have been suffering too long."
5. Monitor: This is essential to change and to the particulars of the intervention. "Let's see how your week is so we can plan to monitor."
6. Change emotional climate: Listen and be empathic, allow time to vent, provide psychoeducation, again and again.

7. Use brain pathology as metaphor: This allows for a shared vulnerability and understanding of what can be addressed from a more medical/physical perspective.
8. Link problems to achievable reality: "This is where we are going and what we can do."
9. Make haste slowly: "We need a little time to position ourselves for the best chance for change. So, we will take 2 to 3 weeks and see about our options and make plans for best care. This is a very active period and you will be in the most active stage of treatment, the planning stages. Most treatment fails because this treatment part is missing and you are thrown into an intervention too quickly."
10. Provide a plan: "Here are the steps for change." This is based on the case-based model that has been formulated.

The implication is that patience is a virtue and validation is engaging and soothing. Perhaps the lesson from Dr. House applies. In one of the episodes of *House*, the irritable doctor, who is always correct but rarely empathetic, is responding to his psychiatrist after a frustrating session. It goes something like this:

> *House:* Oh, you're just a fake.
> *Psychiatrist:* What!
> *House:* You just help those that want to be helped?

This no doubt was both obvious and irritating to House, as he is outcome-centered and, even though a strategist, very impatient. House never figured out that behavior problems involve the art and science of human patience and validation. Data on human behavior, what is researched and "treated," do not follow a linear progression from point A to point B. Most of human behavior is better understood as being nonlinear and dynamic, or unstable and periodic. We all know that, even within linear statistics, the misapplication of a statistical method can lead to very mistaken conclusions, even if the findings are replicable.

In the model, efforts at human change, especially with older adults, are best done with an activation of the biopsychosocial model. In therapy, these efforts involve the human aspects of psychotherapy and change. They involve a necessary grounding to make the modules viable. The idea is not to force treatment, but rather to apply workable talk components that allow for the better acceptance of care.

Given the model outlined previously, we depend on the value of communication. First, we note that communication between older adults and health care professionals is important. It is generally hindered by age-specific problems (e.g., impaired hearing/vision, slower processing of data) or by psychological adjustments to aging (e.g., loss of identity, less influence over one's life, retirement). Unclear communication can disrupt the entire health care encounter. Breakdowns of communication have been cited as contributors to health care disparities and other counterproductive variations in rates of health care use by all patients, not just older adults.

Basic communication assists older adults in psychotherapy. The suggestions below encompass basic interaction and communication with an older adult who needs help. Although some are trite, all apply and can be helpful in the context of treatment. Communication is key in therapy, as it is in most life areas. For the therapist, how he or she does anything is how he or she does everything. Communication is the bedrock of this process.

---

1. Recognize the tendency to stereotype older adults, and then assess.
2. Avoid speech that might be stereotyping (elder speak).
3. Monitor and control nonverbal behavior (maintain eye contact).
4. Minimize background noise.
5. Face older adults when you speak to them.
6. Pay close attention to complex sentence structure (long and complex sentences challenge memory).
7. Use visual aids such as pictures or diagrams.
8. Ask open-ended questions and then listen.
9. Express understanding and compassion to help older adults manage fear and uncertainty.
10. Ask questions about living situations and social contacts.
11. Include the older person in the conversation when a companion is in the room.
12. Customize care by seeking information about cultural beliefs and values.
13. Engage in shared decision making (be factual about pros and cons).
14. Strike a balance between respecting the patient's autonomy and stimulating their active participation in health care.
15. Avoid ageist assumptions when providing information and recommendations about preventive care.
16. Providing information is important, but how this is done is more so (simplify).
17. Use direct, concrete, actionable language when talking to older adults.
18. Verify listener comprehension during a conversation (teach back).
19. Set specific goals for listener comprehension (assure the mastery of data).
20. Incorporate both technical knowledge and emotional appeal when discussing treatment regimens with older adults.
21. To provide quality health care, focus on enhancing patient satisfaction.
22. Use humor.
23. Help savvy older adults with chronic diseases find reputable referrals.
24. If computers are used, consider switching to models that facilitate collaborative use.
25. Maintain a positive communication tone when speaking about dementia.
26. Avoid speaking slowly with dementia patients.
27. Pose different types of questions to dementia patients according to conversational goals.
28. When conversing with dementia patients, use simple right-branching sentences.
29. In dementia, use verbatim repetition or paraphrases.

Gerontological Society of America (2012)

There is more to enhance the Yin and Yang of care from the Watch and Wait perspective. Caring communication and, again, validation set the stage for the modules that follow. In later chapters, we address many of these background factors as well as the modules.

Background Factors in the Watch and Wait Model

- Motivational interviewing
- Psychoeducation
- Monitoring
- Emotional awareness highlighting
- Cognitive appraisal possibilities
- Emotional avoidance as problem
- Emotion-driven behaviors as natural
- Awareness of physical sensations
- Interoceptive and situation-based exposures
- Relapse prevention

Let's return to our case. The Watch and Wait model worked well. Mr. C was able to handle issues of better socialization and depression-based living and thinking. He did well. Mr. C seemed to especially benefit from the deliberative psychoeducation and waiting for the intervention to unfold. The therapist was careful to apply the checklist for the Watch and Wait model.

Mr. C—WATCH AND WAIT:
PROFILE: He is responding well cognitively but has depression and anxiety, as well as some somatic issues. He is living by himself but does reasonably well. His psychiatric problems with depression and anxiety are longstanding. He is inactive and can be depressionogenic in his outlook.

He was assessed and given this feedback. A problem list was formulated involving core issues and a priority of goals. We interacted with his primary care physician as well as his pastor, who felt he could help. Mr. C was to identify what he enjoyed and how he could better structure his day. He was to consider exercise, and a target for a reduction in meds over time. He had negative thinking and a plan was suggested that this could be a target going forward (cognitive therapy). He was also challenged to see the current perspective as a problem in his life.

Watch and Wait Category	Check
Validate Problem	×
Psychoeducation of Model	×
Assessment	×
Monitoring	×
Case Formulation	×
Check Alliance	×

Sessions 4 to 12:
All of the above targets were addressed and unfolded well. (These are core features of the Watch and Wait model, which have been checked by the treating clinician, and will be discussed further in the next chapter.) He became more active, exercised, and was able to reduce some medications. His depression scores lowered but remained at mild for many weeks until the DTR (dysfunctional thought record) and cognitive challenges were entered. Issues also involved more and more behavioral activation, continued mood ratings, as well as self-rewards. In time, relapse issues were discussed and he is seen every 3 months.

PERSPECTIVE

There is a bigger picture here. Recall that older patients have "psychosomatic" illnesses that are embellished by and presented in concert with real problems. The two can easily be mixed. Panic disorder, IBS (irritable bowel syndrome), and noncardiac chest pain (NCCP), for example, account for a substantial proportion of referrals as well as increased use of urgent care or emergency care services. Common presenting symptoms in primary care, where rule-outs can be quite expensive, can take up much time and attention and persist without resolution or progress for a very long while if the psychological aspects are unrecognized or ignored. The key is to make clinical practice an acceptable mode of providing psychological treatment to patients. We need a paradigm shift in which unexplained symptoms are reexamined around the notion of functional disturbance of the nervous system and treatments currently considered psychiatric are integrated into general medical care.

In 2009, the White House Counsel on Aging advocated for several positions. They noted that health reform must include psychological services as part of primary care. The importance of an integrated health care system that fully cares for mind and body was noted. Mental health and substance abuse need to be treated like other disorders. They also measurably add to costs. The interest for the whole person was advocated. In fact, the argument held that psychological services need to be viewed as treatment options for conditions beyond mental disorders. Chronic illnesses can be prevented or better managed through lifestyle and behavior changes. The presence of a mental health provider in primary care settings would assist key problems of holistic care: difficulty in making lifestyle changes, lack of motivation, and lack of treatment compliance. Mental health is, therefore, not separate from behavioral health and changing behavior is about prevention.

So, we should accept that older adults are best treated with a mind–body connection. With older persons, though, there are still other problems. A few years ago Blazer (2003) posited a dilemma: What allows us to understand how an 85-year-old man with an arthritic arm, declining energy, and loneliness is really doing, when asked the question, "How are you feeling today?" He says "Fine." He actually may be living a full and meaningful life in spite of pain, fatigue, and isolation. Yet if he parrots how most of us respond in 21st-century America, he is likely to say, "Great, just great!" Feeling great has almost become the expected response to inquiries about how we are feeling or doing. In fact, most older adults do feel good about life, but not "great." Similarly, when someone states that he or she would not change anything in his or her life, this could be construed as a positive and good perspective on life, or as a lack of ego complexity, denial, or lack of sophistication (Loevinger & Blasi, 1976). Regardless, an understanding of "what is the good?" is not an easy one.

Perhaps this dilemma highlights the difficulty inherent in the nuanced perspective provided by the constructs of well-being and what matters in life. These are value-laden constructs at late life. The meaning and the very quality of "happiness" can change in a person and over time (Hicks & King, 2007); the health care community struggles with what the "good life" is. Happiness or just normal adjustment in an individual who is high in ego development differs qualitatively from that of one whose ego development is low. Such happiness may be based on a realistic perception of one's life, and, as such, may be more resilient in the face of life's difficulties. Happiness in such instances is bittersweet, involving the recognition of loss and the fragility of human intention. It is also problematic to find accurate representations of well-being in aging.

Psychotherapy outcomes, then, need to be multimodal and comprehensive, at both the broad and specific levels. Inclusiveness is the order of the day in consideration of the goals of therapy. There needs to be an outcome target for each problem, practical and psychological but also global enough to translate into better QoL. Different outcomes provide different information, even in long-term care facilities where residents with diabetes, for example, should have different end points from those with physical disabilities and depression (Degenholtz, Rosen, Castle, Mittal, & Liu, 2008). We know that the basic psychometrics of any assessment scale are not just an integral feature of the measurement instrument; rather, they are a product of the context and population in which the psychometrics were produced. Thinking narrowly works for targets in therapy but not for life.

Successful Aging

We are getting older and struggle with the best formulation of our constructs to make this understandable and not problematic. Aging is a highly variable process: Individual differences generally outweigh chronological differences. Life expectancy (the average number of years lived by a group of people born in the same year), along with a growing burden of chronic diseases, keeps rising. Aging itself is characterized by the decline of anatomical integrity and function across multiple organ systems and a related ability to respond to stress. This decline is associated with increasing pathology, disease, and a progressively higher risk of death. Both genetics and environment are responsible for this (resulting in aging phenotype). Aging is thus a part of a modulation of gene–environment interaction. Biologically, old age is associated with progressive impairment of mitochondrial function, increased oxidative stress, and immune activation. Psychologically, old age is associated with the increased propensity to understand and view things in less than optimal ways. But, as we intimated earlier, aging may not be the most salient causal variable in explaining outcomes. What the person can do and how it is done are more important.

Theories are always instructive. Aging is an old discipline but a young science. What started as theories that view aging problems as a response to loss and deficit with disengagement and inactivity quickly segued some short decades ago to issues of competence based on the ecology (Lawton & Nahemow, 1973), a person–environment fit (related to social exchange and age stratification; Kahana, 1982), or life span ideas based on differentiating components of maturity as a result of aging (see Hyer & Intrieri, 2006). Older people use emotions (Carstensen & Turk-Charles, 1994) and intelligence (see Hyer & Intrieri, 2006) in different ways, for example. In general, as Baltes and Carstensen (1996) argued, older people have problems but accommodate well in most circumstances.

Successful aging does exist. Rowe and Kahn (1998), a decade plus ago, characterized successful aging as involving freedom from disability along with high cognitive, social, and physical functioning. The ways an older adult responds to aging problems or avoids morbidity are also markers of successful aging. Depp and Jeste (2006) looked at 29 definitions of successful aging and noted that virtually all identified the absence of physical disability and reduced functioning. Most definitions included being among the young-old and not smoking, as well as the absence of disability, arthritis, and diabetes. Lagging behind were many lifestyle habits related to activity, social contacts, and income and marital status. Only one third were seen as successful agers.

FIGURE 2.2   Assessment of Successful Aging

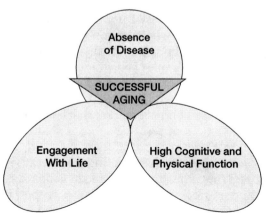

Source: Rowe and Kahn (1998).

In the past decade we have come to know that we are indeed getting older and that we do not fully know what we are doing to make this work. It is not that we do not have guidelines and exhortation, but rather that we may have too many and too much dissonance. One way is related to aging research, involving the struggle for change, best explained by the dual-process model of coping (Rothermund & Brandstädter, 2003). It bases self-regulation on two developmental processes: the offensive process of assimilation and the defensive process of accommodation (see Brandstädter, 1999). Assimilation helps individuals to manage life experiences in ways that are beneficial to the self through coping efforts that involve direct action, problem solving, and active modification of the environment. In contrast, accommodation shapes the self to correspond to the realities of life experience and is often invoked when assimilation fails. Parsing this further, Heckhausen and Schulz (1995) articulate the processes through which individuals strive to maximize control over the external world. One process is termed *primary control*, which is directed at the external world. Secondary control refers to an internal process evoked to minimize developmental losses and increase one's primary control. With age, the presence of secondary control increases, but often needs "therapy" to fully activate.

On the positive side, Carstensen and colleagues contend that selective information processing plays a constructive role in well-being at late life (Carstensen, Fung, & Charles, 2003). When life expectancy is seen as finite, older adults shift their goals to regulating emotional states in order to improve mood and optimize well-being. They essentially avoid negative memories simply as a function of aging. This has also been labeled a positivity bias, which may influence cognitive load (Mather & Knight, 2005). As a group, older adults are more cognitively impaired, not stupid. As a group, most respond in their own ways to change. This involves the iterative process of becoming aware, assimilating (internalizing), and eventually accommodating (changing). Clinicians need to know how to optimize these constructs, as they have operational value in clinical settings. Constructs such as, "I'm a worrier," do not seem to change much. But this feeling does not have to be the barrier that it appears. It is possible for an individual to make an alteration of what is important, learn what is required for this to happen, and take the needed steps for change. In fact, even small changes in core capacities can lead to large changes in complex behavior (Salthouse, 2001).

Since paradigms of aging have emerged in the form of extended life as "compression of morbidity" and "effective aging expectancy," as well as "successful aging," is there a clinical marker that best represents these phenomena? Perhaps the axiom of positive aging is that the aggregate effect of life habits at middle age (or across life) is most important for QoL at advanced ages. We do have problems in this area because we do not have precise phenotypes: What is healthy aging and how do we measure it? There are no universal agreed-upon biomarkers or phenotypes. If we take centenarians as a marker of health, the variance attributed to health, cognition, and social experience accounts for only 14% of survival (Hagberg & Sameulson, 2008). These authors found that high lean body weight; high HDL (high-density lipoprotein) cholesterol; moderate wine consumption; independence in ADL; good verbal ability, memory, and learning ability; better economic condition than peers when growing up; being married or cohabitating; and independent home living are survival-promoting factors. Mortality was related to number of drugs taken, hearing or vision impairment, low ADL capability, education less than 7 years, low job satisfaction, and living in an institution (Hagberg & Sameulson, 2008). What you do in life matters! The savvy clinician, perhaps above all else, needs a perspective on this life span process to value and better understand the older person being treated.

CONCLUSION

Perhaps this book is really about suggesting that the geriatric field needs to reduce variability in care and move toward more consistency in effective care. We know that some patients do better than others and that some therapists do better in outcomes than others, even with patients who have more case-based problems. At present, where older adults are concerned, there is insufficient evidence that techniques make a big difference in outcomes. Health care providers need to act as creators, synthesizers, and consumers of research evidence.

In this book, we deal with the dark side, depression/anxiety and cognition problems, as well as somatic and life issues. At late late-life, disease and frailty are the rule, and these factors often trump the potential positive influence of psychological and self-protective processes. We believe that we can make a difference with older adults who have health/mental health problems. We require a good-enough level of science that can be practiced by practitioners, driven by clinical and service utility, and still be accepted by academics and policy makers alike as a legitimate complement to trials methodology. We need to know to what extent treatment matches shared social construction about what it means to be remoralized within a culture.

We know that depression and anxiety in particular, especially at late life, are not treated with enough power or dosage. The duration also is inadequate. Few older adults access mental health care in primary care clinics (PCCs). Substantial strides have been made in the array and effectiveness of mental illness treatments, but despite all this, outcomes have changed only minimally. The promise of a cure for any mental illness is a chimera or distant accomplishment because of a variety of imposing scientific challenges. Mental illnesses are multivaried and, therefore, not available to specific diagnostic tests. The remission of a mental problem is usually partial or short lived and more than one third of patients do not respond to the recommended treatments.

Unfortunately, we are in good (or bad) company. Few chronic physical diseases are amenable to cures; therefore, they need to be put into perspective in other ways. Mental illness is a chronic condition. We believe that we now have the good-enough conditions for its understanding and treatment.

CHAPTER 3

Psychotherapy

Lee Hyer and Maria Anastasiades

We have come a long way from the initial position of psychotherapy for older adults, when old people were considered no longer educable nor able to benefit from psychotherapy (Freud, 1905). We once "knew" that our ways of being in the world were determined by the struggle among id, ego, and superego; that only thoughts determined our psychological health; and now, that we seem to be victims of genetic or neurotransmitter configurations, unregulated amygdalas, or overdeveloped frontal lobes.

In the 21st century, the therapist can provide more than "symbolic giving." The special needs of the elderly are no longer best encapsulated in distinctive themes (e.g., loss, increased dependency, and existential approach of death), age-specific reactions (e.g., survivor guilt at having outlasted others), and "aging" therapy needs (e.g., more time-limited goals, greater amount of positive benefit, as well as a slower pace and lack of termination). These issues now matter only at the margins.

Psychotherapy Changes Over the Past Two Decades

- The therapist knows and does all
- The client is ignorant and needs the therapist to tell him or her what to do
- Only techniques are helpful
- Common factors are not important, and we should seek winners in therapy
- Outcomes are unimportant
- Only medication is effective
- No empirically supported psychotherapies exist

Psychotherapy with older adults has altered measurably in the past decades. The process has become very egalitarian and cooperative. As psychotherapies merge owing to time and feedback in all systems, cognitive behavioral therapy (CBT)/problem-solving therapy (PST) has had the impact of humanizing its agenda and more traditional or psychodynamic psychotherapy has had the impact of goal directing its efforts with operationalized targets. Both have the advantage of motivational interviewing. Both have the advantage of the vast field of care-based interventions, modern medicine, and learning from the many problems of psychiatric models.

Over 50 years of research have suggested that the following are more true than not:

- The differential effectiveness of competing therapeutic approaches does not seem to exist. Medications and psychotherapies are essentially equal.
- The utility of psychiatric classification as determining the course of medication is poor.
- The *Diagnostic and Statistical Manual* (*DSM*) nosology is a gift to reliability.
- Dimensions of distinct pathologies represent a better model for determining problems than one diagnosis. A profile of a person's problems is optimal.
- The "mores" apply: the more intense the psychiatric problem, and the more general problems there are in the person's life, the less likely it is that change will occur.

In this chapter, we discuss the issue of the science of psychotherapy. We consider the vagaries of life as they apply to changes owing to psychotherapy, its science, and how care evolves from adults to older adults. We address the value of medication. We then present an embellishment of the model given in the previous chapter. We highlight this chapter with core and recommended treatment factors.

PROBLEMS OF SCIENCE

There is a remarkable gap between medical research and practice (Institute of Medicine, 2001). Whereas there are many reasons for this gap, a major problem involves the process of basic implementation, such as the challenge of translation of results into practice (Fixen, Naoom, Blasé, Friedman, & Wallace, 2005).

Kessler and colleagues (2005) found that over the course of 12-month periods there is a 26% chance of a mental disorder occurring in all of us, and most of these are anxiety disorders. This comes to approximately 46% lifetime prevalence. Subclinical levels add even more. This sets the scaffold on which the treatment effects to unfold. We also need to know that empirically based treatments (EBTs) alone are insufficient to account for much of the variance in care. Treatments only partially alleviate disease burden. The maximum health attributable to treatment relieves only 34% of years lived with disability. Spontaneous remission occurs in 23% of new cases. EBT is often not practical.

With older adults, perhaps the most emphasis should be on helping the patients use their resources, with less placed on EBTs. Context is important: both psychological context and psychosocial context. Many patients get better before they begin the actual therapy. This suggests, at least in part, that the active ingredients in the therapy include the reassuring context of the therapeutic situation itself.

Psychotherapy is complex. There are too many moving parts. For starters, therapist effects—how the health care provider affects the patient—are most often more important than treatment effects; the alliance is a good part of this outcome. Psychotherapy works because of alliance, but this alliance is not adequately accounted for. Therapists need to believe that the patient is motivated and thereby foster involvement. Frank and Frank (1993) hold that therapy works because the patient believes that the therapist cares about him or her and is competent. In depression, Beck himself advocated for the cognitive therapist to first be a good psychotherapist. Long ago Hans Strupp noted that "patients progress at their own pace."

- All forms of therapy address two features at least: a new understanding and a new experience.
- Change originates from within and from without.
- Techniques are mostly placebo delivery devices.
- Success depends on the extent to which treatment matches shared social constructions about what it means to be remoralized or cured in a specific culture.
- Success depends on the patient's conviction that the therapist cares and is competent.

To add to this, there is few data that a particular patient will benefit from a particular treatment. Small differences are exaggerated when the researcher uses LOCF (last observation carried forward), continuous variables, and secondary end points. Wampold (2001) noted that only 13% of the variance of change in therapy is owing to the treatment; of that, 8% is owing to the actual technique. Therefore, roughly 87% of the variance of psychotherapy outcome is the result of extratherapeutic factors. In short, we need a good-enough level of science, a practice-based science that can be relevant to older adults and driven by clinical utility.

In addition, the best studies suggest that there are potent effects from placebo. Stone et al. (2009) used Food and Drug Administration (FDA) data and showed that of the 189 studies with more than 53,000 people, "50% of subjects who received active drug and 40% of subjects who receive placebo were designated as responders" (p. 31). In other chapters we note that STAR*D (Sequenced Treatment Alternatives to Relieve Depression), perhaps the best study that maximized the clinical situation and research, showed that remission rates over the four iterations of the trial go from 28% to 13%. Relapse was 56% in 12 months; the dropout rate was 24%. In general, dropout rates are 47% (Wierzbicki & Pekarik, 1993). Perhaps treatment techniques are placebo delivery devices.

Perhaps a broader definition of what constitutes empirically supported therapies (ESTs) in an understanding of psychotherapy can be had. Dattilio, Edwards, and Fishman (2010) argued for no less than a paradigm shift, a mandate for the integrated package of methodological approaches to study psychotherapy that includes both qualitative and quantitative methods, experimental and quasi-experimental strategies, approaches that would allow for the development for both nomothetic, universal cause-and-effect law and idiographic, context-specific knowledge. The field of psychotherapy is indeed in flux.

There are other aspects of therapy that deserve mention, that are effective, and that do not get measured. Shedler (2010) presented ingredients of psychodynamic therapy that address psychological health and not merely the absence of symptoms. They involve the positive presence of inner capacities and resources that allow people to live life better. This includes the ability to use one's talents, enjoy challenges, sustain a meaningful love relationship, find meaning in the larger community, to assert self, and to have an active sex life, among many others. Symptom-free outcomes do not measure such inner capacities. Is there anyone who does not think these apply to older adults?

Psychodynamic Ingredients

Focus on affect

Exploration of attempts to avoid distressing thoughts and feelings

Identification of recurring themes and patterns

Discussion of past experience (developmental focus)

Focus on interpersonal relations

Focus on therapy relationship

Exploration of fantasy life

GENERAL REVIEWS: DATA RELATED TO OLDER ADULTS

As a general comment, support for psychotherapy registers at acceptable levels, but psychotherapy far from truly validated. Westen and Morrison (2001), in a major meta-analysis of high-quality studies on the efficacy of manualized psychotherapies on the short- and long-term effects of depression, Generalized Anxiety Disorder (GAD), and Panic Disorders (PDs)—all studies between 1990 and 1998—showed that roughly two thirds of patients were excluded from studies; only 25% of depressed patients who do not abuse alcohol, are not suicidal, and pass rigorous screening recover after 2 years. In the short run, only about 50% do well who pass through a rigorous series of inclusion and exclusion criteria. The average patient does not continue to do well over 2 years. A careful read of the data supports the idea that our science is wanting, even lame, when it comes to fully accepting our therapies as valid. The Consolidated Standards of Reporting Trials (CONSORT) criteria reveal gaps in even our best studies.

The continuance and maintenance phases of therapy have not been assessed carefully in older adults. Studies on the continuation and maintenance phase for psychotherapy highlight CBT (Blackburn, Bishop, Glen, Whalley, & Christie, 1981; Moore & Blackburn, 1997), as well as interpersonal therapy (IPT) (Frank et al., 1990; File, 2001; Klerman, DiMascio, & Weisman, 1974; Reynolds et al., 1999). Some studies have examined the efficacy of brief psychotherapy following acute-phase pharmacotherapy in patients, who have not recovered fully or only partially from Major Depressive Disorder (MDD) (Fava, Grandi, Zielezny, & Rafanelli, 1996; Fava, Rafanelli, Cazzaro, Conti, & Grandi, 1998; Keller et al., 2004; Paykel et al., 1999; Teasdale et al., 2000). These have involved adults but not older adults.

Of interest, the relative merits of cognitive versus behavioral techniques do not appear superior to one another. Longmore and Worrell (2007) reviewed the evidence regarding the relative contributions of cognitive and behavioral strategies to treatment outcomes. They concluded that there was no strong evidence that cognitive approaches produced better results than behavioral approaches (i.e., behavioral activation and exposure therapy) alone or that cognitive approaches added to the benefit of behavioral approaches. Similarly, a meta-analysis by Norton and Price (2007) found no differences across cognitive therapy, exposure therapy, relaxation, or their combination for anxiety disorders. Even self-reported cognitive appraisals and beliefs are changed to the same degree by either cognitive or behavioral methods of intervention.

In general, psychotherapy works. Psychotherapy does not work as medicine; nonspecific factors are integral to both but critical for mental health care. As noted, success of therapies depends on the patient's conviction that the therapist cares about him or her and is competent to help. Fortunately, most patients who are older have mild symptoms that can best be addressed in psychotherapy. Initially, to be effective, treatment must match a shared social construction about what it means to be remoralized within the culture in which it is practiced. The effective therapist then incorporates expectancy-based strategies into her or his clinical repertoire. This allows the patient to generate change, whatever the reason (from self-generated change to placebo effects).

Goodheart and Lansing (1997) provide a simple template for the assessment of adults in response to the stress of a disorder or disease. Older adults will respond differently based on answers to core questions. Many manage reality through the filter of their personalities (introversion, extraversion), anxiety by excessive worry or repression, relationships by internal learned patterns or objects, cognition by styles that are rigid or loose, synthetic or integrative, and mastery-competence by levels of the GAF (global assessment of function). A person who has a disease filters his or her response through his or her psychological template.

Psychological Template for Disease

How does the person manage reality?
How does the person handle anxiety/depression/stress?
How does the person manage relationships?
How does the person manage cognition?
What is the person's mastery-competence level?

For a true understanding of psychotherapy, our experimental science is incomplete where older adults are at issue. Psychotherapy outcomes are often wanting, being neither multimodal nor comprehensive, neither fully broad nor specific. Different outcomes do indeed provide different information, even in long-term care facilities where residents with diabetes, for example, have different end points from those with physical disabilities and depression (Kane, Lum, Cutler, Degenholtz, & Yu, 2007).

But we believe that psychotherapy for all adults works for older adults. We offer the following as reasonable rubrics of psychotherapy that we believe apply to older adults. They are generally hopeful.

Rubrics of Psychotherapy

- Psychotherapy is effective; effect size is approximately 0.8, indicating that the average treated person is better off than 80% of those not in treatment (Ogles, Lambert, & Sawyer, 1995).
- The apparent existence of specific psychological treatments for specific disorders is suspect (Miller, Duncan, & Hubble, 1997).
- People increasingly accept mental health programs as a normal mode of treatment. Also, most people will admit to emotional or lifestyle problems in the last year.
- The quality of the patient's participation is most determinant of outcome (Orlinsky, Grawe, & Parks, 1994).
- Change as a result of psychotherapy derives from key ingredients or elements that transcend all approaches.
- Nonspecific components of the alliance, the placebo, and the person of the therapist are critical for change in mental health. Allegiance effects by the therapist are also substantial.
- The comparative effectiveness shown by drug studies versus psychosocial therapies is virtually equal. The combined use of both types of therapies is more helpful only to some (e.g., treatment resistant or in acute phase only).
- The placebo effect closely approximates the effect size of both psychotherapy and medication.
- Up to 10% deteriorate in psychotherapy and another 25% do not benefit at all (Ogles, Lambert, & Fields, 2002).
- Monitoring or tracking patient outcome alone has an effect size of at least 0.4 (Lambert & Bergin, 1994).
- Between 6 and 9 weeks seems to be an initial marker for change; if no change occurs by then, problems will likely continue.

- Clinicians practicing in multidisciplinary settings do better than sole-practice models.
- Dropout rates in outpatient clinics total as high as 47%.
- How one copes with problems over time to prevent relapse is more critical than initial changes. Change, then, is not just managing symptoms.
- Particular treatments work because the patient is motivated, the therapist is likeable and competent, the alliance is firm, and feedback is applied.
- The psychiatric treatment with medication is really a psychological intervention.
- There are no specific effects of any of the psychiatric meds, especially the antidepressants.
- Most people with mental disorders remain untreated or poorly treated (Mojtabai & Olfson, 2004).
- Patients given "usual care" have a very high likelihood of remaining depressed.

Perhaps the message here is clear. We need other models for older adults when the issue is psychiatric care. Some are given in the following list.

Key Alternative Treatments

Develop briefer, more cost-effective psychological treatments
Develop self-help books
Use the Internet
Develop other high-volume CBT approaches (e.g., group, day centers, phone use, e-mails)
Apply step care
Always have a patient-centered orientation

LATE-LIFE PSYCHOTHERAPY OVERVIEW

The research literature on the psychological treatment of older adults is small in comparison to the intervention literature on other populations. However, a number of older general reviews are available for the treatment of depression in older adults (e.g., Gallagher-Thompson & Thompson, 1995; Scogin & Shah, 2012; Scogin, Welsh, Hanson, Stump, & Coates, 2005; Teri, Curtis, Gallagher-Thompson, & Thompson, 1994). They are universally favorable. The American Psychological Association (APA) Division 12 task force on depression at later life identified six different psychological treatments as evidence based: behavioral therapy, CBT, problem (group) solving, IPT, cognitive bibliotherapy, and (group) reminiscence (Hartman-Stein & LaRue, 2011).

CBT especially has been proffered as a treatment of choice for many disorders in later life: sexual dysfunction (e.g., Kennedy, Martinez, & Garo, 2012), sleep problems (e.g., Lichstein, Wilson, & Johnson, 2000), and tension (Burish et al., 1984; Scogin, Rickard, Keith, Wilson, & McElreath, 1992), applied both individually (Thompson, Gallagher, & Breckenridge, 1987), with groups (Hyer, Yeager, Hilton, & Sacks, 2009), and in various venues (e.g., Baltes & Carstensen, 1996). Positive results also have been shown in regard to medical illness, with such factors as control/choice (Wallston, Wallston, Smith, & Dobbins, 1987), relaxation training (Burish, Snyder & Jenkins, 1991; Vasterling, Jenkins, Tope, & Burish, 1993), difficult psychological problems (Hanley-Peterson et al., 1990; Gallagher, Rose, Rivera, Lovett, & Thompson, 1989), and older adults with cognitive difficulties (Snow, Powers & Liles, 2006; Snow, 1999). The same results apply (but to a lesser extent) to interpersonal psychotherapy (Benek-Higgins, McReynolds, Hogan, & Savickas, 2008). CBT has also been associated with improved psychological functioning in patients undergoing chemotherapy (Areán et al., 1993; Burish et al., 1984; Nezu, Nezu, Friedman, Faddis, & Houts, 1998).

Treatments that share therapeutic components with CBT have also demonstrated efficacy for late-life depression, and bear mention here. These treatments include PST (Alexopoulos, Raue, & Areán, 2003), dialectical behavioral therapy (DBT; Lynch, Morse, Mendelson, & Robins, 2003), interpersonal therapy (Karel & Hinrichsen, 2000; Reynolds et al., 1999), and behavioral activation (Teri, Logsdon, Uomoto, & McCurry, 1997), as well as a modified CBT for chronic and severely depressed older patients (McCullough, Root, & Cohen, 2006). PST addresses core action tendencies in a structured way, which reflects a core treatment component of CBT. Dialectical behavioral therapy highlights elements of radical acceptance, mindfulness, distress tolerance, and assertiveness training. Interpersonal therapy addresses interpersonally relevant factors in a context of education, goal setting, and socialization. Behavioral activation uses traditional behavioral techniques, including mastery and pleasurable activities, graded task assignments, and goal setting. Additionally, the CBT elements of bibliotherapy (Smith, Floyd, Jamison & Scogin, 1997) and wellness interventions in classroom and home settings for older adults, such as relaxation, cognitive restructuring, problem solving, communication, and behavior activation (Rybarczyk, DeMarco, DeLaCruz & Lapidos, & Fortner, 2001) have also been evaluated as efficacious.

Unfortunately, outcome studies explain only 40% to 50% of total outcome variance. The effect sizes are generally moderate to good but do not generally surpass many medication studies. Although promising, then, psychotherapy, even CBT, for older adults may have reached a sort of asymptote with few newer studies and lessened practice. The resting pulse of psychotherapy now may be supplied more by elements of IPT and PST studies, as these are plentiful. New studies tend to be done in primary care (e.g., Roy-Byrne, Post, Uhde, Porcu, & Davis, 2007; Serfaty et al., 2009).

The question of the efficacy of psychotherapy when combined with medication has been addressed. Several labs have shown that psychotherapies work with medication (e.g., Alexopoulos, 2005; Lebowitz et al., 1997; Reynolds et al., 2006; Thase et al., 1997) but have a limited effect on select patients, like those with executive function (EF) problems with a late-life depression (see Chapters 4 and/or 6). There are also reviews that support the value of both treatments. It is important to note that although we believe both treatments can prove effective for any given individual, in the main, CBT-like therapies are necessary for better and longer lasting results.

ACT

There is one other promising therapy that has not been evaluated to any extent with older adults; this is acceptance and commitment (ACT). To our knowledge, there is one study on this approach (Kiosses, Arean, Teri, & Alexopoulos, 2010). A meta-analysis of the evidence for adults up until 2007 was published by Ost (2008). He concluded that "no third wave therapy fulfills the criteria for empirically supported treatments." This has changed: If we apply the criterion that a psychotherapy method should be supported by at least two randomized controlled trials (RCTs) of sufficient size and quality showing superiority to waiting list or treatment as usual or similar effects to another bona fide treatment and that there should be additional evidence supporting the method and no evidence of relevant harmful effects, ACT holds promise among younger age groups.

ACT is a method of behavioral therapy that is based on functional contextualism and the relational frame theory. It posits the following psychopathological processes as central to mental disorders: (a) cognitive fusion, (b) experiential avoidance, (c) attachment to a verbally conceptualized self and a verbally conceptualized past, (d) lack of values or confusion of goals with values, and (e) absence of committed behavior that moves in the direction of chosen values. The treatment contains psychoeducation about key mechanisms, as well as exercises in mindfulness and cognitive defusion. This last technique is perhaps most appealing to older adults, as it requires less cognitive load. Importantly, for older adults, the value orientation of the patient is elicited and discussed, and patients are supported in value-driven behavior in contrast to behavior driven by emotional or experiential avoidance.

There are several RCTs that test the efficacy of ACT in heterogeneous clinical conditions. ACT was associated with a reduction of depressive symptoms in men and women with subclinical depression, is superior to progressive relaxation training in reducing symptoms of obsessive-compulsive disorder in 79 patients, works well on smoking cessation, promotes physical activity in adults, and reduces levels of stress and burnout. It is also useful in in pain, eating disorders, marijuana dependence, GAD, and affective symptoms in psychotic disorders (see Robinson, Gould, & Strosahl, 2010).

With some reservations, we believe that ACT could be an excellent therapy for older adults. This, along with mindfulness-based interventions (MBCT [mindfulness-based cognitive therapy] and MBSR [mindfulness-based stress reduction]), are apt for older adults, as they focus on self-regulation of attention and an orientation in the present moment; they have also been shown to be effective for any number of health and psychological problems (see Edenfield & Saeed, 2012). Interestingly, both ACT and mindfulness-based interventions involve changes in brain functioning. As mentioned, these have a low cognitive load, are easy to learn and practice, are appealing, and can be incorporated in the modules of psychotherapy with no difficulty. In addition, therapists like these techniques as they fit in well with Watch and Wait as well as monitoring.

MEDICATIONS

Psychiatric care is most often provided in a primary care clinic (PCC) context. This is both good and bad. It is good because this context for treatment is as efficacious as psychiatry clinics; it is bad because it often involves primary care physicians (PCPs) doing the assessment and treatment in PC—a problem that has been identified for over a decade with many studies on depression, anxiety, pain, sleep, dementia, and quality of life. Mitchel, Vaze, and Rao (2009), for example, showed that of 100 cases, 10 are caught, 10 are missed, and 15 are seen as false positives where depression is concerned. Recently, Maust and colleagues (2011) showed this same problem in primary care in which many older adults were given one intervention: Physicians apply the one tool available to them, psychiatric medication, in spite of little diagnosis or, in many cases, need.

If the default standard of care for older adults in the 21st century is the PCC, then the treatment of the moment is pharmacology, a truly blunt instrument with both helpful and harmful effects. In 2006, 79% of mental health care was addressed in primary care. Depression diagnoses among the 65-plus crowd have become more commonplace, rising from 3.2% to 6.3% from 1992 to 2005, according to a nationally representative survey of Medicare enrollees; so too have medication-only treatments. Over that same time, the percentage of Medicare enrollees diagnosed with depression who were treated with antidepressants rose from 53.7% to 67.1%. Furthermore, only 15% of complaints are clearly linked to a biological cause. The proportion of those who received psychotherapy, on the other hand, dropped from 26.1% to 14.8% (Akincigil et al., 2011). Olfson and colleagues (2002) showed that the percentage of adults receiving psychiatric medication over the past decade increased to 57%, up from 44% just a few years prior. The percentage who received psychotherapy alone dropped to 10%, from 16%. This is owing to many factors, not the least of which is the fact that primary care has become the center of treatment and the pharmaceutical companies have lobbied heavily that medications are safe and effective to the exclusion of all else. This latter contention is largely untrue.

Lenze and colleagues (2005) noted several problems with medications: the optimal duration of acute psychopharmacology at late life is unknown, type and timing of changes of therapies are unclear, the best augmentation strategies of any treatment remain a mystery, predictors of treatment response are not settled, indications for and duration of maintenance therapies are also in doubt, and what constitutes the best mediators and moderators of therapy are cloudy. Primary care physicians are paid to think and diagnose; the prescription pad is the chief counterweapon. This process also seems to increase the percentage of poor compliance (60%).

Serotonergic antidepressants are the most widely used group of antidepressant medications. Although generally considered to have a favorable adverse-effect profile (low-affinity drugs), serotonergic antidepressants are associated with potentially dangerous medical complications, some of which have only recently become apparent to patients and clinicians. The association of serotonergic antidepressants and the following medical complications are noted: syndrome of inappropriate antidiuretic hormone secretion, bleeding, serotonin syndrome, serotonin-discontinuation syndrome, and adverse pregnancy and neonatal effects. Regarding older adults, hyponatremia, bradycardia, syncope, and vision problems have been especially noted. Physicians need to remain aware of these potential medical complications and integrate this information into their clinical decision making, informed-consent process, baseline assessment, and follow-up monitoring (Looper & Kirmayer, 2002).

A growing body of research suggests that antidepressants aren't as valuable as many people have claimed. An analysis of FDA clinical trials for four selective serotonin reuptake inhibitor (SSRI) antidepressants found that the drugs didn't perform significantly better than placebos in treating mild or moderate depression (Kirsch, 2000). It is not infrequent that FDA-registered studies paint a different picture than the published data. Of 74 studies in the FDA data bank, most studies with negative results were not published; the FDA database shows that only half of the studies are positive, even though 94% of the published literature is positive. This occurs in a new world where primary care and drugs have become paramount.

Clearly, medication is part of the treatment of depression for older adults. The best admixture of this intervention and psychosocial treatments is unfolding but important to address. Which older adult can be treated with which treatment for what effect? Still, this is the unanswerable question of therapy for any adult, especially an older one.

The interesting thing about this is that all treatment offerings for depression are reasonably equal, except for relapse and quality of life. CBT and other cognitive or behavioral therapies have the advantage of actually teaching coping strategies or a problem-solving method. Antidepressants may actually initiate change more quickly. They may also be attempted at the gate and reinforced or switched to CBT after a period.

We rarely know the dismantling components in the global therapies that address a given population, in this case older adults. Collins, Murphy, and Strecher (2007) espoused a multiphase optimization strategy that operates by the effect of the intervention before completing a large confirmatory trial. We may need more of this in depression research. Regardless, we need to evaluate the importance of psychosocial interventions as a more nuanced view, whether in concert with medications or not. This is a real epigenetic unfolding of person, events, and outcomes.

Summary of Medications and Psychotherapy

- Antidepressants and CBT are effective but CBT sustained improvements better than meds over time.
- If they are effective, antidepressants probably work faster than CBT until about 8 to 10 weeks.
- After a course of medication only, patients must remain on meds. They are as likely to be anxious or depressed as before—even after 3 years on meds.
- The combination of medication and psychotherapy may work better than either one alone for treatment-resistant older adults.

OUR POSITION

The Institute of Medicine's landmark report in 2001, *Crossing the Quality Chasm: A New Health Care System for the 21st Century,* cited person centeredness and control of health as primary aims of a transformed quality health care system. Under this idea, the therapist fosters integrated care with both disease management and health promotion. With older adults as well as health care in general, a shift is occurring from a provider-driven focus on specific interventions for specific symptoms to a person-centered focus on response/remission, recovery, wellness, resilience, and community integration. Implied is the interplay between data and the person. This interplay may be concretized in the form of a road map, not necessarily sequentially but logically and strategically.

At late life, the melding of a commitment to person-centered care and the use of evidence-based practice is at issue. The ultimate demonstration of evidence is the fit between the individual at a particular point in time as judged by the participation and response of that person. To date, there are really few data articulating the exact sequential road map of using EBP, despite its appeal. However, the core problems of late-life continue to be depression, anxiety, somatic and health issues, as well as cognitive decline, and just living as an older person. In effect, the broadening of the full range of depression and anxiety problems in the context of these other issues embraces a greater range of maintaining mechanisms that extend most current theories concerning these problem states. The overwhelming and overlapping mechanisms (social withdrawal and avoidance, negative views of self and cognitive distortions) represent some core psychopathological maintaining mechanisms beyond the current *DSM* symptom cluster of just a depression or anxiety disorder.

Here is the dynamic. There is more here than providing an intervention. In this schema we attempt to provide "other stuff" that mediates the outcome (Figure 3.1).

From the 45,000-foot level of care, CBT and empirically supported therapies have articulated three common threads. Almost all get the attention of the patient and promote emotional and cognitive openness. In addition, they have subtly or more blatantly argued for a mindful awareness of the present moment. This can be seen as a core marker of health. People who can do this

FIGURE 3.1 Model of Psychosocial Intervention

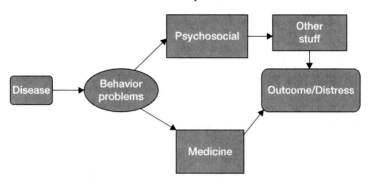

have a robust emotional and cognitive variability. Finally, a values-based behavioral engagement has been proffered. Psychological flexibility has been the goal; inflexibility is the problem child that incubates psychopathology. One can immediately see or at least sense problems with cognitive decline, as this is the one issue that results in less flexibility, whatever the status of the emotional problem. With older adults, flexibility can be attained in many ways.

What can providers do? After all, there is not a hue and cry for the laborious task of psychotherapy. Down in the pits, clinicians try to pay attention to the nuanced differences in treatment (one antidepressant vs. another, one psychotherapy versus another, meds vs. psychotherapy). These help providers very little. Published reports suggest that attending to novel "significantly better," or "evidence based," methods will result in better patient outcomes, but doing so with older adults often diverts attention from the real-world issues, and has only marginal evidence of benefit. Instead of presenting a comprehensive algorithm for treating depression in older adults, or offering a canonical framework for describing or incorporating the complex interplay of medical, psychological, and social services into treatment planning, perhaps attention to the basics is more important (Thielke, Vannoy, & Unützer, 2007).

At late life, necessary treatment is best considered in some form of nonpharmacological intervention. This form of treatment is not so much better than meds or the combo, but it almost never causes harm and always leads to better results. It provides a toolkit for change. It is also needed to make medications work, or at least work better. We have articulated that the Watch and Wait strategy is most important here. The judicious application of monitoring and waiting for success or failure to be expressed is important. As we have indicated, this is not ignoring symptoms. On the contrary, it entails discussing with the patient the risks and benefits of treatments, agreeing on an observation period as a part of the treatment plan, and the continuance of monitoring.

The recent studies in primary care regarding depression (e.g., IMPACT or CALM) have spoken. The value of a step-care model (with a Watch and

Wait background) administered by a case manager works in a primary care setting. Problems regarding mental health occur when decisions are made too quickly, dosage is not appropriate, follow-up is cursory, and problems are not anticipated. Under these conditions, empirical science is suspect and commitment (of the patient) is not optimal. Watching and waiting in the form of a step-care model establishes a slow pattern of treatment in which the problem is assessed and monitored, and problem-solving interventions are slowly but deliberatively introduced. Problems become apparent at some point. The social reality of the patient is of equal concern to the psychiatric problems and requires intervention.

Feedback for the therapist also has benefits. Lambert, Harmon, Slade, Whipple, and Hawkins (2005) noted that patient progress should be tracked on a weekly basis. There is also a time limit on good care, a period within which change should take place for remission. For example, patients who do not respond to treatment in the first three sessions need to be targeted. The resultant feedback is helpful to the therapists, as well as for outcomes of the patient. Patients who rate the therapy as successful are likely to succeed over time. And success breeds success; at least the inexorable decline process without change is retarded.

Global Basics of Care for the Older Adult

Assuming that social reality is in place (home, no alcohol, social care, etc.):

1. Assure that the dosage is appropriate (medications especially).
2. Most mental health problems with older adults are mild.
3. Consider nonpharm treatment first. Efficacious treatment always involves some aspect of nonpharm treatment.
4. Make sure a mental health professional is involved. The Healthcare Effectiveness Data and Information Set (HEDIS) study showed that a mental health professional made a difference in only half the cases, but this modality is always involved in the change in outcomes.
5. Remission rates occur at about 20%. But this can be improved when a long-term focus is in play.
6. That said, do something—some therapy is better than nothing.
7. Consider partial changes in context and empower the older adult to appreciate small changes and to continue on the same path.
8. Symptom problems such as depression will impact adjustment downstream. That is, the use of other meds later in the course of treatment may be discussed.
9. The differences among the core depression problems (MDD, mixed depression and anxiety, subsyndromal depression) are subtle and of less importance than most clinicians think. All involve respect, monitoring, and a clinical watch.
10. Risk factors account for only a small portion of the variance in the cause and persistence of depression in older adults, and attempting to uncover exactly why someone has become depressed has little advantage for clinicians.
11. Dementia changes little in the way of care, if the therapist can allow himself or herself to deal with the whole person and psychiatric/real/medical issues as if dementia is only a part of the problem.

12. Patients at late life come in too late for treatment. When there is a brain disorder, behavior and cognition are the last to change. More in the way of an intervention is required.
13. Psychiatric problems in a dementia result in conceptually similar symptoms to those outside of the degenerative disease, but the expression and phenomena are different. People who present with depression and dementia have both problems. They have depression in dementia, a distinctive profile of problems.

NECESSARY PSYCHOTHERAPY FEATURES

We provide treatment factors for Watch and Wait. Under this model, psychotherapy is indeed a corrective emotional experience. Watch and Wait holds that knowledge of the whole person and the vagaries of the setting are critical for care. Although symptom-based modules are applied and important, a symptom-oriented diagnosis is only a cog in the whole care process.

We discuss therapy components that are involved during the opening 2 to 4 weeks before the formal treatment plan is initiated. Several are core and are needed in the early stage of the Watch and Wait model. They *must* be applied if it is to work. Others represent the treatment itself; they can be initiated during the early phase of treatment, but are more likely to be used during the formal treatment itself. Recommended components then can be selected for the treatment proper. We identify these in the following sections.

CORE TREATMENT FACTOR: PSYCHOEDUCATION

There is no more important element in the therapy of a patient than psychoeducation. This is the buttress for care. It is the core of Watch and Wait. It allows the intervention to take place with appropriate information and a sense of direction and perspective, as well as an increased sense of commitment.

Regarding depression, for example, there are, undeniably, important gaps in the theory of medication use. Depression may be a complex, diverse illness, with different antecedent causes and manifestations, but clinical trials show that medication work best on depressives who are seriously ill. Still, only a fraction of the most severely depressed patients respond to serotonin-enhancing antidepressants. Antidepressants fail to work on a large percentage of mild to moderate depressives for many reasons. Perhaps the cause of the problem is different for different people; certainly, the expression of depression symptoms also varies from person to person. Placing some perspective on medications and what can be expected and what is ideal in terms of a response and a remission is important. Going over depressive symptoms and showing the connection to living, coping, and biological markers is invaluable.

Setting the stage for treatment:

"Your treatment is important and we will address all aspects of care. We need to assess your particular problem and rule out all the other possible noise. We need to see what else is involved with your unique problem. I have several things in mind; psychotherapy, case management, perhaps medication, as well as some cognitive training. We will monitor you carefully over the months ahead. This therapy is likely to work, but it may take longer and it may have to be added to and adjusted."

At a practical level, a key in most of the therapies at late life is to assure the connection between current symptoms and problems in living. The older adult is sometimes mystified by psychological symptoms and cannot translate these to real problems. That is one reason for psychoeducation and why the overall models of CBT, PST, and IPT are so critical. They facilitate therapy in the conceptual realm; in fact, understanding real problems is a signature feature of these therapies. If this is done within an empathetic frame, the possibility of change increases. As therapists who work with older adults know, therapy ruptures are subtle but influential. Antennae need to be extended for older adults where problems may be concerned. This starts with psychoeducation.

In this regard also, education helps with the perspective of psychotherapy evolving in stages. First, there is remoralization, a sense of a passionate reaction to the possibility of change. It is in this stage that psychoeducation can take hold. It provides perspective and incentive for change, along with its possibility. Second, remediation involves the work of therapy as the patient makes changes in strategy and coping. The third and final stage involves rehabilitation, where changes become solidified and permanent.

In the effort to jump-start this process, Alvidrez, Areán, and Stewart (2005) examined the impact of a brief psychoeducational intervention on treatment entry and attendance for clients referred for psychotherapy. This included a 15-minute individual psychoeducational session of what therapy is about, tailored for African Americans. This brief intervention proved helpful in the numbers who entered therapy and those who dropped out. This pre-intervention is potentially important, as the Watch and Wait strategy implies that careful preparation is necessary and at times sufficient for change.

Psychotherapy Ideas for Psychoeducation

- Advocate therapeutic alliance
- Integrate care
- Strategic long-term perspective—the more treatment continues, the more that happens
- Assess brain/health literacy/compliance
- Watch out for pain, sleep, comorbidities
- Attitude counts
- Home care is a possibility

- Consider pretherapy preparations
- Self-help helps
- Problems of old-old are more difficult, therefore, take more time and effort
- Stressors have an impact: They are orthogonal to cerebral vascular risk factors (CVRF—which reduce treatment efficacy) in predicting depression
- Foster compassionate awareness (mindfulness)
- Be free to "therapize": our distinctions are not that clear
- Change is good; small change is also good; change comes from context
- All depression and anxiety behaviors make sense: "They are better than even more pain of… failure, confusion, and so on."

CORE TREATMENT FACTOR: ALLIANCE

A critical task of mental health therapy for older adults is to create an alliance, a relationship. Over 90 studies show that the treatment alliance has a correlation coefficient = 0.46 (Norcross, 2006). Several authors (e.g., Hyer, Kramer, & Sohnle, 2004) have shown that the path from cognition to outcome in older adults in therapy is independently mediated by the alliance and by homework. No surprise here: Get the older adult to like you and to work outside therapy and change is likely. As always, common factors in therapy, as well as the technology of therapy, are both critical for positive outcomes (e.g., Lambert & Hill, 1994). Rapport building and guided intervention strategies should always be in play.

According to APA's Division 29 suggestions, empirically supported relationships (ESRs) involve the therapeutic alliance (0.21 empirical support [ES]; what the client says early in the therapy is most useful), empathy (0.32 ES: promote validation and exploration), goal consensus and collaborative involvement (modest ESs), positive regard (modest ESs related to therapy success), congruence and genuineness (> 77 studies and all positive), among other issues (resistance, aptitude X treatment interactions, and personality). Norcross (2002) notes that the only realities of good therapy involve the therapist, the treatment alliance, and nondiagnostic characteristics of stages of change. The idea is that the need is for ESRs.

The research shows an effective psychotherapist is one who employs specific methods, who offers strong relationships, and who customizes both discrete methods and relationship stances to the individual person and condition. This requires considerable training and experience; the antithesis of "anyone can do psychotherapy."

Norcross (2002)

Hyer, Kramer, and Sohnle (2004) administered a questionnaire to group members asking older adults to rate five cognitive behavioral and five treatment alliance components of CBT on a four-point scale. Once again, the relationship variables were seen as most effective and important. The issue of whether the alliance *is* the therapy, as has been implied (e.g., Norcross, 2002), is moot with older adults. The issue is that this is a necessary component of care that extends beyond the bounds of practice guidelines for younger adults, where the older adult has access and a sense of comfort in the therapeutic contract. It is a covenant in the true sense of the word.

Positive Features of Care

Patients like advice (79%)
Talking to someone interested in me (75%)
Encouragement and reassurance (67%)
Talking to someone who understands (58%)
Instillation of hope (58%) (Norcross, 2010)
Ingredients of successful therapy include:
    Empathetic validation of distress
    A rationale that explains symptoms
    Agreement on goals between patient and therapist
    Maintain agreed-to structure and focus of medication
    Support for new learning and active engagement
    Monitor progress
    Reinforce success and inoculate for future challenges
What do older patients who achieve remission say?
    Meaningful education
    Good interaction with health care provider
    Active engagement with physician who dispenses meds
    Insight into the mechanism of psychopathology
    Confident they could attack their symptoms
    Outlined existing coping strategies
    Actively involved in process, not as observers with less engagement
Barg et al. (2006)

As we have intimated elsewhere, we believe that treatment (medications especially) in a PCC for psychological problems is a psychological intervention. The person of the health care provider counts in a major way for variance reduction of what constitutes change. The ability of the PCP to listen, communicate, motivationally interview, and direct is made easier when the PCP is really involved and provides an understanding and perhaps a script for care. Successful doctors get better results with placebo or SSRI. Patients can sense competence and care. Additionally, the PCP also spends more time, prescribes less, and feels better about the patient when he or she is confident about himself or herself.

These tasks are not done lightly. Psychotherapy is an art, yes, and a science. All good therapists just talk with clients to some degree, as talk is the lifeblood of therapy. When a conversation starts, the therapist has some idea as to where it is going. If you practice CBT, the parameters are more set than most therapies. Regardless, the unspoken self of the client is now engaged.

As therapists, we do not want to be monetized by the therapy model or the insurance company. In fact, as a field we have been unconscious of the nature of the conversation that energizes our models and techniques. It is as if the craft of conversation were a secret weapon that has not been carefully evaluated. The therapeutic art is to establish glue that speaks to the person with a disorder and attaches the symptoms of the problem so that both change. The power of this interchange is not in therapy-speak phrases but in a nonlinear attempt to foster change and keep self-esteem. The alliance and its minions are the staples of this organized human dance.

The argument can be made that, like picking a good surgeon, the better health care providers are those who practice their craft more; the key to health care quality may be the number of times the health care provider administers a treatment. All new treatments involve a learning curve and patients are components on each stage of the learning curve. A core factor, however, is the health care provider "selling" the treatment plan, we hope based on experience and believability. All this involves an alliance that is solid and enduring.

CORE TREATMENT FACTOR: MONITORING

Monitoring or homework plays a central role in Watch and Wait therapy, as it is the vehicle that communicates that therapy exists outside the session, that it is an objective science and needs numbers for clarification, and this activity commits the patient. Sometimes it is enough for change. Homework also provides the structure for the patient to practice outside of therapy itself. It prevents relapse and it teaches problem solving. Use of homework makes recovery the product of the patient's efforts, which is a good thing.

Monitoring Techniques in Depression

1. Identify goals—short- and long-term behavioral goals can be planned at home based on feedback
2. Reward planning—have patient list positive behaviors enjoyed and monitor these
3. Activity scheduling—have patients schedule rewarding activities, rating them for pleasure and mastery and self-monitor
4. Graded-task assignment—have patient assign increasingly demanding tasks
5. Self-reward—have the patient increase use of positive self-statements and identify tangible reinforcers
6. Decrease rumination—have patients develop distractions or active behaviors to replace passivity and rumination
7. Social skills training—help patient develop positive behaviors toward others (for example, complimenting and reinforcing other people)
8. Assertiveness training—help patient deal in clear and assertive communication
9. Problem-solving training—help patient in problem recognition, definition, identifying resources, and generating solutions

---

There are data to suggest the efficacy of this. Persons, Burns, and Perloff (1988), studying depressed patients, found that those who did the homework outside of therapy sessions improved more than those who did not. We also know that even the act of resisting monitoring can be informative and productive. The therapist now has new information and, more importantly, can design a target that can get done, discuss why the current one was not finished, and set the expectation of task-oriented products. A failure at monitoring can be a rich interaction as the therapist can unfold problems and discover solutions, not so much in the problem but in the process of solving the problem.

Older adults often require assistance in the use of monitoring or homework. This is not something they are used to doing. Practice in the session and rewarding little efforts at the tasks can be helpful. Monitoring done well is therapy in process.

Noncompliance With Monitoring

1. What are the costs and benefits of not doing homework?
2. What is a better alternative?
3. What is the evidence for and against as to why homework will not work?
4. How is your resistance toward homework like other thoughts and positions you have?
5. Would you be willing to do a little homework?

CORE TREATMENT FACTOR: CASE-BASED APPROACH

All Watch and Wait roads lead to this place—the case-based approach. This unfolds in several ways: theory driven, diagnosis driven, and multiple causality. The models of care involve a shared approach and testable hypotheses. The most common structure for modeling for a case is provided in Table 3.1. The attachment of problems to outcomes is made simple, as modules are provided as interventions of care. Other models such as stimulus–organism–response–consequence (SORC), goal attainment MAP (strategies, interventions, outcomes), and ABC (antecedents, behaviors, consequences), are often used as supplements to this.

TABLE 3.1   Case Formulation

- Problem List
- Diagnosis
- Working Hypotheses
- Activating Events
- Origins
- Assets
- Treatment Plan
- Obstacles

Patients have many moving parts and much complexity. Problems that occur in the therapy are legion, but the ones noted that limit change are: low levels of patient suffering, diffuse treatment goals, insufficient action orientation, not recognizing the relationship between symptoms and negative consequences, secondary gain from illness, low confidence in positive treatment outcome, fear of change, and inadequate therapist behavior contradicting patient behaviors. Based on Barlow's criteria, the necessary borrowing from the extant literature is only the first stage of change; the patient's "messiness" consisting of age, social situation, chronicity, attitude, and a slew of other factors then must be entered.

Based on the CBT model (Persons, 1989), if the usual application of CBT emphasizing modules is not helpful, then a functional analysis is requisite. This can involve an understanding of the A (antecedents), B (behaviors), and C (consequences). This is often performed by the therapist *after* the formal case evaluation is applied.

FIGURE 3.2 A–B–C Model

```
        A . . . . . . . . . B . . . . . . . . . C
 • A = Antecedent or any event prior to behavior
 • B = Behavior
 • C = Consequence or Outcome
```

The following list presents the necessary components of the Watch and Wait model. These components represent core conditions for the model to be applied. They provide the necessary data for the first 3 to 4 weeks on Watch and Wait (we will discuss assessment in Chapter 12) and or discussed throughout the book. In effect, the therapist needs to use this as a checklist. They are also found in all the cases presented in the book.

Necessary Watch and Wait Categories

1. Validate problem
2. Psychoeducation of model
3. Assessment
4. Monitoring
5. Case formulation
6. Check alliance

RECOMMENDED TREATMENT FACTOR: MOTIVATIONAL INTERVIEWING

Motivational interviewing (MI) is a necessary part of Watch and Wait. The patient is in turmoil, is skeptical, and wants relief. The Eastern guru may say, "Take a deep breath, you have arrived," but the Western therapist has no such luxury and must communicate that making haste is poor care. Monitoring and reflective choices are critical (Rollnick, Miller, & Butler, 2007).

Evidence suggests that MI is synergistic with other therapies; that is, the effects of MI are stronger and more enduring when it is applied in the context of other therapies, particularly CBT and other action therapies. The client also is seen as not deficient or lacking and as possessing all that is required to resolve the issue at hand: "I do not have what you need, but you do. And I will help you find it." Therapy, then, is seen as an emergent quality as clients explore and find sources of motivation, identify key needs and values, and discover alternative perspectives for adjustment.

MI can serve as a foundational framework into which other treatments can be integrated. The extension of MI to supporting action toward change naturally emerges from the underlying spirit or attitude of MI. The spirit constitutes the platform or framework that shows how more action-oriented therapies might be conducted.

Westra (2012)

MI becomes an important factor in the process of care. It is loosely based on stages of change in the model of care. Stages of change, if done well in this context, allow the therapist to appreciate the commitment of the patient and the patient to understand that motivation and commitment are relevant for care. In a sense, stages of change provide the long view that can assist in the registration of change, creating lasting change without wasted effort.

Stages of Change

Precontemplation—no intention to change in next 6 months
Contemplation—intend to change between 30 days and 6 months
Preparation—intend to change within next 30 days
Action—current active, sustained attempt to change
Maintenance—successfully maintained change (for 6 months plus)

But MI is more than just a framework for change. It is a client-centered approach that respects motivation to change and assumes ambivalence in the process. It lovingly respects both sides of the conflict. The idea is that, where there is ambivalence or conflict, there is motivation. It stays the course for stability and elicits change talk. Strategies for the latter include use of reflective listening, asking open-ended questions, asking "low threshold questions," asking for elaboration, and expressing interest selectively as pros/cons of change are explored. REDS (see list below) has also been used to apply MI. The therapist acts like a judo master and deflects issues, avoids freedom-reducing problems, looks for motivational moments, and conveys faith in the patient.

REDS

R → Therapist is like a judo master
- Turn into the skid
- Confrontation breeds defensiveness
- Labeling is unnecessary
- Remember reactance theory

E → Reactance is triggered when freedom is threatened
- Reactance triggers resistance or rebellion (attempt to reassert freedom)
- Reactance leads to overvaluing of forbidden behavior
- Resistance is interpersonal: "How am I contributing to the resistance?"
- Resistance is healthy ("psychological immune system")
- Resistance is feedback
- Resistance is an opportunity to change strategies
  - Expressing empathy
  - Offering simple reflections
  - Emphasizing personal choice

D→ Between current behavior and goals/values
- Look for "motivational moments"
- Reinforce motivational statements
- Express genuine curiosity
- Elicit change talk
  - Remember self-perception theory

S→ Maintain and convey faith in patient's ability to change
- Ask about previous successes
- Ask about positive qualities
- Support personal choice
- Choose interventions consistent with patient preferences, goals, and values

---

In this process, the components of Watch and Wait naturally unfold. The person's base problems that segue from level of importance to confidence to readiness stand as background to the Watch and Wait principles of appropriate expectations, a plan, supports, monitoring, and a general sense of commitment.

As we end this section, we note what does not work.

What does not work:
Confrontations
Negative processes/reactions by therapists
Assumptions by therapists
Therapist centricity (less important than emphasis on patient)
Rigidity
Ostrich behavior for therapy ruptures
Procrustean bed assessment
Reactance misreading
Functional impairment inhibits treatment outcome
Ignoring stages of change

RECOMMENDED TREATMENT FACTOR: BEHAVIORAL ACTIVATION

Several studies have underscored the value of behavioral therapy, chiefly behavioral activation (Cuijpers, Van Straten, & Warmerdam, 2007; Dimidjian et al., 2006; Jacobson, Martell, & Dimidjian, 2001). It has been applied to older adults (e.g., Lichtenberg, 1999; Scogins & McElreath, 1994). The core idea involves the activation of the older adult based on pleasant events, his or her own needs, or just necessity. The model in Figure 3.3 best articulates the process of some event resulting in a decrease of reinforcement, symptoms, and life events loss.

FIGURE 3.3 Jacobson's Model: Depression Is Characterized by Behavior-Context Transactions

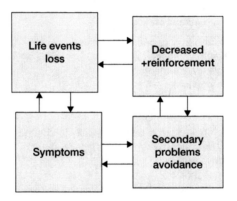

This model by Jacobson has been judiciously applied in several settings of older adults, especially long-term care settings. The importance of common behavior activation, even simple activity, is most relevant. Again, the activity can easily be combined with simple socialization. The target of activity is concrete and tangible. The result can be monitored and altered. The effort for its completion is minimal.

RECOMMENDED TREATMENT FACTOR: IPT

Interpersonally relevant problems increase risk for depression, depression damages interpersonal relationships, and interpersonal relationships play an important role in the clinical course of depression (Hinrichsen & Emery, 2005). IPT is typically delivered weekly for a duration of 16 weeks, in three phases of treatment: initial sessions, intermediate sessions, and termination (see Weissman, Markowitz, & Klerman, 2000). The focus of IPT is on one or two of four interpersonally relevant problem areas: grief (complicated bereavement), interpersonal role disputes (conflict with a significant other), role transitions (life change), and interpersonal deficits (problems in initiating and sustaining relationships). In the initial sessions (weeks 1 to 3), the therapist diagnoses the problem (usually depression), educates the client about depression, reviews current and past significant relationships ("the interpersonal inventory"), determines the problem area(s) that will be the focus of treatment, and outlines therapy goals. In the intermediate sessions (weeks 4 to 13), the therapist implements strategies associated with each of the four problem areas, and uses different therapeutic techniques, to achieve IPT problem-specific goals in tandem with reduction in depressive symptoms. In the termination phase (weeks 14 to 16), the end of treatment is discussed, feelings the client has about ending are explored, treatment progress (or lack of progress) is reviewed, and the possible need for additional treatment is ascertained.

IPT has been shown to be effective with older adults. Distinguishing features include a focus on current interpersonally relevant problems; collaborative, supportive, and optimistic stance of the therapist; psychoeducation about depression; and a regular review of options that the client has to deal with life problems. IPT's therapeutic mantras are: "That's your depression speaking" (i.e., clients feel, think, and act differently when they are depressed but are not always cognizant of the pervasive effects of the disorder); "There are always options" (i.e., depression is disempowering and limits perspective on options to deal with life problems related to the depression); and "You are not to blame" (as the patient is the victim of a disease).

IPT problem areas nicely dovetail with relevant issues in outpatient clinical practice with older adults. The most common problem area among older adults treated with IPT is role transition (Hinrichsen & Clougherty, 2006; Reynolds et al., 1999). The modal late-life role transition is acquisition of responsibility for care of a spouse with physical health problems and/or dementia. Other late-life role transitions include onset of health problems (i.e., transition into the patient role), residential move (e.g., to new community, assisted living, long-term care), retirement or late-life job loss, and care for a grandchild (i.e., acquisition of parenting role). The other problem area commonly encountered is interpersonal role disputes. Among older adults, disputes typically involve spouse or partner and adult children. Others involve siblings and friends. Usually, grief is a problem area.

Key IPT Rubrics

- The client was absolved of blame (e.g., "You have a medical illness; thus, it is not your fault").
- A sense of efficacy and hopefulness was promoted and a commitment to therapy assured.
- An interpersonal area was defined and targeted for therapy (e.g., role transition, interpersonal transition, or grief).
- The therapist acts as a therapy manager.

RECOMMENDED TREATMENT FACTOR: PST

PST is a natural for older adults. It is logical and addresses depression and/or anxiety as a problem to be solved; it is effective for patients who cannot think clearly, especially in executive function; and it has a learning effect as people become more effective in life. This intervention is effective for community-dwelling older adults with MDD (Areán et al., 1993), primary care patients (Gum et al., 2006), homebound and disabled elderly (Kiosses et al., 2010), and treatment-resistant late-life depressives (Alexopoulos, Raue, & Areán, 2003).

Of interest is the fact that PST has been espoused as a treatment of choice for older adults with late-life depression and executive function problems. As we have discussed, the problems with thinking are nicely finessed with PST as the older adult is requested to go through problems and to apply the model. In addition, thinking modules have been attempted with late-life depression in which the patient is again requested to follow the PST model.

Process of Problem-Solving Therapy Session

Orient patient, clarify, and define the problem
Set realistic goals
Generate multiple solutions
Evaluate and compare solutions
Select a feasible solution
Implement the solution
Evaluate the outcome

RECOMMENDED TREATMENT FACTOR: TRANSDIAGNOSTIC MODEL

Recently, a "movement" has begun that attempts to optimize the tripartite model of psychopathology: negative affect, positive affect, and physiological reaction (Clark, Watson, & Mineka, 1994). This model is tied to a dimensional approach to patient classification in lieu of the *DSM* system in which core components of the tripartite variables share factors across disorders. Brown, Antony, and Barlow (1995) found, for example, that patients who receive CBT for Panic Disorder also experience a decline in comorbidities over the course of treatment. The general trend in the past two decades of excessive comorbidities, frequent NOS (not otherwise specified) diagnoses, and problems with subsyndromal domains have presented the *DSM-5* clinical decisions to be more dimensional in the diagnosis process. The tripartite model (Clark & Watson, 1991) explicates this process, holding that many psychiatric disorders are attached to negative affect, positive affect, and physiological reactions to varying degrees. In effect, these three dimensions can account for pathology better than diagnoses.

The transdiagnostic model addresses this. Barlow (2005) held that all emotional disorders have a similar underlying structure and there is a unified approach to treating depression/anxiety. Patients with depression and anxiety especially are served well by this model. A three-factor "tripartite model" outlines a higher order negative affectivity (NA) factor that is common to depression and anxiety problems and two lower-order factors, low-positive affect (mostly specific to depression) and arousal (specific to anxiety/panic) (Teachman, Siedlecki, & Magee, 2007). It holds that an NA vulnerability factor influences the development of an anxiety disorder and depression. Individuals high in NA increase the likelihood of negative life events, have high levels of physical and mental health problems, are prone to multiple Axis I and Axis II disorders, and have multiple negative lifestyle habits (Lahey, 2009). NA individuals undergo multiple learning experiences that promote problems (fears and depression) that manifest in comorbidity.

Day to day, these individuals are excessively irritable, sad, anxious, self-consciousness, and vulnerable—out of proportion to circumstances. A good intervention protocol would therefore indicate a multimodal approach, including psychoeducation, cognitive restructuring, breathing retraining, exposure, and self-monitoring regardless of the presenting *DSM* diagnosis. Procedurally, a case-driven formulation under the umbrella of the transdiagnostic model is given to patients using parallel care strategies (not serial) and a holistic understanding of the person.

Obviously, mental disorders are not discrete events. Most psychological phenomena can be better described and understood according to a dimensional model. Older patients especially experience a high rate of comorbid symptoms. The presence of subsyndromal conditions also is robust and produces uncommonly poor outcomes for older adults (Chopra et al., 2005). This is especially apt for the rather common presentation in late life of depression and anxiety mixed with somatic concerns. The effort of including an Axis II presence in this taxonomy has yet to be adequately evaluated. The question also arises: What should assessment in psychotherapy really measure? Is it more theoretically oriented (e.g., CBT and attributions) or general symptom based (e.g., functional outcomes) (Lambert & Hill, 1994)?

As if designed for older adults, the transdiagnostic model supplements or replaces the *DSM*-based, discrete diagnostic categories with a dimensional approach. Core factors are rated along a continuum of severity. Individual patients can then be treated based on their presentation along these core dimensions, rather than on the basis of their membership in discrete psychopathological categories. The transdiagnostic process is concerned with the psychopathological processes that account for the persistence of the disorder. Based on evidence-based theory of the maintenance of the disorder, ESTs are extended in focus to embrace core-maintaining mechanisms: Clinical features are viewed as being maintained by similar psychopathological processes.

Transdiagnostic approaches to treating patients with anxiety and depression disorders, of which there are now several, hold considerable utility for clinical practice. Common protocols include psychoeducation, cognitive restructuring, progressive muscle relaxation (PMR), breathing retraining, exposure, and self-monitoring (Norton & Phillip, 2008). The common underlying factors related to the development and maintenance of emotional disorders (or general neurotic syndrome; Hudson et al., 2003) is played out. Research in the areas of neuroscience (Etkin & Wager, 2007), emotional science (Fellous & LeDoux, 2002), and psychotherapy (Brown, Hertz, & Barlow, 1992) has begun to elucidate common higher-order dimensions of temperament that underlie emotional disorders, most significantly negative/positive affect and behavioral inhibition/activation (Brown, 2007). These dimensions are closely linked with other shared factors, such as cognitive-emotional processing biases (Beck & Clark, 1997), and increased emotional reactivity and cognitive behavioral avoidance (Campbell-Sills, Barlow, Brown, & Hofmann, 2006).

Barlow's unified protocol (UP) known as the transdiagnostic treatment of emotional disorders (Ellard, Fairholme, Boisseau, Farchione, & Barlow, 2010; Wilamowska, 2010) is one emotion-focused CBT that applies to all anxiety and mood disorders as well as other disorders with strong emotional components (e.g., somatization, dissociation). One recent study by Ellard et al. (2010) suggests efficacy. Its application of case formulation and the transdiagnostic dimensional modules uses deliberative and interacting models for identifying the etiological, precipitant, and maintaining problems of the person and deciding where to treat. It represents the formulation of theory into practice. It is integrative and dynamic, and looks for the whole picture. Symptoms are placed in the context of cyclical patterns, both internally and externally driven. The patient becomes a participant observer, is informed about the therapy, and generally assists in the care process. It is in this process that the whole of treatment is informed and decided. It is here that we can tell whether "treatment receipt" and "treatment enactment" are in place.

Psychotherapist as Transdiagnostician

Module 1: Psychoeducation and Treatment Rationale *(1 to 3 sessions)*
Module 2: Motivation Enhancement for Treatment Engagement
Module 3: Emotional Awareness Training *(1 to 3 sessions)*
Module 4: Cognitive Appraisal and Reappraisal *(1 to 2 sessions)*
Module 5: Emotion-Driven Behaviors (EDBs) and

Emotional Avoidance *(1 to 3 sessions)*
Module 6: Interoceptive and Situational Exposures *(4 to 6 sessions)*
Module 7: Relapse Prevention *(1 session)*

Barlow (2010)

RECOMMENDED TREATMENT FACTOR: PREVENTION

This is an important topic with older adults. In 2009, the Institute of Medicine report, *Preventing Mental, Emotional, and Behavioral Disorders among Young People: Progress and Possibilities* (Institute of Medicine, 2009), listed several randomized trials suggesting that new cases of MDD could be significantly reduced if preventative intervention programs were introduced. Muñoz, Cuijpers, Smit, Barrera, and Leykin (2010) noted that at the beginning of the 21st century, major depression could be prevented if prevention were instituted. This is a major scientific advance. This has not been applied to older adults.

A lifetime prevention of depression with a single intervention is probably not in the cards. At different stages, some factors (spousal death, medical problems) may increase the likelihood of developing difficulties, whereas others (good lifestyle habits) may promote and foster the likelihood of resilience. Vulnerabilities may be expressed in different ways for different developmental periods. Older adults react in different ways to their life quality when the realization is that these elements are serious. In our Memory Clinic Program, almost all will alter at least one lifestyle component when made aware of its importance.

Recently, Cuijpers, Van Straten, Smit, Mihalopoulos, and Beekman (2008) conducted a meta-analysis on 19 studies that fit the prevention paradigm (no depression disorder according to the *DSM* criteria at baseline). The risk of developing a depression in the next year was 22% lower in participants receiving interventions than in those in the control group. Thus, two out of nine cases could be prevented if existing depression-prevention methods were implemented. These data were not specific to older adults. Preventing almost a quarter of the people from depression is quite a feat, however.

A stepped-care study by van't Veer-Tazelaar et al. (2006) showed that elderly participants benefited from an intervention comprising assessment and waiting, followed by bibliotherapy, then by CBT, and finally by a primary care referral. Subjects (*N* = 170) aged 75 or older were randomized to either the intervention or an assessment control only. After a year, participants in the intervention condition developed a depressive disorder at significantly lower rates than controls; at 2 years, similar results applied.

- Step-care approach: assessment and waiting
- Bibliotherapy
- CBT or PST
- Referral
- *N* = 170 age 75 or older randomized to intervention or assessment only
- After 1 year, 7% in intervention condition developed depression and 18% in control condition; 2 years, 10% of intervention and 26% of assessment only

van't Veer-Tazelaar et al. (2006)

In sum, a focus on prevention in the Watch and Wait protocol can be productive. It identifies risk and takes steps to highlight problems and to establish interventions that can make a difference. This can range from awareness to exercise to changing a life habit. Surprisingly, the older adult is receptive if these interventons are given in the context of the total treatment program.

RECOMMENDED TREATMENT FACTOR: CASE MANAGER

One of the roles in the care of an older person is that of case manager (CM). This is an important job that entails thinking out-loud about practical problems, home issues, treatment problems, and compliance. The role of this person is so critical that two meta-analyses noted the case manager's value above all other features of care (Gilbody, Bower, Fletcher, Richards, & Sutton, 2006; Gilhooly, Sweeting, Whittick, & McKee, 1994). The use of a CM is now an effective way to assist in the treatment of depression. Older adults often do not get better unless there is a CM and the CM has had training and supervision. Alexopoulos et al. (2003) have shown that treating depression effectively in this way is a major step in improving the outcomes of most medical illnesses and in reducing mortality. This was also shown in the Prevention of Suicide in Primary Care Elderly Collaborative Trial (PROSPECT) in which the importance of a CM was noted, as this allowed the therapist to be active in treatment, to handle modal problems in the community, and to keep in contact during the week.

Traditionally the CM had three jobs: (a) rehabilitation model, (b) intensive case management, and (c) clinical case management. They all involve a linkage to social services, advocacy, rehabilitation, and ongoing support during recovery from illness. Case management is most often used in PCC. Areán et al. (2005) studied the value of CM tasks. They involve problem solving on health, housing, legal issues, and other social issues. Usually the patient works on interpersonal issues, affect regulation, communication skills, and health behaviors, as well as behavioral activation. An action plan formulates the way. In assessing three groups of depressed patients using CBT, a CM, and a combination of these, she studied 70 low-income subjects with MDD randomly assigned. Over time the values of a depression rating, the Hamilton Depression Rating Scale (HDRS), fell for the combination group most and then for CM and last for CBT. The important point was the value of CM in the context of older adults who had some impairment.

Depression Care Management Strategies

- Education about depression in later life
- Education about the medications used to treat depression in later life
- Education about good sleep practices
- Review of symptoms
- Review of side effects
- Management of side effects
- Education about suicide and assessment of suicidality
- Encouragement to stay the course long enough to benefit from treatment
- Discussions with family members/caregivers to elicit their support for the treatment plan

---

RECOMMENDED TREATMENT FACTOR: EXERCISE

In Chapters 4 and 5 we learn that exercise is effective. It is effective for depression, cognition, virtually all medical problems, and quality of life, as well as anxiety (Herring, O'Connor, & Dishman, 2010). This form of therapy is especially apt for older adults in just about any stage of health care problems. Exercise assists in overall health, especially for people with cardiac problems, even if they are sedentary and first-time exercisers. It also works well as an adjunct or as the main focus of therapy and cognitive health for healthy and impaired older adults.

In long-term care (LTC) facilities, a renewed emphasis has been on activity as well as on exercise. The importance of everyday activity translates to health, to better sleep, to less depression and anxiety, and to better thinking. Insurance companies are now covering this expense, as it has so many proactive elements.

What Helps With Exercise

- Anything over baseline
- Best 30 to 60 minutes per day
- Increases serotonin and norepinephrine and brain-derived neurotrophic factor (BDNF)
- Depression and anxiety; exercise is a reasonable alternative to antidepressants (Bartholomew, Morrison, & Ciccolo, 2005)
- Increases BDNF in hippocampal tissue
- Increases quality of life

RECOMMENDED TREATMENT FACTOR: MODULES

In the Introduction, we noted that the psychological problems at late life are best dealt with by modular interventions. Modal problems at late life (anxiety, depression, somatization (pain), and cognitive decline) are intertwined with emotional disorders having a similar underlying structure. The components of core therapies, like CBT, PST, and IPT, incorporate the best modules for change.

Choice of modules is always a combination of factors—what the client desires, what the therapist is trained in, what the client is likely to agree to, and what can be expected to be the optimal response. Several studies (e.g., Chorpita, Daleiden, & Weisz, 2005; Henin, Otto, & Reilly-Harrington, 2001) showed good results when both the patient and therapist choose the modules. In this context, even use of the phone can be beneficial (Mohr et al., 2005; Simon, VonKorff, Rutter, & Wagner, 2000). In a highly cited study, Wetherell et al. (2009) evaluated 31 older adults with GAD or anxiety, NOS. They received modular or extended-care treatment. Modules included education, relaxation, cognitive restructuring, thought stopping/schedule worry, exposure, behavioral activation (pleasant events), sleep hygiene, problem solving, life review, acceptance (mindfulness), time management, pain management, and relapse prevention. Results indicated that both methods worked well.

The throughput of how to organize the modules for care is, of course, important. This process is best done under a Watch and Wait understanding in which plans are carefully formulated based on the particular patient, reasonable empirically supported therapies, and patient and therapist buy-in. The real advantage of the modules cannot be overstated: They are the techniques of the therapy and they offer a focus for the therapist, as they remain after the intervention has been applied. They are then the toolkit for care.

A related factor, and one of the primary goals in CBT, is to teach the client to "function as his or her own therapist." There is a strong evidence base supporting the effectiveness of CBT in treating depression and increasing coping skills in caregivers (Akkerman & Ostwald, 2004; Gallagher-Thompson & Coon, 2007; Teri, Logsdon, Uomoto, & McCurry, 1997).

Tasks, including general assertive interventions, health homework, assorted behavioral requests, and relational tasks with a friend, apply. The ability to use newly developed skills to help others contributes to a perception of a positive outcome and increased overall self-efficacy.

Modules of Therapy

- Relaxation
- Sleep guidelines
- Problem-solving skills training
- Worry control
- Acceptance/mindfulness
- Behavioral activation
- Pain management
- Pleasant activities
- Mindfulness
- Assertiveness training
- Time management
- Cognitive therapy
- Exposure
- Family involvement

RECOMMENDED TREATMENT FACTOR: COGNITIVE TRAINING

We have noted repeatedly that older adults with a newer-onset depression or anxiety have thinking problems. Interventions help, work on, and facilitate change. We address this issue again in Chapter 6, on cognition. Here we briefly highlight the role of cognitive training as one of the modules.

In a series of studies using PST, it has been reasonably confirmed that training in executive function provides necessary assistance in the psychotherapy itself. Patients who are depressed and have executive-function problems do not respond well to antidepressants (Sneed et al.,

2007). Brodaty, Green, and Koschera (2003) argue that cognitive training techniques are best used as adjuncts to other psychosocial interventions, because improved cognitive functioning appears to help patients to benefit from subsequent skills training and psychoeducation. Also of potentially great importance is the fact that stabilizing or reversing cognitive decline in the elderly is an important step in preventing subsequent functional decline and caregiver burden (Tariot & Ismail, 2002); therefore, the cognitive training approach can be viewed as a preventative strategy as well as a remedial intervention.

Although cognitive training is effective in improving cognitive functions in these populations, with more severely impaired individuals, benefits are sometimes limited in terms of generalizability. There is a negative association of impairment severity and amount of improvement following cognitive training: in patients who are relatively less impaired (e.g., those with mild brain injury who are living independently as compared with those with severe schizophrenia who require assistance with activities of daily living), cognitive training can lead to enhanced cognitive functioning and transfer of skills to new situations (Boman, Lindstedt, Hemmingsson, & Bartfai, 2004; Palmese & Raskin, 2000).

The largest study to date of cognitive training in healthy older adults (ACTIVE, $n = 2,832$) demonstrated that 10 sessions of reasoning, processing speed, or memory training led to an improvement in cognitive abilities equivalent to the amount of decline expected in nondemented elderly over a 7- to 14-year period. Although ceiling effects on measures of daily functioning precluded evidence for transfer of skills, cognitive benefits were durable over a 2-year period (Ball et al., 2002). All of the training groups improved in their task-specific training area, and subjects who were given reasoning training improved in transfer areas, such as IADL.

Other means of achieving similar cognitive benefits have been explored in future trials with older patients. These include vigorous exercise (Kramer, Colcombe, McAuley, Scalf, & Erickson, 2005). (We have discussed the value of exercise and will pick this up again.) Stimulent medications have also been employed (Markis, Rush, Frederich, Taylor, & Kelly, 2007). However, these methods might be more difficult for older clients to use than cognitive training, owing to limits on mobility and drug side and interactive effects. Alternative strategies for promoting and delivering services for older clients, such as through senior centers and meal-delivery programs, should become the norm at some point. Educational settings, such as the popular Oasis program or the PATH (Promoting Alternative Thinking Strategies) program, are worth noting. The Oasis program, for example, is located in 26 U.S. cities (http://www.oasisnet.org) and serves as a means of disseminating information about CBT and other evidence-based therapies, teaching basic mood management skills, and offering referrals to CBT therapists in the community; all these clearly have merit.

In Chapter 7 we present two studies on efficacy for cognitive training and older adults. We believe that the effort to address thinking does several things that provide help in the realm of psychotherapy. They include awareness on the part of the patient that she or he has the ability to think. The patient also sees that this assists in his or her overall treatment and has a generalized effect on life as a whole. He or she also sees that his or her own symptoms are not entirely intractable. Some success breeds more success.

Regarding the ACTIVE trial previously described, it was noted that:

Cognitive training improves cognitive function in well-functioning older adults, and this improvement lasts up to 5 years. These improvements can have a positive effect on daily function.

Ball et al. (2002, p. 2274)

RECOMMENDED TREATMENT FACTOR: PSYCHOTHERAPIST AS NEUROSCIENTIST

We encourage therapists to foster their role(s). This is a new venture for many but one that we endorse highly. As a therapist for older adults, there are three roles to be fostered. They are not mutually exclusive. The therapist can be a neuroscientist, a geropsychologist, or an empirically supported therapist. Each has merit with different patients and times.

Psychotherapist as Neuroscientist

- Encourage neurocognitive knowledge; not a fault of character; Neuroscience is simple and cool: Mind and brain are indivisible.
- Thinking causes problems. All schemas, for good or bad, are personal fabrications. The solution is to question thoughts, be open to feedback, and resist avoidance.
- Encourage psychotherapy: This positively impacts the underlying neural network.
- Any re-regulation of neuronal networks parallels symptomatic changes in psychotherapy.
- Psychotherapy changes the brain: Lower hippocampus related to anxiety and hypometabolism in temporal lobes related to depression creates real brain-related memory problems and resistance to therapy. For MDD, CBT decreased frontal activation/increased limbic; IPT increased activation in right posterior cingulate and decreased activation in prefrontal cortex.
- Activate the left hemisphere: Narratives resculpt neuronal networks throughout life. This is the heart of assimilation/accommodation.
- Enrich environments (cognitive reserve).
- Encourage plasticity: Use cognitive reserve or cognitive training because depression and anxiety are brain-related problems.
- Be an amygdala whisperer: Early stress impairs! Amygdala (50 ms feedback system) is fully developed at birth and begrudgingly shares time and function with the frontal lobes (500 ms) over time.

- Use the placebo rules: Effect depends on the prefrontal lobes in a top-down cortical modulation of mood, emotion, and immune activity. Placebo effect is the core condition of treatment—often necessary and sufficient for change.

RECOMMENDED TREATMENT FACTOR: BOOSTER SESSIONS

There is the longstanding recognition that late-life mental disorders have a heterogeneous and tenacious quality. One might even argue that the chronic disease model fits best for this population—a model in which symptom amelioration or suppression but not complete resolution applies. Concomitantly, it follows that a partial response is a frustrating but nonetheless a frequent outcome leading to recommendations of *multimodal* interventions and extended treatment over time.

Booster sessions can be applied. This has been found to add to the efficacy of CBT with younger groups (Hollon et al., 2002). It makes sense here: More is better than less. As many as 38% of elderly patients who experience a first depression episode will relapse within 6 years, and many more with two or more episodes will relapse (Hyer & Intrieri, 2006). Additionally, many will subclinically wax and wane with depressive symptoms, depending on initial response/remission status, current circumstances, health status, and comorbidities, especially anxiety. In effect, this form of relapse therapy is not only logical but also critical. Bockting and colleagues (2005) reported one of several studies showing that cognitive therapy makes a difference in remitted patients who have had recurrent problems of depression; relapse is reduced considerably with cognitive therapy.

Extratherapy interventions are equally important. They are routine in many primary care studies with older adults (e.g., Unitzer, Patrick, & Simon, 1997). In structured studies with older adults who have anxiety, extratherapy elements (i.e., phone calls, home visits, and longer meetings) can be used to good effect (e.g., Mohlman et al., 2003; Stanley et al., 2011). It is not entirely clear why symptoms of anxiety/depression in the elderly differ from those of younger groups, but this aspect of reassurance and commitment appears helpful, even necessary, for change in older groups.

Let's see another case.

Case: Mr. D

BACKGROUND: Mr. D is a 73-year-old male who indicates that he has had memory problems dating back to 2009. Recently he had successful back surgery. He indicates that he had to stop work in 2008 owing to "problems in the shop." He had been in waste management for over 40 years. He is married, has four children, and lives with his wife. His wife describes him as "very structured and a worrier." He did not want to be in this interview but consented.

Mr. D is a native of Georgia. He is the oldest of three children. He indicates that his growth years were positive and there were no milestone disruptions. He finished high school and went to college. He was married in 1958 and has been married to the same person for almost 54 years.

He relates that his memory is fine. His wife sees this otherwise. She noted several IADL problems in the last year, including problems with finances, driving, and occasional medicine confusion. He indicates that he has had only a few medical procedures (back and hernia repair). He also has had recent heart problems and has had an angioplasty with stents placed. He does not drink alcohol, but did smoke cigars for 40 years. He has not smoked for about 10 years. He also apparently has a history of fear problems, although was never treated for panic attacks and claustrophobia. These have not occurred in the past 2 to 3 years.

TEST RESULTS: Mr. D is fully oriented and functions reasonable well day to day. His Montreal Cognitive Assessment (MoCA) was 22/30, Mini Mental Status Examination (MMSE) 20/30, and Repeatable Battery for the Assessment of Neuropsychological Status (RBANS) Total Index score was 81 (approximately 1 standard deviation low). He has poor memory and responds less than normal on tasks of executive function. He is able to do simple problem solving only. He has reasonable attention skills. He scored 6 on the Functional Activities Questionnaire (FAQ), indicating mild problems on this measure of executive functions in activities of daily living.

He registered problems with anxiety on the MINI. On the GDS-SF (Geriatric Depression Scale-Short Form) he scored 3 and on the BDI-II (Beck Depression Inventory-II), 9, average for no depression. He endorsed problems that had to do with having no energy, sleep, and sex. There were indications of anxiety on the Millon Behavioral Medicine Diagnostic (MBMD). He scored in the anxiety range on the Short Anxiety Screening Test (SAST) (22), as well as the GAD-9 (Generalized Anxiety Disorder-9); (10).

Mr. D's profile indicates that cognition and anxiety are problems and require initial responses. He has a supportive wife and relates that he is handling most issues in life adequately. A problem list focusing on cognition and anxiety were targeted. Medical issues will also be carefully monitored.

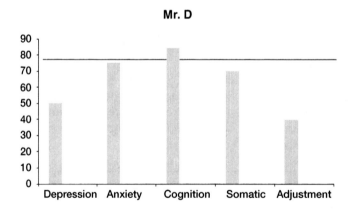

Mr. D

Mr. D—WATCH AND WAIT

Sessions 1 to 3:
Mr. D has mild cognitive problems and is anxious. He is about 1 standard deviation low on cognitive tests. He has a reduced memory especially. He also has substantial anxiety as a worrier. He has minor problems with adjustment (FAQ = 6).

The two areas of cognition and anxiety were highlighted. He was asked to consider the importance of brain health and to enter the 10-week memory program. He was to plan his next 3 months for this. He was also informed about anxiety and the problems with the hippocampus with anxiety and worry. He was to carefully monitor this and see where he had the most anxious concerns. Relaxation, worry psychoeducation, and worry control were to be initiated. Medication was to be considered if these failed. Medical issues were also be carefully monitored, especially any reactivation of pain.

Watch and Wait Category	Check
Validate Problem	×
Psychoeducation of Model	×
Assessment	×
Monitoring	×
Case Formulation	×
Check Alliance	×

Sessions 4 to 12:
The modules were instituted and the therapy went well. He was very responsive to the Memory Clinic and had his wife come to the session. He loved the idea of homework and being a student. This helped with confidence and his anxiety. Relaxation was slow but heart rate variability biofeedback showed a positive result. Self-rewards were very helpful. His wife was very supportive and helpful. Relapse issues were discussed and he is seen every 3 months.

CONCLUSION

We have presented the components in therapy with older adults that can make a difference. Watch and Wait is a method and a message. Involved are the flexible components that foster change—specific and general. Living consciously is a challenge for us all. Psychology teaches us that avoidance is the enemy: passivity, surrender, excessive help, loss of control, surrender, giving in to emotions. The therapy outlined here teaches the older adult to be in charge of self. It teaches us to think clearly, optimizing "the passionate life." This is the heart of psychotherapy.

From another perspective, aging/frailty/cognition resist facile definition and measurement. Aging is related to a number of deficits, not to a particular system. The "syndrome of aging" derives not from singular components of a system but from a system as a whole.

It is, therefore, an emergent construct. Emergence derives its essence from multiple synergies of the components, not from individual ones. Knowledge of aging in effect is rarely complete, rather dynamic, and requires an assay of its behavior as well as factors such as biomarkers and social aspects.

The view espoused of psychotherapy here is, in part, programmatic and simple. It too is an "emergent construct" that provides both direction and passion, as well as meaning.

CHAPTER 4

Depression

Depressive symptoms among older adults are common and costly. For the general population, between 13.1 and 14.2 million people will experience Major Depressive Disorder (MDD) in any given year. Approximately half of these people seek help for this condition, and only 20% of those receive adequate treatment. For those who do initiate treatment for their depression, approximately 50% will not adequately respond following acute-phase treatment; this refractory group has garnered considerable clinical and research interest (treatment-resistant depression [TRD]). For all these data points, older adults can be viewed as equal or worse.

If one were to factor-analyze depression, the bottom line is that there would exist subtypes of problems, but a large common factor would also be present; one would see some commonality and many distinct profiles representing differences. In fact, depression is most likely an epigenetic disease: Environmental acts set in motion the genetic code for some characteristic that leads to depression. Depression is then influenced by social genomics in which common problems in the environment (such as social isolation, trauma, or medical diseases) result in the formation of a depression related to the initiating problem. Regardless, depression at late life is complex.

There is increasing evidence that symptoms of elderly depression may be etiologically distinct (e.g., more psychomotor retardation and anhedonia in vascular depression) and that focusing on subclusters of depressive symptoms, rather than relying on general depression assessment tools may help enhance construct validity. ... (p. 379)

At the least, ... the development of depression and cardiovascular dysfunction share molecular mechanisms, such as stress induced changes in inflammatory markers and neurotransmitter signaling, all related to common genetic elements. (p. 380)

Lu and Ahmed (2010)

In a quixotic way, the best design for the treatment of depression is based on the public-health target "indicated," where prevention is sought for high-risk subjects before they become patients. As a common disorder with devastating outcomes, geriatric depression is a major health hazard. The various antidepressants have similar efficacy, but each agent helps a rather small number of depressed elderly patients. Identification of predictors of treatment response and personalization of treatment (i.e., matching treatment with patient) has long been contemplated as a strategy to increase efficacy, to prevent relapses, and to preempt disability. Unfortunately, antidepressant drugs often worsen medical morbidity and increase cognitive decline. Although we are not yet there, it is prudent to have a "depression watch" on at-risk patients and to monitor therapy so as to make changes in treatment.

These facts, among others, make the treatment of depression difficult at best. But data from standard care make the picture worse. As we have previously indicated, overall, about 10% of adults use antidepressants (Olfson & Marcus, 2009). These medications are the most commonly prescribed in United States; 59% of patients taking psychiatric meds take two, and 33% take three (Olfson & Marcus, 2009).

In this chapter, we discuss the prevalence and biology of depression, the phenomenology of depression and its correlates (suicide, executive function issues, anxiety, and dementia), treatment, predictors of change, a special case of intervention in the home, and our model.

PREVALENCE AND BIOLOGY

The generally accepted prevalence rates for depression in older adults are 3% to 13% depending on the sample and study method. Representative estimates of mood, anxiety, and combined mood and anxiety disorders using a sample of 2,575 survey participants age 55 and older were 43%; 55 to 64, 32%; 65 to 74, 20%; 75 to 84, 20% and 5% for those older than 85 years (Byers et al., 2012). Lifetime prevalence is 20% to 50%. At any given time 20% have depressive symptoms. Women again rule in the world of depression (2:1). Recidivism rates also are high; 50% for one disorder, 70% for two, and 90% for three or more. It is also stated that the genetic load at late life for depression is 16% to 25% of variance. The usual suspects include socioeconomic status (SES), early learning problems, family history, stress, trauma, and sleep. In addition, about 12% of those with an MDD also have an anxiety disorder. Interestingly, 66% of those with MDD have experienced a major negative event in the past 6 months. Unfortunately, older adults make up 60% of all psychiatric hospitalizations, often owing to depression. It has been noted that the incidence of depression (how often it first appears) does not vary with advancing age, but the probability of it resolving decreases. This is generally owing to aging-specific problems. This results in an increase in the overall prevalence of depression in old–old age, but it is not a "normal part" of getting older.

Depression: Primary Care Focus

- 80% to 90% of depression patients are seen in primary care clinics (PCC)
- Prevalence rates 17% to 37%
- Up to one-half of depressed elderly seen by primary care physicians (PCPs) are not identified as depressed

---

There is to date no biological marker for depression, let alone for older adults with depression. But there are indicators. This starts with MRI changes in late life relative to depression. For late-life depression (LLD), there are enlarged ventricles, white matter hyperintensities, periventricular hyperintensities, small putamen, and small caudate. The persistently reduced activation in the cingulate too is evident in remitted LLD during performance of the executive task, which was not related to genetic influence.

General Biology of Depression

- Twin studies (16% of variance in Center for Epidemiological Studies Depression Scale [CES-D] and 19% of somatic items)
- 5-HTTLPRs short allele associated with increased amygdala activation to sad stimuli
- BDNF (brain-derived neurotrophic factor) met allele-modulated activation to sad stimuli
- Increased incidence of homozygous "short" alleles in promoter region of 5-HT transporter
- CRF (corticotrophin-releasing factor) hypersecretes
- HAM-D (Hamilton Depression Rating Scale) factor correlates with distinct brain regions
  - Weight loss
  - Cardiovascular disease
  - Platelet activation is greater
  - T-cell response is lower
  - Poorest blastogenic response to mitogens
  - Highest level of cytokine interleukin 6
  - Elevated homocysteine levels

PHENOMENOLOGY OF DEPRESSION

Depression is not a simple construct of sadness. In the past 10 years the importance of medical care, selective serotonin reuptake inhibitors (SSRIs; and their antidepressant brethren), suicide, subsyndromal states, and unique psychotherapies like cognitive behavioral therapy (CBT)/problem-solving therapy (PST) have taken center stage in terms of discussion. Primary care has also been of high interest. Of importance, older adults with depressive symptoms, but not depressive disorder per se, have functioning comparable to or poorer than those with chronic medical conditions, such as heart and lung disease, arthritis, and diabetes, and are at risk for developing full-blown major depressive episodes. Moreover, treatment is often inadequate in relieving the burden of depressive illness in old age.

There are many problems related to depression at late life that may make a diagnosis suspect. The MDD criteria for depression have been reasonably standard since the *DMS-III* (1980). The *DSM-5* (2013) is very similar. This edition presents essentially like criteria, but slightly more intricate. The core criterion symptoms applied to the diagnosis of major depressive episode and the requisite duration of at least 2 weeks have not changed for the *DSM-5*. Again, one of the symptoms is either depressed mood or loss of interest or pleasure. Issues related to social, occupational, or other life areas also impacted have not been altered. For older adults, the overall criteria make little difference at this level (MDD).

The bereavement exclusion is not present in the *DSM-5* because it is seen as a severe psychological stressor, it lasts longer than 2 months, it tends to be a problem in people who have had depressive concerns in the past, and depressive symptoms associated with bereavement-related depression respond to the same psychosocial and medication treatments as non-bereavement-related depression. The authors of the *DSM-5* hold that the presence of a major depressive episode, in addition to the normal response to a significant loss, should also be carefully considered.

The symptom profile for older adults, is often not typical (heterosyndromal), as symptoms fluctuate and often may be transient in the short term. In point of fact, there are shades of gray in the construct of depression. Minor depression involves two to four symptoms, including low mood or anhedonia. This is highly relevant for older adults. It should last at least 2 weeks and exclude individuals with a history of MDD. Rapoport et al. (2002) noted that minor depression was primarily characterized by mood and cognitive symptoms, not classical neurovegetative signs and symptoms of depression. Having a history of MDD, however, did not influence the severity of the disorder. Other variants are also present.

Subsyndromal depression, which is usually a score of 16 or more on scales like the Cornell (CES-D) and does not meet the criteria of MDD or other depression categories, is also prevalent. Depression in dementia is a unique and ever-changing construct with much variability; and poststroke depression is common in 20% of stroke victims and tied to excess disability. There exist also a number of specificiers characteristic of older adults. These are tied to onset, course, and treatment response. The *DSM-5* broadens the scope with these to a more dimensional view that could add to the richness and mix of the core diagnosis with subthreshold influences. Presumably this more dimensional approach will allow for an improved ability to monitor change over time. Of special relevance for older adults is the presence of mixed anxiety depression, with criteria similar to the *DSM-IV* but requiring three to four criteria from depression and two or more from anxiety with no other diagnosis of depression or anxiety. Mixed depression and anxiety is the most common diagnosis in Great Britain.

There are in addition a slew of unique later-life dysphoric problems such as depression without sadness and suicidal depression. Certainly, we need not forget older patients with medical disorders and multiple somatic complaints: They are plentiful and clinicians should consider the possibility of depression (Drayer et al., 2005).

MDD Diagnosis (*DSM-5*)

- Depressed mood or lack of interest of at least 2 weeks with at least four of the following:
  - Significant change in weight when not dieting
  - Insomnia or hypersomnia
  - Psychomotor agitation or retardation
  - Fatigue or loss of energy
  - Feelings of worthlessness, inappropriate guilt
  - Decreased concentration or thinking, indecisiveness
  - Recurrent thoughts of death or suicide
- No medial/substance etiology/mixed episode/other psych
- Significant distress or impairment
- Not uncomplicated bereavement

Specifiers

With anxious distress
With mixed features
With melancholic features
With atypical features
With mood-congruent psychotic features
With mood-incongruent psychotic features
With catatonia
With peripartum onset
With seasonal patterns

A question can be asked here: "When is a dimensional diagnosis not better than a category?" The answer is simple: virtually never (Slade & Andrews, 2005). Using taxonometric analysis on the question of whether a construct is better considered as two latent discrete variables or one latent continuous variable, Ruscio and Ruscio (2000) noted that continuous wins. The correlates of severity include high pretreatment severity, suicidality, melancholic or psychotic features, and various types of comorbidities (anxiety disorders, neuroticism, and panic disorder). Biomarkers of hypercortisol and changes in regional and cerebral metabolism (increased activation of amygdala, decreased activation of frontal cortical structures, and increased activation of norepinephrine) also play a role. In addition, there is also a slower rate of treatment response, less likely placebo response, and a greater likelihood of a response to both psychotherapy and medications.

Minor Depression

- Appendix B in *DSM-IV*: two to four symptoms, low mood or anhedonia
- After 1 year as a minor depression (MinD), 78% had protracted depression after 1 year, same as MDD (Cole et al., 2006)
- Risk factor for poorer cognitive function after 1 year in PCC

Subsyndromal Depression

- Many do not reach criteria for MinD
- Subsyndromal: more than 16 on CES-D but not full MDD criteria met

Depression Without Sadness

- Unexplained somatic complaints
- Hopelessness
- Helplessness
- Anxiety and worry
- Memory complaints with or without objective markers
- Loss of feeling of pleasure
- Slowed movement
- Irritability
- Lack of interest in personal care
- Personality disorder (dejected, conforming, dependent)

Bereavement

- 800,000 people per year experience bereavement (20% MDD)
- 50% MDD symptoms some time during first year
- Subsyndromal symptoms
  - 27% at 2 months
  - 19% at 3 months
  - 12% at 25 months

Depressive Executive Dysfunction

- Frontostriatal dysfunction appears to contribute to the pathogenesis of some late-life depression
- Proposed clinical features:
  - Psychomotor retardation
  - Reduced interest in activities
  - Suspiciousness
  - Impaired instrumental activities of daily living (IADL)
  - Limited vegetative symptoms
- Treatment response:
  - Suboptimal to antidepressants
  - Better response to problem-solving therapy

Anxiety With Depression

- Accelerates disease process of all diseases
- Worsens pain
- Worsens health outcomes and quality of life (QoL)
- Increases mortality
- Increases long-term care facility (LTC) admission and hospitalization
- Increases caregiver problems
- Risk/prodrome for cognitive decline

Overriding this problem state is the idea that depression exists as adaptation. Fever is a good metaphor for depression. Like a fever, depression can be healthy, as it promotes an analytic thinking style. In sum, the psychiatric emphasis on discerning the nuances of depression has created excessive numbers of diagnoses; the real prevalence may be as low as 1% to 2%.

Poststroke Depression

- Prevalence rates 16% to 61%; 25% have another stroke in 5 years
- Immaterial whether caused by etiology or as a secondary consequence
- Excess disability is a problem
- Results are limited, but CBT modules of psychoeducation, collaborative empiricism, active problem solving, evaluating the nature and quality of supports, and enhancement of the adjustment to the new life appear to be useful
- Cognitive restructuring is important
- 25% have Generalized Anxiety Disorder (GAD)
- CBT programs for poststroke: Kemp et al. (1992), Lincoln et al. (1997), Lincoln and Flannaghan (2003)
- Risk highest in first 2 years after a stroke
- Within 10 years after a stroke, the risk of death is 3.5 times higher in depressed patients

Depression Caused by Dementia

- Depression is common in patients with Alzheimer's disease
- It presents as an atypical affective syndrome
- It can be hard to diagnose
- Its treatment is an essential part of dementia care

Persistent effort, using nonpharmacologic and pharmacologic interventions, is needed for success.

TABLE 4.1 Secondary Causes in Late-Onset Depression

– Vascular disease
  – Stroke
  – Ischemic white matter disease
– Neurodegenerative disease
  – Parkinson's disease
  – Alzheimer's disease
– Anemia
– Cancer
– Macular degeneration
– Chronic pain

Depression as Continuum

- Depression may be present or absent at one point in time but not over time
- Specious to argue that it is gone after a "treatment"
- No evidence of a break at four to five symptoms
- Relationship between number of symptoms and impairment is linear

- No evidence of any natural dichotomy of five out of nine symptoms (Sakashita, Slade, & Andrews, 2007)
- Patients with a depression diagnosis differ from each other in many ways
- Twenty percent of those with major depressive episode (MDE) report being satisfied with life, not distressed

This minority had a lower neuroticism score, had only five symptoms, and reported fewer comorbid symptoms and lower levels of help-seeking characteristics.

- Diagnoses with anxious-depressed co-occurrences lend themselves to dimensions

---

Depression is also an issue at some point for many (most) older adults. The *DSM* and its connection to syndromes are important, but we believe a false front where older adults are concerned. Most older adults have issues with life and have two out of nine depressive symptoms, two of six general anxiety symptoms, and several pain or somatic problems, as well as issues of health and life-based concerns. These are not necessarily Axis I syndromes. Also, recall that most depressions at late life are mild. So, the person at later life needs help in several areas and need not be labeled with an Axis I diagnosis. This places the emphasis on openness, on primary care interconnectedness, on real-life issues, and on the need for perspective.

Softer Depressive Symptoms

DSM symptoms
- Loss of interest
- Fatigue or loss of energy
- Diminished ability
- Physical complaints
- Sleep problems

Geriatric Depression Scale
- Satisfied with life
- Dropped out of activities
- Bored
- Prefers to stay at home
- Others better off than you
- Not in good spirits most of the time

Recently, in the *New York Times*, Abby Ellin echoed this as she praised how psychotherapy can assist in the golden years with both a changed attitude on mental health and a reframe on what mental health really is at late life.

Everybody has a certain amount of heartache in life—it's how you handle the heartache that is the essential core of your life, Mr. Tolkin said. "I have found that my attitude was important, and I had to reinforce positive things all the time."

Ellin (2013, p. 22)

Older patients with depression often present with somatic complaints for which a medical etiology cannot be found or that are disproportionate to the extent of medical illness. In fact, older patients who express somatic symptoms as a manifestation of depression seem to be less willing to mention psychological symptoms to their physician. Patient attributions of symptoms matter: If seen as physical, then a physical diagnosis is provided. Somatic presentations of depression are among the most challenging situations faced by family physicians. The patient may worry that a serious illness underlies the symptoms. Certainly, illnesses such as pancreatic carcinoma or hypothyroidism might cause symptoms that mimic depression. It is important to address the patient's psychological distress while appropriately evaluating the possible diagnoses. The evaluation should always include a careful, critical review of the medications the patient is taking. Family physicians are well situated to consider both the mental and physical aspects of the patient's illness.

In addition, cognition (principally executive function), cerebral vascular problems, and dementia play an important role in LLD. The issue of CVRF (cerebrovascular risk factors) is front and center. Anxiety may be a variable in this organic context. We will address these later, as well as in other chapters.

Again, most older patients do not solicit treatment. Patients present only after there is urging from others. Interestingly, the trajectory of depression after some remission does suggest problems. Deshields, Tibbs, Fan, and Taylor (2006), in a longitudinal study on cancer survivors using the CES-D, identified five distinct subgroups of women (Never Depressed, Recover, Become Depressed, Stay Depressed, and Vacillate). In another cancer study, Dunn et al. (2011) identified four latent classes: Low Decelerating, Intermediate, Late Accelerating, and Parabolic.

Perhaps the best study was conducted by Byers et al. (2012). To characterize the natural course of depressive symptoms among older women (from the young old to the oldest old), participants were followed for almost 20 years. Using latent-class growth-curve analysis, this group analyzed women enrolled in an ongoing prospective cohort study (1988 to 2009) of community-dwelling women ($N = 7240$) 65 years of age or older. The Geriatric Depression Scale short form (score range, 0 to 15) was used to routinely assess depressive symptoms during the follow-up period. Among older women, four latent classes existed during 20 years, with the predicted probabilities of group membership totaling 27.8% with minimal depressive symptoms, 54.0% with persistently low depressive symptoms, 14.8% with increasing depressive symptoms, and 3.4% with persistently high depressive symptoms. Baseline smoking, physical inactivity, small social network, physical impairment, myocardial infarction, diabetes mellitus, and obesity were predictors for the increasing and persistent depressives. During 20 years, then, almost 20% of older women experienced persistently high depressive symptoms or increasing depressive symptoms.

CORRELATIVE SYMPTOMS

The empirical basis for personalizing treatment principally consists of post hoc analyses of unitary treatments (e.g., a course of an antidepressant or psychotherapy). Although this knowledge is necessary, it is insufficient for two reasons. First, depressed elderly persons face a bewildering constellation of health threats and social constraints and thus have many different contributors to poor treatment outcomes. Second, the skills available in various treatment settings and sectors can promote or inhibit treatment success. Therefore, to benefit depressed elderly patients in the community, personalization of care must employ comprehensive care algorithms targeting both modifiable predictors of poor outcomes and organizational barriers to care. Accordingly, the model of geriatric depression must integrate the current biological concepts of depression with patients' unique reactions to adverse experiences and with their unmet social and health care needs. The care algorithms based on this model should (a) target clinical/biological predictors of adverse outcomes of depression, (b) address unmet needs through linkage to appropriate social services, (c) enhance the competencies of elderly persons so that they make use of their resources, and (d) attend to patient psychoeducation needs (Alexopoulos, 2008).

But there is more. Most patients fail in treatment because their problems exceed the ability of the effectiveness of our science, or they or we expect too much from our therapies. We need to know this and apply what we can do with recognition of what we cannot do—and we should know the difference. The "tyranny of reality" is present. There are many causes of depression and its problems. It is an equal-opportunity offender and a leveler of people, seeping through the portals of several medical illnesses, making primary and secondary depression illusory. Its treatment should be readdressed.

Suicide

In the Prevention of Suicide in Primary Care Elderly: Collaborative Trial (PROSPECT) (Bruce, Ten Have, & Reynolds, 2004) study, older primary care patients with major depression who had access to trained care managers were more likely to have their depression treated and to have reduced suicidal ideation (SI) and increased remission rates over a period of 2 years compared with a similar population who received usual care. The study included 599 patients with depression at 20 primary care practices in urban, suburban, and rural settings. Their mean Hamilton Depression Rating Scale score at baseline was 18.1. The subjects were randomized to receive either the intervention (320 patients) or usual care (279 patients).

In the intervention group, patients had access to trained care managers, including social workers, nurses, or psychologists, who helped physicians monitor depressive symptoms and adverse medication effects and offer treatment with an antidepressant medication, as well interpersonal psychotherapy when needed or chosen by patients. The treatment algorithm used by care managers recommended the antidepressant citalopram as the first step of treatment, but physicians could prescribe other medications and refer patients for other types of psychotherapy. Physicians in the usual-care group received information on geriatric depression and were made aware of the patients' depression diagnosis and of suicidal thoughts when present.

Results at 24 months were striking. Treatment rates ranged from 84.9% to 89% with the intervention, compared with 49% to 62% for the usual-care group. In addition, the rate of suicidal ideation dropped more in the intervention group. By 24 months, the decline in suicidal ideation was 2.2 times greater than in the usual-care group—a decline of 18.3% to a rate of 11.4% versus a decline of 8.3% to a rate of 12.1%.

Care-management systems such as the one in PROSPECT are increasingly needed, as primary care physicians do not have the time or resources to provide the necessary care. Improving quality of care and frequency of contacts for people with depression helps over the first 12 months and beyond. Patients with depression and significant comorbidities, such as those in the study, are costly to the health care system.

In another study at multiple sites (IMPACT; Vannoy et al., 2001), efforts were made to describe the course of SI in primary care-based LLD treatment. This was a secondary analysis of a randomized controlled trial comparing collaborative care to usual care for LLD. Participants were 1,801 adults, aged 60 and older, from eight diverse primary care systems. The prevalence of SI was 14%; the cumulative incidence over 24 months was 21%. The likelihood that SI emerged after baseline was highly dependent on change in depression. The effect of collaborative care on SI was mediated by the treatment's effect on depression. SI, then, is not uncommon in depressed older adults being treated in primary care. The likelihood that depressed older adults will report SI is strongly determined by the course of their depression symptoms.

Anxiety

Anxiety cohabits with depression. The prevalence rates for comorbid anxiety and depressive symptoms varied between 4.5% and 9.4% (Wolinsky et al., 2010). Furthermore, all depressive symptoms are made worse with comorbid anxiety. Comorbid anxiety and depressive symptoms especially seem to be related to cognitive decline and follow the pattern of an increasing intensity as cognitive performance declines and, interestingly, a decrease intensity when cognitive functioning is severely impaired.

The associations between risk factors and pure anxiety or depressive symptoms or disorders were summarized and compared (Vink, Aartsen, & Shoevers, 2008). The abstracted risk factors from studies on anxiety ($N = 17$) and depression ($N = 71$) were clustered into the categories biological, psychological, and social. In fact, risk factors for anxiety and depression showed many similarities, but some differences were found. Biological factors may be more important in predicting depression, and a differential effect of social factors was found for depression and anxiety. Further, being older seems to be protective for anxiety, but is a risk factor for depression. Biological factors thus predict the onset of depression and the existence of depression and anxiety, and there is a differential effect of social factors on anxiety and depression is found. This appears to be in line with the idea that depression may be more strongly related to loss events, whereas anxiety may result from actual and more imminent threats.

Nevertheless, the similarities between risk factors for anxiety and depression in the elderly mostly favor a dimensional and less a categorical classification of these disorders. This assumption underlines the importance of clinicians not only to focus on the categorical *DSM* criteria, but also on variations between the different sets of symptoms offered by older adults, in the early recognition of both anxiety and depression.

Executive Function

Depression at late life exists on messy grounds; on the one end, functional and psychological depression exists; on the other, organic problems present themselves. In general, depression presents with a heterogeneous mix of depression, some anxiety, and cognitive decline. Depression is often comorbid with vascular problems, striatofrontal impairment to be specific. This is due largely to CVRF. This may actually be a small-vessel disease. As noted earlier, MRI changes of LLD include enlarged ventricles, cortical atrophy, increased incidence of periventricular hyperintensity, increased incidence of basal ganglia lesions, small caudate nucleus, and a smaller putamen nucleus. As biomarker vulnerabilities and frontal-striatial brain areas are impacted, impaired life events or decreased social support can accentuate stress: depression becomes the final common pathway.

An important step in personalizing treatment is to develop an understanding of the type and nature of brain abnormalities occurring in patients with LLD. This knowledge can be informative in two ways. First, identifying persisting abnormalities during remission may indicate a high risk for relapse or persistent cognitive impairment. Second, finding brain abnormalities predictive of poor outcomes of depression may initiate a search for their clinical correlates, which then can be used to personalize treatment.

A reduced activation of structures that participate in executive function (EF) (the supramarginal gyrus bilaterally, the left anterior cingulate,

FIGURE 4.1 Development of Depressive Disorders

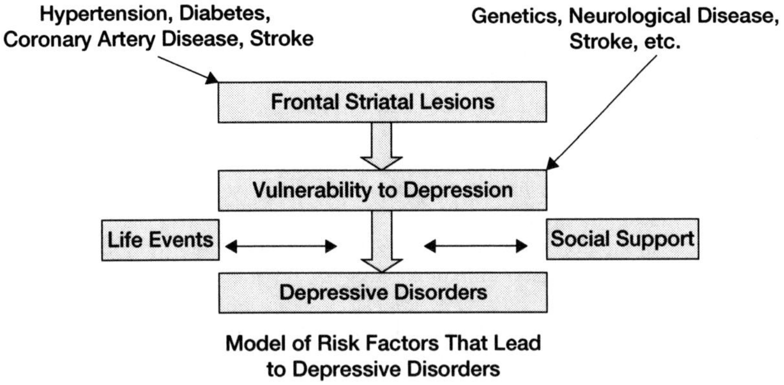

Hypertension, Diabetes,
Coronary Artery Disease, Stroke

Genetics, Neurological Disease,
Stroke, etc.

Frontal Striatal Lesions

Vulnerability to Depression

Life Events ⟷ ⟷ Social Support

Depressive Disorders

Model of Risk Factors That Lead
to Depressive Disorders

Adapted from Krishnan (2002).

and the anterior part of the posterior cingulate) occurs both in depressed and previously depressed (remitted) patients relative to comparison subjects. The persistence of reduced activation in these structures is consistent with the clinical observation that executive dysfunction in depressed elderly patients remains after remission of depression (Alexopoulos, 2005; Lyketsos & Olin, 2002). Executive dysfunction (Lyketsos et al., 2003) and microstructural abnormalities in white matter connecting structures that subserve EFs (De Vasconcelos et al., 2007) have been associated with poor or slow response of geriatric depression to antidepressant treatment. Taken together, these findings suggest that functional and structural abnormalities of networks relevant to executive dysfunction characterize a robust subgroup of depressed elderly patients who experience poor outcomes.

Alexopoulos (2008) has reminded us that geriatric depression is characterized by a slow response to antidepressants, a failure to fully remit, and a high propensity for relapse. Converging evidence suggests that both structural and activation abnormalities in cerebral networks necessary for emotion regulation may not only predispose individuals to depression, but also confer risk for poor antidepressant response. These network abnormalities likely result from a number of influences, including differences in cerebral aging, vascular disease, and genetic influences. Greater activation of select aspects of frontostriatal and limbic networks, including the rostral anterior cingulate cortex, predicts subsequent treatment remission. In a meta-analysis on the use of MRI in older adults with depression volume, Sexton, Mackay, and Ebmeier (2013) found reductions in the orbitofrontal cortex, hippocampus, putamen, and thalamus. In a phrase, EF problems reflect brain issues and wreak havoc on depression.

- Executive dysfunction is present in a considerable number of older individuals with major depression (Alexopoulos et al., 2002, 2005; Elderkin-Thompson et al., 2003, 2008; Lockwood, Alexopoulos, & van Gorp, 2002). Estimates range from 25% to 40% of patients.
- Executive dysfunction predicts poor, slow, and unstable response to antidepressant treatment (Alexopoulos et al., 1997, 2000, 2003, 2005; Murphy & Alexopoulos, 2004; Potter, Kittinger, Wagner, Steffens & Krishnan, 2004; Sneed et al., 2007, 2008), as well as increased current and future disability (Kiosses et al., 2001; Yochim, Lequerica, MacNeill, & Lichtenberg, 2008).
- Relative contribution of lesion severity, executive dysfunction, and late age at onset indicate that only executive dysfunction predicted poor response to citalopram (Sneed et al., 2007).
- Executive dysfunction predicts suicidality, even after controlling for comorbid conditions (Dombrovski et al., 2007).
- Deep white matter lesions appear to be the critical diagnostic factor in identifying a distinct subgroup of late-life depression, BUT deficits in executive dysfunction appear to be more important clinically (Sneed et al., 2010).
- Observations from both acute treatment trials and longer-term follow-up suggest that executive dysfunction persists despite remission of depression (Butters et al., 2000; Murphy & Alexopoulos, 2004).

The measures below are EF scales used in traditional psychology. A poor response echoes the probability of a failure in response to treatment of depression for older adults. Life in the therapy room for depression is different when EF is a problem.

- Lower scores on Mattis Depression Rating Scale (DRS I/P) were associated with poorer response to 6-week antidepressant treatment (Kayalam & Alexopoulos, 1999)
- Among 50 patients with late-onset depression (29 who were responders to antidepressant monotherapy and 21 who were not), nonresponders scored significantly worse than responders on two tests of EF (verbal fluency and Stroop test; Baldwin et al., 2003)
- Perseverative errors on scores of two tests: Animal Naming (AN) and Controlled Oral Word Association (COWA) tests; total perseverative errors (AN + COWA) decreased odds of 3-month remission among actively treated older depressed patients (OR = 0.74, confidence interval = 0.55–0.99, p = .045) (Potter et al., 2004)
- Older depressed patients with lowest quartile performance on Stroop had poorer response to 8 weeks of citalopram (Sneed et al., 2010)
- Those with poor Stroop performance receiving usual care had poor response and remission rate; those assigned to a depression care manager did better (Bogner et al., 2005)

Depression and cognition are coequal and cause problems for each other as well as disability. Many longitudinal studies show that greater numbers of depressive symptoms at baseline predict cognitive decline. Jorm (2001), on evaluating 14 studies, found that the history of depression doubles the risk of dementia (risk ratio = 2.01). Brommelhoff et al. (2009) hold that depression is a prodromal feature of dementia, not a risk factor. Finally, Ownby, Crocco, Acavedo, Veneeth, and Loewenstein (2006), using 13 studies, both case-controlled and cohort, analyzed the relationship between interval length and diagnosis of depression and AD, and found that the length of the interval between the diagnosis of depression and AD is associated with increased risk of AD; depression leads to dementia.

It is now reasonably recognized that a cognitive pattern of memory, EF and information processing deficits is characteristic of depression at late life and occurs to a greater or lesser extent in virtually all people with clinical depression. Thus, relevant research has progressed to examine the relative contribution of different domains of cognitive impairment, their relationship to each other, changes over time and in response to treatment, and what neurobiological changes underpin these cognitive deficits. Impaired information processing is then an important mediating factor for other neurocognitive impairments in depression. It follows then that people with more severe neurocognitive impairments when depressed are both less likely to remit and more likely to remain significantly cognitively impaired after a period of antidepressant treatment. This is the challenge of depression treatment at later life.

Executive dysfunction makes a difference in LLD and is associated with poor treatment response with antidepressants. This deficit does not appear to change even after an effective course of medication. We are then confronted with the issue of the value of assessing EF. Would treating EF deficits improve clinical outcomes? The answer seems to be a resounding YES! Abnormal performance on some tests of EF moderates (negatively) response to SSRI. Assuming that cognitive retraining (CR) changes EF by changing underlying brain abnormalities, a change in depressive symptoms will probably ensue. Further, CR improves both targeted functions and related but not directly targeted functions (near transfer) in older adults (Bherer et al., 2008; Persson & Reuter Lorenz, 2008; Smith et al., 2009). Remediation of EF deficits may decrease disability, improve functioning, and reduce depression. Neurobiologically informed computerized cognitive remediation may then improve targeted executive functions. In sum, cognitive remediation targeted to specific cognitive functions found to be associated with poor treatment response may improve both cognitive and affective symptoms associated with geriatric depression.

We should also note that depression is different in a dementia. Among the atypical depressive features are increased severity of motivational symptoms (Janzing, Hooijer, van't Hof, & Zitman, 2002) and the presence of delusions (Mizrahi, Starkstein, Jorge, & Robinson, 2006), as well as symptoms that are distinctive of dementia (more middle or terminal insomnia and irritability) relative to younger groups (Husain et al., 2005). Depression in a dementia consists of anhedonia, irritability, anxiety, nonspecific worry, apathy, and neurovegetative change; even "psychotic" features like delusions (30% to 40%) are pervasive.

Depression in the context of dementia has an impact on functional competence also. Comorbid depression and dementia, through their impact on motivation, attention, and processing speed, may also affect performance of more complex IADL (Attix & Welsh-Bohmer, 2006), such as managing finances, shopping, and managing medication routines (Duffy & Coffey, 1996). Alexopoulos et al. (1996), for example, reported an association between geriatric depression and deficits in basic self-maintenance skills (e.g., ability to eat, dress, groom, bathe, use toilet, etc.) and IADL. Executive function was implicated as the mediator. Boyle et al. (2003) also demonstrated that EF and frontal behavioral impairment independently contribute to functional deficits in patients with mild to moderate dementia.

TREATMENT STUDIES

Psychological Treatment

In the past 5 years, little has been published to add to the value or content of the empirically supported therapies (Shah, Scogin, & Floyd, 2012). Those treatments that remain empirically supported include behavior therapy, CBT, cognitive bibliotherapy, PST, brief psychodynamic therapy, and reminiscence therapy. That said, we review these after a discussion of the overall efficacy and, to some extent, the history of treatment for older adults.

Over the past 30 years, a consensus has evolved that psychotherapy can be an effective treatment for depression in older adults. Several meta-analyses have been conducted confirming the efficacy of such interventions. In one early analysis, Scogin and McElreath (1994) found a large effect size ($d = 0.78$) for psychotherapeutic treatments. Using a more conservative effect-size estimation procedure that involved correcting for pretest differences between treatment and control conditions, Engels and Vermey (1997) examined 17 psychological treatments for geriatric depression, and found a mean effect size of $d = 0.63$. Regarding the specific efficacy of CBT for the treatment of depression, one review using American Psychological Association (APA) criteria for empirically validated treatments concluded that CBT was a well-established treatment for depression in older adults (Gatz et al., 1998; Scogin, Welsh, Hanson, Stump, & Coates, 2005). Other reviews that endorse the efficacy of psychotherapy, especially CBT, include a meta-analysis on psychotherapy and pharmacology, as well as reviews on the role of caregivers in late-life depression (see Hyer & Intrieri, 2006), and the important influence of primary care in this process (Andel, Kåreholt, Parker, Thorslund, & Gatz, 2007). CBT is also efficacious for depressive disorders in a wide variety of older adult patients (Boone et al., 1995; Lesser, Boone,

Mehringer, & Wohl, 1996), including affective disorders in the frail elderly (van Ojen et al., 1995).

Although not without limitations, meta-analyses have been helpful in drawing conclusions on the current state of psychosocial interventions for late-life depression. Cuijpers, van Straten, and Smit (2006) analyzed 25 randomized studies and found that these treatments had a moderate to large mean effect size. This meta-analysis reported no significant differences in the effects among psychological interventions (i.e., CBT, behavioral therapy [BT]), reminiscence therapy, IPT, PST, and others), no significant difference in effect of antidepressant medication versus psychological intervention, and a significantly larger effect of combined antidepressant and psychological intervention than antidepressant medication alone. In another meta-analysis that included nonrandomized studies but accounted for quality of study, Pinquart, Duberstein, and Lyness (2007) reported that CBT and reminiscence therapy had large effects, whereas most of the remaining psychosocial interventions had moderate effects.

Furthermore, studies comparing CBT or other evaluated psychotherapies against psychopharmacology for depression show that psychotherapy delivered in conjunction with pharmacotherapy is significantly more efficacious in treating depression and other mental health problems than is pharmacotherapy alone (Bhalla et al., 2009; Köhler, Thomas, Barnett, & O'Brien, 2010). Indeed, in regard to older age groups specifically, CBT and interpersonal therapy have been found to be at least as efficacious in treating depression as pharmacotherapy (Alexopoulos, Raue, & Aren, 2003; Nebes et al., 2003; Rosenberg, Mielke, Xue & Carson, 2010).

Health care policy restructuring is placing greater demands on the use of treatment interventions that can be empirically supported. Using the criteria for evidence-based treatments set forth by the Committee on Science and Practice of the Society for Clinical Psychology (Division 12) of the American Psychological Association, several psychosocial interventions can be defined as evidence based: BT, CBT, cognitive bibliotherapy, PST, brief psychodynamic therapy, and reminiscence therapy (Scogin, 2005). Using more focused criteria, Mackin and Arean (2005) identified CBT (including PST), brief psychodynamic therapy, and to some extent reminiscence therapy, as evidence-based interventions for late-life depression.

In addition, treatments that share therapeutic components with CBT have demonstrated efficacy for LLD, and bear brief mention here. These treatments include PST (Alexopoulos, Raue, & Areán, 2003), dialectical behavioral therapy (DBT; Lynch, Morse, Mendelson, & Robins, 2003), interpersonal therapy (Karel & Hinrichsen, 2000; Miller, Frank, Cornes, Houck, & Reynolds, 2003), and behavioral activation (BA; Teri, Logsdon, Uomoto, & McCurry, 1997), as well as a modified CBT for chronic and severely depressed older patients (McCullough, 2000). PST addresses core action tendencies in a structured way, which reflects a core treatment component of CBT. Dialectical behavior therapy highlights elements of radical acceptance, mindfulness, distress tolerance, and assertiveness training. Interpersonal therapy addresses interpersonally relevant factors in a context of education, goal setting, and socialization. Behavioral activation uses traditional behavioral techniques, including mastery and pleasurable activities, graded task assignments, and goal setting.

Additionally, we note that the CBT elements of bibliotherapy (Jamison & Scogin, 1995) and wellness interventions in classroom and home settings for older adults, such as relaxation, cognitive restructuring, problem solving, communication, and behavior activation (Rybarczyk, Lopez, Benson, Alsten & Stepanski, 2002), have also been evaluated as efficacious. Finally, combining pharmacotherapy and CBT for late-life depression has demonstrated efficacy (Gerson, Belin, Kaufman, Mintz, & Jarvick, 1999).

The effectiveness of CBT does not stop at depression in later life; CBT has been efficacious in sexual dysfunction (e.g., Zeiss, Delmonico, Zeiss & Dornbrand, 1991), sleep problems (e.g., Lichstein & Johnson, 1993), and tension (e.g., Scogin, Rickard, Keith, Wilson & McElreath, 1992), applied both individually (Thompson, Gallagher, & Breckenridge, 1987), with groups (Hyer, & Intrieri, 2006), and in various venues (e.g., Carstensen, 1993). CBT also has been associated with improved psychological functioning in patients undergoing chemotherapy (Areán et al., 1993; Carey & Burish, 1988; Nezu, Nezu, Friedman, Faddis, & Houts, 1998).

There has been no appreciable improvement in the impact of CBTs since the mid-1990s, suggesting that traditional CBT has reached a plateau in terms of what it has to offer.

Robinson, Gould, and Strosahl (2010, p. 13)

CBT has been adapted for depressed older adults with mild stages of dementia, but efficacy data are hard to come by (Teri & Gallagher-Thompson, 1991). The CBT–mild dementia protocol is 16 to 20 sessions long and includes a comprehensive neuropsychological battery to assess the cognitive deficits and the cognitive strengths of the patient. The treatment consists of behavioral activation (BA) and the incorporation of memory aids (e.g., notepads and audiotaping of sessions), as well as the cognitive components of examination of the evidence for and against a specific condition, listing the pros and cons of situations, and experimenting with new attitudes and cognitions in stressful situations (Teri & Gallagher-Thompson, 1991).

Effective Therapies for Older Adults

- Meds, both anxiolytic and SSRI (e.g., Lenze et al., 2008; Pinquart, Duberstein & Lyness, 2007)
- CBT (Stanley et al., 2009)

- Control your depression (Lewinsohn et al., 1986)
- Behavioral activation (Martell, Addis & Jacobson, 2001)
- IPT (Rounsaville, Chevron, & Weissman, 1984)
- Integration of CBT and IPT (Newman et al., 2008)
- Problem solving (Nezu, Nezu, & Perri, 1989)
- Acceptance and commitment therapy (ACT)/Mindfulness (Hayes/Teasdale)
- Exercise
- Attention Training (Mohlman, 2007; Papageorgiou & Wells, 2001)
- Intolerance of uncertainty (Ladouceur et al., 2004)
- Emotional dysregulation (Mennin, 2006; Newman et al., 2008)
- Metacognition (Wells & King, 2006)

The oft-cited study by Alexopouplos et al. (2003) found that PST improved over supportive therapy (ST) using 221 older patients with MDD. These were patients with EF problems, all of whom had depression. Using PST, those with EF problems got better.

FIGURE 4.2 Problem-Solving Therapy Versus Supportive Therapy in Older Depressed Patients With Executive Dysfunction

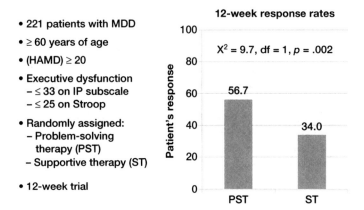

Adapted from Alexopoulos et al. (2003), p. 2; Mackin and Arean (2005), p. 3; Thompson, Hermann, Rapoport, and Lanctôt (2007).

There is considerable interest in fast-pacing and generalizing treatment for older adults. Dakin and Arean (2013) acknowledge this and in a qualitative study on late-life depressives posit several effective treatment ingredients for efficient and effective care. They stress that integration of behavioral activation, problem solving, and cognitive skills should be considered in the development of efficient treatments.

Effective Treatment Ingredients

1. Collaborative relationship, not reflective
2. Problem solving is active, not just talk
3. Integrate patient spirituality
4. Discuss awkwardness/shame in seeking mental health treatment
5. Address problems common in older adults like social functioning, finances, family counseling, and so on
6. Extend treatment
7. Give patients a choice in treatment strategies as in CBT, PST, and so on

---

Medication Plus

In the two large-scale studies mentioned previously, IMPACT and PROSPECT, the use of collaborative care management in primary care found that less than half of older patients with major depression who underwent intervention experienced a 50% reduction in depressive symptoms (Harman et al., 2002; Uebelacker, Wang, Berglund, & Kessler, 2006). In these studies patients received medication plus other interventions depending on the treatment result. In the IMPACT study, only about one-quarter of patients became completely free of depressive symptoms (Harman, 2002). Similarly, Andrews et al. (cited in Blazer, Hybels, Fillenbaum, & Pieper, 2005) estimate that under optimal evidence-based depression treatment, only 34% of years lived with disability could be averted. The limitations of treatment, even under optimal conditions, point to a need to develop public health–relevant approaches to prevent depression in high-risk elderly people.

In the following list, Nelson and Papakostas and Fournier tell us something very important: drugs are barely better than placebo and the more severe the depression, the better medication may work. We need more than medication, even when severity is at stake.

Two Key Medication Studies

1. Meta-analysis: acute-phase, parallel group, double-blinded, placebo-controlled with random assignment, for second-generation antidepressants not associated with a med disorder and 60 or > (Cochrane and MEDLINE)
   - Ten unique trials with 13 contrasts (N = 2,377 active drug and 1,788 placebo)
   - Nelson and Papakostas (2009):
     - Response rate for drug = 44.4%
     - Response rate for placebo = 34.7%
     - Placebo rates vary 19% to 47%. Lots of heterogeneity: nonspecific effects 10 to 12 weeks > 6 to 8 weeks
     - For every 100 treated, 8 show response and 5 show remission in excess of placebo

Nelson and Papakostas (2009)

2. 6 randomized placebo-controlled trials (N = 718) → magnitude of benefits vary as a function of severity of MDD

Fournier et al. (2010)

Additionally, physicians are taught to treat to remission or alter treatment after a short period if a robust response is not forthcoming. If there is little or no response by 12 weeks, problems will likely remain and a new course is in order.

- Treat to remission, not to response.
- If patients are partial responders at 6 weeks, they have a reasonable chance to be full responders by 12 weeks: stay the course; don't change medication.
- If patients are partial responders at 12 weeks, switch tactics.
- For meds: Switching is as effective as augmentation (about 50% respond) but is associated with fewer side effects. Adherence is easier, and prescription costs are lower. All patients, even those with first episodes, are candidates for at least 1 year, and preferably 2 years, of maintenance pharmacotherapy.

This lack of efficacy applies in spades in PCCs. There is recent evidence that even when older adults receive care, they often receive an insufficient amount of treatment (including both pharmacotherapy and psychotherapy); that is, treatment is below recommended guidelines (Harman, Edlund, Fortney, & Kallas, 2005; Unutzer et al., 2002). A review of 30 years of health services research on depression outcomes in PCC concluded that major depression has a poor outcome, especially for older adults (Callahan, 2001). Mitchell et al.'s (2009) study in *The Lancet* pointed to problems in PC like no other. The problem is PCP misdiagnoses and overdiagnoses; patients who may or may not be depressed.

Primary Care Facts

- Meta-analysis of 50,000 across the world
- For every 20 true cases
    - 10 were correct
    - 10 were missed
    - 15 nondepressed were seen as depressed
- Varied by countries: the United States and the UK had most problems

Mitchell, Vaze, and Rao (2009)

Finally, we note that there are other therapies for depression, especially TRD. Several old drugs are now new again, including MDMA and ketamine, among others. Deep-brain stimulation, transcranial magnetic stimulation, and electroconvusive therapy (ECT) also are around. Gardner and O'Connor examined the impact of ECT on cognitive functioning in depressed older people. Twenty-seven studies met our criteria. Apart from evidence of inter-ictal slowing of information-processing speed, there were mixed results with regard to the impact of ECT on other cognitive domains. Factors contributing to this variability in results include the lack of discrimination among unilateral, bilateral, or mixed electrode placement; the inclusion of patients with dementia; the small sample sizes; and the use of tests insensitive to subtle cognitive changes. The effect of ECT in elderly recipients remains unclear at present.

PREDICTORS OF DEPRESSION AT LATE LIFE AND WHEN TO CHANGE

Clinical and psychosocial predictors of response to single antidepressants or comprehensive interventions have been identified. These include anxiety, hopelessness, executive dysfunction, limitations in physical and emotional functions, chronicity of the current episode, and low income (Charlson & Peterson, 2002). Such predictors can help in personalizing the first step of treatment for a given patient. Ideally, a patient with one or more predictors of poor outcome will receive interventions targeting each modifiable predictor as well as more vigilant follow-up. For example, a low-income depressed elderly patient whose symptoms did not respond to an adequate trial of an antidepressant and who is experiencing hopelessness may benefit from a trial of a different antidepressant, therapy focusing on hopelessness, or case management connecting him or her with social services.

Although personalization of treatment is promising in the management of geriatric depression, its actual impact in clinical practice has yet to be tested. Important clinical questions include how long to maintain a given treatment and which patients are candidates for making a treatment change before much time is lost and the patient is exposed to the accumulation of many noxious effects of depression. As already indicated, we do know that depression is different for older adults than younger adults. Older adults have more middle and terminal insomnia, less irritability, less hypersomnia, less fatigue, more length of illness, more med comorbidities, less anxiety, and less bulimia (STAR*D [Sequenced Treatment Alternatives to Relieve Depression], 2008; Gaynes et al., 2008). There is, however, a similar factor structure for depression (Blazer, 2003).

Poor Depression Response to Treatment

- History of psychiatric problems
- Pretreatment depression
- Poor expectations
- Little satisfaction with life's roles
- Concurrent Rx

- Lack of perceived social support, or stressors
- Physical problems
- Older-old age
- EF problems
- Poor response after 4 weeks
- Suicide attempts
- No perceived mastery
- Not tired of being depressed

Predictors of full response both at baseline and on change in depressive symptoms after treatment are a growing and sometimes elusive target. Andreescu et al. (2008) addressed these questions, using signal detection theory on pooled data from three acute treatment trials of either nortriptyline or paroxetine. They found that response by the fourth week of treatment was a critical factor in determining the probability of response by 12 weeks. Of course, a strong treatment response by the fourth week suggests that the treatment should continue. However, if only a moderate response has occurred by that time, the clinician has to choose whether to continue the same treatment or do something different—switch to another treatment, for example, or augment the first treatment with another drug or a nonbiological intervention. A moderate response by week 4 predicted full response by week 12 in 43% of all patients. However, patients who had low levels of anxiety at baseline had a 61% chance of full response, whereas those with moderate or severe anxiety at baseline had a 39% chance of response. The probability of full response was even lower (33%) in patients who had experienced depressive episodes from early life. Of course, using the probability of full response in treatment decisions can spare patients from long exposure to treatments that have a low likelihood of success, as well as from premature discontinuation of treatments that would likely be helpful.

RECOMMENDED TREATMENT

There is much to consider when it comes to older adults. The variables are myriad and the complexity can be daunting. The figure that follows points out this complexity—issues related to the person, the biology, psychosocial and clinical factors, and the psychosocial–environmental factors. The health care provider must keep an open mind and antennae out for problems. Additionally, because older adults are typically coping with more than depressive symptoms, that is, illness and QoL issues, outcomes should focus more broadly on other functional domains, such as QoL, activities of daily living, and better management of illness, and not just on decrements in depressive symptoms. In addition, older adults are rarely treated by mental health professionals; fewer than 10% see such a person. Roughly 50% do not follow through on these consults.

Figure 4.3 Nested Potential Predictors of Treatment Response in Late-Life Depression

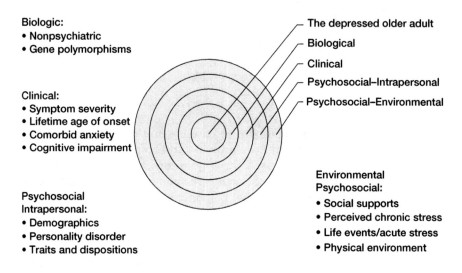

Biologic:
• Nonpsychiatric
• Gene polymorphisms

Clinical:
• Symptom severity
• Lifetime age of onset
• Comorbid anxiety
• Cognitive impairment

Psychosocial
Intrapersonal:
• Demographics
• Personality disorder
• Traits and dispositions

The depressed older adult
Biological
Clinical
Psychosocial–Intrapersonal
Psychosocial–Environmental

Environmental
Psychosocial:
• Social supports
• Perceived chronic stress
• Life events/acute stress
• Physical environment

The ideas put forth in this book are simple: evaluate the complexity of the person and outline a priority of issues, watch and wait by providing support, education, and direction for care. The idea is to set the table so that the person is committed and the main focus is on self-improvement. Also, another focus is on support, help from all concerned in a way that fosters growth and adequate coping. This can take many forms; hence the need to watch and wait at the beginning of care.

Let us be clear here. We note throughout this book that psychotherapy works; medication also works. But, psychotherapy does not work as medicine; nonspecific factors are integral to both but prepotent for mental health care. As noted, success of therapies depends on the patient's conviction that the therapist cares about him or her, communicates this, and is competent to help. This, we believe, is best done with the careful setting of the table at the beginning, watching and waiting. The patient needs to commit to this program. Fortunately, most patients who are older have mild symptoms that can be adequately addressed in psychotherapy. Initially, to be effective, treatment must match a shared social construction about what it means to be remoralized within the culture where it is practiced. The effective therapist then incorporates expectancy-based strategies into his or her clinical repertoires. This allows the patient to generate change for any of a number of reasons. At the risk of some repetition, we address Watch and Wait as it applies to depression. As this is the most common symptom at late life, a careful application is important. In many ways the process is the treatment.

Core Treatment Ideas

Nonpharmacologic treatment should be considered first. Period. It is true that these forms of Rx are not so much better than meds or the combo, BUT they are the least harmful and always some form of treatment involves nonpharmacologic treatments.

Watch and wait. Monitor and wait for issues to confess themselves. There is an annoying lack of clinically significant differences between treatment and placebo in depressed patients. So, frequent monitoring of patients' symptoms and the frequent reconsideration of treatments may produce as much benefit for patients as a medication or psychotherapy and may fit better with the patient's desires.

This is not ignoring symptoms: on the contrary, it entails discussing with the patient the risks and benefits of treatments, agreeing on an observation period as a part of the treatment plan, and the continuance of monitoring.

The differences among the core depression problems (MDD, subsyndromal depression) are subtle and of less importance than most clinicians think. All involve respect, monitoring, and a clinical watch.

Risk factors account for only a small portion of the variance in the cause and persistence of depression in older adults, and attempting to uncover exactly why someone has become depressed has little advantage for clinicians.

People with depression have problems with concentration but most do not have the memory problems seen in dementia. People who are depressed and dementing have both problems. This means they are demented and have a depression in dementia.

DO NOT pick one best treatment at the outset. Rather, recognize how patients present with and experience depression, apply and reapply objective measures of treatment response, and make changes until the patient improves.

Establishing rapport is critical.

Build in commitment from the patient; "I am willing to try this with you as my health care provider. I am committed to this."

Depression ALWAYS involves negative thinking. Whether this is accessible and amenable to change is another issue. Patients only rarely present with "I am depressed."

Patients with "usual care" have a very high likelihood of remaining depressed.

Case: Mrs. B, depressed, grieving, widowed, health and cognition problems

BACKGROUND: Mrs. B is an 86-year-old White female who presents with primary pathogenic components of depression, grief, and cognitive slowness. She is living with her son but also stays with her daughter at least once a week. She has been widowed for just over 2 years. She is a college-educated female who married a minister whose career was in the Air Force. Her husband retired from the Air Force and opened up several churches, where he was very popular. She was the dutiful pastor's wife. During her marriage it became clear that she could not have children. She and her husband adopted one child and then a set of twins. She believes that she was excessively permissive, which led to drug problems for the oldest child and subsequent divorces for the twins. She feels guilty about this. Currently, her older son, now in his 50s, is in a rehab home and the twins have taken a protective stance toward their mother, as the older son has "abused" her financially over the years.

Mrs. B has been forlorn since her husband's death. This is expressed by her yearning after her husband, but also by being inactive, unable to make a decision, cognitively confused, and, on occasion, experiencing visual hallucinations. She has been dealing with these problems for at least the 2 years since his death. Medically she has arthritis and hypertension, as well as parkinsonism, but she does not attend any primary care clinic. She is depressed, and anxiety is also part of this, and she seems to have cognitive problems.

Surprisingly, Mrs. B handles all her household tasks. On occasion she requires assistance as she cannot fix things, lift heavy objects, and handle complex tasks like taxes. She handles her medications and she drives. She is social and is connected with church members but is not happy. She has also been a peacemaker in the family with her children.

OVERALL COGNITIVE FUNCTIONING: Data on Mrs. B's pre- and postassessment are given below. Mrs. B's cognitive profile was set by her score on the Oklahoma Premorbid Intelligence Estimate—Vocabulary (OPIE-V IQ) of 98, placing her in the average area intellectually. There was, however, a wide confidence interval (~12 points) in Wechsler Adult Intelligence Scale (WAIS-IV) test scores. Currently, Mrs. B also scored a Repeated Battery for the Assessment of Neurological Status-Form (RBANS) Index of 80, placing her at the 5% level for other people her age. Her Montreal Cognitive Assessment (MoCA; 23) is moderately impaired and suggests difficulty on overall cognitive functioning, slightly lower than her premorbid state. On executive functions, Mrs. B's performance was poor. This included the Stroop, the Trail Making Test, semantic fluency, and several working memory tasks on the WAIS-IV. There were mild deficits on the Functional Assessment Questionnaire (FAQ) (see below), a measure of executive functions in activities of daily living. She currently has sufficient skills to handle her day-to-day requirements. She is cognitively competent for all decisions, medical or otherwise.

Her diagnoses were set initially by the MINI (Mini-International Neurospsychiatric Interview), as well as clinician ratings and selected cognitive tests. Her current depression was a repeat from an earlier period in her life when she had problems with her children. She also is still grieving over the loss of her husband. Recently she has become concerned about her health, about being a burden, and about her son's condition. She does not feel in control of her situation. She filled out several self-report measures that confirmed all interviews. She also showed a lower QoL, had sleep problems, but was not in pain (to any degree). She was loosely suicidal (General Suicide Index Scale [GSIS] [Factor I]—no operative plans). As noted, for the most part she handled her day-to-day functioning well.

She was also given the Millon Behavioral Medicine Diagnostic (MBMD) to determine personality styles as well as treatment issues (treatment prognostics and stress moderators). She possesses a cooperative and inhibited personality style, and treatment concerns about her functioning and illness apprehension and social isolation, as well as concerns about interventional fragility and problematic compliance. These are face valid, given her history and can be folded into her treatment. She had a 4 on the Charslon Comorbidity Index, a predictor of further morbidity and probable mortality within 2 years.

Mrs. B

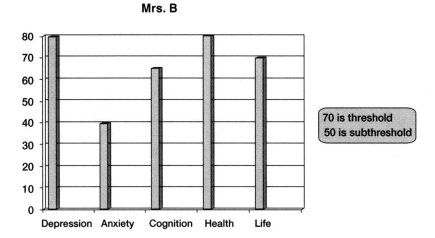

70 is threshold
50 is subthreshold

Depression   Anxiety   Cognition   Health   Life

Mrs. B—WATCH AND WAIT

Sessions 1 to 3:
Based on the model, she has several areas of concern. She is depressed, is still grieving, and has increasing practical and health problems. She has cognitive issues related to executive function. Three sessions were spent in the formation of her treatment plan. She was apprised of the following areas of concern as a result of the interview and testing. These included problems related to: (a) depression, notably to increase behavioral activation and positive events, improve problem solving and emotional awareness, as well as to positively priming her image, and monitor death ideation; (b) interpersonal functioning that is task based, including talking to son and daughter; (c) loss of husband, including monitoring mood and scheduling rituals, as well as time restriction on grief tasks; and (d) medical tasks to acquire labs and attend a neurology consult for possible Parkinson's disease. She was also requested to be involved in EF exercises in treatment sessions (ACTIVE trial exercises as well as a Memory Group). This project lasted for one third to one-half of all sessions. She was taking an antidepressant.

She had a positive attitude and was upbeat about therapy. She could not be more thankful. The initial sessions confirmed the diagnoses and socialized Mrs. B to the problem list. It is important to note that priorities were set. She was encouraged to continue the antidepressant medication for the present but to become proactive in her care according to the problem-list sequence. She indicated her extreme interest in the therapy, agreed-to goals, outlined tasks, and possible barriers.

Watch and Wait Category	Check
Validate Problem	×
Psychoeducation of Model	×
Assessment	×
Monitoring	×
Case Formulation	×
Check Alliance	×

Sessions 4 to 12:
The therapy sessions directly followed from the problem list (below). In addition to EF training, these included activity scheduling and an EF focus (as she is excessively passive and unstructured), monitoring moods so that she would better assess her day and psychological status, relaxation, problem solving (in middle and later sessions), family needs, followed by physician issues, sleep hygiene, grief, and some interpersonal challenges. She would try the tasks, monitor outcomes and change focus, if necessary. The initial sessions stressed the importance of activity scheduling, placing her in control of her situation, and rewarding her challenge to monitor her psychological status. She was also primed with several positive identity images. This had a very positive effect.

Ongoing sessions:
Treatment never closed for her over the years. In time she became more frail and eventually died (after 2 years).

TABLE 4.2 Pretreatment to Posttreatment Changes on Key Measures

Pretreatment

Axis I: 296.30 Major Depressive Disorder, Recurrent

R/O 294.9 Cognitive Disorder, NOS (not otherwise specified)

Axis II: Deferred

Axis III: CHF, HTN, MCI

Axis IV: Lack of resources: social support, family problem

Axis V: GAF: 55

Posttreatment (2 weeks after Rx of 12th session)

Axis I: 296.30 Major Depressive Disorder, Recurrent (subsyndromal)

294.9 Cognitive Disorder, NOS

Axis II: Deferred

Axis III: CHF, HTN, arthritis, "MCI"

Axis IV: Social support, family problem

Axis V: GAF: 60

Six-Month Follow-Up (MINI interview administered)

Axis I: 296.30 Major Depressive Disorder, Recurrent (subsyndromal)

294.9 Cognitive Disorder, NOS

Axis II: Deferred

Axis III: CHF, HTN, arthritis, Parkinsonism, "MCI"

Axis IV: Family problem

Axis V: GAF: 60

(continued)

TABLE 4.2 Pretreatment to Posttreatment Changes on Key Measures (*continued*)

Measure	Prescore	Postscore (2 wks)
Cognitive		
RBANS (total)	80 (below average)	88 (low average)
MoCA	23 (below average)	24 (average)
Stroop Color-Word	15 (low average)	42 (average)
Phonemic Fluency (FAS)	24 (low)	48 (average)
Affective		
HAM-D	24 (high)	7 (normal)
HARS	28 (high)	9 (normal)
BDI-II	28 (high/ moderate)	12 (minor problem)
PSWQ	67 (moderate)	42 (normal)
GSIS	22 (moderate)	14 (normal)
SWLS	12 (low)	27 (normal)
Pain Rating	3/10 (low)	2/10 (low)
Sleep (ESS)	12 (high)	6 (average)
Functional		
ADCS-ADL	7 (normal)	8 (normal)
FAQ	8 (problem normal)	9 (high normal)
Charlson Comorbidity Index	6 (problem)	
Personality and Treatment Issues		
MBMD: Personality styles		
Cooperative and inhibited		
MBMD: Stress Moderators		
Functional deficits		
Illness apprehension		
Social isolation		
MBMD: Treatment Prognostics		
Interventional fragility		
Problematic compliance		

ADCS-ADL, Alzheimer's Disease Cooperative Studies Scale-Activities of Daily Living; BDI-II, Beck Depression Inventory-II; CHF, congestive heart failure; ESS, Epworth Sleep Scale; FAQ, Functional Assessment Questionnaire; FAS, Letter Fluency; GAF, Global Assessment of Functioning; GSIS, Geriatric Suicide Ideation Scale; HARS, Hamilton Anxiety Rating Scale; HTN, hypertension; MBMD, Millon Behavioral Medicine Diagnostic; MCI, mild cognitive impairment; MoCA, Montreal Cognitive Assessment; NOS, not otherwise specified; P HAM-D, Hamilton Depression Scale; RBANS, Repeated Battery for the Assessment of Neurological Status-Form A; SWLS, life satisfaction; SWS, Penn State Worry Scale.

Therapy Sessions

Session 1 to 3: Discussion of case, transdiagnostic targets, socialize to EF training

Monitor moods

Activity scheduling

Increase pleasant experiences (three of them)

MD consult/Med labs (bring in physician)

EF training discussed

Session 4: Monitor moods/Activity scheduling/Increase PE

Decrease avoidance

Positive aging image priming

Involve son

Emotional awareness

Sleep diary: Sleep hygiene—option of meds

Belly breathing

Session 5: EF training

Monitor moods/Activity scheduling/Increase PE/Decrease avoidance

Positive aging image priming

Worry schedule

Sleep diary: Sleep hygiene

Emotional awareness

All interpersonal tasks (role play)

Breathing

Session 6: EF training

Monitor moods/Increase PE/Activity schedule/Avoidance/Worry schedule

Positive aging image priming

Emotional awareness

Sleep monitoring and hygiene

Bring in family (all interpersonal issues)

Breathing

Session 7: EF training

Monitor moods/Increase PE/Decrease avoidance/Worry schedule

Improve problem solving (target family issues)

Death ideation challenge (monitor GSIS)

Sleep monitoring and hygiene

Breathing

Session 8:   EF training

Monitor moods/Increase PE/Decrease avoidance/Worry schedule

Problem solving

Death ideation challenge (monitor GSIS)

Sleep hygiene

Breathing

Session 9:   EF training

Monitor moods/Increase PE/Activity schedule/Worry schedule

Problem solving

Death ideation challenge (monitor GSIS)

Sleep hygiene (resolved)

Breathing

Session 10:   EF Training

Monitor moods/Increase PE/Activity schedule/Increase PE/Worry schedule

Problem solving

Breathing

MD follow-up/Sleep check-up

Problem solving

Session 11:   EF training

Monitor moods/Increase PE/Decrease avoidance/Worry Schedule

Loss of husband (mood monitoring and ritual)

Activity schedule (family for last session)

Call physician

Problem solving

Breathing

Family issues

Breathing

Session 12:   Sum up

Relapse issues

Ongoing sessions: approximately 6 times per year for 4 years

Figure 4.4 Stroop CW and BDI across Sessions. Therapy Process Measures on the Stroop Color-Word Trial (Stroop CW) and the Beck Depression Inventory (BDI) over 12 Therapy Sessions of Treatment

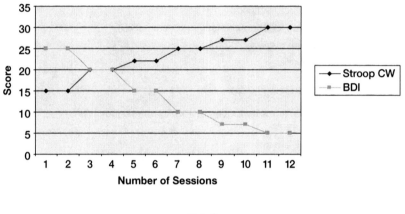

Grief

Grieving is a natural process of life. It represents not an illness but a multidimensional, unique, dynamic process characterized by pervasive distress to a perceived loss. The stage models of grief, so widely promulgated, are inadequate. At base, the task of change in the grieving person is to rebuild the assumptive world that included the missing person and open an enlarged sense of self, associated with the timeless flow of life, rather than with previous roles. Despite the contentiousness of the new *DSM-5* (American Psychiatric Association, 2013) regarding the relationship with depression (is it part of depression, orthogonal, cohabitating?), grief involves a process of change. The goal of therapy in grief, if that is even the appropriate word, is not to never experience a state of loss-related sadness, but to have a sense of integrated loss in the context of living and what life is about.

We will not dwell on grief, but we will mention issues. Roughly half the patients complete the grief process after a short time (at least accommodate to life in seemingly acceptable ways); one-quarter have a sense of relief in the loss, and do not experience problems; and one-quarter have immediate and undulating psychological problems. Grief itself interfaces with elements of possible depression (and, for that matter, posttraumatic stress disorder [PTSD]) and the specific feature of the type of grief itself. For years we have known that there are types of grief that are largely a function of who the person is and what his or her relationship to the departed was. Problems in the relationship, guilt, unfinished business, and previous psychiatric problems predict problems.

Risk Factors for Complicated Grief

What the loss was and who the deceased person was

Nature of attachment

Mode of loss of the death

Historical antecedents

Personality variables

Social factors

Concurrent stressors

Types of Grief

Chronic—grief is static

Delayed—expression of grief is suppressed and later triggered

Masked—avoidance of emotions, occult anxiety and depression, numbness, self-destructive behaviors

Exaggerated—feel completely overwhelmed by pain

One pervasive problem is complicated grief. Here, the troubling symptoms of protracted yearning and lower quality of living are most noticeable. The risk factors below might lead one to expect problems of this sort. Whatever unfolds, the health care provider needs to develop a wide scope, a sense of real and human empathy, as well as a preparation for the longer haul for this process. Clearly grief is not depression, but it can become so, given elongated issues or complications.

Challenges of Therapy

Accept the reality of the loss

Experience the pain of the loss

Adjust to the environment without the deceased

Emotionally relocate the departed and move on with life

SPECIAL CASE OF HOME CARE

Psychosocial interventions for depressed older adults with mild cognitive deficits have been an issue for years. There is promising research on the efficacy of telephone-based and in-home psychotherapy for older or disabled adults. PST was adapted for depressed older adults with mild executive dysfunction, and, as noted, helps this population. IPT was modified for depressed older adults with mild cognitive impairment (MCI) by including the systematic incorporation of concerned caregivers into the treatment process, with joint patient–caregiver sessions to promote better understanding, communication, and respect (Miller, 2008; Miller & Reynolds, 2007). In addition, IPT-cognitive impairment helps both the older adult and his or her caregiver through his or her role transitions that result from cognitive deficits and functional limitations.

Problem adaptation therapy (PATH) is a relatively new 12-week home-delivered intervention specifically developed to treat late-life major depression presenting with significant cognitive impairment (including mild to moderate dementia) and disability (Kiosses, Arean, Teri, & Alexopoulos, 2010; Kiosses, Teri, Velligan, & Alexopoulos, 2010). PATH focuses on the patients' ecosystem, which involves the patient, the caregiver, and the home environment. PATH uses PST as its basic framework to promote adaptive functioning and integrates environmental adaptation tools, including calendars, checklists, notepads, signs, and timers, to bypass the functional and behavioral limitations of these patients. Preliminary efficacy data suggest that PATH is effective, compared with a control condition of home-delivered supportive therapy, in reducing both depression and disability (Kiosses et al., 2010).

The evidence for combined treatments for LLD is still preliminary. Good support exists for the combination of medication and IPT as a means for preventing relapse and recurrence of major depression in older adults, particularly older adults who have recurrent major depression. Although promising, the research on medication with IPT suffers from the same set of limitations seen in the IPT literature; only one research group has studied this approach with adequately powered study designs, and thus the generalizability of these findings is unclear. Similarly, with regard to CBT trials, the finding that few differences exist between the CBT alone and a combined CBT and medication condition indicates that further research is necessary to evaluate the efficacy of combined interventions compared with specific monotherapies to determine the overall efficacy of these approaches. Indications are not empirically supported facts.

CONCLUSION

When the issue of LLD is viewed from some distance, things seem clearer, especially from a psychotherapy perspective. The context of the person can be specified and an intervention outlined. The patient is then brought on board by a renewed view of self: "I can give this treatment a try." Ideally, the patient eventually gives up living in the past, reconnects with values, becomes less impulsive and fearful, reduces negative self-stories, and experiences himself or herself as a partner in care. Coping becomes easier.

The extant literature is unfortunately wanting where older adults are concerned. New studies have been entered into the record, but few real changes have been made in the last decade. Medication also has improved on side effect profiles but not on efficacy. The case formulation of a particular older adult makes manifest the road map. The Watch and Wait model of care, with the profile of the person and the five components, makes visible the core issues, the needed interventions, requested assists, and outcomes. This is also the case for anxiety, discussed in our next chapter.

CHAPTER 5

Anxiety at Later Life

Pigeon-holing anxiety is not an easy task. It is a sign, a symptom, and a syndrome. It is comorbid with many other disorders and medical problems. What are "true anxiety" and "secondary anxiety" is often difficult to discern, especially in older adults. At later life, too, the phenotypic models of anxiety do not conform to the *DSM*. The usual pattern is one that expresses itself in irritability, anger, sadness, anxiety, self-consciousness, and vulnerability that are frequent and out of proportion to circumstances. Worry is also a big issue. For older adults, there is often no functional attachment of symptoms with real-world issues (medical, social, financial, family). This is considerable, as the older adult never fully grasps the connection between a problem/symptom and anxiety/worry. And, as if all these were not sufficient for concern, response rates in the most common symptoms/problems of older adults, generalized anxiety disorder (GAD), are lower (~30%) than those in younger samples (~50%) (Wetherell, Gatz, & Craske, 2003).

It was the *DSM-III-R* (American Psychiatric Association [APA], 1987), where for the first time, anxiety had its own diagnostic distinction with a formula of excessive and unrealistic worry unrelated to another Axis I disorder. This involved three symptom areas (motor tension, vigilance and scanning, and autonomic hyperactivity), and 6 months duration. According to the *DSM-IV-TR* (APA, 2000), worry was excessive but also difficult to control. The autonomic symptoms were removed and impairment added. To qualify for the diagnosis, one had to have experienced at least 6 months of frequent, uncontrollable worrying about several real-life issues and have three of six accompanying symptoms (muscle tension, insomnia, irritability, fatigue, restlessness). GAD/worry is the best marker of older-adult problems and can be viewed as a dimensional construct. In fact, the subthreshold levels of anxiety are serious, leading to many problems, but usually occur over time.

In the *DSM-5* (2013), the core features of anxiety remain but differences exist in the placement of some of the disorders, for instance posttraumatic stress disorder (PTSD) and obsessive compulsive disorder (OCD). Where older adults are concerned, specific phobia and social anxiety criteria have been altered; panic disorder and agoraphobia remain the same. At the heart of syndromes for older adults, however, is GAD, and the number of associated physical symptoms has been reduced from six to two with minor wording changes. It has even been espoused that GAD should be changed to "generalized worry disorder," as GAD could be considered the basic anxiety disorder; worry is the defining feature that reflects a basic process of anxiety. Worry is generalized to a number of future events and activities, is excessive, and is a negatively enforced avoidant coping strategy that is associated with symptoms of feelings of restlessness, feeling keyed up or on edge, and muscle tension, and with consequent behaviors (avoidance, procrastination, reassurance) that attempt to reduce worry and/or emotional/affective distress.

Older adults especially have problems with anxiety. They have excessive amounts of anxiety; even when not in clear evidence, worry asserts an influence. Anxiety may not seem to be a problem for many, but it appears that as many as 20% of older adults experience anxiety in one form or other at clinical levels. Worry is an intrusive negative habit; a disorder of uncertainty: It is a verbal sell and it works ... for a while.

In this chapter, we address several issues. Most importantly, we present a model of treatment for anxiety. First, however, we discuss its prevalence. Second, we consider the phenomenology of anxiety in its many forms at later life. Third, we discuss cognition in the context of anxiety. We also consider dementia, and endorse the use of treatment modules and medication. Treatment studies and a treatment model are presented. We conclude with a discussion on PTSD as a special case for older adults.

PREVALENCE

GAD, the marker disorder for anxiety among older adults, is highly prevalent among the elderly. In the previous chapter, we cited the Byers study (2010). This group held that anxiety diagnoses accumulated to 12%. This is twice as prevalent as dementias and more prevalent than Major Depressive Disorder (MDD). In the National Comorbidity Study, this number was 5.1%, but the construct for GAD was eliminated as it is an exclusionary diagnosis. Furthermore, 20% were seen as having problems, 65% comorbid. Cohort trajectory of anxiety is curvilinear (up [before 65], down [66–75], and up [> 75]). For contrast, GAD levels (e.g., Montorio, Nuevo, Márquez, Izal, & Losada, 2003) as well as depression and anxiety in general are lower in older age than in other ages (e.g., George, Blazer, Winfield-Laird, Leaf, & Fischback, 1988).

In fact, GAD actually accounts for at least 50% of anxiety cases; this includes 50% to 97% that are early-onset disorders with late-life exacerbations. This problem, then, is more common than depression (Flint, 1994). Indeed, anxiety disorders are the most common psychiatric illnesses in the United States, with approximately 30% of the population experiencing anxiety-related symptoms in their lifetime (Kessler, Lloyd, Lewis, Gray, & Heath, 1996). Estimates are that 30% to 40% of the variance contributing to these disorders is heritable. Only 33% of GAD patients reported using mental health resources (Blazer, George, & Hughes, 1991). Unfortunately, the prevalence rates may be an underestimate of true population values, as older adults tend to minimize anxiety or depressive symptoms or simply not recognize them.

As with depression, however, problems with anxiety show first at primary care clinics (PCCs); both use and medication numbers are up. It is important to note that older individuals might provide responses that are significantly different from those of younger adults, potentially requiring special attention in psychiatric care. Equally important, older adults with GAD are more disabled, and have a worse quality of life. They also have greater health care usage than nonanxious groups (Porensky et al., 2009). In general, the type of disorder varied: early-onset disorders tended to be GAD, OCD (obsessive compulsive disorder), panic disorder (PD), and specific phobias; whereas late-onset disorders tended to consist of PTSD, agoraphobia, or adjustment with anxiety. The fact that anxiety may attack in early or late life is probably unremarkable, except for medical problems. Late onset had more medical symptoms.

PHENOMENA OF ANXIETY

Anxiety influences many aspects of functioning that prevent any connection to the real issues that produced the problem. The inability of the person to dialogue with himself or herself and access data is apparent. The box below provides a listing of problems that occur in the process of one who has anxiety. Imagery, cognition, and a reduction in problem solving co-occur with frequency.

What Happens With Anxiety at Late Life

- Suppresses imagery
- Blocks "real" fear structures from being accessed
- Inhibits performance
- Constructs negative models of future
- Acts as an availability heuristic
- Requires high evidence
- Low threshold for danger
- Procrastinates

- Needs certainty to act
- More distressing problems are not attended to
- Reduces problem solving
- Becomes passive and excessively "nice"

One relevant model regarding fear is Mineka and Zinbarg's (2006) model of fear learning. They argue that relevant differences in people's lives may occur before, during, and after the fear-conditioning experience, which acts singly or in combination to affect how much fear is initially experienced and maintained (i.e., resistance to extinction) over time. Additionally, certain fears are more likely to resist extinction (Öhman & Mineka, 2001). For example, initial panic attacks associated with a fear-inducing event set the stage for conditioning of a generalized panic response to internal and external cues associated with the event and its initial sequelae, thus setting in motion a cascade of cues that kindle and sensitize the person to further anticipatory anxiety and fear. Learned associations remain intact even though the expression of fear in a given context has subsided. We continue to fear what we were initially afraid of. Associations are revived by the passage of time, changes in context, and reexposure to an aversive stimulus. Continuation of associations may contribute to return of fear and resurgence of anxiety symptoms (panic) in the long term (Bouton & King, 1983; Delamater, 2004)

So, if this is how fear/anxiety is initiated and fostered, how does it continue? One path is through negative affectivity, or a high N. This is more characteristic of females than males. It is also probably heritable (50% to 60%). High N is not unique to anxiety disorders, as it is also correlated with mood disorders, somatoform disorders, schizophrenia, eating disorders, and ETOH (alcohol) problems, as well as most Axis II disorders. High N also leads to more deaths over age 65 controlling for everything else.

It is known that each anxiety disorder has its own signature issue but has attached the underlying feature of high N. In effect, there is a core fear and an expression that is distinct.

Each anxiety disorder has a unique component:

- GAD: chronic uncontrolled worry
- Panic: somatic overconcern/avoidance
- Phobias: fearful avoidance
- Social anxiety: cognitive self-evaluation and avoidance
- OCD: obsessions and compulsions
- PTSD: numbing, reexperiencing, avoidance, and arousal
- GAD: Worry (*DSM-5*)

The anxiety and worry are associated with one (or more) of the following symptoms:

(a) restlessness or feeling keyed up or on edge
(b) muscle tension

The anxiety and worry lead to changes in behavior:

(a) marked avoidance of potentially negative events or activities
(b) marked time and effort preparing for possible negative outcomes of events or activities
(c) marked procrastination in behavior or decision making due to worries
(d) repeatedly seeking reassurance due to worries

This unfolds according to the *DSM* distinctions. Older individuals actually seem to provide responses that are significantly different from those of younger adults, potentially requiring special attention in psychiatric care. According to Erskine, Kvavilashvili, Conway, and Myers (2007), the frequent findings of lower psychopathology in later life are due, at least partially, to lower levels of rumination and intrusive thoughts, as well as higher positivity and repressive coping common in older age. It may also be that the rates at late life are actually high in large part because they do not remit at later life as easily as other ages.

Expression of Anxiety at Late Life

- OCD → prevalence declines and lessens with age
- 1.3% males and 1.0% females
- GAD → 1% to 7%; up 60% in past 5 years: Graves's disease, chronic obstructive pulmonary disease (COPD)
  - Often presents with ETOH use
- PTSD → Lower prevalence than other ages but high for acute stress disorder (ASD) (50% motor vehicle accidents [MVAs]):
  - 20% of all men older than 65 were exposed to combat
  - PTSD features numbing, reexperience, avoidance, and arousal
- Phobias → 3.3% males and 7.0% females
  - Most prevalent disorder in late life
- PD → 0% males and .2% females: if panic attack involves medical reasons, then rates are high—COPD 8% to 24%
- Secondary anxiety for medical problems
- Thyroid, endocrine, vitamin, hypoglycemia, cancer, Parkinson's (21%)
- Waiting for a transplant (16%) and stroke (25% + 33% worried)

Research on subthreshold disorders with nonclinical older samples also is a problem. This state is prevalent at later life. The general belief that mental health is better at older age may be contradicted at a subthreshold level. Anxiety may be subthreshold but present in the context of a depression in old age and make both disorders difficult to treat. Higher levels of anxiety symptoms (especially worry) also predict longer time to remission, lower rates of remission, and increased risk for recurrent major depressive episodes. The evidence base informing pharmacotherapy for comorbid depression and anxiety in older adults is limited and controlled studies are needed.

The comorbidity of anxiety disorders suggests that *DSM* disorders can be classified according to higher-order dimensions, and may suggest a higher genetic load. Slade and Watson (2006) recently described a best-fit structure for 10 common *DSM-IV* disorders, such that disorders were classified according to *distress* or *fear* factors. The authors classified major depression, dysthymia, GAD, and PTSD as *distress* disorders, whereas social phobia, agoraphobia, PD, and OCD were classified as *fear* disorders. This type of psychiatric classification may improve the efficacy and generalizability of future genetic analyses.

Depression is a special problem. Up to 65% of older adults with depression have comorbid symptoms of anxiety. This was discussed in Chapter 4. Modal problems in addition to the actual diagnoses include physical complications, lower well-being, increased mortality, cardiac problems, and an overuse of services. Moreover, like depression, there appear to be phenotypic differences (not adhered to in the *DSM*) between young and old (Cassidy, Baird, & Sheikh, 2001).

Comorbid Depression and Anxiety

- Poorer treatment outcomes
- More severe presentation of depressive illness (including suicidality)
- Delayed/diminished response to treatment
- Increased likelihood of nonadherence
- Increased disability
- Increased risk of relapse and treatment resistance
- Continued psychosocial limitations
- Decreased ability to work and decreased workplace productivity
- Increased cost for medical treatment
- Sustained depression may worsen morbidity/mortality of other conditions

---

Anxiety disorders especially wreak havoc on physical complications and vice versa. Symptoms like a decreased sense of well-being and reduced life satisfaction have been linked to anxiety in older adults (Brenes et al., 2004). Often there is a masking or exacerbation of symptoms by physical complications, lower well-being, increased mortality, cardiac problems, and the overuse of services. Anxiety is also associated with increased mortality and greater risk of coronary artery disease in men (Kawachi, Sparrow, Vokonas, & Weiss, 1994).

We note one more problem: falls. There are functional motor impairments that cohabitate with anxiety and depression. Zijlstra et al. (2007) used a community-dwelling elderly sample ($n = 311$) and assessed them every 6 weeks for 36 weeks; 17% had one fall, 16% had more than two falls. The falls were predicted by number of falls in a previous year, abnormal postural sway, and poor handgrip strength, as well as depression. Substantial levels of older adults (perhaps as high as 10%) truncate their lives because of fear of falling; some even become agoraphobic. We will see this again in Chapter 10 on primary care clinics (PCCs).

ANXIETY AND COGNITION

An anxiety disorder is associated with cognitive dysfunction whether in the context of an LLD or not. We are aware of the inverted-U relationship between anxiety and cognitive performance in younger individuals; with older adults, a linear relationship between anxiety and cognitive performance has been reported with increased anxiety leading to poor cognitive performance (Beaudreau & O'Hara, 2008). For simple tasks, mild anxiety enhances cognitive performance (Bierman, Comijs, Rijmen, Jonker, & Beekman, 2005; Powlishta et al., 2004). Because of reduced working memory and processing resources especially, older adults may be more vulnerable than younger adults to the effects of state anxiety on cognitive functioning. Two longitudinal studies that also adjust for baseline performance show that clinically significant anxiety predicted accelerated cognitive decline (DeLuca et al., 2005; Sinoff & Werner, 2003). As intimated, comorbid depression and GAD present a special problem (Beaudreau & O'Hara, 2008). This even occurs in community-dwelling elderly where cognitive impairment is associated with a decline in activities of daily living (Hyer, 2009).

In an often-cited study, Beaudreau and O'Hara (2009) showed that clinical depression with anxiety was associated with cognitive problems; clinical depression with no anxiety, less so. Episodic memory deficits are unique to depression. The authors looked at 102 seniors in a community. People with increased anxiety only had problems with speed of processing, attention, and inhibition. Depression symptoms were not associated with any cognitive factors. Again, up to 65% of older adults with depression have comorbid symptoms of anxiety, making the distinctions between the two problematic. Mantella et al. (2007) found similar deficits in elderly patients with GAD, as compared with normal comparison subjects and patients with major depression.

In a recent study from Germany, subjects with subjective memory impairment, and anxiety had considerably more problems than those with no memory complaints when conversion to a dementia was at issue. Those with an MCI had still more problems. Again, this suggests that anxiety is a problem for cognitive decline in general.

2010 Study on Subjective Memory Impairment and Anxiety

Subject memory impairment (SMI) seniors were more likely than people without SMI to show changes in brain activity resembling those seen in the early stages of Alzheimer's disease (AD; MRI).

- Not all people with SMI convert to dementia
- Not all people with dementia went through SMI

Study:
- Adults 75 and older (*N* = 2,415) asked whether memory was a problem
- And, if so, did they worry?
- Subjects with SMI and no worry → 2× to develop AD as no SMI
- Subjects with SMI and worry → 6× to develop AD as no SMI
- Subjects with MCI → 10× risk of any dementia and 20× for AD

Archives of General Psychiatry (2010)

Worry, in the context of some depression, is especially a problem; anxious depression predicts a faster decline in memory than late-life depression alone. Teng et al. (2012) showed that a decline in the quality of life in patients with MCI was more associated with neuropsychiatric and functional changes than cognition: anxiety especially made a difference. Recently Price, Seigle, and Mohlman (2012) showed that older adults who worry frequently exhibited a pattern of emotional Stroop performance, suggesting that selective attention toward threat-related information may be seen as a relevant factor in older, as in younger, groups of anxious people. Conversely, those with mild or moderate worry showed the opposite pattern. Worry makes older adults more rigid.

ANXIETY AND THE BRAIN

So what do we know about the brain and anxiety? Like depression, anxiety is a brain problem. The emotional-processing brain structures historically are referred to as the "limbic system." The limbic cortex is part of the phylogenetically ancient cortex. It includes the insular cortex and cingulate cortex. The limbic cortex integrates the sensory, affective, and cognitive components of pain and processes information regarding the internal bodily state. The hippocampus is another limbic system structure; hippocampal volume and neurogenesis (growth of new cells) in this structure have been implicated in stress sensitivity and resiliency in relationship to mood and anxiety disorders. An evolutionarily ancient limbic system structure, the amygdala, processes emotionally salient external stimuli and initiates the appropriate behavioral response. The amygdala is responsible for the expression of fear and aggression as well as the species-specific defensive behavior, and it plays a role in the formation and retrieval of emotional and fear-related memories. The central nucleus of the amygdala (CeA) is heavily interconnected with cortical regions, including the limbic cortex. It also receives input from the hippocampus, thalamus, and hypothalamus.

The higher cognitive centers of the brain reside in the frontal lobe, the most phylogenetically recent brain region. The prefrontal frontal cortex (PFC) is responsible for executive functions such as planning, decision making, predicting consequences of potential behaviors, and understanding and moderating social behavior. The orbitofrontal cortex (OFC) codes information, controls impulses, and regulates mood. The ventromedial PFC is involved in reward processing and in the visceral response to emotions. In the healthy brain, these frontal cortical regions regulate impulses, emotions, and behavior via inhibitory top-down control of emotional-processing structures. These regulatory activities are down in patients with GAD.

At a more clinical level, PTSD and phobia have an underactive prefrontal cortex and disinhibited amygdala; GAD and OCD (now no longer an anxiety disorder) have an overactive prefrontal cortex. For anxiety problems, emotional regulation and understanding are problematic. For general anxiety, there is a common abnormality in anterior cingulate cortex (ACC)–amygdala circuitry and a disconnect between the frontal lobes and amygdala; for panic, there is an amygdala regulation problem. Symptoms of mood and anxiety disorders are thought to result, in part, from disruption in the balance of activity in the emotional centers of the brain rather than in the higher cognitive centers.

In addition to the activity of each brain region, it also is important to consider the neurotransmitters providing communication among these regions. Increased activity in emotion-processing brain regions in patients who have an anxiety disorder could result from decreased inhibitory signaling by g-amino butyric acid (GABA) or increased excitatory neurotransmission by glutamate. Well-documented anxiolytic and antidepressant properties of drugs that act primarily on monoaminergic systems have implicated serotonin (5-hydroxytryptamine, 5-HT), norepinephrine (NE), and dopamine (DA) in the pathogenesis of mood and anxiety disorders (Craft et al., 2012).

TREATMENT STUDIES

GAD has been assessed more than any other type of anxiety condition at late life. It is *the* anxiety problem at late life. Anxiety disorders in older adults are associated with increased disability, diminished well-being, and excessive and inappropriate use of medical services (Wetherell, Gatz, & Craske, 2003). Ayers, Sorrell, Thorp, and Wetherell (2007) examined empirically supported psychotherapies for older adults with GAD. The authors conducted a review of the geriatric anxiety treatment outcome literature by using specific coding criteria and identified 17 studies that met criteria for evidence-based treatments (EBTs). These studies reflected samples of adults with GAD or samples with mixed anxiety disorders or symptoms. Evidence of efficacy was found for four types of EBTs: relaxation training, cognitive behavioral therapy (CBT), and, to a lesser extent, supportive therapy and cognitive therapy. CBT for late-life GAD has garnered the most consistent support, and relaxation training represents an efficacious, relatively low-cost intervention. Treatment effects of GAD are typically 10% to 20% lower than in younger samples, regardless of disorder.

Other studies dating back more than 15 years support CBT's efficacy with elders suffering from anxiety disorders (Areán & Cook, 2002; Beck & Stanley, 1998; Scogin, Rickard, Keith, Wilson, & McElreath, 1992). Previously, Wetherell (1998) conducted a broad review of psychological literature on psychodynamic therapy and life review as alternatives to pharmacological approaches to treatment of anxiety. Mohlman and Gorman (2005) also investigated an integration of CBT and executive function (EF) training in older adults with anxiety and executive dysfunction. Although preliminary, other studies (e.g., Areán et al., 2010) suggest that both CBT and EF training are promising for older adults who have anxiety and cognitive decline. Interestingly, Ayers et al. (2007) found that relaxation training was as effective in the treatment of anxiety in older adults as CBT or CBT combined with relaxation.

Other relevant and related therapies, such as problem-solving therapy (PST; D'Zurilla & Nezu, 2010), metacognitive therapy (Wells, 2000), intolerance of uncertainty (Dugas, Gagnon, Ladouceur, & Freeston, 1998), and life review (Haight, 1988) have been evaluated in adults with anxiety, but not older adults. Acceptance and commitment therapy (ACT) has been applied to older clients with GAD (Wetherell et al., 2011) and results were largely positive. The same conclusion can be applied to mindfulness (Segal, Williams, & Teasdale, 2012), as well as well-being therapy (e.g., Frisch, 1998) and positive psychotherapy (Seligman, Rashid, & Parks, 2006). These last three have not been applied to older adults. In general, however, CBT has not been compared with other psychotherapies in regard to older adults for PTSD.

Interestingly, there have been relatively few randomized controlled trials with combined medication and psychotherapy at later life. Combined medication and CBT or interpersonal therapy (IPT) have had some support in the literature for older adults (Thase et al., 1997; Thompson, Coon, Gallagher-Thompson, Sommer, & Koin, 2001). In one key meta-analysis, Pinquart, Duberstein, and Lyness (2006) reviewed 32 studies of treatments focused on anxiety disorders in older adults in which subjects received either behavioral interventions or pharmacotherapy. Although more robust effects were found for pharmacotherapy, they concluded that both pharmacotherapy and behavioral interventions are reasonably effective. The use of selective serotonin reuptake inhibitors (SSRI) with psychotherapy may be especially beneficial, as the efficacy of SSRIs for older adults with anxiety has been suggested (Lenze et al., 2005; Schuurmans et al., 2006).

On the basis of the preceding data, evidence supports relaxation training, CBT (or cognitive therapy), PST, supportive therapy, and IPT, as well as medication. CBT was the most robust of the grouping. It is reasonable to speculate that the combined use of CBT, IPT, and PST, along with the judicious application of medication, may provide the best chance of change. Typical CBT protocols seem to do this, as they include education about anxiety, self-monitoring, relaxation training, exposure to anxiety-provoking thoughts and situations using systematic desensitization, and cognitive restructuring. Some protocols also included problem-solving skills training, behavioral activation, sleep hygiene, reflective listening, life review, and memory aids. CBT can be conducted in both individual and group formats.

Effective Therapies for Older Adults

- CBT
- Cognitive therapy
- Relaxation therapy
- PST
- Medication
- Medication and psychotherapy
- Supportive therapy
- Executive function training added to CBT

MEDICATION

Pharmacology is a blunt instrument, but perhaps that is all that is needed, at least for a while. The one advantage of meds is that, if individualized well, the patient can be calmed down and made to feel better. In fact, even benzodiazepines work. Studies suggest that there is a relationship between a reduction in anxiety or anxious depression and a reduction in somatic symptoms. In terms of the biology of anxiety and treatment, the immediate response (to the cortex) forces the person to secrete epinephrine in less than 1 second. Kindling occurs in 15 seconds or, in repeated conditioning, very quickly. In effect, the amygdala and cortex interact and cortisol flows quickly. Often the person chooses to avoid and this behavior is reinforced. It now is seen as something that works, and is firmly believed.

In two studies on anxiety at later life, the evidence showed that anxiety medications kicked in more quickly than other treatments (Pinquart et al., 2006), and that medication was more effective than psychotherapy (Pinquart, Duberstein, & Lyness, 2007). This is an important finding, as it shows that, even if for only 10 weeks, medication use in combination with psychotherapy is often effective. However, the treatment response was slower than in patients without anxiety.

Benzodiazepine use remains high among older adults despite the risk of adverse events, such as falls and cognitive decline (Klap, Unroe, & Unutzer, 2003; Paterniti, Dufouil, & Alperovitch, 2002; Rapoport, Mamdani, Shulman, Herrmann, & Rochon, 2005). Safer SSRI medications are available and appear to be effective for geriatric anxiety in the short term, but insufficient data exist on long-term risks and benefits (Katz, Reynolds, Alexopoulos, & Hackett, 2002; Lenze et al., 2003; Schuurmans et al., 2006). Many older adults prefer not to take anxiolytic medications because of side effects or a reluctance to

FIGURE 5.1 Meta-Analyses Comparing Psychotherapy and Medication for Geriatric Depression and Anxiety

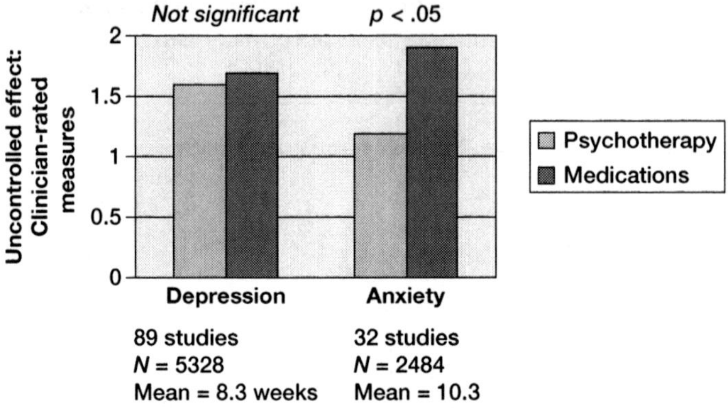

Adapted from Pinquart et al. (2006); Pinquart and Duberstein (2007).

add to an already extensive medication regime (Wetherell et al., 2004). Thus, the availability of effective psychosocial treatments as an alternative to or in combination with pharmacotherapy for late-life anxiety remains an important priority.

In another important study, Drayer et al. (2005), provided a systematic review of the literature on somatic symptoms in older patients with anxiety disorders. Additionally, the hypothesis was tested that somatic symptoms would respond to SSRI treatment in 30 anxious patients aged 60 years and older who participated in a 32-week trial of citalopram. In the analysis, citalopram treatment was associated with a significant decrease in several somatic symptoms from pretreatment baseline. It is concluded that somatic symptoms in older adults with anxiety disorders or anxious depression often improve with successful antidepressant treatment. This was also found to apply for venlafaxine ER (Staab & Evans, 2000).

What we can export here is that medication works. Medication can enhance the effect of psychotherapies, especially CBT and IPT. The psychotherapies also may enhance the effects of the medication. Medication also results in a quicker response and seems to interface well with modules. But the effect sizes have not been consistent or robust enough to suggest that medication is sufficient. The judicious application of modules, with medication being one module, seem especially appealing. Also, a planned use of the sequence of psychotherapy interventions is requisite.

MODULES AND VENUES AND OTHER THERAPIES

Like depression, anxiety in older adults has presented at PCCs for almost a decade, and a change needs to occur. In the CALM study ($N = 52$), the use of modules and case management were applied to good effect (Snowden, Sato, & Roy-Byrne, 2003). The lessons learned are that the treatment model requires flexibility, involving the spouse, applying more time to treatment, using behavioral activation, and attending to memory issues.

Wetherell and Gatz (2001) applied CBT in "Worry Reduction Classes." Participants were taught the nature of anxiety, how to monitor anxiety symptoms, relaxation (progressive muscle relaxation [PMR]), risk estimation, decatastrophizing, imaginal and in vivo desensitization, and worry-behavior prevention. Homework was assigned (30-minute assignments per day). Results were positive for patients but also for the support group. Mohlman et al. (2003) also applied an enhanced CBT framework that increased homework compliance, strengthened memory, and facilitated the use of these techniques: Weekly readings in an anxiety workbook (meant to enhance in-session prescription), with graphing exercises, midweek homework reminders, troubleshooting any problems, and no more than three missed assignments. There was a review at the end of each session of methods learned to date (using dysfunctional thought records [DTRs]). In both studies, success was shown for the enhanced modules.

Modular Intervention Use: A Menu

• Relaxation	• Pain mangement
• Sleep guidelines	• Time mangement
• Problem-solving skills training	• Pleasant activities
• Worry control	• Assertiveness training
• Acceptance/mindfulness	• Cognitive therapy
• Behavioral activation	• Exposure
• Tolerance of uncertainty	• Family involvement

The use of modules in studies has been growing. The application of manuals, then, comes in the form of modules. We should also add that data on joining patients interpersonally and emotionally are also produced and discussed more frequently. Treatment can also be done in several venues and forms. This is all good news. Although success is not always experienced, the idea of practical care with modules is unfolding.

Alternate Therapies With Value

• Bibliotherapy
• Home-based video (Steffen, 2000)
• Caregiver emphasis: REACH (Schulz et al., 2003)

- Telephone-based CBT (Glueckauf et al., 2007)
- Phone and home: Mohr et al. (2005); Simon, Ludman, Tutty, Operskalski, and Von Korff (2004)
- Hospice (Day, Demiris, Oliver, Courtney, & Hensel, 2007)
- Pleasant-events schedule (Cernin & Lichenberg, 2009)
- CBT in home (Scogin, Welsh, Hanson, Stump, & Coates, 2005)
- Medical units (COPD, Kunik et al., 2008)
- New models: Low-intensity CBT
- STEPS model → PCC basis, community, self-help, lectures
- Day care, screens
- Prepsychoeducational interventions

The issue of modules has implications for other aspects of treatment as well as the application of other modules. The importance of collaboration is stressed, as is the contract for homework. In addition, simple but important issues like managing time, assertiveness, and general acceptance of what anxiety is are stressed. Acceptance too is considered. This involves an awareness of the positive aspects of what anxiety is all about, an inner focus as seeing the big picture, distress tolerance, and the need for ongoing commitment to the practice of skills learned (Wetherell et al., 2011).

EXERCISE

One treatment module that, like relaxation, seems to stand on its own is exercise. This has been discussed previously, but it merits special treatment for anxiety. Exercise works. It is effective for depression, cognition, virtually all medical problems, and quality of life, as well as anxiety. It seems to work for people who have rarely exercised, who exercise at late life only, and who do so aerobically or by means of weight training (Institute of Medicine, 2012).

In a meta-analysis of 40 English-language articles published from January 1995 to December 2008 in scholarly journals involving sedentary adults with chronic illness, Herring, O'Connor, and Dishman (2010) revealed the importance of exercise on anxiety. Coauthors independently calculated the Hedges g effect size from studies of 2,914 patients and extracted information regarding potential moderating variables. Compared with no-treatment conditions, exercise training significantly reduced anxiety symptoms by a mean Delta effect of 0.29 with a 95% confidence interval between 0.23 and 0.36. Largest anxiety improvements resulted from exercise programs lasting no more than 12 weeks, using session durations of at least 30 minutes and an anxiety report time frame greater than the past week. This program reduced anxiety symptoms among sedentary patients who had a chronic illness.

TREATMENT SUMMARY

Psychologists must start with the best available research and individualize it to meet the needs of our clients, and they must continue to develop and test efficacious, cost-effective interventions as the aging population in need of treatment continues to increase in coming decades.

Teri, McCurry, Logsdon, and Gibbons (2005)

As we have been arguing, treatment is done best when done carefully and slowly. van't Veer-Tazelaar et al. (2009), for example, suggested that a stepped-care approach using bibliotherapy as a first-line treatment strategy was effective at preventing the onset of anxiety and depression among older adults with subsyndromal symptoms. Like depression, this applies to anxiety. Too often effective therapies are not applied. The figure below suggests what many anxiety patients have seen in the treatment of late-life anxiety: adequate treatment does not happen easily. The typical patient comes into the PCC with vague symptoms, almost always physical. Unless the primary care physician (PCP) inquires about worry and the connection between problems and symptoms, no designation of an anxiety disorder or referral is forthcoming from the patient. In fact, it is often at that moment when the PCP or therapist first discovers an anxiety/depression problem that makes all the difference in therapy's eventual progress. Should the right questions be asked and the right treatment be introduced, treatment will usually be successful, at least partially.

We believe that the better treatment offerings for anxiety directly involve the Watch and Wait model. Messages at the beginning enhance interventions. What is important is that there is respect for anxiety. Unlike depression,

Figure 5.2 Recognizing and Treating Anxiety at Late Life

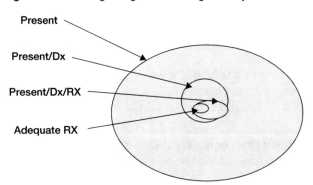

Dx, diagnosis; RX, prescription.

medication seems to provide some relief and can be applied initially. Then the use of modules with monitoring and a perspective are applied.

Overall Treatment for Anxiety

Anxiety is an important dimension of mood in old age and frequently a marker of difficult-to-treat depression:

- Higher levels of anxiety symptoms (especially worry) predict longer time to remission, lower rates of remission, and increased risk for recurrent major depressive episodes
- The evidence base informing pharmacotherapy for comorbid depression and anxiety in older adults is limited and controlled studies are needed
- Most patients are seen in primary care
- Many go undiagnosed and without treatment

Obviously, there are many commonalities in the treatment of depression and anxiety. One difference is that the first line of treatment for anxiety often should involve medication. This is followed by many of the standard efforts for depression: psychoeducation, monitoring, then the use of modules, and perhaps the use of a case manager. Medication is paramount with anxiety because relief at the beginning is important.

Watch and Wait Philosophy

Assess in a usual way plus cognition (EF)

- Treat depression first
- First-line treatment is SSRI/SNRI (serotonin–norepinephrine reuptake inhibitor)
- Psychoeducation
- Choose modules
  - First line: relaxation training
  - Second line: CBT
  - If problems: motivational interviewing to encourage a medication trial
  plus
  - Always include supportive contact and communication with prescriber/CM (case manager)
  - Monitor, see periodically, and watch for relapse
- Use case manager, if needed

Before we look at a case, one point needs to be made: We are dealing with a person. Psychiatry/psychology used to be the discipline that was singular, because it dealt with the person who was perturbed with many symptoms/problems/idiosyncratic expressions/complexities. Somewhere after the death of psychoanalysis this idea was lost. It is always worth highlighting.

Psychiatrists are urged to remain aware that a diagnosis does not define the whole person.... Psychiatry has its own epistemology, which states that the person is primary in relation to its contributory subjects such as biology, psychology, sociology, and so on.

Cox and Gray (2009)

FORMAL TREATMENT PACKAGE

Let's look at a case. Anxiety is always hurried and challenging. In this case, Mrs. K is first and foremost anxious, but also suffers from life issues of excessive caring for others and time management, as well as some depression. She has adequate cognitive skills, is reasonably healthy, and takes care of herself. She also has a respectful and dependent personality.

Case: Mrs. K, anxious, possibly depressed, lives alone

BACKGROUND: The patient is a 75-year-old White female who lives alone. She is married, raised all her children, and has a son who has severe disabilities due to a car accident. Her husband is now in the Veterans Administration (VA) nursing home with dementia and her son has been placed with a local family. She divides her time trying to see these two people. She also lives in a senior apartment complex, has a rent-controlled apartment, and relates no problems there.

She was an only child and experienced problems during her growth years. She indicated no milestone disruptions. She graduated from high school, migrated to this area, and went to beauty school. She was married at age 18 and had five children. Her husband died at age 30 when she was pregnant with her fifth child. She was married shortly thereafter to another gentleman and had two more children with him. A strange situation occurred at age 30 when she was psychiatrically hospitalized during the transition between her first and second husbands, receiving shock treatments for a short period of time. She was unclear about this. She did not work and was a housewife for most of her life.

At present, she takes medications for blood pressure, diabetes, thyroid disease, and takes vitamins B12, E, and D, as well as fish oil. She indicates she takes Cymbalta 60 mg. She states she does not drink alcohol and does not smoke. Her sleep is good, but she is tired during the day. She has hearing problems and wears hearing aids. She also indicates that she has pain in the back of her head that is a 3 out of 10. She indicates that she feels stressed, at times depressed, and she feels like she has had a memory problem or "felt stupid" most of her life. She indicated that she does errands for others excessively as she is the community driver. Her memory, she notes, has gotten worse over the past year. She does all of her activities of daily living (ADL) and instrumental activities of daily living (IADL), and has been a guardian for her son and husband.

She presents rather well. She looks her stated age. She had no difficulties with word-finding problems, but clearly had problems with circumlocution and being focused. She often would answer things in a very roundabout way. She indicated she felt stressed, and that her mind is in a fog. She appears to show good judgment and reasonable insight into her current situation. She was also able to provide reasonable dates for things. Her mind was sharp but distracted.

OVERALL COGNITIVE FUNCTIONING: Mrs. K has a premorbid intelligence score placing her in the average area intellectually. She is a high school graduate. Currently Mrs. K also scored low average on the Repeatable Battery for the Assessment of Neuropsychological Status (RBANS) index 92, 30%. She has a 22/30 Montreal Cognitive Assessment (MoCA), which is mildly impaired. Her other scores suggest mild difficulty on overall cognitive functioning, slightly lower than her premorbid state. Her attention, visuospatial, and language skills are adequate, all being normal. She also has normal new-learning skills as well as an average memory doing better on gist and figure memory. She has largely adequate retrieval skills. Her EF abilities are lower, as she has problems with more complex problem solving. Her complex adjustment scores are good.

She scored highest on anxiety scales (GAD-7 and the Millon Behavioral Medicine Diagnostic [MBMD]). She has a high score for depression (BDI-II [Beck Depression Inventory-II]). She scored as one with GAD on the MINI (Mini-International Neuropsychiatric Interview). On the MBMD she scored high on anxiety and concerns about cognitive dysfunction. Her personality profile shows a pattern of cooperation and respectfulness. This is a highly compliant personality code. She reports no problems with sleep. She is also in minor pain as she has problems in several areas. She is active but does not exercise. She relates that she has problems with stress in her life as she is always doing for others.

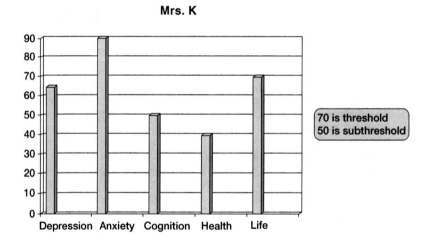

Mrs. K

70 is threshold
50 is subthreshold

Mrs. K—WATCH AND WAIT

Sessions 1 to 3:
She is a worrier and has overinvolved herself in many day-to-day tasks to which she feels overcommitted and taken advantage of. She was asked to monitor her week for hassles and worry. She was also asked to review when she responded positively in her life; what she enjoyed. She was also informed about anxiety and the need to organize her day and, at times, to be assertive and set boundaries. Her cooperative personality was an issue, as she would simply acquiesce to any request. She was also informed that her memory was fine but that she could improve with some cognitive training. She was taking Cymbalta and that seemed to be helping with any depression.

She was to ready herself for the treatment to come, which would involve monitoring, relaxation training, memory training, a structured day, assertiveness training, and pleasant events exposure. She agreed. She endorsed interest in the therapy, the identified goals and tasks, as well as possible barriers.

Watch and Wait Core Category	Check
Validate Problem	×
Psychoeducation of Model	×
Assessment	×
Monitoring	×
Case Formulation	×
Check Alliance	×

Sessions 4 to 10:
The plan was carried out. She complied with all the target treatments but still sensed that she was taken advantage of by family. She especially enjoyed memory training. Specific social events were targeted and practiced with anxiety management training (AMT) and assertion training. She got better at making her needs known. Relaxation and time alone were especially helpful. She was also more involved with her church and with knitting, a skill she had given up. She was pleased at her progress.

Sessions 11 to 12:
She was provided feedback on her problem list as core tests were repeated. She had no changes in cognition or health areas. She did better on depression and anxiety problems, so much so that both were subclinical. She remained the same on life issues as she continued to feel stress and was a caregiver. She was, however, more optimistic about these areas, too, while doing less for others, but still being overtaxed.

Now we discuss the anxiety-specific treatment procedure. This is incorporated into the Watch and Wait model. The lengthy outline indicates that there are many options in Watch and Wait. There are many parts to this outline. Not all are required. The idea that the therapist can choose from this menu is one that has merit. The latter phases of exposure, cognition, worry control, acceptance, and commitment modules, as well as interpersonal interventions, can be applied as needed.

Treatment

Watch and Wait for Anxiety

1. Psychoeducation: Persuade patients to go out into the world and seek

   - Opportunities to get anxious; learn to tolerate anxiety
     - Resist (Oh no!)
     - Permit (It is okay)
     - Provoke (More!)
   - Counterproductive to stay relaxed

- Do not take care of self so intensely
- Let emotions come forward with no resistance
- Learn to tolerate anxiety/uncertainty
- Collaborate, collaborate, collaborate
- Manage time effectively
- Primary care means multiple health partners and conditions
- Be altruistic
- Practice empathy

2. Monitor

- Use GAD-7, State Trait Scale or BAI (Beck Anxiety Inventory)
- Do not wait for the patient to report anxiety

3. Intervention period

- Apply meds
- Use modules
- Use relaxation
  - Use multiple methods (as relaxation-induced anxiety may cause problems)
  - Rehearse relaxation response
  - Find the moment of absorption and find the spot
  - "Recognize the spot" → Just use a technique to get to the spot
  - If problems: Stay the course and use multiple channels
- Meditate or self-monitor: live in the now, the present moment

4. Exercise

- 30 minutes four times per week
- Get commitment
- Gym
- Get social

5. Exposure

- Facing the fear
- Do Fear/Symptom hierarchy
- Do interoceptive exercises
- Do Activities Hierarchy Form (real world)
- Do Facing Activities Form (real world)
- Distraction ratings
- Tasks of exposure:
  - Choose one situation from Situation Hierarchy (SUDs = 50)
  - Identify day and time of practice
  - Identify scary thought
- Imagine being anxious and then coping
  - Do not distract—Be objective
  - Practice for 1 hour
  - Proceed slowly
  - Practice abdominal breathing
  - If overwhelmed, leave but return soon
  - Rate your fear—must go down—hopefully more than 50%
  - Reward self
  - Do again without any safety signals and close to exact fear situation

- One model: self-control desensitization (SCD)
  - Hierarchy
  - Image for 20 seconds
  - Develop and use coping image
  - Postanxiety cue
  - Postimage relaxation
  - Repeat SCD
  - Incorporate cognitive coping statements and perspective shifts

6. Cognitive

   - Strategies: All cognitive distortions are a rush to judgment
   - Educate on the psychology of threat
   - Demonstrate that thoughts → affect
   - List pros and cons of worry beliefs: Do you need this?

7. Stimulus control of worry

   - 20 minutes worry time
   - Distinguish easy worries from difficult ones

8. Interpersonal

   - GAD is inherently interpersonal
   - Social phobia is most frequent comorbidity
   - Assertiveness is one method

9. ACT willingness

   - Being willing to engage in the experience you are already having
   - Will you feel what you feel when you feel it?
   - Are you willing to think the thoughts you are already thinking?
   - Willingness is not about a belief of whether or not you are able to do something but rather about whether you are willing to experience the moment.

SPECIAL CASE: PTSD

We begin by noting that PTSD and acute stress disorder (ASD) are no longer regarded as anxiety disorders in the *DSM-5* (2013). Older people tend to be no more vulnerable or reactive to psychological trauma than younger individuals, despite high stress rates (Hyer, Kramer, & Sohnle, 2004). Recent studies have confirmed earlier ones (Norman et al., 2006) which show that age is not a problem where (a) gender is at issue (Acierno et al., 2007), (b) acute hospital stays are assessed (Zatzick et al., 2004), or (c) primary care is the venue (Magruder et al., 2004). The variable age, in a word, does not seem to negatively relate to prevalence rates (Creamer & Parslow, 2008).

That said, older adults are prone to developing ASD. The most studied acute trauma at late life involves motor vehicle accidents (MVAs; Norris, 1992). For perspective, estimates of PTSD secondary to MVAs range from 10% to 46% for all ages (Blanchard & Hickling, 2004), in addition to other psychiatric symptoms at 1-year follow-up. Notably, MVAs are the second leading cause of injury in geriatric patients, resulting in the highest crash fatality rate of any age group, with most accidents related to driver error (Mandavia & Newton, 1998). MVAs are associated with increased morbidity and mortality in older drivers as well as older pedestrians, owing to their inability to hear traffic, to attain speeds, and poor judgment. When elders are victims, not only may they sustain more serious injuries than other age groups, but they also heal more slowly after injury (Brown, Streubert, & Burgess, 2004). These kinds of vulnerabilities put elders at substantially higher risk of developing ASD/PTSD.

Several other common sources of elder-specific trauma have been reported. For example, the incidence of PTSD following the completion of cancer treatment ranges from 0% to 32% (Kangas, Henry, & Bryant, 2002). Other serious health problems, loss of a spouse, and victimization by crime also have been cited as severe stressors at late life. Elder abuse, which refers to many types of maltreatment, including neglect, physical, emotional, financial, and sexual abuse, is a major trauma as well (McCartney & Severson, 1997; Newton, 2010). In the PCC and even in the mental health clinic, these kinds of traumas are often overlooked as producing ASD/PTSD in older adults, thereby preventing or delaying effective intervention. Even in cardiac care, from coronary artery bypass graft (CABG) to congestive heart failure (CHF) to the new use of VADs (ventricular assist devices), PTSD is a likely outcome when mental problems ensue.

When trauma is linked to poor health habits or to medical comorbidities, the response to treatment for any psychiatric problem is less robust in older adults than in other age groups (Hyer et al., 2004). Over time, PTSD has been linked to smoking and alcohol abuse, suicidal ideation, high rates of primary care use, and behavioral disturbances in long-term care (Cook, O'Donnell, Moltzen, Ruzek, & Sheikh, 2006). Kessler et al. (1996) showed that a substantial proportion of adults with established PTSD (40%) do not recover even decades later. Several studies have shown that a variety of health problems and physical disability are more common in men and women with PTSD than in their unaffected peers. Sareen et al. (2007) surveyed almost 37,000 community-dwelling adults, of whom 478 had been diagnosed with PTSD (1%). Despite low prevalence, PTSD was associated with significantly greater odds of chronic illness, including asthma, COPD, chronic fatigue syndrome, arthritis, fibromyalgia, migraines, cardiovascular disease, gastrointestinal disorders, pain disorders, and cancer. These findings underscore the importance of careful screening for PTSD symptoms among older patients presenting with medical problems.

One issue has been debated regarding older adults and trauma: whether older adults are more vulnerable or have increased inoculation as a result of a stressor. As just intimated, because of reduced adaptive capacities, coping resources, and external resources (e.g., low income and lack of social supports), and increased exposure to traumatic events through aging (e.g., health-related events or elder abuse), older adults may be more likely than younger people to develop psychiatric disorders, including PTSD, and/or problems with psychosocial functioning. This has been labeled the *vulnerability* or *additive burden* hypothesis (Dohrenwend & Dohrenwend, 1981), and more recently, *stress proliferation* (Pearlin, Schieman, Fazio, & Meersman, 2005). The *stress inoculation* hypothesis has also been proffered. This theory argues that age is protective against the development of PTSD. This occurs particularly when older people have dealt successfully with previous traumas, were able to reexperience a trauma with a high degree of voluntary control, or were able to find meaning in the outcome of the trauma, and/or to find social support (Hyer et al., 2004). Clearly, the older adult who is resilient in the face of trauma is more likely to respond favorably to psychotherapy (if even needed) or to be a good candidate for "indicated" public health interventions.

There are no empirically based therapies for older adults with PTSD. In addition, there is no solid evidence that any of the components of CBT work better than others (Arch & Craske, 2009). Data emanating from treatment studies of older adults with anxiety and depression, or younger adults with PTSD, show that components of CBT, especially relaxation, are apt for older adults. In the treatment of older adults, the clinician also must consider PTSD-specific concerns of an altered stressor; use of exposure; aging-related issues of health, cognition, resilience, and emotions; treatment concerns of the alliance; health care use/compliance; and the interface with integrated therapies.

Hyer et al. (2004) argued that four therapies have special merit for the treatment of PTSD symptoms: (a) AMT; (b) stress inoculation therapy, representing a coping model; (c) eye movement desensitization and retraining (EMDR), providing a dosed exposure that targets state-specific information related to the trauma and has applicability with older people (Hyer & Kushner, 2008); and (d) cognitive processing therapy, applying gradual and multiple exposure to the trauma and consisting largely of rescripting and altering distortions (Felder, Monson, & Friedman, 2007). Rygh and Sanderson (2004) nicely outlined a complete package for the treatment of anxiety problems that we believe relates to PTSD. They include a cognitive component (cognitive restructuring, worry exposure, psychoeducation, etc.), physiologic aspects (progressive muscle relaxation, self-control, desensitization, etc.), behavioral component (pleasurable activity scheduling, behavioral response prevention, etc.), and ancillary interventions (mindfulness, emotional processing, interpersonal effectiveness, and time management). Increasingly, the use of modules is being recommended for the care of anxiety disorders in older adults (Wetherell, Lenze, & Stanley, 2005).

To this, Hyer and colleagues (2004) added a specification of the components of PTSD treatment for older adults. They created a six-step model of treatment, highlighting the issues noted above. In general, the more intense the person's perturbation, the more focus is placed on therapeutic tasks staged at the beginning of the treatment model. In contrast, the less the person is impacted by the trauma, the more the therapist can address the latter parts of the model and achieve lasting change. The rationale for the ordering of these tasks is to keep clients committed, encourage experimentation, and create cognitive change. But be aware that older adults do well on the application of the first few parts of the model, but struggle with, or even resist working on, the latter tasks. Again, it is emphasized these components are considered modules for treatments that have a logic in sequence but remain flexible.

Treatment Model

1. Stabilize symptoms → Treat comorbid disorders or stressors (including health).
2. Relationship building → Build trust, reinforce the client's ability to confront trauma with a trusted therapist. Apply the client rated Working Alliance Inventory (WAI).
3. Attend to necessary developmental, treatment, and education (normalization) factors → Assure social supports, daily coping, social skills, and treatment compliance.
4. Apply cognitive restructuring (CR) → Teach the five-step program of CR and consider tactics of personality style as therapy-guided treatment.
5. Elicit positive core memories (PCM) → Foster a re-narration of self with core memories that can generalize to current life situations.
6. Decondition trauma memories → Apply AMT.

CONCLUSION

Worry or anxiety is problematic in older adults at about a 20% rate, with more severe problems at about half that rate. Older adults who have been worried all their lives put this trait in overdrive as they age. As we have seen, anxiety has an impact on the brain and on a person's quality of life. In addition, anxiety is not easily treated. As a disorder it is generally resistant to change.

That said, therapy is ultimately an exercise in self-improvement, in perspective, and in toleration of the throes of life. The goal is to keep the anxious person apprised of his or her plight, to keep him or her engaged in the world, and to be persistent at change. Anxiety is a disorder or problem state that hangs around but at reasonably mild to moderate levels; because it is so, it can be altered over time. The pursuit of normalizing is one in which being symptom free is a misnomer, even heresy, as living demands more of the person. Anxiety, like depression, is one of the problem states in which the older adult wrestles with real life, using worry strategies that no longer work.

CHAPTER 6

Cognition

Scientists are not going to solve the problem of recovery from brain damage to the brain with cellular, molecular or pharmaceutical treatments alone. We're going to have to figure out how to get learning to occur in combination with that, whether it is cognitive, sensory, or motor learning.

—*Newport* (2013)

The modeling of a complex system of behavior best involves a schema that incorporates aging. Aging, frailty, and cognition resist facile definition and measurement. Aging is related to a number of deficits, not to a particular system. The "syndrome of aging," if you will, derives not from singular components of a system, but from a system as a whole. It is, therefore, an emergent construct. Emergence derives its essence from multiple synergies of the components, not from individual ones. Knowledge of aging in effect is rarely complete, but rather dynamic, and requires an assay of its behavior as well as factors, such as biomarkers and social aspects. All that said, distinct memory and cognitive deficits are now recognized as core to the broader phenotype of many late-life problems and clearly many late-life psychiatric disorders.

Cognitive aging is messy. Cognitive decline, particularly in late adulthood, is becoming the nation's top public health problem. According to the National Institute on Aging, as many as 2.4 million to 5.1 million Americans have Alzheimer's disease (AD). AD is now the seventh leading cause of death across all ages in the United States and the fifth leading cause of death in Americans aged 65 and older. Meanwhile, the prevalence of mild cognitive impairment (MCI)—problems with memory, language, or other mental functions that do not yet interfere with daily living—is thought to be higher. Even for normal aging, the question is what health care providers can do about the natural or pathological state of cognitive decline (LeCouteur & Sinclair, 2010). Small changes in core capacities can lead to large changes in complex behavior (Salthouse, 2001).

We are receiving minimal help from consensus guidelines. The National Institutes of Health's Alzheimer's and Cognitive Decline Prevention (Sperling et al., 2011) study was most cautious in their recommendations of what really assists in this process—exercise, leisure, and cognitive activity. In *The Lancet Neurology* there was a suggestion that early identification and intervention of these seven factors may result in a 10% to 25% reduction in the incidence of AD.

---

1. Diabetes mellitus
2. Midlife hypertension
3. Obesity
4. Present smoking
5. Depression
6. Physical inactivity
7. Cognitive inactivity

Source: The Lancet Neurology.

In addition, the update to the CDC (Centers for Disease Control) Healthy Brain Initiative (2012) emphasized the importance of a healthy brain. It outlined a road map for healthy brains and highlighted physical activity and vascular factors. However, cerebrovascular risk factors (CVRFs), especially diabetes, smoking, depression/anxiety, metabolic syndrome, and apolipoprotein E4 (ApoE4), do raise red flags. At least 22% of people older than age 70 have memory impairment. This often is apart from plaques and tangles. In fact, it is best to remember that a balance of positive and negative genetic factors affect the brain in early/middle life to determine the degree of cognitive agility or impairment at late life. These factors increase or decrease in the cerebrospinal fluid, and cause problems with oxidative stress, inflammation, insulin signaling components, size and frequency of infarcts, concentration of growth factors, cortisol, and other hormones. It cannot be emphasized enough: behaviors across the life span matter.

Cognition has taken on a whole new emphasis in the past year. This construct is now operative in the formation of psychiatric problems, phenomenology, understanding, and, it is important to note, the care and change of the brain. Furthermore, the cognitive domains most consistently related to aging are also the ones most impaired in late-life psychiatric disorders. This is new; although it has been part of the complexity of psychopathological formation for some time, it now is evident and transparent.

- Traditional cognitive models are increasingly employed as a window to understanding psychiatric disorders.
- Cognitive dysfunction and neural circuitry may play a key role in understanding the etiology of behavior and psychiatric symptoms.
- Distinct memory and cognitive deficits are increasingly recognized as part of the broader phenotype of many psychiatric illnesses.
- Cognitive dysfunction may be a significant risk factor for development of psychiatric illnesses, particularly in older adults.
- Cognitive and memory dysfunction may exacerbate psychiatric symptoms in all populations.
- Cognitive dysfunction is increasingly documented to negatively impact response to pharmacological and psychological interventions such as cognnitive behavioral therapy (CBT).
- Cognitive impairments offer a potentially effective target for addressing psychiatric illness through cognitive rehabilitation and augmentation of pharmacotherapies.

Neural plasticity facilitates healthy development across a vast continuum of child-rearing conditions and might help to account for the resiliency often seen even when children experience nonoptimal parenting or conditions of social and economic adversity. However, adaptive neural plasticity might also finesse vulnerability under certain circumstances. There is increasing evidence that exposure to stress levels that overwhelm the organism's ability to manage that stress may negatively affect brain development (Fisher & Gunnar, 2010). Researchers have documented neuroanatomical changes after exposure to enriched environments, including increased brain weight and size, increased dendritic branching and length, changes in synaptic size and number, and behavioral improvements on long-term spatial memory tasks. The two core components of an enriched environment seem to be complexity and novelty (Sale, Berardi, & Maffei, 2009). Voluntary exercises that maximize these areas, among other interventions, seem to help. Exercise itself increases brain-derived neurotrophic factor (BDNF) as well as improving spatial memory tasks (Erickson et al., 2011).

However, there are limits. Owen (2010) expressed concerns about the "fetishization" of brain health and noted that the data are insufficient for any recommended benefits of cognitive therapy for older adults. In the 21st century, we may be victims of our technopathologies. We have been given to poor attention habits (continuous partial attention), cognition (digital fog), overload (frazzing), and addiction (online compulsive disorder). Firm conclusions cannot be drawn on our current level of knowledge.

Firm conclusions cannot be drawn about the association of any modifiable risk factor with cognitive decline or AD.

National Institutes of Health (2010)

The Dark Side of Brain Health: Consequences of Reductionism

In the past 5 years, 20 candidate compounds for AD have failed—Dimebon, Alzmed, Flurizan

Effect sizes for acetylcholinesterase inhibitors (AChEIs) low

Big switch → Brain health is "in"

    300 million (2010) – 8 billion (2015)

Excessive focus → "fetishization"

    Brain as separate, must stimulate and rewire

Bottom line: Data are insufficient for now

    11,430 subjects – 6-week program → No transfer effects

Adapted from Owen (2012)

NORMAL AGING: WHAT IS UP WITH COGNITION?

Greater variability in tasks may be due initially to very small inefficiencies in the transmission of information or lapses of attention. These inefficiencies accumulate as pathology accumulates. In other words these inefficiencies and inconsistencies may build up over time and slowly worsen until they become clinical-level disorders.

Hultsch (2008)

Reasons for the continuation of cognitive problems at later life are many. Perhaps all have merit, as older age is the final common pathway to problems in life. Older age is the time when biomarkers collude against the system and, even in very healthy people, problems unfold with regularity (Beekman et al., 2005). Aging is not for sissies.

Reasons for Memory Problems

- Common cause: Neurobiological factor causes decline. Ninety-three percent of variance of age-related decline is owing to loss of visual and auditory acuity
- Use it or lose it: Reduced sensory input
- Cognitive permeation: Tasks are more cognitively demanding
- Extraneous factor: Difficulty in perceiving the relevant stimulus

---

And, of course there are brain problems across the life span. In the past 30 years, human development as a field has become aware of the importance of the "life span developmental" perspective, which conceptualizes human development across the entire life span. From this perspective, development is embedded in multiple contexts and is conceived of as a dynamic process in which the ontogeny of development interacts with the social environment, a set of interconnected social settings, embedded in a multilayered social and cultural context. At late life, these build and result in problems. Synaptogenesis, the synaptic density in the infrastructure of the human system, declines over time. There are also considerable structural brain damage and neurotransmitter deficiencies. If problems segue toward AD, then plaques and tangles result.

Brain Problems at Late Life

- Synaptogenesis goes down
- Neuronal loss
- Structural brain changes
  - Reduced hippocampal volume
  - Reduced brain volume
  - White matter lesions and hyperintensities
  - Prefrontal cortex deficits
  - Frontostriatal dysfunction
  - Anterior cingulate deficits and posterior cingulate deficits
- Neurotransmitter deficiencies
  - Cholinergic deficits
  - Serotonergic deficits
  - Dopaminergic deficits
  - Norepinephrine deficits
  - Glutaminergic deficits
- Neurofibrillary tangles and deposits of beta-amyloid plaques

---

But what about the normal aging brain? Old brains work harder and engage in more distributed, compensatory processing to perform a task that is focal for younger adults. In general, older adults function reasonably well. Despite pathology, older adults can compensate by scaffolding (Park & Reuter-Lorenz, 2009); this is the recruitment of additional circuitry that shores up declining structures whose functioning is noisy. Generally this is bilateral activation. Scaffolding or secondary networks are an important part of normal aging. It allows for the maintenance of cognitive functioning as age-associated structural deterioration occurs. This process is very efficient in youth and stands at the ready at late life. With age, the scaffolding process may be invoked to perform familiar tasks as done in youth as these processes become increasingly more challenging.

This is the brain's response to challenges (see Figure 6.1). A common theme in the decline of performance involves executive function and the frontal lobes. Data from one model, the Compensation-Related Utilization of Neural Circuits Hypothesis (CRUNCH), provides one framework for this understanding. This model shows that relative to younger adults, older adults activate at lower levels of task demand where performance differences are minimal, but underactivate at higher levels of task demand where there is a corresponding drop in performance.

The figure expands on the CRUNCH model. At base (upper left box), dopaminergic receptors decline (attention and modulation of responses) and brain structures show volumetric shrinkage (caudate, cerebellum, hippocampus, and prefrontal); less gray and white matter result; and there is cortical thinning. There are also white matter areas that are less dense (diffusion tensor imaging), and neurofibrillary plaques and tangles.

That said, the brain responds with continuous reorganization and repair to support cognitive function (lower right box). Dedifferentiation becomes a core vehicle for compensation: younger adults have focused activation in the fusiform face area, parahippocampal area, and lateral occipital area for tasks related to these areas, for example; older adults use more of the brain area. The default network too is less suppressed in older adults. That is, the usual areas of the brain remain at rest when they should be activated. This is especially a problem because the default network is key to attention and concentration; when present, the older adult is in reverie or is not attending.

Finally, the boxes on the right of the figure portray the complexity of the brain's adjustment. Generally, this involves an overactivation of the prefrontal sites owing to the underactivation of the posterior sites of occipital and parietal lobes (upper right). Frontal lobe activation increases although the hippocampus and parahippocampal areas decrease. Both hemispheres are involved. A recruitment of additional circuitry shores up declining structures whose functioning is noisy. Neurogenesis also applies. However, the external actions (lower right) that can make a difference include physical fitness, cognitive stimulation, occupational attainment, and education. Brain reserve consists of using brain networks that are less susceptible to disruption.

FIGURE 6.1   Normal Aging Brain Dynamics

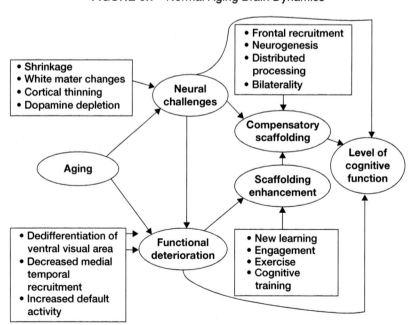

Source: Park and Reuter-Lorenz (2009).

In effect, extrinsically, the brain is confronted with novel or increased demands; intrinsically, there can be issues like sleep deprivation or more continuous problems (biological aging). Scaffolding is not a sign of pathology. It is compensatory in design. At some point scaffolding may meet its limit due to pathology, as in AD, as pathology increases and the reparative processes wither.

The pathophysiology of decline is predictable. Synaptogenesis—the synaptic density in the infrastructure of the human system—is the most accurate biophysical correlate of cognitive impairment and hippocampal atrophy; the brain's memory marker over the lifetime also increases. This structure more than anything is related to cognitive activity in healthy adults. On the positive side, environmental enrichment, involving occupation, leisure, complexity in life, and mental training, makes a difference; how and with whom are yet to be fully fleshed out. Unfortunately, now there is more chaos in the brain health field as dementia biomarkers keep changing: amyloid-beta markers, white matter hyperintensities, proinflammatory cytokines, number of neuritic plaques, and so on.

The extent of cognitive decline over time has only recently been studied. Older adults with MCI are thought to convert to a dementia at high rates; what is involved with MCI decline predicts dementia. In other words, the pathological processes related to AD are directly related to the decline process in MCI. Obviously, this assumes that the person has no other medical or predictor problems like cerebrovascular problems in which the trajectory is more precipitous.

In fact, dementia risk is different from dementia progression. The latter was studied by Wilson and colleagues (2012). Using a battery of 18 cognitive tests, his group followed more than 200 healthy older adults over a decade. The list below portrays the results: Pathological measures of AD and vascular dementia were not strongly related to cognitive trajectories. The trajectory was slow for 5 to 7 years and then increased.

- Mean cognitive decline over 10 years initiated at 7.5 years before dementia was diagnosed
- Global cognitive decline measure declined −0.87 unit per year
- At 2 years before diagnosis, decline increased by a factor of 4 of 0.37 unit per year
- Cognitive decline in AD is nonlinear and precedes dementia
- Data support an accelerating model of cognitive decline lasting approximately 5 years and then accelerating

Wilson et al. (2012)

The reciprocal relationship of neurocognitive and functional problems is a substantial issue. Rajan et al. (2013) found that disability and cognitive decline are highly interrelated. Results from this group support the hypothesis that disability in old age is associated with accelerated cognitive decline.

As part of a longitudinal population-based study, change in cognitive function was assessed in older people and after the onset of disability. During a mean of more than 9 years of observation, 37% of participants developed at least one ADL limitation and 48% developed IADL limitations. The cognitive function declined by 158% after onset of ADL disability and 115% after IADL disability onset. These findings persist after controlling for demographic variables, chronic health conditions, and depression.

Rajan et al. (2013, p. 629)

Also, neuropsychiatric symptoms in later life cohabitate with cognitive decline. This is also not surprising. The shared neurophysiological features of cognitive aging and mental health problem symptoms in older adults are apparent. These include neuronal loss and neurotransmitter dysregulation. Older adults also experience medical problems. The extent to which moderators like Apo-E or neuroticism influence this process is just now unfolding (O'Hara et al., 2005).

CONTINUUM OF COGNITIVE DECLINE

First, we need to appreciate the continuum of cognition at late life. The cognitive continuum represents the dance of normal aging, followed by age-associated memory impairment (AAMI), MCI, and the dementia. There are components to each: AAMI is best seen as largely normal with little conversion to dementia; MCI has many definitions but represents an amnestic or nonamnestic decline of 1 to 2 standard deviations (mostly for working memory [WM] or executive function [EF]) from norm with normal functioning; and dementia results in problems with memory and function.

FIGURE 6.2 Continuum of Cognitive Decline

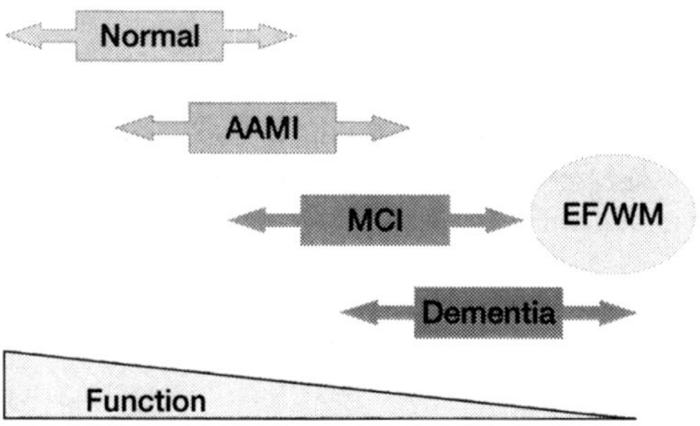

In terms of the specifics of decline at late life, most cognitive problems lead to lower functioning. The brain areas that subserve fluid intelligence are hardest hit. Naturally, these skills are subject to the many mediators across life, including the more salient ones, like socioeconomic status (SES), education, and life habits.

Memory at Late Life

Declines
- WM (keep irrelevant info)
- Executive function
- Speed of processing
- Long-term memory
- Less controlled processing (elaborative processing)
- Effortful tasks are poorly done
- Poor source memory
- Senses (visual and verbal)
- Dedifferentiation (less neural specificity)

Remains
- Verbal

Memory is best understood from the dissociations brought into light by different neuropsychological syndromes. Assessment of memory is at best an approximation, as it is contaminated with typologies, other cognitive domains, and the personality of the older patient. There are at least five memory systems based on Baddeley's model of WM, Tulving's serial parallel independent (SPI) model, or MNESIS (Memory NEo-Structural Inter-Systemic model; see Eustache & Desgranges, 2008), that are based on long-term representation, as well as reactions to them that foster the reconstructive nature of human memory. This can get interesting, as the models integrate the interactions between the extant systems and WM but also newer features.

In recent years, four areas and global functioning have been targets of cognitive training. These include memory, reasoning, speed of processing, and executive function. Each seems to predict function in different ways and amounts. Reasoning tends to be the best predictor of initial functioning and memory the best predictor of changes in everyday functioning over time (Gross et al., 2011). But, memory is at the heart of one's psyche. This is self-awareness that generates a subjective impression of self in time, linked to feelings of wholeness, continuity, and coherence. The relations between cognition and affect become a core schema for any one person. These are models, painstakingly incorrect, but positively heuristic as the person self-evaluates over time.

There are, of course, many other mediating or moderating variables. They are all complex and interactive; nothing is simple. If we just look at education, it is annoyingly subtle and un-simple.

Overall the results of this review suggest that the education–dementia relationship may be more complex than earlier suggested in the aging literature. The results suggest that lower education is associated with an increased risk for dementia for some but not all studies. Further, the level of education that was most associated with dementia risk varied considerably by study region, and by age, sex, and race/ethnicity.... The existence of an education–dementia relationship seems strongly tied to the unique demands of an individual's environment. We suggest that education is best described as a proxy for a trajectory of life events, beginning before and extending beyond the years of formal education and that either increases or decreases an individual's risk for dementia.

Sharp and Gatz (2011)

MCI

Terms such as *AAMI* and *benign senescent forgetfulness* (BSF) have been around for many years and fall on the aging side of the forgetting spectrum; terms like *malignant forgetfulness* and *questionable dementia* fall on the dementia side. The terms *MCI* or minor neurocognitive disorder are somewhere in the middle. Over the years, the *Diagnostic and Statistical Manual of Mental Disorders (DSM)* and National Institute of Neurological and Communicative Disorders and Stroke and AD and Related Disorders Association (NINCDS-ADRDA) have been widely used in research and clinical settings. Now the *DSM-5* and the National Institute on Aging and the Alzheimer's Association (NIA–AA) are seeking change. MCI will be labeled as a "minor neurocognitive disorder." As just indicated, the NIA–AA has now labeled AD into three phases and a heavy emphasis is placed on biomarkers.

MCI is a kind of strategic construct used to allow health care providers the luxury of placing the identified patient into a holding area where time can sort out the eventual diagnosis. The number of persons in the United States who have MCI by age 70 is estimated to be 6 million. Conversion rates to dementia have been estimated for over a decade to be about 12% to 15% per year. But it depends on the sample, the measures, and the clinician. Morris et al. (2001) noted that 100% of MCI subjects in memory disorders clinics progressed to dementia over 9.5 years, and 84% met neuropathological criteria for AD. In contrast, reviewing epidemiological studies, one researcher found that the reversion rate of MCI to normal is as much as 30% (Lowenstein, 2011). Remember, too, that everyday people—community adults—also have problems. Lowenstein, Acevedo, Czaja, and Duara (2004) and Jak et al. (2009) suggested that using just clinical historical evaluation suggestive of memory decline but with normal psychological testing is not as accurate as using those with a normal clinical history, but who have the addition of two or more tests; 1 to 2 standard deviations is low.

MCI Facts

- MCI differs from normal aging
- Objective memory low by 1.0, 1.5, or 1.96 SDs on one or two tests
- There are many types of MCI
- Neuropsychological assessment helps
- Neuropathology consistent with AD
- Biomarkers suggest that MCI is more like dementia
- Progression: 10% to 15% per year convert to AD
- There are many false positives, especially in community samples
- Treatment: No FDA-approved treatment

This issue of course is not simple. The percentage of normal aging with mild AD pathology is higher than anyone cares to absolutely know. This can mean that the person is able to depend on brain reserve or the environment is uncomplicated. We are still in new territories.

Percentage of Normal Aging With AD Pathology

- 27% (age > 75; Price & Morris, 1999)
- 45% (age > 66; Hulette et al., 1998)
- 34% (mean age 85; Katzman et al., 1988)
- 33% (age > 47; Braak & Braak, 1991)

Regardless, the odds are that any careful diagnosis of MCI represents a state closer to dementia and has a biomarker profile representative of this.

MCI Biomarker Profile

- Hypometabolism on PET (positron emission tomography) (Caselli, Chen, Lee, Alexander, & Reiman, 2008; Mosconi, Pupi, & De Leon, 2008)
- Abnormal fMRI (functional MRI) activation (Xu, Zuo, Wang, & Han, 2009)
- Elevated tau/aβ ratios in the CSF (cerebrospinal fluid) (Petrie et al., 2009)
- Hippocampus and entorhinal cortex atrophy; Yuan et al. (2009) showed that hippocampal volume on MRI alone could identify 73% of MCIs

---

The Sperling Workgroup (2011) also believed that those with MCI were likely to have problems (we address this in the context of dementia). They attached their criteria to biomarkers, including neuronal injury.

MCI Owing to AD: Categories

- MCI with AD unlikely: no positive biomarkers
- MCI with AD intermediate: either a positive biomarker of AB or neuronal injury
- MCI with AD likely: positive biomarkers in both AB and neuronal injury

---

A summary of the issue of the value of an MCI concept or diagnosis at present follows.

- Is MCI a useful concept in that it has generated interest in studying diseases in their early stages (important implications for diagnosis and treatment)? — Yes
- Is MCI necessarily AD? — No; MCI and etiological underpinnings must be established through comprehensive clinical evaluation and neuropsychological testing
- Will certain cognitive profiles and biomarkers increase the probability that we are dealing with an underlying Alzheimer's process? — Yes
- Are we ready to make research diagnosis of AD at the MCI stage based on cognitive and biomarker data? — Yes
- Is the clinical diagnosis of MCI—AD now ready? — Probably too early

---

Brain Reserve

This construct is critical in the understanding of cognitive decline. It is especially noteworthy where MCI is concerned. As an influencing construct, it is now more than 10 years old. It represents the protective brain areas owing to life skills, like intelligence, occupational complexity, "thick" leisure, computer games, less stress, and healthy living. Patients with more education, for example, require more brain problems (degeneration) to show the same level of cognitive burden as someone with less education or brain reserve. Required for brain reserve estimation are measures of brain deterioration, cognition, and some marker of reserve.

Whatever the ultimate brain reserve, it is clear that this skill needs to be considered when diagnosing a patient. An understanding of this construct as well as personality and current problems becomes most relevant in the assessment and treatment of an older adult with apparent dementia values of MCI problems.

Brain Reserve Models

1. Moderation—brain reserve influences the relationship between cognitive measures and neuropathologic burden
2. Neuroprotection model—brain reserve retards the rate of brain deterioration
3. Compensatory model—brain reserve moderates the relationship between brain burden and cognitive functioning

---

DEMENTIA CRITERIA AND CONFUSION

The current diagnosis of dementia is wanting. It is categorical, exclusive, and arbitrary. Creating a dichotomy between dementia and non-dementia ignores the spectrum of cognitive impairment. Converting soft data into hard categories fails to capture the complexity of the common coexistence and probable interaction of cerebrovascular impairments/dementias and AD on the moving background of aging. While it is time to shift the focus from thresholds to a continuum of cognitive impairment, from the late to the early stages, and from effects to causes, this is not helpful, in the present moment, to health care providers who are on the front lines.

The literature on dementia abounds in overlapping, contradictory, and confusing descriptive association studies. The dominant explanations for causes, that AD is amyloidopathy or tauopathy, have established only that these are important components, but far downstream from whatever triggers the spreading causal cascade. In the meantime, mounting and persuasive evidence suggests that stroke and dementia share similar risk factors and that the lifetime risk of developing one or both is one in three. As noted previously, cerebrovascular disease and AD often occur together and may potentiate each other, at least in a subset of patients.

AD is a chronic disease that begins decades before clinical manifestations. The challenge is to identify those destined to develop AD in the future. All technology that involves biomarkers also depends on cognition as an endpoint. Cognition currently lags behind biomarkers (AB and tau) in preclinical detection accuracy, followed by behaviors. The understanding is that the AB amyloid pathology precedes the neuronal injury by 20 years. The result is that AB is low in the CSF early and as the disease progresses biomarkers of neuronal injury, such as CSF tau, fluorodeoxyglucose (FDG-PET), or atrophy on MRI of the brain, become informative. This model is yet to be validated.

Over time there have been improvements in the identification of other variables, such as cognition, that predict the conversion of MCI to dementia. Devanand et al. (2010) showed that a health care provider can be

---

Predictor Algorithm MCI → AD

- 0–24%   → < 3 predictors abnormal
- 35%–67% → if 3 predictors abnormal
- 84%–92% → if 4 predictors abnormal
- 98%   → 5 predictors abnormal
- SRT (speech recognition threshold), UPSIT (University of Pennsylvania Smell Identification Test), FAQ (Functional Assessment Questionnaire), Hippocampal volume, Entorhinal volume

Adapted from Devanand (2008).

---

accurate to over 90%, but a memory task was involved along with function scale and odor test as well as two scans. Despite advances in scans, then, developing more measures of cognition will also be a benefit in the discovery and diagnosis of AD and other dementias (Ashford & Borson, 2008).

Effort to identify new biomarkers are underway; the criteria for a new diagnostic approach include genetic testing, molecular imaging, and body fluid biomarkers (Dubois et al., 2010). The holy grail of assessment is the identification of patients in the earliest stage of AD, before clinical manifestation of dementia, to provide effective early intervention that aims at delaying significant impairment. A definitive diagnosis of AD requires a detailed postmortem microscopic examination of the brain. But nowadays, AD can be diagnosed by taking a careful history from patients and their families, and assessing cognitive function by neuropsychologic tests. Other causes of dementia must be ruled out, such as low thyroid function, vitamin deficiencies, infections, cancer, and depression. It is also crucial to differentiate AD from other neurodegenerative dementias.

In the dementia screening process sequence, that resulting assessment should involve a preliminary examination by a trained professional and include a more extensive cognitive evaluation, interview of an informant knowledgeable about the patient's daily function, appropriate neuropsychological assessment, and a summary rating, followed by a discussion of the implications of the conclusions with the subject and caregiver.

Ashford (2008, p. 419)

The emphasis for finding dementia has been on seeking biomarkers to replace functional markers. Functional markers, such as index functional ability, decline with many age, fitness, and health conditions, and lots of cognitive markers have been taking a back seat to biomarkers. These have included histopathological counts of plaques and tangles; oxidative stress, derived from blood assays; genetic markers such as ApoE4; white matter hyperintensities; whole-brain atrophy; dopamine receptor binding; and amyloid load, among others.

Biomarkers for AD

- Beta-amyloid markers are reductions in CSF AB42 and increased amyloid PET tracer retention
- After a lag, neuronal dysfunction and neurodegeneration become the dominant biomarkers
- Biomarkers now are increased in CSF tau and structural MRI measures of cerebral atrophy
- Neurodegeneration → synaptic dysfunction, which is marked by uptake on PET

Jack et al. (2011)

The *DSM-5* has made a change in the area of Neurocognitive Disorders. The term *dementia* is subsumed under Major Neurocognitive Disorder. This disorder pulls together a set of existing mental disorder diagnoses from the *DSM-IV*, including dementia and amnestic disorder. Its criteria have not changed to any degree. The generic cognitive areas at issue include complex attention, executive function, learning and memory, language, perceptual motor, and social cognition. Mild Neurocognitive Disorder (Mild NCD) now takes the place of Cognitive Disorder, NOS (or MCI). It goes beyond normal issues of aging, but doesn't yet rise to the level of a major neurocognitive disorder. Mild NCD describes a level of cognitive decline that requires the person to be engaging in compensatory strategies and accommodations to help maintain independence and perform activities of daily living. To be diagnosed with mild NCD, there must be changes that impact cognitive functioning. The APA (2013) noted that there is substantial clinical need to recognize individuals who require care for cognitive issues that go beyond normal aging. Recent studies suggest that identifying mild NCD as early as possible may allow interventions to be more effective.

Regarding etiological subtypes, clinicians formerly could use a number of different criteria sets to designate whether the dementia was of the AD type, vascular dementia, or substance-induced dementia, for example. This has changed somewhat in the *DSM-5*. According to the *DSM-5*, major or mild vascular NCD and major or mild NCD due to AD have been retained, but newer separate criteria are now presented for major or mild NCD due to frontotemporal NCD, Lewy bodies, traumatic brain injury, Parkinson's disease, HIV infection, Huntington's disease, prion disease, and conditions with multiple etiologies like substance/medication-induced NCD or unspecified NCD. We will continue to use the term *MCI*.

Also, the *DSM-5* workgroups suggested three categories of dementia starting long before any formal diagnosis was made. They intended to incorporate biomarkers, formalize different stages of AD, and use criteria for MCI and AD not dependent on biomarkers.

***DSM-5* Workgroup Categories for Dementia (AD)**

- Asymptomatic Phase (Preclinical)
- Predementia Phase (MCI)
- Diagnostic Phase (AD)

Sperling et al. (2011)

Regarding the asymptomatic phase, it was emphasized that there was a problem prior to any symptoms related to AD. This was evident because of the general lack of biomarker specificity and that upward of 30% normal at autopsy have AD-P (no clinical symptoms). The reverse can also be true: a reconversion from MCI to normal. The workgroup addressed and focused on research recommendations. Thus, front-line practitioners continue to walk a tightrope between regarding AD as a chronic condition that starts well before symptom onset and knowing that an AD's underlying pathology may exist even in an asymptomatic period.

Preclinical Phase

- AD-P (pathophysiological)
- AD-C (clinical)

Sperling et al. (2011)

Currently, the diagnosis of a dementia has been reformatted, such that memory is respected but allowed to be partnered with other deficits in cognition, including reasoning, visual-spatial, language, and personality change.

Diagnosis of Dementia

Cognitive or neuropsychiatric symptoms that:

1. Interfere with the ability to function in usual activities
2. Represent a decline from previous functioning
3. Are not due to delirium or major psychiatric disorder
4. Cognitive impairment detected through history and objective assessment
5. Are a problem in at least two domains (memory, reasoning, visuospatial, language, personality change)

Special Contamination

There is a large overlap between AD and vascular dementia (VaD) pathologies. Autopsy studies have found that up to 90% of patients with AD exhibited cerebrovascular pathology and about one third of VaD patients showed AD pathology (Kalaria, 2000). Although the NINCDS-ADRDA and the *DSM-IV-TR* (APA, 2000) criteria for AD are the prevailing diagnostic standards in research. However, they have fallen behind the unprecedented growth of scientific knowledge. Now, a "vasculopathic complex" has been identified. These are vascular-related factors that negatively impact cerebral perfusion to a critical level of dysfunction.

Vascular Problems Relating to AD

1. Epidemiological studies have demonstrated that known risk factors of AD have a vascular basis
2. Shared risk factors exist for both AD and VaD
3. Medications used to slow the development of AD improve cerebral perfusion

4. Regional cerebral perfusion deficits can predict preclinical AD
5. Cerebrovascular pathological lesions frequently overlap in AD and VaD
6. Similar symptomatology in VaD and AD
7. Cerebral hypoperfusion may precede AD-related hypometabolic and neurodegenerative pathology

---

This contamination is not a small issue at the diagnostic or treatment phase. The current emphasis in the literature of both cerebrovascular pathology and AD is on the late stages, that is, clinical stroke and symptomatic AD. The most common type of cerebrovascular disease is probably silent stroke, manifesting with subtle cognitive and physical findings. Individuals who later develop AD may show subtle cognitive changes as early as two decades before diagnosis. By the time patients become symptomatic, it may be too late to slow the relentless progression of AD. To make a difference in outcomes, recognition of early signs of these disorders must occur much sooner. We have more to say about vascular problems and their special relationship to EF in this and other chapters, especially where depression is at issue.

TABLE 6.3   Vascular Dementia

- Cumulative decline due to
  - Strategic infarcts
  - Ischemic injury
  - Hemorrhagic lesions
- Gait disturbance, falls, incontinence
- Autopsy studies show that pure vascular dementia is rare; typically mixed type

---

Memory impairment is usually part of the diagnosis for a dementia. The memory requirement works fairly well for AD but misses most cases of vascular cognitive impairment (VCI), that is, any cognitive impairment associated with or caused by vascular causes. The earliest cognitive manifestations of cerebrovascular disease are changes in executive function, such as planning, organizing, and deciding. Moreover, most epidemiologic and clinical studies of cognition use the Mini Mental State Examination. This test is sensitive to memory disorders but insensitive to the executive function impairment typical of VCI (Richter, Hyer, Nooni, & Toole, 2008), thus, systematically biasing the literature in favor of the ascertainment of AD and to the exclusion of vascular disorders.

Individual sets of criteria fail to work, and none are used universally, precluding comparisons across studies using different criteria. Cognitive impairment is not a threshold, but a continuum, affecting different cognitive domains, at different rates, from different causes. As noted, this occurs on the evolving canvas of aging. To achieve clarity of thought and unity of purpose, current thinking about these disorders must shift. We will identify more screens in Chapter 12.

Finally, we note something interesting, perhaps another contamination: The aging brain is similar to the brains of persons with attention-deficit disorder (ADD). In the list that follows you can see how there is considerable intraindividuality, that the default network is faulty, dopamine is reduced, the prefrontal cortex is relied on, differentiation occurs, and attention is deficient. To our knowledge, extant data do not support the use of methylphenidate for dementia. Clearly many AD patients appear as ADD patients with the addition of memory issues.

ADD or Aging Brain

- High intraindividual variability
- Failure to suppress neural-default-attention network
- Sustained attention actually increases over time but RT (recognition threshold) goes down. Also there is a failure on increased filtering challenges. Response inhibition and EF also go down.
- Reduced dopamine
- Activation of PFC (prefrontal cortex; linked to IIV)
- Emotional simplification
- Dedifferentiation

MEMORY

Memory appears more equal than other cognitive domains at late life. A general taxonomy regarding memory is presented later. Episodic memory represents the episodes in one's life and is thought to decline early in the stages of a dementia. Semantic memory is also about explicit and declarative areas, but has more to do with facts. The procedural memory involves procedures, habits, and overlearned acts. WM is the soul of functioning, as it does problem solving and complex tasks. It is in that aspect of memory, data are taken in, stored, and retrieved along with other information in short periods of time. It is the area of memory with the most generalization.

The role of episodic memory is important. All memories start as episodes and later converge to semantic properties as the particulars become cloudier. It was Schacter and Addis (2007) who spelled out the vagaries of memory, noting that postevent misinformation, gist-based memory errors, and imagination inflation contaminate veridical memories. Regardless, memory is critical. It is certainly relevant in the understanding and rating of a person in the throes of a decline, as in a determination of MCI and dementia diagnoses. In a meta-analysis, Schmand, Huizenga, and Van Gool (2010) showed that episodic memory scores are more predictive in detecting preclinical AD than CSF biomarkers. Dubois et al. (2010) noted that there must be a decline in episodic memory over a 6-month period and evidence of one or more abnormal biomarkers to be given a diagnosis of AD.

Episodic and Semantic Memory Transformation

- Initially memories are tied to context in how they are experienced.
- Context-dependent memories (episodic) are formed in the hippocampus (HPC) and the HPC is needed to recover them.
- Over time, episodic memory is transformed into semantic memories that are less tied to context and capture only essential features of the experience (gist). Statistical regularities are extracted and/or memories are incorporated into preexisting schemas.
- Semantic memories reside in neocortical structures and the HPC is not needed to recall them.

TABLE 6.4 Components and Examples of Memory Systems

Memory System	Major Anatomical Structures Involved	Length of Storage of Memory	Type of Awareness	Examples
Episodic memory	Medial temporal lobes, anterior or thalamic nucleus, mamillary body, fornix, prefrontal cortex	Minutes to years	Explicit, declarative	Remembering a short story, what you had for dinner last night, and what you did on your last birthday
Semantic memory	Inferolateral temporal lobes	Minutes to years	Explicit, declarative	Knowing who was the first president of the United States, the color of a lion, and how a fork differs from a comb
Procedural memory	Basal ganglia, cerebellum, supplementary motor area	Minutes to years	Explicit, or implicit, nondeclarative	Driving a car with a standard transmission (explicit) and learning the sequence of numbers on a touch-tone phone without trying (implicit)
Working memory	Phonologic: prefrontal cortex, Broca's area, Wernicke's area Spatial: prefrontal cortex, visual-association areas	Seconds to minutes; information actively rehearsed or manipulated	Explicit, declarative	Phonologic: keeping a phone number "in your head" before dialing Spatial: mentally following a route or rotating an object in your mind

EF PROBLEMS (AND DEPRESSION)

EF is core to learning in so many ways. It clearly is the marker that accounts for most of the variance of WM, a considerable amount of episodic memory, and semantic memory. Unfortunately, it has been defined in many ways. As such, it has many measures, some so global that it incorporates many components and even other cognitive domains. Recently, Barkley and Murphy (2010) discussed four core features of EF, noting that its definition, assessment, theory, and adaptive ability or problem-solving extensions have been lacking in precision. For these authors, the idea of EF is one of extended phenotype, acting as an emergent property with a self and a motivated and self-directed component, suggesting the amplified importance of this construct and its evolutionary capacity to adjust to the environment.

Executive Function Tasks

- Cognitive flexibility, problem solving, and response maintenance (Greve et al., 2002)
- Volition, planning, purposive action, and effective performance (Lezak, 1983)
- Inhibition and switching, WM, sustained and selective attention (Alvarez & Emory, 2006)
- Shifting, updating, and inhibition (Miyake et al., 2000)
- Word-fluency performance, shifting, updating, and inhibition (Fisk & Sharp, 2004)
- Reasoning and perceptual speed (Salthouse & Babcock, 1991; Salthouse, 2001)
- Inhibition and WM (Pennington & Ozonoff, 1996)
- Behavioral inhibition (Barkley, 1997)

When problems with EF are addressed regarding older adults, two issues are raised: dementia and depression. Regarding dementia, this cognitive area is one of the first to decline and one of the first to cause functional problems. EF and memory are the two most used cognitive areas where decline is evident.

As we saw in Chapter 4, older depressed patients most often have EF problems, psychomotor retardation, apathy, and reduced agitation and guilt. Consequences are considerable. There is a poor response to antidepressants, relapse is high, prefrontal systems are disrupted, and subcortical lesions and cortical lesions (especially left frontal) are noted and associated with depression. In the left frontal area, serotonin is decreased and metabolites are dumped into CSF. Late-onset depression, one consequence of this cascade, is itself associated with neurological disorders, cognitive problems, long P-300 auditory evoked potential latencies, other medical problems, and lower familial prevalence of depressions than younger groups. Cognitive impairment is also present with white matter hyperintensities, stroke, HTN (hypertension), cardiovascular problems, and hypercholesterolemia.

The Duke concept of "Subcortical Ischemic Depression" (Krishnan et al., 2004) and the Cornell concept of "Depression Executive Dysfunction" (Alexopoulos, 2005b; Alexopoulos et al., 2000) have led the charge, positing that the frontal ganglia–thalamocortical networks are impacted because of vascular problems (white matter hyperintensities, small-vessel disease, and occlusions) and predispose one to depression and later dementia. In fact, the vascular depression hypotheses have been in existence now for over 15 years (Blazer, 2003). Depression at later life is thought to be striatofrontal impairment. Cardiovascular risk factors (CVRFs), involving high blood pressure, diabetes, atherosclerotic heart disease, as well as small-vessel disease—usher in depression. In a sense, depression can be construed as a vascular disease at late life (see Alexopoulos, 2005a).

Depression may even be a marker of cognitive impairment. This applies to normal aging as well as MCI (Royall, Chiodo, & Polk, 2004). Factually, subclinical structural brain disease has been noted in 30% to 100% of community-based older adults (Cook et al., 2004). Older people with any of these physical problems may be depressed for many reasons, but one of them is almost certainly organic.

- The question is no longer asked whether depression is a risk factor for dementia but rather whether dysthymia is as well and what might be the pathophysiological substrates underpinning depression as a risk factor.
- Depression does increase the risk of dementia in old age by about twofold and this risk extends for many years.

Thomas (2012, pp. 641–643)

We add that EF problems have a special relationship to trauma-related problems like posttraumatic stress disorder (PTSD). The neuropsychological status of older trauma victims has been examined for the past decade at least. Several investigators have suggested that severe or prolonged trauma, or a history of such exposure, places the aging individual at increased risk for cognitive decline or dementia (Cook, Ruzek, & Cassedy, 2003). Most older adults, unlike younger groups, develop deficits in binding and retrieval access to recollective information. This deficit demands additional EF strategies to overcome recall deficits. Given the role of EF in aiding memory, then, older adults with poorer frontal functioning are at heightened risk for cognitive failures and memory problems. This occurs in everyday acts, as when older adults are reminded to perform at selected times during the day (Kane et al., 2007), and also affects how traumatic experiences are recollected.

EF and Treatment

Direct targeting of cognitive impairments in late-life psychiatric disorders through cognitive training or rehabilitation may be an effective approach for improving symptoms. There has been increasing recognition that cognitive control is a key factor in the development or exacerbation of psychiatric disorders.

O'Hara (2012, p. 1003)

There is a difference between treatments aimed at symptomatic improvements for some of the mild deficits of cognitive aging versus disease-modifying drugs that slow the course of a neurodegenerative process. The best data today show that this distinction is hard to make in the real world. That said, there are interventions that can make a difference in treatment/slowing the disease/increasing quality of life.

Studies of neuropsychological function in elderly anxious subjects may be informative in developing treatment interventions that mitigate cognitive dysfunction and illuminate the course of illness and underlying neural pathways (Lavretsky, 2009). But questions remain. The success of CBT, the most assessed treatment for older adults, hinges on the client's ability to engage in focusing, dividing, and shifting attention, self-monitoring, metacognition, and perspective taking, all of which involve executive abilities. Clearly older adults with EF problems will have trouble accessing needed skills for this treatment method. Studies in general have fallen short of showing an improvement between a form of cognitive rehabilitation (CR) and problem-solving cognitive therapy with older depressed adults. There are many reasons why this is the case.

- Abnormal performance on some tests of EF moderates (negatively) response to SSRIs.
- Neurobiologically informed computerized cognitive remediation (CCR) may improve targeted executive functions.
- Assuming that CCR changes EFs by changing underlying brain abnormalities, we may expect a change in depressive symptoms.
- Neural plasticity-based CCR interventions in animals and humans produce neuroplastic change, and correlate with improved performance (de Villers-Sedani et al., 2010).
- CCR improves both targeted functions and related, but not directly targeted, functions (near transfer) in older adults (Persson & Reuter Lorenz, 2008).
- Remediation of EFs may decrease disability, improve functioning, and reduce depression.

Using the APT-II, a series of modules that address EF and attention, Mohlman et al. (2009) did something novel in therapy, even for older adults: the application of CR conjointly with CBT modules. In one of the few studies on this area, Mohlman and colleagues had experimental participants practice executive function tasks, APT-II, in sessions for 45 minutes (sessions 1 to 4), and as homework (sessions 1 to 8), with the remainder of each session devoted to CBT, whereas control subjects received CBT only. The CBT/APT-II group showed a significant improvement in executive skills following the intervention, relative to the control group. Alexopoulos et al. (2000) also showed that older adults who are depressed and have EF problems do remit regarding depression, but show no changes in EF as a result of this therapy change.

Whether the cognitive retraining process can be considered an EST (empirically supported treatment) with older adults (or just for those compromised in EF) has yet to be fully studied. Many studies have suggested that cognitively stimulating activity preserves mental performance and prevents cognitive decline in later life (see Chapter 7). It is likely that positive changes in cognitive functioning are critical to having a beneficial impact on neuropsychiatric symptoms, especially mood and anxiety symptoms. In effect, successfully managing the psychiatric aspects of the disease depends on optimizing the patient's cognitive and functional capacities. Neuropsychiatric problems and adjustment are, then, necessarily cognitively mediated and reflect the outcomes of cognitive training in patients.

Critical Questions

- Do neuropsychological and neuroimaging findings and their effects on treatment outcome represent a biomarker for a subtype of geriatric depression?
- Why does executive dysfunction lead to lower antidepressant treatment response? Are there other pharmacological agents that can be used to reduce depression in older depressed patients with executive impairment?
- What is the underlying pathophysiology in the brain of patients with cognitive and imaging changes?
- What are long-term mood, cognitive, and functional consequences of neuropsychological and neuroimaging changes?

MEDICAL TREATMENT FOR DEMENTIA

In this section, we discuss the standard treatment of dementia. We are talking, of course, about AD and VaD. Cerebrovascular disease and AD share similar risk factors, most of them treatable. The vascular component of cognitive impairment is the only aspect currently treatable and preventable. Treating vascular risk factors can prevent stroke and possibly may delay the onset of dementia.

Pointedly, there was no effective therapy for AD before the approval of the cholinesterase inhibitors and memantine. These agents are associated with detectable symptomatic improvement, and have a modest effect at best on the progression of MCI to AD to disabling dementia and death (Grossberg, 2009). Factually, medicines currently prescribed for AD fall into three groups: inhibitors of acetylcholinesterase (ChEIs; according to the cholinergic hypothesis of AD, memory impairments result from death of cholinergic neurons in the basal forebrain), an antagonist of a receptor for the neurotransmitter glutamate, and drugs from the psychiatric toolbox to control depression and behavioral abnormalities (Hachinski, 2008).

We will not belabor this, but several studies have suggested that treatment of AD with these medications is suspect at best (e.g., Grossberg, 2009; Sink et al., 2007). There is a role for ChEIs, but it is limited. The best we can say is that if the caregiver and patient are willing to use the medication, are enthusiastic, have the money, and are committed to a trial, the benefit can be positive—fewer behavior problems, some cognitive stability, and a lessened chance of long-term care facility (LTC) entry. This is rather "iffy" and if any parts of the patient commitment are absent, then a nonrobust responce can be expected. There are also side effects.

- For symptomatic improvement, an individual patient may have a robust response, rather than the average
- Use ChEIs to stabilize function rather than improve cognition
- Treatment may occur throughout the entire course of illness
- Choice of a specific ChEI is guided by tolerability and ease of use, not efficacy
- Assessment of efficacy relies heavily on the physician and the caregiver's "clinical global impression"

Do Patients Want to Know?

As a relevant footnote, we ask this question: Do patients want to know about their diagnosis of dementia? Perhaps the best study for this information was by Carpenter et al. (2000) studying 90 pairs of patients and caregivers; the overwhelming response was that patients and caregivers desired to be informed about this state. They wanted the immediate family to know but not other people. They also did not recall the data from the doctor. The issues of concern about knowing were firearms and driving, as well as needing care or being treated differently.

Study

- Studied 90 pairs: Caregivers were spouses (61%) and children (22%)
- Diagnostic disclosure preferences:
  - Patients and caregivers wanted to know
    - three-fourths wanted other children to know
    - less than half wanted other family to know

Reasons not to know

- Driving (40%)
- Work (12%)
- Relocation (31%)
- Firearms (50%)
- Being treated differently (40%)
- Social limitations (31%)
- Needing care (50%)

Carpenter et al. (2000)

Case: Mr. H

BACKGROUND: Mr. H is a 70-year-old male with Parkinson's disease, diabetes, and memory complaints. He is living in Georgia with his daughter as the result of medical problems incurred and alcohol abuse in the last few months. Approximately 5 years ago, he developed hydrocephalus and 2 years subsequent to that, fell and developed a brain bleed. He underwent rehabilitation that produced only mixed results. He also had difficulty in Maryland, where he was living with his significant other. He abused alcohol and migrated south to live with his daughter to address his problems better. This in combination with his decline and alcohol history resulted in problems.

He is a native of northern Virginia and is the oldest of three children; he has two younger sisters. His father was a musician, and his mother was a stay-at-home mom who is currently still alive. He describes his growth years as very good, and there were no developmental disruptions. He graduated high school and attended college for several years, but did not graduate. He went to work for an airline and did so for 37 years, retiring 10 years ago. He was married at age 26 and had one daughter. This marriage did not last very long. He assisted in the raising of his daughter. He had been living in Maryland, where he was taking care of his mother and aunt.

He has had a history of colon, prostate, as well as throat cancer. He also, as noted, had hydrocephalus 5 years ago and a fall 3 years ago. This fall resulted in a brain bleed in which he had considerable damage. His rehabilitation, although not formal at present, continues to this day. He has problems with handwriting and speech. He takes only a few medications, including Sinemet and Lexapro, which he has taken now for approximately 8 years. He also has abused alcohol across his years, and this has caused difficulty with his significant other and daughter. He indicates that he sleeps well, that he is not in pain, and that before 6 months ago he was exercising.

Mr. H is a 70-year-old Caucasian male who had difficulty walking into the appointment. He walks with very short steps clearly reflective of Parkinson's disease. His daughter accompanied him. He was upbeat, funny, laughed, and had some insight into his condition. He did not show any word-finding problems and was specific regarding dates in his life. He indicated that he is mildly depressed, but that he does not feel this is his major problem. Memory and Parkinson's disease are concerns. Although problems with alcohol have raised issues, he is not drinking now (at least not around his daughter), his judgment now appears to be reasonable, and his insight seems appropriate.

OVERALL COGNITIVE FUNCTIONING: Mr. H shows variability on the WAIS IV (Wechsler Adult Intelligence Scale IV) subtests. He has an 11 on Vocabulary (OPIE Vocabulary = high average intelligence). Currently, Mr. H scored a Repeatable Battery for the Assessment of Neuropsychological Status (RBANS) index of 76, placing him at the 3% level compared to other people of his age and education. His Montreal Cognitive Assessment (MoCA) was 20/30, also impaired. These scores are below average and suggest difficulty on overall cognitive functioning. He is fully oriented, but has problems adjusting day to day. He is not able to do all his independent activities of daily living (IADL) due to limits of Parkinson's disease. In summary, he scores at a level considerably lower than probable premorbid state. This man had problems with hearing. He also has a gait problem and has difficulty with scanning and sequencing.

In regard to specific cognitive domains, he scored in the low-average range on index of attention and language. He was lower on new learning but had some skills here. He did poorly on WAIS-IV Picture Completion, indicating that he has problems with perception and attention. He processed information slowly. He does, however, read well and has reasonable information skills. He had lower skills on visuospatial tasks, doing poorly on complex designs from command. He was also not able to draw a clock on command.

New learning and memory are issues. On delayed memory he had real problems. He was able to recall 0/10 words, 5/12 story-recall bits, and 5/20 figural recall data points. He scored below average on the recognition task (11/20). All EF scores were below normal (Trials B, WAIS-IV subscales subserving these skills, Wisconsin Card Sort). He does not encode new data well and cannot think well on his feet. There were deficits on the FAQ (Functional Assessment Questionnaire) (14), a measure of executive functions in activities of daily living. His IADL are suspect.

He was given a Parkinson's Disease Rating Scale (UPDRS). On the global areas, he has problems with intellectual impairment and motivation. In activities of daily living, he is lower on speech, swallowing, handwriting, falling, and walking. In motor areas, he has difficulties with speech, rigidity, finger taps, hand movements, rapid alternating of hands, leg agility, gait, and body bradykinesia. He has no dyskinesias and no "off" periods. His Hoehn Yahr is 2.

Regarding affect, he was administered the Mini-International Neuropsychiatric Interview (MINI), which showed problems with depression. He also had problems with this on all self-report scales and on both omnibus measures of depression as well as somatic issues. On these measures, he endorsed use of alcohol as having a negative impact on his life. He also endorsed an unusual degree of concern about physical functioning and health matters and probable impairment arising from somatic symptoms. He describes his thought processes as marked by confusion, distractibility, and difficulty concentrating.

The Millon Behavioral Medicine Diagnostic (MBMD) was given, and indicates problems. He is concerned about his thinking and his control of thoughts as well as rating himself as depressed. He has a cooperative, respectful, and sociable personality profile, all positive. His stress moderators were all normal except for illness apprehension and functional deficits. He endorsed problems with eating, inactivity, and alcohol (ETOH). Pain and sleep are not problems.

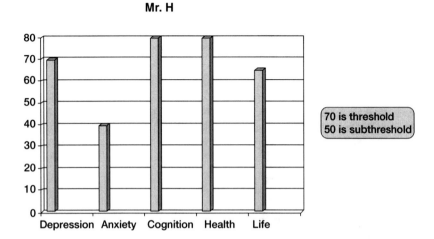

Mr. H — WATCH AND WAIT MODEL

Sessions 1 to 3:
Current scores reflect evident ongoing cognitive, health, and life problems intertwined with depression. He is having problems with Parkinson's disease (PD) as well as cognitive problems from brain insults and alcohol. His life issues, although important, are largely handled at present; issues of caregiving, housing, and transportation are now addressed by his family. He is now a captive in his daughter's home. In the past he had problems with alcohol use. Officially one can make the case for MCI. He is at high risk for conversion to dementia (~80 in later stages). He has had PD for several years, increasing chances of a conversion to dementia. He has a cooperative and social personality that allows him to comply and to be concerned about his life.

He was apprised of his status and the need for action in the ensuing weeks. His daughter was present. He has MCI and a plan was made for him to join the Memory Clinic. This will get him out of the house and initiate behavioral activation. His cognition and mood will be monitored as part of this. Life issues are less immediately important now, as he has transportation and has no access to ETOH. He will remain with his daughter for the near future. All his needs are met. Health is an issue, as he feels constricted and embarrassed with PD and has no positive lifestyle involvement. He and family were invited to think about a CBT group for depression. He indicated his interest in the therapy, the goals, identified tasks, and barriers.

Watch and Wait Category	Check
Validate problem	×
Psychoeducation of model	×
Assessment	×
Monitoring	×
Case formulation	×
Check alliance	×

Sessions 4 onward
He was admitted to the Memory Clinic, which took a few months. His memory tests improved by half, as he could now recall several words and understand data in recall tests. He also did better on EF tests. He was active in that he was able to get out once/ day. He was increasingly more optimistic. He had his PD medications adjusted several times and now shows less rigidity and movement problems.

Session 12 onward
He was entered in the CBT Depression Clinic. His affect scores are now in the high normal ranges. His UPDRS is stable. His cognition actually has improved. That said, he had a fall and was hospitalized. He is now back in the group and more positive about his goals.

CONCLUSION

One way to conceive of cognitive abilities is as an intermediate phenotype of biological age, because cognitive ability, in aggregate, reliably declines with age, and a greater decline in cognitive function predicts mortality and morbidity better than chronological age does. Ultimately, determining cognitive health also depends on which brain regions are altered with age, when these declines begin, what cognitive abilities are modifiable, and which, if modifiable, could enhance functioning and well-being the most (Depp, Vahia, & Jeste, 2010).

Science is arrogant, as it assumes that nature is predicable, has a rhyme and reason, and that we can discover it. The brain is resisting this. There will be fits and starts for many years until we have a good theory of the aging brain that can be validated. Until then, we must act prudently if we address memory in the older adult based on reasonable cognitive abilities and function, and also apply the necessary other medical features, such as correlated scans and other biomarkers. This in turn helps everything for the older adult. We hope this is communicated here.

CHAPTER 7

Cognitive Training

Cognitive rehabilitation: Any intervention strategy or technique which intends to enable clients or patients, and their families, to live with, manage, by-pass, reduce or come to terms with deficits.
—*Barbara Wilson*

There is a disagreement between the advocates of brain training and those who are skeptical. In 2011, Americans spent $265 million on brain-fitness software and web-based programs that claim to boost brainpower. This is likely to increase considerably, despite many studies that suggest caution in the application of cognitive training (CT). One recent study assessed 430 volunteers of 18 to 60 years of age and found that computer-based brain training did not significantly improve mental fitness (Owen et al., 2010). This study is in contrast to the recent findings from the National Institutes of Health (NIH) Conference for Alzheimer's Disease and Cognitive Decline. Of the 6,713 studies on risks and protective factors for cognitive decline examined by the NIH, only CT and protective factors were found to be associated with sizable reduction of the risk for cognitive decline. A recent Cochrane summary (2011) also found that cognitive stimulation works on older adults with dementia.

As we have indicated elsewhere, if aging compromises the basic operating characteristics of biological hardware, then training and experience may well assist the software of the cognitive system (Mayr, 2008). There is a constantly adapting central nervous system (CNS)—plasticity, brain reserve, and enriched environments (Reuter-Lorenz & Park, 2010). Targeting tasks that are more encompassing, as in executive functioning, as well as the neural basis of transfer effects with set shifting, inhibition, and updating (Dahlin, Neely, Larsson, Bäckman, & Nyberg, 2008), can make a difference in some outcomes. More "holistic" training also can provide benefits that extend beyond attention and working memory (WM) if applied to complex goal-directed activity (Basak, Boot, Voss, & Kramer, 2008; Stine-Morrow, Parisi, Morrow, & Park 2008). In addition, environmental enrichment tasks (e.g., occupation, leisure, complexity in life, mental training) and a health focus notably enhanced cardiovascular health and neurocognitive function (Hertzog, Kramer, Wilson, & Linderberger, 2009), and exercise (Kramer, Erickson, & Colcombe, 2009) has a positive impact. This has also been labeled as brain reserve. Interestingly, selective psychotherapies, such as cognitive behavioral therapy (CBT), in older adults also change brain function (Cozolino, 2010; Mohlman et al., 2009).

CT programs offer promise.... They are easily implemented across a variety of settings, including aged-care facilities, community centers or individual homes by facilitators who require relatively uncomplicated training. They engage participants and therefore offer an enjoyable experience. Training can be conducted in one-on-one or group settings, with the latter offering the additional benefit of social interaction. Additionally, data suggest that older adults are increasingly opting for non-pharmacological forms of therapy for psychological and cognitive difficulties.

Mowszowski, Batcheltor, and Naismith (2010, p. 545)

Overall, CT appears to be an asset in improving attention and WM for older adults. Research appears to show that mental activity can reduce a person's risk for dementia, although the effect size of mental training on healthy older people is not well understood. In this chapter, we briefly present the results of two studies on the use of cognitive rehabilitation (CR) for older adults with memory complaints and depression or anxiety symptoms, or both. We attempt to be clinically practical, as it is believed that this training is critical for changes to occur in most domains of importance, as already outlined in this book. We discuss the types of interventions and the context of therapy and conclude with thoughts on self-regulation.

COGNITION TRAINING

Memory training for older adults is both "in" and evolving as far as efficacy is concerned, especially for normal older adults. There are many types. The laboratory-based training is often applied in clinics with special programs and involves computers and often specific cognitive domains. Neurobiologically informed interventions strengthen compensatory processes. They also address self-regulation. Neurorehabilitation involves the rehab of brain-injured patients and addresses neural systems that can work. Generic approaches, which constitute the bulk of CT, include reality orientation, as well as external assists in life. Group-based cognitive stimulation is also used with dementia patients and includes stimulation and structure.

Types of Memory Training

- Laboratory-based training often involves repeated performance, typically computer training or speed-choice tasks. These approaches tend to target a particular cognitive domain (often labeled as a specific process or direct intervention) rather than take a domain-general approach aimed at overall improvement in well-being, improved symptoms, and better behaviors.
- General cognitive stimulation, mnemonic strategies, or games for older adults who are normal but show aging-associated memory problems.
- Neurobiologically informed ecological interventions address social emotional skills that are based on executive function (EF) neural substrates. These skills include self-regulation, effortful control, and working memory.
- Neurorehabilitation therapies for patients with traumatic brain injury (TBI) are aimed at improving cognitive functioning by using strategic training techniques to offset rather than restore lost functionality. Generally the underlying neural systems supporting a given function are assumed to be damaged beyond repair. The rerouting of neural circuitry is done so that individuals learn new methods of handling older problems or goals. The target is usually a specific cognitive area, attention, memory, or even vision. Vulnerable populations may benefit especially from these approaches.
- Generic approaches include reminiscence, reality orientation, and cognitive stimulation therapy. Reality orientation, which involves reteaching information related to orientation to everyday life, has been largely superseded by cognitive stimulation, which uses more implicit methods, with activities such as categorization and word association.

Which training is chosen is a function of the type of problem and the goal. The typical problem with older adults involves complaints of loss of memory in the service of some organic, functional, or situational tasks. The diagnosis is often age-associated memory impairment, mild cognitive impairment (MCI), or dementia. Depression, anxiety, and somatic problems are usually associated. In the other chapters we have espoused the role of the therapist as a manager and an informed clinician to apply a Watch and Wait treatment method. In fact, we advocate the role of the therapist as a neuroscientist in which the friendly confines of the brain are borrowed for the purposes of targeted metaphor and structured change. This assists in the Watch and Wait model.

Rebok et al. (2012) added to this mix. He parsed apart the complexity of CT among older adults. Training differs in population (community dwelling or impaired), goals (immediate, based on specific training or broader, as in improving functional competence, quality of life), self-guided or formally guided training, and type of training. The type of training can be simple (association, categorization, visual imagery, bizarreness, rehearsed) or more complex (method of loci, face name recognition, number and story mnemonics). There is also training for types of memory, including procedural (spaced retrieval, errorless), external aids, and reality orientation.

It was Cozolino (2010) (see Figure 7.1) who encouraged the therapist to apply neurocognitive knowledge to the therapy in which the patient is liberated from the position of excessive self-responsibility. The therapist uses neurocognitive knowledge to provide perspective on the problem for support, to alleviate the condition, and to provide interventions. This especially applies to the role of the therapist as a neuroscientist. This therapy is supported in the use of brain metaphors, especially the activation of the left hemisphere and frontal lobes, and provides a perspective on the amygdala and use of CR.

OVERVIEW

When it comes to the development of treatments for neurocognitive aging, it would help to clarify exactly what one intends to treat. Potential indications include an improvement in cognitive performance, an attenuation in cognitive decline, and/ or a reduction in the risk of an age-related disorder.

Reiman et al. (2012, p. 769)

Interestingly, normal aging requires adaptation, as brains develop new neural circuits, or "scaffolds." This scaffolding protects cognitive function and may be strengthened by cognitive and social engagement and physical exercise (Park & Reuter-Lorenz, 2009). To test this scaffolding theory, Park and colleagues have assessed whether acquiring new, real-life skills (unlike some of the computer-based brain training exercises) can preserve cognitive function among older adults. In the Synapse Study, randomly assigned participants are assigned to one of six activity groups: learning digital photography; learning how to quilt; learning both digital photography and quilting; spending time in fun social settings, such as museum tours; completing self-paced learning tasks at home; or a control group, which does not participate in any activities. Participants agree to spend a minimum of 16 hours a week for 3 months working in groups on their assigned projects. They undergo fMRI scans and written tests to measure their brain function before and after the 12-week sessions, and again 1 year after the intervention ends. Synapse teaches people how to learn new things, so that even after they leave the Synapse setting they can continue to develop new skills. To date, more than 250 older adults have participated. Pilot results showed that this program a significantly increased older adults' WM. A similar training with similar results has been done in China. Participants between 65 and 75 years old received 24 hours of training over 12 weeks on a multi-approach system tackling memory, reasoning, problem solving, map reading, handicrafts, health education and exercise, or focusing on reasoning only. Li and Wu (2012) noted that cognitive training improved mental ability over 1 year.

Several recent reviews on CT have also been positive, indicating that CT can have a positive impact on memory for older adults (e.g., Li et al., 2008; Rebok, 2008; Sitzer, Twamley, Patterson, & Jeste, 2008). These studies are largely done on healthy older adults. Clinical trials on the effects of specific memory strategies, such as visualization and association, have proven effective in healthy older adults (Ball et al., 2002; Cavallini, Pagnin, & Vecchi, 2003; Ercoli et al., 2007; Ercoli, Siddarth, Harrison, Jimenez, & Jarvik, 2005; Smith et al., 2009; Valentijn et al., 2005; Willis et al., 2006). In a meta-analysis on (episodic) memory training in older adults, Verhaeghen, Marcoen, and Goossens (1992) showed that memory gains are large (0.73 ES [effect size]) compared with control (0.37) and placebo (0.38). Research on CT has mostly focused on interventions for episodic memory (e.g., Craik et al., 2007) and has largely targeted younger adults as well as healthy older adults (e.g., West, Dark-Freudeman, & Bagwell, 2009). Results show that episodic memory can be improved by training, and that the effects are well maintained (Verhaeghen & Marcoen, 1996). Other studies have also suggested that cognitively stimulating activity preserves mental performance and prevents cognitive decline in later life (Ball et al., 2002; Ercoli et al., 2005; Scarmeas, Stern, Tang, Mayeux, & Luchsinger, 2006; Studenski et al., 2006; Wilson et al., 2002, 2003, 2005, 2007).

In 2009, Valenzuela and Sachdev evaluated 54 studies, later reduced to 7, on cognitive exercises for healthy older adults. Cognitive exercise interventions were compared with the Watch and Wait method with follow-up at 2 years. Results indicated strong and persistent effects on neuropsychological testing. Transfer of training was also evident. Older adults also reported improvements in everyday attention. In another review, Rebok (2008) examined the empirical basis for classifying memory-training methods as evidence based. This review examined evidence for both normal and cognitively impaired elders. Using criteria similar to those of the American Psychological Association's Division 12 task force for empirically supported treatments (ESTs) in psychotherapy (number of studies, number of subjects, use of measures, use of manuals, and so on—see Chambless & Ollendick, 2001), Rebok reviewed almost 300 studies. Of these, 39 gave preliminary support for 16 treatments to qualify as evidence based. These included studies involving instruction in multiple mnemonic techniques and in specific techniques, such as visual memory support, story mnemonic, method of loci, and cognitive restructuring. The authors concluded that although there are several promising methods that improve memory in normal older adults, the question of use and efficacy with impaired elders or in real-world situations has yet to be answered. Also, most training effects are often largely task specific and not durable (see Saczynski, Willis, & Schaie, 2002).

One study involving a 2006 investigation led by Pennsylvania State University psychologist Sherry Willis has suggested that brain training can improve cognitive function in elderly patients, even those in the early stages of Alzheimer's disease (AD). This Advanced Cognitive Training for Independent and Vital Elderly (ACTIVE) study involved three different interventions (reasoning training, memory training, and speed of processing training) and compared these with a control group. Each intervention improved its target function and the training effects were maintained for 2 years (Ball et al., 2002). This was later updated to 5 years (Wolinsky et al., 2009). Reasoning training provided a transfer between tasks. In fact, there are now over 20 studies on this subject.

Perhaps the biggest component of change is later-life engagement in intellectually and socially stimulating activities (e.g., reading books, doing puzzles, performing volunteer work, traveling, playing card games, and so on). These activities have been shown to enhance thinking, memory, and attention control processes, thereby increasing brain reserve capacity (e.g., Carlson et al., 2008; Fabrigoule et al., 1995; Schooler, Mulatu, & Oates, 1999; Staff, Murray, Deary, & Whalley, 2004; Wang, Karp, Winblad, & Fratiglioni, 2002). Using the Cache County Dementia Progression Study, Treiber et al. (2011) showed an interaction between dementia duration and number of activities in predicting cognitive decline. In a 6-week program addressing memory and also healthy lifestyle issues, Miller et al. (2012) showed that encoding and recalling of new verbal information had improved as well as self-perceptions of memory ability in older adults residing in the community.

HOLISTIC PROGRAMS

Memory training unfolds best, it seems, when it is combined with other related life habits that foster good health and quality of life. In separate studies, Ercoli et al. (2005, 2007) showed that a 2-week healthy lifestyle intervention, including daily physical conditioning, healthy diet, and relaxation and memory training exercise, led to improvements in verbal fluency and cerebral glucose metabolism measured by positron emission tomography (PET). Multifactorial approaches and targeted programs therefore seem promising for healthy adults and perhaps for impaired elders as well. Pointedly, Nusbaum (2008) designed a pilot investigation with 26 healthy, independent older adults. Sixteen of them consumed a special "brain health" diet; took part in activities such as walking, dancing, and learning sign language; went on field trips with other older adults; and practiced meditation and other relaxation techniques. After 6 weeks, participants in the brain-health lifestyle group were able to recall presented information after a 20-minute delay better than they could at the start of the study. They also reported a higher quality of life than the 10 participants in the control group who did not follow the holistic intervention.

Scaffolding (discussed in the previous chapter) protects cognitive function and may be strengthened by cognitive and social engagement and physical exercise (Park & Reuter-Lorenz, 2009). To test this scaffolding theory, Park and colleagues assessed whether acquiring new, real-life skills (unlike some of the computer-based brain-training exercises) can preserve cognitive function among older adults. In the Synapse Study discussed earlier in this chapter, pilot results showed that the activity program significantly increased older adults' WM. A similar study, using similar training and yielding similar results was done in China. Cheng et al. (2012) noted that this CT improved mental ability over 1 year.

Other programs have been applied with success in more impaired older adults, including those with dementia (Carlson et al., 2008; Hyer, Damon, & Nizam, 2008; Logsdon et al., 2010; Zarit, Femia, Kim, & Whitlach, 2010). A growing body of research seems to show that early support groups can be beneficial (e.g., Goldsilver & Gruneir, 2001; Snyder, Bower, Arneson, Shepherd, & Quayhagen, 1993; Snyder, Jenkins, & Joosten, 2007). Logsdon et al. (2010) demonstrated the utility of a holistic approach in overall cognitive health. Often this involves the caregiver, as well as the other family members. The focus is psychoeducation, behavioral activation, and monitoring of targeted problem areas. More "holistic" training can provide benefits that extend beyond attention and WM if applied to complex goal-directed activity (Basak et al., 2008; Stine-Morrow et al., 2008). In addition, general environmental enrichment (occupation, leisure, complexity in life, mental training) and a health focus notably enhanced cardiovascular health and neurocognitive function (Hertzog et al., 2009), and exercise (Kramer et al., 2006) is also beneficial.

WORKING MEMORY AND OLDER ADULTS

Training of WM is both problematic and a sensitive marker of cognitive decline. It has been identified as one of the main factors underlying cognitive impairment in old age and in dementia (Backman, Jones, Berger, Laukka, & Small, 2005; Backman & Small, 2007; Baddeley, Bressi, Dellasala, Logie, & Spinnler, 1991; Craik & Bialystok, 2006; Salthouse & Babcock, 1991). Some years ago WM was defined as a mental workspace that is capacity limited (Morrison & Chein, 2011). Early models of WM posited the existence of material-specific slave systems under the management of an active manipulation component (Baddeley & Hitch, 1974). More recent models propose a single memory store in which specific information can be brought up into WM (e.g., Cowan, 2005). WM now refers to active "online" and short-term maintenance of information in the service of more complex tasks, such as mental arithmetic, language comprehension, planning, or problem solving (Cowan, 2005; Shah & Miyake, 1999).

Whatever the case, WM seems to exert an influence over other cognitive spheres. WM training affects individual differences in fluid intelligence and executive function (Engle, Kane, & Tuholski, 1999), language acquisition (Baddeley, 2003), reading comprehension (Chein & Morison, 2010; Daneman & Carpenter, 1980), problem solving (Logie, Gilhooly, & Wynn, 1994), reasoning (Kane et al., 2004), cognitive control (Chein & Morrison, 2010; Klingberg et al., 2005; Klingberg, Frossberg, & Westerberg, 2002), and reading comprehension. There are also studies that support a "far transfer" effect (generalizability, in the real world) (Buschkuehl et al., 2008; Mahncke et al., 2006; Richmond, Morrison, Chein, & Olson, 2011). Richmond et al. (2011) also trained older adults in WM to good effect. WM may therefore serve as a domain-general cognitive resource that modulates ability in a number of seemingly disparate areas of cognitive performance. Training in one area can benefit many others.

That said, there are problems when older adults are studied. Several studies have shown little or no effects on older adults but have shown fruitful results for younger people (Buschkuehl et al., 2008; Dahlin et al., 2008; Li et al., 2008; Mahncke et al., 2006; Schmiedek, Lovden, & Lidenberger, 2010). Noack, Lovden, Schmiedek, and Lindenberger (2009) noted that "few studies report transfer effects for tasks dissimilar enough from the trained tasks to suggest transfer at a broad level of abilities."

COGNITIVE COMPROMISE: MCI OR MILD DEMENTIA

There is a surprising number of studies addressing the CT of older adults with MCI or mild dementia (e.g., Belleville, Chertkow, & Gauthier, 2007; Greenaway, Hanna, Lepore, & Smith, 2008; Hampstead, Sathian, Moore, Nalisnick, & Stringer, 2008; Loewenstein, Acevedo, Czaja, & Dura, 2004; Troyer, Murphy, Anderson, Moscovitch, & Craik, 2008; Unverzagt et al., 2008; Yesavage et al., 2008). For many years, there have been memory applications for procedural memory in dementia patients, and more recently these have also been applied in the form of strategy acquisition in this population (Rothi et al., 2009; Souchay, 2007). Of course there has been interest in the combination of psychosocial interventions along with pharmacological ones (Meguro et al., 2008; Rothi et al., 2009). Interestingly, these studies have been largely positive and indicate that training can make a difference with impaired older adults.

Caregivers, when enlisted, can help with compensation strategies (Yeager, Hyer, Hobbs, & Coyne, 2010), especially with impaired older adults. Multimethod packages with caregivers are especially helpful, as is a focus on brain reserve (Karp et al., 2009; Perneczky et al., 2011). Over the last two decades, success has been found with comprehensive group training programs (Ball et al., 2002; Floyd & Scogin, 1997; Rebok, 2008; Verhaeghen et al., 1992). Valenzuela et al. (2011) showed that CT helps subjects tolerate more brain damage before clinical symptoms are expressed. Finally, the field of geropsychiatry has come to appreciate that selective serotonin reuptake inhibitors (SSRIs) work best on older adults with depression who have no general WM, or more specifically, executive functioning, problems (Sneed et al., 2010).

It is further likely that positive changes in cognitive functioning are critical to having a beneficial impact on neuropsychiatric symptoms, especially mood and anxiety symptoms. In effect, successfully managing the psychiatric aspects of the disease depends on optimizing the patient's cognitive and functional capacities. Neuropsychiatric problems and adjustment are then cognitively mediated and reflect the outcomes of CT in patients. Sitzer, Twamley, and Jeste (2006) suggested as much in their review of dementia studies: cognitive rehabilitation assists with medium effect sizes in multiple functional domains, such as learning, memory, executive functioning, activities of daily living (ADL), general cognitive problems, depression, and self-rated general functioning. As noted earlier in this chapter, perhaps the biggest component of change is later-life engagement in intellectually and socially stimulating activities that enhance thinking, memory, and attention control processes, thereby increasing brain reserve capacity.

Finally, another factor is important here: Over the years authors have emphasized the role of self-regulatory factors in training improvement (Bissig & Lustig, 2007; Lachman, Weaver, Bandura, Elliott & Lewkowicz, 1992; Rebok & Balcerak, 1989; Valentijn et al., 2005). Cogmed, a computer training program (see p. 190), emphasizes coaching as a necessary part of the training process. Low memory self-efficacy undermines memory-change possibilities. West and Hasting's (2011) approach showed that successful training outcomes depend on self-regulation, that is, the extent to which individuals applied themselves in terms of information processing and adaptive beliefs. Self-efficacy empowerment and change showed the best relationship to memory change (West & Hastings, 2011).

Study 1: Memory Clinic

This study involved a practical clinical program (Hyer et al., in press), findings for which are reviewed here. It is intended to show that such training programs work in the messy real world. Evidence is now suggesting that a more holistic behavioral approach to improving brain performance—a combination of diet, exercise, socialization, stress reduction, and mental stimulation—may delay the onset of neurodegenerative diseases such as dementia.

In this study, we targeted several areas in addition to memory training. We assume that socialization has its place, as lonely individuals are twice as likely to be diagnosed with AD as those who are not lonely. In addition, diet was discussed, notably a Mediterranean-type diet that is rich in fruits, vegetables, and omega-3 fatty acids. Using this diet, participants experienced a 38% less chance of developing AD over the next 4 years (Scarmeas et al., 2006). We focus also on stress reduction, following research showing that a reduction in short-term stress leads to a decrease in the amount of beta-amyloid protein in the brains of mice (Mahncke et al., 2006).

We placed a special emphasis on exercise and meditation. Exercise is now universally accepted as a positive marker in both health and cognition. The issue is really commitment and finding which dose is best for specific older adults, many of whom have physical problems. In just one study, older adults with MCI showed significant improvements on tests of executive function after 6 months of 4-days-a-week aerobic exercise (Baker et al., 2010). Exercise also has been helpful for various health components, psychiatric problems, and for the younger-old and the older-old, and even those older adults who had been sedentary for a long period of time. Meditation too is now recognized as important to good health, well-being, lessened depression, and anxiety, as well as cognition.

In the context of these interrelated components, we also emphasized identity or purpose-in-being as a strategy for a better life and improved cognition. We target the individual identity of each person and request that each participant evaluate this, and we foster core values, as this will improve compliance with the program, especially memory training. These strategies and techniques are based on the findings from the Longevity Project (Friedman & Martin, 2011).

Core Components of Lifestyle

Socialization: Lonely individuals are twice as likely to be diagnosed with AD as those who are not lonely, according to a 2007 study in the *Archives of General Psychiatry* (Vol. 64, No. 2).

Exercise: Older adults with mild cognitive impairment showed significant improvements on tests of executive function after 6 months of 4-day-a-week aerobic exercise, according to a January study in the *Archives of Neurology* (Vol. 67, No. 1).

Diet: People who eat a Mediterranean-type diet, rich in fruits, vegetables, and omega-3 fatty acids, were 38% less likely to develop AD over the next 4 years, according to a study published online in April in the journal *Archives of Neurology.*

Stress reduction: Researchers led by neurologist David Holtzman, MD, at Washington University in St. Louis, reported that short-term stress leads to an increase in the amount of beta-amyloid protein—a key component in the development of AD—in the brains of mice, according to a 2007 study published in *Proceedings of the National Academy of Sciences* (Vol. 104, No. 25).

Relaxation/Meditation: Data now suggest that some form of relaxation can improve cognition. This includes mindfulness where there is a focus on being in the present.

Identity: People who have purpose in life respond better in several areas of their lives. In fact, they perform all the other core components of life better. Values clarification allows this.

Mental stimulation: Research links higher education and occupational levels to a lower incidence of dementia (*Journal of the American Medical Association*, Vol. 271, No. 13). The more complex and novel the environment, the lower the risk of getting ailments like AD.

A holistic approach with a special emphasis on memory was undertaken in some studies (e.g., Bendheim, 2009; West, Bagwell, & Dark-Freuderman, 2008). Older adults living in the community were assessed. All the participants had memory complaints and showed some memory impairment, such as AAMI, MCI, or early dementia, upon screening and a cognitive profile matching. Participants were not randomized, as all were given the Memory Clinic intervention. Additional subjects were recruited as controls. These subjects did not receive any training and were tested at times commensurate with the memory group. Pre-/postintervention measures included a battery of cognitive measures, as well as memory complaints and function measures. This program is expanded on in Appendix A.

Method: We have had a total of 14 cohorts in the Memory Clinic for which data are provided in this study. Assessing the first three cohorts resulted in our manualizing of the program and assessing succeeding cohorts. Ten to 15 older adults commit to participating in each group. Each Memory Clinic session focuses on one of the six tenets noted in Appendix A, with the topic of memory permeating every discussion. The group convenes once a week for 6 weeks for approximately 2 hours at a time, and then receives a booster session a month later. All the participants report initially as having mild memory problems, with many of them presenting with more severe cognitive deficits.

There were 135 subjects, of whom 112 were in the memory group and 23 in the control group. All participants were older adults (65 years or older) who had memory complaints. The subjects came from referrals in the community. Each was given a standard battery of tests and then referred to the Memory Clinic or, after about halfway through the cohorts, to the control group. For the study measures, there were a total of 112 Memory Clinic subjects and as a secondary issue we also had 25 control subjects. The average age of all was just over 74 years and the groups were evenly matched in terms of marital status, gender, ethnicity, and medicine taking.

Subjects in the memory group were placed into risk status groups based on preassessment scores before the initial evaluations were administered using an alternative form of the Repeatable Battery for the Assessment of Neuropsychological Status (RBANS). Subjects were placed into high- (<3/10 words recalled on list recall), medium- (3–4 words recalled on list recall), and low- (>4 words recalled on list recall) risk groups. Participants in the high-risk group met criteria for MCI or mild dementia. Of the 33 participants in the high-risk group, 27 were considered MCI or early dementia; of the 60 in the medium-risk group, 11 could be construed as MCI. None in the low-risk group met criteria for either designation. These ratings were based on a formal clinical interview and a rating of the Clinical Dementia Scale as well as the memory indices done prior to the trial. All the subjects also had access to a caregiver.

TABLE 7.1 Descriptive Data on Sample

Variable	Memory (n = 112)	Control (n = 23)
Age	75.5	74.3
Male	37%	33%
Married	60%	59%
White	93%	91%
Number of meds	4.8	4.9
PsychMeds	5%	4%

TABLE 7.2 Frequency and Percentage by Risk Status and Control

Risk status	Frequency	Percentage
Low Risk	19	14.1
Medium Risk	60	44.4
High Risk	33	24.4
Control	23	17.0

Pre- and postmeasures included the RBANS (Randolph, Pearson, 2008). In addition, participants were given the Cognitive Failures Questionnaire (CFQ; Broadbent, Cooper, Fitzgerald, & Parkes, 1982) and Functional Activities Questionnaire (FAQ; Pfeffer, Kurosaki, Chance, Filos, & Bates, 1984). Again, measures were given pre- and postmemory sessions.

Intervention: The groups had booster sessions that lasted 1.5 to 2 hours each time for 6 weeks successively. The core technique in the Memory Clinic is memory, emphasizing attention and concentration. The method that is promoted during Memory Clinic is a technique known as "GUP+L." The GUP (Get it, Use it, and Practice/Picture it Plus Link) procedure emphasizes concentration and retrieval as well as the method of linking. Throughout the sessions, the participants perform various mental exercises related to GUP+L, as well as the method of linking. They are requested to practice this hourly (see Appendix A). They have day-minders to encourage this. To foster this, the facilitator uses behavior-modification techniques, such as self-monitoring, to promote more ownership of memory in participants.

Results: There were no differences in the premeasures or demographics for the cognitive scales between the memory group and the control group. This was not the case for postmeasures. For these, three differences were noted in the memory group (List Learning, Story Memory, and Story Recall), with the trends consistently in their favor. The differences involved two learning tasks and a recall measure (words learned previously). The memory group, then, as a whole, improved relative to a control.

We then calculated paired t-tests for pre- and postmeasures for each group separately. For the control group, there were no changes. When we looked at the memory group only, several measures were significant, but all the scores were in the positive direction. As before, the significant measures included List Learning, Story Learning (both learning tasks given during the postintervention time period), and Story Recall (a memory task). Once again, these subjects included everyone, even those at high risk.

TABLE 7.3 Pre- and Postvalues for Memory Group Only

Variable	Prescores	Postscores
List Learning*	22.2 (6.1)	24 (6.3)
Story Memory*	14.5 (4.8)	16.1 (3.9)
Coding	35.1 (9.0)	35.6 (8.6)
Digit Span	10.8 (4.6)	10.0 (2.6)
List Recall	3.9 (2.6)	4.3 (3.0)
List Recognition	18.2 (2.0)	18.4 (1.8)
Story Recall*	7.1 (3.3)	8.5 (2.8)

Note. Paired *t*-tests: $p < .05$.

There were several differences when the memory group was broken down by risk status with the control goup added. The low- or medium-risk groups did significantly better than the other groups. For List Learning, low- and medium-risk groups scored better than control, who scored better than the high-risk group; for Story Memory, the low- and medium-risk groups were superior to control; for List Recall, low- and medium-risk groups were better than high-risk and control groups; for List Recognition, low- and medium-risk groups scored higher than the controls, who were better than the high-risk group; and for Story Recall, low- and medium-risk groups were better than the high-risk and control groups.

For the final cognitive analysis, we conducted a series of regressions controlling for the prescore on the cognitive measures. We added group (risk and control) status as the second predictor variable in the regression equation. We did this for all the cognitive measures. For all measures, there was significance for the whole equation. For three of the measures, however—Story Memory ($F = 23.0$, $p < .001$, Beta for group = −3.77), List Recognition ($F = 36.8$, $p < .001$, Beta = −0.306), and Story Recall ($F = 38.2$, $p < .001$, Beta = −1.45)—there was significance for each group. In effect, the low- and medium-risk groups outperformed the other two groups, high-risk and control, on these cognitive measures.

Finally, we addressed adjustment with a regression analysis. This is an important issue because it represents a marker of "far transfer" in the sense that it translates to a real-life event, as in less complaints and better

TABLE 7.4 Means and *SD* of Postscores by Risk Status or Control

Variable		Postscores						
		List Learning	Story Memory	Coding	Digit Span	List Recall	List Recognition	Story Recall
	n				M (*SD*)			
Low Risk	10	27.30 (4.52)	16.70 (4.79)	40.50 (10.51)	10.60 (3.50)	5.60 (2.91)	19.50 (0.97)	9.60 (2.46)
Medium Risk	29	25.79 (5.41)	16.90 (3.44)	34.83 (7.87)	10.51 (2.13)	4.93 (2.79)	18.76 (1.50)	9.14 (2.17)
High Risk	12	17.00 (4.45)	13.75 (3.60)	33.00 (7.77)	9.42 (2.75)	1.58 (2.02)	16.50 (1.73)	5.92 (2.84)
Control	16	21.69 (5.04)	11.25 (3.64)	32.75 (12.60)	10.51 (8.01)	3.93 (3.09)	17.25 (2.49)	5.31 (2.73)
Total	67	23.46 (6.11)	14.96 (4.36)	34.88 (9.72)	10.88 (4.56)	4.19 (3.02)	18.10 (2.03)	7.72 (3.04)

Note. List Learning ($F = 11.3$, $p < .001$): Low and Med Risk > Control > High; Story Memory ($F = 9.1$, $p < .001$): Low and Med > Control; List Recall ($F = 5.3$, $p < .003$): Low and Med > High and Control; List Recognition ($F = 7.9$, $p < .001$): Low and Med > Con > High; Story Recall (12.2, $p < .001$): Low and Med > High and Control.

adjustment. We had no data on these variables for the control group, so we evaluated only the risk groups. We note at the outset that there were no differences among risk groups on the premeasures for FAQ. There was a significant difference among the risk groups for post-FAQ ($F = 23.1$, $p < .001$, Beta = 0.227), such that the low-risk group had less adjustment problems than the other two groups.

Conclusion: We applied a newer model of a holistic Memory Clinic to older adults with memory complaints. There were differences in favor of the memory group over the control group, and differences before and after for the memory group. Most importantly, the subjects differed as a function of risk status, with the low- or medium-risk groups doing significantly better than either the high-risk group or the control group. These results also were confirmed when we looked at adjustment. This far transfer revealed that memory training for the low-risk group did indeed translate into better adjustment. Again, we note that the overall trends were favorable for the low-risk group.

Aging is unavoidable, but the associated decline does not necessarily mean a degenerative brain. Memory functions do decline with age, but several older adults show well-preserved functioning apparently related to putative factors, including brain reserve. Education and complex learning challenges help, but those benefits quickly dwindle after a period of inactivity, as in retirement. Constant engagement appears to be one secret to success (Nyberg, Lövden, Riklund, Lindenberger, & Bäckman, 2012). Those who are socially, mentally, and physically stimulated tend to show greater cognitive performance with a brain that appears younger than its years. This was our effort here.

The fact that the memory group improved over the control group supports a wave of other literature indicating that cognitive stimulation is advantageous for healthy older adults and increasingly more impaired elders. Although we did not formally assess the other brain-reserve components (e.g., education, leisure), we did see a few differences in the groups by intervention or by risk status. Roughly half of the subjects in this study met the criteria for an MCI diagnosis or worse (mild dementia).

Our training on memory was specific. For several years the focus of training for adults has been on core components of WM. This has involved attention and concentration, some elaboration, use of retrieval, and practice. We developed the GUP + L (contents) technique as a method for optimizing concentration. The group was trained to identify a stimulus in a dramatic way; to start by asking self-questions about the target (G); to carefully encode the data (U) in any way necessary, including use of writing or standing or reading out loud; to look away and retrieve the topic from memory (P, which really meant practice without the stimulus [retrieval]); and then to elaborate on the contents (L). The targets for the memory group were to identify markers different from autopilot functioning, to hold and manipulate information for short periods of time (integrity of the prefrontal cortex), and to do so using multiple stimuli at the same time (even using short delays during which the representation of stimuli stressed WM). The change in the difficulty level as a function of individual performance was also stressed. Several computer techniques (e.g., Cogmed) were applied to these WM tasks.

Of the more recent studies on impaired older adults cited previously (e.g., Cochran Report), this result suggests that although most impaired older adults do well if some treatment or intervention is done, those with more skills do better. The core issue is to select those older adults who possess minimal skills and receive a validated procedure. That said, it is believed that all older adults can improve if given the right zone of proximal development or zone of friendly difficulty. These findings also loosely support the idea that a caregiver who is engaged can make a difference. It may be recalled that multimethod packages with caregivers are especially helpful. The subjects in this study had an active caregiver who saw to compliance that rewarded success.

It is important to note that this study showed that for the low-risk subjects there was a significant impact, which was adjustment. This has been considered a positive transfer indicator in CT. The FAQ is especially important, as it assesses important instrumental activities of daily living (IADL) tasks. Participants who were at low risk had fewer problems after this intervention, whereas those at more risk had more. The complexity of this connection to a meaningful far transfer, however, is at present unknown.

The low-risk group, as with all the groups, qualified as having AAMI or subjective memory impairment.

This study was intended to be a clinical study and every effort was made to make this a clinically practical intervention. This was therefore a real-world study. Older adults were very receptive to this type of training. Positive lifestyles are important for older adults. The extent to which lifestyle components outside of memory training contributed to the positive results are unknown. This remains to be assessed with further study.

Study 2: Cogmed

Cogmed is a computer program that addresses WM. Currently there are more than 20 studies published on Cogmed and at least double that number are in the pipeline (see www.cogmed.com). These studies have addressed attention-deficit problems, largely in children. Recent studies using Cogmed or Cogmed-like tasks have shown that training leads to improvements on trained tasks and also generalizes to improvements on tasks that are not part of the training (Buschkuehl et al., 2008; Dahlin et al., 2008; Jaeggi, Buschkuehl, Jonides, & Perrig, 2008; Klingberg et al., 2005; Persson & Reuter-Loreenz, 2008; Westerberg et al., 2007). Work on older adults, however, has been limited to only a few studies on community samples (McNab et al., 2009; Olesen, Westerberg, & Klingberg, 2004) or on adults after stroke (Westerberg et al., 2007). WM training using Cogmed with older adults remains very scarce.

In this study, we report on findings from a clinical trial that examined the effectiveness of Cogmed (Hyer et al., in submission). We assess this program against a sham program and (as an afterthought) a control group in older adults. Older adults living in the community were assessed. All participants had memory complaints and showed memory impairment on screening, but had normal screens for dementia (Mini Mental State Examination [MMSE], ADL, and IADL). All met criteria for MCI. In effect, this study complements the first one in that it addresses the value of one particular method that has clinical appeal as it is not labor intensive for the clinician. Subjects, however, all have impairment (MCI).

Method: All participants were older adults (65 years or older) who had memory complaints and showed memory impairment on screening (RBANS), but had normal ADL/IADL. Other neuropsychological domains were generally in the average range. Potential participants were residents of the local community, had an MMSE greater than 24, and had an RBANS Delayed Memory score with at least 1 standard deviation below average (Index score < 86). All subjects also had access to a caregiver. The screen for all patients involved the MMSE and RBANS (Delayed Memory Index). To rule out dementia in suspected subjects, the *Diagnostic and Statistical Manual of Mental Disorders (DSM-IV-TR)*;

American Psychiatric Association, 2000, and National Institute of Neurological and Communicative Disorders and Stroke and Alzheimer's Disease and Related Disorders Association (NINCDS-ADRDA) were applied as diagnostic criteria. Also, all subjects were screened for current depression or anxiety diagnoses.

After meeting study requirements, each subject was randomly assigned to one of the two groups, Cogmed or Sham. Sessions ($n = 25$) were completed over a 5- to 7-week period. Subjects were engaged in training on a variety of WM tasks in a computerized game for approximately 40 min/day for 25 days. The trials were divided among eight different tasks each day, selected from a bank of 13 tasks. For Cogmed, each training task involved the temporary storage and manipulation of sequential visuospatial and/ or verbal information. One week after training, posttesting was applied to the cognitive scales and then at 3 months for the affect and adjustment measures (post-posttesting). A patient is considered a "completer" when he or she attends 80% of the training sessions and is assessed at the various times posttreatment.

There was a total of 68 subjects: 34 Cogmed and 34 Sham, plus another 25 subjects in a control group. There were no differences among the groups on the demographic markers (including control, see text that follows). The average age for all was 74 years; 61% were married, 27% widowed, and 8% single; 47% were male and 53% female; 90% were White; 68% had a high school or greater education; 6% were on psychiatric medications; 17% had pain problems; 34% and 36% had greater than one depression or anxiety symptom, respectively; and none of the subjects were on cholinesterase inhibitors (ChEIs). In addition, this group took on average five medications and rated their personal health as good. The mean Delayed Memory Index was 80.6 and the average MMSE was 26. No one scored lower than 2 standard deviations for the RBANS.

The control group was measured before and after only on the RBANS. Due to study constraints, the control group was given only five of the test's cognitive measures, and none of the other measures.

Measures: Pre- and post-measures were taken on the cognitive scales, RBANS. Subjects were also given affect, adjustment, and satisfaction measures. These scales were assessed pre and post as well as post-post (3 months). The affect scales included the Geriatric Depression Scale-Short Form (GDS-SF) and the Short Anxiety Screening Test (SAST). The FAQ and Cognitive Failures Questionnaire (CFQ), as well as the Cogmed Satisfaction Questionnaire (6 questions), were given. The Cogmed Satisfaction Scale has an internal consistency of 0.84. All other scales are well known and established.

Intervention: Cogmed trains on WM focusing specifically on the ability to hold and manipulate information for short periods of time. It draws on the integrity of the prefrontal cortex, an area of the brain, which shows pronounced morphological alterations across the adult life span. The training is a software product (Cogmed QM©), which is used at the clinic or at home on a personal computer (PC). The intervention software involves intense and adaptive computerized training on various verbal and nonverbal WM tasks (Westerberg et al., 2007). All tasks involve: (a) maintenance of multiple stimuli at the same time, (b) short delays during which the representation of stimuli should be held in WM, (c) unique sequencing of stimuli order in each trial, and (d) the difficulty level adapting as a function of individual performance. The Cogmed group showed a percentage change of 27%. The comparison condition (Sham) involves training with the same software, but there is no adaptability—the difficulty level remains constant across the intervention period. To ensure blindness to condition, we removed all brand names from the training software. Appendix A provides a representation of many Cogmed tasks.

In addition, both groups (Cogmed and Sham) had a coach, a person who ensured that the tasks were being done properly, in a timely manner, and received rewards as part of the process. The caregiver coach was a spouse or a significant other (82%), an adult child (16%), or a good friend (2%). There was also a study-group coach who monitored the results daily and could respond immediately to the day's results. This coach worked with the significant-other coach on a weekly basis. This was done for Sham also. The control group of course received no activity.

Results: There were no differences on any of the premeasures for any of the groups. Cogmed proved to be superior to Sham and control on two of the cognitive measures (Story Recall and List Recall), and Cogmed and Sham improved over Control on Coding. These differences were in selected areas, but important ones representing speed of processing and memory. Cogmed was significantly higher than Sham on Story Recall for post measures, as well as for Story Memory for the post-post time.

In data not shown that addressed the post-post time period, Cogmed was also higher than Sham on 9 out of 12 postcognitive measures and 8 out of 12 on post-post cognitive measures. Only a few of these were significant, however. In effect, it can be said that both interventions made a difference for the MCI group, with the Cogmed group demonstrating slightly more improvement.

Interestingly, Cogmed did better on affect. The participants using Cogmed had less depression and anxiety symptoms at post-post than Sham. This was not the case at post, although the trend for Cogmed was again in the more healthy direction relative to Sham. Cogmed thus resulted in less anxiety and depression, but whether this influenced cognition is unknown. In addition, Cogmed performed better than Sham on adjustment as measured by everyday function (see Table 7.5). Again, as with the Memory Clinic study, this is important, as "far transfer" is a core issue in CT. At time 3, the adjustment of Cogmed improved, whereas that of Sham got worse. Cogmed also had improved satisfaction scores relative to Sham.

TABLE 7.5 Means, Standard Deviations, ANOVA, and Scheffé's Method Between Cogmed, Sham, and Control RBANS Posttest Scores

Group	Coding	RBANS Subscale Raw Scores			
		Story Memory	Story Recall	List Recall	List Recognition
Cogmed					
Mean	49.88	14.06	8.42	3.00	18.15
SD	14.04	5.47	2.15	1.35	1.99
Sham					
Mean	50.03	13.15	6.58	2.48	17.77
SD	12.96	5.84	2.41	1.65	1.54
Control					
Mean	32.75	11.25	5.31	2.09	16.26
SD	12.60	3.64	2.73	2.39	1.84
ANOVA					
F	10.76	1.50	10.46	5.48	.569
Sig.	.000**	.230	.000**	.006**	.568

**p < .01.
Notes: Scheffe: Coding: Cogmed, Sham > Control.
Story Recall: Cogmed > Sham, Control.
List Recall: Cogmed > Sham, Control.

Implications: Cogmed is a newer software program that targets non-verbal WM. Older adults who have MCI were selected for this training. This is the first study using this program with this type of older group. The fact that Cogmed and Sham improved over controls supports other literature indicating that cognitive stimulation is advantageous for both healthy older adults and increasingly more impaired elders. These data especially support research in which older subjects with MCI or mild dementia improved.

FIGURE 7.1 Estimated Marginal Means of Measure

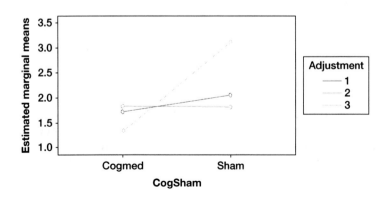

There are a few messages here from the data shown and not shown. First, anything is better than nothing, even in this impaired population: Train older adults using virtually anything. Second, the more skilled they are, the greater the effect (the more the training seems to take). We actually parsed those who did well at post-post in the Sham group and looked at their prescore profiles for help. Of the measures where there were differences, it was apparent that those who did well were those MCI subjects who had existing cognitive skills. When this analysis was done on the more versus the less successful Cogmed subjects, there was no profile of prescore tasks that was significant. In effect, most or all Cogmed subjects improved, but among the Sham group, those with the better cognitive skills performed well.

Third, the findings also support the idea that a caregiver who is engaged can make a difference. Recall that multimethod packages with caregivers are especially helpful. Both Cogmed and Sham had an active caregiver as well as a coach who saw to compliance and rewarded success. Of course, the extent to which this component influenced success is unknown.

Fourth, Cogmed was superior to the nonadaptive intervention in affect: Cogmed had less depression and anxiety symptoms at the 3-month period than Sham. None of the subjects had clinical depression or anxiety at entry into the study. The literature on cognition and depression has pointed to executive function as a problem for treatment response in both depression and anxiety. Cogmed targets WM, which is highly related to executive function. Some have taken to training older adults in executive function tasks as a treatment for late-life affect problems (e.g., Alexopoulos, 2003; Mohlman et al., 2009). Perhaps Cogmed serves as a filter so that improved cognition influences depression or anxiety symptoms.

Fifth, the area where there was a significant impact was adjustment. Again, Cogmed performed better than Sham. This has been considered a "far transfer" indicator in CT. Participants who had Cogmed had less than one problem after this intervention, whereas those in Sham actually got worse over time with five problems. Similar to affect, the value of Cogmed seems to support a total package of care in which, when cognition is improved, both adjustment and affect show gains. The complexity of this interaction is at present unknown. Transfer, it must be said, is rather difficult to produce (Green & Bavelier, 2008), and usually training that is intended to be transferred is complex, such as video games. Perhaps training with Cogmed that targets WM may be especially appealing to the older brain, where this type of cognitive challenge will yield the most change and transfer.

Even for normal aging, the question is how can we prevent the harmful aspects of old age related to cognition (LeCouteur & Sinclair, 2010)—and we do not know the answer. Even small changes in core capacities can lead to large changes in complex behavior. From this study, it cannot be definitively said that Cogmed improves older adults with cognitive impairment better than other cognitive-stimulation interventions. It can be said, however, that Cogmed had several advantages over nonadaptive interventions. Cogmed was better received, affected adjustment and affect outcomes better, and showed some advantages over nonadaptive interventions on cognition.

Special Case: Self-Regulation

Training has been widely studied as a potential means to improve memory for older adults, and most research has supported the effectiveness of such programs. Cognitive success is driven by information-processing skills (strategy use, attention allocation, perceptual speed, WM) and self-regulatory factors (meta-memory, self-monitoring, motivation, self-efficacy, performance anxiety), as well as individual-difference factors that might covary with these (age and education). We add these as postscripts, as they are critical for change in memory training.

West and Hastings (2011) highlighted the self-regulation aspects of this equation, specifically information processing (strategy use) and adaptive beliefs (increased locus of control). Individual differences were also highlighted. With several individual differences, results show that the potential exists for targeting and testing the impact of self-regulatory factors in intervention programs designed to improve memory skills.

Self-Regulatory Factors in Training Improvement

- Low memory self-efficacy undermines memory-change possibilities (Bissig & Lustig, 2007; Lachman et al., 1992; Rebok & Balcerak, 1989; Valentijn et al., 2005).
- Successful training outcomes depend on self-regulation, that is, the extent to which individuals applied themselves in terms of information processing and adaptive beliefs. Self-efficacy empowerment and change showed the best relationship to memory change (West & Hastings, 2011).
- Recall that individuals with larger WM capacities can better regulate emotions.

FIGURE 7.2 Self-Regulation Perspective

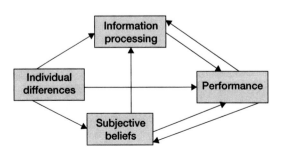

CONCLUSION

In their comprehensive review of the value of CT for MCI patients, Simon, Yokomizo, and Bottino (2012) noted something important: The interaction between biomarkers and cognitive-reserve factors determines, interacts with, or influences functional and adaptive outcomes in later life. Cognition, then, as we have argued elsewhere, is an epigenetic phenotype for the transition across time. It accounts for more than age.

We believe that there is a complex interaction between cognitive reserve factors (educational background, occupational attainment, premorbid intelligence quotient, leisure, and cognitively stimulating activities) and each biomarker of neuronal injury and neurodegeneration, modulating the benefits from cognitive interventions.

Simon, Yokomizo, and Bottino (2012, p. 1176)

Cognitive decline is not, then, due merely to chronological age per se, but rather reflects multiple causal factors from a broad range of biological and health domains that operate along the age continuum. In time we will develop a better "explanation sketch" using improved psychological theories that are helpful in the explanation of natural phenomena. Moderators are always in play. Perhaps we can loosen up our causal density and find options that lead to prediction.

We now know that training in cognition matters. It matters if one is anxious and/or depressed, if one has memory complaints, and if one is beset with disorders/diseases related to the brain. It is one of several things that can be done to assist in health at later life. It is one of the necessary things to be done for quality-of-life improvement. It probably assists in affect problems also.

CHAPTER 8

Health Issues

Aging is complex and clinically variable. We do not know what causes aging or how we can prevent the harmful aspects of old age. Older age itself increases the possibility of acquiring maladies, or at least makes one less able to defend against outside or inside intruders. The big three of impairment—mitochondrial function, increased oxidative stress, and immune activation—are less reactive as one ages. The decline of anatomical integrity and function across multiple organ systems and a related decrease in ability to respond to stress unfold. This decline is associated with increasing pathology, disease, and a progressively higher risk of death. Cell senescence and the allostatic load are simply not processed well. Both genetics and environment are responsible for this (resulting in aging phenotype). Aging is, then, a part of a modulation of gene/environment interaction.

Indeed, variability is itself an optimal sign at older ages (Lehrer, 2012). This decreases across systems. Intraindividual variability (IIV) is associated with developing cognitive deficits, especially in working memory (WM), brain volumetric decline, demyelination, reduced blood flow, vascular injury, and many other neurological conditions. The more variability in the cognitive system, the more medical problems are likely to arise. In fact, a discrepancy among cognitive measures (for example, verbal and performance) is a marker for cognitive decline. This applies to all markers in the older person, biological or functional.

There is no "centenarian lifestyle" that is common to all centenarians. It is this recognition that human populations are a highly heterogeneous mixture of subgroups that, besides socioeconomic, educational, and ethnic diversity, also includes numerous biologically defined subgroups (of which centenarians are the only one) that is missing from the information used to inform demographic models of longevity or life expectancy.

Carnes, Olshansky, and Hayflick (2012, p. 139)

As regards challenges, we have noted that even small changes in core capacities can lead to large changes in complex behavior. The pathways to a long life are just now unfolding (see the list below). Presumably the true savings in "number of years added" for most of our treatment efforts will be important and known at some point. In time, we may know also the "real" upper limit of cure for most disorders. Just the idea of an 85-year-old individual who is optimally healthy, coming for care, is problematic. Within 5 years, 80% of the healthy oldest-old will still develop considerable medical issues (Beckman, Parker, & Thorslund, 2005).

Aging Components to Be Developed for Longevity

Delay initiation of cell senescence
Improve lifestyle habits (smoking, alcohol [ETOH] use, exercise, cognitive training, diet)
Stabilize telomere length
Control apoptosis
Explore calorie restriction
Intervene in insulin-like growth factor 1 pathway (IIS)
Enhance adenosine monophosphate–activated protein kinase and forkhead (FOXO)
Promote systemic antioxidant activities
Inhibit target of rapamycin signaling
Diminish activation of inflammatory cytokines
Express longevity-enhancing genes
Identify new candidate genes and pathways

Stessman, Hammerman-Rozenberg, Cohen, Ein-Mor, and Jacobs (2009)

Clinically, common problems when working with elders run the gamut from basic safety issues to reasonable prevention, as well as issues related to the specific disease(s) itself. Clinical areas of focus include polypharmacy, adverse drug events, medication compliance, falls prevention, continence care, and caregiver management of problem behaviors. They are often based on reasonable lifestyle habits as well as the experience of core medical problems; chief among these problems are pain and sleep. These issues can significantly impact the quality of everyday life of older adults and therefore need to be addressed aggressively.

This chapter and the two others that follow directly address medical and health issues. Drs. Ackermann and Yeager outline issues related to primary care. Here we address the context of integrated care, the strategy of best practice in care, mental health in this context, and several lifestyle and medical correlates in the care process. They are very much a part of the care algorithm advocated in this book.

INTEGRATED CARE

Integrated care is not achieved simply by placing a mental health professional in a primary care clinic (PCC). The providers need to be medically savvy, to see patients more quickly, to make decisions timely, to assess with validated tests, and to be flexible. The cost savings are there; at least two dozen studies show this model to be cost-effective (Cummings, O'Donohue, & Ferguson, 2002). Often the integrated model is considered "treatment light." Although this is so, there are other "high-touch" treatments that can be applied for serious psychiatric problems such as bipolar I, schizophrenia, autism, and suicidal patients. Finally, integrated care attempts to handle therapy problems at the margins, such as compliance, help with acute and chronic pain management, intense-disease management, help with lifestyle change, help with general stress, help with caregiving, and case management. We will see more of this in the following chapters.

Patients need to be empowered to participate in the management of their health. We have a sickness care system, not a health care system. It is also not clear that we have the technology to prevent behavioral health problems. Yaffe and colleagues (2001) evaluated determinants of successful cognitive aging in men and women; 30% were maintainers, 53% were decliners, and 16% were major decliners. Many older adults, then, are not thriving as age takes its toll on life quality.

TOO MANY BEST CARE PRACTICES

We start this chapter with unsettling input: Too much of a good thing is not a good thing. In a *Journal of the American Medical Association* article of a few years ago, Boyd et al. (2005) presented the case of a 79-year-old female with the usual medical problems at later life (see list below). When her situation was carefully placed in perspective, problems related to her care became obvious. She was receiving 13 medications daily (pills were taken multiple times a day) and she was subjected to 18 nonpharmacological interventions. This woman represents the other side of the coin, excessive care that is not coordinated. Best-practice guidelines do not comment on the time or burden of self-management, or raise the issue of likely poor compliance due to burden.

79-Year-Old Female: osteoporosis, type 2 diabetes, arthritis, hypertension, chronic obstructive pulmonary disease (COPD), and depression

- 13 medications, dosed for 21 times per day
- Medications costs were greater than $400/month
- 18 nonpharmacological activities, such as dieting, self-monitoring
- Medications had a 100% chance of drug/drug interactions and 100% for nonpharmacological intervention interactions

Boyd et al. (2005)

This case is not meant to cause providers to shelve diagnostic best practices, but rather to be prudent about them, to develop a coordinating team process, and to monitor progress. The typical older adult has more than four medical conditions, has sensory problems, and has subsyndromal mental health symptoms. Many have limited means, are isolated, and have a high need to develop and maintain good lifestyle habits (socialization, cognitive retraining, exercise, health, etc.). This person is likely to have health literacy issues and may be unable to afford medications or comply with suggestions/prescriptions. Cost also increases in these situations.

This medicalization of life has been excessive. Consumerism and the medical/industrial complex have made us a bundle of risk factors to be plucked. In effect, there is little effective transformation of health care to disease care. With the increase of chronic diseases, with the effective treatment we currently have for these diseases, and with the way we can prevent illnesses, health care has become tertiary, even reductive. This rise in expectations causes problems because we have less self-responsibility and more demands on the system. Health care is not only a right but is also wedded to the position that more is better. The results are not good; we rank last in health care and health system performance relative to the seven other most industrial countries' spending. We spent $7,290 per capita on health care in 2007 compared to $3,837 per capita in European countries with better care (Davis, Schoen, & Stremikis, 2010). Health in this sense has become an end in itself, not a means to an end.

When there is multimorbidity or complexity of problems, there are additional problems. High-quality clinical practice guidelines can help improve care, but (as we have just seen) can have a downside. Multimorbidity is normal. More than half of older adults have at least three chronic diseases, and, as a result, problems ensue. The American Geriatrics Society (AGS) is sensitive to this, and has recommended that guiding *principles* be applied, not so much guidelines per se. This better allows for an approach that clinicians can follow for optimal care. These principles emphasize the uniqueness of the patient, the preferences of the patient, interactions among the treatments, multifactorial geriatric issues and syndromes, and the feasibility of each management decision and its implementation (AGS Viewpoint, 2012).

Optimal Care

Attention to patient preferences
Implementation of evidence base
Framing of clinical decisions in the context of risks, patient benefits, burdens, and prognosis
Assessment of feasibility in light of treatment options
Optimization of treatments and care plans

AGS (2012)

Several models have been developed that espouse these ideas. The Wisconsin Star Method was developed over a number of years to assist health care providers in the complexity of geriatrics. It is supported by heuristics, cognitive science, information visualization, ecological interface design, team functioning, and network theory. The method involves the use of a star and a paper/whiteboard and the mapping of the clinical data regarding a patient. The primary clinical challenge is written in the center. This target also may change. The medication arm includes all medications taken, including over-the-counter medications. The medical arm addresses all diagnoses; the behavioral arm, all activities of daily living (ADL) and independent activities of daily living (IADL) components; the personal arm includes values, traits, and coping styles; and the social arm covers interpersonal problems, environmental problems, assets, and access to needed resources.

Data are written down, as this is a communication tool. In effect, this is an extension of the user's WM. It also provides a benefit for multiple interacting variables. It is intended especially to consider when one factor causes problems with another, as in the need for blood pressure medications and the inability to afford them. Our PCC has a $4.00 medication list that all patients are taught to use. It can also be nicely applied to more specific problems, such as Parkinson's disease with poor gait, falls, poor coping, depression, cognitive problems, and social isolation. Finally, it allows the identification of vicious cycles among domains. One example is a "fall": This sets in motion a cascade of events: falls → embarrassed with walker → decreased activity → physical debility → falls (Leveille et al., 2002).

FIGURE 8.1 Wisconsin Star Method

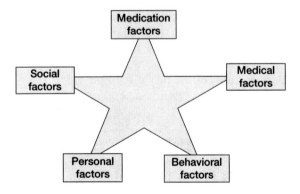

Compliance of course is a problem. Patients make suboptimal health decisions because they disproportionately value benefits and risks of medical interventions based on the perception of gain and loss, as well as poorly understood clinical information. Patients expect clinicians to make the diagnosis, determine the treatment, and outline the pros and cons. Most want participation in decision making. Effective care now involves the use of electronic prescribing and use of electronic health records so that all care providers are aware of prescribed meds; a perspective respecting reduced costs; dosing and appointment reminders as well as dosing aids; and better monitoring by doctors and patients. Effective positive communication and shared decision-centered accountable care are important steps in keeping informed consent and better clinical outcomes. Communication should account for literacy limits, avoid technical terms, and simplify complex risk–benefit data. Honoring patient preferences is always critical. The patient knowledge of his/her condition and management are improved at least in the short term by incorporating talkback strategies and postvisit summaries.

Otherwise, self-care behaviors are compromised. Most problematic is medication being taken as prescribed. Adherence to lifestyle modifications, which may include exercise, diet, and stress relief (Bodenheimer, Lorig, Holman, & Grumbach, 2002), is not far behind. We know that optimal heart health in middle age, for example, allows one to live up to 14 years longer, free of cardiovascular disease, than peers who have two or more cardiovascular disease risk factors (see sciencedaily.com, November 5, 2012). Depression may decrease the motivation and energy needed to perform self-management behaviors and may also adversely impact interpersonal relationships, including collaboration with caregivers, physicians, and other health care providers (Lin et al., 2004). A meta-analysis indicated that the odds of noncompliance with medical treatment regimens are three times greater for depressed patients in comparison to nondepressed patients (DiMatteo, Lepper, & Croghan, 2000).

In Chapter 3, we discussed case management. This is mentioned here as it is naturally related to best practice and can take the sting out of excessive care rubrics. This is a complex area, but the role of the case manager is core to the care of many older adults, period. Fortunately, this role can be assumed by a real case manager or the health care provider dealing with the patient. The tasks/duties of a case manager encompass many features of the reality on the ground, including the complexity of the diagnoses and the necessary features of the treatment mandates. It involves a goodly amount of education as well as hands-on common clinical sense.

MENTAL HEALTH

Medical care is directly related to mental health. When older adults do seek help for mental health problems, they go to their family physicians or attend PCCs. It is estimated that over 70% of medical problems, especially unexplained ones, are attributable to mental health issues (Escobar et al., 1987). Common problems for older adults in the areas of cognitive decline, depressive symptoms, anxiety issues, or unexplained somatic concerns are well over 50%. Patients with depression and significant comorbidities are especially costly to the health care system. The acronym MUPS has been applied to medically unexplained symptoms. Diabetic patients with depression, for example, have more trouble adhering to their diets and checking blood glucose levels, plus they exercise less, smoke more, and die at about twice the rate of those without depression. It is not hard to argue that it is more costly *not* to treat the depression.

As we have seen in other chapters, older adults have historically used mental health services at substantially lower rates than other groups. Older adults are three times less likely than their younger counterparts to receive any outpatient mental health treatment. The low rate of usage by older adults may be partly a function of limited subjective mental health need. It is important, then, to recognize that mental health problems appear to be significantly undertreated in older age groups.

The pathways leading to comorbidity of mental and medical disorders are complex and bidirectional (Lin et al., 2004). Medical disorders may lead to mental health conditions, mental health conditions may place a person at risk for medical disorders, and mental health and medical disorders may share common risk factors. Therefore, we should expect comorbidity between medical and mental health conditions to be the rule rather than the exception. In the 2001 to 2003 National Comorbidity Survey Replication (NCS-R), a nationally representative epidemiological survey, more than 68% of adults with a mental health condition (diagnosed through structured clinical interview) reported having at least one general medical disorder, and 29% of those with a medical disorder had a comorbid mental health condition (Ortega, Feldman, Canino, Steinman, & Alegría, 2006). In addition to the high prevalence of these conditions, there also is evidence that having each type of disorder is a risk factor for developing the other.

It is an interesting fact that medical conditions are most often grouped into "triads" (i.e., common co-occurrences of three diseases together). Notably, psychiatric disorders were among 7 of the top 10 most frequent diagnostic comorbidity triads. This category of disorders resulted in the most expensive 5% of Medicaid beneficiaries with disabilities. The commonest triad was (a) a psychiatric condition, (b) cardiovascular disease, and (c) central nervous system disorders. This triad was present in 9.5% of all beneficiaries and 24% of the most expensive group of beneficiaries. Indeed, at least in the United States, one of the most important drivers of the high numbers of individuals with comorbid mental and medical conditions is the combination of a psychiatric condition and a chronic disease. The 2001 to 2003 National Comorbidity Survey Replication found that approximately 25% of American adults meet criteria for at least one diagnosable mental disorder in any given year (Kessler et al., 2005).

When mental and medical conditions co-occur, this combination is associated with elevated symptom burden, functional impairment, decreased longevity and quality of life, and increased cost (Elhai, Grubaugh, Richardson, Egede, & Creamer, 2008; Lin et al., 2004; Roy-Byrne et al., 1999). The impact of having comorbid mental and medical conditions is at least additive and at times may be synergistic, with the cumulative burden greater than the sum of the individual conditions. Comorbid mental and medical conditions are associated with substantial individual and societal costs as well (Kessler, 2008). Melek and Norris (2008) analyzed the expenditures for comorbid medical conditions and mental disorders using the 2005 Medstat Market Scan national claims database (Melek & Norris, 2008). They found that the presence of comorbid depression or anxiety significantly increased medical and mental health care expenditures, with over 80% of the increase occurring in medical expenditures. For example, the average total monthly expenditure for a person with a chronic disease and depression is $560 more than for a person without depression; the cost difference for people with comorbid anxiety is $710.

Yes, we may be beating a dead horse here, as this topic is a refrain. But it underlines the fact that the role of the behavioral health provider will only become more essential. Currently, only 7% of health care expenditures go to mental health treatment. This is despite the fact that over 70% of people dually eligible for Medicare and Medicaid have mental illness. We also know that 67% of adults and more than 92% of people with serious mental illness do not receive effective mental health and substance-use treatment. This is due to multiple variables that affect success and acceptability of care. The Institute of Medicine (IOM) estimates that excessive costs stemming from waste and inefficiency within the nation's health care system currently total between $750 and $785 *billion* annually. Much of this is due to ignoring mental health.

Of course, there are larger ethical concerns. Callahan and Nuland (2011), two bioethicists, argue that our health care is not sustainable. We must prioritize and emphasize public health. We also need to apply looser standards to the young. Their position is that death and disease are now treated as targets of unlimited medical welfare: We have great human and economic cost but little progress. The major diseases such as heart disease, cancer, stroke, and Alzheimer's disease (AD) are present and will be with us for many years. There are indeed worse things than death that can happen to an older person.

Recommendations for a Sustainable Health System

- Improve the provision of medicines at the public health level
- Shift resources for the elderly to greater economic and social security and away from medical care
- Subsidize the education of physicians, especially those in primary care, and decrease specialization
- Train physicians in less aggressive medical care, especially with end of life
- Conduct a full study of the American health system emphasizing humanism, science, economics, and social issues

Callahan and Nuland (2011)

CORE PROBLEMS

As we have done in other chapters, we consider core issues of health as they apply to the health care provider and the best understanding of the patient. We start with general health, as this is almost always part of the holistic care equation. We then discuss lifestyle habits as necessary components of psychological care. Stress, pain, and sleep round out the issues of the substance of health.

Medical Problems/Physical Functioning

We cannot emphasize enough the throughput problems of medical issues related to older adults. The percentage of older adults with medical problems is substantial: 49% have arthritis, 41% hypertension, 31% heart disease, and the list goes on. The inability of the older adult to do ADL and IADL becomes increasingly important the older the person is: it impacts all of living (A Profile of Older Americans, 2010).

What happens in the quiet of the physician's office is often a "prescribing cascade": "The problem is that you are overmedicated. We have medications to help with that." We have previously noted that the number of psychiatric medications prescribed has increased measurably in this setting as well as in general psychiatry. It is always a concern when most older adults are taking more than five medications and are focused on the nuances of their success, whether for pain, diabetes, or blood pressure. It creates a kind of self-regulation that becomes overly reliant on medications, thus overengaging biology, and subverts personal responsibility for other health and lifestyle factors.

Scope of the Problem

- 66% of medication users 70 years and older take 2 to 4
- 20% take 5 or more medications
- 5 medications – 50% interaction probability
- 7 medications – 100% probability (Bjerrum, Sogarrd, Hallas, & Kragstrup, 1998, as cited in Rollason & Vogt, 2003)
- More medicines equals greater risk (e.g., Flaherty et al., 2000; Walker & Wyne, 1994; Zhan et al., 2005)
- Nonpharmacological approach – first-line option (Molinari, Chiriboga, Branch, et al., 2010)

Prescriptions can be a problem because older adults make up 13% of the population but take more than 30% of all prescriptions and just under 40% of over-the-counter agents. Simply, the more medical conditions, the more the demand for medicaments, the more the dependence on chemistry, and, of course, the more medications are involved.

FIGURE 8.2 Physical Functioning

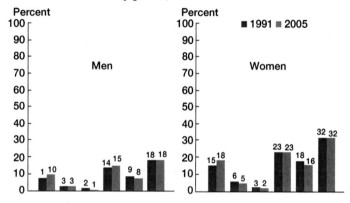

Percentage of Medicare enrollees age 65 and
over who are unable to perform certain physical functions,
by gender, 1991 and 2005

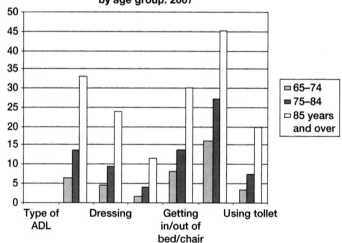

Percentage of persons with
limitations in activities of daily living
by age group: 2007

Source: A Profile of Older Americans (2010).

TABLE 8.1 Conditions X Prescriptions

Chronic Conditions	Annual Prescriptions
– None	– 10.9
– One or two	– 24.6
– Three or four	– 44.0
– Five or more	– 60.6

Source: http://www.agingstats.gov

It seems both trite and obvious to say that medicine-based problems can be substantial. They impact the overall picture of care, from diagnosis, clinical interpretation, and treatment. They also result in substantial problems, as they are the number one iatrogenic problem in health care. Marcia Angell (2006) noted that "even when changes in lifestyle would be more effective, doctors and their patients often believe that for every ailment and discontent there is a drug" (Angell, 2006). Worse, cosmetic psychopharmacology seeks to move a person from one normal but disfavored personality state, like humility and diffidence, to another normal but rewarded state, like self-assertion. If difference confers some degree of vulnerability, then all of us are vulnerable.

Medication's Direct and Indirect Effects

- Change(s) in clinical presentation
- Unnecessary hospitalization
- Unnecessary costs
- Overuse of services
- Poorer health outcomes
- Loss of independent living
- Quality of life
- Death

Perhaps the last station on the lifestyle route is frailty. It is a multisystem progressive impairment of decreased physiologic reserve, and is caused by aging, social factors, health issues, and medical problems. Function matters at late life (Keeler, Guralnik, Tian, Wallace, & Reuben, 2010). Frailty is a physiological construct best identified by weakness, wasting, losing weight, and decreasing grip strength, among other problems. More than 50% of females over 65 have three or more chronic conditions, and for males the number is 40%. Getting older means having to deal with health problems. But it does not necessarily mean dealing with the side effects of often unnecessary medications.

There are, of course, many measures of health, often disease specific. Self-rated health (SRH), however, remains a reliable and valid marker of morbidity, mortality, and quality of life at later life. It is a predictor of chronic disease onset, health decline, and probable trajectory of problems (Latham & Peek, 2013). It is also a marker of functional decline (except for perhaps cancer). An evaluation of SRH is a valid part of the assessment array of the health care professional.

At a practical level, health care measures are best situated in problematic biomarkers. Most often they include insulin resistance, metabolic syndrome, oxidative stress, and inflammation. These issues are ripe for biomedical research that is ongoing. These issues are also the scaffold for the metabolic syndrome. Patients are considered to have the metabolic syndrome if they meet three out of five criteria (see below; Craft et al., 2012). These components result in mortality and poorer mental health.

Metabolic Syndrome

Abdominal obesity (waist circumference > 88 cm for women and 102 cm for men)
Low high-density lipoprotein cholesterol (< 40 mg for men and < 50 mg for women)
High blood pressure (systolic > or = 130 mmHg, diastolic > = 85 mmHg; high fasting blood sugar) = 110 mg/dL
Use of antidiabetic medication

Craft et al. (2012)

Lifestyle/Prevention

A soft axiom of public health is that the best chance for real change in outcomes involves a preventive model for mild or subthreshold problems of older adults. Mental health syndromes carry comorbidities with them (Schoevers, Smit, Deeg, et al., 2006) and make change more problematic. We have touched on these in other chapters. Here, we directly highlight the importance of lifestyle factors in the context of general health issues. The frequent medical care users or the "indicated group" are especially ripe for preventive measures (Pluijm et al., 2006).

Simple prevention can make a big difference in care. We start this section with a global and societal view of this problem, specifying more global risk factors that can be transmuted into better health outcomes.

- Specific risk factors: like first-degree relatives or previous Major Depressive Disorder
- Nonspecific factors: exposure to violence, poverty
- Starting point: (a) identifying high-risk individuals, (b) reducing incidence
- Long-term goals: intervention programs that show evidence for prevention, test interventions with growing evidence of effectiveness, implement interventions effective at the small scale in bigger trials, create nurturing environments, develop infrastructure and funding

Munoz, Beardslee, and Leykin (2012)

Lifestyle habits, as we have argued, make a difference in the life of a person. Although government argues that officially there is very little that can be recommended strongly for the care of AD or cognitive decline, for example, there should be a focus on prevention. This includes exercise, leisure, cognitive activity, as well as a therapeutic emphasis on cerebrovascular risk factors. It is also noteworthy that enriched environments assist in the delay of cognitive decline, as synaptic connectivity at least is increased. This even applies to diabetes, as schooling, for example, mediates the relationship of glucose hypometabolism and impaired ADL performance. Cognitive retraining too has an impact on all older adults, including those with MCI (see Chapter 7).

Health rests on our daily behavioral routines. Five habits lead to 70% of morbidity and mortality: How much we eat, what we eat, do we exercise, do we smoke, and do we consume alcohol excessively (deVol & Bedrosian, 2007). These lifestyle behaviors are significantly and positively related to quality of health and mental health. Delivering care for chronic diseases resulting from these habits accounts for more than 75% of medical health care costs (Scott, 2009). If we added sleeping, mating, drug use, and relationship habits, we account for another significant proportion of the burden of chronic and infectious diseases (Chorpita et al., 2011). Other noted risk factors include age, lower socioeconomic status (SES), health status, medication usage, apolipoproteinE (APOE) status, unhealthy behaviors, and neuroticism, as well as gene–environment interactions (Hagger-Johnson, Shickle, Deary, & Roberts, 2010).

Similarly addressing dementia, Margie Gatz, using a longitudinal view of the Swedish Twin Registry and looking at a sample of nearly 12,000 twins now over 65, found that diabetes and obesity are among the most significant nongenetic risk factors for AD and dementia (Chamberlin, 2011). Although genetics account for a majority of the variance for AD, diabetes is a particularly potent risk factor when its onset is in middle life. Modifiable factors of concern in this sample were noted.

- Diabetes
- Obesity
- Periodontal disease
- Cardiovascular disease
- Depression
- Poor education
- No leisure activity
- No light exercise
- No complex work

Health professionals have significantly underestimated the importance of lifestyle for mental health. Recent data suggest that better lifestyle habits spread to others (Walsh, 2011). Want a better life and health? Develop a lifestyle change. This is preventive medicine at its best. The conditions that cause the most problems in terms of cost are respiratory disorders, cardiac disease, cancer, metabolic disease, and mental disorders. Mental health issues have risen more than the others by substantial amounts in the last few decades. Thus, as we have been arguing, it is not far-fetched to see that even a reduction in mental health problems would assist in the overall cost of health care.

Exercise especially is important. We have already alluded to the Herring, O'Connor, and Dishman (2010) review of 40 studies on sedentary adults with chronic illness. Compared with no-treatment conditions, exercise training significantly reduced anxiety symptoms. The authors concluded that exercise training reduces mental health symptoms among sedentary patients who have a chronic illness. In addition, 1 year of moderate physical exercise can increase the size of the brain's hippocampus in older adults, leading to an improvement in spatial memory (Hillman, Erickson, & Kramer, 2008). The aerobic exercise group demonstrated an increase in volume of the left and right hippocampus of 2.12% and 1.97%, respectively. The American College of Sports Medicine and the American Heart Association noted over 15 health benefits of exercising for 150 minutes a week (Warburton, Nicol, & Bredin, 2006).

Exercise seems to do everything: It prevents or delays AD (Hamer & Chida, 2009); it reduces cardiopathology, diabetes, and maladies in general; it fosters less depression and anxiety, as well as reduced pain levels; and it increases activity and quality of life. Although there is a probable session effect (30 minutes), any effort seems helpful. And, moving the body demands a lot from the brain. Exercise activates countless neurons, which generate, receive, and interpret repeated, rapid-fire messages from the nervous system, coordinating muscle contractions, vision, balance, organ function, and all of the complex interactions of bodily systems that allow you to take one step, then another.

The critical question for exercise is "Does exercise prevent or treat disease in older adults?" This can be answered simply "Yes." More accurately, this quandary can be resolved only when exercise is described in terms of modality, dose, duration of exposure, compliance with the prescription and in relation to a specific disease, disorder, or biological change of aging. We are getting better at this.

Meditation, nutrition, social interaction, low levels of stress, and personal meaning-making are coincident with exercise in the application of good health habits and better quality of life. Meditation, for example, has an effect on brain health. After 5 weeks, Moyer et al. (2011) showed changes in EEG; even with a little meditation effort, people who complied had positive changes in the left frontal lobe. This is associated with positive mood. Increasingly, the amount of exercise required for changes in cognitive activity is decreasing.

Diet, to name another lifestyle component, also deserves highlighting. Scarmeas et al. (2009) used 1,880 subjects who followed a Mediterranean diet and were 40% less likely to incur AD after 5.4 years. Similarly, in another group, 44% of newly diagnosed diabetic patients on this diet versus 70% on a low-fat diet required drug therapy. The patients on the Mediterranean diet also showed greater improvement in cardiovascular risk factors. In a meta-analysis of 50 studies, this diet improved metabolic syndrome, waist circumference, high-density lipoprotein (HDL) cholesterol levels, triglycerides, blood pressure markers, as well as glucose metabolism (Kastorini et al., 2011). Perhaps the message is that good diets trump bad genes.

We have devoted two chapters to cognition (6 and 7). Nevertheless, cognitive decline deserves additional mention here because it is perhaps the most significant predictor of all-cause and cause-specific mortality. Loss of cognitive function is the most feared aspect of aging. Last year, Americans spent millions on "brain fitness" software and web-based programs that claim to boost brainpower. But can playing Word Scramble or Rock, Paper, Scissors on a computer really fend off dementia? These exercises may or may not work. We have already addressed the most cited study in cognitive health: a 2006 investigation led by Pennsylvania State University psychologist Sherry Willis suggested that brain training can improve cognitive function in elderly patients and those in the early stages of AD (Boron, Willis, & Schaie, 2007).

The hard fact is that researchers still don't know exactly what works. A recently published study with over 11,000 volunteers ages 18 to 60 years found that computer-based brain training did not significantly improve mental fitness (Katsnelson, 2010). We noted previously that the NIH concluded that there is no clear evidence to support most interventions (Plassman, Williams, Burke, Holsinger, & Benjamin, 2010). The softer line is that there is considerable promise in memory clinics and memory training, at least for healthy older adults. In the real world, consideration of the problems related to cognition while developing cost-of-care models is time well spent, as this variable is highly related to just about all outcomes. We believe that a focus on cognition is important and useful, as cognitive training activates the older adult, often provides socialization (at least), and probably improves brain health. Cognition, like exercise, diet, and meditation, influences adjustment, functionality, and quality of life across the entire gamut of settings—from home to nursing home. We presented two studies in which this training did matter (Chapter 7).

There are other important lifestyle components. Socialization and religious coping, along with one's attitude, are especially important. The use of any of these can be very important depending on the patient. Retirement is one core issue. Doing this too early can be a problem; problems are less in evidence when it is done "too late." For every year that retirement is delayed, one has a 3% less probability of obtaining AD. Timing perhaps is everything. In this context, volunteering makes a difference. National studies clearly show that this activity is especially effective for those who retire with few friends (Silverstein, 2013). Similarly, older adults who involve themselves in social support in religious institutions have fewer mental health problems than those who find support in secular settings (Hayward & Krause, 2013).

According to functional specificity theory (Weiss, 1974), relationships fulfill basic human needs for security, intimacy, and self-esteem. Specific types of relationships become specialized in terms of the functions they serve. In our culture, for example, a spouse fulfills the need for security; a spouse and/or confident generally meets the needs for intimacy; and secondary friends and organizations help maintain self-esteem. Relationships, then, are critical. The health risks of social isolation are comparable to those of smoking, high blood pressure, and obesity (Jetten, Haslam, Haslam, & Branscombe, 2009). There is a sort of social capital—the sum benefit of community connections and networks—that links people and fosters beneficial social engagement and support (Bhandari & Yasunobu, 2009).

Social networks may also provide a vector for positive or negative states of health, as identified in innovative social network analyses of dynamic spreading of obesity, smoking, and even happiness in the Framingham Cohort. Thus, linking social relationships with physiological markers, as well as viewing health as a function of the social network and of the individual, helps to explain how social factors determine positive health states. Finally, social activity has also been linked to reduced risk of dementia, which may be due to its cognitive demands and/or through its stress buffering effects.

Depp, Vahia, and Jeste (2010, p. 538)

Religious practices also have a powerful impact on quality of life. In the United States, more than 140,000,000 people (52% of the entire population) attend 260,000 religious congregations, which in turn affiliate with 149 different denominational groups (Milstein, Manierre, & Yali, 2010). We know that the practice of a religion involves many factors—socialization, spirituality, networking, and so forth—and often translates into better and longer living. Whatever it is in the practice of a religion, be it socialization or spirituality or some element of psychological comfort, the result seems to be helpful. Regarding the related issue of end-of-life care, roughly 30% of decedents require treatment decisions that they cannot make. For these decisions they require assistance and social help. So, although we will not be labor the issue of end of life, attention to planning (living will, durable power of attorney for health care [DPAHC]) is not only relevant but even critical for good care. This is often done in a social or religious setting.

Finally, attitude makes a difference. Levy, Slade, and Kasl (2002) indicate that older adults can live as long as 7 years more just due to attitude. A "can do" attitude is the key to a healthy lifestyle. Researchers analyzed data on the diet, exercise, and personality types of more than 660 people in 2002. Findings were that those who believe their life can be changed by their own actions ate healthier food, exercised more, smoked less, and avoided binge drinking. Cobb-Clark, Kassenboehmer, and Schurer (2012) showed a direct link between the type of personality a person has and a healthy lifestyle. The Longevity Project endorses this position.

There are large differences in susceptibility to injury and disease. Some of these are a function of personality. Others are tied to social relations, including marriage, family, friendship, and religious observance. Most eye opening is our finding that the risk factors and protective shields do not occur in isolation, but bunch together in patterns. For example, the unconscientious boys—even though very bright—were more likely to grow up to have poor marriages, to smoke and drink more, and be relatively unsuccessful at work. And they died at younger ages.

Friedman (2012, p. 37)

Again, the physician/health care provider is challenged to foster the implementation of these life habits or care ideals, given the case mix and reality of the older adult. From a "pie-in-the-sky" view, these habits represent quality care. They also imply indirect effects: the recruitment and training of a competent behavioral health workforce; the development of better service delivery models, bridging science and service and facilitating the dynamic, iterative learning process resulting from their interplay; fostering intervention designs; developing basic and applied research; implementing decisional algorithms for referral to specialty services; and applying outcome-driven, culturally informed, evidence-based intervention strategies are all beneficial. (See Appendix A for cognitive and lifestyle markers.)

Stress

There are continua over which components of the stress universe assert an influence: acute or chronic, macro level or micro level, life-course onset of stressor, and severity. Stress is contemporaneously or temporally contextualized. An implication is that acute and chronic stressors are experienced in concert with one another rather than individually. Stress is very individual and context specific. This indicates that any one stressful experience is not the sole determinant of well-being; rather, there are constellations of stressors that become problems (Scott, Whitehead, Bergeman, & Pitzer, 2013).

The primary implication is that stress can have quite a large impact. Out of a scale of 1 to 10 (1 is good), most Americans report stress levels at 4.9 in 2012, down from 5.2 in 2011. They believe that 3.6 is a healthy level of stress (Bothune, 2013). One can see that although real stress leaves a real marker in life, stress is ultimately perceived, especially in late life. And there is enough of it. At the least, it involves life events, financial strain, neighborhood strain, ageism, loneliness, and chronic and somatic health problems. Americans also often have a global perception of stress.

Almost three quarters (72 percent) of respondents say their stress has increased or stayed the same over the past five years, and 80 percent say their stress level has increased or stayed the same in the past year. Only 20 percent say their stress level has decreased in the past year.

Bothune (2013, p. 23)

Stress leads to all kinds of psychiatric problems, most notable of which is depression. Depression can also precipitate stress (Holahan, Moos, Holahan, Brennan, & Schutte, 2005). It is also true that stress has a greater impact on low-income homes, but low stress is positive for self-regulation and learning. Stress from health-related and financial problems affects decline trajectories among those with greater biological frailty (Peek, Howrey, Ternent, Ray, & Ottenbacher, 2012).

Stress Components of Older Adults

Life Stress: There are many features here, including widowhood and retirement, as well as the death of a loved one. Generally studies on these issues focus on mental health outcomes, as in depression and anxiety (e.g., Beekman et al., 2000), physical health and mortality (Alloy & Clements, 1992), and disease symptoms (Mitsonis, Potagas, Zervas, & Sfagos, 2009).

Financial Strain: Lower SES is associated with increased rates of depression (Pinquart, Silbereisen, & Korner, 2010), as well as detrimental health behaviors, such as smoking, inactivity, and poor diet (Rosengren et al., 2004). Financial strain, in particular above one's SES, is its impact (Kahn & Pearlin, 2006).

Neighborhood Strain: Neighborhoods provide both physical and social contexts and have implications for health and well-being (Yen, Michael, & Perdue, 2009). This has been referred to as ambient strain, a marker for increasing feelings of vulnerability due to safety or limits in access to services (Krause, 1996).

Ageism: This threatens the well-being and health of older adults (Levy & Banaji, 2002). Being a victim of negative stereotypes of aging has been linked to cardiovascular health (Levy, Hausdorff, Hencke, & Wei, 2000), greater psychological distress, and lower positive well-being (Vogt Yuan, 2007). It has also been attached to a variety of psychosocial domains, such as social involvement and responsibility, physical activity, SRH, and subjective age (Sánchez Palacios, Torres, & Blanca Mena, 2009).

Loneliness: Feelings of loneliness are associated with a myriad of negative outcomes. These include health, depression, poorer-rated quality of life, poor physical activity, sleep problems, several biomarkers such as cortisol, and immune response, among others (Scott, Jackson, & Bergamen, 2011). Loneliness is consistently associated with morbidity and mortality across demographic characteristics (Penninx et al., 1999).

Acute stress is known to negatively affect hypertension, suppression of anabolic processes, and hippocampal atrophy. This response becomes toxic through adaptation, as sustained levels can present a serious health risk, especially neuroendocrine function through the hypothalamic–pituitary–adrenal (HPA) axis. Something as simple as poor sleep disrupts IL6 and consequent mental and physical health. IL-6 levels are also related to encoding and recall after controlling for age; C-reactive protein also has an influence, but less so. This appears to be especially so for depression. Knowledge of the serum levels of IL-6 among older individuals can assist in a determination of cognitive or depression levels (Lavretsky & Newhouse, 2012). Aging itself also is accompanied by a two- to four-fold increase in plasma/serum levels of inflammatory mediators such as cytokines and acute phase proteins. That said, simple interventions can make a difference: Tai Chi, for example, can reverse the cellular inflammation trend (Irwin & Olmstead, 2012).

Stress always has an impact. Decades of research have linked stress to adverse physical and emotional health outcomes of aging adults. Stress is both a cause and a consequence of cognitive aging. Stress affects quality of life across the life span. Early childhood adversity, for example, predicts both age 20 cognitive ability and age 55 cortisol levels (Kremen, Lachman, Pruessner, Slowinski, & Wilson, 2012). We have been arguing that quality of life is the sum of the aggregate actions of the person: General cognitive ability predicts later symptoms and problems in life.

Stress, then, is a psychosocial phenomenon. It is too difficult a construct to clearly isolate and operationalize. Some promising mechanisms linked to social and stress factors and cognition involve the following. These, as can be seen, encompass more than a simple intervention.

---

1. Hormonal factors (cortisol, oxytocin)
2. Allostatic load (multisystem dysregulation including inflammation and metabolic parameters)
3. Neural plasticity
4. Motivation
5. Effort
6. Strategy use
7. Rumination (negative thinking)
8. Intrusive thinking

9. Distraction
10. Repetitive thought
11. Emotional factors (depression and anxiety)

Lifestyle change is critical for good quality of life. Most Americans believe that stress has increased in the last 5 years. Concerns about money, work, and the economy are paramount. The chief reason that older adults do not change is that they do not sense the willpower or the inner strength to do so. This is a myth; the job of the gerotherapist is to help the older adult structure his or her environment to increase the likelihood of making healthy choices at any given time. The idea is self-control.

The health care provider can assist with stress problems. Stress can be measured and the clinician can make decisions about a response. Developing plans for a reduction in stressful situations, maximizing distraction and pleasant events, as well as the psychological powerhouses of mastery and self-control, are important. Where older adults are concerned, the key to reducing stress is to tolerate the anxiety, to encourage patients to relinquish defenses, and to facilitate the direct experience and expression of feelings, needs, and desires. Work on stress reduction can mobilize the approach system. In general, people will pay attention to more positive information than to negative data. Stress may attune people to attend to positive feedback. Stress is normal; suffering and agonizing are optional.

A method used with older adults in the CBT clinics, as well as in the Memory Clinic, is AWARE. It teaches acceptance of the situation through awareness and monitoring and, eventually, coping.

AWARE Model

A: Accept the anxiety and agree to commit to it in a positive way
W: Watch the stress in your life and monitor it. Give it a number 0 to 10. Watch the values vacillate. Be one with the numbers.
A: Act with the anxiety as if it were not a problem.
R: Repeat the above steps.
E: Expect the best.

Pain

Pain, especially chronic pain, is a disease in its own right. This is from the IOM (2011), and has led many professionals to consider the alleviation of pain to be a moral imperative. Yet all too often barriers impede the effective management of pain. This raises ethical issues, including the undertreatment of pain, the availability of opioids, and conflicts between health care providers and consumers.

For starters, pain is pervasive and debilitating, and can be the driving agent in remission of psychiatric problems. Pain is an unpleasant, subjective, multifaceted, biopsychosocial experience. It encompasses sensory–discriminative, affective–motivational, and cognitive–interpretive dimensions. It is classified into nociceptive, neuropathic, psychosocial, visceral, and mixed categories. To achieve effective pain control, much is required: All factors—physical, psychological, social, and spiritual—must be addressed. It especially influences sleep. Life quality itself is a victim.

In general, for patients older than 75 years of age, 66% have pain, 50% have pain in multiple sites, and 33% rate pain as severe in at least one site. This causes limitations in activities of daily living (walking, bathing, dressing, etc.). This interaction increases with age. Prevalence rates are especially high for those living in long-term care: 59% to 80% of nursing home residents report experiencing persistent pain. With 30% to 60% of adults having two or more health problems, pain is going to be a problem.

TABLE 8.2 Some Facts About Pain

• One of the most common symptoms reported among older adults
• 70–85% of people aged 65 and older experience a significant health problem predisposing to persistent pain

Source: Karp, Rudy, and Weiner (2008).

Of high interest is the fact that pain is a subjective experience. It causes the very things that create problems with depression and anxiety: rumination, catastrophic thinking, and helplessness. Given pain, usual Axis I problems occur easily and readily, especially anxiety and depression. Pain also interacts with cognition, as both are equal contributors to decreases in ADL and IADL functioning (Shega, Hougham, Stocking, Cox-Hayley, & Sachs, 2004).

TABLE 8.3 Pain Is a Subjective Experience

• Suffering amplifies the pain experience
– Catastrophizing
• Rumination
• Helplessness
• Magnification
– Anxiety
– Fear
– Depression
– Hostility

Source: Keefe, Rumble, Scipio, Giordano, and Perri (2004); Ong, Zautra, and Carrington (2010).

Another cause for concern is that the throughput of the person is impacted by pain: The person enters the fray and subjectively makes sense of the problem; he/she does not think well, cope well, adapt well, or function well, and in general develops a passive and external locus through which to control life. The person defers to time and postpones living. In an interesting finding, Berman (2011) examined the influence of mastery (how one regards one's life chances as being under one's control in contrast to being fatalistically ruled) on the relationship between pain and depression in older adults. For younger-old people, mastery had no influence on the relationship between pain and depression, but for the older-old mastery reduces the influence of pain on symptoms of depression. Being older and having some control (internal locus of control) of pain matters.

TABLE 8.4   Pain and Control as Coping

• Perceived Control–Key Mediator
  – Influences
    • Copying strategies * Adaptation * Outcomes
  – Low Control Beliefs
    • Psychological and functional impairment
    • Poor health perception
    • Higher pain intensity levels
    • Distress * Anxiety * Depression
    • Longer disease duration
• Pain Locus of Control Measure

Source: Hadjistavropoulos, Herr, Turk, Fine, Dworkin, et al. (2007).

Pain assessment is key to optimal pain control as well as a determination of its mechanism. Patient self-reporting is the most reliable form of pain assessment and assessment is ongoing. In general, the multidimensional scales are important and reliable. Pain assessment generally best consists of a self-report, behavioral assessment, caregiver reports, and a listing of analgesic trials and nonpharmacological interventions and outcomes. In general, too, data on pain care are absent from studies of older adults.

Patient Variables Most Related to Pain Experience

• Misconceptions—increasing disease and pain as part of aging; pain as nontreatable
• Fear—of addiction, masking disease progression, loss of independence
• Personality—noncompliance, negative attitudes
• Personal—cultural and religious beliefs, language, comfort with health care setting, social support
• Comorbidities—depression, dementia, anxiety

This stance is seen in the case below. The patient has cognitive and depressive problems. Pain, however, runs amok with these psychological problems and makes life worse. We can also see how the Watch and Wait model assists in the formulation and care of these problems.

Case: Mr. H, health issues, married, retired, depressed

BACKGROUND: Mr. H is a 75-year-old African American man who has health and apparent depression problems. He has been married for 38 years and has two children. He retired at age 65 from the company that he worked at for 45 years. Now he lives with his wife and he sits at home inactive and watching TV. He previously enjoyed socializing with neighbors and his church group. His wife notes that the patient's mother was "frequently depressed." The patient is unsure of why he is here.

Mr. H was accompanied to office visit by wife. The patient acknowledges "tough" experiences in his life but does not elaborate. His life story was communicated apathetically with general paucity of content. He denies feeling depressed but shows no enthusiasm for what his wife has described as "prime interests." He relates minor sleep problems. He is not reading anymore. He has a loss of interest in seeing neighborhood friends and generally feels "withdrawn" and does not enjoy former pleasures like softball. He has no history of depression.

He does complain of poor concentration. His wife reports that husband's memory has become faulty and "disturbed." She also notes that there are changes in behavior: he is irritable and raises his voice frequently, is less talkative, and is not like himself. She notes that he has "never been this way before." There are no apparent ADL/IADL difficulties but she complains that "everything just takes longer now."

Mr. H has a history of smoking (he quit 6 years ago). He has had hypertension for over two decades. He has type 2 diabetes, which has been labile in the last 6 months. He also has had hypercholesterolemia treated with atorvastatin. He has had angina on and off but is now symptom free. He also has osteoarthritis, has been treated with nonsteroidal anti-inflammatory drugs (NSAIDs), and has been in chronic pain. He has sleep problems. He is also hearing impaired, with delayed but adequate comprehension at increased volume.

OVERALL FUNCTIONING: His testing shows cognitive problems. His Montreal Cognitive Assessment (MoCA) is 21 of 30 and Repeatable Battery for the Assessment of Neuropsychological Status (RBANS) Total Index is 89 with specific deficits in Delayed Memory. He is low on Stroop C/W = 28 and slow on Trials B (2.1 standard deviations low). He had problems with the Wisconsin Card Sort (not complete categories and Learn to Learn problems).

Affectively he is depressed; Beck Depression Inventory (BDI-II) = 19 and Patient Health Questionnaire (PHQ-9) = 16. He is not anxious; Generalized Anxiety Disorder (GAD-7) = 3 and Short Anxiety Screening Test (SAST) = 17. He endorses apathy (Apathy Scale items). His pain is a problem; Brief Pain Inventory (BPI) Pain Scale = 7 of 10. Sleep is also a problem both at night and during the day (Epworth Sleepiness Scale

[ESS] = 11). The Millon Behavioral Medicine Diagnostic (MBMD) shows an introverted and confident personality style with a high depression. Information discomfort and compliance are issues of concern. His Functional Activities Questionnaire (FAQ) = 4, mild problems. The Mini-International Neuropsychiatric Interview (MINI) was positive for MDD.

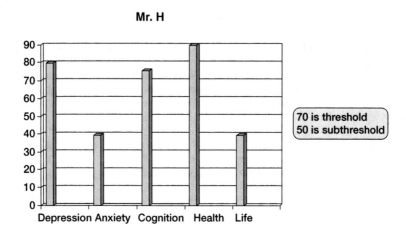

Mr. H—WATCH AND WAIT MODEL

Sessions 1 to 3:
Mr. H has several problems. He has health issues around CVRFs (cerebrovascular risk factors) that need better care and constant monitoring. He has pain and sleep is an issue. His cognition suffers from memory and some executive function problems. He would qualify for diagnosis of mild cognitive impairment (MCI) (vascular based). There is clear evidence of impairment of anterograde memory and executive function. He is at high risk for dementia (vascular). He is also depressed. He has good support and is functioning reasonably well. He is inactive.

This man has three substantial issues: health, cognition, and depression. He also has a wary attitude toward treatment. His wife is supportive. In the session, he was validated. His problems of depression, reduced cognition, increasing health issues, and a sensible attitude for self-protection were actually made clear and understandable. He was asked to commit for three sessions and monitor his moods and levels of pain/sleep. He was to be taught pain techniques, including behavior rest intervals, relaxation, and coping statements. His monitoring revealed day-to-day problems that were eye opening to him. He was told about the Memory Clinic and his possible role in this. He was provided much psychoeducation as to how this would influence his brain health. He was asked to consider behavior activation for periods in the day as well as exercise. He was to consider these and how he would apply them and any possible problems. He was also told about selective serotonin reuptake inhibitors (SSRIs) and their possible role. He indicated his skepticism regarding the therapy, but was willing to try with stated goals, tasks, and possible barriers.

Initial Core Watch and Wait Category	Check
Validate problem	×
Psychoeducation of model	×
Assessment	×
Monitoring	×
Case formulation	×
Check alliance	In doubt

Sessions 4 to 12:

A problem list is produced here along with possible modules:

1. Depression (Geriatric Depression Scale [GDS]):
   a. Psychoeducation ("You have depression and some anxiety"). Need to monitor.
   b. Increase behavioral activation
   c. Increase positive events
   d. Improve problem solving
   e. Positive priming of image
   f. Emotional awareness training
2. Pain Intervention: relaxation, rest periods, coping, interface with pain clinic
3. Interpersonal Functioning (Task Based)
   a. Talk to wife and pastor
4. Executive Function/Memory Training (Home Calls)
   a. Memory group
   b. ACTIVE forms
5. Medical Problems (Feedback)
   a. Parkinson's disease consult
   b. Labs
   c. Pain consult
6. Exercise
7. Sleep Problems (Hygiene and Diary)
8. Relapse Issues

Pretreatment Diagnosis

Axis I: 296.30 Major Depressive Disorder, Recurrent
308.07 Psychological factors influencing pain
R/O 294.9 Cognitive disorder, NOS (not otherwise specified) (MCI)
R/O Vascular dementia
Axis II: Deferred
Axis III: CVRF
Axis IV: Inactivity
Axis V: GAF: 60

Sessions 13 to 14:

He made progress everywhere, including on the MoCA (25/30) and affect scales. Pain became more acute and his walking was more impaired, so exercise had to be altered and a referral to the pain physician established. He was now more active, less depressed, cognitively sharper and involved, and was actually sleeping better. His attitude was more upbeat. He was in more pain. At 6 months his test scores were improved:

TABLE 8.5   Pretreatment to Posttreatment Changes on Key Measures

Measure	Prescore	Postscore (6 months)
Cognitive		
RBANS 89	94 (average)	
MoCA 21	25 (low average)	
Stroop Color-Word	28 (low)	42 (average)
Controlled Oral Word Association Test	24 (low)	48 (average)
Affective		
BDI-II	19 (moderate)	9
SAST	26 (moderate)	16
GAD-7	16	6
Pain	3/10 (low)	5/10
Sleep (ESS)	11 (high)	6

Yes, pain matters. Pain is interactive with mental health and quality-of-life issues. Chronic pain increases the risk of depression in elderly subjects; depression increases the risk for development of chronic pain; they are highly comorbid. Chronic pain and depression share a similar disease course characterized by worsening symptoms over time and increased treatment resistance. In chronic pain, this pattern of increased vulnerability has been labeled "central sensitization"; in depression, an analogous process has been called "kindling." Chronic pain and depression share underlying abnormalities in brain function that are believed to lead over time to similar changes in brain architecture. The shared neurobiology of pain and depression likely accounts for the high degree of comorbidity of these conditions, as well as the ability of several types of antidepressants to improve chronic pain. Pain and depression, then, are bidirectional and highly comorbid (GSA [Gerontological Society of America] Panel on Persistent Pain in Older Adults, 2009).

Therapy with depression and pain is made more complicated by the presence of both. In the table below are the usual treatments advocated for pain. Clearly these can make a difference. There are very little data on the efficacy for older adults and pain, even with opioids. In a study in submission (Hyer, Scott, & McKensie, 2013), duloxetine made a difference in pain for older adults undergoing back surgeries, though not as much for younger patients. This translated into less depressive symptoms. There are, of course, recommendations from various medical associations regarding the order of medications for pain patients, which progress through opioids and morphine-based drugs. In general, as with most problems at later life, the need for a multidisciplinary approach is obvious. In fact, such an approach is critical, as pain often does not remit with psychological strategies alone. They are necessary but not sufficient in the care of the older pain patient. Also, the likelihood of having only a pain patient is remote.

TABLE 8.6 Treating Pain

Complementary/Alternative Treatments	CBT/Mind–Body Therapies
– Patient Education – Weight Loss – Physical Activity – Acupuncture	– Biofeedback – Relaxation – Meditation – Guided Imagery – Hypnosis – Tai Chi – Yoga

In this context, it is important to be an empathetic and caring listener and to pursue a goal both as a scientist and a practitioner. In this case, it involves empathy, an understanding of the interaction, a plan of care, and patience. The role of the psychologist especially is important and involves strategies that reflect the mind–body connection, *in the context of* a person who is evaluated and for whom a care plan is developed.

General Pain Management

- Provide a rational, individualized plan of care
- Assess comprehensively
- Use physical therapy (PT) and occupational therapy (OT)
- Avoid high-risk medication, as recommended by Beers criteria
- Avoid polypharmacy
- Use lowest effective dose and evaluate constantly
- Adjust for renal and hepatic problems
- Adjust one medication at a time
- Use a nonpharmocological method for all patients
- Monitor

It is now axiomatic that psychosocial problems such as loneliness, financial concerns, or practical issues pile on when pain is present. The symptoms of pain and then anxiety or depression or both lead to more stress and the inability to encode data logically (Satre, Knight, & David, 2006). Providing help in the form of an empathetic presence, and use of pain supports (medication plus) as well as the use of teams makes a difference in outcomes.

- Listen to the patient and get his or her view of pain intensity and what needs to be done for change
- Establish a diagnosis
- Educate the patient
  - All pain is "real"

- Focus on functional impairment
  - What does the pain keep you from doing?
  - How do you cope with this?

Support medication/medical management

A. Antidepressant medication: usually serotonin-norepinephrine reuptake inhibitor (SNRI) or other newer antidepressants
B. Analgesic medications: acetaminophen, NSAIDs, opioids
C. Medication teaching, diary, stepped care
D. Foster surgery possibilities, if needed.

Psychosocial care: Behavioral activation/pleasant events scheduling.

Problem-solving treatment in primary care (PST-PCC 6 to 8 sessions).

- Encourage; foster hope
  - Regular physical activity
  - Adequate trials of analgesic medications
    - How bad does the pain need to be?
- Consult
  - Primary care, orthopedics, rheumatology, PT/OT
- Coordinate care with all providers

Adapted from AGS (2002); Bernabei et al. (2009); Gibson, Katz, Corran, Farrell, and Helme (1994); Hadjistavropoulos et al. (2007)

Sleep

We now enjoy almost 2 less hours of sleep per night than we did 50 years ago. As a culture, we lose 11.3 days or $2,280 in lost productivity every year to sleep problems. Sleep is required to rebuild the brain's cache of neurotransmitters, neural growth factors, and cell-building proteins that gradually become depleted during waking hours. It appears that with less sleep, the amygdala response to emotional images is unchecked and goes into overdrive. We also know that insomniacs have different brains than noninsomniacs; the gray matter has less density and has a different appearance. Cognition suffers to a considerable degree, with 30% loss of motor functioning also. Chronic insomniacs who slept less than 6 hours are more likely to die during the 14-year follow-up period. Interestingly, the old-old also relate that they have fewer problems when they sleep better. Sleep is not trivial.

Complaints of insomnia are common among older adults. As many as 45% of individuals between the ages of 65 and 79 years report mild to severe problems falling and staying asleep, and such reports are associated with poor daytime functioning. As many as 80% of older adults report some sleep disturbance (Harper et al., 2005). Typically, a patient's complaints fall into the broad categories of insomnia, excessive sleepiness, and parasomnias. In order to discern the problem, a careful sleep history is required; a sleep diary is important, perhaps actigraphy, and maybe a polysomnographic evaluation can all be used, if there exists a parasomnia or excessive persistence of sleep problems. Primary insomnia accounts for 10% of complaints among older patients, but secondary or comorbid insomnia is as high as 90%. Sleep problems, then, are associated with other medical or psychiatric problems.

Insomnia is the core problem for older adults. It is defined as having difficulties succeeding at falling asleep or maintaining sleep during the night, or early-morning wakening and consequently experiencing impairments in daytime functioning for at least 4 weeks. Consequently, patients worry and ruminate about their symptoms at night and are concerned about the expected negative consequences during daytime. These symptoms are very common, frequently occurring comorbidly with almost any mental or organic disorder, and also as an independent sleep disorder. The *Diagnostic and Statistical Manual of Mental Disorders, Fourth Edition, Text Revision (DSM-IV-TR)* of the American Psychiatric Association (APA) differentiates three types of insomnia: Primary Insomnia, insomnia related to a medical or mental disease, and insomnia related to the intake or abuse/dependency from substances (APA, 2000). If the symptoms persist for at least 6 months, chronic insomnia is diagnosed.

The *DSM-5* makes several changes but seems to retain the core criteria for the modal sleep problems of older adults, and we will not dwell on the new *DSM-5* (2013) here. The current *DSM-IV* puts too much emphasis on presumed causes of symptoms. Primary and commonly diagnosed sleep disorders are being organized in the *DSM-5* into three major categories: insomnia, hypersomnia, and arousal disorder. The new *DSM* will allow professionals to choose among subtypes in each category. The core diagnoses related to older adults of primary insomnia involve the occurrence of insomnia three or more times weekly; duration of 1 month or longer is retained. Another older adult offender is breathing-related sleep disorder and the criteria for this have been updated. Restless leg syndrome is retained, as is REM sleep behavior disorder. Other problem states, less related to older adults, are also outlined with differences; circadian rhythm sleep disorder text and criteria are updated; parasomnia disorders and diagnostic criteria are updated to include REM sleep behavior disorder and confusional arousal disorder; insomnia comorbid with either another mental disorder or with a substance abuse disorder is also in the manual; and primary hypersomnia now lumps together a rather heterogeneous group of disorders.

Although insomnia is a component of numerous psychiatric disorders, including mood and anxiety disturbances, much of the published research concerning insomnia in psychiatric disorders has been in the context of major depression; less attention has been paid to insomnia in anxiety disorders. This is somewhat surprising, given that anxiety and arousal are closely related, and that arousal reduction is a core component of some of the most prominent nonpharmacological treatments for insomnia (e.g., cognitive/behavioral, stimulus control, and relaxation therapies). It is interesting to note that even levels of anxiety that failed to meet diagnostic criteria for a clinical disorder were associated with noteworthy "distress and impairment" in older adults. However, anxiety disorders and depressive disorders are highly comorbid (transdiagnostic), and this has likely complicated investigators' ability to assess the independent relationships of anxiety and depression to sleep disturbances.

We have suggested that it is usual for older adults with anxiety and depression to have sleep problems. For older adults, both insomnia complaints and anxiety disorders are common and are associated with poor daytime functioning (APA, 2000). For anxiety, elevated state anxiety was associated with higher levels of waking after sleep onset (measured by both actigraphy and sleep log) and shorter sleep-onset latency (measured by sleep log). Higher levels of trait anxiety were associated with greater waking after sleep onset (measured by sleep log). Elevated state and trait anxiety were associated with worse social functioning, and higher levels of trait anxiety were associated with worse role functioning. Thus, subclinical anxiety symptoms may be an important target for clinical intervention to improve sleep and functioning in older adults with primary insomnia (Spira et al., 2008).

For depression, insomnia is also a problem (it is part of the diagnosis). In addition, insomnia persists after remission of depressive symptoms (Iovieno, van Nieuwenhuizen, Clain, Baer, & Nierenberg, 2011), is a marker for depression recurrence (Perlis, Giles, Buysse, & Tu, 1997), is associated with nonresponse to antidepressant medication (Casper et al., 1985), is independently associated with poor quality of life in depressed patients (McCall, Reboussin, & Cohen, 2001), and is related to an increased risk of suicidal behavior (Ağargün, Kara, & Solmaz, 1997).

Where do the insomnia patients go?

69%: Never discuss their problem
5%: Primary reason for a health care consultation
28%: Secondary reason for a health care consultation

Of those discussing the problem:

58%: Family practitioner or internist
8%: Psychiatrist
5%: OB/GYN
1%: Sleep specialist
28%: Other practitioners

As part of the symptomatology of insomnia, patients experience impairments during the day after nights of poor sleep. Insomnia has been proven to exert a negative impact on health-related quality of life, limiting domains like energy and vitality, and also aspects of social, physical, and mental functioning. These impairments are linearly associated with the severity of insomnia. A recently published meta-analysis by Shekleton, Rogers, and Rajaratnam (2010) evaluated the few studies that can be found investigating neurobehavioral performance deficits in insomnia patients. The results are inconsistent and findings conflict. According to the authors, deficits seem to be only subtle. WM tasks and attention tasks appear to reveal performance deficits. The inability to prove distinct daytime impairments is assumed to be due to heterogeneous patient populations, differing test protocols and conditions, and also unsuitable cognitive tasks in the primary literature.

Sleep is, however, a major problem with older adults.

Sleep Study

- Determine the occurrence and recognition of common sleep-related problems and their relationship to health-related quality-of-life measures in the elderly.
- Study included 1,503 participants with a mean age of 75.5 years from 11 primary care sites.
- Subjects completed a five-item sleep questionnaire, among other measures.
- Of patients, 68.9% reported at least one sleep complaint and 40% had two or more.
- Participants most commonly endorsed (45%): "difficulty falling asleep, staying asleep, or being able to sleep."
- Problems endorsed were associated with both physical and mental health quality-of-life status.
- Excessive daytime sleepiness was the best predictor of poor mental and physical health-related quality of life.
- Even when all five sleep questions were endorsed, a sleep complaint was only reported in the chart 19.2% of the time.
- Sleep complaints predicted the general physical and mental health-related quality-of-life status in elderly populations with comorbid medical and mental illnesses.
- Questions regarding sleep are not an integral component of most clinical evaluations.

Reid et al. (2006)

Treatment: There is compelling evidence that psychological and pharmacological treatment of insomnia is effective. Hypnotic medications are evaluated adequately for short-term usage and, therefore, should only be used for a short period of time in clinical practice, until more long-term studies are published in the future. The occurrence and management of side effects is an important issue for insomnia patients and must be appreciated in a pharmacological treatment strategy.

Cognitive behavioral therapy-Insomnia (CBT-I) is the first-line option for insomnia, as long-term effects have been shown conclusively. Overall, it can be said that CBT-I treatments for people aged 60 and older are mildly effective for some aspects of sleep (according to the patient diaries) in the short term, but the effect of these treatments is not always durable.

In general, beneficial effects from these treatments are not as great as when used with younger adults, CBT-I seems to be best used for sleep-maintenance problems in older adults. CBT-I encompasses education about sleep and sleep hygiene, sleep restriction, stimulus control, relaxation techniques, and cognitive strategies to combat nocturnal ruminations. These treatments are mildly effective but not always durable. Total sleep duration especially appears to show a modest improvement at posttreatment, which declines with time. Early meta-analyses and systematic reviews on studies with elderly people also found this to be the case (Lunde, Nordhus, & Pallesen, 2009; Montgomery & Denis, 2004). Internet-based treatment options and stepped-care models might be feasible options for the future.

A major problem of CBT is its accessibility for most insomnia patients. Internet-based therapy might be a solution for this; in addition, face-to-face treatment could be administered through a stepped-care approach, as recently proposed by Espie, Inglis, and Harvey (2001). They developed a hierarchy of delivering CBT on five levels, starting with a self-administered CBT as a basis and moving through a manualized, small-group CBT delivered by nurses, and eventually "referring" further upstream. More experience with this health care model for insomnia patients is necessary to draw further conclusions on availability for a larger proportion of society and cost-effectiveness. Generally, research supports the idea that when informed of options for the treatment of chronic insomnia, CBT treatments are welcomed (Vincent, 2001).

There have been no controlled studies using CBT to treat insomnia in persons diagnosed with major depression, anxiety disorders, or other significant psychiatric disease. However, uncontrolled studies suggest that sleep can be improved using CBT in persons with or without depression. Depressed persons receiving CBT show clinically significant improvements in depression. CBT in persons with other psychiatric comorbidity (e.g., anxiety disorders) may need additions or modifications to the behavioral components.

The main elements of cognitive psychological therapy of insomnia are psychoeducation, stimulus control, sleep restriction, relaxation therapies, and cognitive techniques. At the beginning of the therapy, providing information and presenting a working model of sleep is important. Regarding the efficacy of sleep hygiene recommendations in the treatment of insomnia, Morin, Culbert, and Schwartz (1994) concluded in their review that sleep hygiene education is a necessary part of therapy but not a sufficient treatment approach. Many insomniacs suffer from ruminating when they are lying in bed and cannot sleep. In this case, CBT can be applied. Writing down the thoughts a few hours before going to bed or using a "ruminating chair" in the living room for rumination instead of doing it in bed are only the two of common techniques.

Relaxation techniques are well-tried methods in the treatment of insomnia. In particular, autogenic training, progressive muscle relaxation, and mindfulness exercises have a positive influence on emotional and cognitive and physiological arousals, which disturb the process of falling asleep. The advantages of progressive muscle relaxation are that patients can learn it quite quickly, and afterward, they have an effective method they can use before falling asleep and during longer wake time at night. The effectiveness of mindfulness meditation for treating insomnia has been examined in several studies. For example, Ong, Shapiro, and Manber (2009) used a combination of mindfulness exercises and typical CBT methods and found significant improvements in insomnia. Finally, self-help therapy in the form of nonpharmacological, standardized psychological treatment manuals, which can be worked through by the patients themselves, appear to be an inexpensive and accessible alternative for mild to moderate severity insomnia disorders.

TABLE 8.7 Sleep Therapy

Technique	Aim
Sleep hygiene	Promote habits that help sleep; provide rationale for subsequent instructions
Stimulus control	Strengthen bed and bedroom as sleep stimuli
Sleep restriction	Restrict time in bed to improve sleep depth and consolidation
Relaxation training	Reduce arousal and decrease anxiety
Cognitive therapy	Address thoughts and beliefs that interfere with sleep
Circadian-rhythm entrainment	Reset or reinforce biological rhythm

Sleep and dementia: As a footnote, patients with dementia can have a variety of underlying sleep disturbances consisting of insomnia, hypersomnia, circadian-rhythm disturbances, excessive motor activity at night, nocturnal agitation, and wandering and abnormal nocturnal behaviors. Increased irritability, impaired motor and cognitive skills, depression, and fatigue are also common. Many of these symptoms have multiple underlying causes and pathophysiologies. Patients with dementia are at risk for additional sleep disturbances, such as obstructive sleep apnea and periodic limb movement disorder of sleep, which occur at higher incidence with aging. Many of these sleep disruptions can cause considerable caregiver burden and may put the patient at increased risk for institutionalization in nursing home facilities. Sleep fragmentation is also common.

The management of irregular sleep–wake rhythm begins with behavioral and environmental strategies. In addition to increased bright-light exposure, structured social and physical activities and avoidance of naps during the day have been shown to improve sleep. During the sleep period, the environment should be conducive to sleep and consist of minimal noise, a darkened room, and a comfortable room temperature. Hypnotic or sedating psychoactive medications should be used with caution in patients with dementia. Time exposure to bright light in the morning may be helpful in some patients. Evening bright-light pulses ameliorated sleep–wake cycle disturbances in some patients with AD (Ancoli-Israel et al., 1997). See Appendix C for more sleep hygiene information.

CONCLUSION

We presented three major areas of focus: general health, lifestyle components, and problems of pain and sleep. These components should be part of the psychotherapy dialogue. Sleep, pain, and, in general, poor health care habits will exacerbate psychiatric problems and take their toll. There are, of course, other health and life concerns. Sex, for example, remains an important issue, with 30% still active sexually well into their 80s; 43% have sexual problems. This can become rather complicated, as a history of sexual assault is associated with greater declines in executive function in older adults but only in the presence of an Apoe4 issue (Petkus, Wetherell, Stein, Liu, & Barrett-Connor, 2012). We also highlight sensory problems, notably hearing and vision, as key markers in quality of life and as predictors of decline. Change has to come from the top down and from common sense programs in PCCs. This is happening, but slowly.

Clay Christensen (2009) of the Obama administration noted that the way to handle the problems in health care is not by disseminating the same traditional care as has been applied. We need to redesign the system. In regard to health care for older adults, we do need more. We become mired in our own biases and care beliefs. Too often the response is one based on the practitioner's bias, convenience, differences in availability, lack of an informed patient, and overconcern for cost. Psychotherapy, for example, has been bogged down in its own rigid ideas of the 50-minute hour, in an office, and with little science. Changes in the focus of the behavioral treatment of sleep and pain, in the use of meds, and in the application of a health care system, especially to mental health, as well as in the preventive use of lifestyle habits, can make a difference. The use of lifestyle habits and the careful integration of care for sleep and pain especially deserve consideration of the first order.

CHAPTER 9

Medical Problems

Richard Ackermann

Older adults, usually defined as those 65 years of age and older, account for about 13% of the U.S. population, but they also account for 20% of physician services, 40% of hospital days, and over 90% of nursing home days. Per capita medical expenditures for older adults are about $10,000 per year, contrasted with $3,500 per year for those younger than 65 years. By 2030, older adults will account for 20% of the population. The most common chronic conditions of the elderly include hypertension, arthritis, and heart disease, and most patients have more than one disease. A wide range of physician specialties are needed to help manage these conditions: Of the 200 million physician visits by older Americans in 1998, 23% were to family physicians and 24% to general internists—these two groups, not specially trained geriatricians, provide the bulk of primary care to older adults. Clinicians working with older adults need special medical knowledge and need to work successfully in teams to maximize health and function of this population (Ham et al., 2006; Pacala, 2010).

This chapter reviews general principles of caring for the geriatric population, followed by discussions of common chronic conditions and geriatric syndromes, with special emphasis on maintaining function and preventing premature institutionalization. Ideally, mental health professionals are integrated into primary care and collaborate with physicians to ensure optimal diagnosis, treatment, and function of older adults.

PRINCIPLES OF GERIATRIC HEALTH CARE

Providing medical care for older adults requires a healthy mix of science and art. One needs to respect the unique physiology of aging as well as

231

evidence of the effectiveness of drug and procedural interventions in the elderly. But because very old adults and those with substantial comorbidities are often excluded from clinical studies, the geriatrician is left to use art and experience to decide how to help the patient in front of him or her. Start a drug, stop a drug, make a referral for an ambulatory assistive device or hearing evaluation, or just listen and think about the complexity of the case—all of these may be important interventions.

Perhaps our number one rule is the most obvious: When older adults become sick, always consider whether the cause could be iatrogenic, that is, caused by a medication. For example, an 88-year-old man with moderately advanced dementia and hypertension lives in an assisted-living facility. Over a period of 1 month, he has three rides to the emergency department, including one hospitalization, for near-syncopal episodes. His only medications were amlodipine and aspirin. An extensive workup, including blood tests, brain CT, carotid ultrasound, echocardiogram, and prolonged EKG monitoring, showed either normal or minor abnormalities. On further questioning in the geriatric clinic, the daughter volunteered that all three of the episodes occurred immediately after supper, and that her father did not actually lose consciousness any of the times. This led to a diagnosis of postprandial hypotension, a drop in blood pressure because blood is shunted to the mesenteric blood supply during a meal. The physician stopped the amlodipine, and no further "spells" occurred.

Another unique aspect of geriatric medicine is atypical presentation of disease. The most common symptom of myocardial infarction in older adults is dyspnea, not chest pain, and some patients simply present with delirium. Serious infections may present without fever or with a subnormal temperature. Elders with aortic stenosis may present with decreased activity, rather than the classic symptoms of dyspnea or chest pain. Older adults with hypoglycemia may not experience adrenergic symptoms like sweating and tachycardia; rather, they just present with seizure, coma, or increasing confusion.

Common, normal findings of older adults may be wrongly attributed to disease. Up to 50% of older adults living in nursing homes have asymptomatic bacteriuria—that is, a properly collected urine culture will demonstrate bacteria. This asymptomatic bacteriuria is independently associated with neither morbidity nor mortality and it usually should not be treated. But if a frail nursing home patient presents with fever and bacteriuria, it is very easy to (mis)diagnose a urinary tract infecion, when the cause of the fever may be something else.

Finally, informed decision making for frail older adults requires an honest discussion of the potential risks and benefits of the intervention, in addition to the patient's preferences. For example, we generally stop doing screening mammography in vigorous older women about age 85 years, because the benefits of early detection are largely outweighed by the complications of false positive tests. As another example, a vigorous 70-year-old woman would definitely consider warfarin anticoagulation therapy if she developed atrial fibrillation, but a frail 85-year-old woman with advanced dementia who is bed-bound would likely not be a good candidate for this intervention, on the basis of both clinical and ethical considerations (Ham et al., 2006; Pacala, 2010).

Art and Science of Medicine for Common Problems in Primary Care

1. Iatrogenic problems caused by a medication
2. Atypical presentation of disease
3. Normal findings of older adults are often attributed to disease
4. Potential risks and benefits of the intervention, patient's preferences

---

Hypertension

Normal aging is associated with a rise in systolic blood pressure (BP), with either no change or a small decrease in diastolic blood pressure. For this reason, diastolic hypertension is not common among older adults, whereas isolated systolic hypertension becomes increasingly common as we age, reaching a prevalence of over 70% by age 85 years. Elevated systolic blood pressure is strongly correlated with adverse outcomes, such as heart failure, kidney failure, myocardial infarction, and stroke (Chobanian, 2007).

The large majority of hypertension is "essential," that is, of primary origin, but sometimes other diseases or medications may be responsible. The most common causes of secondary hypertension in older adults are the use of nonsteroidal anti-inflammatory drugs (NSAIDs) and alcohol ingestion, but other causes of hypertension include sleep apnea, medical renal disease, renovascular disease, hyperthyroidism, and hyperaldosteronism.

Multiple high-quality randomized trials have demonstrated that older adults with a systolic blood pressure above 160 mmHg benefit from reduction of their blood pressure. This relation becomes tenuous in the very old and frail, as clinical trials generally omit the very old (over age 85 years) and those with substantial comorbidities. The geriatrician must use judgment, looking at the big picture, to decide in these cases.

Nonpharmacologic, or lifestyle interventions, can be effective in causing mild reduction in blood pressure and may reduce the number of blood pressure pills that are needed. The most effective interventions to reduce blood pressure are weight reduction, dietary restriction of sodium and alcohol intake, adequate potassium intake, and regular exercise (Sacks & Campus, 2010).

The pharmacologic mantra of geriatrics is "start low and go slow." Elevated blood pressure is rarely a medical emergency, and high systolic blood pressure, particularly blood pressure that is very high (over 220 mmHg), require slow correction, to allow impaired baroreceptors and other impairments of homeostasis time to adjust. Explain this to patients: "Your elevated blood pressure is like a faulty air conditioning system. The blood pressure is too high, but if we lower it too quickly, we may burn up the system. Our goal is to gradually and safely lower your blood pressure, probably over weeks to months." Reduce systolic blood pressure to below 160 mmHg; there is no convincing evidence that getting to a "normal" systolic blood pressure of less than 140 mmHg, or further to goals used in younger diabetics (< 125 to 130 mmHg) is helpful in older adults. As the blood pressure is lowered, the clinician should monitor the standing blood pressure, as many older adults have orthostatic changes in their pressures—a substantial drop when standing. When this happens, the risk of falls and other adverse consequences increases, and the clinician may have to settle for a less than optimal sitting blood pressure (e.g., 175/75 mmHg), because the standing pressure drops to 115/50 mmHg (Chobanian, 2007).

New evidence suggests that the benefit of lowering systolic blood pressure may be largely isolated to vigorous patients. One author suggests that if the patient can walk reasonably well and at a normal rate down the hallway, then antihypertensive therapy is likely to reduce vascular endpoints such as stroke and heart failure. In contrast, if the patient walks very slowly or cannot walk, lowering blood pressure may either provide no benefit or increase the risk of death. For some patients, tight control of blood pressure may no longer be clinically or ethically indicated (Goodwin, 2003; Odden, Peralta, Haan, & Covinsky, 2012). For example, a 78-year-old woman with severe dementia who is bed-bound and lives in a nursing home would be a poor candidate for tight control of hypertension.

Preferred initial medications for older adults are either a thiazide diuretic like hydrochlorothiazide or an angiotensin-converting-enzyme (ACE) inhibitor, or perhaps a combination of the two, which tends to reduce metabolic side effects (Ernst & Moser, 2009). Beta blockers should not be a first choice unless the person has another reason to use them, such as underlying coronary artery disease. Calcium blockers are reasonable. Many older adults will need two, three, or even four or more antihypertensive agents to control blood pressure. Agents to avoid include reserpine and clonidine, because they cause sedation; methyldopa, because it is relatively ineffective; and alpha blockers, because they are associated with increased cardiovascular side effects when compared with other choices. Older adults on antihypertensive medications need blood tests and a doctor's visit every 3 to 6 months (Chobanian, 2007).

Control of hypertension may reduce the incidence of vascular dementia. In one large European randomized trial of systolic hypertension in older adults, a calcium blocker-based regimen reduced the risk of dementia by about 50% (Beckett, Peters, Fletcher, & Staessen, 2008).

Tips on Treating Hypertension in Older Adults

- First, try nonpharmacologic treatments, such as weight reduction, exercise, dietary restriction of sodium and alcohol, increased potassium intake, and stress reduction.
- In average and vigorous older adults, slowly reduce the systolic blood pressure below 160 mmHg, usually starting with either a thiazide diuretic or an ACE inhibitor.
- Monitor patients for side effects, including an orthostatic drop in blood pressure.
- Consult a physician if the BP remains above 180/100 mmHg, or if the patient appears to suffering from medication side effects.

Diabetes

Type 2 diabetes, in which the problem is mainly insulin resistance rather than a deficiency of insulin, is increasingly common among older adults, reaching a prevalence of up to 40% by age 85 years, if one uses the newer diagnostic criteria for diabetes, which include a fasting blood glucose ≥126 mg/dL.

After emphasizing weight loss, exercise, and dietary modification, general first-line pharmacologic agents for diabetes in older adults include metformin and the newer sulfonylurea agents, such as glipizide. Pioglitazone (trade name Actos) should probably be avoided in most older adults, because of its association with heart failure and other adverse effects. Older sulfonylurea agents such as chlorpropamide (Diabinese) should not be used, because of that drug's very long half-life, which can lead to severe hypoglycemia, and its unique association with hyponatremia. Newer agents have very little track record in older adults, particularly those who are frail or who have concomitant heart or kidney failure (Kirkman et al., 2012).

If the patient has uncontrolled diabetes after a combination of metformin and a newer sulfonylurea, the usual next step is a long-acting insulin, such as Lantus or Levemir. These agents are highly effective, but the incidence of hypoglycemia increases dramatically, and patients/caregivers need much more skill in monitoring blood glucoses and reacting to potential hypoglycemia if insulin is prescribed (Durso, 2006; Kirkman, 2012).

The level of control appropriate for frail older adults has undergone substantial relaxation over the last several years, because multiple clinical trials have demonstrated that tight control (HA$_1$C levels < 6.5 or 7%) either does not reduce mortality or may actually increase cardiovascular morbidity and mortality (ADVANCE, 2008). Part of this risk is due to increased risks of hypoglycemia. If an older adult is placed on an insulin product, he must be able to monitor his blood sugar and be able to react swiftly to hypoglycemia. Indeed, common symptoms of hypoglycemia such as sweating and tachycardia are much less common in older adults, who may instead present with arrhythmias, severe confusion, or coma. There is strong evidence that even a single episode of insulin-associated hypoglycemia severe enough to lead to an emergency department visit is permanently associated with an increased risk of dementia (Whitmer et al., 2009).

Most geriatricians "loosen" control of diabetes as patients become very old and frail, particularly for patients who are in the last few years of their lives, for whom long-term reduction of micro- and macrovascular complications of diabetes are not important. Translating guidelines into a patient-centered plan is particularly important in geriatrics. For each patient, the geriatrician's role is to (a) ask what the major health threats are to the older diabetic patient and (b) prioritize health recommendations based on the health status and preferences of the individual patient. It is likely that for most elderly patients, a HA_1C goal of 7% to 8% should be recommended (Kirkman, 2012).

Tips on Treating Diabetes in Older Adults

- After maximizing diet and weight loss, the first-line drug for treating diabetes in older adults is usually metformin.
- Control of diabetes, as measured by the HA_1C level, should take into consideration age, comorbidities, and function.
- Overcontrol of diabetes in frail older adults leads not only to hypoglycemia but also to an increased risk of cardiovascular disease, death, and dementia.
- Assess for depression or cognitive problems with a mental health provider.

Coronary Artery Disease

Coronary artery disease (CAD) is also strikingly age related, and most coronary artery bypass surgeries and coronary angioplasty and stents now occur in patients insured by Medicare. Indeed, it is now common for patients to get their second or third stent, or a repeat bypass procedure. CAD is the most common cause of death in both older men and women, and aggressive management and risk factor reduction is indicated for many older adults. For example, a vigorous 70-year-old man with hypertension, hyperlipidemia, and diabetes and without cognitive impairment or any other life-limiting illness who presents to the hospital with unstable angina pectoris is an excellent candidate for coronary arteriography and state-of-the art procedural and pharmacologic treatment. On the other hand, a frail 88-year-old man with advanced dementia living in a nursing home is likely not a candidate for either invasive procedures such as heart catheterization or even aggressive risk factor reduction with medications; in this case, the goal is likely to be comfort, not prevention of sudden cardiac death.

On the other hand, the simple drug, aspirin, is likely the most underused drug in geriatrics. Aspirin at relatively low doses, typically 81 mg/day, can reduce vascular events by 15% to 25% in a wide range of patients, including those with a history of CAD, stroke, or peripheral arterial disease. Aspirin treatment in these patients is safe, effective, and may even reduce disabilities and lower the need for nursing home placement. There is weak evidence that cardioprotective aspirin might actually reduce the risk of dementia (at least vascular dementia), but recent high-quality randomized trials have not been able to confirm this link. So you prescribe aspirin to patients with cardiovascular risk factors or established disease to prevent vascular events, but not primarily to prevent dementia.

Medical management of stable coronary disease usually requires multiple medications, including medications from at least three key classes: lipid-lowering, antihypertensive, and antiplatelet drugs. In average and healthy older adults with CAD, attempt to get the LDL cholesterol below 100 or even 70 mg/dL; control blood pressure, primarily with ACE inhibitors and beta blockers; and prescribe low-dose aspirin. If the older adult has an acute coronary syndrome or undergoes coronary angioplasty, then clopidogrel should generally be added to the aspirin regimen (Pflieger, 2011). One small but rigorous randomized trial showed that patients older than 75 years with chronic symptomatic CAD, despite aggressive medical management, benefited more from revascularization than from optimized medical treatments (Strandberg, 2006). However, other trials have suggested that although aggressive pharmacologic management of patients with established CAD can improve cholesterol and blood pressure levels, this does not always translate into improvement in real benefits, such as lower rates of myocardial infarction or death. It does seem clear that patients with stable CAD (those who do not currently have myocardial infarction [MI] or unstable angina) do not need to progress directly to percutaneous interventions; they can safely be managed initially with optimal medical therapy, reserving angioplasty for later indications (TIME, 2001).

Older adults presenting with acute myocardial infarction generally have higher complications and mortality, as compared with younger patients. Age alone is rarely helpful in deciding whether to proceed with aggressive intervention. Vigorous older patients who undergo informed consent may be excellent candidates for cardiac catheterization, angioplasty, or coronary artery bypass surgery.

There remains controversy as to whether permanent cognitive dysfunction is caused by exposure to the extracorporeal cardiopulmonary pump used when patients undergo coronary artery bypass graft (CABG) surgery. Techniques were developed for performing CABG without the use of cardiopulmonary bypass (off-pump), but interestingly, the rates of adverse neurologic outcomes were not improved. Currently, bypass is not thought to directly contribute to neurologic impairment. But older patients undergoing CABG should probably be assessed for cognitive impairment before and after the procedure, and selected patients may benefit from aggressive treatment of blood pressure and cholesterol, as well as by enhancing a healthy diet and exercise.

Tips on Treating CAD in Older Adults

- Ensure that appropriate patients with established vascular disease are taking cardioprotective doses of aspirin, usually 81 mg per day.
- Polypharmacy is generally the rule for the treatment of congestive heart failure in older adults, usually including an ACE inhibitor or angiotensin receptor blocker, diuretic, and a beta blocker.
- Older adults with vascular disease are at high risk of cognitive impairment, especially if they are undergoing coronary artery bypass grafting.
- Be on the lookout for depression and cognitive decline, especially after CABG or change in health status.

Vitamin B_{12} (Cobalamin) Deficiency

This disease affects up to 20% of all older adults, if one includes mild degrees of deficiency. B12 deficiency causes protean manifestations, including cognitive dysfunction, neuropathy, and anemia. Some experts recommend periodic routine screening of older adults for this vitamin. If the level is greater than 400 µg/dL, deficiency is excluded. Levels less than 100 µg/dL are clearly abnormal, but this leaves a gray area in the 100 to 400 µg/dL zone. For these patients, checking levels of intermediate metabolites such as methylmalonic acid or homocysteine can be useful, or one can simply replace the vitamin. There is no known toxicity from B12 replacement, so this is reasonable. Certainly all patients with any degree of cognitive dysfunction, including mild cognitive impairment (MCI) and depression, as well as patients with peripheral neuropathy or macrocytosis, should be assessed for vitamin B_{12} deficiency.

Anemia is caused by either a decrease in production of red blood cells or hemoglobin, or an increase in loss or destruction of red blood cells, and vitamin B_{12} deficiency is only one of dozens of potential causes of anemia in older adults. Some patients with anemia have no symptoms. Others may feel tired, be easily fatigued, appear pale, feel their heart racing, feel short of breath, and/or have worsening of heart problems. Anemia can be detected by a simple blood test called a complete blood cell count (CBC). It is worth noting that if anemia is longstanding (chronic anemia), the body may adjust to low oxygen levels and the individual may not feel different unless the anemia becomes severe. On the other hand, if the anemia occurs rapidly (acute anemia), the patient may experience significant symptoms relatively quickly.

The most common cause of B_{12} deficiency in older adults is not pernicious anemia, but rather achlorhydria, which reduces the ability of the organism to cleave R factors from the B_{12} found in food. Without this cleavage, the R factor–B_{12} conjugate cannot bind to intrinsic factor, and then the B_{12} cannot be adequately absorbed in the distal ileum.

Treatment is straightforward and is independent of the cause of the B_{12} deficiency. Although intramuscular vitamin B_{12} shots are very beautiful (a deep red color) and have a placebo effect, multiple studies have demonstrated that oral supplementation with megadoses (100 to 2,000 µg, or 0.1 to 2 mg) per day will work for almost all patients, even in the absence of intrinsic factor or an ileum. There appears to be an intrinsic factor–independent pathway of B_{12} absorption that works if you flood the bowel with enough cobalamin (Langan, 2011).

Tips on Treating Vitamin B_{12} Deficiency in Older Adults

- Screen all older adults with cognitive impairment (including both dementia and depression) for B_{12} deficiency.
- Oral treatment with 1 mg of B_{12} daily will almost always correct deficiency.

Vitamin D Deficiency

Probably the second most important vitamin deficiency to consider in older adults is vitamin D deficiency. This is still controversial, but many experts use less than 10 ng/mL as frank deficiency, less than 20 ng/mL as suboptimal, and greater than 30 ng/mL as normal. The same normal values can be applied to both men and women of all races. Vitamin D deficiency has definitely been linked to bone disorders such as osteopenia, osteoporosis, and osteomalacia, but there are indirect links to many other nonbone diseases, although this area of research is still unclear (Rosen, 2011).

For older adults who present with any kind of pain, bone, or muscle problem (which is the vast majority), it is reasonable to check a vitamin D level. In humans, vitamin D comes either from the diet or from conversion of precursors by sunlight in the skin—this vitamin D must be twice hydroxylated—first in the liver (25-hydroxylation) and then in the kidney (1-hydroxylation) to become the active 1,25 $(OH)_2$-vitamin D. The proper test to order is 25(OH) vitamin D, which is the storage form of vitamin D in humans.

There are several options for vitamin D replacement. Although vitamin D can be replaced parenterally, this is only necessary in critically ill patients who have no enteral source of nutrition. For the vast majority of older adults, oral vitamin D will replace a deficiency: if the level is very low, say at 14 ng/mL, prescribe 2,000 IU of either vitamin D_2 or D_3; prescribe smaller amounts if the levels are higher. After several weeks or months, the physician can check the 25(OH) vitamin D level again, to ensure that it has risen to normal. Some patients may have poor absorption of vitamin D and may need larger doses (Pearcer & Cheatham, 2010).

Another option, especially for noncompliant patients, is to give big doses less often. For example, an 88-year-old woman with severe osteoporosis and multiple thoracic compression fractures with chronic back pain is found to have a low 25(OH) vitamin D level, at 12 ng/mL. The geriatrician can prescribe vitamin D 50,000 units (this is prescription only) once per month, which can be administered by a family member. Very large doses of vitamin D (e.g., 300,000 units every 6 months) should not be prescribed, as these have paradoxically been associated with an *increased* risk of falls and fractures (Sanders et al., 2010).

It is particularly important for older adults with chronic kidney disease to have normal vitamin D status, because even subtle levels of vitamin D deficiency accelerate the hyperparathyroidism of renal disease, which can lead to multiple complications, even worsening of the renal disease. Use the same goal level of 30 ng/mL; higher doses of vitamin D may be necessary because the patient has reduced 1-hydroxylase activity. Some patients may require special forms of vitamin D, such as 1,25 $(OH)_2$ vitamin D or calcitriol, but this is expensive.

There may be a link between vitamin D deficiency and cognitive impairment, but the evidence is weak. It is reasonable to screen cognitively impaired patients for vitamin D deficiency, although routine replacement has not been shown to improve outcomes (Pearce & Cheatham, 2010).

Tips on Treating Vitamin D Deficiency in Older Adults

- Screen all older adults with falls, chronic pain, or muscle and bone problems for vitamin D deficiency with a 25(OH) vitamin D level.
- The optimal serum level of vitamin D in older adults is greater than 30 ng/mL.
- Replacement of calcium and vitamin D in frail older adults, especially those living in nursing homes, has been clearly shown to reduce falls and fractures.
- After prescribing oral vitamin D replacement, recheck the level to verify compliance and ensure absorption.
- Consider a cognitive screen on patients low in vitamin D.

Osteoarthritis

Osteoarthritis, also called degenerative joint disease (DJD), is the second most common chronic condition of older adults, after hypertension. Although the disease is common, not all aches and pains in older adults are due to DJD. After a good history and physical, consider x-raying the one or two most symptomatic joints, and check screening labs—CBC, chemistry, sedimentation rate, vitamin D level—to look for other diseases such as myeloma, other malignancies, Paget's disease of bone, polymyalgia, myositis, and osteomalacia, which may mimic arthritis.

Treatment of osteoarthritis is multifactorial and should not lead to an automatic prescription for an NSAID. NSAIDs do not affect the natural history of the disease (they don't prevent joint damage or delay joint replacement); they aren't that effective as pain medications; and they have serious toxicities, mainly gastrointestinal and renal. First, consider nonpharmacologic approaches such as exercise and rest periods, physical therapy assessment for an ambulatory assistive device, or occupational therapy assessment for upper extremity symptoms (Sinusas, 2012).

Some patients obtain substantial benefit from acetaminophen, and the toxicity risk is minimal, as long as the total dose is kept below 2 or 3 grams per day. The FDA recommends that no more than 500 mg of acetaminophen be taken at one time. Next might be consideration of glucosamine/chondroitin—although the evidence of effectiveness for this drug combination is weak, it is worth trying because it has almost no toxicity.

If NSAIDs are considered, choose generic drugs such as ibuprofen or naproxen, and use the lowest doses possible. If a trial of an NSAID does not help pain and mobility, then discontinue it, because the drug has no other benefit than relief of symptoms. For older adults with only intermittent pain, like when it rains or when the grandchildren come over, then intermittent use of the NSAID is worth a try. For every older adult taking NSAIDs, consider co-administering a proton pump inhibitor like generic omeprazole, because this strategy reduces the risk of gastrointestinal bleeding by about 50%. Warn patients taking chronic NSAIDs that there is a risk of about 2% to 3% per year of life-threatening renal or gastrointestinal (GI) complications.

Some patients will benefit from other analgesics, such as tramadol, at a dose of 50 to 100 mg, up to 300 mg per day. This drug can rarely cause seizures, and so should be avoided in patients with seizure disorders or structural brain diseases such as a previous stroke or a meningioma. Also, tramadol may raise the level of the neurotransmitter serotonin, and if the patient takes other drugs that do this, such as the serotonin reuptake inhibitor antidepressants, then the life-threatening serotonin syndrome can rarely be induced.

For a subset of frail older adults, particularly those with renal disease, careful use of opioids may be appropriate in the treatment of osteoarthritis. For example, a 90-year-old moderately demented woman with chronic kidney disease stage 3 lives in a nursing home. Her joint pain leads her to cry out and become agitated. A reasonable approach would be the use of a low-dose sustained-release morphine product like Kadian, 10 or 20 mg per day, which may completely relieve her DJD pain, as well as allay her "behavioral problems," without posing any risk of renal or gastrointestinal toxicity. Indeed, for older adults living in the nursing home with severe chronic pain, carefully monitored opioids are often a better choice than NSAIDs (Sinusas, 2012).

Injections and major orthopedic procedures have a definite place in the management of DJD in older adults, and not just after one has tried everything else. Steroid injections into the knee can be very effective for several weeks or months, but they will usually need to be repeated. Steroids should generally not be injected into the hip. New agents, such as hyaluronic acid, are promoted for intra-articular treatment of knee DJD in older adults, but results of rigorous randomized trials have actually been disappointing, and the agents are expensive (Rutjes et al., 2012). On the other hand, total replacement of either the knee or hip is extremely safe and effective: about 90% of well-selected patients will have either complete or substantial resolution of their pain after surgery (Pivec et al., 2012; Carr et al., 2012).

For example, consider a 78-year-old woman with hypertension, hyperlipidemia, and hypothyroidism who has no cognitive impairment or any life-limiting illness. She also has severe bone-on-bone DJD of her left knee. She has mild symptoms of DJD in other joints, but nothing like the knee. When you ask her what her life would be like if her left knee didn't hurt, she says, "I'd be a new woman." Pharmacologic treatment of this woman is unlikely to be effective, and would expose her to toxicity. She should be referred early to orthopedics to consider total joint replacement. Patients referred for total joint replacement should have a comprehensive preoperative evaluation, in order to minimize risk and maximize functional recovery.

Tips on Treating Osteoarthritis in Older Adults

- Use a stepwise approach in choosing medications to treat osteoarthritis in older adults, usually starting with acetaminophen or glucosamine/chondroitin, but also consider limited use of NSAIDs, tramadol, and even opioids.
- When using analgesics, stay with a low dose, monitor for side effects, and stop the drug if pain relief does not occur, especially with NSAIDs.
- Orthopedic replacement of knee and hip joints is highly effective in reducing pain and increasing function among properly selected older adults.

Falls

One of the classic syndromes of geriatrics is falls. As we have noted elsewhere, more than a third of community-dwelling adults over age 65 years fall each year. Although most falls are trivial, some cause severe injuries, such as fractures or central nervous system (CNS) injuries, and falls remain a common cause of death in the very old and frail.

Not all falls can be prevented, and the evidence base for prevention and treatment of falls is weak, but there are reasonable approaches. First, primary care clinicians and perhaps other providers should screen for fall risk; the best question is to routinely ask older adults if they have experienced a fall in the last 6 months. If the answer is yes, get details of the fall—where did it happen, what were the circumstances, was there an injury, has the patient changed his or her behavior since, and so on. For these patients, carefully review medications, look for orthostatic hypotension and cognitive impairment, and consider baseline labs and tests.

Another useful office test is the Tinetti get-up-and-go test. In this maneuver, you ask the patient to rise from a chair without using her hands, walk briskly 10 feet, turn around, return to the chair, and sit again. If this can be accomplished safely within 30 seconds, the patient is at low risk of injurious falls. Patients who fail this test and many others may benefit from referral to a physical therapist, for assessment of an appropriate ambulatory assistive device (Moncada, 2011; Tinetti et al., 1994).

Finally, there is evidence that reducing restraints among older adults in nursing homes may reduce the risk of injurious falls (Gulpers et al., 2013).

Tips for Treating Falls in Older Adults

- Screen every older adult with a simple question: Have you fallen in the last 6 months?
- Watch the patient rise from a chair, walk across the room, and come back (Tinetti get-up-and-go test).
- Refer patients at risk for falls to physical therapy.

Polypharmacy

Polpharmacy, or the use of more than one drug at a time, is common in older adults and by itself is not a problem. Many older adults have multiple diseases that require pharmacologic treatment, and some diseases, like systolic heart failure, require multiple medications for evidence-based treatment (Milton, 2008).

Previously, we have indicated that alleviating the patient's load of already-onboard medications is a goal of care. Obviously this requires a careful evaluation. Do not prescribe drugs that have opposing mechanisms of action. For example, cholinesterase inhibitors (donepezil, rivastigmine, galantamine) work by increasing the neurotransmitter acetylcholine in the synaptic cleft; they have only modest effects in older adults with Alzheimer's disease (see Chapter 6). Drugs that are anticholinergic (antimuscarinic) blockers should thus be avoided. These include the directly anticholinergic drugs used to treat urge incontinence, such as oxybutynin, tolterodine, and newer agents, as well as a large number of drugs that have anticholinergic side effects (Hall et al., 2009).

Selected Drugs With Anticholinergic Effect That Are Commonly Prescribed to Older Adults

Directly anticholinergic drugs—benztropine, trihexyphenidyl
Antinausea medicines—meclizine, prochloperazine
Antihistamines—chlorpheniramine, brompheniramine, cyproheptadine, diphenhydramine
Antidepressants—amitriptyline, nortriptyline, desipramine, imipramine, doxepin
Antipsychotics—haloperidol, chlorpromazine, olanzapine, risperidone
Smooth muscle relaxants—cyclobenzaprine, flavoxate
Drugs for urinary incontinence—oxybutynin, tolterodine, darifenacin
Cardiac medicines—captopril, digoxin, diltiazem, furosemide, nifedipine
H_2 blockers—cimetidine, ranitidine
Opioid analgesics—codeine, oxycodone
Corticosteroids—dexamethasone, hydrocortisone, prednisolone

An important role for the geriatric population is to coordinate care. For example, a neurologist prescribes donepezil to an 84-year-old woman with moderate Alzheimer's disease, first 5 mg per day and then 10 mg per day. She also sees an urologist for urge urinary incontinence, who prescribes darifenacin. These drugs have opposite mechanisms of action; each interferes with the other's action. In this case, the most appropriate action is to decide which disease is most important (probably the dementia), and to treat that with a medication, using a nonpharmacologic approach for the incontinence.

Another example of opposing mechanism is the combination of Parkinson drugs with antipsychotics. Parkinson's disease is caused by a deficiency of the central neurotransmitter dopamine, and the main drug strategies in this disease are to increase the level of dopamine—for example, by giving the dopa precursor (carbidopa-levodopa, Sinemet), dopamine agonists (pramipexole or ropinirole), or by inhibiting the metabolism of dopamine (catechol-O-methyltransferase [COMT] or monoamine-oxidase [MAO] inhibitors). All of these treatments seek to either increase the level of dopamine or increase its duration of action. In contrast, all antipsychotics work by acting as dopamine antagonists. These include the first generation, or typical antipsychotics, such as haloperidol or chlorpromazine, as well as the newer atypical antipsychotics, such as risperidone, quetiapine, or ziprasidone. Combining dopamine agonists and antagonists doesn't make any pharmacologic sense, yet it happens commonly in medicine, often with tragic results.

Often, medication is not discontinued after a short interval for its intended purpose. As an example: During an acute hospitalization of an 85-year-old woman with pneumonia, she became delirious and was prescribed risperidone, 0.5 mg, by mouth twice daily. This was likely meant to be a transient pharmacologic intervention, with weaning of the medicine once the delirium resolved and she returned to her assisted-living facility. However, it was continued, and she started showing signs of bradykinesia and rigidity. She was diagnosed with Parkinson's disease and placed on Sinemet. This is incorrect on two accounts. First, she doesn't have Parkinson's disease but rather drug-induced Parkinsonism (DIP). Second, the treatment won't work—you can't fix the dopamine deficit caused by a dopamine antagonist, which is blocking the dopamine receptor, by simply adding back dopamine. The initial drug must be stopped. In this particular case, the drug interaction was not recognized, and she was eventually admitted to a nursing home for hospice care of end-stage Parkinson's disease. Fortunately, the geriatrician at the facility recognized DIP and weaned her off the risperidone. Over the next few weeks, her Parkinson symptoms completely resolved, and the Sinemet was also stopped. Due to the drug combination, she had become remarkably deconditioned, so several weeks of physical therapy ensued, and she was able to return to her assisted-living facility, with much improved function.

On the other hand, polypharmacy is not itself a bad thing. The large majority of older adults with systolic heart failure should take several medications, generally including a loop diuretic, an ACE inhibitor, and a beta blocker. Some should also take aldactone or eplerenone, or even other medications. It is unwise to add multiple cardiac drugs at the same time; much better is stepwise addition of drugs with careful clinical and laboratory monitoring. Also, many older adults have multiple diseases for which pharmacotherapy has clear benefits with acceptable risks. The geriatrician needs to weigh the pros and cons of each drug, particularly as the patient ages and accumulates more disabilities (Milton et al., 2008; Schiff et al., 2011; Steinman & Hanlon, 2010).

Tips in Prescribing Medications for Older Adults

- Avoid combinations of drugs that have opposing mechanisms of action.
- Start low, go slow, but get there, titrating medications to appropriate effect.
- Polypharmacy may be necessary due to multiple medical problems and when evidence demands such an approach, as with systolic heart failure.
- When an older patient becomes ill, always survey the drug list for possible culprits.

Hearing and Visual Impairment

Hearing impairment affects one third of older adults in their 60s and more than 80% of those over age 85 years, although they may not recognize or acknowledge this fact. Medicare will cover a screening audiogram if a physician refers for this test, although Medicare does not cover the cost of hearing aids, which can run to several thousand dollars.

Age-related hearing loss is mostly sensorineural, usually caused by damage to the organ of Corti from aging, noise damage, and genetic causes. Conductive loss is less common, but an example of this would be bilateral cerumen impaction, which is potentially reversible. Sensorineural loss manifests as a loss of high frequencies, where much normal conversation occurs. Hearing loss among older adults is strongly associated with quality of life, cognitive decline, and depression. Sudden unilateral hearing loss suggests more serious pathology and deserves an urgent ear/nose/throat (ENT) referral.

A variety of screening tests have been recommended, including response to a whispered voice, a single question (do you have difficulty hearing?), and a 10-item self-administered questionnaire called the Hearing Handicap Inventory for the Elderly. The best test is an audiogram, which can be accomplished in a primary care physician's office or more commonly by an audiologist. Psychologists can attempt the whisper test or the rubbing fingers test behind the ear, but only as a screen.

Audiologists may recommend a wide range of hearing aids, including behind-the-ear, in-the-ear, and in-the-canal models. These may require substantial dexterity and cognitive abilities, and older adults must be encouraged to make several visits to the audiologist to adjust these complex devices properly, or they will end up in a drawer, unused. Only a minority of older adults who could benefit from hearing aids acquire them, and many of those who do receive them don't use them. There are also other assistive listening devices to help with using the telephone or watching television (Pacala & Yueh, 2012; Walling & Dickson, 2012).

Visual impairment is also a disease of aging: 70% of Americans with severe visual impairment are over age 80 years. Visual loss is associated with depression, social withdrawal, isolation, and falls, and older adults with visual impairment are more likely to be institutionalized.

Screening for visual impairment is easier than for hearing impairment. The use of a standard Snellen chart, available in almost every physician office, is important. Common causes of visual impairment among older adults include age-related macular degeneration, cataracts, glaucoma, and diabetic retinopathy. All of these cause slowly progressive visual loss and require regular visits to an ophthalmologist. For example, patients with macular degeneration are often given an Amsler grid, which is a card with closely spaced horizontal and vertical lines. The patient is urged to look directly at the middle of the grid every day, and if he notes distortion of the lines or scotoma (areas of visual loss), an urgent follow-up is needed. Patients with sudden vision loss also need urgent referral to an ophthalmologist. Primary care physicians can encourage older adults to keep up with these specialist visits, which are covered by the Medicare program.

There are no specific treatments for age-related macular degeneration, although most patients will be prescribed a mixture of antioxidant vitamins, which may reduce progression of the most destructive type of this disease (Lim et al., 2012). Cataracts also have no medical treatment; rather, they are treated surgically, and today this is an office procedure in which the cataract is extracted and an intraocular lens is implanted. This is the most common procedure performed on Medicare patients. Older adults with open angle glaucoma are often prescribed topical eye drops, some of which may cause systemic side effects. For example, topical beta blockers can cause wheezing, heart block, or heart failure, whereas topical sympathomimetics may exacerbate hypertension or CAD. Therefore, the primary care physician needs to include all ocular medications on the drug list of older adults.

Tips for Managing Visual and Hearing Impairment in Older Adults

- Routinely assess for these sensory impairments, because treatment may dramatically improve the quality of life.
- Hearing impairment is best screened with an audiogram, but if you have any suspicion of hearing loss, refer to an audiologist for testing.
- Visual acuity is best screened with a Snellen chart.
- Eye drops can have systemic side effects in older adults.

CONCLUSION

In most cases, primary care of older adults involves coordination of a substantial number of diagnoses and medications. These patients often have multiple physicians, but ideally there is one primary care physician (geriatrician, family physician, or internist) who can coordinate care, often from many clinics and providers. When assessing older adults with cognitive problems, a thorough history must include the medical history and medications. If you suspect that a medical diagnosis or a medication side effect may be causing cognitive impairment, collaborate with the physician. Ideally, mental health professionals would work in teams with primary care physicians, to seamlessly integrate physical and cognitive/emotional aspects of care. This is particularly true for patients with cognitive disorders or affective problems, and for those living in institutions. The next chapter will elaborate on many other problems, as well as these. Careful collaboration, accurate diagnosis, and careful consideration of every drug on the medication list can improve the care of frail older adults.

CHAPTER 10

Behavioral Health Treatment of Older Adults in Primary Care

Catherine Yeager

Primary care is the provision of integrated, accessible health care services by clinicians who are accountable for addressing a large majority of personal health care for all ages.

—*Institute of Medicine* (1996)

It is well known that family physicians and primary care clinics (PCCs) are the "first responders" for individuals in psychological distress, whatever their age and often whatever their condition. To appreciate the scope of the issue, between 1998 and 2003 the percentage of patients receiving mental and behavioral health care in PCCs increased by 154% (Kessler et al., 2005; Mauer & Druss, 2010). What is more, as we have been arguing, over 75% of prescriptions for psychotropic medications are written by nonpsychiatry physicians or other providers (Mark, Levit, & Buck, 2009). Seventy-five percent of individuals seeking help for problems arising from depression do so through their primary care physician (PCP), and it is probably closer to 100% for depressed older adults (Goldman et al., 1999; Institute of Medicine, 2012). As many as 37% of older adults seen in PCCs for other reasons are discovered to have significant depressive symptoms (U.S. Department of Health and Human Services, 1999). Although the stigma regarding mental health treatment certainly contributes to the pervasiveness of undetected mental health problems among older adults, the chief culprit is a combination of (a) lack of access to specialty care, (b) limited transportation, (c) higher Medicare copays for outpatient treatment (i.e., psychotherapy[1]), and (d) lack of awareness that one's symptoms can have a psychiatric undercurrent (Mickus et al., 2000; Unützer et al., 1999; U.S. Department of Health and Humans Services [USDHHS], 1999).

249

So, given that the PCC is the de facto community mental health system in the United States, especially for elders, the question of note is: How well do PCPs diagnose mental and behavioral health conditions? In most studies of adult primary care patients, successful diagnosis of psychological/psychiatric problems has *not* exceeded 50% to 60% (U.S. Preventive Task Force, 2002). Studies focusing only on older adults show similar findings (e.g., Callahan, 2001). Certain mental health issues also go undetected. With older men having the highest suicide rates in the United States (about 30 per 100,000 people), PCPs are unlikely to ask older patients about suicidal thinking (Feldman, Franks, & Duberstein, 2007; Institute of Medicine [IOM], 2012). Indeed, studies of depressed, suicidal older adults have shown that about 70% had made contact with their PCPs within the month before attempting suicide, but their mental status went undetected by their doctors (e.g., Conwell, 1994; Pearson, Conwell, & Lyness, 1997; Simning, Richardson, & Friedman, 2010).

PCPs seem to have good reasons for this state of affairs. They have attributed inadequate identification of mood disorders among elders to lack of time, lack of knowledge, and competing demands of addressing many physical problems in a brief visit (IOM, 1996; Sudak, Roy, & Sudak, 2007). In addition, depressive symptoms and grief, especially, are often misattributed to normal aging (Unützer et al., 1999) and the assumption that the patient "will eventually get over it." With these kinds of assumptions and attitudes, opportunities for effective interventions are lost. Even when older adults receive treatment for mental and behavioral health problems (hereafter referred to as behavioral health care), most receive insufficient care because medication—the treatment of choice in PCC settings—or dosage is inadequate or is not adjusted properly, is stopped too soon, and/or follow-ups are too far apart (USDHHS, 1999; Williams et al., 1999; Young, Klap, Sherbourne, & Wells, 2001).

It is therefore increasingly clear that to reach older adults suffering from psychological distress and frank psychiatric conditions, psychologists and other behavioral health providers must relinquish their private practice offices and specialty care institutions, become proactive, and join the fast-paced, sometimes unpredictable, but real world of true interdisciplinary behavioral health care.

The purpose of this chapter is to describe what psychologists do as members of an interdisciplinary team or a "patient-centered medical home" (PCMH) in the provision of behavioral health care for older adults. First, the history of the PCMH is reviewed and several models that integrate behavioral health care into the PCC to a greater or lesser degree are highlighted. Second, the role of psychologists in PCMH settings, as well as essential areas of expertise, is described. Third, psychological interventions that are brief and effective in PCC settings are presented. And fourth, common problems and crises in PCC and rubrics for stepped care are addressed. Again, this chapter amplifies the core features of health issues raised in Chapter 8 as well as the central medical issues discussed in Chapter 9.

THE DEVELOPMENT OF THE PATIENT-CENTERED MEDICAL HOME

The notion of a medical home has been around since the 1960s (American Academy of Pediatrics [AAP], 1967), created for children with complex medical needs. AAP's medical home model envisioned coordinated, family-centered, continuous, culturally sensitive, whole-person care by a physician-led interdisciplinary team for children with chronic severe illnesses and developmental disabilities. The goal was to increase access to care and decrease the use of emergency rooms for routine or preventable problems. As a result of the medical home, patient outcomes improved, patient and provider satisfaction increased, and health care costs were contained (Sia, Tonniges, & Osterhus, 2004). The medical home model did not spread beyond pediatrics until the past decade, in large measure because the usual fee-for-service arrangement does not reimburse clinicians working as a team. Interest in the medical home model has increased substantially in recent years as a way to contain the national health care budget and improve outcomes for people with multiple chronic medical comorbidities—that comparatively small group of patients who incur the most health care expenditures (Gawande, 2011). About 1% of high-use adults account for over 25% of the whole medical budget. Older adults are a major segment of that population.

Depression is the best example for understanding behavioral health issues that present in PCCs, because depression is so prevalent and is comorbid with most other problems, mental and physical. Depressed older adults, as a group, tend to be physically sicker with multiple medical comorbidities and pain, are frequent overusers of medical services, are less compliant with medical prescriptives, and are more likely to die earlier than their nondepressed peers from medical complications (Elhai, Grubaugh, Richardson, Egede, & Creamer, 2008; Merikangus et al., 2007). Unützer and colleagues (2002; IMPACT[2]) applied the medical home model to treat late-life depression in the PCC. The IMPACT trial targeted depressed elders in PCCs by offering access to a "depression care manager," either a nurse or a psychologist trained to provide education and apply a brief psychotherapy intervention for depression. The depression care manager and PCP collaborated to optimize treatment (including antidepressant medication and/or brief problem-solving therapy). Patients were followed regularly for 12 months. IMPACT showed that the medical home approach had a significant positive effect on depressive symptoms up to 12 months posttrial and beyond (Bruce, Ten Have, Reynolds, Katz, & Schulberg, 2004; Jaeckles, 2009; Nutting et al., 2008; Unützer, Katon, Fan, Schoenbaum, et al., 2009), as well as on cost containment (see Hyer, Scott, & Yeager, 2011).

The AAP, American Academy of Family Physicians, American College of Physicians, and the American Osteopathic Association have jointly produced *Joint Principles of the "Patient Centered Medical Home"* (March 2007), followed by a set of guidelines for PCMH by the National Committee for

Quality Assurance (NCQA, 2011). NCQA defines a PCMH as a model of care that strengthens the clinician–patient relationship by replacing episodic care with coordinated care and a long-term relationship in the PCC setting with a team headed by a PCP. The core of the PCMH is the chronic care model. The team takes collective responsibility for the patient, provides for the patient's health care needs, and arranges for specialty care with other clinicians. A true PCMH will offer embedded behavioral health services. Some PCMHs focus their services on a target group, such as patients with multiple chronic medical comorbidities who also have behavioral health needs that are contributing to: (1) worsening medical condition, (2) poor functioning, (3) treatment noncompliance, and/or (4) overuse of the system. Whether or not a particular PCMH targets the sickest patients, or anyone with behavioral health needs, it is ultimately intended to result in more personalized, coordinated, effective, and efficient care. Integral to the PCMH is the care manager, who coordinates care within the team and with outside specialists, and ensures that the patient complies with treatments and appointments.

In general, the behavioral health professional (BHP) in the PCMH is a clinical psychologist, a licensed professional counselor, or licensed medical social worker who collaborates with the PCMH team in different ways depending on the structure of the model. The PCMH also may retain a psychiatric nurse practitioner or consulting psychiatrist for as-needed assistance for psychotropic medication management or for hands-on management of complex psychiatric cases or serious mental illness with significant medical comorbidities (for these especially difficult-to-manage individuals, see Mauer and Druss [2010] for a description of the *Four Quadrant Model* medical home).

The gold standard for behavioral health in PCCs is the onsite, embedded, collaborative care model in which the BHP is fully integrated into the PCMH team. This enables the PCMH to maintain care continuity for the patient, to increase acceptability of behavioral health services and decrease stigma, and to increase ease of service—especially for older adults who have limited transportation—while realizing cost containment or savings (Blount, 1998; Blount, Schoenbaum, Kathol, Rollman, Thomas, et al., 2007; Hunter & Goodie, 2010). The PRISM-E[3] trial (Krahn, Bartels, Coakley, et al., 2006) evaluated a fully integrated PCMH model against traditional referrals to physically separate, clearly identified behavioral health or substance abuse clinics. Subjects were older adults with depression. Study findings showed that, except for elders with severe depression who had better outcomes in specialty care, remission rates were similar in both groups at 6 and 12 months, suggesting that PCMH offers elderly patients with less severe depression the access and convenience of "one-stop shopping" and comparable clinical outcomes. This was the experience of IMPACT also.

In the gold-standard model, the PCMH psychologist addresses the full spectrum of behavioral health issues that present in PCC settings:

depression; anxiety spectrum disorders; serious mental illness and psychosis; eating disorders; chronic pain; attention-deficit hyperactivity disorder (ADHD) and learning disorders; sleep disorders; sexual dysfunction and relationship problems; bereavement; abuse and domestic violence; health-risk behaviors, such as smoking, substance abuse/addictions, and obesity; as well as dementia-related problems and caregiver burden. Not only is there regular communication among all PCMH team members via daily face-to-face contact in "huddles," in which that day's patients are reviewed before clinic starts, or on-the-fly consultations, but there also is a shared treatment plan and medical record.

If fully embedded behavioral health care is not possible, an alternative model is behavioral health coordination by the PCC care manager with BHPs either co-located in the same physical structure or at separate nearby locations. Unfortunately, this arrangement does not allow for a shared medical record, and standards of care are not necessarily the same because both the health care entities and BHPs may be in independent practices. Given these realities, excellent communication and care coordination are essential to achieving the tenets of PCMH.

Alternatively, the Care Management Model, a less comprehensive version of the PCMH, can be adopted in smaller PCC settings. The BHP (often a master's-level counselor, medical social worker, or nurse) focuses on specific problems, such as depression (Williams et al., 2007). This model is typified by the IMPACT trial mentioned previously and the RESPECT-Depression[4] trial (Dietrich, et al., 2004), which used a care manager to apply specific brief interventions and psychoeducation to depressed adults. In this scenario, the PCP refers the patient to the care manager, who follows a standard protocol for assessment, planning, and care facilitation, and communicates back to the PCP and possibly to a consulting prescriber—psychiatrist or advanced practice nurse. The treatment plan and medical record are shared among the team members. This model, although shown to be effective for specific subpopulations of patients in need of behavioral health care, does not meet the goals of PCMH and cannot offer comprehensive behavioral health services to the patient.

Gold-Standard Model: Embedded Behavioral Health Care

- Collaborative care model: physician, nurse case manager, allied health staff
- BHP is licensed, onsite, and fully integrated into the PCMH team
- BHP sees full spectrum of patients and problems; collaborates on psychopharmacology as needed
- Daily huddles and on-the-fly communications about the team's patients
- Shared treatment plan uses "Watch and Wait" as well as stepped-care models
- Nurse case manager arranges for specialty care as needed and communicates findings back to the PCMH team
- Shared medical record

Intermediate Model: Co-Located Behavioral Health Care

- Collaborative care model: physician, nurse case manager, ±allied health staff
- BHP is licensed and co-located in same building or nearby location
- BHP *may* see full spectrum of patients and problems
- Nurse case manager arranges for specialty care as needed and communicates findings back to the team; communication with BHP may be weekly or biweekly
- Treatment plan *may* be collaborative
- Medical record is not shared between PCC setting and BHP

Care Management Model

- Collaborative care model: physician, nurse case manager
- BHP is master's-level counselor
- May have consulting psychopharmacology prescriber (e.g., nurse practitioner)
- BHP targets brief, scripted interventions for specific problems (e.g., depression)
- Nurse case manager arranges for specialty care as needed and communicates findings back to the physician
- Shared treatment plan for patients with the target behavioral health problem
- Shared medical record

ROLE AND EXPERTISE OF THE PRIMARY CARE PSYCHOLOGIST

The American Psychological Association recognizes the increasingly important and diverse roles of psychologists practicing in the medical profession and has recently published *Guidelines for Psychological Practice in Health Care Delivery Systems* (APA, 2013). These guidelines address professional identity, privileges, integrative and collaborative care responsibilities, and competency related to scope of practice within the health care delivery system. Few specifics are offered at this time, however, including issues of patient privacy, confidentiality, and information disclosure in the context of team care.

The psychologist who works in the PCMH wears a number of hats, some of which tap established skills and others that demand new skills relevant to PCC. Below is a brief list of responsibilities in no particular order (from McDaniel and Fogarty, 2009). The issues of quick assessment, supportive care, determining what can be done at the moment, triaging for later care, behavioral interventions, and interacting with families are especially important.

Psychologist Responsibilities in the PCMH

1. Identify and address emotional concomitants to medical disorders.
2. Advise PCMH team about the best ways to interact with a difficult-to-manage patient because of psychiatric comorbidities, low cognitive functioning/dementia, and/or personality-based resistance.
3. Consult with medical and behavioral health specialists outside the PCMH regarding a particular patient.

4. Determine whether a patient's behavioral health needs exceed the services available in the PCC and oversee referral for specialty services in psychopharmaco-therapy, psychotherapy, or health psychology.
5. Screen for mood disorders, anxiety, substance abuse, cognitive impairment, and other biopsychosocial disorders that may be overlooked in PCC evaluations.
6. Provide supportive care and educational services to patients who are having difficulty participating effectively in their medical care.
7. Offer specialized interventions for smoking, obesity, and other common behavioral problems in the general PCC population.
8. Offer specialized interventions for older adults, such as capacity assessment, group cognitive retraining, and caregiver support.
9. Work with family members and with the sequelae of family dynamics when the family is not or cannot be present.
10. Offer behavioral interventions for individuals whose medical diagnoses call for treatments that require a substantial behavioral component, such as diabetes, asthma, chronic infectious disease, heart disease, traumatic brain injury.
11. Develop outcomes assessment and program evaluation systems.
12. Aid in the design of research protocols.

The PCMH psychologist typically will see patients in the same examination rooms used by medical staff, and visits are limited to 30 minutes or less. That said, older adults may require more time (e.g., 45 minutes) in session both to ensure that the patient has processed the gist of the work in session, and because older adults expect and appreciate conversation/storytelling. The typical behavioral health intervention is brief and problem focused. The intervention and follow-up might take place in four or fewer sessions that may occur as infrequently as one time per month. If the presenting problem is predicted to need a more intensive level of care, the psychologist must then determine whether the patient has transportation to attend specialty care appointments in another setting and whether the patient is willing to seek behavioral health care outside the PCC office.

Older adults often have problems with behavioral health professionals in general. Some older patients would rather refuse behavioral health care than be referred out to a specialty practice. Attitudes are hardened by fears of loss of independence and concerns about decline, especially cognitive decline, as well as annoyance at having life unduly disrupted. If the older adult does agree to a specialty referral, the transfer should be a warm hand-off to the next provider with progress monitoring by the PCMH care coordinator; if not, a record of possible problems and an alertness for future interventions must be communicated to the next behavioral health professional.

Core Competencies

To practice competently in PCC settings, psychologists will have core training in clinical health psychology/behavioral medicine and integrated health care in which acute problem solving is emphasized. They will have developed clinical competencies in evidence-based assessment, suicide risk assessment, psychopharmacology, brief treatment interventions, relaxation, biofeedback, and/or hypnosis, preventive interventions and health behavior change, group therapy, and outcomes assessment (see Belar, 2011; Blount, 2008; Kelly & Coons, 2012; McDaniel & Forgarty, 2009). For PCC settings with a large geriatric population, proficiency in geropsychology, including cognitive assessment, capacity determination, bereavement, and caregiver interventions for patients with dementia, as well as knowledge of the biopsychosocial aspects of normal aging, are essential for competent practice. The typical interaction, assessment, and intervention with an older adult matches other age problems in process and form but differs in the sensitivity to and practice of the later-life issues described here.

Perhaps the most important professional competency is the ability for the psychologist to communicate and work collaboratively with PCPs, physician specialists, and allied health professionals. Psychologists and PCPs determine a patient's care together. This approach is very different from private practice, in which the psychologist alone determines the behavioral health care provided to the patient, and may not be involved at all with a patient's medical comorbidities, or perhaps involved in a consultative way. Integral to the psychologist's role in integrated care settings is the ability to assist medical providers in appreciating the patient's illness, and her ability to manage it, in the context of the patient's psychiatric comorbidities, her self-perception and developmental stage, her family, culture, and community. Essentially, the psychologist in the PCMH not only needs to have excellent patient care and problem-solving skills, but also skills that enhance the medical team's approach to diagnosis, treatment, and measurement of outcomes.

For those psychologists who are part of a primarily geriatric PCMH, the Geriatric Interdisciplinary Team Training Program (GITT; Fulmer, Hyer, & Flaherty, 2005) may be useful. The GITT program is designed to promote the development of effective patient management across multiple disciplines, with an emphasis on older patients who have multiple comorbidities. Teams are capable of creating good or bad outcomes. A well-functioning team is capable of achieving results with patients that individuals who constitute the team cannot achieve in isolation. The same variables that affect functioning are ones that apply to the team, internally (personal/professional and intrateam) and externally (organizational and team maintenance). At some point, well-functioning teams learn from themselves and react better to conflict.

Clearly, the information listed in Table 10.1 is excessive for many clinics. That said, it is a model for optimal care, as it posits that all professionals have a place at the table, all require respect, conflict is present and natural in even the best of teams, and a process for clarification and communication is important.

TABLE 10.1 Geriatric Interdisciplinary Team Training Example

Generic GITT Goals	PCMH GITT Targets	Team Modifications
Clarify objectives	Team identified target goals	Leader requested and identified targets
Review team roles	Advanced nurse practitioners conduct meetings with input from all team members Physicians make strategic input	Pharmacist, hospice asked to partake in meetings; new team members oriented and introduced
Set agenda	Issues set for current group and for past incomplete targets	Leader sets agenda
Work through agenda	Agenda followed for average 20 cases/wk	Focus on time and on key problem/return patients
Evaluate meeting	Feedback from members on day as well as follow-up issues	Leader requests input on meeting
Participate	Leader encourages all to partake	All requested to make input
Address/handle conflict	Conflict was minimal and often not addressed	Conflict was minimal
Team communication	Team communicates in meeting and sets a "footprint" for all communication for 24-hr/7-day week	Team improves on communication over the months
Care planning	Team makes input and decides on division of labor	Leader sets the tasks, although members may volunteer
Multidimensional assessment	Disciplines accept tasks and make input; this is both family based and medically based	All make input regarding assessment issues

Psychopharmacology

Working knowledge of psychopharmacology is essential to integrated practice, as psychologists are frequently called on by PCPs to provide information about specific medications for various psychiatric conditions, to assess for side effects, to measure effectiveness, and to evaluate alternatives when the drug of choice is less than effective (McGrath & Sammons, 2011). As mentioned earlier, upward of 70% of psychotropic medications are prescribed by PCPs, but the majority of family medicine residencies offer no formal training in clinical psychopharmacology (Bazaldua et al., 2005). At the least, PCMH psychologists should be familiar with classes of psychotropic medications; their uses, adverse reactions and side effects; methods and routes of administration; and dosing ranges.

The effects of aging cause older adults' bodies to metabolize and clear medicines differently compared with younger people. Age-related changes in the liver, kidneys, central nervous system (CNS), and heart are among the contributing factors that cause older adults to be more vulnerable to side effects and overdose. It is especially important to be familiar with the CNS side effects of commonly prescribed drugs, such as sedation, agitation/anxiety, balance problems, mood alteration, or cognitive clouding. Knowledge of common drug–drug interactions is useful as well; two drugs taken together can cause unwanted effects or make either medicine's effects more or less potent. Drug–drug interactions also may be caused by mixing alcohol, nutritional supplements or herbal products, or over-the-counter medicines with prescribed drugs (see American Geriatrics Society (2012); Beers Criteria Update Expert Panel and the Improved Prescribing in the Elderly Tool or IPET (Naugler, Brymer, Stolee, & Arcese, 2000).

The issue of polypharmacy is of particular concern for older patients who, compared with younger individuals, have more medical conditions for which drug therapies are prescribed. It has been estimated that 20% of Medicare beneficiaries have five or more chronic conditions and 50% take five or more medications (Tinetti, Bogardus, & Agostini, 2004). And older adults are especially impacted by polypharmacy.

- Polypharmacy increases the potential for drug–drug interactions.
- Polypharmacy is independently associated with increased risk of an adverse drug event.
- Polypharmacy is an independent risk factor for hip fractures in older adults, especially if one of the drugs is associated with falls risk (e.g., CNS-active drugs).
- Polypharmacy increases the possibility of prescribing "cascades," that is, an adverse drug effect is misinterpreted as a new medical condition and additional drugs are then prescribed to treat it.
- Polypharmacy can lead to medication nonadherence.
- Nonadherence can be exacerbated by cognitive deficits resulting from polypharmacy.

A balance is required between over- and underprescribing medication and PCPs are often challenged by the need to match the complex needs of their older patients with those of disease-specific clinical practice guidelines. The Boyd et al. (2005) study was cited previously as one example in which professional guidelines and reasonable care clash; several medical diagnoses suggest several medications. An older woman with this constellation of four or more diseases is at twice the risk of having a depressive disorder or depression plus anxiety than her healthy peers. Her PCP, therefore, is concerned about the risks of adding an antidepressant and/or anxiolytic to the medication mix. In PCMH, a psychologist will be consulted and a careful unfolding of a care plan can be applied. Brief behavioral interventions will be indispensible in these all-too-common PCC cases.

Assessment

Integral to PCMH is evidence-based initial, follow-up, and outcome behavioral health assessments. There are six major clinical domains that are relevant to the PCMH psychologist who sees older adults: mood, behavior, cognition, daily functioning, quality of life, and caregiver burden. These domains can be assessed in clinic by the screening staff (medical technician, RN, or LPN) while the patient is waiting, so that the psychologist has data in hand at the start of the visit. Many of these scales are also addressed in Chapter 12.

As depression and anxiety are the most common presenting behavioral health problems, and there is a mandate by the U.S. Preventive Task Force (2009) for all PCC settings to screen for depression, numerous evidence-based screening tools are now available. As outlined in the assessment chapter, we apply several common scales. They include the Patient Health Questionnaire (PHQ) family of measures: the PHQ-9 for Depression or the very brief PHQ-2; the Generalized Anxiety Disorder-7 (GAD-7) for generalized anxiety; and the PHQ-15 for somatic symptoms (see systematic review of all PHQ measures: Kroenke, Spitzer, Williams, & Löwe, 2010). The Geriatric Depression Scale (GDS; Yesavage, Brink, Rose, et al., 1983) was developed specifically to assess depressive symptoms in older adults. There is a short form, the GDS 5/15, a 15-item questionnaire that uses the first five items as a screener (Weeks, McGann, Michaels, & Pennix, 2003). The GDS and GDS 5/15 are preferred for older patients because the measures take into account the fact that depressive symptoms can present somewhat differently in this age group, with less irritability and negative thinking, and more sleep and health problems. Indeed, if the older patient does not meet a cut score for a depressive disorder in a given measure, attention still should be paid to the types of symptoms endorsed—insomnia and increased pain or malaise could indicate subsyndromal depression (Hyer, Yeager, Hyer, & Scott, 2010).

Assessment of anxiety in older adults can be accomplished with several brief measures, most of which were developed on younger adults, including the GAD-7, mentioned above, and the Beck Anxiety Inventory-Primary Care (BAI-PC; Beck, Steer, Ball, Ciervo, & Kabat, 1997). The BAI-PC is notable for assessing symptoms of posttraumatic stress disorder (PTSD) in addition to generalized anxiety (Mori et al., 2003). A newer, 20-item self-report measure, the Geriatric Anxiety Inventory (Pachana et al., 2007), also can be used in PCC. This measure has been evaluated on elders with cognitive impairment and delivers results similar to that of cognitively intact elders regarding the presence/absence of anxiety (Boddice, Pachana, & Byrne, 2008). Worry, a hallmark symptom of generalized anxiety in the elderly, can be assessed with the 16-item Penn State Worry Questionnaire (PSWQ; Meyer, Miller, Metzger, & Borkovec, 1990). Norms for older adults for the PSWQ are lacking, however. The Panic Frequency Questionnaire (PFQ; Antony & Swinson, 2000) is a qualitative measure of nature, number, intensity, and frequency of panic symptoms. The PFQ is useful for formulating treatment targets and collecting outcome data, and is brief enough for PCC settings.

TABLE 10.2 Brief Depression and Anxiety Scales

Name	Purpose	Age Range	Citation
Beck Depression Inventory-Primary Care (BDI-PC)	Depression: 7 items, 5 min	Adult self-report	Beck, Guth, Steer & Ball, 1997
Center for Epidemiologic Studies Depression Scale (CESD-20)	Depression: 20 items, 5 min	Adult, older adult self-report	Eaton, Smith Ybarra, et al., 2004
Composite International Diagnostic Interview-Primary Care (CIDI-PC)	Depression & anxiety: 10 items, 5 min	Adult self-report	Goldberg, Prisciandaro, Williams, 2012
Beck Anxiety Inventory-Primary Care (BAI-PC)	Anxiety: 7 items, 5 min.	Adult self-report	Beck, Steer, Ball, Ciervo, & Kabat, 1997
Panic Frequency Questionnaire (PFQ)	Panic: 6 items, 5 min	Adult self-report	Antony & Swinson, 2000

Screening for cognitive impairment should be routine in PCCs. These measures would be administered by the psychologist in session and not by support staff. The Montreal Cognitive Assessment (MoCA; Nasreddine, Phillips, Bédirian, et al., 2005) is recommended for older adults over the Mini-Mental Status Exam (MMSE; Folstein, Folstein, & McHugh, 1975) because the MoCA provides a broader picture of neuropsychological functioning by assessing eight domains (attention and concentration, executive skills (cognitive flexibility and verbal fluency), abstraction, memory, language, visuoconstructional skills, calculations, and orientation); it is also more sensitive and specific than the MMSE in detecting mild cognitive impairment and early dementia (Luis, Keegan, & Mullin, 2009; Smith, Gildeh, & Holmes 2007). The MoCA takes 10 to 15 minutes to administer and offers three versions to retest for cognitive changes over time. The MMSE remains a staple in PCCs to assess cognition in individuals who are more impaired.

On occasion, the PCMH psychologist may be asked to do a more extensive cognitive assessment of the older adult. The Wechsler Abbreviated Scale of Intelligence-Second Edition (WASI-IV; Wechsler, 2011) and Repeatable Battery of the Assessment of Neuropsychological Status (RBANS; Randolph,

Tierney, Mohr, & Chase, 1997) are adequate for this task and together will take approximately 1.5 hours to administer depending on the patient's degree of impairment. Most often, a full neuropsychological assessment is not necessary to obtain sufficient data to make an MCI (mild cognitive impairment) or dementia diagnosis and to create a practical treatment plan for patient and caregiver. Again, these are addressed in Chapter 12.

TABLE 10.3 Brief Cognitive Assessments

Name	Purpose	Age Range	Citation
Montreal Cognitive Assessment (MoCA)	Cognitive dysfunction: 8 subtests, 15–20 min	Adult, older adult—clinician administered	Nasreddine et al., 2005
Mini-Mental Status Exam (MMSE)	Cognitive dysfunction: 11 tasks, 10 min	Adult, older adult—clinician administered	Folstein et al., 1975
The 7-Minute Cognitive Screen	Cognitive dysfunction: 4 subtests, 7 min	Older adult—clinician administered	Solomon et al., 1998
Mini-Cog	Cognitive dysfunction: 2 subtests, 5 min	Older adult—clinician administered	Borson, Scanlan, Brush, Vitallano, & Dokmak, 2000

The screen must include an assessment of functional impairment. There are several brief measures that can target activities of daily living (ADL). As a rule, measures of functioning require an informant who knows the patient well. The Functional Activities Questionnaire (FAQ; Pfeffer, Kurosaki, Harrah, Chance, & Filos, 1982) assesses independent ADL that require good executive skills. The Caregiver Assessment of Function and Upset (CAFU; Gitlin et al., 2005) assesses both independent and basic ADL, as well as caregiver burden. In addition, the PCMH psychologist who sees dementia patients will be mindful of the caregiver's level of stress and, perhaps in a separate visit, assess the caregiver for degree of burden, depression and anxiety, and safety (e.g., elder abuse). There are a variety of measures that tap caregiver burden, the most commonly used of which is the Zarit Caregiver Burden Interview (Zarit, Reever, & Bach-Peterson, 1980). For caregiving spouses, it is also necessary to keep a lookout for any change in mood, cognition, and functional ability, as the spouse also may be covertly deteriorating. Any of the measures listed in this chapter also can be administered to the caregiver. For a compendium of caregiver assessment measures that are practical and that address the multidimensional aspects of the caregiving experience, see *Selected Caregiver Assessment Measures: A Resource Inventory for Practitioners*, 2nd Edition (Family Caregiver Alliance, 2012).

TABLE 10.4 Brief Measures of Functioning and Caregiver Burden

Name	Purpose	Age Range	Citation
Functional Activities Questionnaire (FAQ)	IADL: 10 items, 5 min	Adult, older adult—informant report	Pfeffer et al., 1982
Caregiver Assessment of Function and Upset (CAFU)	IADL, ADL, caregiver burden: 11 tasks, 10 min	Adult, older adult—informant report	Gitlin et al., 2005
Lawton Instrumental Activities of Daily Living Scale	IADL: 8 items, 5 min	Adult, older adult—informant report	Lawton & Brody, 1969
Activities of Daily Living-Prevention Instrument (ADL-PI)	IADL and mobility: 20 items, 10 min	Older adult, caregiver report	Ferris et al., 2006
Activities of Daily Living Scale	ADL: 6 items, 5 min	Adult, older adult—informant report	Katz, Ford, Moskowitz, Jackson, & Jaffe, 1963
Zarit Caregiver Burden Interview	Caregiver burden	Adult, older adult—self report	Zarit et al., 1980

There are a number of other self-report measures that can be used to gather data quickly in the first visit and further on in treatment. The measures chosen should be based on the referral question or chief complaint. Many of the brief, evidence-based measures have not been designed specifically for older adults, so the psychologist will have to decide the appropriateness of a given measure based on the patient's age, cognitive functioning, and the likelihood that it can capture the signs, symptoms, and behaviors as manifested by older adults.

TABLE 10.5 Other Brief Psychological Measures for Older Adults in Primary Care

Name	Purpose	Age Range	Citation
Epworth Sleepiness Scale (ESS)	Daytime sleepiness: 8 items, 5 minutes	Adult self-report	Johns, 1994
Pittsburgh Sleep Quality Index (PSQI)	Sleep quality, insomnia: 19 items, 5–10 minutes	Adult self-report	Buysse, Reynolds, Monk, Berman, & Kupfer, 1989
Alcohol Use Disorders Identification Test (AUDIT-C)	Alcohol use: 10 items, 5 minutes	Adult self-report	Bush, Kivlahan, McDonell, Fihn, & Bradley, 1998
Quality of Life Inventory (QoLI)	QoL: 16 items: 5 minutes	Adult self-report	Frisch et al., 2005
Behavior and Symptom Identification Scale (BASIS-32)	QoL and distressing behaviors: 32 items, 10 minutes	Adult self-report	Eisen, Wilcox, Leff, Schaefer, & Culhane, 1999

Until recently, fear of falling was little appreciated as a cause of increased fall risk in elders. About one third of those 65 years and older will experience at least one fall each year and almost 40% of them will be admitted to a hospital for treatment (Centers for Disease Control [CDC], 2008). Furthermore, falls are the leading cause of injury-related death and the most common cause of nonfatal injuries and hospital admissions for trauma (CDC, 2011). Suffering a fall, even when injury does not occur, often causes the older adult to restrict activities to avoid the risk of another fall. Fear of falling may develop, especially among patients with anxiety, and this has been found to increase the probability of falling again, irrespective of the actual risk. Similarly, disparity between actual and perceived fall risk contributes to risk mainly through psychological pathways (Gagnon & Flint, 2003). Lachman, Howland, and Tennstedt (1998) developed the Survey of Activities and Fear of Falling in the Elderly (SAFE), which examines 11 activities of daily living, instrumental activities of daily living, mobility tasks, and social activities, using the questions listed below for each activity. (See Chapters 8 and 9 for more falls discussion.)

Survey of Activities and Fear of Falling in the Elderly (SAFE)

1. Do you currently do [the activity]? (yes/no)
2. If you do the activity, when you do it how worried are you that you might fall? (not at all, a little, somewhat, or very worried)
3. If you do not do the activity, do you not do it because you are worried that you might fall? (not at all, a little, somewhat, or very worried)
4. If you do not do the activity because of worry, are there also other reasons that you do not do it? (specify)
5. If you are not worried, what are the reasons you do not do it? (specify)
6. Compared to five years ago, would you say that you do it more, about the same, or less than you used to?

ADL to assess with the above questions:

Go to the store	Visit a friend or relative
Prepare simple meals	Reach for something over your head
Take a tub bath	Go to a place with crowds
Get out of bed	Walk several blocks outside
Take a walk for exercise	Bend down to get something
Go out when it is slippery	

Lachman et al. (1998)

Watch and Wait Versus Assessment/Treatment in 30 Minutes or Less

In this chapter, we discussed the need for clear-headed and quick input regarding delicate and often ongoing problems in the PCCs. This may fly in the face of the Watch and Wait model, as "wait" is the Janus-face standard that makes a difference in care. In fact, the model is the same. The core interventions of Watch and Wait involve psychoeducation, monitoring, allying, motivational interviewing, and formulating a case. These do not change. The psychologist is dealing with the patient/family and the other staff as well as coordinating care for behavioral health issues. This is not easy, and requires a "making haste slowly" approach. Setting the stage, gathering commitment, fostering hope, and modeling tolerance are critical skills. If the psychologist is unfamiliar with Watch and Wait, and unclear about brief, problem-focused assessment and intervention in a PCC setting, the experience will be frustrating at the least, and even overwhelming.

A beauty of the stepped-care and Watch and Wait models is that they embrace subsyndromal symptoms that often respond very well to brief interventions. One model used in PCC that applies a stepped-care strategy that included Watch and Wait is delineated by O'Donohue et al. (2006) and Hunter et al. (2009). They propose an heuristic for understanding and intervening effectively in the PCMH: The 5A's—Assess, Advise, Agree, Assist, and Arrange. The 5A's are based on the Goldstein, Whitlock, and DePue (2004) model for assessment and intervention across a range of problems seen in PCC. Use of this approach is an iterative process; the 5A's help keep the focus of visits on the referral question/chief complaint and enable the patient and/or caregiver to leave the visit with a plan of action. Subsequent visits are guided by the patient's progress with the agreed-upon *action plan*.

TABLE 10.6 The 5A's of Assessment and Intervention for Behavioral Health in Primary Care

Assess	Gather information on the physical symptoms, emotions, thoughts, behaviors, and environmental context to determine variables associated with patient's symptoms and functioning. On the basis of patient's values and degree of control over his environment, determine what is changeable to improve symptoms and functioning.
Advise	Describe to patient the options for intervention and the anticipated outcomes based on the data gathered during assessment.
Agree	Patient decides on a course of action based on the options discussed. Or patient rejects the options presented, he/she generates alternatives. Patient also may defer deciding on an action plan to discuss options with family.
Assist	This is the formal intervention. Help patient implement behavior change through learning new information, developing new skills, and/or overcoming environmental or personal barriers. Reinforcement and occasional retrenchment can occur over several visits, often several weeks apart. Interim outcome assessments (e.g., PHQ-9, GAD-7) are helpful here.
Arrange	The follow-up plan is determined here. Will follow-up be with the PCMH psychologist? The PCP? Will the patient need a referral to specialty behavioral health? These questions should be addressed at each subsequent visit should the patient remain with the BHP. For BHP follow-up, the psychologist should discuss the focus of the next appointment (e.g., homework).

In addition, the already mentioned stepped-care model means that services are provided, outcomes are tracked, and then services are adjusted—lack of improvement or worsening status suggests that additional or different biopsychosocial approaches may be needed in the care plan. Care, therefore, is not static, but rather responsive to individual needs. Watching a patient over time is *not* nontreatment; to the contrary, especially with the use of nurses or the telephone, it is good care, every bit as effective as individual care in a psychiatry clinic. So at each visit, the psychologist will consider whether the degree of progress, or lack thereof, necessitates referral to specialty behavioral health care or additional special services, such as nutrition counseling, sleep study, physical therapy, neuropsychological assessment, and so on. The action plan that emerges from the 5A's approach should be concise, personalized, and integrated into the patient's overall treatment plan. The psychologist reviews the care plan with the rest of the PCMH team, including sharing ancillary information that may impact the patient's follow-through, so all team members can monitor and coach the patient at subsequent visits.

COMMON BEHAVIORAL HEALTH INTERVENTIONS IN PRIMARY CARE

Given the goal of applying brief, targeted treatments in PCC, certain behavioral health interventions are more effective than others in this setting. Described below are 11 interventions that are especially useful in PCC for a wide range of problems (see DiTomasso, Golden, & Morris, 2010; Hunter, Goodie, Oordt, & Dobmeyer, 2009; O'Donohue, Cummings, Cucciare, Runyan, & Cummings, 2007; Robinson & Reiter, 2007). Throughout the book, we have attended to these in various ways.

- Behavior activation/pleasant events scheduling
- Relaxation training
- Mindfulness
- Goal setting
- Cognitive disputation
- Problem solving
- ABC analysis (e.g., thought records, behavior tracking)
- Self-monitoring
- Motivational interviewing
- Stimulus control
- Assertive communication

Behavior Activation/Pleasant Events

Two very important interventions in brief treatment settings are behavioral activation and scheduling pleasant activities, including socialization. In fact, behavioral activation, especially exercise, is an essential component of any PCC intervention for depression, anxiety, poor sleep, chronic pain, cognitive decline, fear of falling, weight gain, and/or chronic disease management, such as diabetes and cardiovascular disease. At times this intervention should be made with PCP input, as it is best designed within the scope of a patient's physical capacity and almost always helps. The focus of pleasant events scheduling is to motivate the patient to move, to get distracted from stress and negative perspectives, to attain a sense of joy and calm, to gain a sense of belonging through social inclusion, and to improve overall quality of life. Often older adults need assistance in coming up with activities; family members can be very helpful here.

Relaxation Training

Relaxation training is among the easiest and most versatile interventions to teach patients. Techniques include diaphragmatic breathing (especially heart rate variability [HRV] breathing biofeedback—see Lehrer & Vaschillo, 2008; Song & Lehrer, 2003), progressive muscle relaxation, and visual imagery. Relaxation is effective in the treatment of anxiety, panic, rumination associated with depression, insomnia, anger, PTSD, chronic pain, and other issues in which physiological arousal is a problem. When the patient's spouse or caregiver is taught these techniques alongside the patient, the spouse or caregiver becomes a coach who can remind and encourage the patient to practice outside the exam room. Indeed, relaxation training is so versatile that it can be taught to individuals with mild-to-moderate dementia, with their caregivers as coaches (Kraus et al., 2008; O'Connor, Ames, Gardner, & King, 2009).

It is important to note that many older adults have no experience with relaxation training and in fact have never developed focused attention on their physiology, including awareness and control of muscle tension and controlling breathing rate and volume. For them, it is important to take adequate time to teach body awareness so that they can buy into and benefit from relaxation training. A before/after relaxation self-rating exercise (rate tension/anxiety on a scale of 0–10) can be especially helpful to increase body awareness. For all patients, relaxation techniques should be taught and practiced during the office visit. A few moments should be taken in subsequent visits to ensure that the patient continues to do the technique correctly.

Mindfulness Practice

Mindfulness describes a special kind of attention that directs the person to experience not the past, not the future, but the present moment. Baer's definition (2003, p. 125) is apt: "Mindfulness is the nonjudgmental observation of the ongoing stream of internal and external stimuli as they arise." Acceptance of what "is" is integral to the concept of mindfulness. Steven Hayes (Acceptance and Commitment Therapy: 2004) and others (e.g., Dialectical Behavior Therapy: Linehan, 1993) have developed interventions that draw on principles of mindful thinking, acceptance of the self "as is," and training oneself to stop experiential avoidance and increase emotional flexibility. Mindfulness meditation, which requires practice to prevent attention from wandering, can be cultivated through diaphragmatic breathing by having the patient focus on changes in muscle tension or other physical sensations as breath flows through the body. This can be done through movement, too. The practice of mindfulness meditation is typically applied in group format (see Kabat-Zinn, 2005). Mindfulness training is especially effective when the goal is to reduce emotional reactivity; for example, anxiety, chronic pain, chronic disease management, and cancer. Indeed, a recent study by Rosenkranz and colleagues (2013) showed that mindfulness meditation techniques reduce poststress inflammatory cytokines, tumor necrosis factor-alpha, and interleukin-8, which are sensitive to psychological stress. They propose that mindfulness meditation can have a positive impact on chronic inflammatory conditions, such as rheumatoid arthritis, psoriasis, inflammatory bowel disease, and asthma. For more on introducing mindfulness-based interventions in PCC, see Robinson, Gould, and Strosahl (2010).

Goal Setting

This intervention works with fast- or slow-paced case formulation. It is a staple in PCC because goal setting is useful for a wide variety of problems, including illness management, social isolation, and poor lifestyle habits. Goal setting is broadly applicable, and is especially useful for older adults who are showing cognitive dysfunction. Often the patient can state the complaint, but cannot see the way clear to make a change. The patient can be assisted in several ways: operationalize the goal into a doable form with the patient's help, redefine unrealistic or long-term goals into attainable small or short-term goals, assess with the patient whether stated goals are value driven or are supposed to satisfy someone or something else, clarify priorities, define realistic time frames, and recruit family members to support the patient. With the PCMH team available as coaches and cheerleaders to whom the patient will be accountable, important behavioral and physical health goals are more likely to be achieved.

Cognitive Disputation

Cognitive disputation—the use of direct questions, logical reasoning, and persuasion—is an abridged approach to cognitive behavioral therapy (CBT) that is more appropriate than traditional CBT in PCC settings, as CBT requires more time and depth than is practical. Hunter and colleagues (2009) recommend assessing relevant cognitions in three areas: predictions, expectations, and evaluations. Distorted or obstructive thinking patterns that may be contributing to the complaint are then examined with the patient. If the patient is open to questioning unhelpful thoughts, the psychologist can teach how to examine and dispute these thoughts and give homework (e.g., thought records or Activating Event–Belief or Behavior–Consequence [ABC] exercises; see Appendix B). The psychologist can then coach the patient how to recognize and dispute negative thought patterns and adopt other ways of thinking and behaving that are more consistent with the patient's values and goals. This intervention is most effective with older adults who are psychologically minded.

Problem-Solving Strategies

Teaching simple problem-solving skills and modeling problem solving for patients can be highly effective for poor compliance, interpersonal difficulties, poor assertiveness or communication, and for jump-starting a care plan for depression treatment. SOLVED (Cully & Teten, 2008) is a six-step problem-solving model that is easily applied in PCC settings.

SOLVED Rubric for Problem Solving

S: Select the problem.

O: Open yourself (brainstorm) to all possible solutions without being critical.

L: List the pros and cons of each option, eliminating solutions that are impractical.

V: Verify the best solution through rank ordering of logical options.

E: Enact the plan by identifying the steps necessary to carry out the solution. Actions may need to be broken down into small steps to encourage goal attainment.

D: Decide if the plan works. If the outcome is positive, tweak as necessary and monitor patient for improvement in symptoms.

Cully and Teten (2008)

After selecting and implementing the action plan, if the outcome is not favorable, have the patient select another option and go through the steps again. This intervention will span at least two visits. When the problem is treatment compliance, outcome markers—such as blood pressure, blood sugar, weight/body mass index (BMI), or decreased medication dosages—are easily available in the PCMH and sharing these markers with the patient is reinforcing. When the problem is interpersonal, invite the involved person, often a family member, to come to a visit so that the patient and the other person might solve the problem together. For depression treatment, problem solving with the patient is especially effective when implementing behavioral-activation interventions.

ABC Analysis

Self-analysis is one of the tenets of cognitive therapy and a core intervention in brief therapy. In PCC, self-analysis is made simple by teaching the patient the ABC model: Activating Event—Belief or Behavior—Consequences. Set out as a table, the ABC model would look like this:

TABLE 10.7   ABC Model

(A) Activating Event	(B) Beliefs/Behavior	(C) Consequences
Write down the event or situation that triggered your thoughts and feelings	Write down the thoughts that went through your head when the activating event occurred (or after it)	**Actions** How did you act then? **Emotions** What did you feel then?

The ABC model is an appropriate intervention when the chief complaint is lifestyle change, disease management, anger, anxiety, and others. Self-analysis is contraindicated for patients with significant cognitive impairment.

Self-Monitoring

Self-monitoring is intended to help patients reach their goals. This intervention is commonly used to track habit and lifestyle changes (e.g., sleep diaries, exercise logs, food diaries, smoking logs, blood sugar and blood pressure logs). Indeed, self-monitoring is a core intervention in PCC. With the availability of portable electronic devices, such as smartphones, notebook computers, and tablet computers, self-monitoring has never been easier. There are countless "apps" to choose from, a number of which permit the monitoring of multiple behavior-change targets and provide built-in reinforcers and rewards.

TABLE 10.8   Self-Monitoring Apps and Websites

Smartphone Apps	Websites for Computers
Nutrition/Diet/Exercise	*Nutrition/Diet/Exercise*
MyFitnessPal.com	MyFitnessPal.com
RestaurantNutrition.com	HealthCoach4Me.com
Fooducate.com	Diet.com
FastFoodCalories.com	Mypyramidtracker.gov
MyNetDiary.com	Sparkpeople.com
NikeBOOM.com	Livestrong.com
iMapMyrun.com	
Specialized	*Specialized*
dLife.com (diabetes)	HealthCoach4Me.com
OnTrack.com (diabetes)	OnTrack.com (diabetes)
Breathe2Relax.com (relaxation breathing pacer)	EZAir.com (breathing pacer)
BloodPressureMonitor.com	

For older adults who are not technically savvy, there are simple tools they can use to self-monitor: paper-and-pencil worksheets supplied by the psychologist, a calendar to mark off each day the target change is met, and simple daily tallies of target behaviors.

Motivational Interviewing Strategies

We have advocated for this intervention again and again. Motivational interviewing (Rollnick, Miller, & Butler, 2007) can be especially useful for nonadherence to medical prescriptives; alcohol and prescription-drug misuse; and lifestyle problems, such as overeating, smoking, and poor sleep hygiene. Barriers to compliance are numerous and can be related to patient beliefs (e.g., the medical condition is of low priority), nonsupport by family, other psychosocial or cultural influences, complexity of treatment, medication side effects, lack of patient understanding, and inadequate communication between provider and patient. Rarely, nonadherence can result from an occult wish for a negative outcome. The psychologist, therefore, identifies with the patient those factors contributing to inadequate follow-through and poor self-efficacy, and works with the patient to improve confidence and self-efficacy via select motivational interviewing strategies, problem solving, self-monitoring, and creating accountability to self and to the PCMH team. Several motivational interviewing strategies are suited to the brief PCC visit.

Motivational Interviewing Topics

- Importance of change
- Readiness to change
- One's confidence to change
- Barriers to change
- The pros and cons of change

One can work on identifying a patient's strengths, areas of ambivalence or barriers, and the benefits versus risks of change in one session and in the next develop problem-solving strategies and self-monitoring exercises to help the patient make the changes he or she is willing to commit to. Commitments are shared with the PCMH team so that the patient will be accountable and encouraged by all members at each visit.

Stimulus Control

Stimulus control is a means for the psychologist and patient to identify the stimulus or trigger that precedes a target unhealthy behavior and to alter or control the stimulus so that the target behavior is less likely to occur. Stimuli could be environmental, interpersonal, or antecedent thoughts, emotions, and behaviors. For example, one can better control overeating (target) by using a smaller plate (stimulus) at every meal and preparing just enough food (stimulus) for one serving. Between visits, the patient will work on identifying all the stimuli that trigger the undesired behavior so that the psychologist and patient can work together to alter the stimulus–response relationship. Self-monitoring, accountability to the PCMH team, and positive reinforcement are important feature components that make this intervention effective.

Assertive Communication

Poor communication with others is usually not a chief complaint in PCC settings. However, poor communication (e.g., anger, withdrawal) and lack of assertiveness are not infrequently components of the patient's psychological and medical symptoms, and can impede functioning as well as goal attainment. Assertiveness training can be an effective part of treatment for many conditions, such as depression, social anxiety, family conflicts, and problems resulting from unexpressed anger. This issue can be addressed in the PCC by teaching the patient the difference between passive (or nonassertive), aggressive, and assertive communication styles, as well as how to set boundaries (see Alberti & Emmons, 2001). Hunter and colleagues (2009) suggest the HARD technique (**H**onest, **A**ppropriate, **R**espectful, **D**irect) in which the patient rates her or his interactions regarding the target problem (see below). The patient is then taught to apply the XYZ formula for changing maladaptive styles to appropriately assertive.

TABLE 10.9   Exercise: How Was My Communication?

Passive		Assertive		Aggressive	
Honest?	No	Honest?	Yes	Honest?	Yes
Appropriate?	Yes	Appropriate?	Yes	Appropriate?	No
Respectful	Yes	Respectful	Yes	Respectful	No
Direct	No	Direct	Yes	Direct	Yes

TABLE 10.10 XYZ Formula for Effective Communication and Examples

I feel **X**	When you do **Y**	In situation **Z**	And I would like…
I feel angry	When you interrupt me	You are with friends	…you to let me finish my thought
I feel frightened	When you yell	You are frustrated	…you to count to 10 to calm down before addressing me

COMMON PRESENTING PROBLEMS IN PRIMARY CARE

Increasingly, it is clear that the PCC is the best setting to offer behavioral health care for older adults. The typical U.S. older adult is not accepting of psychiatric problems or treatment. Older adults are often not psychologically minded. Fear of being told that he or she has a "mental" problem and the embarrassment evoked by the possibility of others finding out that he or she is seeing a "shrink" are sufficient to prevent the average older adult from ever seeking help at a mental health clinic, even when quality of life is markedly reduced or functional ability is severely compromised. Elders of U.S. minority cultures are especially reticent about visiting behavioral health professionals, and their family members too may hesitate to address their loved ones' behavioral health problems because of shame and stigma that can be experienced within their communities.

This is, of course, a problem. In the PCC setting the trust in one's doctor, the familiarity with the medical staff, and the comfort of procedure that are part of an office visit (temperature, blood pressure, and weight taken each time—included in visits with the psychologist, too—banter with the nurses, waiting in the exam room) are familiar and even comforting. This routine is expected. Seeing a BHP for the first time in such a setting is thus made easier. The first visit with the psychologist is the most important visit because the older adult will have to be convinced in 30 minutes that behavioral health problems are common; that treatment can be brief, problem focused, and practical; and that intervening at this time will improve quality of life and functioning in the near future if the patient agrees to stick to the plan. This is especially the case when the psychologist can apply "healthy brain talk" to show how a given intervention is most helpful for cerebral health. Older adults know that this is a universal problem and a "medical" clinic is now helping to address this in a reasonable way. This can be applicable to depression and anxiety as well as to a cognitive problem.

When working in a PCC setting with a large number of older adults, it becomes necessary to accommodate the physical changes that come with age, especially vision, hearing, memory, and ambulation. Hunter and colleagues (2009) provide a number of excellent suggestions for addressing the practical needs of older adults.

- Any handouts should be printed in font sizes of 14 to 16 points to improve readability. Availability of magnifying glasses during a visit can be helpful, too.
- Because of wide variations in literacy among older adults, assess whether the patient can read and understand self-report measures and handouts.
- Consider keeping a pocket sound amplifier (small amplifier with headphones and/or earbuds) in the exam room for those who are hard of hearing or who have left their hearing aids at home.
- Patients should be able to supplement their hearing by reading the BHP's lips—therefore, ambient lighting should be bright and the provider should remember to face the patient when talking.
- Slow the rate of speech and simplify questions (i.e., avoid asking multipart or complex questions).
- Write down and/or offer handouts of recommendations and prescriptives that include the steps needed to accomplish them.
- Goals for change should be concise and specific. Ask the patient to repeat back the agreed-upon goals and steps for reaching them.
- Always consider the impact of medication side effects on functioning. Review the patient's medication schedule and make sure his or her routine follows the prescriber's intent. If any of the prescribed drugs have known CNS effects that are manifesting in the patient, a consultation back to the PCP to investigate further is indicated. Sometimes a simple change in medication or in the daily dosing of a medication can have a positive impact on the patient's mental status, functioning, and quality of life.
- Ensure that there is space in the exam room for wheelchair and walker access. Also, the exam room should be able to accommodate anyone accompanying the patient (spouse, adult, child/children, professional caregiver).
- Physical activity is an important recommendation for older adults. The exercise routine under consideration should be discussed with the PCP before the patient attempts it. Special consideration also should be given to risk for falling and fear of falling.
- For many older patients who have trouble exercising because of physical limitations or pain, water exercise via physical therapy or water aerobics classes can be quite effective.

Crisis Interventions in PCCs

Here we identify three common problems in PCCs. For space reasons, we have picked only three, leaving out substance abuse, elder abuse, and family crises, among others. These are crises in the psychological sense; they present as urgent issues but can be dealt with by a Watch and Wait strategy. In fact, this is an optimal intervention process, as the crisis has to be tempered, placed in perspective, and deliberatively responded to. If the crisis cannot be handled in this way, a referral to a specialty behavioral health provider is appropriate.

Depression and Suicide Risk

We add this as an addendum to the depression chapter as it plays out in PCCs. Most, if not all, PCMH initiatives focus on treating depression because of the broad scope of the problem. About 30% to 40% of depressed individuals in PCCs are not identified as such, and about 10% of these patients are treated with benzodiazepines only (Ford, 2004). There is a growing understanding in medicine of the reciprocal relationship between depression and chronic health conditions, such as cardiovascular disease, chronic pulmonary disease, and diabetes. These diseases are suspected in activating depressive symptoms via inflammatory processes (Wium-Andersen, Ørsted, Nielsen, & Nordestgaard, 2012), and depression in turn makes it very difficult for the patient with a chronic medical condition to perform self-care activities that keep the disease process under control. In these cases, the psychologist will expect to address medical treatment compliance and lifestyle problems (e.g., sleep, overeating) over and above depression.

Depression

- *Assess:* PHQ-9 or other brief depression measure
  Functional measure such as BASIS-32 or QoLI (Quality of Life Index)
- *Advise:*
  - Use the stepped-care approach. Based on degree of depression exhibited, manage in PCC with or without medication, or refer to specialty care based on severity and complexity (e.g., psychotic features, multiple treatment failures, level of suicidal thinking that requires more monitoring than can be managed in PCCs).
  - Offer a focused care plan that includes, at a minimum, behavioral activation plus one or more brief psychological interventions that address specific signs, symptoms, and behaviors, such as sleep and eating dysregulation, anhedonia, or negative thinking. Problem solving, goal setting, self-monitoring, cognitive disputation, and/or assertiveness training are applicable interventions.
- *Agree:* Get buy-in at first visit; may need to offer choices to get buy-in. If patient is ambivalent about engaging in brief therapy, offer a second appointment to do motivational interviewing to increase likelihood of buy-in.
- *Assist:* Use functional assessment to identify activities that have been decreased or stopped to create a behavioral activation plan. It should include some form of exercise; walking, or for patients with chronic joint pain, swimming or aqua aerobics. Apply brief psychological interventions as agreed upon; all should include some form of homework that will be reviewed at next visit. If antidepressants are prescribed, review dosing instructions and monitor for side effects/adverse events and effectiveness. Then watch and wait.
- *Arrange:* Frequency of follow-up visits will vary from patient to patient. The first two visits should be no more than 2 weeks apart. Subsequent visits may spread out depending on progress in treatment. If patient is not progressing, discuss with her or him a referral to specialty BH care for more intense treatment.

Suicide risk must be probed carefully when working with older adults. As mentioned earlier, males 75 years and older have the highest rates of suicide in the United States and clinically depressed mood is associated with the vast majority of suicides by the elderly. Conversely, although it is not uncommon for elders to talk about wishing for death when health is failing, when there is chronic severe pain, or when there is significant loss, this kind of talk does not necessarily lead to suicidal intent or plan. In fact, death ideation (e.g., life is not worth living) is reasonably common (Britton, et al., 2008). There are other risk factors:

TABLE 10.11 Risk Factors for Suicide in Older Adults

Biopsychosocial Risk Factors	Demographics	Personal History	Environmental Risk Factors
Depression	Male	History of mental illness	Availability of lethal agent
Serious medical comorbidities	Widowed, divorced	Previous attempts	Financial problems
Somatic complaints	White	Family suicide	Residing in long-term care facility
Severe pain	Older age	History of violence	Desensitized to suicide
Frailty or perceived health decline		Intrafamily conflicts	Isolation, poor social connectedness
Medications (amount and type)		Cumulative losses	Elder abuse
High caregiver burden		History of physical, sexual, or emotional abuse	Barriers to mental health services
Inflexible and/or impulsive thinking			
Traumatic grief			
Hopelessness			
Substance abuse			
Ongoing high stress			
Loss of social roles			

The Watch and Wait approach can work for suicidal or death ideation. The plan is to highlight the problem, validate it, assess for excessive intensity or comorbid problems as well as social concerns (the five factors), and apply a careful case-based approach in the confines of the PCC setting. If appropriate, the older patient can be seen daily as needed for monitoring until acuity diminishes. As always, if frequent monitoring is not viable or workable, a referral is made to specialty behavioral health. The Preventing Risk of Suicide in Primary Care: Collaborative Trial (PROSPECT; Alexopoulos et al., 2009) showed that, with regular contact by the PCMH team, subjects' suicidal thinking as well as depressive symptoms decreased and adherence to treatment improved over the 24-month study period.

Bryan and Rudd (2011) have devised an heuristic that can assist when assessing risk of self-harm and the need to move the patient to a higher level of care. That said, the PCC must have a standard operating procedure in place when psychiatric hospitalization is indicated, which includes a plan for transportation (ambulance, police car, family member) and a list of hospitals in the area with psychiatric units.

TABLE 10.12 Degree of Suicidality

Nonexistent	No suicidal thinking
Mild	Limited ideation, no intent, limited risk factors, and good protective factors
Moderate	Frequent ideation, vague plan, or fantasy, but no intent; good self-control, limited distress, other risk factors, but also protective factors
Severe	Frequent and intense ideation that is enduring; some preparatory behaviors and access to a method, but intent may not be expressed; multiple risk factors and few protective factors
Extreme	Frequent and intense ideation that is enduring; plan with preparatory behaviors and access to a method; impaired impulse control, multiple risk factors, and no protective factors

Late-Life Psychosis

Psychosis encapsulates delusions, hallucinations, paranoia, disorganized thinking, and/or disorganized behavior. Late-life psychosis is more common than one might expect and it is anticipated to become more common as the U.S. population grows older. Its prevalence is between 4% and 10% regardless of cause, and it is even more common among the oldest old (Gareri, DeFazio, & Stilo, 2003; Ostling, Borjesson-Hanson, & Skoog, 2007; Ostling & Skoog, 2002; Sigström, Skoog, & Sacuiu, 2009). Psychosis at this stage of life is attributable to a number of factors and combinations thereof, such as, age-related deterioration of cortical areas, particularly the temporal and frontal lobes; abnormalities in neurotransmitter systems; delirium; a resurgence of the positive symptoms associated with chronic serious mental illness; hearing loss and other sensory deficits; alcohol or other substance use or withdrawal; social isolation; long-term sequelae of chronic medical diseases; and polypharmacy. Individuals who develop late-onset psychosis may be brought into the PCC by a spouse or other family member for assessment. Note especially that it is not unusual for patients with dementia or Parkinson's disease to present to the PCC with hallucinations and delusions. Visual hallucinations in particular are a sign of neurodegeneration.

Work-up of the patient with late-life psychosis becomes a truly collaborative venture in PCMH because medical concerns and culture-bound syndromes must be ruled out or treated, and psychological and family concerns must be addressed expeditiously.

Late-Life Psychosis

- *Assess:* Rule out acute medical causes in collaboration with PCMH team
    Rule out or address culture-bound syndromes (see case vignette that follows)

Administer MMSE or MoCA
Administer PHQ-9, BDI-PC, or other brief depression measures
Assess for suicidal ideation and/or command hallucinations
Assess for mania
Add functional measure such as BASIS-32 or QoLI
What are the antecedents to psychosis (e.g., unfamiliar environment, pain, dehydration, sleep deprivation)?
Determine as a team the level of care and type of care (medical vs. psychiatric) needed. Can the psychotic symptoms be managed in PCC?
Assess spouse/caregiver's response to psychosis

- *Advise:*
  - Offer care options to patient and family based on severity and acuity of symptoms.
  - If hallucinations and delusions are relatively benign, and the family is willing to keep patient at home, frequent visits to PCC can be scheduled for medication management, and monitoring until symptom remission (i.e., Watch and Wait). Ensure that weapons or other lethal means are not in the home.
  - Stepped care: Should patient require a higher level of care, a warm hand-off should occur between the psychologist and receiving psychiatrist.
- *Agree:* Buy-in by patient may or may not occur, especially if hospitalization is recommended. The health care proxy person will need to step in to make a decision in case the patient cannot.
- *Assist:* Provide psychoeducation on late-life psychosis. Help patient/family reduce stress and specific antecedents to psychotic symptoms. Ensure adequate sleep. Help family minimize emotional reactivity. Mindfulness, relaxation training, and goal setting for the patient and caregiver are helpful. If possible, teach patient to question his or her internal stimuli via cognitive-therapy techniques (see Chadwick, 2006).
- *Arrange:* Assist nurse case manager for referral to specialty care such as psychiatry, or admission to psychiatric inpatient hospital if needed. Follow-up visits will be frequent initially to track acuity and degree of patient and family/caregiver distress. Caregiver may be seen separately if he or she is having difficulty coping.

Case Example: Mr. E

Mr. E is a 68-year-old Latino who was raised in Puerto Rico and came to the United States alone at age 17 years. He did not complete high school and joined the military at age 21 years. He retired about 25 years ago and has worked in construction to supplement his pension. He is married and estranged from his wife, but they still live together. They are raising a 14-year-old foster son. Mr. E came alone to see his PCP (a geriatrician) with a complaint of visual hallucinations and an urge to hang himself as well as an urge to grab a gun and kill a man he "sees" [hallucinates]. He emphasized that he does not want to do either, but he becomes overwhelmed with these visions and urges. He denies auditory hallucinations.

Mr. E's vitals were taken, labs were drawn, and the PCP checked him out both physically and neurologically, and found nothing untoward, including no alcohol or drugs. Medical conditions include gastroesophageal reflux disease (GERD), mild asthma, hyperlipidemia, prediabetes (HbA1c = 6.2). Medications are esomeprazole for GERD and albuterol spray for asthma.

The PCMH psychologist was called in emergently by the geriatrician to assess Mr. E's mental status and safety risk.

Watch and Wait: *The 5A's*

Assess: Mr. E was alert and fully oriented, with no evidence initially of impaired thought processes or content. He denied alcohol or drug use. Mr. E described seeing himself "pulling on a rope to hang myself and I'm hanging." He also sees himself "getting a gun and shooting this person over and over and over—the man is on the floor with blood all over." Mr. E said that the hallucinations started about 6 months ago and they can occur anywhere from once per day to once per week. He feels like he is "possessed by spirits" during these episodes and experiences bodily sensations coincident with feeling possessed. Mr. E could not provide any information about antecedents before the visions manifest. The visions were incongruent with Mr. E's desire to live and to raise his foster son, with whom he is very close. Mr. E also complained of insomnia with nighttime awakenings, psychomotor agitation, and anhedonia. He was most concerned about having Alzheimer's disease, like his mother, and has noticed that he is more forgetful these days. His neuropsychiatric history was significant for a mild traumatic brain injury as a teenager; possible hypnagogic hallucinations of a woman in a silk dress calling his name, also as a teen; and recent tactile hallucinations of bugs crawling on his back, arms, and legs, for which he asks his son to look. There was early life adversity, with a cousin and a neighbor committing suicide by hanging. During the history taking, Mr. E suddenly cried out that the vision of seeing himself hanging was happening again and he clutched his chest and became unresponsive to the psychologist's voice. He appeared to be immersed in the hallucination and then came around in about 5 minutes reporting that he felt possessed for that short time, noting tachycardia and derealization. Afterward, Mr. E was fully oriented, showed good memory for the event, and exhibited a clear, linear thought process and content. We asked that he call a family member to be with him while we decide next steps in his care.

PHQ-9 = 15 (moderately severe depression)
BASIS 32 = 29/78 – IADL were reported as WNL (within normal limits)
MoCA = 22/30 – significant for poor list recall, calculations, and verbal fluency
Working Diagnoses: Major Depression w/ psychotic features; Psychosis-NOS (not otherwise specified); Psychosis due to general medical condition; Ataque de Nervios (culture-bound syndrome associated with Latin cultures); R/O Mild Cognitive Impairment (MCI)

Psychologist and PCP met informally to determine stepped-care options for patient, which include the following:

1. Outpatient care in PCMH with head CT (computed tomography) and frequent monitoring
2. Outpatient care as above plus trial of low-dose antipsychotic medication
3. Hospitalization for further medical work-up, including head CT
4. Psychiatric hospitalization
5. Cognitive assessment regardless of the next level of care

Advise: Working diagnoses were discussed with Mr. E and his brother (wife was unavailable). Care options also were discussed. Mr. E did not want to go to a hospital because he did not want to harm himself and wanted to be with his foster son. Brother assured us that any weapons would be removed from the home. He agreed to monitor Mr. E closely and bring him to all outpatient appointments. Safety risk was determined to be mild–moderate.

Agree: Mr. E and his brother agreed to outpatient follow-up with a head CT. They agreed too that Mr. E would be started on a small dose of antipsychotic medication if the CT was normal. Mr. E was eager to have cognitive testing because he worried about Alzheimer's disease.

Assist: The PCMH psychologist worked with Mr. E on improving sleep (thus addressing sleep deprivation as a factor in his psychosis), using sleep hygiene and ABC analysis around the visual hallucinations/derealization episodes. It became clear that Mr. E was more likely to experience frightening hallucinations when stressed, leading to a more targeted working diagnosis of Ataque de Nervios. The hallucinatory episodes continued to occur, but they were more benign. The PCP added 0.5 mg of haloperidol to the treatment plan, which addressed the hallucinations better and eliminated his subjective feeling of being possessed. At this point the PCMH team used Watch and Wait.

At 4 weeks:
PHQ-9 = 7 (mild depression)
BASIS 32 = 15/78

Arrange: The nurse case manager arranged for the head CT, which was normal. She also scheduled a cognitive assessment with the PCMH psychologist, which showed deficits in attention and delayed memory. Once patient was stable, follow-up appointments with the PCP were scheduled monthly and with the psychologist, as needed with repeat cognitive testing at 9 months.

Managing Dementia in PCC

Older adults commonly come to their PCPs rather than to specialty medical professionals with worries about forgetfulness. That said, between 26% and 76% of patients presenting in PCC, in whom dementia may be present, are not diagnosed (Holsinger, Deveau, Boustani, & Williams, 2007; Wilkins et al., 2007). In a recent Danish study of older patients who complained of memory problems to their PCPs, 28% were diagnosed with dementia within 4 years of disclosure to their doctors, suggesting that subjective memory complaints are an independent predictor for a subsequent dementia diagnosis (Waldorff, Siersma, Vogel, & Waldemar, 2012). Clearly, every older adult who presents to PCC with concerns about memory or other cognitive functions deserves to be screened for MCI/dementia. Too, when family members raise concerns to the PCMH team, attention must be paid.

The Cognitively Impaired Patient

- *Assess:* MoCA or similar cognitive screen
  Functional measure such as FAQ or CAFU
  GDS 5/15 to detect concomitant depressive symptoms
- *Advise:*
  - Use Watch and Wait for patients who do not meet threshold for MCI or dementia, but show some decline in cognition compared with same-age peers. Recommend

follow-up visit for cognitive monitoring every 6–9 months or sooner if there is a change in health or cognitive status. Address depression if present. For all, regardless of mild cognitive problems or normal cognitive aging, encourage exercise, as this is the only "brain" intervention that has a clear positive effect on cognition.

- Use the stepped-care approach for patients with good evidence of MCI or dementia. A more thorough cognitive assessment can be done in PCMH with the RBANS, or the team may decide to refer for full neuropsychological assessment under certain circumstances, such as younger age (forties, fifties, and sixties). Address depression if present. The team also must decide whether they can manage the patient's condition solely in PCMH or refer to specialty care, such as neurology or psychiatry.

- Offer a focused care plan that includes psychoeducation for patient and family, behavioral activation, and techniques for accommodating memory deficits. For patients with MCI or mild dementia, cognitive retraining, if available, can be helpful. May also need to address depressive and anxiety symptoms and caregiver distress. Problem solving, goal setting, relaxation training, mindfulness, and self-monitoring are applicable interventions for MCI and early dementia. Patients with moderate dementia may benefit from goal-setting interventions with the assistance of the caregiver.

- *Agree:* Buy-in from patient and family may be difficult to achieve initially because they may be overwhelmed by a diagnosis of MCI or dementia. Remain available and offer follow-up as needed to discuss options for further testing, developing accommodations in the home, goal setting, discussing the future, and so on. For those who do not meet criteria for a cognitive disorder, obtain buy-in for making lifestyle changes that will support brain health, such as exercise, smoking cessation, weight loss and nutrition improvement, engagement in social and thinking activities.

- *Assist:* Apply psychological interventions as agreed upon. Work with the family and caregiver. Monitor the caregiver for distress (see below). If medication is involved (e.g., cognitive enhancers), review dosing instructions and monitor for side effects/adverse events and effectiveness. Then watch and wait.

- *Arrange:* Assist nurse case manager with referral for neuropsychological testing as needed. As dementia is a progressive disease, have a resource list available for the PCMH team of specialty providers (e.g., geropsychiatrist, geropsychologist, neurologist who specializes in neurodegenerative diseases, elder care consultant, hospice staff). Frequency of follow-up visits will vary depending on the needs of the patient as well as the caregiver. Caregiver may be seen separately if monitoring suggests that he or she is having difficulty coping (see below).

Caregivers of dementia patients are most often spouses, and they may or may not have the assistance of other family members or friends. Caring for a loved one with significant cognitive and/or medical problems is a chronic stressor and many caregivers do not seek help for themselves. When their own mental and physical health is neglected, caregivers are at high risk of neglecting or adversely affecting the care recipient. The PCMH psychologist is therefore in a good position to monitor the caregiver at each patient visit.

The Caregiver

- *Assess:* CAFU or Zarit Burden Interview
   GDS 5/15 to detect depressive symptoms
   Other measures as indicated (e.g., BAI-PC, ESS)
- *Advise:*
  - Use Watch and Wait for caregivers who are showing resilience. Continue to monitor at each patient visit with PCP and/or psychologist. Offer community resources such as caregiver self-help groups and respite-care opportunities.
  - Use the stepped-care approach for caregivers who are showing burden, declining physical health, and/or frank psychiatric symptoms, such as clinical depression, anxiety/panic, increased substance use, cognitive difficulties. The PCMH team is fully involved. Offer community resources such as caregiver self-help groups and respite care opportunities, in addition to interventions that can build resilience (e.g., goal setting, problem solving, relaxation, and mindfulness). Encourage the caregiver to seek assistance from family and friends to decrease burden.
  - Patients who exhibit difficult behaviors such as shadowing (following the caregiver), agitation, aggression, and dysinhibition need special assistance. Medical causes of the behavior (e.g., adverse drug effects, urinary tract infection) must be ruled out. Behavior modification techniques can be taught, but the caregiver will likely need hand-holding to do this well. Mindfulness and Acceptance Therapy (ACT) interventions also can be useful here to assist the caregiver to accept the loved one as is and let her or his values inform her or his reaction to the patient's difficult behaviors.
- *Agree:* Work with caregiver on acceptable options; this may ultimately include discussion of transferring the patient to assisted living or nursing home. That discussion should be done collaboratively with the PCP, who joins the visit.
- *Assist:* Apply psychological and other interventions as agreed upon. If teaching the caregiver behavioral modification for the patient, work through modified ABC worksheets so the caregiver can identify the antecedents or triggers, maintaining factors, and consequences of the noxious behavior. Offer behavioral strategies to address the behaviors (see Warner, 2000). Then watch and wait. Monitor for worsening of caregiver symptoms and consider referral to specialty care.
- *Arrange:* Frequency of follow-up visits will vary depending on the needs of the caregiver. Arrange for respite care as needed, including day care.

CONCLUSION

This chapter is a compendium of two others. We have seen that health issues are critical in the holistic care of older adults. Dr Ackermann provided necessary information on common medical issues. This chapter focused on the application of behavioral health interventions in primary care as part of a patient-centered medical home team. The goals of PCMH for older adults are to provide holistic, person-centered care; to increase access to care; to address behavioral health needs in a familiar and friendly atmosphere; and to contain health care costs through care coordination and decreasing health care overuse through Watch and Wait as well as stepped-care. Indeed, as the U.S. population grows older over the next decades and chronic medical conditions become more prevalent as well, the PCMH will offer the best opportunity for stable health, optimal behavioral health, and good quality of life for older adults who suffer from multiple medical and psychological/psychiatric comorbidities.

NOTES

1. See http://www.medicare.gov/your-medicare-costs/costs-at-a-glance/costs-at-glance.html
2. Improving Mood-Promoting Access to Collaborative Treatment (IMPACT) collaborative care management program for late-life depression.
3. Primary Care Research in Substance Abuse and Mental Health for the Elderly (PRISM).
4. Re-Engineering Systems for the Primary Care Treatment of Depression (RESPECT-Depression).

CHAPTER 11

Life Issues

Lee Hyer, Maria Anastasiades, and Sanna Catherine Tillitski

> There is now a vast amount of data demonstrating the relationship between gene expression and anatomical features in early brain development . . . . [W]e suggest that similar genetic and epigenetic mechanisms continue to impact the structure and function of the brain throughout life . . . . Late in life, similar genetic mechanisms may be involved in the breakdown of brain microstructure, AND changes in experience, as in early development, can advance and ameliorate the deleterious effects of aging. Data from multiple laboratories around the world suggest that calorific restriction and environmental enrichment can impact on gene expression in the aging brain . . . .
>
> —*Huffman* (2012)

This chapter addresses adjustment as it applies to general life issues. We must be selective and target those highly relevant problems related to medical and general care. In this effort we consider some overall concepts related to adjustment as well as issues of living. Again, these are important at later life because they influence the psychological and cognitive symptoms of living in substantial ways.

For starters, there are differing trends in diseases and symptoms over time as compared with disability. The implication is that problems at late life are multifaceted and complex. Mental health is one issue, for example. Substantial strides have been made in the array and effectiveness of mental health treatments, but there is a remarkable gap between research and practice (Institute of Medicine [IOM], 2011). The promise of a cure for any mental illness may be a chimera or distant accomplishment because of a variety of imposing scientific challenges. Mental disorders continue to be identified as variegated syndromes and may, therefore, never be amenable to specific diagnostic tests. As we have emphasized, the remission of mental illness using current pharmacological or psychotherapies is partial or short lived; as much as one third of patients do not respond to the recommended treatments. A quixotic and foolish search for and discovery of a cure for mental illness, and the advent of universal insurance coverage for its accoutrements, could further financially unbalance the U.S. health care system and impede the necessary paradigm shift in health care.

The goals of cures and eradication of illness are relics of pre-epidemiological transition, when a nation confronted infectious diseases and medical conditions that fit the classic definition of a disease (Szasz, 1997) with an underlying physical or physiological lesion or pathology. Few chronic physical conditions have shown themselves amenable to cures, but some have been approached in terms of latter stages of prevention. This is, of course, another way of emphasizing the cost-effectiveness of primary prevention. If there are problems with type 2 diabetes, then we can manage the condition, but we miss the opportunity to identify the person as high risk and provide preventive interventions. Although mental illness prevention efforts have reasonable efficacy (Muñoz & Mendelson, 2010), all prevention efforts are aimed at reducing cases of mental illness and have yet to turn any attention to investigating whether those interventions really work.

Nebulous concepts of morbidity have clouded discussion on, and research about, health trends. Studies have shown that during a single time period there are different trends for different components of health in the elderly population and that the correlations between different components also change. . . . [T]he prevalence of symptoms, disease, and functional limitations is expanding at the same time that disability is being compressed, or at least postponed. Researchers must clarify the implications of these different trends. Symptoms and disease imply need and demand for medical services. Functional limitations imply rehabilitative and compensatory measures, whereas disability among elderly people often entails need for social services and/or long-term care.

Parker and Thorslund (2007)

In this chapter we identify problems of living both broadly and practically. We start with a perspective on older adults. They have more opportunity to have more problems. This starts with a view of society. Next, we request a longer view at the point of contact, as this will assist in opening up care. We continue advocating for better prisms of care, addressing a better taxonomy of psychopathology, a better view of prevention (evidence-based therapeutic and preventive intervention programs [EBI]), and flourishing, a novel idea born from positive psychology. We provide practical care suggestions ranging from the burden of socioeconomic status (SES) and home models to the lament of caregiving, as well as a cursory look at the many other problems that can occur in the community. We end with a discussion on long-term care (LTC). A case is also provided.

OLD-AGE PERSPECTIVE

Where age is concerned, America has experienced an extraordinary shift. We have lamented this before. For further perspective, there is a cost for the growth in life expectancy. More than one fifth of hospitalized patients in 2008 were born in 1933 or earlier. Twenty-two percent of all admissions to U.S. hospitals in 2008 were for patients born the year that Franklin D. Roosevelt was first inaugurated as president of the United States—or earlier. Those who ranged in age from 75 to 84 years accounted for almost 14% of the 40 million admissions to U.S. hospitals that year, and patients 85 years and older made up another 8%. Together, these most senior of America's older adults accounted for 8.7 million hospital admissions in 2008 compared with the 5.3 million admissions of relatively younger seniors—that is, those between 65 and 74 years of age (Gliklich & Dreyer, 2010).

Use of health care services increased only slightly in 2007: 336/1,000 in 2007 from 306/1,000 in 1992, but skilled nursing care went from 28/1,000 to 81/1,000 in 2007. Also, the number of physician visits and consultations increased to just over 13 per year; but the number of home health visits decreased from 8.4 in 1996 to 3.4 in 2007. This decrease occurred during a time when home health was viewed as beneficial. Significantly, average health care costs per year were directly related to income: those living in poverty cost $21,033 compared with those with more means at $12,440. Of these monies, inpatient health care accounted for 25% (down from 32% in 1994) and prescription costs for 16% (up from 8% in 1997). Older adults paid 60% of prescription costs out of pocket, compared with public programs at 35% and private insurers at 38%. Finally, virtually every older person was paying some out-of-pocket expenses (95%). From 1977 to 2006, the percentage of household income that people of 65 years and older allocated to out-of-pocket spending for health care services increased from 12% to 28%. Today, over 50% of out-of-pocket health care spending goes toward medication (Gliklich & Dreyer, 2010).

Compared with other age groups, older adults have the highest numbers of doctor visits, hospital stays, and prescription medication usage. In 2004, the average annual cost per older person 65 years or older was $3,899 (Blount et al., 2010). Left unchecked, health care expenditures will likely rise from the current level of ~15% to 29% of gross domestic product (GDP) in 2040. As intimated, medication use is high among the elderly. Adverse drug reactions account for a substantial amount of emergency room use, hospital admissions, and other health care expenditures. Only 50% of medication is taken properly, and there are 1.9 million drug-related injuries (Cogbill, Dinson, & Duthie, 2010). Taking just blood pressure medication as an example, only 25% of older patients remain in treatment and consistently take their medications in sufficient amounts for blood pressure control. Several barriers have been attributed to poor medication use. These include physical illness, medication side effects, cognitive dysfunction, psychiatric conditions (mood disorders), functional loss, social loss, and inability to afford the medication at full dosing (Cogbill et al., 2010).

These data dovetail with the reality of the functional limitations of older age. In the year 2000 U.S. census, the most prevalent type of limitation or disability among Americans older than 65 years was physical (28.6%), followed by limitations that affect leaving the house (20.8%), then sensory limitations (14.2%), followed by cognitive (10.6%) and self-care limits (Freedman, Martin, & Schoeni, 2002). The overall prevalence of disability among older adults was 41.9%, and that rate was even higher for elders living in poverty (Hurwicz & Tumosa, 2011). As people age, activities of daily living (ADL) decline dramatically between 65 and 74 years—a fourfold change in ADL and threefold change in instrumental activities of daily living (IADL). Looking more closely at functional decline, adults older than 75 years account for 59% of fall-related deaths, but make up only 5% of the population (Haber, Logan, & Schumacher, 2011). Also, a sedentary lifestyle leaves older adults at risk for just about everything. Both obesity and malnutrition increase with age; currently, about one third are obese and one fifth are malnourished (Haber, 2010). Fortunately, smoking and alcohol use are lower (15%) than in younger groups, but are still a concern. Finally, although only 5% of those over 65 years reside in a nursing home (NH), between 10% and 15% of community-dwelling older adults require considerable support and assistance to remain in their own homes.

TABLE 11.1   What Are Old People Like?

Age	% No Disability	% Long-Term Care	% Married
65–69	83	3	70
70–74	83	5	60
75–79	78	7	52
80–84	62	10	38
85–89	45	17	24
90–94	35	32	16
95–99	20	42	10
100+	18	48	9

Older adults, then, have problems that rest in a variety of places, all of which have social implications. All have an influence on living. This, then, becomes part of the problem list and of the intervention process.

EVALUATION: POINT OF CARE AND LONG VIEW

Given the need to have a perspective on care, perhaps a useful concept is point of care. This concept addresses issues and procedures associated with face-to-face patient care. According to a report by the Association of American Medical Colleges and the American Association of Colleges of Nursing (2010), *point-of-care learning* is defined as learning that occurs at the time and place of a health provider–patient encounter. It is most often distinguished by its context, that is, the active encounter between the clinician and the patient at the health care site, home, or elsewhere. It is during this process that information needs are identified and the opportunities for clinician and patient education, clinical decisions, and patient management all intersect. The provider–patient encounter traditionally has occurred face to face in a clinical setting; however, in this age of growing information and communication technologies and new approaches to health care delivery, patient encounters may also occur through telephone calls, e-mail communications, and video conferencing. The most basic of provider skills in the point-of-care environment is knowledge management, including the ability to identify learning needs, know and understand what resources to use, understand how to access and critically appraise information, and know how to apply it. A second basic skill is the ability to self-assess, that is, to accurately assess one's own learning needs, impact on patient outcomes, and need for performance change.

Related is the fact that patients' psychiatric problems wax and wane over time, but do not extinguish easily. The mood or behaviors that influence illness presentation may be malleable but not substantially alterable in any easy way. On the one hand, normal adults vary in their expression of problems. They are, if anything, variable. On the other hand, older adults do repeat with problems. They experience repeated depression at levels as high as 80%, depending on the number of earlier incidents of depression (Barlow, 2004).

In short, the provider needs to keep the long view in mind and focus on mitigating the impact of psychiatric vulnerabilities on medical conditions. So the busy health care provider is really tasked at the point of care to maximize the intervention for the current incident while keeping the long view of care in mind. This requires developing a care mentality that is not short sighted cost limiting, or validation poor. After all, a solitary, acute response to developing medical issues would be very short sighted. Several models noted earlier have suggested as much. And, as described in this book, the primary care movement in the last decade also reaches deep and seeks interdisciplinary collaborative care, home-based care, social care, and the integration of psychiatric care.

We believe that something like this is necessary for the full gamut of the issues at late life. There needs to be a fuller perspective and a longer view of care. In effect, the health care clinician needs to be a Watch and Wait provider, one with efficacy and vision.

DIFFERENT PRISMS OF TREATMENT

In the opening chapters we addressed successful aging. We pick this up here and drill down in a more specific way. Well-being is complex. There are many prisms to this construct. Older adults need more and different health care models, and there are many good models of care that foster better practices. We address newer models that apply. We start with preventive ideas in the form of the newer ideas of the taxonomy for normal/abnormal aging, and then discuss EBIs and the construct of flourishing. We see these as methods/technologies of optimal health.

Taxonomy for Normal and Clinical Aging

Any clear demarcation between normal aging and clinical aging is at present unclear. Most medical conditions that have a slow onset can be viewed as a chronic condition. This implies two fundamental needs for health care providers: (1) the need for ever-increasing specificity of syndromes and familiarity with these syndromes as they evolve; and (2) the need for good normative data across multiple health domains and health assessment tools. A strategy for effective assessment and treatment of chronic conditions is to identify changes early in the syndrome and intervene. With older individuals, pathological changes are hypothesized to begin during what would be classified as normal aging and go undetected. In studying pathways toward disability, Fried, Bandeen-Roche, Chaves, and Johnson (2000) posited that changes in the ability to complete tasks of daily living are preceded by changes in physical functioning, suggesting that the concept of predisability or subclinical disability status, a stage that lies before "dependence" on the disability spectrum, should be attended to by providers. Predisability and MCI provide clinical-like categories for older adults whose symptoms do not yet meet the criteria for a geriatric syndrome.

The question of norms therefore becomes important: What, for instance, is the normal range of scores for older adults in domains such as sleep, pain, gait speed, and flexibility? How much daily variability can one expect in scores on assessments of depression, cognition, and pain, for example? Normative data are commonly influenced by age, education, and historical and/or ethnocultural factors, so we must be careful when applying what norms we have to our patients.

In medicine, Oslerian teachings hold to "Occam's razor," an idea that fosters the distillation of a disease presentation into a single diagnosis. This can be for the good or for the bad. Such simplification often leads to a poor outcome, especially in a typical older adult patient in whom chronic, multimorbid conditions and deficits in both health and well-being are present. Often these are lumped into one International Classification of Diseases (ICD) or *Diagnostic and Statistical Manual of Mental Disorders (DSM)* diagnosis.

Any given older patient might have a combination of hypertension, type 2 diabetes, new-onset shortness of breath, allergies, cognitive impairment, depression, and pain, as well as social isolation, impaired IADL, and limited family support. But the interplay of chronic disease and external factors may create a very different clinical picture from patient to patient. In fact, just minimal increases in allostatic load correlate greatly with frailty over a 3-year period (Gruenewald, Seeman, Karlamangla, & Sarkisian, 2009).

Looking at cognitive decline specifically, the issue of whether a dimensional or categorical model best represents the neuropsychiatric construct of "dementia" crystallizes this problem. Dementia is prevalent. As it is currently defined in the *DSM-5* (American Psychiatric Association, 2000), dementia is too categorical, exclusive, and arbitrary for ascertaining and addressing cognitive impairment. It is unfortunate that there is no objective taxonomic boundary separating those who do and those who do not meet criteria for dementia. By creating a dichotomy between dementia and nondementia, we do not do justice to the spectrum of cognitive problems seen at older ages.

For instance, over 22% of people older than 70 years have memory impairment. This is quite apart from the plaques and tangles we associate with Alzheimer's disease (AD). Although we commonly use cut scores to connote dementia, they do not represent the taxonomic boundary between health and pathology. Converting what is observed in the way of soft signs and symptoms into hard categories fails to capture the complexity of the common coexistence (and probable interaction) of cerebrovascular disease and AD, as well as other contaminants. Sperling et al. (2011) noted how the value of biomarkers changes in AD over time. The focus, as we have said previously, should be on identifying signs, symptoms, and behaviors that place a person on the continuum of cognitive decline, not whether that person qualifies to be in a particular diagnostic group. It is time to shift the focus from thresholds of dementia/no dementia to a continuum of cognitive impairment, from the late to the early stages, and from effects to causes.

Other psychiatric constructs (e.g., depression, anxiety) also are best thought of as dimensional. The idea that one can be depressed and be like other depressives with five of nine signs and symptoms is not realistic. Likewise, the idea that "subsyndromal" problems are different from syndromes is also fallacious. With older adults, the mix of psychiatric problem states with medical conditions as well as with situational stressors requires a broad view—one that respects common sense and empirically based interventions as well as cost. Treatment of such a complex person requires a team, requires vision, and requires a cost-offset mindset.

Evidence-Based Therapeutic and Preventive Intervention Programs

One model we have not discussed is the evidence-based interventions (EBIs), which have become more popular. Health rests on behavioral routines. EBIs provide a way for this to occur. Psychologists' primary technology for influencing behavior consists of EBIs. This includes both prevention and treatment. There are literally hundreds of these. Rotheram-Borus, Swendeman, and Chorpita (2012) considered the most robust features of the EBIs and suggested that providers apply them. This serves more people at lower cost. EBIs provide a simpler and less expensive alternative that meets the essential needs of consumers and are accessible, scalable, replicable, and sustainable.

So what are they? Examples include telemedicine, $2 eyeglasses, and automated machines. The application of EBIs also eases the silo mentality of the empirically supported rigors of care. In the main, mental health providers have overcompartmentalized our expertise. The web of causation can be applied more simply. This has been discussed in public health but not discussed in psychology or psychiatry to any degree. Given the costs of medications and procedures, it would seem that a better approach would be to identify which patients would benefit from a specific treatment. This requires thought, time, and a plan for potential options. The issue is not to deny the service or drug, but to stop using a shotgun approach and begin using more science for treatment.

Flourishing

Substantial strides have been made in the array and effectiveness of mental health treatments. However, as we noted earlier, the promise of a cure for any mental illness still lies in the distance, because of a variety of imposing scientific challenges. The absence of mental illness does not imply the presence of mental health. Keyes, Shmotkin, and Ryff (2002) held that mental health is best studied through a combination of assessments of mental health and mental illness. In the following table, the combination of both the diagnosis and positive markers of mental health is more important than either alone. Mental health is the result of positive emotions, positive psychological functioning, and positive social functioning. This two-factor model hypothesizes that the measure of mental illness represents the latent factor of mental health that is distinct from but correlated with the latent factor of mental illness. In a sense, the focus is on positive emotional, psychological, and social functioning as evidenced primarily by quality of life, active prevention, and upbeat functioning. Flourishing and languishing are polar ends of the process. Independent of any mental illness diagnosis, quality of life is improved with flourishing.

This view of personhood bypasses the *DSM* and holds to a different ideal. The idea that identity and growth can be identified or fostered in the process of living and adjusting is relevant. On the one hand, many older adults' lives are suboptimal; they are languishing or "just making it" in life. They are not depressed, but they are not happy or living optimally. Adaptation occurs quickly. Clinical syndromes develop when pathological processes become part of the adaptation course. If illness is sustained, the adaptive process becomes part of the person and thereby becomes a problem independent of the physical condition. This is the natural phenomenon that occurs in a cognitive decline process: the pathological processes become part of the adaptation course. If illness is sustained, the person now has an additional difficulty. Self-regulatory processes eventually overtake and regulate stress. Individual differences of course play a critical role. These differences include current cognitive status and appraisals, personality (coping type and abilities), and emotions (down-regulation as in reappraisal or avoidance).

On the other hand, many older adults are content and flourish, whether or not they have problems. Diener and Eunkook Suh (1997) have indicated that the various types of well-being are affected by different processes involved in life satisfaction, positive feelings, and negative feelings. These run the gamut of interventions to increase happiness, to identify personality traits that portend happiness. Older adults are in the main happy and satisfied, despite having problems. When older adults are at issue, perhaps constructs should be stretched.

TABLE 11.2 *DSM* Diagnosis and Languishing/Flourishing

DSM 12-Month Diagnosis	Languishing	Moderately Mentally Healthy	Flourishing
No	Languishing	Moderate mental health	Complete mental health
Yes	Mental illness and languishing	Mental illness moderately mentally healthy	Mental illness and flourishing

The core message of this book is to treat according to the profile of the patient and consider all aspects of the patient. The model provided by Keys et al. expands on this. For example, treating depressive symptoms in isolation of the patient's cognitive and physical limitations risks slower or less-effective reduction in depressive symptoms. However, simultaneously targeting a profile of depression, cognitive impairment, and physical disability provides a multipronged approach to helping patients cope with their problems, which in turn increases the likelihood of a successful outcome for depression treatment.

This newer perspective of the older adult should provide reasons for change. It allows the health care provider to treat outside the box. The issues being addressed are many: physical, mental, lifestyle, practical, and human. We now know, too, that the conditions that cause the most problems in terms of cost are respiratory disorders, cardiac disease, cancer, metabolic disease, and mental disorders. It is the last of these that captures our interest. Mental health disorders have risen in prevalence more than the others by substantial amounts in the last few decades. It is not far-fetched to say that even a slight reduction in mental health spending would assist in the overall cost of health care. If reducing symptom burden is paramount at later life and mental health is core to this, the issue is treating both. This is holistic care at its best.

Happiness Matters, But...

Happiness is a real, objective phenomenon. In fact, happiness, whatever it is, has an impact on bad feelings; it runs the gamut from pain and depression on one side to contentment on the other. In general, what makes us happy is also good for us. EEG measurements show that positive feelings occur with activation of the left frontal lobe; the right frontal area is dedicated to negative feelings (Davidson, 2004). There is also evidence that when one is happy, the body chemistry (e.g., blood pressure, heart rate variability) is in optimal ranges.

So what is happiness? Where Aristotle advocated for the good life in virtue, Ryff (1995) provided us with refined measures of purpose in life, autonomy, positive relationships, personal growth, and self-acceptance. Layard (2006; see the following list) presents seven factors that influence happiness. Issues that are closely related to these (divorce rate, unemployment rate, level of trust, membership in nonreligious organizations, quality of government, and fraction believing in God; Helliwell, 2003) result in problems with reduced happiness. It is interesting to note that data suggest that age, education, gender, and intelligence have only a negligible effect on happiness (Layard, 2006). As Adam Smith advocated, we want to be happy and seek to provide our present and future with opportunity for this; we also make mistakes (smoking) or are ignorant of our situations (get cancer from some exposure). We seem to vacillate in the pursuit of better living and our subjective assay of this state.

Big Seven Factors Affecting Happiness

Family relationships
Financial situation
Work
Community and friends
Health
Personal freedom
Personal values

Layard (2006)

We are subject, then, to a hedonic treadmill: initially we feel positive about good news, but quickly revert to baseline. We seem to try to exact from the gift or advantage we are given more than it can provide, and demand more of it. Happiness is elusive, and for it to be maximal we need an admixture of comfort and discomfort. Above all, we seem to require a clear concept of the common good, to be able to promote it. This involves a social structure for comfort and progress.

Sources of Happiness

We are social beings
We want to trust one another
We do best when we accept what is good enough and not feel that we need the best
We also generally accept the status quo and dislike losses
We are status conscious and seek equity in education and social zero-sum games
We are very adaptable; we enjoy success, but only for a little while
We get happiness from both inner life and outer life

There are, of course, no answers here. Whatever the final result, happiness demands an inner life that leads to uplifting of the spirit. Perhaps the secret is not to distort our perception of reality by unhelpful comparisons and accept things as they are without comparing them to anything better. Perhaps, too, we require values clarification, as we often do not know which things really make us happy. If we run into the happenstance of mental issues, we certainly should not lose sight of perspective, inner power, and reasonable social interventions.

PRACTICAL ISSUES FOR COMMUNITY CARE

Socioeconomic Status of Older Adults

Socioeconomic status (SES) factors such as low income and poor educational attainment are associated with comorbid mental disorders and medical conditions. A consistent inverse association exists between low SES and a variety of health indicators, health behaviors, and mortality (Harper & Lynch, 2007; Lantz, 1998; Lorant et al., 2003). For example, one meta-analysis showed that people of low SES are 1.8 times more likely to report being depressed than people who have a higher status (Lorant et al., 2003). Low SES may both contribute to the onset of mental disorders and be a consequence of the "downward drift" associated with a history of psychiatric disorders (Eaton & Muntaner, 1999). Crimmins, Kim, and Seeman (2009) examined poverty and biological risk, and their findings provide some plausible explanations for why age and mortality are not linearly related in clinical settings. Their data were collected from two National Health and Nutrition Examination Survey (NHANES) samples, which they then linked to the National Death Index. The NHANES data revealed that poor people in each decade of life (twenties to seventies) had higher levels of biological risk than people of similar age who are not poor, thus supporting the notion of premature aging in those who endure poverty. Figure 11.1 reflects this problem. Decline in mean cognition scores as we age is inevitable, but it is biased against those with a psychiatric history or with a disadvantaged childhood, or both. Although there are certainly independent moderating effects at later life, it is clear that this trend bodes ill for older adults, especially those with psychiatric histories or current problems, or with built-in socioeconomic disadvantages.

Whatever problems people may have, the older adult and especially older adults who are poor have more of them. Low SES is a well-documented determinant of obesity, heart problems, and cancer, as well as other health markers. In fact, it may be that there are sensitive periods in which certain ages experience more problems than others (childhood vs. adults). This may especially apply to mental health issues. As we have indicated in other chapters, anxiety and depression in socioeconomically disadvantaged older adults frequently go unrecognized and untreated. Mental health care need is always associated with impairments in IADL; more medical illness; decreased mobility; smaller social network size; more severe life events; and increased use of medical, human, and informal services. Most of those with mental health care needs were not receiving help. Compared with residents receiving mental health care, residents with untreated needs were more likely to be men and have more IADL impairment, medical illness, severe life events, onsite social worker use, and human services use. Mental illness is most common and largely untreated in public housing residents. Increasing collaboration among medical, mental, and human services is needed to improve identification, treatment, and ultimately prevention of late-life mental illness in this community setting (Simning, van Wijngaarden, Fisher, Richardson, & Conwell, 2012).

FIGURE 11.1 Declines in Mean Cognition Scores by Psychiatric History and Childhood Disadvantage, Health and Retirement Study/AHEAD

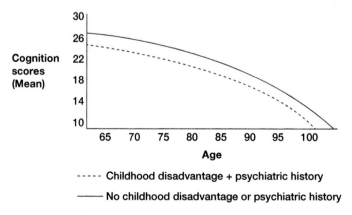

Adjustment/Functioning in Community

Well-being is complex. The psychological process of assimilation and accommodation allows for the preservation of positive emotions despite significant age-related losses. In general, older adults conserve resources and disengage from unattainable goals. Regarding degenerative diseases, the decline in function is progressive, starting out with more sophisticated IADL (managing finances, driving, handling medications) and segues to a faltering in ADL. The decline is reasonably linear and progressive.

In the main, there is no more important function in life than good adjustment. This is a marker for healthy living as well as adapting to problems. ADL and IADL are the best markers of adjustment and are measured in many ways. They differently predict frequency of hospital contact, LTC facility placement, and mortality. Knowledge of these is critical and impacts everything in care for the older adult. These variables are discussed in Chapter 12.

There is one other issue that we have so far avoided: late-life psychotic episodes independent of dementia. In general, the median lifetime risk of schizophrenia is 0.4%, peaking in adolescence, midlife, or late life. It is unknown whether aging has an influence on psychotoform symptoms, either positive or negative. But what is important is that the frequency of psychotic symptoms (most commonly paranoid delusions), which stands at a 13% level (Kohler et al., 2013), is not trivial. These data also indicate more of a problem if one belongs to a minority, has some cognitive impairment, is older, female, has low SES, or has previous mental illness.

FIGURE 11.2 Progressive Loss of ADL

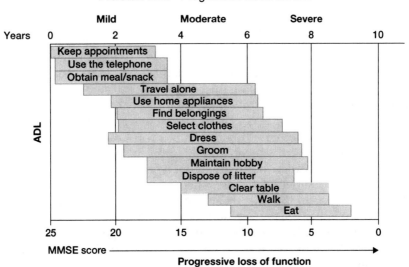

MMSE, Mini Mental State Examination.

This is important because the older, severely mentally ill can be monitored by their levels of adjustment. Older psychotic-level adults do not seem to cognitively decline any more than healthy older adults (Rajji et al., 2013), but are at high risk for dementia (Kohler et al., 2013). However, their service needs (life issues) are likely to be high (Meesters et al., 2013). It is noteworthy that most older adults who possess these problems at late life have sufficient cognitive strength and skill to appreciate the Watch and Wait model and be dealt with according to the five factors posited here.

Finally, we note, again, that *prevention rules*. Without a shift away from the focus on individual problems to a focus on an understanding of nurturing environments, progress in mental health will be slow. This involves the big picture of education, preventive health, crime prevention, and abuse/ neglect, among other factors. The IOM report emphasized a developmental perspective on risk and protective factors (National Research Council [NRC] & IOM, 2009). At different stages of development, some factors (divorce, medical illness) may increase the likelihood of a person developing difficulties, whereas others (stable parental relationship, positive parenting) may promote resilience. Integrative models suggest that depression may be determined in part by familial and genetic factors and in part by life adversities. One intervention that has been successful is that of Clarke and colleagues (1995), who showed that the Coping With Stress model was successful intervention in preventing depression in the elderly. Assessment and waiting (Watch and Wait) made a difference.

Caregiving

On the basis of the experiences of 1,480 family caregivers, AARP and the National Alliance for Caregiving compiled a report titled "Caregiving in the United States," which posits that an estimated 65.7 million Americans served as caregivers in the year 2012. This is 28% of the population. Nearly one third of American households reported at least one person serving in an unpaid caregiving role. Now there are over 2,000 studies on caregivers of persons with dementia/stroke/medical illness. The psychological condition of the caregiver also is critical. Depression is present in 28%, and 34% have depressive symptoms. This results in poorer caregiving, more problems with the identified patient, and big problems for care receivers (CR). As the strain and burden of caregiving for a person with AD increases, the likelihood of a caregiver developing depressive symptoms also increases. Although 57% report that their health is excellent or very good, 17% report that it is only fair or poor (compared with 13% of the total population).

As mentioned earlier, the longer the caregiving goes on, the more of a toll it takes: 23% of those who have been providing care for 5 years or longer report fair or poor health, 31% report feeling stressed by their situation, and 15% report financial strain. Spousal caregivers report more depression than nonspouse caregivers. Less-educated caregivers also report more depression. Family caregivers report chronic health conditions at a rate of two times that of same-age noncaregivers. Caregiving-related stress in chronically ill spouses is associated with 63% higher mortality rate than noncaregivers. Stress from caring for a relative with dementia impacts the caregiver's immune system up to 3 years after the experience. It has been estimated that this type of caregiving can age a person by 10 years (Braun, Mikulincer, Rydall, Walsh, & Rodin, 2007).

The added burden of a loved one's cognitive deterioration has been attributed to increased intensity of caregiving in terms of: (a) time involved in caregiving over the course of a day, and (b) degree of assistance needed for basic and complex ADL (Russo, Vitaliano, Brewer, Katon, & Becker, 1995). In their meta-analysis, Pinquart and Sörensen (2003b) also found that patient behavior problems were more strongly related to caregiver burden than were patient physical and cognitive impairments, the amount of care provided, or duration of caregiving. Caregiver burden also is problematic in the context of dementia, as there are many correlates and moderators. Indeed, there appears to be a recursive interaction that engages the strengths and problems present within both the patient and the caregiver, thus contributing to increased burden. Type and severity of the patient's neuropsychiatric problems intensify both caregiver involvement and distress, and eventually lead to early placement of the patient in long-term care (Black & Almeida, 2004; Covinsky et al., 2003).

The weight of evidence, then, indicates that certain caregiver characteristics are associated with increased psychiatric morbidity, especially having concomitant health problems (Brodaty, Griffin, & Hadzi-Pavlovic, 1990), being female (Mausbach et al., 2006), having poor coping behaviors (Mausbach et al., 2006), showing high expressed emotion (Vitaliano, Russo, Young, Teri, & Maiuro, 1991), and, as noted, being the care recipient's spouse (Lyons, Zarit, Sayer, & Whitlatch, 2002). Other caregiver characteristics that increase psychiatric difficulties include caregiver "overload," poor life satisfaction, role captivity, and depression. One study that examined the relationship of caregiver depression to burden found that caregiver burden mediated the relationship between patient problem behaviors and caregiver depression (Clyburn, Stones, Hadjistavropoulos, & Tuokko, 2000).

Treatment

Caregiving is far from a simple area when treatment is at issue (Schultz et al., 1999). Data from the Resources for Enhancing Alzheimer's Health (REACH; Harrow et al., 2004) caregiver project have shown that the caregiving spouse can actually receive valuable help from the patient. When the patient is responding well, the caregiver thrives. When caregivers are distressed, the patient almost invariably does poorly, so adjunctive care for the caregiver is beneficial to both. In this context, caregiving in the home has been expanded with telephone support (Smith & Toseland, 2011) and adult day respite services (ADS-Plus; Gitlin, Reever, Dennis, Mathieu, & Hauck, 2006), among others. Adult day services programs target the primary stressors of caregiving: behavior problems of the care recipient and the physical, mental, and social health of the caregiver. Family caregivers initially meet face to face with the service director to (a) identify areas of concerns and needs, (b) develop a care plan to minimize identified areas of difficulty, and (c) implement an agreed-upon care plan with four components (counseling, education, referral, and periodic supportive contact with the site's family service director).

In general, there are three categories of evidence-based therapies (EBTs) for caregivers. They include psychoeducational programs (behavioral management, depression management, anger management, progressively lower stress); psychotherapy, involving cognitive behavioral therapy (CBT) especially; and multicomponent programs using a combination of two or more approaches (e.g., counseling, support group attendance). Using a patient goal, intervention desired, comparison to other interventions, and outcome (PICO) format, Gaughler (2011) showed that psychoeducation and multicomponent domains are effective.

- Psychoeducation: Effective
  - In a meta-analysis, group-based supportive interventions based on a psychoeducational framework were effective in reducing psychological morbidity (Gallagher-Thompson, & Coon, 2007).
  - In a meta-analysis, psychoeducational interventions had consistent short-term benefits across outcomes (Pinquart & Sörensen, 2003a).
  - In a systematic review, individual strategies were more effective than group or education-based approaches, although teaching coping strategies in group or individual settings seemed to provide short-term psychological benefits (Selwood, Johnston, Katona, Lyketsos, & Livingston, 2007).
  - In a systematic review, combining social support and problem-solving approaches appeared effective (Areán & Cook, 2002).
  - In a systematic review, a brief education intervention appeared to reduce caregiver depression (Peacock & Forbes, 2003).
- Supportive Interventions: Possibly Effective
  - In a systematic review, combining social support and problem-solving approaches appeared effective (Areán & Cook, 2002).
  - In a meta-analysis, supportive interventions had some effect on burden and ability/knowledge but not on other outcomes (Sörensen, Pinquart, & Duberstein, 2002).
- Respite: Possibly Effective
  - In a meta-analysis, respite had some effect on burden, depression, and well-being of caregivers (Sörensen, Pinquart, & Duberstein, 2002).
  - In a systematic review, respite appeared to reduce burden and depression in some studies, but this trend tended to occur among lower-quality studies (Shaw et al., 2009).
- Psychotherapy: Effective
  - In a meta-analysis, psychotherapy had an effect on all outcome variables (Sörensen, Pinquart, & Duberstein, 2002).

- In a systematic review, CBT (along with relaxation-based therapy) appeared effective in reducing caregiver anxiety (Cooper et al., 2007).
- In a systematic review, individual strategies, such as multisession behavior management therapy, were found to be effective (Selwood, Johnston, Katona, Lyketsos, & Livingston, 2007).
- Multicomponent: Effective
  - An evidence-based guideline found that interventions with several components are important in dementia treatment.
  - A meta-analysis found that only multicomponent interventions were effective

Acton and Kang (2001).

Specific Interventions

The interconnection of problems can be complex, even to the extent that progress is made problematic. Problems can actually increase if progress is made. A study of 130 depressed older adults and their spouses or adult children examined the impact of caregiver burden specific to patients' depressive symptoms or patients' response to antidepressant treatment. Primary care patients completed medical, psychiatric, and neuropsychological assessments prior to treatment, and interviews were conducted with their identified family member. As hypothesized, caregivers' depression-specific burden predicted greater depression severity for the patient at week 6 of treatment after accounting for patients' pretreatment characteristics, caregivers' depressive symptoms, and caregivers' relationship satisfaction (Martire et al., 2008).

Resilience also is a factor. From the caregiving perspective, caregivers can be resilient (Gaugler, Kane, & Newcomer, 2007) and experience uplifts (Fulton Picot, Youngblut, & Zeller, 1997) in the face of dementia. In this context, support can also cause problems. Findings on 948 older people who were classified as demented, frail, or healthy were convincing: Treatments that slow the progression of dementia did not necessarily relieve caregiver strain (Holley, Murrell, & Mast, 2006).

Below is a listing of several concepts about caregiving. The list starts with overall caregiving tasks: what needs to be done and what can be done. It builds on the core relationship that the identified patient has: Is the relationship a good one? It extends to aspects of exemplary care: Is the relationship one of love and respect worthy of special consideration (Dooley & Hinojosa, 2004)? Exemplary behavior mediates the relationships between subjective appraisals (daily bother, burden, and behavioral bother) and emotional outcomes (depression and positive aspects of caregiving). Willingness is also a feature: Can the caregiver accept, or is the caregiver willing to undertake, difficult tasks? Finally, practical issues are never far from the mix. It is interesting to note that several studies have shown that objective problems are not as impactful as subjective ones. As will be shown in Chapter 12, caregiving can be assessed in many ways: we apply the Zarit Burden Scale (Zarit & Zarit, 1983).

---

1. Overall Caregiver Tasks
   - Acknowledge the disease
   - Make a cognitive shift
   - Develop emotional tolerance
   - Take control
   - Establish a realistic goal
   - Gauge the recipient's capacities
   - Design opportunities for satisfying work
   - Become a sleuth

2. Patient's Relationship Skills
   Self-efficacy
   I believe that I have good skills when it comes to my care situation.
   Relational coping with caregivers
   I often tell my caregiver that I appreciate him/her.
   Perceptions of dependence
   People tend to think I cannot do things that I can do.
   Performance-related quality of life
   I can still do a number of things that I have enjoyed all my life.
   Accepting help
   I just accept the fact that that I need help.

3. Caregiver's Exemplary Care:
   I take the time to sit and talk with the CR.
   I make sure that food is what is desired and nutritious.

4. Cope with Willingness
   ✓ Will you feel what you feel when you feel it?
   ✓ Are you willing to think the thoughts you are already thinking?
   ✓ Are you willing to engage in the experience that you are already in?
   ✓ Remember that willingness is not about a belief of whether or not you are able to do something, but rather whether you are willing in the moment?
   ✓ Do not use "if" statements or self-deception.
   ✓ Never ask someone "if" they would enter an anxiety-provoking situation.

5. Practical Problems
   - Shifting of power and renegotiation of roles
   - Financial and legal concerns
   - Palliative care
   - The question of institutionalization

Values also add something to the caregiving experience. They concern choices of what the caregiver wants life to be about and what is important. Each of us chooses values for living. Values are important to recognize in caregiving because the caregiver has a better chance of feeling like a whole person if the sense is that he or she is being consistent with the values held. Values that have been important throughout life may include such things as the family is important, taking care of self is important, or being a loving person is important. The belief is that adherence to values can help with acceptance of thoughts and feelings. The task is to identify the caregiver's values. Set a range of small to bigger goals, which will help the caregiver progress slowly in that direction.

Anticipatory Grief

Anticipatory grief is the experience of the pangs of grief before the actual loss. It often occurs as a prelude to an ugly death caused by the degenerative process. Sadness starts early in the caregiving process. Support can also cause problems. Findings on 948 older people who were classified as demented, frail, or healthy were convincing: Treatments that slow the progression of dementia did not necessarily relieve caregiver strain, as two thirds of caregivers reported grief before the death of the DR, resulting from ambiguity about the relationship, loss of previously established roles, loss of intimacy, and loss of control (Holley et al., 2006). Meuser, Marwit, and Sanders (2004) noted that anticipatory grief explained an additional 12% to 21% of the variance of burden beyond background characteristics, primary stressors, and depressive symptoms.

Figure 11.4 offers a schema of the normal throes of grief after a CR's death. It indicates that the process of grieving undulates over time but can include grief experiences at many points in time. Grief is a real problem and the *DSM-5* (2013) has removed this as an exception for depression, suggesting that it is prevalent and needs to be treated more aggressively.

Home Care

One model regarding interventions for older adults who have impairment considers home care. This model has been labeled "medical homes." Perhaps above all, prevention is emphasized: Early identification and intervention, chronic disease management, and person-centered approaches are based on the adoption of evidence-based practice (EBP). There are now several compelling examples of integrated care interventions targeting mental health and substance use in elderly adults that include psychological interventions/supervision. We have discussed IMPACT and PROSPECT in other chapters.

FIGURE 11.3 Grief Patterns

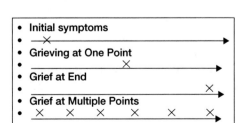

The core issue involves home care with a caregiver emphasis. Hicken and Plowhead (2010) outlined the effective use of home care for depression, anxiety, and many health-related conditions, such as type 2 diabetes and heart disease, as well as traumatic brain injury. In 2007, the Veterans Administration (VA) Office of Mental Health Services began offering home-based psychological services. The typical home-care patient in this system has eight or more chronic medical conditions, and 47% have reached *dependent* status on two or more ADL. Depression and/or anxiety are typically part of the picture. Interventions involved environmental distractions, role clarification, boundaries, time management, safety, and provider competence.

The PATH (Home Delivered Problem Adaptation Therapy for Depressed, Cognitively Impaired, Disabled Elders; Kiosses, Arean, Teri, & Alexopoulos, 2010) model has been studied in this context. This model focuses on the patient's ecosystem: patient, caregiver, and home. Problem-solving therapy is applied. Environmental adaptation tools and caregiver participation are required. Environmental tools are designed to bypass any behavioral and functional limitations identified in the patient. The PATH tools include calendars, checklists, pictures, notebooks, notepads, alarms, signs, colored tags, diaries, timers, timed prerecorded messages, voice alarms, customized audiotapes, and a step-by-step division of tasks. This intervention is done in the home in 12 sessions with the caregiver's participation. A trial comparing PATH with standard treatment revealed that the PATH care model was more efficacious than standard treatment in reducing depression and disability in these especially vulnerable patients (Kiosses et al., 2010). At this time, cost data that compare PATH to usual care point in the direction of savings in terms of usage and quality of life.

As noted, most older adults with dementia will be cared for by primary care physicians, but the primary care practice setting presents numerous challenges to providing quality care for these individuals. Callahan et al. (2006) conducted a clinical trial of 153 older adults with AD and their caregivers, with the dyad randomized by physician to receive collaborative care management ($n = 84$) or augmented usual care ($n = 69$) at primary care practices within two U.S. university-affiliated health care systems. Intervention patients received 1 year of care management by an interdisciplinary team led by an advanced practice nurse working with the patient's caregiver. The team used standard protocols to initiate treatment and identify, monitor, and treat behavioral and psychological symptoms of dementia, stressing nonpharmacological management. The Neuropsychiatric Inventory (NPI) was administered at baseline and at 6, 12, and 18 months. Secondary outcomes included the Cornell Scale for Depression in Dementia (CSDD), cognition, ADL, resource use, and caregiver's depression severity.

Initiated by caregivers' reports, 89% of intervention patients triggered at least one protocol for behavioral and psychological symptoms of dementia, with a mean of four protocols per patient from a total of eight possible protocols. Intervention patients were more likely to receive cholinesterase inhibitors and antidepressants than patients receiving usual care. Intervention patients had significantly fewer behavioral and psychological symptoms of dementia. Intervention caregivers also reported significant improvements in distress. Collaborative care for the treatment of AD, therefore, resulted in substantial improvement in the quality of care, in behavioral and psychological symptoms of dementia among primary care patients, and in reduced symptoms of depression among their caregivers.

This form of care is increasingly important. At our primary care clinic (PCC), we see more than 100 patients in their homes. They cannot come to the clinic due to transportation, physical limitations, resistance, and logistics barriers. We send a team with a physician assistant (PA) and aide, as well as a geriatric fellow. Four results have evolved. First, this is universally appreciated and valued. Second, we are able to see conditions at home and provide substantial input and provide recommendations, from nutrition to basic issues of heat and hygiene. Third, we become friends and confidants for such a service. Last but not least, we improve on cost and hospital admissions, as well as medication administration. In most cases, we also identify psychological problems and can reduce medications, especially regarding the use of antipsychotics or sedative-hypnotics.

Other Problems

This section could be a book in and of itself. The list that follows highlights many "other problems," but not all. In addition to the issues already discussed, the panorama of money problems; basic life concerns like transportation (driving especially), housing, and food; and idiosyncratic issues are not to be taken lightly. Of course, any of these can be major problems, especially if there are other issues such as cognitive decline and little social support.

Community Problems

Finances
Competence
Transportation
Medical insurance
Iatrogenic disease
Housing needs
Meals on wheels
Nutrition

Driving
Elder abuse
Practical functioning
Relapse issues

Abuse in any of these areas leads to real or iatrogenic problems. Prevalence for such problems varies between 10% and 40%. Problems can be subtle, as in medical and cognitive decline in older adults who still drive (Emerson, Johnson, Dawson, Anderson, & Rizzo, 2011); or more obvious, as in medical emergencies. Many problems are often born in hospital settings. Common problems can include excessive medicine and emergency room (ER) use, rehospitalization, drug effects, falls, nosocomial infections, pressure ulcers, delirium, and surgery complications. In 2003, Peyriere et al. reported that the rate of adverse drug events as a cause for hospital admission was 57%. Studies of U.S. patients 65 years and older indicate that each year more than 180,000 life-threatening or fatal adverse drug effects occur in the outpatient setting. The bottom line is that, generally, intervention and support are available for most problems, if only there is awareness and an early warning system.

Case: Mr. V, alone, depressed, possible cognitive problems, pain, has issues with the government.

BACKGROUND: The patient is a 65-year-old man who indicates that approximately 8 years ago he started noticing problems with his memory. More recently he has had difficulty that involves being inattentive, getting discouraged easily, being apathetic, as well as having difficulty with concentration. He also related that he has been very stressed over his treatment from the military after 25 years. Over the past 5 years, however, he has had considerable problems with practical and health issues, including loss of a job, need for a caregiver, and pain. He has chronic back problems. Currently, he is not married, lives locally, and is fighting retirement issues with the Air Force and the VA. He is having problems with transportation, finances, getting help at home with shopping, and in general caregiving. He does not yet receive Social Security disability but has 10% VA disability. He complains of transportation difficulty, money, and the need for assistance with health care.

The patient is a native of Puerto Rico. He is the second of four children and his father died when he was 6 years old. He notes that his early life was very positive and upbeat. That said, when he was 15 years, he went to visit New York City and remained there to attend high school. He was married at age 18 years and had two children from that union; his wife died after 3 years. He worked on Wall Street for a while, then returned to Puerto Rico, and at age 30 years he went into the Air Force. He remained there for 4 years, took a break, and then returned to the Air Force and finished out his service after 25 years. He had no combat action. He was married three more times, once at age 23 for approximately 26 years, and has a total of five children. He also has several grandchildren. When in the Air Force he worked as an accountant. He has been out of the Air Force for 5 years. He indicates he is very inactive.

He had several operations throughout the years: both shoulders, gallbladder, and umbilical hernia. He indicates that he has back problems with problems at L1–L5. He had one nerve block in 2010. He also has difficulty with sleep and suffers from sleep apnea, restless leg syndrome, and possibly rapid eye movement (REM) behavior disorder. He indicated that between 2005 and 2012 he had difficulty with his pancreas and lymph nodes. He is in pain and is depressed. Prior to this, while in the military, he incurred tuberculosis (TB) after being in Saudi Arabia, causing health problems in 2001–2002. He denies alcohol or tobacco use, and indicates that he spends his day being very inactive, staying in the house alone. He can do most of the ADL but has some problems with IADL. He needs some assistance from others for basic needs. Family is not available. He has 126 credits from various universities across the years, having been in the Air Force, but has no degree. He is taking several psychiatric medications, including antidepressants. He is also on Provigil. He is on ibuprofen or Toradol for pain.

RESULTS: Mr. V's scores (Wechsler Adult Intelligence Scale [WAIS IV] subtests) are varied (scale score range 7–14). On the basis of the Oklahoma Premorbid Intelligence Estimate (OPIE-Vocabulary (9) subtest), his intelligence is low average. Although culture may be an issue, he has been in this country since adolescence. Given his other scores and past achievements, he is considered to now be lower than his level of premorbid intelligence. Mr. V scored a Repeatable Battery for the Assessment of Neuropsychological Status (RBANS) index of 84 (mildly impaired), placing him at the 14% level compared with other people his age and education. He had problems with new learning, less with attention and language. On Delayed Memory he was able to recall 5 of 10 words, 7 of 12 story-recall bits, and 18 of 20 figural recall data points. He scored low average on the recognition task (18 of 20). He did well on tests of executive function. His Montreal Cognitive Assessment (MoCA) is 25 of 30; his MMSE was 28 of 30, and he lost points on both tests for memory. These scores indicate that he is scoring at slightly below average levels but within his mean level. Several deficits were registered on the Functional Activities Questionnaire. He is inactive around the house. He calls for rides or he drives himself.

This man had no evident problems with vision. He can see adequately and does not wear glasses. He had no problems with hearing. He was in pain when at rest. He is in pain too when he walks and he walks with a cane. Driving at present is a problem for him.

Emotional self-report scales indicate mild depression and no anxiety. He was administered the Mini-International Neuropsychiatric Interview (MINI), which showed depression. The Personality Assessment Inventory (PAI) indicated suspiciousness and mistrust in his relations with others that is unusual even in clinical samples. He is a hypervigilant individual who often questions and mistrusts the motives of those around him. He does demonstrate an unusual degree of concern about physical functioning and health matters and probable impairment arising from somatic symptoms. He reported that his daily functioning has been compromised by numerous and varied physical problems.

The Millon Behavioral Medicine Diagnostic (MBMD) indicates problems. He scored as depressed. He has an introversive personality and is dejected, as well as oppositional and self-denigrating as a personality profile. His self-concept appears to involve a generally negative self-evaluation that may vary from states of harsh self-criticism and self-doubt to periods of relative self-confidence and intact self-esteem. His interpersonal style seems best characterized as withdrawn and introverted. He seems to have little interest in socializing, and his passive style in relationships probably does not invite social interaction with others. His stress moderators indicated problems in functional deficits, illness apprehension, pain sensitivity, and pessimism; his treatment prognostics indicate problems in information fragility and utilization excess. He rated pain at present as 5 out of 10; average 6 out of 10. Sleep currently is a problem as he has sleep apnea, restless leg syndrome (RLS), and perhaps REM Behavior Disorder. He is not napping during the day but is tired (Epworth Sleepiness Scale [ESS] = 13).

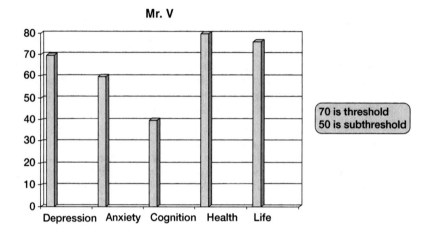

Mr. V

70 is threshold
50 is subthreshold

Mr. V—WATCH AND WAIT MODEL

Sessions 1–3:
He is a 65-year-old man who was referred for an evaluation for cognitive and affect status. He has problems with living, being alone, and needing assistance from others. His last few months have been a problem with day-to-day living issues especially. He lives at home alone. He is cognitively stable and able to handle his needs intellectually. Affectively he has some problems. He is depressed. He does not enjoy simple things, has become sloppy in his life, excessively irritable, and nonaffectionate. He is also suspicious of others. He has a depressive and isolative as well as self-denigrating personality profile. He mostly does his ADL but needs help with IADL and living issues. He may not be eating well. He has no goals and has no real friends. He does sleep excessively.

Plans were made to address his life and get help during the week with some local family.

Permission was requested to call them and enlist help. He agreed. He was also to get out of the house one time a day and call on some military friends. He was asked to provide reasons for this. He was to monitor this as well as his mood. He was also to make an appointment with the VA representative whom he trusted and have set questions for him to ask. He did trust his one son who was to assist with money confusion. Pain and sleep were also issues that would be addressed. He was taught relaxation, pacing, and self-rewards.

Mr. V agreed to the plans and discussed the problems with compliance. He seems to have been the victim of a cascade of events that led to his being lost in a maze of medical confusion and living problems. He sees himself as unable to handle tasks and is inclined to give up. This was to be challenged. He feels disavowed by the military and angry/irritable/confused/helpless because of this. His family is not available for him.

Watch and Wait Category	Check
Validate problem	×
Psychoeducation of model	×
Assessment	×
Monitoring	×
Case formulation	×
Check alliance	×

Sessions 4–12:
Issues of first concern involve coordinating his living needs (nutrition, transportation, appointments, and shopping), mood, and personality concerns of isolation and suspiciousness. He was presented a plan that involved use of a paid caregiver for several hours/day who would assist with shopping, meals, and organizing his day; monitoring his mood and positive events; interfacing with a pain program; and developing a plan to overcome self-defeating thoughts and behaviors. He will continue to take his antidepressant meds and be evaluated in the future. He agreed, and is committed to the program.

The treatment plan was pursued. The caregiver became a part of the treatment for portions of the time. Monitoring was very helpful, as he was able to see that his depression was highest in the afternoon when he was least active and prone to sleep. A sleep hygiene program was initiated and he responded well. Pain issues were less successful but he accommodated better. He was more active and applied relaxation well. Key personnel in the VA were involved to clear up confusion as to his health status. He also responded better to frustrations and was able to seek goals that were actually more positive to him.

Booster sessions: He continues to be seen every other month. He is less depressed, more active, and is reacting to pain better. More importantly, he has a less negative attitude toward life and a more positive plan for his future. He is actually dating again.

LONG-TERM CARE

Nursing home has a factory culture.

Jiska Cohen Mansfield

No one wants to enter a nursing home (NH). There are ~1.43 million residents in 15,850 licensed NHs and 2.5 million yearly discharges: 86% occupancy rate (a decline over a decade). In 30 years, NH went from 79 average beds to 107 and short stay (< 30 days) residents now equal 10%, with 9.5% staying 30 to 90 days and 80% having long-term stays. About 10% stay for more than 3 years. In addition, 50% have five or more ADL problems and 75% require help in three or more ADL. The typical resident is a White, unmarried woman, >85 years old, with few social supports, who is widowed. Residents are sicker: On admission, 3.9% have pressure sores, 40% have congestive heart failure (CHF), 22% diabetes, and 26% stroke.

There is more. Over $231 billion is spent for long-term care (LTC), resulting in $76,000/year/resident. Medicaid pays for 65% and Medicare 14%. There are more than 3 million direct-care workers. The biggest problems for workers (based on 1,147 expert respondents) are workforce staffing, financing, and quality achievement. There is also general agreement that there should be a rebalancing away from LTC to home-care-based services (see Hyer & Intrieri, 2006). The movements of the last two decades in LTC include Culture Change, Wellspring Initiative, Pioneers, Eden Alternative, Benedictine, and Social Culture. These initiatives have made a concerted effort to ameliorate the excessive regulation and scrutiny of these facilities.

Facts Related to Nursing Homes

- Federal guidelines: Licensed nurse on each shift: RN on duty at least 8 hr/7 d/wk; no federal requirements for staff/resident ratios.
- 9 of 10 inadequately staffed: $8 billion to correct this.
- Once a person is 65 years old, 40% chance of NH admittance.
- Nine percent of NH residents are under 65 years of age. This group comes at age 50 years and stays for 2 years.
- Many residents are in subacute care with delirium and psychiatric problems.
- Predictors of NH admission: age, low income, poor social supports, low social activity, cognitive impairment, incontinence, functional impairment.
- Minorities are underrepresented in LTC, but African American residents are increasing in numbers.
- NH residents are getting sicker: On admission, 3.9% have pressure sores, 40% CHF, 22% diabetes, 26% stroke.
- Persistent use of antidepressants (79%), antipsychotics (75%), or another psychotropic drug (88%) is common.
- Changes are small and hard to detect regarding the course of psychosis, agitation, or depression over time.
- Conclusion: Lots of psychiatric symptoms; most are chronically present, but individual symptoms often show an intermittent course.

Selbæk, Kirkevold, and Engedal (2007)

Prevalence of Psychiatric Problems

The prevalence of depression among NH residents is well established, with estimates ranging between 6% and 25% for major depression (e.g., Parmelee, Katz, & Lawton, 1991; Teresi, Abrams, Holmes, Ramirez, & Eimicke, 2001) compared with community estimates of 2% to 8% (Robins & Regier 1991).

Minor or subsyndromal depressive syndromes may be as prevalent as 50% (Kim & Rovner, 1995; Parmelee et al., 1991; Samuels & Katz, 1995; Teresi et al., 2001). Despite this prevalence, and the fact that many evidence-based treatments are available for depression in late life (e.g., Lebowitz et al., 1997; Scogin, Welsh, Hanson, Stump, & Coates, 2005), relatively little is known about the effectiveness or acceptability of depression treatments in NHs (Snowden, Sato, & Roy-Byrne, 2003).

The most common approach to treatment is to use antidepressant medications. Data from the Centers for Medicare & Medicaid Services suggest that, nationwide, an average of 43.3% of NH residents take these medications (American Society of Consulting Pharmacists, 2006). However, there is evidence that, as they are presently being used, antidepressants are not fully effective in dealing with depressive symptoms of NH residents (Weintraub, Datto, Streim, & Katz, 2002), and that potential side effects pose particular dangers in this frail population (Butters et al., 1997; Katz, Parmelee, Beaston-Wimmer, & Smith, 1994; Thapa, Gideon, Cost, Milam, & Ray, 1998). Furthermore, older adults have expressed preference for psychotherapy over medication in the treatment of depression (Gum et al., 2006). Additional treatment options are needed, either as supplemental or alternative approaches, for depressed NH residents.

It is well known that a significant number of older adults receive little or no treatment for depression. We have learned that depression diminishes overall quality of life and has been associated with significant disability in physical, interpersonal, and social role functioning. In LTC, depression exacerbates other problems, such as functional deficits, behavioral disturbances, poor nutrition, noncompliance with treatment, pain, excess disability in dementia, morbidity, and even mortality (see Hyer & Intrieri, 2006).

Increasingly, newer psychotherapy models have been applied in LTC. In Appendix B, we outline one of these: the Group, Individual, and Family Treatment/Group, Individual, and Staff Therapy model. The idea is to keep the therapy simple and to optimize the core problems in a depression (an underrepresentation of pleasant events and negative mood). In addition, BE-ACTIVE is a therapy applied effectively in LTC (Meeks et al., 2011). This is a 10-session intervention with four components: (1) individual weekly meetings between the depressed resident and a mental health consultant; (2) involvement of facility staff, particularly from the activities department, including a 3-hour staff training component and ongoing collaboration throughout the intervention period; (3) systematic assessment and increase of pleasant events; and (4) assessment and removal of barriers through behavioral problem solving and weekly communication between the mental health consultant and activities staff. Other models have emphasized use of the A–B–C behavioral method (Teri et al., 2006) to understand obstacles and, if necessary, to develop a behavior plan to overcome them.

CONCLUSION

Case studies cry out for more innovative and less costly models of care for older adults. These are being developed under the aegis of primary care and integrated health, with mental health as the fulcrum. As we have argued, mental health has a wide swath of influences/causes and an increasing number of available interventions. In this process, we have not addressed newer models involving telehealth and medical recordkeeping. We have kept our eye on the ball, placing emphases on prevention, personal participation, and case-managed interdisciplinary care. Mental health treatment must be broad and effective. Single specialty clinics are not the answer, as they are no more effective than many other options and are more costly; single mental health professionals also are anachronistic, because effective responses require more.

In this chapter, we highlight the function and adjustment needs of the older adult. Again, we have argued that a new look at the care of older adults is in order, one that addresses the coincident mental health and physical health of older adults. Absent this, we will see increased cost and continued problems. A reasonable design for the treatment of medical and mental health comorbidities is based on the public health target "indicated," in which prevention is sought for high-risk individuals before they become patients. This includes geriatric mental problems. Identification of predictors of treatment response and personalization of treatment (i.e., matching the treatment to the patient) have long been contemplated as a strategy to increase efficacy, to prevent relapses, to preempt disability, and to obviate a worsening of medical morbidity and cognitive decline. It is prudent to have a "problem watch" for at-risk patients and to carefully monitor interventions regarding the need for treatment changes, discontinuations, or implementation of different interventions.

Objectively, the additive effect of both genetic and environmental risk factors likely best accounts for the data. All of life is a stochastic process, in which one component leads to another. In fact, a balance of positive and negative genetic and good-living factors affects the brain throughout life to influence the degree of cognitive agility or impairment at late life. Internally, these factors increase or decrease oxidative stress, inflammation, insulin-signaling components, size and frequency of infarcts, and concentration of growth factors, cortisol, and other hormones. Externally, a kind of social genomics unfolds, and the person thrives or not based on supports, perspective, resources, and reasonable interventions. In effect, an older individual's "fate" unfolds as we would expect based on personal actions and integrated preventive care. This occurs for mental as well as physical problems, and represents a good treatment paradigm.

All that said, older adults want life to be fulfilling. With a low SES, stress, and difficult life circumstances, older adults become victims of living and often perceive problems as greater than the sum of their parts.

The experience of living, the nature of what makes people happy, and the ability to accommodate and assimilate make for a self that is vibrant and searching, even if worn and unrewarded. These situations make psychotherapy important, and for many necessary.

Perhaps we are really pawns of our brains and these externals of living are simply phantasms of the soul, signifying little. Regardless, the health care clinician needs to respect all.

After exploring various definitions of self—a soul, an agent with free will, some essential or unique set of qualities—Hood (in *The Self Illusion*) concludes that what we experience as a self is actually a narrative spun by our brain ... [N]eural activity reveals what an individual will do before that person becomes conscious of having made a decision. Perhaps our sense of free will is just a way for our brain to organize our actions and memories. Our sense of self is just an after-the-fact organization trick of the brain. As with a just-so story, our brain synthesizes the complex interactions of biology and environment to create a simplified explanation of who we are.

Yuhas (2012)

CHAPTER 12

Assessment

Lee Hyer and Sanna Catherine Tillitski

Assessment is an eminent theoretical process which requires a weighting of this and a disqualifying of that across the idiosyncrasies and commonalities of methods and data sources through multiple iterations of hypothesis generation and testing. The ideal result is a "theory of the client," a theory in which every loose end has been tied up in a logic so compelling that it seems to follow from a logic of the client's own psyche, so convincing that one gets the feeling that things could not be otherwise.

—*Millon and Bloom* (2008)

Psychological assessment is at least as valid as most medical tests (Meyer et al., 2001). As a prelude to and follow-up after psychotherapy, psychological assessment can enhance the therapeutic process in several ways, including (a) the delineation of clinical symptomatology, (b) hypothesis testing and decision making regarding differential diagnoses, (c) assisting in case formulation, (d) predicting a client's ability to participate as well as degree of participation in psychotherapy, (e) predicting health care usage, (f) hypothesis testing for therapy impasses or looming therapy failure, (g) monitoring treatment effects over time, (h) the confirmation (or disconfirmation) of perceived psychotherapy outcomes, (i) improving prediction of relapse, and (j) enabling the clinician to respond to managed care and other external pressures (Antony & Barlow, 2002). These have special meaning for older adults.

The most common method that psychologists use for clinical data collection is the unstructured interview, coupled with informal observation (Mash & Foster, 2001; Mash & Hunsley, 1993; Meyer et al., 2001). Older adults, however, are relentlessly complex beings, so these methods, though seemingly time efficient, can have significant limitations. In fact, Fennig, Craig, Tanenberg-Karant, and Bromet (1994) long ago showed that diagnoses derived from clinical interviews alone agreed only about 50% of the time with diagnoses derived from multimethod assessments. Rates of agreement among physicians regarding dementia and depression are not much better.

Indeed, there are a number of shortcomings associated with unstructured, single-method approaches to information gathering. First, reliance solely on the unstructured interview can mislead clinicians into overlooking potentially important areas of distress or dysfunction while focusing too much on others (e.g., the chief complaint). A second shortcoming is the client himself/herself, who may be a poor historian, have issues to hide from the assessor, or have personality characteristics that bias his or her self-presentation. Third, if the clinician's therapy objectives are at odds with those of the client, or if the client lacks motivation for psychotherapy, the interview will almost invariably be unrevealing. Fourth, certain neuropsychiatric conditions, such as anosognosia, amnesia or confabulation, paranoia, or delusions and other subtle psychotic symptoms, interfere with the accurate reporting of information. This is especially true with regard to elders, who may present with occult cognitive problems that cloud or distort the history and clinical picture. On the other hand, using a semi-structured clinical interview alone (e.g., Structured Clinical Interview for *DSM-IV* Axis I Disorders [SCID]; First & Gibbon, 2004), can mislead the clinician into focusing too much on the yes/no response to the question at hand and ignoring clues that point to less obvious biopsychosocial inputs to the symptom picture. Multimethod assessments, in contrast, enable the clinician to "deconstruct" the client in terms of cognitive/neuropsychological, personality, and behavioral/functional contributions to the chief complaint using standardized, quantifiable, norm-referenced tests coupled with self-report and input from significant others.

Why Assess Baseline Functioning and Outcomes?

The reliance on a single clinician using a single method to obtain information from a patient (interview) will lead to generally unreliable and erroneous understanding of the patient.

Millon and Bloom (2008)

There is also the need, however, for care and accuracy when using multiple measures so that one does not miss the forest for the trees. In the main, tests are often sensitive but not very specific, so sound clinical judgment is vital in "reconstructing" the person from multiple sources of data. One must be especially prudent when assessing older adults, because there often can be a serious disconnect between raters on target symptoms or behaviors, even when markers are quite specific. For example, when one compares depression ratings on the Geriatric Depression Scale (GDS; Yesavage et al., 1982) for a client with cognitive decline, clients and caregivers part company on just about every item. Similarly, in dementia, caregivers almost always overrate problems, whereas patients generally underrate them (perhaps due to patient anosognosia). Regarding functional assessments, caregivers and clients also are at odds, with the caregiver typically reporting that the client is less functional than the client perceives himself or herself to be.

At late life, constructs interact in ways that are not problematic at younger ages. For example, cross-sectional investigations generally support the hypothesis that the presence and severity of anxiety in an older adult is associated with lower cognitive performance. An older adult who is anxious has a reasonable probability of having cognitive problems as well, especially in processing speed and/or executive functioning. Comorbid depression and generalized anxiety also are special problems to attend to in the assessment of older adults. It now appears that there is reasonable, even probable, likelihood that the brain is involved, either subtly (as in working-memory dysfunction), or more globally (as in an underactive prefrontal cortex and disinhibited amygdala) (Beaudreau & O'Hara, 2008). Therefore, a thorough pretherapy assessment for the elder who presents with depression and/or anxiety is vital for understanding the full complement of issues that may be playing a role in the chief complaint.

Psychological assessment also can be a rich short-term therapeutic intervention in its own right. Regardless of age, sharing test results with the client has been found to increase hope and motivation to change, increase self-awareness, decrease the sense of aloneness and isolation with one's condition, confirm one's self-efficacy, and enhance the therapeutic alliance (Finn & Butcher, 1991). Caregivers and family members who participate in the assessment process also benefit from testing feedback; they, too, can experience a healthier appreciation of their loved one's strengths and weaknesses, and are empowered to meet their loved one's needs in a more compassionate, competent, and realistic way. Finn and Tonsager (1997, 2002) describe a major goal of the "therapeutic" style of assessment as making it possible for the client to leave the assessor's office having gained new information or experiences about himself or herself that will increase hope and facilitate change.

This point has not escaped us that the personality-based (Millon & Bloom, 2008) or case-based (Persons, 2005) therapy formulations depend on buy-in from the older patient. One cannot discount the placebo effect of an empathetic connection with the client, but this connection also creates a collaborative environment in which the client (and caregiver) is encouraged to actively participate in answering the questions that brought him or her to the office in the first place. Testing older adults requires special sensitivity toward this cohort's suspicion of mental health providers in general and toward the strangeness of undergoing performance and personality testing specifically (Karlin & Duffy, 2004). When used therapeutically, the tests serve to stimulate discussion about the client's self-perceived strengths and weaknesses as well as his or her response patterns to novel or problematic situations. Although the need for standard administration is respected, older adults are often confused by the assessment process, test instructions, or test items. Furthermore, elders, who may be anxious and who may feel disrespected by an "all business" professional stance, will indeed be put off by a strictly standard administration that doesn't allow for interjections by the client or caregiver, or explanation and encouragement by the assessor. Hence, non-standard test administration is often necessary to draw out the client's best performance, as well as to gain an accurate understanding of the ways in which symptoms or deficits get in the way of day-to-day functioning.

In the end, the goal of an assessment is not to predict that event, but to place a person along a putative risk continuum; to evaluate the problem, especially in the period immediately following recognition of the probable existence of the problem; and to allow for a more informed intervention. Another goal is to find the right battery of tests, interviews, adjustment ratings, and background factors that will yield an overview of the person and problems. Better tests may not be as valuable as these other assessment features. Incremental validity is important, and this is so at all stages of a dementia. In the earliest phase of a possible dementia, less and less distinction is often made between normal and pathological conditions, thus creating a dilemma of diagnostic uncertainty. The nuances at this stage of possible problems may be too uncertain or come too early in our predictive science to allow us to be absolutely certain of our conclusions. We also need to know what exactly we are testing, or we may need to add more function-based tests, or both.

For AD, the fundamental focus is memory on a unidimensional continuum. However, other causes of a dementia (those that result from posterior-temporal, inferior parietal type of cognitive disruption) may follow a similar pattern, while other causes (e.g., those that cause frontal-temporal type of dementia) may lead to a different continuum. A dementia syndrome may appear heterogeneous due to disruption of diverse cognitive processes until the vulnerable factor is determined.

Ashford (2008, p. 410)

THE WHOLE PERSON

Psychiatry . . . is a discipline concerned with patients as persons. Meaningful philosophical constructs are "extricates" from persons—that is, the "person" is the primary category, and constructs of brain and body are derived from the person and not vice versa. The patient, rather than mind or a body, is logically and historically at the center of psychiatric practice.

Cox and Gay (2009, p. 589)

In addition to client benefits, there are, benefits for the psychologist who uses the assessment process as a therapeutic intervention. Test results are no longer a composite of scores reflecting performance in light of age-based norms. Rather, you now *know* your client, and can make a difference in his or her experience of the world and the self (see Hyer, Molinari, Mills, & Yeager,

2008). Mast, Yochim, Carmasin, and Rowe (2011) even argued that the assessment of a dementing patient involves care and a sense of the person and his or her situation. Efforts need to be made toward an understanding of the whole person (Mast, 2011).

Whole-Person Assessment

- Work collaboratively
- Understand how normal processes impact self-perception
- Assess subjective experience of the assessment
- Dialogue with person about ways to address cognitive challenges

Mast (2011)

This is an important issue for many reasons. The health care provider who can assess the declining or dementing patient well adds something to the care equation; he or she becomes part of the care process and is needed for information on trajectories of decline and for continued trust in the treatment process. Executive functioning is perhaps one of the best markers of this problem, as it includes so many features of the thinking/now-declining person. Barkley (2012), in his book on the value of EF, laments this issue from the perspective of this more advanced brain construct. Executive function is best represented in an evolutionary perspective involving cognition and emotions. It is a sort of extended phenotype, a suite of neuropsychological abilities that create profound effects at considerable distance and across time spans from the genotype that initially forms them. The person is often missing in assessment.

Where Is the Person?

Who chooses? I do. What is to be valued and pursued? What I choose to do. How is it to be pursued? The way I decide to do. The "I" has been almost entirely jettisoned from cognitive theories of EF, replaced by some unknown, undefined central executive holed up in some penthouse office suite in the frontal lobes. This conscious capacity to consider who and what we are, what we will value, and how and when it will be pursued originates in self-awareness.

[T]his active agency of the self exists in philosophy but seems lost to or intentionally avoided by the field of neuropsychology. Perhaps this is because it is seen as unscientific or just difficult to measure.

Barkley (2012, p. 29)

Yes, the person is missing. Mast again notes that we need to know the person's traits. Is this a trait of the person? Is it a long-standing trait that was there prior to dementia, or is it a new, stable behavior that has arisen since the onset of dementia? Is it context behavior: Is this a relatively context-specific or situation-specific behavior that is related to the underlying need? In what situations does it occur? Is it a part of the life story: Is this an aspect of the person's enduring life story? How might it be an expression of "This is who I am"? Perhaps this issue is best expressed in the following way: The person who is the patient is concerned about his or her life, values, and memory; the caregiver is concerned with his or her burden and fears. Both are relevant.

FIGURE 12.1   Whole-Person Dementia Assessment Approach

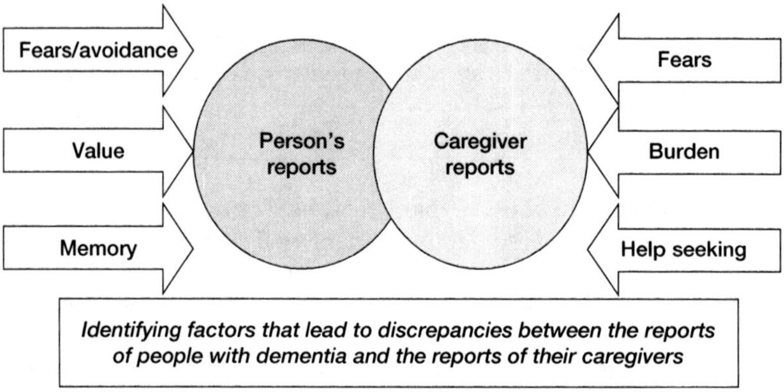

Fears/avoidance

Value

Memory

Person's reports

Caregiver reports

Fears

Burden

Help seeking

Identifying factors that lead to discrepancies between the reports of people with dementia and the reports of their caregivers

COGNITION

Cognition is *the* core area of assessment for older adults. It is the marker for adjustment in virtually all areas of life for an older adult. It is the key reflector of the biomarkers for dementia and mild cognitive impairment (MCI). Cognitive testing is based on the cognitive and behavioral manifestations of brain damage, of possible lesion localization and, more recently, integrated subsystems of brain function, and of clinical diagnoses. Of course, any test is an approximation of real-world performance, and this can be affected by issues related to the test and the person's unique situation and style of responding. Testing also subserves many cognitive areas.

Test Issues (Assessment Issues):

– Many neuropsychological tests measure more than one cognitive function (i.e., Trails B).
– Neuropsychological testing emphasizes optimal performance, which often does not parallel the real world.
– Neuropsychological testing provides a snapshot of behavior.
– Environmental tasks have multiple cognitive determinants.

Person Issues (Ecological Validity):

– Veridicality—Extent to which test results predict real-world performance.
– Verisimilitude—Topographical similarity of data-collection method to a task in the free environment.

Neuropsychological or psychological assessment has assumed a central place in the detection of dementia, the identification of MCI, the identification of rehab strategies for cognitive problems, and, in general, an understanding of skill/ability levels for many later-life purposes (including competence). It is required for a diagnosis of Alzheimer's disease (AD) using the National Institute of Neurological and Communicative Diseases and Stroke–Alzheimer's Disease and Related Disorders Association (NINCDS–ADRDA) criteria (McKann et al., 1984).

Table 12.1 shows the functional areas related to a typical testing.

TABLE 12.1 Functional Areas in Neuropsychological Assessment

- Sensory–motor: Graphomotor, fine/gross motor, visual–spatial perception, eye–hand coordination
- Attention: Sustained attention, impulsivity
- Language: Receptive and expressive
- Learning: Both verbal and nonverbal
- Memory: Long and short term, verbal and visual
- Executive functions: Problem solving, cognition set
- Intelligence: General intelligence (e.g., "IQ")
- Achievement: School-related abilities: fact/skill

Psychological testing of older adults seeks to estimate premorbid intelligence, for obvious reasons: At what level had this person been previously functioning? The standard geriatric/neuropsychological report considers the functional areas of cognition as well as function and mood-based problems. Much has been written about the best approximation for such a fair measure of skills before problems set in: strategies include use of reading scales, vocabulary, algorithms of background factors, and education and achievement, as well as newer psychological scales. For older adults, for example, reading mediates cognitive tests to rather high levels, and often provides a better measure than just education. In a real sense, education is not education. We should remember that educational factors other than years of education influence cognitive performance in later life. Understanding the role of education in cognitive aging, then, has substantial implications for prevention efforts, in addition to assisting in the accurate identification of older adults with cognitive impairment. Higher student–teacher ratio, for example, is associated with worse cognitive function and greater school-year length was associated with better cognitive function (Crowe et al., 2012).

In like fashion, screens are applied to assess current functioning both to identify problem patients (sensitivity) and to assist those who are not in the identified group (specificity). The concern is also not to excessively evaluate and assess. In the list that follows we see typical screens applied in clinics across the country. In fact, the variance accounted for by the various screens is reasonably robust relative to the time that is taken for administration. Sensitivity and specificity vary with each test.

Premorbid Functioning Measures

Wechsler Test of Adult Reading

The Wechsler Test of Adult Reading (WTAR) was developed to assess premorbid functioning of adults. This 50-item instrument requires the subject to read aloud irregularly spelled words, a function that has been demonstrated to be resistant to brain insult. The WTAR is co-normed with the Wechsler Adult Intelligence Scale-III (WAIS-III) and Wechsler Memory Scale-III (WMS-III), and has demonstrated high correlations with the American National Adult Reading Test (AMNART; 0.90) and the WTAR-3 (0.73).

National Adult Reading Test

The National Adult Reading Test (NART) has several versions, including the American National Adult Reading Test (AMNART), which is standardized for use in the United States. The 50-item test requires the subject to read irregularly spelled words aloud to assess for premorbid intellectual ability. The NART is deemed one of the most reliable tests currently in use, with a test–retest reliability of 0.98 and interrater reliability above 0.88; it is also a good predictor of the WAIS full-scale IQ and verbal IQ.

Oklahoma Premorbid Intelligence Estimate — Verbal

This is one of a suite of assessments of premorbid intellectual functioning. The Oklahoma Premorbid Intelligence Estimate — Verbal uses an algorithm for premorbid intelligence based on the WAIS-III Vocabulary score and selected background factors.

Barona Index of Intelligence

This is an index of premorbid intellectual functioning based solely on background factors of age, education, and race, among others. It has a high error variance and therefore is only a rough estimate.

Cognitive Screen Tests

Mini Mental State Examination

The Mini Mental State Examination (MMSE) is one of the most widely used brief screening assessments for cognitive impairment. Modest to high correlations have been reported between total MMSE scores and other cognitive screening measures. Test–retest reliability ranges from 0.83 to 0.99. The cutoff score for sensitivity and specificity studies was 24 out of 30, resulting in ranges of 0.90 to 0.96 and 0.63 to 0.69; respectively, however, cutoff scores of 26 and 27 are now recommended. This test is subject to the influence of ethnicity and education.

Montreal Cognitive Assessment

The Montreal Cognitive Assessment (MoCA) was designed as a rapid screening instrument for mild cognitive dysfunction. It assesses different cognitive domains: attention and concentration, executive functions, memory, language, visuoconstructional skills, conceptual thinking, calculations, and orientation. Time to administer the MoCA is approximately 10 minutes. The total possible score is 30 points; a score of 26 or above is considered normal.

Mini-Cog

The Mini-Cog is a brief screening instrument for cognitive decline that assesses recognition and recall of three unrelated words and clock drawing. The scoring algorithm dictates that a recall of zero words classifies the subject as "demented" regardless of clock drawing, one- to two-word recall with normal clock drawing as "nondemented" or "demented" with any impairment in clock drawing, and recall of all three words as "nondemented." The screen has sensitivity of approximately 0.75 and specificity of 0.90 and has been found to perform as well as the MMSE.

Cognistat

The Cognistat, formally known as Neurobehavioral Cognitive Status Examination, is a brief assessment used to screen for cognitive dysfunction. The test comprises 10 subtests that provide a cognitive profile: Orientation, Attention Span, Language (Comprehension, Repetition, Naming), Constructional Ability, Memory, Calculation Skills, and Reasoning (Similarities/Judgment). The subtests correlate with the respective domains of the Luria-Nebraska Neuropsychological Battery ranging from 0.40 to 0.83. Studies have demonstrated specificity of 0.47 to 1.00 and sensitivity of 0.72 to 0.83 in detecting organic disturbance.

Alzheimer's Disease Assessment Scale: Cognitive and Noncognitive Sections

The Alzheimer's Disease Assessment Scale (ADAS) has both cognitive and noncognitive sections and is typically used to assess change in cognitive functioning for clinical drug trials. ADAS is designed to assess all aspects of Alzheimer's disease (AD), including mood and behavioral changes; each subsection is added to produce a final score up to 120, indicating greater impairment. The lengthy administration time of 35–40 minutes tends to yield higher specificity than the MMSE in regard to levels of cognitive impairment. Despite this strength, the interrater reliability is significantly lower for the noncognitive section in comparison to the cognitive section; 0.42 to 0.45 and 0.82 to 0.90, respectively.

Clock Drawing Test

The Clock Drawing Test is one of the most frequently used screening measures for dementia. The subject is required to freehand draw a clock face, properly placing the numbers in the correct orientation, and draw the hands at the correct provided time. The accuracy of the drawing is rated; the most popularly used rating system is a 10-point scale, 1 being worst and 10 being best. This specific categorical scale version has been found to have 0.86 interrater reliability, 78% sensitivity, and 96% specificity.

Brief Cognitive Rating Scale

The Brief Cognitive Rating Scale (BCRS) is a two-part rating scale that contains mental status questions and qualitative observations obtained through a semi-structured interview, which is part of the Global Deterioration Scale (GDS). Typically, testers use the mental status questions, which have five axes: concentration and calculation, recent memory, remote memory, orientation, and functioning and self-care. Each part, including the three scales of the qualitative observations (i.e., language, motoric, and mood concomitants), varies on a 7-point rating metric. Reliability is approximately 0.90 for all of the five axes.

Saint Louis University Mental Status

The Saint Louis University Mental Status examination (SLUMS) is a 30-point screening tool used to assess MCI and dementia. Classifications (i.e., normal, mild neurocognitive disorder, and dementia) have different values in accordance with education level. The developers found the assessment to have comparable sensitivity to the MMSE, but the SLUMS has better specificity for detecting mild neurocognitive disorder.

Dementia Rating Scale

The Dementia Rating Scale (DRS), also known as the Mattis Dementia Rating Scale, assesses five areas of functioning that are sensitive to behavioral changes representative of senile dementia, Alzheimer's type. The scoring of these domains (i.e., attention, initiation and preservation, construction, conceptual, memory) allows comparison of test–retest for the subscales and total scores. The individual subtests range in test–retest reliability between 0.75 and 0.95, whereas total score is 0.97. There is much debate about appropriate cutoff scores, ranging from 123 to 129 out of 144, which results in 83% to 96% sensitivity and 92% to 100% specificity.

Short Portable Mental Status Questionnaire

The Short Portable Mental Status Questionnaire (SPMSQ) is a brief cognitive screening measure developed for the geriatric population. Test–retest reliability ranges between 0.82 and 0.85. Seven out of the 10-question assessment items strictly relate to orientation. Thus, it has been suggested that the SPMSQ is potentially a better assessor for identifying functional impairment within a population.

7-Minute Screen

The 7-Minute Screen (7MS) was developed as a rapid screen for early stages of AD. The assessment comprises four tests: Enhanced Cued Recall, Semantic Fluency, Benton Orientation Task, and Clock Drawing. Despite high sensitivity and specificity (> 0.90), a scoring algorithm is required to find the overall score.

The MMSE is the most used test in the world. It has several subparts and can be given in about 5 minutes. There are literally thousands of studies about this test or that use this test, as it has become the standard for determining dementias. Based on the Crum norms, a score of 24 or below suggests problems related to dementia. This test too must be adjusted for ethnicity, education, and reading if careful decisions are to be made. Of course, there are many problems with the MMSE: discrepant instructions, use of two tasks that lead to different outcomes ("world" backward and serial 7s), and a heavy influence on language. Thankfully, the test does stand up well in both psychiatric and primary care clinics and accounts for about half the variance of functionality (Freilich & Hyer, 2007). Typically, older adults with cognitive problems have difficulty with recall and calculations initially.

TABLE 12.2 Mini Mental State Exam

- Orientation – Temporal, Place
- Registration – Repeat 3 objects
- Calculations – Serial 7s, WORLD
- Recall
- Language – Naming, Repetition, Comprehension
- Copying

It is worthwhile to view the details of the Schafer–Johnson study. Reading skills matter. Many older people do not read well, and this has implications for the test given. Among the tests noted in Table 12.3 on the next page, all show a high percentage in the relationship between the test and education as accounted for by reading. In effect, knowledge of the older adult's reading ability is a key to full knowledge of his or her current cognitive status.

TABLE 12.3 Schafer–Johnson Details

- Education, reading ability, and executive functioning
- WRAT-3
- Age 72, educ 12, 81% women, 94% African American
  - 73% read below grade level
  - 19% read at grade level
  - 7% read above grade level

- % of relationship between education and test mediated by reading ability
  - Letter-Number 80%
  - COWAT 99%
  - CPM 47%
  - Similarities 65%
  - Trails A & B 46% and 96%

Of course, psychological testing for cognition eventually involves more extended batteries. We provide just some of the more popular measures applied in various clinics for older adults. Below and elsewhere we consider function in the mix of important data for the evaluation of older adults. Note that the incremental validity for a test battery lasting much beyond 3 hours is very small and should be avoided when testing older adults.

1. Test Batteries
   a. RBANS: Subserves five domains of cognitive function; well normed, brief, and has alternate forms.
   b. WAIS-III or IV: standard for cognitive testing. WAIS-IV does not provide Verbal and Performance IQs; rather, information is given for Verbal Comprehension, Perceptual Reasoning, Working Memory, and Processing Speed.
   c. WMS Scale-IV: Revised battery with older adults in mind. It has a brief cognitive screen. It measures verbal and nonverbal memory and has indices for immediate and delayed memory as well as working memory.
   d. California Verbal Learning Test (CVLT): This is one of several memory scales. This uses 16 words repeated five times and has short and long delay as well as a second trial.
   e. Fuld Memory Evaluation (FOME): Standardized on older adults in both long-term care (LTC) and in the community. It assesses both immediate and delayed memory and is a robust marker for normal and dementia groups.
2. Specific Test Areas
   Attention—Continuous Performance Test, Trails A, Digits Forward and Backward, Dot test
   Visuospatial—Rey-O Test, Benton Figures, Hooper Visual-Spatial
   Language—Boston Naming Test, WAIS-IV Vocabulary/Similarities/Information, Wide Range Achievement Test-IV (WRAT-IV), Word Fluencies, Hooper Abstraction
   New learning/memory—Alzheimer's Disease Assessment Scale-Cognitive (ADASCog), AVALT, California Learning Test-Second Edition (CVLT-II), Rey-Osterrieth Complex Figure (Rey-O)
   Executive functioning—Wisconsin Card Sort, Trials B, Stroop Color Word Test (StroopC/W), Delis–Kaplan Executive Function System (DKEFS), Executive Interview (EXIT-25).

Table 12.4 gives a profile of a person who presents with a memory complaint and has poor memory and executive functioning. This person is functioning reasonably well (100% is high) but has problems in executive function (EF) and memory. Whether this person has dementia or has an MCI largely depends on functioning. The interesting feature of this profile in that the person could be functional depending on the environment, and this support/scaffold can make the difference. The designation of a dementia can be problematic when there is advanced age, caregiver bias, cultural resistance, confusing education issues, and a general social facility. As noted, having a good fit of an environment makes a difference also.

TABLE 12.4   Percentage Correct for Cognitive Domains of an Early Dementia Patient

Variable	% Correct
Remote personal memory	95
Attention	90
Visuospatial	70
Language	60
Abstraction	60
Praxis	70
Processing speed	80
Executive functioning	40
Delayed memory	20

FUNCTION: THINK OUTSIDE THE BOX

The *Diagnostic and Statistical Manual of Mental Disorders-5* (*DSM-5*; American Psychiatric Association [APA], 2013) is here. Depending on your bias, this is good news, bad news, or more of the same. It continues in the tradition of the *DSM-III* (APA, 1980) as a paradigm shift. It alters many diagnoses (e.g., substance abuse), reifies subclinical problems (attention deficit disorder [ADD]), and creates new weird-science designations (Attenuated Psychotic Syndrome). It is a prescription for an iatrogenic epidemic. So, the mental health community may be in for a rough ride.

Three Types of Psychopathologies

1. Descriptive: to account for experiences or phenomena through observation.
2. Clinical: to use for pragmatic diagnostic purposes.
3. Structural: to identify for a global level of intelligibility of synthetic knowledge.

Stanghellini (2009)

Regarding dementia, the new *DSM-5* places an emphasis on biomarkers (see Chapter 6). Cognition and behaviors are forms of biomarkers, however. Indeed, they are functional markers, but clearly add to the extant bioindicators currently in use. They add to the conversion rates from MCI to dementia, for example. In meta-analyses, episodic memory scores are more predictive in detecting preclinical AD than cerebrospinal fluid (CSF) biomarkers (Schmand, Huizenga, & Van Gool, 2010). According also to Dubois et al. (2007), memory must be followed over a 6-month period for any diagnosis to be considered. Other data sets show that the value of memory is central to the core of measures for any prediction of who converts to dementia from MCI (Devanand, 2010).

Regardless, the careful clinician needs to think outside the box. As one example, MacNeill and Lichtenberg (2000) evaluated the utility of a unique scale that not only evaluates cognitive status, but also considers psychosocial factors and emotional status in older adults. It provides a simple "decision tree" that identifies potential mental health problems in older medical patients and guides decision making for referrals. In a stroke and geriatric unit of a freestanding urban medical rehabilitation hospital, the authors assessed 1,173 older, consecutively admitted medical rehabilitation patients for purposes of triage. A decision tree accurately triaged 87% of mental health problems and allowed for deferral of 41% of cases, for whom further assessment was unnecessary. The test (MacNeill–Lichtenberg Decision Tree [MLDT]) was superior to the MMSE, with higher sensitivity and a lower failure rate. In a subsequent study, a separate sample of 313 older adults was used. The MLDT was compared with the MMSE, the Mattis Dementia Rating Scale, and the 30-item Geriatric Depression Scale (GDRS). The emotional status component of the MLDT was useful in triaging cases for depression evaluation. In effect, this test was useful in prioritizing cases with regard to mental health problems (e.g., dementia, depression) and making quick referral decisions.

As another example, behavioral triggers may become useful. Imagine that you are in primary care and any of the following occurs over time. These would become red flags at some point. Lichtenberg (2012) again suggested these as behavioral triggers for the primary care physician (PCP) to use in the formulation of clear adjustment problems reflective of a cognitive problem.

Communication
- Missed office appointments
- Confusion about medication/treatment instructions
- Calling office frequently

Accidents
- Motor vehicle accidents
- Fractures
- Falls

Delirium
- History of delirium
- Delirium during hospitalization

Change in Functional Status
- Decrease in instrumental activities of daily living
- Move to senior housing or assisted living
- Presentation of self-neglect (i.e., hygiene, grooming, weight loss)

Cognition Changes
- Patient/family/office staff report memory problems
- Unable to list current medications
- Unable to recall recommendations from prior visit

Previously, we noted the importance of functional competence. The relationships between cognitive performance and functional behaviors explain less than 50% of observed variability in regression models (Loewenstein & Lerner, 2003). This is often because real-world outcomes are not frequently employed. In addition, prediction is often based on global levels of severity rather than specific cognitive predictors of cognitive tasks. Hence, there is typically a lack of sensitivity and specificity analyses (associated with specific base rates) that guide the clinician in making individualized treatment decisions. Being unable to handle day-to-day tasks, especially instrumental activities of daily living (IADL), is important and reflective of a dementia. In the Barberger-Gateau study, an IADL scale accounted for most of the variance of a dementia (Barberger-Gateau, Fabrigoule, Helmer, Rouch, & Dartigues, 1999). In addition, we note that EF measures, such as the Functional Assessment Questionnaire (FAQ; Pfeffer, Kurosaki, Harrah, Chance, & Filos, 1982) and Behavioral Dyscontrol Scale (BDS; Grigsby, Kaye, & Robbins, 1992), are also very helpful in identifying problems in types of functioning.

The overlap of cognition and functional scales is substantial, but they also work independently, indicating that both scales should be applied. IADL are most accounted for by fluid reasoning, which emerges as the strongest longitudinal predictor of everyday competence (52% of variance), and crystallized intelligence (accounting for 11% of variance; Willis, Jay, Diehl, & Marsiske, 1992). It is interesting to note that baseline scores of IADL scales predict 3-year incident dementia in 1,582 community-dwelling older adults, even after adjusting for MMSE (Barberger-Gateau et al., 1999). In general, 40% of variance of functional decline is accounted for by cognitive decline, indicating that cognition and functional capacity reflect distinct, parallel features of the disease process (Mortimer, Ebbitt, Jun, & Finch, 1992). Leckey and Beatty (2002) initially found a robust correlation between measures of global cognitive status (i.e., MMSE) and activities of daily living (ADL)/IADL (ADL = 0.51, IADL = 0.69) for dementia-diagnostic clinic samples. These relationships were reduced considerably when patients with severe dementia were removed from the analysis. This finding suggests that the relationship between global cognition and ADL/IADL may not be exactly linear, and that intact cognition is a necessary but not sufficient condition for successful performance of everyday tasks in normal and abnormal aging.

TABLE 12.5 Functional Competence

- Baseline scores of IADL scales predict dementia.
- About 40% of variance of elements is accounted for by functional measures; therefore, functional scales best accompany cognitive scales.
- Intact cognition is a necessary but not sufficient condition for successful performance of everyday tasks in normal and abnormal aging.

Increasingly there are performance-based scales. Competency scales reflect this, in that they test for skill-based understanding that is attached to situation-specific performance. The University of California, San Diego (UCSD) Performance-Based Skills Assessment (UPSA) (see below), a scale of functional capacity, stands as an example of a performance scale that is applied in geriatric settings to good effect. This scale is a test of functional capacity for people with schizophrenia, but is widely used with older adults.

- ADL performance: underpinned by automatic processing and procedural memory; poor ADL performance is more closely related to cognitive status, caregiver burden, higher rates of institutionalization, and subsequent mortality.
- IADL functioning: effortful, controlled processing and good executive functioning, as well as procedural memory. IADL performance is associated with frontal lobe activation. Similar to ADL competence, declines in IADL functioning also predict frequency of hospital contact, nursing home placement, and mortality.

UPSA assesses everyday activities:

Communication.
Finance.
Transportation.
Household management.
Comprehension (e.g., planning, organizing)

Patterson, Goldman, McKibbin, Hughs, and Jeste (2001)

Neuroimaging techniques in all modalities have a great allure with respect to their potential to improve diagnosis and care. New tools are now available. The Alzheimer's Disease Neuroimaging Initiative (ADNI) has provided clinicians and imagers with acquisition protocols that are standardized across sites. The ADNI data have been made available to researchers across the world: Now there are MRI protocols for spectroscopy, diffusion tensor imaging, and arterial spin labeling. Much is happening in this arena (Ashford et al., 2011).

DEPRESSION

Depression is easily measured . . . almost. There are now more than 30 review articles on the measurement of depression at later life (see Gould, Edelstein, & Ciliberti, 2010). Several points should be made. First, there are now dedicated scales for older adults. Second, that said, most of the scales used for adults have not been validated on older adults. Third, culture and ethnicity mess everything up. The ability of a scale to target a specific ethnicity with a specific acculturation and a specific education is impossible to determine accurately. Fourth, an understanding of what sadness means to the older person and what can be important/goal oriented are very relevant, always. This especially applies in a dementia. Fifth, as we have argued, measures of the transdiagnostic pathways to depression are relevant and can represent a generic perturbation of which depression is a salient feature. This is rather important and may represent the best way to assess depression as an orthogonal variable. We need more global scales. Sixth, clinical ratings are always welcome in the assessment process; the more specific, the better. Problems occur when they are not valid or when bias enters into the assessment. This happens with consistency when culture is a factor or the clinician's bias asserts itself.

Seventh, and most important, measures of depression are connected to quality of life (QoL). This involves all features of the person's life, such as medical problems, sleep, pain, stress, relationships, therapy factors, and attitude, and these factors are central to measurement. Practically speaking, a therapist usually does not rely on one treatment approach for a given set of symptoms, but rather reviews the range of possible strategies and tactics and applies them for a given client. A goal attainment map (GAM) can be formulated for the individual that includes potential intervention strategies, treatment targets, and ultimate outcomes. The GAM specifies what is most important for each goal. A Pleasant Events Schedule (PES) is often applied. This provides a goal-specific assessment tool (e.g., PES for the target of increasing positive reinforcement) and goal-specific potential interventions (e.g., behavior activation) that are focused, monitored, and collaborative. Here, empirical research gives way to real-world practice in the actual clinical situation.

The list below presents assessment choices for depression in older adults. It argues for an overall focus (medical, social support, cognition, sleep, pain, and so on); use of an omnibus measure such as the Millon Behavioral Medicine Diagnostic (MBMD) where Axis I, Axis II, treatment prognostics, stress moderators, health habits, and response styles are provided; clinician ratings of depression or correlative problems; use of self-report scales; use of cognitive style measures; overall monitoring; and a special focus on dementia and depression, if warranted.

General Assessment for Depression for Older Adults

- Overall:
  - Assess medical and psychiatric comorbidities: Charlson Index
  - Assess social support, cognition, sensory function, sleep, pain, meds
- Consider Omnibus Measures: MBMD, Personality Assessment Inventory (PAI), NEO-PI (Neuroticism–Extroversion–Openness Personality Inventory), Minnesota Multiphasic Personality Inventory (MMPI-II), MCMI-III
- Clinician Ratings
  - HAM-D (Hamilton Depression Scale: 17 or 24, use 10), MINI (Mini-International Neuropsychiatric Interview), PHQ-2 (Patient Health Questionnaire), GDRS (use 20), MADRS (Montgomery–Åsberg Depression Rating Scale)
- Self-Report Scales
  - PHQ-9, BDI-I or II (10), GDS (11), GDS-SF (5), CESD (Center for Epidemiologic Studies Depression Scale; 20 item, cutoff 16: 10 item, use 10), Zung Depression Self Rating Scale (50), Visual Analogue Mood Scales
- Overall monitoring
- Cognitive Style Problems
  - ATQ (AutomaticThoughts Questionnaire; 21 items)
- Dementia and Depression
  - Cornell Scale for Depression in Dementia (19 items used to determine severity after depression is established)
- Dementia Mood Assessment Scale (17 items)
- Provisional Depression in Dementia Scale (Olin et al., 2002)

Finally, we endorse one other type of measure, omnibus scales, as most helpful. There are several noted in the boxes that follow. The MBMD is especially helpful. Along with lifestyle habits and response styles, personality traits and Axis I symptoms are featured. It is important to note that, stress moderators and treatment prognostics are measured. We can tell whether the client has problems with stress moderators, such as illness apprehension, functional deficits, pain sensitivity, and pessimism; or treatment prognostics, which can involve relevant problems such as compliance. An example of a client with various strengths and weaknesses is given below.

Stress Moderators: Intrapersonal and extrapersonal characteristics that affect medical problems. They target cognitive appraisals, resources, and context factors.

Moderator			Weakness	Strength
Illness apprehension	vs.	Illness acceptance	×	
Functional deficits	vs.	Functional competence	×	
Pain sensitivity	vs.	Pain tolerance	×	
Social isolation	vs.	Social support		×
Future pessimism	vs.	Future optimism	×	
Spiritual absence	vs.	Spiritual faith		×

Treatment Prognostics: Behaviors and attitudinal aspects that may complicate or enhance treatment efficacy.

Treatment + Prognostic			Weakness	Strength
Interventional fragility	vs.	Interventional resilience		×
Medication abuse	vs.	Medication consciousness		×
Information discomfort	vs.	Information receipt		×
Utilization excess	vs.	Appropriate utilization		×
Problematic compliance	vs.	Optimal compliance	×	

ANXIETY

The issues that apply to depression also adhere to the construct of anxiety. As we have indicated in Chapter 5, this is a broad construct and addresses different parts of the brain based on symptoms (e.g., posttraumatic stress disorder [PTSD] or obsessive-compulsive disorder [OCD]). Anxiety has many forms and is most often attached to depression. Treatment plans should reflect this, both the specificity of the problem and the general nature of the co-occurring problem.

As for depression, the assessment covers the same areas. Added features include anxiety-specific measures.

General Assessment of Anxiety for Older Adults

- Overall:
  - Assess medical and psychiatric comorbidities: Charlson Index
  - Assess social support, cognition, sensory function, sleep, pain, meds
- Clinician Ratings
  - Anxiety Disorder Interview Scale-IV (ADIS-IV), Structured Clinical Interview for *DSM-IV* Axis-I Disorders (SCID), MINI, Hamilton Anxiety Rating Scale (HARS; 13 items)
  - Barlow: One Q: Do you worry excessively about minor matters?
- Behavioral Assessments
  - Self-monitoring
- Self-Report Measures
  - Penn State Worry Questionnaire (PSWQ), Generalized Anxiety Disorder-7 (GAD-7), State-Trait Anxiety Inventory (STAI), Multidimensional Anxiety Questionnaire (MAQ), Short Anxiety Screening Test (SAST), Worry Questionnaire, Worry Scale for Older

Adults, Depression Anxiety Stress Scale (DASS), Addiction Severity Index (ASI), Profile of Mood States (POMS), BAI, Positive and Negative Affect Schedule (PANAS)

- Omnibus measures: MBMD, PAI, Millon Clinical Multiaxial Inventory-III (MCMI-III), MMPI-II, NEO-PI
- Specific Anxiety Scales:
  - Anxiety and Aging Scale (AAS)
  - Death Anxiety Scale (DAS)
  - Fear scales
- Cognitive Style Problems
  - ATQ (Automatic Thoughts Questionnaire, 21 items)
- Overall monitoring
  - Diary (interpersonal avoidance issues)

PSYCHOTHERAPY MEASURES

The assessment of psychotherapy outcomes is tiered, global, symptom based, and target specific. In cognitive behavioral therapy (CBT), for example, evidence suggests that adjustment can be measured by QoL or overall adjustment scales; depression can be measured by a focused psychological instrument such as the BDI-II, and targeted specifically in the form of scales unique to cognitive change. In CBT, cognitive change is associated with changes in depressive symptomatology, assessed for the prevention of relapse, and involved for QoL. This unique therapy thus requires specific assessments if it is applied.

We are being redundant here intentionally. We present common assessment measures used in psychotherapy. We begin with recommended measures of depression and general anxiety for older adults. Fortunately, where older adults are concerned, most of the measures that apply to younger adults have applicability to them. Differences have to do with norms or with constructs that require an aging emphasis. As for the former, we do not yet have adequate norms on symptom-based measures to assert that clinical significance represents some measure of change. As for the latter, the constructs relevant to aging are many and change even as a function of young-old to oldest-old.

The measurement and treatment of specific anxiety disorders (panic, agoraphobia, PTSD, OCD, and phobias) in older adults are not very different from those applied to younger adults. Regarding depression and generalized anxiety, however, the measures used with older adults demand more consideration. Although the factor structure of both the constructs remains similar across age groups (Blazer, 2003), there are differing cutoff points and different features unique to each. Depressed older adults, for example, have less irritability and negative cognitions, but show more sleep and health problems. In Table 12.2 we provide a listing of measures that can serve for the initial session and diagnoses, as well as markers for change. In the initial session we establish the diagnosis (or diagnoses), its severity, and possible related problems, such as treatment issues (e.g., MBMD), suicidal thinking (General Suicide Index Scale [GSIS]), and function (IADL). We also establish the possible existence of cognitive problems with a short battery that tests multiple domains. In each session, the clinician can apply short forms of these scales that are sensitive to change. Monthly measures also can be applied to determine the status of the diagnosis and symptom severity. Discharge and follow-up sessions largely do the same. The hope is that the patient will be diagnosis free and have a substantial reduction in symptom severity.

TABLE 12.6 Measures for Initial Session and Diagnosis of Depression and/or Anxiety

Session	Depression: Recommended Instruments	Anxiety: Recommended Instruments
Initial session	HAM-D MINI MADRS BDI-II/GDS Beck Hopelessness Scale GSIS MBMD MoCA and/or RBANS Stroop Color Word Test ADCS-ADL, FAQ QoL	ADIS-IV-L MINI Penn State Worry Scale MBMD MoCA and/or RBANS Stroop Color Word Test ADCS/FAQ QoL
Each Session	BDI-II, GDS QoL	Penn State Worry Scale QoL
Discharge Session	HAM-D MADRS BDI-II/GDS MINI QoL	Penn State Worry Scale HAM-A/HARS ADIS-IV-L MINI QoL
Follow-up assessment	MINI MADRS BDI-II HAM-D	MINI HAM-A/HARS Penn State Worry Scale

ADCS-ADL, Alzheimer's Disease Cooperative Studies Scale-Activities of Daily Living; ADIS-L, Anxiety Disorder Interview Scale-Lifetime; BDI-II, beck depression inventory-II; FAQ, Functional Assessment Questionnaire; GDS, geriatric depression scale; GSIS, General Suicide Index Scale; HAM-A, Hamilton Anxiety Scale; HAM-D, Hamilton Depression Scale; HARS, Hamilton Anxiety Rating Scale; MADRS, Montgomery-Åsberg Depression Rating Scale; MBMD, Millon Behavioral Medical Diagnostic; MINI, Mini-International Neuropsychiatric Interview; MoCA, Montreal Cognitive Assessment; QoL, Quality of Life; RBANS, Repeated Battery for the Assessment of Neurological Status.

PERSONALITY ASSESSMENT

The major factors involved in negative personality change at midlife are the same factors that caused negative aging at 70: bad habits, bad marriage, maladaptive defenses, and disease.

Vaillant and Sharp (2002)

This construct varies in importance. This is too bad, as information on this construct can be helpful. The issue of whether to measure is, then, one of concern. An equally important concern is what to measure: more global personality traits based on the Big 5, or more specific traits that can become dysfunctional, based on the Axis II? For the former, neuroticism especially is a harbinger of problems over time, both cognitive and affective, whereas openness to experience and, to a lesser extent, conscientiousness and agreeableness provide a more positive trajectory. For the latter, the profile of trait-based behaviors echoes eloquently in a person's life and provides important data on probable adjustment and problems. It is interesting to note that personality stability may actually serve as a protective resource throughout the aging process (Graham &Lachman, 2012).

The Axis II indicators or personality disorders (PDs) are another matter. In general, the assessment issues concerning PDs in younger age groups also apply at later life. They include the following: (a) a high degree of comorbidity, (b) the temporal instability of Axis II disorders, (c) a lack of discrete boundaries between individual PDs and PD clusters, (d) heterogeneity within diagnoses due to a polythetic classification system, (e) differing threshold levels of PDs, (f) redundant criteria for each disorder, and (g) nonweighted diagnostic criteria that vary from core to periphery with little specification of level of severity. In addition, as with any area of study, the many methodological problems inherent in personality research influence the nature of results. Confounds in personality research include where the sample was acquired, use of cross-sectional data, diagnostic criteria used (as noted earlier, heterotypic continuity of behaviors in a given personality are not adequately reflected in older age), type of measurement (self-report vs. clinical interview), the nature of the cutoff between trait and disorder, and masking biological and cultural issues.

There is no gold standard for the measurement of PDs at late life. Indeed, no PD measures have been specifically developed for this age group. Structured interviews are more reliable than unstructured ones or self-report measures, but self-reports can be very helpful, assuming that problems of false positives and false negatives can be clinically understood. Livesley (2001) specifies that a two-stage process for PD evaluation is preferred: an interview based on *DSM* to establish the PD category and later a self-report scale to determine the severity. Paris (2004) also notes that early diagnosis of a PD has considerable clinical advantage: necessary adjustments for care can be made early in treatment.

It is ironic that such a case must be made for older adults, because assessment traditionally has been a hallmark of geropsychological practice (Segal, Coolidge, & Hersen, 1998). The dynamic interplay of comorbidities, medical problems, situational stressors, and functional decline adds considerable confusion to any attempts at determining the presence of a PD. In general, measurement of PDs at late life is made more difficult due to the already hardened myths of aging, which foster a brittle adaptation or developmental stagnation view (Zweig & Agronin, 2006); to the absence of longitudinal data; and to unreliable measurement instruments.

That said, there are several suggestions for the assessment of older adults in general. Clearly, best practice includes a multiassessment package that contains chart/record review, clinical review with the patient, interview with informants, self-report objective personality inventories, and semi-structured interviews (Segal et al., 2006). This can be a daunting and time-consuming enterprise. However, given the often dubious ability of clinicians to diagnose and treat older adults who may have a PD (Sadavoy, 1996), a certain amount of structure and prudence is important for accurate assessment.

Personality Disorder Measures

PACL

The Personality Adjective Check List (PACL) is a self-report measure of Millon's eight personality patterns, consisting of 153 items. The PACL may be used in the assessment of PD as well as a problem indicator of three severe patterns: schizoid, cycloid, and paranoid (Strack, 1991).

MBMD

The Millon Behavioral Medicine Diagnostic (MBMD) aids clinicians in assessing patients with psychological problems and physical illnesses. The 165-item test includes response patterns, negative health habits, psychiatric indicators, coping styles, and stress moderators to help create successful treatment plans for patients (Millon, Antoni, Millon, Meagher, & Grossman, 2001).

Semi-Structured or Structured Interviews

There are a number of validated PD instruments tied to *DSM* criteria; however, none of these instruments have been validated on older adults.

SCID-II

The Structured Clinical Interview for *DSM-IV* Axis II Personality Disorders (SCID-II) was designed to diagnose the *DSM-IV* standard PDs as well as depressive PD, passive–aggressive PD, and PD NOS (not otherwise specified). The instrument characterizes the patient's inner experience through an overview of typical behavior, relationships, and capability of self-reflection (First, Gibbon, Spitzer, Williams, & Benjamin, 1997).

As the rules of assessment apply to later life and PDs, it may be best to diagnose and treat from a "double think" perspective: the clinician uses Axis II considerations to assist in the case formulation and treatment and, at the same time, the clinician respects cognitive problems, seeks parsimony in diagnoses, respects more longstanding psychosocial problems as well as history (relative to recent behavior), and is suspicious about crisis behaviors. Collateral information and objective measures are also important to the systematic assessment of PDs. We believe that objective measures are prepotent in the understanding of late-life problems.

Differential Diagnoses Axioms

1. Double think for assessment: Axis II and Axis I.
2. With older adults, comorbidity is the rule, not the exception.
3. Use structured interviews initially.
4. Cognitive disorder trumps all other diagnoses. Assess neurocognitive status.
5. Axis I symptomatology (i.e., irritable depression) could be mistaken for Axis II (e.g., borderline, dependent) pathology.
6. Priority is given to the disorder that has been present longest.
7. Apply the parsimony rule—be prudent with diagnostic implications.
8. Developmental history is essential.
9. Use Axis IV and V as markers for functioning.
10. Recent history is better than ancient history.
11. Crisis-generated data are suspect.
12. Collateral information is at least equal to history from the patient.
13. Objective assessments are better than subjective judgments.

CAREGIVERS

The term *caregiving* subsumes a wide range of activities from overall management of the patient, medication input, appointments, and ADL/ IADL negotiation, to focus on surrogate issues of choice at the end of life. This term was barely known 30 years ago. Research over this period has shown that the care process in dementia is critical, and it is both dynamic and challenging (Aneshensel, Pearlin, Mullan, Zarit, & Whilatch, 1995; Max, Weber, & Fox, 1995; Pruchno, Kleban, Michaels, & Dempsey, 1990; Wright, Clipp, & George, 1993). Caregivers of individuals with dementia often experience high levels of stress and it is not uncommon for them to experience depression and anxiety symptoms as well (Schultz, 1998). Percentages of common problems can reach as high as 50% for caregivers (Williamson & Schultz, 1993). In fact, as we indicated in Chapter 11, in addition to burden, estimates show that 40% to 70% of caregivers of older adults with various medical conditions experience clinically significant depressive symptoms, with approximately one quarter to one half of caregivers meeting criteria for a depressive disorder (Zarit, 2006). There is reasonable evidence, too, that older caregivers, who are mostly female, and who are spouses with health problems are especially at risk (see Mausbach et al., 2006).

Two core issues regarding assessment come to mind when working with a caregiver of an older adult. The first involves assessment of the caregiver regarding the identified patient. As noted, caregiving is commonly associated with depression and burden, especially when both the caregiver and care receiver are older adults. The usual measures related to caregiving are caregiver burden; the caregiver–care receiver relationship; ADL and IADL ratings of the care receiver; and, increasingly, scales related to the care receiver's executive functioning, such as FAQ and the Disability Assessment for Dementia (DAD). In addition, depression and anxiety markers also are highly relevant for caregiver status and should be applied. Norms should be adjusted for age at least, but also for gender and ethnicity, and perhaps for education. Local norms are always best, and these can easily be developed after assessing approximately 100 cases.

The second issue concerns the caregiver role and what we know as it relates to the caregiver's health status and therapy with the identified patient. Recent studies demonstrate that if the caregiver is depressed, the identified patient becomes depressed and more impaired (Martire et al., 2008). The added burden of the care receiver's cognitive deterioration has been attributed to increased problems in caregiving over the course of a day and degree of assistance needed for basic and complex activities of daily living (Russo & Vitaliano, 1995). In their meta-analysis, Pinquart and Sörensen (2003a) found that patient behavior problems were more strongly related to caregiver burden than were the patient's physical and cognitive impairments, the amount of care provided, or the duration of caregiving. In addition, the subjective view of the caregiver situation is often more relevant than the objective problems. Vitaliano and colleagues (2009) recently showed that the caregiver who is stressed and depressed is at risk for cognitive decline herself or himself. Assessment may therefore involve more than just the usual markers of burden in caregiving.

One other issue is relevant here: The lack of concordance between caregiver and care receiver is a concern for the practitioner. As we have suggested, estimates of the patient's problems typically result in the caregiver seeing a worse situation, whereas the care receiver sees less pathology. Inflated scores on extant measures of patient insight also insinuate that there may be distorted ratings of current functional status (Hyer, Scott, Yeager, & Hyer, 2010). Often, too, the caregiver can overstate problems because of frustration and burden. So, the practitioner must be wary, obtain data from multiple sources over time, and pay attention to outcomes.

Idiographic assessment is most relevant to caregiving, as this allows for measurement in each individual setting. This can occur with basic caregiving tasks as well as values. There can never be too many questions for this purpose; the qualitative questions are invaluable. For interventions, the practical issues of living, tasks, and problems with adjusting to the rigors of living are queried. Among caregiver studies, the issue of diversity has been an important consideration. The Resources for Enhancing Alzheimer's Caregivers Health (REACH) project addresses this issue specifically and endorses psychoeducation, counseling, and multicomponent interventions as effective, but they must be tailored to the culture mores of the caregiver (see Gallagher-Thompson & Coon, 2007).

General Clinical Interview and Interventions

Systematic Care Program for Dementia Screening Tool (Spijker et al., 2012)

Sense of Competence:
Do you feel stressed by trying to do enough for your care recipient?
Do you have enough privacy?
Do you wish that you had a better relationship with your care recipient?
Do you feel that your care recipient tries to manipulate/annoy you?
Do you feel that your care recipient tries to have his or her own way?

Goals of Involvement:
Do you have an open dialogue regarding expectations, resources, conflicts, and feelings of guilt?
Can you organize additional help?

Caregiver Management Strategy:
Nonadapters: Lack of understanding and feeling irritated and angry.
Nurturers: Parent–child approach in which the dementing person is treated as a child.
Supporters: Adapt to the level of functioning of the person with dementia.

Stage of Dementia:
Mild: Person can live on his or her own with reasonable judgment and ADL skill.
Moderate: Independent living is a problem and limited supervision is required.
Severe: Impairment in ADL, continued supervision is required.

Suggestions:
- Assist family members to identify how the illness has had an impact on their daily schedule.
- Ask the family members to identify what they miss the most about their old schedule (e.g., time for reading, going shopping, playing on a sports team).
- Ask the family members to identify how much time they would need to incorporate this activity back into their lifestyle.
- Have family members negotiate with other members of the family or friends circle to determine if some caregiving responsibilities could be assumed by another person for that period of time.
- Assist family members to write a list of all necessary caregiving responsibilities and negotiate with others who are best suited to provide the care.
- Determine who can be relied on to provide these caregiving responsibilities as a "back up" relief person to lessen the burden on the primary caregiver(s).
- Have family members evaluate how satisfactorily the relief or "back up" system is working after a 1-week trial.
- Assist family members to identify what is working and what needs to be reworked.
- Revise plan as necessary.
- Advise parents that it is often helpful for teachers to know that children are dealing with serious illness in the home if there are school-age children in the family. This information sharing with teachers may alert teachers to potential changes in children's usual academic performance and social behavior, and may avert problems at school.

For more objective markers, the Zarit Burden Scale (Zarit & Zarit, 1983) has been applied to caregivers for many years. In addition, there are hassle scales, depression measures, and QoL assessments that have been used with caregivers. Adjustment measures such as the FAQ have also been applied. Most studies assess caregiver burden, depression, and anxiety, in addition to cognition (see Gallagher-Thompson & Coon, 2007). Below we also highlight several related constructs that have been used as outcomes for caregivers.

Idiographic Assessment—Goal-Attainment Markers for the Caregiver

Core Problems
    Burden—Zarit Caregiver Burden Interview
    Depression—CES-D, GDS, POMS
    Anxiety—STAI, BAI
    Cognition—MoCA, Revised Memory and Behavior Checklist, reaction–response
Related Constructs
    Social support—Perceived Social Support Scale
    Caregiver health—General Health Questionnaire (GHQ)
    Coping, especially avoidance—Revised Ways of Coping Scale
    Quality-of-Life Scale (WHOQOL)
    Cultural specificity—Language-specific measures

Center for Epidemiological Scale-Depression (CES-D), Geriatric Depression Scale (GDS), Profile of Mood Scale (POMS), State Trait Anxiety Inventory (STAI), Beck Anxiety Inventory (BAI), Montreal Cognitive Assessment (MoCA), WHO Quality of Life (WHOQOL).

GENERAL ADJUSTMENT

Several omnibus measures are often applied in research related to older adults, both as screens and as outcome measures. These relate to general functioning, psychiatric problems, QoL, health, and coping. It is important to note that these measures can be summed or disaggregated and applied for general or specific purposes. These measures also provide reasonable reliability, as the structure of the interview or self-report allows for feedback and checking. The cost of in-depth information is always an issue with these shorter general measures (bandwidth vs. fidelity).

Several measures have been consistently applied to outcome studies related to older adults. These include the Montgomery–Åsberg Depression Rating Scale (MADRS), the Generalized Anxiety Disorder Symptoms Scale (GADSS), Clinician Administered PTSD Scale (CAPS), Psychiatric Diagnostic Screening Questionnaire (PDSQ), and Personal Health Questionnaire (PHQ-9), among many others. Finally, there are several other structured or semi-structured measures that address the *DSM* for Axis I diagnoses (e.g., ADIS, Schedule for Affective Disorders and Disease States [SADS], SCID), which have high kappa coefficients for the general population.

TABLE 12.7 Psychosocial Outcome Measures: Psychometric Information

Measure	Content	Reliability	Comment
General Health Questionnaire (GHQ)	60 items for severity of psychiatric symptoms	0.8 test–retest	15-minute self-report; problem is underreporting
Symptom Checklist-90-Revised (SCL-90-R)	90 items for general psychopathology and subscales	0.7–0.85 test–retest	20-minute self-report, not disorder based
Multidimensional Health Profile-Psychosocial Functioning	58 items assessing mental health, social resources, stress, and coping	0.7–0.8 test–retest	20-minute brief screen for primary care
Medical Outcomes Study 36	36 items for social functioning, body pain, mental health, roles, vitality, general health	0.8 test–retest	10-minute assessment of medical (and mental health) outcomes; Likert scale
Behavior and Symptom Identification Scale	32 items assessing symptoms and functional abilities	0.7–0.8 test–retest	10-minute with excellent use for inpatient and outpatient settings
Treatment Outcome Package	Depression, anxiety, thought problems, paranoid ideas	0.8 test–retest	20–30 minute self-report: useful for outpatient settings; based on *DSM-IV*
Mini-International Neuropsychiatric Interview (MINI)	Comprehensive *DSM* criteria	High interrater reliability (kappas)	15–20 minutes, training necessary
Primary Care Evaluation of Mental Disorders	Matched to *DSM-IV*, generates specific diagnoses	Interrater reliability is suspect	10–20 minutes; inadequate provision of accurate diagnoses

For measures cited in this table, see Hyer, Yeager, Scott, and Hyer (2010).

In the era of the Affordable Care Act and patient-centered medical homes, the issue of quality improvement is paramount. In 2001, the Institute of Medicine (IOM) report indicated that the health care system should ensure that care is patient-centered, safe, effective, timely, efficient, and equitable (IOM, 2001). The focus on quality care is that a person in Atlanta receives the same care as one in New York. The quality field has provided models for change involving input from several sources, most importantly the patient. Common models of the quality-improvement cycle include "plan–do–study–act" (PDSA), and "define–measure–analyze–improve–control" (DMAIC). These models provide a simple methodology that emphasizes the data-driven, iterative nature of quality improvement. They improve care because the patient is onboard.

Regardless of the direction that the country is taking, there is an emphasis on patient-reported outcomes, that is, ones reported by the patient directly. This is a marker not just of whether symptoms are lowered but of how the patient really experiences those symptoms, as well as the experience of how the therapy is proceeding. There is substantial scientific evidence that feedback to clinicians on patient-reported outcomes is associated with better retention in treatment and clinical outcomes for the patient (Azocar et al., 2007; Brodey et al., 2005).

TESTING IN DIFFERENT SETTINGS

We briefly address two settings here, primary care and long-term care. The two are the most common venues in which mental health issues present and in some ways are the least understood. Perhaps we have beaten this issue to death, as Dr. Yeager discussed the importance of primary care (PC). We only re-remind the reader of the importance of assessment in this setting. Recall that primary care continues to have high psychiatric comorbidities (17%–37% for depression alone), which are frequently missed by primary care physicians (Miller, Paschall, & Svendson, 2006). Missed psychiatric diagnoses (false negatives) can be as high as 50%, whereas false positives are approximately 75%. Proper diagnosis of dementia and anxiety fares no better in these settings. The integration of psychology into primary care is increasingly recommended and effective, especially when focused case management models are applied (see Areán, Hegel, Vannoy, Fan, & Unutzer, 2008). Fortunately, all the measures noted above have applicability for PCCs. There are some unique measures related to medical care that can be incorporated into the mix (see Hunter, Goodie, Oordt, & Dobmeyer, 2009), largely medical gero-assessments for medical issues such as nutrition, compliance, and home care.

Long-term care, both in nursing homes and assisted-living facilities (ALFs), provides unique settings for assessment. In recent years, ALFs have become more like nursing homes in prevalence rates of psychopathology, including dementia. In comparison, nursing homes have fewer numbers of long-stay residents, more frail elders, and increased numbers with psychiatric problems (Hyer & Intrieri, 2006). Measures in this setting are increasingly prescribed by insurance and Centers for Medicare & Medicaid Services (CMS) regulations (e.g., Minimum Data Set). All residents must be evaluated by facility staff at set times during the year and these ratings tend to be more accurate than otherwise (Hawes et al., 2005). Reviews on cognition, depression, anxiety, adjustment, and QoL in long-term care (see Reichman & Katz, 2008) have fostered the use of common measures with careful attention to purpose of testing and norms. Domains of sleep and pain, as well as behavior disruptions, require attention in these settings because close to 80% of residents will have these problems (Kim & Rovner, 1997). Any evaluation must account for the unique phenomenology of the long-term care setting, where activity and sleep are compromised, as well as the fit between the construct measured and requirements to do tasks in a setting where there is considerable help.

OTHER RELEVANT VARIABLES

Assessment is never done. Health care providers spend less than 1 minute of a 15-minute period with a patient in the discussion of treatment plans. Health literacy and compliance skills then become important. Ideally, the best care involves assessing the patient's values, goals, and capabilities as well as conviction and level of confidence, offering options, and arriving at mutually agreed-to goals. Of course, there are always patients who want to defer to the health care provider.

Assuming reasonable health literacy and some commitment, the effect of optimizing participation in the care equation is equal to the effects of empirically supported treatments (ESTs). Nothing gets done unless these minimal conditions are met.

Participatory Decision Making

Self-management
  Take meds
  Exercise regularly
  Adhere to diet
  Blood pressure and diabetes info or monitor
  Check all health needs
Physician communication
  Tell patient all info
  Share test results
  Explain treatment alternatives
  Explain what to expect from treatment
Participatory decision making
  Ask patient for ideas when making treatment plan
  Give choices about treatment

Discern patient's goals for care
Provider thoughts about patient's values in treatment choices
Treatment plan can be attained in patient's life
Help to set a treatment goal with provider

Heisler, Cole, Weir, Herr, and Hayward (2007)

CONCLUSION

This chapter highlighted the importance of assessment in older adults. Assessment is the sine qua non for good care, whether it is done for just a formulation of the person or for a treatment regimen. "There are many roads to Rome." The fields of psychology and, for that matter, psychiatry have rediscovered the value of monitoring and measuring, as they provide perspective, a course for care, and markers for success. In this chapter we have provided input for many levels of evaluation in the care process, and made suggestions as to how to foster change.

Ultimately, an unearthing of the biological and behavioral mechanisms that mediate psychological disturbances will be necessary for a full understanding of the origin, symptomatology, cultural context, maintenance, treatment, and course of a mental disorder. This may yet be a distant vision, but one that is ever nearer on the horizon for older adults.

CHAPTER 13

Summary

The Watch and Wait model provides the infrastructure for care plans to be activated meaningfully and deliberately. It is served economically by the five problem-based components that require an understanding of their assessment and eventual treatment plans. The Watch and Wait model effectively represents a best fit for the content of the patient's problem and possible interventions to be applied. It melds further stage-treatment matching and patient-treatment matching. Careful work is done upfront.

Watch and Wait holds to the ideal that the patient is not broken, is not a medical anomaly, and does not need to be rescued. The patient is trapped in rigid patterns of living that at later life prevent the pursuit of normal living. The patient is not a mechanistic creature who requires someone to figure out his or her feelings and eliminate causes of problems. Rather, each lives in a context with teachings that can be used for the better, given the right atmosphere and support. All too frequently, the older person does have deficits, but most often these have been assimilated into the context of age and into the context of living. One does not postpone living, even in the throes of a dementia. Watch and Wait fosters commonsense living with plans that elicit the help of the patient. Life is a journey and this is but one experience on the road.

This message of Watch and Wait is not easy to apply, as "stamp out the problem and provide immediate relief" is the usual mantra. The health care system too conspires against this model. Yeager, in Chapter 10, nicely walked the line between reactionary responding and deliberative planning in primary care (PC). The health care landscape is rife with confusion and unsubstantial change. Older adults are caught in the civil wars of vying philosophies of care. Regarding health care, everyone has weighed in from the president to congress, even the Supreme Court: All is opinion.

We have variously addressed health care costs as they relate to older adults. These have been increasing and reached $2.6 trillion in 2010. This is now more than 17% of the gross domestic product (GDP) and is expected to rise to almost 20% in a few years. Medicare costs as a ratio of all health care is 49%. Unfortunately, the share of spending for psychologists and counselors is only 8% of all mental health spending. Psychotherapy fees are only 0.05% of all health expenditures; 14% goes to physicians. Medication costs are now 30% of mental health expenditures (Nordal, 2012).

It is against this background that the Watch and Wait model can be delivered. It plays out best in a PC and with a team. As noted, required data include information and prioritization of five areas: depression, anxiety, cognition, health issues, and life issues. We have presented much data and more than a few cases to suggest the importance of this model. We hope the geropsychologist/psychiatrist/social worker/rehab specialist/nurse will incorporate these ideas and reconsider the world of an older person.

SUMMARY OF WATCH AND WAIT MODEL

Below is a replication, compendium, and summary of the core treatment tables/ideas presented in the book. We begin with the Watch and Wait model itself, segue to the contents of the psychotherapy chapter, and then to depression, anxiety, cognition, health, and life issues.

I. Overall Model: Watch and Wait Checklist

Watch and Wait Core Category	Check
Validate problem	
Psychoeducation of model	
Assessment	
Monitoring	
Case formulation	
Check alliance	

II. Overall Psychotherapy Components

Core Model Factors

Psychoeducation
Alliance
Assessment
Monitoring
Case-based approach

Recommended Treatment Factors

Motivational interviewing
Behavioral activation
Interpersonal process therapy
Problem-solving therapy
Transdiagnostic application
Prevention
Case manager
Exercise
Modules
Cognitive training
Booster sessions
Neuroscience input

_____

_____

Core Psychotherapy Ideas for Psychoeducation

- Protect the therapeutic alliance.
- Integrate care.
- Persist with strategic long-term interventions—the more treatment continues, the less nothing happens.
- Assess brain/health literacy/compliance.
- Watch out for pain, sleep, comorbidities.
- Attitude counts.
- Home care is a possibility.
- Consider pretherapy preparations.
- Self-help helps.
- Problems of the old-old are more difficult. Therefore, take more time and effort.
- Stressors have an impact: They are orthogonal to cerebrovascular risk factors (CVRF) in predicting depression.
- Foster compassionate awareness (mindfulness).
- Be free to "therapize": our distinctions in the nuances of therapy are not that robust.
- Change is good; small change is good; change comes from context.
- All depression and anxiety behaviors make sense: "They are better than even more pain of… failure, confusion, etc."

_____

_____

Treatment Ideas

1. Validate the problem: "What you are doing is okay, even normal, if one sees things from your perspective. If I think as you do and have the issues you have, I would react the same. Now let's see if we can make some changes."
2. Psychoeducation: "This is what seems to be going on. Again, it is common and we can make a difference. Depression is…"

3. Get on the same page: Let patients know about the Watch and Wait model. Speed kills. Small changes are important; being in the present is critical; homework and monitoring are necessary. Let the patient know that he/she is actually getting treatment now (assessment, perspective, monitoring, task clarification, and so on).
4. Offer direction and leadership empathically: "I can help. You have been suffering too long."
5. Monitor: This is essential to change and to the particulars of the intervention. "Let's see how your week is so we can plan to monitor."
6. Change emotional climate: Listen and be empathetic, allow time for the patient to vent, provide psychoeducation, again and again.
7. Use brain pathology as metaphor. This allows for a shared vulnerability and understanding of what can be addressed from a more medical/physical perspective.
8. Link problems to achievable reality: "This is where we are going and what we can do."
9. Make haste slowly: "We need a little time to position ourselves for the best chance for change. So, we will take 2 to 3 weeks and see about our options and make plans for best care. This is a very active period and you will be in the most active stage of treatment, the planning stages. Most treatment fails because this treatment part is missing and you are thrown into an intervention too quickly."
10. Provide a plan: "Here are the steps for change." This plan is drawn from the case-based model that has been formulated.
11. Choose and apply modules.

III. Five Core Issues

A. Depression

Core Treatment Ideas

Nonpharm treatment should be considered first, period. It is true that these forms of prescription are not so much better than meds or the combo, BUT they are the least noxious and always some form of treatment involves nonpharm treatments.

Watch and wait. Monitor and wait for issues to confess themselves. There is an annoying lack of clinically significant differences between treatment and placebo with depressed patients. So, frequent monitoring of patients' symptoms and the consideration/ reconsideration of treatments may produce as much benefit for patients as a medication or psychotherapy and may fit better with the patient's desires.

This is not ignoring symptoms; on the contrary, it entails discussion with the patient of the risks and benefits of treatments, agreement on an observation period as a part of the treatment plan, and the continuance of monitoring.

The differences among the core depression problems (Major Depressive Disorder [MDD], Mood Disorder [MD]), subsyndromal depression) are subtle and of less importance than most clinicians think. All these problems require respect, monitoring, and a clinical watch.

Risk factors account for only a small portion of the variance in the cause and persistence of depression in older adults, and attempting to uncover exactly why someone has become depressed has little advantage for clinicians.

People with depression have problems with concentration, but most do not have the memory problems seen in dementia. People who present as depressed and dementing have both problems. This means they are demented and have a depression in dementia. This is a different form of depression, is variable, and requires more planning.

DO NOT pick one best treatment at the outset. Rather, recognize how patients present with and experience depression; then apply and reapply objective measures of treatment response, and make changes until the patient improves.

Establishing rapport is critical.

Build in commitment from the patient; "I am willing to try this with you as my health care provider. I am committed to this."

Depression ALWAYS involves negative thinking; whether this thinking is accessible and amenable to change is another issue. Patients often do not present with "I am depressed."

Patients who get "usual care" have a very high likelihood of remaining depressed.

B. Anxiety

Watch and wait philosophy
Assess in usual way plus cognition (executive function [EF])
Treat depression as the first consideration
First-line treatment is selective serotonin reuptake inhibitor (SSRI)/serotonin-norepinephrine reuptake inhibitor (SNRI)
 Psychoeducation
 Choose modules
 • First line: relaxation training
 • Second line: cognitive behavioral therapy (CBT)
 • If problems: Motivational interviewing to encourage a medication trial, plus
   ◦ Always: Supportive contact and communication with prescriber/case manager (CM)
   ◦ Monitor, see periodically, and watch for relapse
   ◦ Use case manager, if needed

Treatment rubrics—Watch and Wait
– Most patients seen in primary care
– Many unrecognized and without treatment
– Medication may be first consideration
– Respect side effects, fears, and preferences
– CBT, computed tomography (CT), interpersonal therapy (IPT), relaxation, and problem-solving therapy (PST) work and should be used
– Use modules
– Exercise helps
– Alternative therapies may be appealing
– Take time for intervention choice

C. Cognition

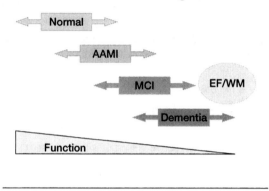

FIGURE 13.1 Continuum of Cognitive Decline

Types of Memory Training

1. Laboratory-based training often involves repeated performance, typically computer training or speed-choice tweaks. These approaches tend to target a particular cognitive domain (often labeled a specific process or direct intervention) rather than taking a domain-general approach aimed at overall improvement with increased well-being, improved symptoms, and better behaviors.
2. General cognitive stimulation, mnemonic strategies, or games tend to work well for older adults who are normal but show aging-associated memory problems.
3. Neurobiologically informed ecological interventions address social-emotional skills that are based on EF neural substrates. These skills include self-regulation, effortful control, and working memory.
4. Neurorehabilitation therapies for patients with traumatic brain injury (TBI) are aimed at improving cognitive functioning by using strategic training techniques to offset rather than reconstitute lost functionality. Generally, the underlying neural systems supporting a given function are assumed to be damaged beyond repair. The rerouting of neural circuitry allows individuals to learn new methods of handling older problems or goals. The target is usually a specific cognitive area, attention, memory, or even vision. Vulnerable populations may benefit especially from these approaches.
5. Generic approaches include reminiscence, reality orientation, and cognitive stimulation therapy. Reality orientation, which involves reteaching information related to orientation to everyday life, has been largely superseded by cognitive stimulation, which uses more implicit methods, with activities including categorization and word association (see Figure 13.1).

D. Health Issues

Core Health Issues

Medical Problems
Lifestyle/Prevention

Stress
Pain
Sleep

_____

_____

Lifestyle

Core Components of Lifestyle

Socialization: Lonely individuals are twice as likely to be diagnosed with Alzheimer's disease as those who are not lonely.

Exercise: Older adults with mild cognitive impairment showed significant improvements on tests of executive function after 6 months of 4-day-a-week aerobic exercise.

Diet: People who eat a Mediterranean-type diet, rich in fruits, vegetables, and omega-3 fatty acids, were 38% less likely to develop Alzheimer's disease over the next 4 years.

Stress reduction: Researchers led by neurologist David Holtzman, MD, at Washington University in St. Louis, reported that short-term stress leads to an increase in the amount of beta-amyloid protein—a key component in the development of Alzheimer's—in the brains of mice.

Relaxation/Meditation: Data now suggest that some form of relaxation can improve cognition. This includes mindfulness, in which there is a focus on being in the present.

Identity: People who have purpose in life respond better in several areas of life. In fact, they perform all the other core components of life better. Values clarification allows for this.

Mental stimulation: Research links higher education and occupational levels to a lower incidence of dementia. The more complex and novel the environment, the lower the risk you have of getting diseases such as Alzheimer's.

_____

_____

Primary Care Core Issues

1. Identify and address emotional concomitants to medical disorders.
2. Advise primary care mental health (PCMH) team about best ways to interact with a patient who is difficult to manage because of psychiatric comorbidities, low cognitive functioning/dementia, and/or personality-based resistance.
3. Consult with medical and behavioral health specialists outside the PCMH regarding a particular patient.
4. Determine whether a patient's behavioral health needs exceed the services available in PC and oversee referral for specialty services in psychopharmacotherapy, psychotherapy, or health psychology.
5. Screen for mood disorders, anxiety, substance abuse, cognitive impairment, and other biopsychosocial disorders that may be overlooked in PC evaluations.
6. Provide supportive care and educational services to patients who are having difficulty participating effectively in their medical care.
7. Offer specialized interventions for smoking, obesity, and other common behavioral problems in the general PC population.

8. Offer specialized interventions for older adults, such as capacity assessment, group cognitive retraining, and caregiver support.
9. Work with family members and with the sequelae of family dynamics when the family may not be present.
10. Offer behavioral interventions for individuals whose medical diagnoses call for treatments that require a substantial behavioral component, such as diabetes, asthma, chronic infectious disease, heart disease, or traumatic brain injury.
11. Develop outcomes assessment and program evaluation systems.
12. Aid in the design of research protocols.

Concerns About Polypharmacy

- Polypharmacy increases the potential for drug–drug interactions.
- Polypharmacy is independently associated with increased risk of an adverse drug event.
- Polypharmacy is an independent risk factor for hip fractures in older adults, especially if one of the drugs is associated with falls risk (e.g., central nervous system [CNS] active drugs).
- Polypharmacy increases the possibility of prescribing "cascades"; that is, an adverse drug effect is misinterpreted as a new medical condition and additional drugs are then prescribed to treat it.
- Polypharmacy can lead to medication nonadherence.
- Nonadherence can be exacerbated by cognitive deficits resulting from polypharmacy.

Watch and Wait With 5A's in PC

Assess   Gather information on the physical symptoms, emotions, thoughts, behaviors, and environmental context to determine variables associated with patient's symptoms and functioning. On the basis of patient's values and degree of control over environment, determine what is changeable to improve symptoms and functioning.

Advise   Describe to patient the options for intervention and the anticipated outcomes based on the data gathered during assessment.

Agree   Patient decides on a course of action based on the options discussed. Or patient rejects the options presented and generates alternatives. Patient also may defer deciding on an action plan to discuss options with family.

Assist   This is the formal intervention. Help patient implement behavior change through learning new information, developing new skills, and/or overcoming environmental or personal barriers. Reinforcement and occasional retrenchment can occur over several visits, often several weeks apart. Interim outcome assessments (e.g., Patient Health Questionnaire-9 [PHQ-9], Generalized Anxiety Disorder-7 [GAD-7]) are helpful here.

Arrange   The follow-up plan is determined here. Will follow-up be with the psychologist? The primary care provider (PCP)? Will the patient need to be referred to specialty behavioral health care? These questions should be addressed at each subsequent visit should the patient remain with the provider. For behavioral health plan (BHP) follow-up, the psychologist should discuss the focus of the next appointment.

Common Interventions in Primary Care

- Relaxation training
- Goal setting
- Cognitive disputation
- Problem solving
- Self-analysis (e.g., automatic or dysfunctional thought records, behavior tracking)
- Self-monitoring
- Motivational interviewing strategies
- Stimulus control
- Assertive communication

E. Life Issues

Socioeconomic status
Adjustment in community
Caregiving
Home care
Community problems
    Finances
    Competence
    Transportation
    Medical insurance
    Iatrogenic disease
    Housing needs
    Meals on Wheels
    Nutrition
    Practical functioning
Relapse issues
Long-term care

POSTSCRIPT

We need changes in the treatment of mental health for older adults. We need a newer and broader definition of what constitutes empirically supported treatments (ESTs) in psychotherapy for older adults. Dattilio, Edwards, and Fishman (2010) argued for no less than a paradigm shift, a mandate for an integrated package of methodological approaches to study psychotherapy that includes both qualitative and quantitative methods, experimental and quasi-experimental strategies—approaches that would allow the development of both nomothetic, universal, cause-and-effect law, and idiographic, context-specific knowledge. This makes sense to us. We see a revolution in mental health care unfolding. This is occurring at the national level. Teams in primary care, savvy mental health workers, and a mix of philosophies related to the ideas of improved care and common sense are now in place. Mental health can be most respected, best appreciated, and most validly adhered to in a setting where the whole person is treated. Professionals see the merit of tolerance for possible problems: a weighing of *this* and a casting aside of *that* with the input of patients and family. Validation and psychoeducation are now considered important, as are the monitoring and the specification of plans. Tinkering is not merely allowed, but appreciated. Outcomes are not eschewed.

Whatever happens in the 21st century for care—stem cells, genomics, nanotechnology, personal medicine, among many others—an improved quality of life will best be achieved if there is an informed and caring professional who knows the better components of care, knows that all components have a role in the care equation, and understands that monitoring and integration of therapies can make a difference. The biopsychosocial model takes on new meaning and new importance for older adults in this new century. We only need to apply it.

APPENDIX A

Memory Clinic and Cogmed Tasks

MEMORY CLINIC BROCHURE

FIGURE A.1 Holistic Memory Clinic

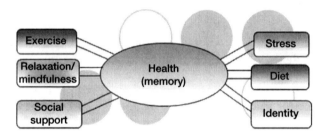

The Memory Clinic consists of a total of six sessions that typically occur two times every month. During each session, we will address MEMORY. This is the core issue of later life problems, which, if addressed correctly, will extend and improve quality of life. We train on a number of validated techniques, practicing on one special system for long-term use. Memory then will be the basis of discussion at every session, and will underlie each supplementary topic that is addressed.

During each session, we will introduce one of the other topics in the model. The last session will serve as a cumulative learning experience to integrate every part of the Memory Clinic model into the lives of each participant. Those in attendance will be expected to participate in open discussions during sessions. In addition, participants will be expected to complete multiple tasks and assignments at home to supplement their knowledge of newly acquired skills to improve their memory.

Overall Module: Memory

The topic of memory will be addressed during each clinic session. Facilitators of each session will introduce various tools that participants can use in order to improve their memory. Below is an image of the parts of the brain that are used when a person is attempting to remember or recall certain pieces of information:

FIGURE A.2   Key Memory Areas in the Brain

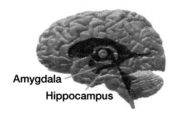

Amygdala
Hippocampus

The method that is promoted during Memory Clinic Group involves a technique called "GUP + Link." Our focus is concentration and attention using a GUP + Link method (Get it, Use it, and Practice it, as well as attempt to Link it) in which we optimize core components of memory. Participants are taught to refocus attention in some distinct way (G; e.g., stand up), to ask questions about the target (G), to read or do the task for a period less than 5 minutes and use helpers, if needed (e.g., write down material) (U), and to look away and retrieve the material (P, practice on the stimuli or picture it), and, if possible, Link it to some associated event). They are then to repeat this until they believe that they can recall the material to a reasonable degree.

Facilitators of each session will emphasize the importance of using these steps to focus on what participants would like to remember and being able to train the brain to recall certain pieces of information.

FIGURE A.3   GUP + Link Method

Get It   **U**se It   **P**icture/Practice It

GUP promotes attention, concentration, repetition, linking, and consistency.

We also add an L for **L**ink It

Throughout the course of the memory clinic, participants will learn many different tools to improve their ability to retain and recall information.

Some of these methods include mnemonics, categorization, imagery, word association, and rehearsal.

Participants will be provided with a monthly planner in which they may write daily activities and events that they would like to remember. In addition, participants will be provided with a deck of playing cards to play "Concentration" (also known as "Memory"). The game of Concentration has been scientifically proven to help improve one's memory!

Module I: Relaxation

FIGURE A.4 Practice Relaxation Robot

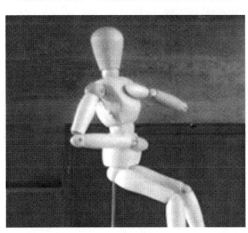

During the course of the Memory Clinic, we will teach you different stress reduction and relaxation techniques that can be used in your everyday life.

One of the most successful relaxation techniques is deep-belly breathing. Here are the steps involved with deep-belly breathing:

1. Sit upright in a chair with both feet placed firmly in front of you on the floor.
2. Try to calm your mind. If you do happen to have a thought pass through your mind, acknowledge the thought, but let it go.
3. Place one hand flat against your abdomen.
4. Breathe in through your nose at an even rate.
5. Allow your abdomen to expand, rather than your upper chest. You should feel the hand on your abdomen being pushed away from your body as your abdomen rises.
6. Breathe out slowly and evenly through your mouth.
7. Repeat this process. You should aim to perform five to six "breathe in/breathe out" revolutions per minute.

Module II: Social Support

Each person's social circle should provide a positive environment for personal growth, fulfilling interactions, and encouraging support. Below are a few ideas to help improve social life and increase the amount of positive interactions with your family, friends, and coworkers:

- Join a book club.
- Invite friends or family over for a potluck dinner.
- Become a member of a Bible study group at a local church.
- Begin volunteering to support a cause that you believe in.
- Start a weekly movie night event for your friends at your home.
- Visit a senior citizen center.
- Attend a free salsa-dancing seminar.
- Plan weekly outings with a group of close friends. You can meet at your home, the mall, a restaurant, or any other favorite place to enjoy each other's company.
- Search for free cooking lessons at local grocery stores and invite your friends to join you.
- Attend a free wine-and-cheese tasting.
- Seek out cultural fairs and festivals that interest you or your friends.

We also ask that you fill out a Pleasant Events Schedule so that you are aware of what makes you feel positive and engaged. Below is a list of some simple activities that may bring a ray of happiness into your day:

- Tea in the afternoon
- Day visit with your grandchildren
- Crocheting/quilting
- Playing bridge
- Reading the newspaper
- Watching your favorite soap opera
- Taking a leisurely stroll in your favorite park
- Phone call with best friend
- Tending to your garden
- Going window shopping in local boutiques
- Preparing a family favorite for dinner
- Catching your favorite program on television every day

Life is full of ups and downs. Being social helps coping. In life, many situations or incidents necessitate strong coping mechanisms—divorce, death of a loved one, relocating homes, job loss, health issues, or other problems. Below there are several avenues that allow for better coping with life's troubles:

- Prayer
- Meditation
- Journaling
- Seeking counseling/therapy
- Joining support groups

Module III: Stress

> Our greatest glory is not in never falling, but in rising every time
> we fall.
> —*Confucius, Chinese Philosopher*

> If you are distressed by anything external, the pain is not due to the
> thing itself but to your own estimate of it; and this you have the power
> to revoke at any moment.
> —*Marcus Aurelius, Roman Emperor*

Cognition refers to one's thought processes. Some people are not aware of the strong impact that one's thoughts can have on one's mood, motivation, and attitudes toward everyday life.

Facilitators of the Memory Clinic will present different techniques to help improve cognition and further aid in better managing stress and worry. We stress the AWARE technique discussed in Chapter 7. Other techniques include mindfulness, cognitive restructuring, and thought stopping, among others.

Module IV: Exercise

The National Institutes of Health recommend that adults engage in some form of moderate physical activity at least 2½ hours each week. This would equate to exercising 30 minutes 5 days a week. There is strong scientific evidence that supports immense health benefits in engaging in physical activity.

Some of these benefits include:

- Lower risk of:
  - Early death
  - Heart disease
  - Stroke
  - Type 2 diabetes
  - High blood pressure
  - Colon and breast cancers
- Reduced depression

- Increased bone density
- Improved sleep quality
- Better cognitive function
- Reduced abdominal obesity
- Better functional health

Below is a list of different forms of exercise that participants can implement into their daily routines:

Walking	Biking	Swimming
Weight Training	Yoga	Tennis
Running	Golf	Martial Arts

Module V: Diet

Diet is now established as a core feature of good health. While this has always been the case, it is only in the last five years that this health component has become critical to good living, and not just a preventative strategy against diseases like diabetes or celiac intolerance.

We stress the Mediterranean Diet, as there is considerable evidence for its merit for overall health and especially cognitive health.

- **Heart Disease and Stroke:** Diet alone can reverse heart disease.
- **High Cholesterol:** Recent studies confirmed that diet can lower cholesterol without medications.
- **High Blood Pressure:** Eating a low-sodium diet will help people suffering from hypertension.
- **Weight Loss:** People following a Mediterranean-style diet have more long-term benefits and lose weight safely.
- **Type 2 Diabetes:** A Mediterranean-style diet can help prevent diabetes and help reduce the need to use diabetes drugs.
- **Cancer:** A lot of studies confirm that some foods may modify estrogens level. Consuming dairy foods may increase the risk of prostate cancer.
- **Osteoporosis:** People from the Mediterranean countries have lower rates of hip fractures.
- **Alzheimer's:** Antioxidants found in fruits and vegetables play an important role in cognitive capacity.

We will provide helpful information sheets on foods to consider, as well as strategies for better food intake.

Module VI: Identity

It is essential to our well-being, and to our lives, that we play and enjoy life. Every single day do something that makes your heart sing.
—*Marcia Wieder, American Motivational Speaker & Author*

In order to succeed, we must first believe that we can.
—*Michael Korda, English Novelist and Publisher*

Let yourself be silently drawn by the stronger pull of what you truly love.
—*Rumi, Persian Poet, Theologian, and Mystic*

Every day of one's life journey should be filled with moments that define one. We will provide some methods that can better develop a personal value system and better identify a purpose in life. It is important also that one takes time to enjoy life, no matter how large or small these moments may be. As humans, we are unique in our interests, and as a result each person's idea of a pleasurable moment may be different from someone else's.

A healthy self attitude is a BELIEF IN YOURSELF. This is the first step to improving your memory! Research studies have demonstrated the power of belief in one's ability to better themselves.

We will provide a values orientation and exercises relating to self-definition, as well as a perspective on self-control and self-efficacy. How problems are approached and what your self-beliefs are matter.

COGMED TESTS

TABLE A.1   Sample Cogmed Tasks

Task	Description
Reproduce a light sequence in a visuospatial grid	Lamps arranged in a four-by-four grid are displayed. Participants watch several lights go on and then reproduce the same sequence.
Indicate numbers in reverse order	A keyboard with numbers is displayed and then digits are read aloud. Participants responded by indicating the same numbers *but* in reverse order.
Identify letter positions in a sequence	Letters are read aloud, one at a time. Participants have to remember the letters and the order in which the letters are read. A row of lights is then visible, and a flashing light cues the participant to indicate the letter that was read in the sequence. For example, if light number 3 lit, then participants report the third letter that they had just heard.
Identify a letter sequence in pseudowords	Participants keep track of letters displayed in columns. A sequence of letters is vocalized while a light (above each column) flashes for each letter that is spoken. Participants click on the letter that was said first, then the second, third, and so on—until the entire pseudoword is reproduced.

(continued)

TABLE A.1 Sample Cogmed Tasks (*continued*)

Task	Description
Find mismatched letters	Two sequences of letters (pseudowords) are vocalized. Each sequence is nearly the same, but there is one difference in the second sequence. Participants have to click on a button, which indicates the letter that did not match the first sequence. For example, if P D A is said first and then P D I, then they click the button above "I".
Reproduce a light sequence in a rotated grid	A rotating version of the visuospatial grid task described above. After the sequence of lights is lit, the grid panel rotates 90° clockwise and participants have to reproduce the sequence in the panel's new position
Reproduce a light sequence in a 3D visuospatial grid	Lights are symmetrically positioned in a 3D room with five inner walls. Participants watch several lights go on and then reproduce the same sequence.

APPENDIX B

CBT and Related Interventions

This appendix presents a mix of case-based and cognitive behavioral therapy (CBT) suggestions. We start with a case formulation model often used in CBT. We discuss the rationale for CBT; basic principles of CBT; stages of CBT; a Watch and Wait session format (a 12+ session format of CBT therapy); and typical CBT interventions, modules, and modal problem areas. We also address other related therapies and suggestions. Then we present the Group, Individual, and Family Treatment (GIFT)/Group, Individual, and Staff Therapy (GIST) model. This is a streamlined CBT program that we have assessed for efficacy. Finally, we provide some help with therapy adaptation for older adults.

CASE FORMULATION

Identifying Information
Problem List
Diagnostic List
Origins and History of Problem Behaviors
Beliefs
Current Precipitants
Personality Formulation
Hypothesis
Treatment Plan
   Obstacles
   Strengths

The unfolding of the care equation starts with the case formulation. This has been much discussed in CBT. Here we use this outline to highlight one process for the Problem List and consequent Treatment Plan that address the five problem areas of this book. The result is a profile of these five areas as discussed in several places in the book.

MODEL OF CBT

The target of therapy as conceptualized by the patient can be any of the four domains highlighted below. Generally therapists tend to target problems within the emotional domain. Facilitating changes in behaviors and/or cognitions is posited to be the most effective way to bring about changes in emotions. The change targets of the cognition domain are unhelpful thoughts (sometimes referred to as dysfunctional or irrational thoughts), several major categories of which have been identified for ease in teaching the concept to patients. Many of these thoughts are "automatic," occurring too quickly to notice. The goals in therapy would be to help the patient identify these thoughts, understand why they are unhelpful, learn how to be more aware of these thoughts, and learn how to modify these thoughts. The change targets in the behavior domain are maladaptive/dysfunctional behaviors. As with unhelpful thoughts, these behaviors may not be fully in awareness.

An action step in therapy could be to help the patient identify these behaviors and replace them with incompatible adaptive behaviors (e.g., planning pleasant events, introducing pleasant reinforcers, changing maladaptive interpersonal behavior). For example, a patient with depression may react to feelings of decreased energy by staying home, refusing social invitations, and failing to exercise. An action step in therapy would be to help the patient understand how these behaviors contribute to and sustain depressed feelings, and develop a plan to become more active and seek social support. In sum, in CBT unhelpful thoughts and maladaptive behaviors are conceptualized as responsible for causing and sustaining emotional disturbances; therefore, changing thoughts and/or behaviors will lead to changes in emotions.

FIGURE B.1 CBT Process

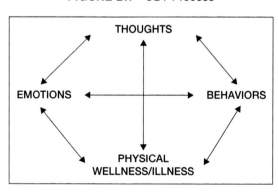

BASIC PRINCIPLES OF BEHAVIORAL THERAPY

Cognitive Distortions

Ultimately, any valid "matching" of specific treatments to particular patients is suspect. Still, effective efforts will hinge on understanding mechanisms that maintain clinical disorders and mechanisms whereby treatment methods work. The essential tension of feeling better versus getting better is very much in play: What is the clinician really doing? One big scientific issue is that what really goes on in CBT is unknown. Are people really changing, compensating, diverting, stumbling through, and so on?

The core idea of CBT is that thinking is the problem (reality does not cause depression). The idea that depression ALWAYS involves negative thinking: whether this thinking is accessible and amenable to change is important but not critical. Patients only rarely present with "I am depressed." The attack on cognition may not bear fruit, but an awareness of this problem is important. The issue of what is happening is relevant and theoretical: For Beck, we change the disordered thinking; for Abramson, we change thought questionnaires, ASQ (Attribubutional Style Questionnaire) and DAS (Dysfunctional Attitude Scale); for Teasdale, we change "events in the mind"; for Nolen-Hoeksema, we stop ruminating; and for Jacobson, we behave better by setting up reinforcement contingencies that work for us.

The critical features of change in thinking involve:

CBT Thinking Tasks

1. Accept model: I have automatic thoughts (ATs) and they influence my life
2. Parse apart: Examine evidence/cognitive distortions/alternative hypotheses
3. Develop rational response or challenge
4. Test it out/Hy testing
5. If true, a problem-solving mode (action plan)

```
A            B              C
S ------------ AT ------------ Emotion
S ------------ AT ------------ Emotion
```

In addition, the importance of cognitive distortions with older adults is at present unknown. While there are data to the contrary (see Chapter 4), the level and types of distortions can be a problem with this group as with younger ones. The problem occurs in the challenge stage of the dysfunctional thought records, often necessitating more psychoeducational effort (Thompson, 2007). Homework in the form of bibliotherapy (even in the form of structured exercises) helps. This has promise for older adults (Scogin,

Jamison, & Gochneaur, 1989). The use of pleasant events too is pervasive in aging literature and used well here (Teri & McCurry, 2000).

Of course, the requirements for change can sometimes be tedious for older adults. But they can work. The person must first accept the model ("I have automatic thoughts") that thoughts influence life. Second, the person must parse apart or examine evidence for cognitive distortions as well as alternative hypotheses. Next, the person must provide a rational response or challenge and then test it out. If there are problems, then the person institutes a true problem-solving mode (action plan). Nicely, CBT is not a cognitively demanding series of tasks (Laidlaw, 2011).

- Core Cogitive Tenets
- Cognitive Theory of Disorder (ABC)
    Beliefs influence feelings and behaviors
    Causal influences go in all directions
- Beliefs More Often Used Than Motivations
    Negative beliefs not aberrant motivations
    Don't infer motivations from consequences
- Beliefs and Behaviors Can Be Changed
    Beliefs and behaviors are learned and can be unlearned
- Emphasis on "Here and Now"
    Focus on present in early sessions and past in later sessions
    May use personality traits as assists
- Emphasis on Rapid Symptom Change
    Action leads to insight (don't wait to get started)
    Attend to underlying beliefs to ensure stability
- Preference for Concrete Examples
    Don't get lost in philosophical discussions early
    More attention to abstract beliefs in later sessions
- Reliance on "Socratic" Questioning
    Ask questions to explore beliefs
    Four-sentence rule (don't talk too much)
- Inductive Approach Preferred
    Move from specific to abstract across sessions
    Explore the abstract earlier with personality disorders
- Empirical Approach to Test Beliefs
    Not your beliefs versus your client's
    Pit unsystematic beliefs versus systematic tests

STRUCTURE OF INDIVIDUAL SESSION

- Brief Update and Check on Mood
    Get the "lay of land" before plunging in
    Hopelessness or suicide may need attention

- Bridge From Previous Session
    - Session-bridging sheet may be useful
    - Encourage client to establish themes
- Set the Agenda
    - Be collaborative in setting the agenda
    - Encourage client to participate
    - Be flexible in following agenda
- Review of Homework
    - Always review homework assigned
    - Troubleshoot if problems encountered
    - Do in session if left undone (if client agrees)
- Discussion of Issues on Agenda
    - Discuss issues of interest on agenda
    - Assign homework relevant to issues
    - Capsule summary of issues discussed
- Final Summary and Feedback
    - Review homework assigned
    - Invite client to summarize key points
    - Ask for feedback about session (even negative)

STAGES OF TREATMENT

- Provide a Rationale
- Train in Self-Monitoring
- Behavioral Activation Strategies
- Identify Beliefs and Biases
- Evaluate and Change Beliefs
- Core Beliefs/Underlying Assumptions
- Relapse Prevention/Termination

PROTOTYPE OF SESSIONS

Watch and Wait Sessions: The first three sessions can have any of the features of the following three sessions. As the therapy segues into approximately Session IV, more direct therapy or modules can be applied. We focus on cognition here.

Session I: Introduction to the Model

- Socialize Client to Therapy
    - Skills-training approach (make therapist obsolete)
    - Emphasize importance of work between sessions
    - Explore expectations for therapy
    - Reactions to "Coping with Depression"
    - Assess hearing and vision

- Listen to Client's Concerns
    - Invite client to tell story in own terms
    - Generate list of specific problems to be solved
- Introduce Cognitive Model
    - Inquire about client's explanations (stable trait)
    - Examine beliefs that underlie feelings and behaviors
    - Provide alternative rationale (bad strategy)
    - Self-fulfilling prophecy (beliefs drive behaviors)
    - Inverted "U" model of performance (arousal and performance)
- Show How Therapy Works
    - Work through example from recent experience
    - Relate change in belief to affect and behavior
    - Suggest how process could apply to other problems
- Assign Homework
    - Base on problem list or example worked above
    - Work through assignment in session
    - Anticipate any problems that might arise
- Summary and Feedback
    - Case-base the proposed therapy so patient is fully aware of treatment plan
    - Invite client to summarize key points
    - Ask for feedback about session

Session II: Training in Self-Monitoring

- Rationale for Self-Monitoring
    - Get a picture of what life is like "in the trenches"
    - Explore hypotheses about what's driving mood
    - Protect against cognitive biases in memory
- Specific Training in Self-Monitoring
    - Moods and activities easiest to monitor
    - Mastery and pleasure often useful
    - Modify as needed to maximize information
    - Monitor on regular basis (about once an hour)
- Set up Homework as "No Lose"
    - Anticipate what might get in way
    - If forget to do, just fill in later
    - If can't be done, see what makes it tough
- Review Self-Monitoring With Client
    - Start next session by reviewing homework
    - Invite client to identify what stood out
    - Encourage client to "walk you through"
    - Look for places to intervene behaviorally
    - Look for places to examine role of beliefs
    - Invite client to summarize what's been learned

Session III: Pleasant Events/Behavioral Activation Strategies

- Basics of Behavioral Activation
  - The more depressed, the more behavioral
  - Use behaviors to test beliefs (helps generalization)
  - Keep it simple and concrete (helps compliance)
  - Act first and motivation will follow (and confidence)
- Activity Scheduling
  - "Plan your work and work your plan"
  - Schedule each hour or schedule selectively
  - "What would you do if you weren't...?"
  - Be realistic about what can be accomplished
  - Build in time for pleasure or relaxation
- Graded Task Assignment (Chunking)
  - Break big tasks into constituent parts
  - Only focus on one step at a time
  - Write steps down and cross them off
  - "Going up a slippery slope" metaphor
- "Success" Therapy
  - Start with something easy and concrete
  - Initial task can be wholly unrelated
  - Sense of accomplishment usually boosts morale
  - Then go on to more difficult task
- Mastery and Pleasure
  - Review self-monitoring for balance in life
  - Assign mastery or pleasure if either lacking
  - Different people respond to different things
- Problem-Solving Therapy
  - Brainstorm solutions without censor
  - Act on most promising solution despite odds

Sessions IV–VI: Identifying Beliefs and Biases

- Identify ATs
  - ATs versus underlying beliefs
  - Recognizing ATs, such as driving a car
  - Link specific thoughts to feelings and behaviors
  - In vivo situations and role-play to identify thoughts
  - Use "orphaned" thoughts to search for affects
- Dysfunctional Thought Record (DTR)
  - Introduce first three columns of DTR
  - Be sure client doesn't contaminate categories
  - Rate intensity of affect and degree of belief
- Exploring Underlying Belief System
  - Use "downward arrow" to explore meaning
  - Identify "hot cognitions" and link to specific affects

See whether underlying beliefs make better sense of affect
Use empathy (self or other) to assess adequacy
- Identify Distortions and Biases
  Look for examples of distortions in client's thinking
  Describe other types of distortions and look for them
  Encourage client to label distortions on DTR
  Examples: all-or-none thinking
  overgeneralizing
  discounting the positives
  jumping to conclusions
  mind-reading
  fortune-telling
  magnifying/minimizing
  emotional reasoning
  making "should" statements
  labeling
  inappropriate blaming

Sessions VII–X: Evaluate and Change Beliefs

- Distraction and Thought Stopping
  Interrupt thoughts with stimulus (involve senses)
  Focus attention on another topic (deliberate)
  Schedule time for ruminating (thought-suppression)
- Distancing From Beliefs
  Beliefs not necessarily facts (maintain distinction)
  Write down beliefs or use board in sessions
- Three Questions (Examining Beliefs)
  What is the *evidence* for that belief?
  Is there an *alternative explanation* for that event?
  What are the real *implications,* if true?
- Other Useful Questions
  Is it *functional* for me to think about this right now?
  What would I *tell a friend* in this same situation?
- Dysfunctional Thought Record
  Question existing beliefs/form alternative responses
  Rate degree of belief in alternative responses
  Rerate intensity of affect and belief in thoughts
- Empirical Hypothesis Testing
  Use own behaviors to test beliefs
  Try new strategies (just to see)
  Opposite action: Do what you've been avoiding
- Other Useful Strategies
  List "pros" and "cons" (for and against action)
  Reattribution therapy for causes ("pie" diagram)
  Task-interfering/task-orienting thoughts (TIC/TOC)
  Rational-emotive role-play (practice rapid response)

Sessions XI–XII: Core Beliefs/Underlying Assumptions

- Form Cognitive Conceptualization
    Infer from ATs
    Historical reconstruction highlights genesis
    Present as hypotheses, not as facts
    Invite client to join in process of exploration
    Defines larger "schema" (beliefs and behaviors)
    Makes sense out of "self-defeating" behaviors
- Cognitive Conceptualization Diagram
    Childhood events and earlier life experiences
    Core beliefs (stable traits about self/world/future)
    Underlying assumptions/conditional beliefs/rules
    Compensatory strategies (behavioral patterns)
- Identify Core Beliefs
    Often infer from "downward arrow"
    More central and abstract than ATs
    Unlovable versus incompetent (love and work)
    Show clients sample list of beliefs if things get stuck
- Identifying Conditional Assumptions
    Typically "if/then" quality (conditional)
    Rules and assumptions people live by
    Often manifest as "should" statements
    People usually surprised others don't live by same assumptions
    Major source of problems in relationships
- Concretize and Test Like Any Belief
    Use "Core Beliefs Worksheet" (CBW) to test beliefs
    Relate ATs to underlying beliefs
    Reconsider assumptions from a mature perspective
    Substitute action plans for compensatory strategies
    "Every new action chips away at old beliefs"

Final Session: Relapse Prevention/Termination

- Relapse-Prevention Strategies
    Focus on relapse prevention well before last session
    Role-play potential problems (stress inoculation)
    Sensitize clients to look for early signs of problems
    Rehearse what client would do if problems arise
    Emphasize skills-training notion (shower analogy)
    Complete "relapse-prevention plan" in session
- Preparation for Termination
    Prepare client for termination from first session on
    Use as rationale for skills-training approach
    Encourage clients to keep homework notebook
    Practice termination when session frequency is reduced
    Use self-sessions to prepare for termination

Termination as an opportunity to develop resources
Explore "pros and cons" of continuing
Examine affective reactions to termination fully
Renegotiate contract if indicated but keep focus
Schedule "booster sessions" as indicated

MODULES

Modules of Therapy

- Relaxation
- Sleep guidelines
- Problem-solving skills training
- Worry control
- Acceptance/mindful
- Behavioral activation
- Pain management
- Pleasant activities
- Mindfulness
- Assertiveness training
- Time management
- Cognitive therapy
- Exposure
- Family involvement

SPECIAL PROBLEM ISSUES

Sleep (see Appendix C)
Pain (see Chapter 8)
Assertiveness: This is an empirically supported method that has not been discussed to any degree previously. It is optimal for passive and dependent older adults, pleasers, and those with boundary issues. When applied well, it is a meta-communication technique that addresses one's values and beliefs in a structured way, thereby allowing clarity for needs and identity

FIGURE B.2 Assertiveness Training

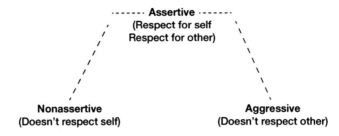

Assertive Communication

Describe	(When you...)
Express	(I feel...because I think it means...)
Ask	(What I would like is for you to...)
Reinforce	(And if you do, I will...)

HELPFUL INTERVENTIONS

FIGURE B.3 Model of Depression

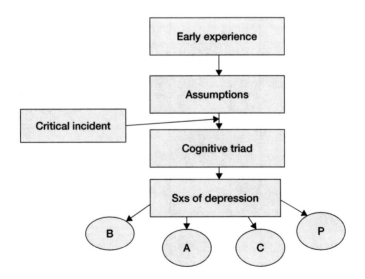

Weekly Activity Schedule

Time of day	M	T	W	Th	F	Sa	Su
9–10 a.m.							
10–11 a.m.							
11–12 a.m.							
12 a.m.–1 p.m.							
1–2 p.m.							
2–3 p.m.							
3–4 p.m.							
4–5 p.m.							
5–6 p.m.							
6–7 p.m.							
7–8 p.m.							
8–12 p.m.							

Note. Grade activities "M" for Mastery and "P" for Pleasure.

Thought Record

Directions: When you notice your mood getting worse, ask yourself, "What's going through my mind right now?" and as soon as possible jot down the thought or mental image in the Automatic Thoughts column. Then consider how realistic those thoughts are.

Date	Situation	Emotions	Automatic Thoughts	Alternative Responses	Outcome
	Where were you—and what was going on— when you got upset?	What emotions did you feel (sad, anxious, angry, and others.)? Rate intensity (0%–100%).	What thoughts and/or images went through your mind? Rate your belief in each (0%–100%).	Use the questions at the bottom to compose responses to the automatic thoughts. Rate your belief in each (0%–100%). Also, consult the list of possible distortions.	Rerate belief in your automatic thoughts (0%–100%) and in the intensity of your emotions (0%–100%).

(1) What is the **evidence** that the automatic thought is true? What is the evidence that it is not true?

(2) Are there **alternative explanations** for that event, or alternative ways to view the situation?

(3) What are the **implications** if the thought is true? What's most upsetting about it? What's most realistic? What can I do about it?

(4) What would I tell a good friend in the same situation?

Possible Distortions: All-or-None Thinking, Overgeneralizing, Discounting the Positives, Jumping to Conclusions, Mind-Reading, Fortune-Telling, Magnifying/Minimizing, Emotional Reasoning, Making "Should" Statements, Labeling, Inappropriate Blaming.

FIGURE B.4 Cognitive Model Revisited (Historical)

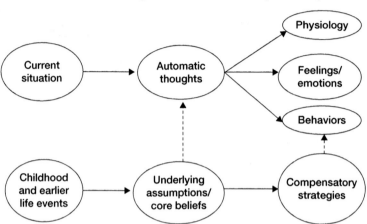

FIGURE B.5 Cognitive Conceptualization Diagram

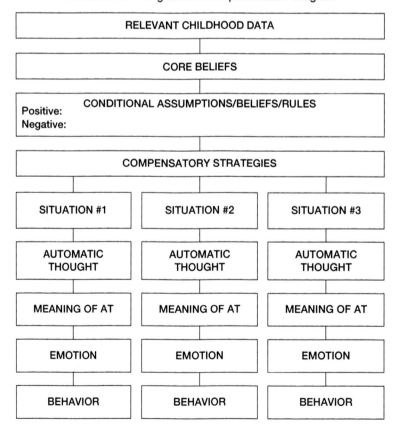

CORE BELIEF WORKSHEET

Old core belief: _____

How much do you believe the old core belief right now? (0–100) ____
    *What's the most you've believed it this week?   (0–100) ____
    *What's the least you've believed it this week?   (0–100) ____

New core belief: _____

How much do you believe the new core belief right now? (0–100) ____

Evidence that contradicts old belief and supports new one.	Evidence that supports old belief with reframe (alt. explanation).

Behavioral Activation

FIGURE B.6 Jacobson's Model: Depression Is Characterized by Behavior-Context Transactions

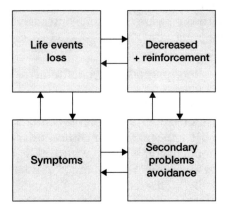

OTHER RELATED THERAPIES

Reminiscence Therapy

Reminiscence therapy is a longstanding treatment modality that has been used to address depression in older adults. Based on Erikson's psychosocial developmental theory, reminiscence therapy emphasizes the review of life and identification of meaning and purpose in one's life. This is done through a process of inspection of one's life through memories, focusing on both positive and negative experiences, and developing perspective. Reminiscence therapy, with its emphasis on personal experiences and history, lends itself to the older adult context.

    Reminiscence therapy emphasizes the review of life and identification of meaning and purpose in one's life. This is done through a process of inspection of one's life through memories, focusing on both positive and negative experiences, and developing perspective. This can be done formally, progressing through the years of informally targeting aspects of the person (e.g., incident related to control issues; see Hyer & Sohnle, 2001). It can be quite helpful.

Brief Psychodynamic Therapy

Psychodynamic therapy, particularly in its brief form, has empirical findings that support its effectiveness in treating late-life depression. Brief psychodynamic therapy focuses on the identification of conflicts and unconscious processes, often originating from early developmental stages. Brief psychodynamic therapy encourages the development of insight and gives importance to the relationship and interactions between the therapist and the client.

The therapist can focus on the client's identity; skills with emotions; themes in the person's life; as well as successes, goals, and future aspirations. The therapist looks for themes, emotional conflicts, and resistance, identifies defenses for change, and is aware of personal internal reactions to problems. See Shedler in Chapter 3.

Interpersonal Psychotherapy

Interpersonal psychotherapy (IPT) focuses on interpersonal problems in four areas: role transitions, interpersonal role conflicts, grief, and interpersonal skills deficits. IPT appears to have clinical utility in treating late-life depression and potential in combination with antidepressant medication.

The client can be absolved of blame (e.g., "You have a medical illness; thus, it is not your fault"). This technique can be used in conjunction with medication. As the target is one of the interpersonal issues, flexibility is maximized and support can be directed at the issues of the therapist. The therapist identifies one of four targets that are interpersonally based and drills down on issues related to this problem state (see Chapter 3).

Problem-Solving Therapy

This therapy has been addressed in various chapters. It applies a problem-solving model of problem identification, brainstorming, barriers, and solutions and follow-through. The GIFT/GIST model, described below, explicates one form.

GIFT/GIST: An Efficient and Effective Cognitive Behavioral Therapy

In recent years, efforts have focused on simplifying empirically supported components in psychotherapy, especially for older adults. GIST is one such model. It is adapted from the GIFT program, a therapy for depression based on CBT theories and techniques, developed to increase cost-effectiveness and transportability. GIFT is really an "emotional fitness model of mental health," which is based on the idea that physical fitness (i.e., eat healthily and exercise regularly) is not inherently complicated but is often difficult to implement consistently. GIFT consists of 10 to 14 group sessions, three individual sessions, and two family sessions to implement coping strategies and build the foundation to maintain these new skills. It relies more on behavioral than cognitive approaches to target a specific coping process, such as behavioral activation or problem solving. GIFT stands in contrast to cognitive approaches that emphasize learning an array of more complex skills (e.g., linking underlying cognitive schemas to automatic negative thoughts) to facilitate recovery. Thus, the emphasis of GIFT lies in identifying more positive behaviors and a focused set of skills that an individual can become increasingly adept at implementing in the face of adverse situations or negative mood. Once an individual is able to identify the behaviors that improve mood, he or she is then more able to regularly engage in them to influence mood.

We applied GIST in a long-term care (LTC) setting with success. We labeled this intervention, substituting "S" for "F" as we used staff instead of family. The principle was the same. *This technique can be applied for outpatients.* The GIST program uses a single, repeated group session that emphasizes the reapplication of the same skills from week to week. Thus, patients at the beginning of their treatment are participating in the same group session as those individuals who have participated in numerous sessions. The difference is that the more experienced group members have developed some expertise in the skills being taught to the newer group members. Because the format is the same in each group, residents can enter the group at any point. Also, individual-based interventions complement the group sessions. The concept of integrating individual and group-based psychotherapy has a long tradition in the clinical literature and has been proposed for integrating patients into open-group CBT for depression.

The three essential interventions in GIST are behavioral activation, increasing positive mood, and modifying behaviors. These are achieved by focusing on pleasant activities and setting up easy-to-attain goals. The program's focus of change is on increasing mood by developing positive short-term goals and life goals, and managing negative mood through experience mapping, or understanding the cycles of cognitions, emotions, and behaviors.

Goal Selection: Goals are to be simple, doable, important, and measurable. Two kinds of goals are identified: *positive* and *meaningful,* and these are explored with participants during their initial individual sessions. By the end of session one, participants are expected to have at least one short-term positive goal identified. Positive goals are intended to provide a motivated focus for the group member that results in improved mood and behavior. Meaningful or life goals include tasks that are important in life but not

FIGURE B.7 GIST Model

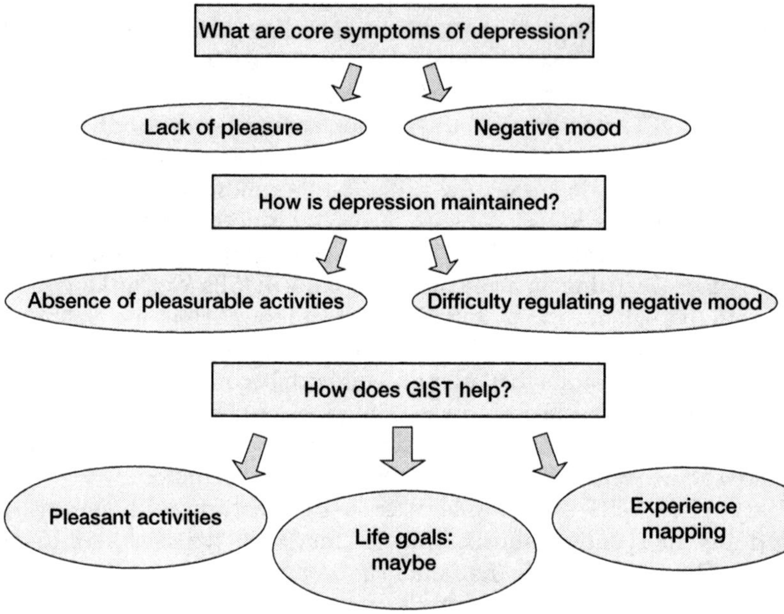

necessarily rewarding (e.g., seeing a special doctor, calling an unavailable son, and so on). In GIST, life goals are optional, as some group members cannot formulate such goals, especially early in the GIST experience.

Group-Session Content: The core of the GIST program is 13 weekly group sessions, which last 75 to 90 minutes each. These sessions are designed to further develop and reinforce members' goals for behavioral activation of pleasure and/or life goals (60 minutes), and to a lesser extent, attend to negative experiences, called *experience mapping* (30 minutes). The format for each session is as follows: (1) check-in, in which participants share their perspectives regarding general well-being; (2) the therapist explains the GIST model, and group members help explain or share examples of common emotional and behavioral experiences; (3) group members review their goals; and (4) the group problem solves and offers support for other members who are having difficulty attaining goals. In GIST, goals serve as the cornerstone of the group. Every member identifies at least one goal for discussion. Goals are written onto a *Goal Sheet* form. A whiteboard also is used during group sessions for this purpose. Goals should be referred to as much as possible in all sessions as they become the target for group discussion and intervention. Behavioral Activation of Positive or Meaningful Goals, then, constitutes the first and longest session component.

Next comes validation.

- Validation. "Okay, now that we have identified what is happening, let's move to validation. Why do we validate? Depressed individuals spend so much time debating whether they are crazy/defective that they feel bad about themselves and never get past that issue to cope more effectively. It is very rare that an emotion comes from nowhere—it is much more likely to be based on reality. It may not be an adaptive emotional reaction, but it is reality based, and valid."
  - What were the environmental, thought, and behavioral factors that most closely linked to your negative mood?
  - If you were X, Y, and Z, does it make sense that you were feeling A?
  - Ask others—if anyone says no, then say, "Well, let's see, maybe we haven't gotten everything up here."
- Change Experience. "Okay, now we have identified and validated what is happening, let's move to change what you are feeling."
- Identify positive mood goal. "Okay, how do you want to feel in this situation?" This may be different across situations—for example, when trying to sleep, person may want to feel relaxed. At a party, confident, and so on.
- We identify a positive mood goal because most of the time, we cope with negative mood by avoiding experience, which doesn't necessarily get us where we want to be. Also, thinking of positive mood helps break focus on negative emotion.
- Alternative coping strategies. "What are possible ways of getting to this positive mood goal?"
- Here is where you have all the group participate.
- Make sure to get plenty of behaviors, thoughts, and environmental strategies.
- Intervention: Watch out for patient negating options. "Okay, we will have plenty of time to decide something won't work. But when we are depressed, we have a tendency to assume things won't work before giving them a chance. Let's do the exercise of considering all options, and then choosing."
  - Strategies used
    - "What did you actually do? What did you wind up feeling?"
    - If this was what person wanted, congratulate them.
    - If not, "What could you do next time? We know for sure that this situation will come up again, let's plan for it."
    - Get others' opinion, or congratulations

Behavioral Activation of Positive or Meaningful Goals: Members begin the behavioral-activation exercise by reviewing their positive or life goals. Then each participant is asked to consider how the group can provide him or her with support. This enables the group to be flexible in how it meets each member's needs (e.g., one group member wants the group to provide her with encouragement to strive toward a particular goal). Several methods have been developed in GIST to identify goals, attach mood to goal activation, and assure that goal-related tasks are being done. These include social support, motivation, peer/staff-assistance, and a narrative understanding of the member.

Social support involves asking the member to do something simple and basic, such as leaving the bedroom and interacting with other people. This intervention can be very low-key, as in encouraging the member to just get out of the room. Sometimes it requires "instruction," in which the group reminds a participant of the value of engaging with other people even if he or she prefers to be alone. This is especially helpful when a member feels sad. *Motivation* involves an exposition of the reasons for this particular goal. It is important to take some time to discuss how motivation can be elusive, but, if thought through, will emerge. It is also important to discuss how motivation feeds off of action. Depression, for example, follows this dynamic: Depressive symptoms tend to remit quicker following behavioral activation—not the other way around. The use of *peer/staff/family assistance* is helpful to ensure that the member can (will) do this task. Finally, a *narrative understanding* of each group member is important. This allows the group facilitator to place goals and problems with goal attainment in context and in perspective.

The GIST/GIFT model enables the therapist to choose among several additional interventions in the behavioral-activation process. One intervention asks the group member to complete mood ratings and attach them to pleasant events to encourage behavioral activation. The group member may need peer/staff assistance to accomplish this task. Other CBT techniques (individual and group models) also may be applied, such as the depression spiral model, use of external rewards, acting "as if," functional analysis, monitoring, structuring the day, and relaxation methods. Finally, breathing relaxation is also applied, as most members can appreciate this and readily comply.

One other feature of the GIST model is applied in the group sessions, called *Experience Mapping* (EM). It is an optional but highly valuable intervention when problems are identified during the week by a group member. The EM is intended to be a problem-solving method for the issue raised. It is a "slow presentation" of a point in time surrounding the problem. Staff should always assist in its formulation. The group facilitator should also tell and retell the group why this is an important group activity—it enables members to fully see and appreciate the ways in which the problem unfolded. So, following the behavior activation/life goals component of the group, the facilitator asks one group member to share a problem with the group. The facilitator begins with a description of the experience map, and then pulls out the thoughts/feelings/behaviors the member experienced when the problem occurred. With the member presenting each component of the experience map (e.g., situation, behavior, negative mood, alternative coping strategies), the facilitator guides the discussion to incorporate the group's reactions. The facilitator then elicits the environmental, cognitive, and behavioral factors that may have contributed to negative mood.

Creating the EM is a three-stage process: (1) identify/validate—the target member is allowed to feel safe and normal, given this "logical" problem and

FIGURE B.8   Negative Emotion: Experience Map

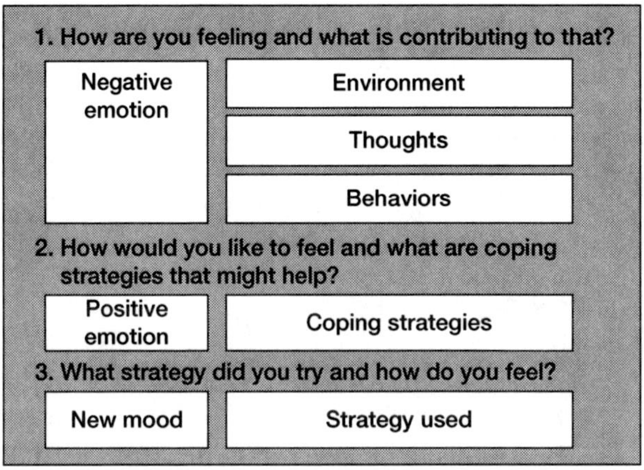

1. How are you feeling and what is contributing to that?		
Negative emotion	Environment	
	Thoughts	
	Behaviors	

2. How would you like to feel and what are coping strategies that might help?

Positive emotion	Coping strategies

3. What strategy did you try and how do you feel?

New mood	Strategy used

his or her "reasonable" response; (2) brainstorming—all possible options are considered by the target member and the group; and (3) change—the target member chooses a strategy to manage the next similar problem. As part of this process, the member identifies a positive mood goal and then generates strategies for attaining that goal. The group also is encouraged to become active in generating alternative potential coping strategies. At the end of the exercise, both the target member and the group have a better understanding of how coping is influenced by a given mood state. Also, more concretely, there is a "lesson learned" (take-home message) for both the target member and the group.

- GIST is *simple* and *repetitive*.
- The *open group format* accommodates those persons who, because of health problems, cannot attend each week.
- *Peer modeling* motivates higher-functioning group members to assist lower-functioning members during the week between group sessions.
- Furnishing a *dry-erase memory board* to each participant works as a visual reminder of positive behavioral goals for group members and staff throughout the week.
- The social connections forged from the group therapy format increase a sense of *emotional support* among participants.
- *Therapist skill* is an important variable in treatment success, given participants' sometimes difficult personalities and/or cognitive factors. The therapist must be active in engaging members who tend to withdraw or tune out in group.
- A *reward system* for staff participation assists in the pregroup actions (gathering members) as well as postgroup actions (assisting members with goal achievment).
- GIST accommodates difficult individuals. Frail and compromised individuals can participate in groups, provided they are not moderately demented or they do not make up the majority of the members. Hearing impairment must be attended to.

Therapy Adaptation

If adaptations are required, then we need to know if this is due to developmental changes, cohort differences, or the environment in which the intervention occurs. Older adults have been shown to respond favorably to the present-focused nature of CBT and enjoy its skill acquisition and educative components. Thompson (1996) and others (e.g., Gallagher-Thompson & Coon, 1996) have advanced specific modifications to CBT for depression for use in older patient populations. These may have special application to older adults who exhibit cognitive decline (Snow, Powers, & Liles, 2006). In fact, the cognitive load of CBT on older adults does not have to be high.

In spite of the lack of solid information about which adaptations are most effective, researchers have identified the benefits of some stock CBT techniques with older adults. For example, the use of handouts and homework for older patients is particularly recommended to facilitate learning and remembering. Homework has been shown to predict treatment outcome in CBT for late-life depression among those with good homework compliance (Coon & Thompson, 2003). Zeiss and Steffen (1996) have urged clinicians using homework assignments with older adults to help clients find ways to "say it, show it, do it." For example, in teaching older clients communication skills, the clinician first explains one principle or tenet of effective communication. The clinician then role-plays the client employing this communication technique in a scenario relevant to the client's life. Next, the client is prompted to practice the technique (as himself or herself) in the same role-play (Gallagher-Thompson & Coon, 1996). The clinician then gives the older client constructive feedback, and the sequence can then be repeated through successive approximation.

Additionally, as in CBT for clients of all ages, the clinician can audiotape each session for the older adult to review between sessions to facilitate the therapeutic and skill-acquisition process. Last, to facilitate and maintain active engagement in the therapeutic process and enhance learning, the older adult is frequently prompted to summarize the material out loud during the session. Similarly, offering a brief review of the session's highlights to conclude and begin each session is particularly important in this patient population (see Thompson, Gallagher-Thompson, & Dick, 1995). As with the treatment of any psychiatric condition in late life, the active involvement of family members and other health care providers (especially physicians) is at times critical for effective CBT of late-life depression.

Modifications to CBT for Dementia

- Content changes
- Simpler skills
- More behavioral, less cognitive
- Core procedures: Clear education, breathing
- Simple coping statements, behavioral activation, sleep skills
- Structure changes
- 1 to 2 topics per session
- Collateral involvement (spouse, adult, child)
- Learning and memory tenets applied
- Cueing procedures
- Simpler practice exercises
- Repetition and practice
- Spaced retrieval

APPENDIX C

Insomnia Manual

BASIC FACTS ABOUT SLEEP

1. Approximately 20% to 40% of the adult population complains of sleep difficulties and about one in six individuals (17%) considers sleeplessness a serious problem. Insomnia is the second most prevalent health complaint after pain.

2. There is some evidence that chronic insomnia leads to major health problems and that it affects longevity. However, no one has ever died from insomnia!

3. Insomnia is usually defined as either: (a) sleep-onset latency averaging more than 30 minutes per night, (b) total time awake after sleep onset averaging more than 30 minutes per night, (c) early-morning awakening before the desired wake-up time with an inability to fall back asleep, and (d) poor quality of sleep. To meet the criteria for insomnia, an individual must also complain of impaired mood, performance, or daytime functioning.

4. The belief that everyone must have 8 hours of sleep every night is a myth. Adults average about 7 to 7.5 hours of sleep per night and many individuals function effectively with 4 to 6 hours of sleep. Twenty percent of the population (slightly higher in men) sleeps less than 6 hours per night.

5. Total sleep time declines with age from an average of about 7.5 hours per night during adolescence to 6.5 hours per night after approximately 60 years of age. Additionally, deep sleep decreases and light sleep increases as we get older, making arousals more common.

6. Sleep efficiency, or the ratio of time asleep divided by time in bed, begins to decline at about 35 years of age. As a consequence, sleep difficulties gradually increase with age.

7. Sleep is divided into five basic stages: Stages 1, 2, 3, 4, and REM (rapid-eye movement) or (dream) sleep. Stage 1 represents the lightest stage of sleep and it marks the transition from wakefulness to sleep. In good sleepers, this stage ranges from 1 to 7 minutes. If awakened from this stage, most individuals will report wakefulness, not sleep. Stage 2 is the

first "true" sleep stage. This is still considered a "lighter" stage of sleep. Stages 3 and 4 are called "delta sleep" and are distinguished by the appearance of delta waves on the electroencephalogram (EEG). These are the deepest stages of sleep. In REM sleep, the eyes move because we "look" around while we dream. REM sleep is also termed "paradoxical" sleep because the EEG pattern resembles wakefulness. During REM sleep, the large muscles of the body are paralyzed. The brain and nervous system are quite active during REM sleep, making awakenings more likely during this stage.

8. During sleep, we progress from stage 1 to stage 4, then back to stage 2, and then to REM sleep. This entire cycle is about 90 minutes long and the typical sleeper will go through four to six of these cycles per night. During the first half of the night, REM cycles are very short and delta sleep cycles are long. As the night progresses, delta cycles become shorter and the length of REM cycles increases. Thus, almost all deep sleep is obtained during the first half of the night while the second half of the night is predominantly dream sleep. Because dream sleep is a lighter stage of sleep, awakenings are more common during the second half of the night.

SLEEP EDUCATION/COGNITIVE RESTRUCTURING

1. One night of total sleep deprivation makes healthy young volunteers sleepy, but has remarkably little effect on daytime performance. Even extended sleeplessness causes remarkably little pathology aside from extreme sleepiness. One volunteer stayed awake for 264 hours, or 11 days, and showed no demonstrable abnormalities! Even after this length of sleeplessness, 2 to 3 nights of extended sleep returns volunteers to normal.

2. For most individuals, performance can usually be maintained with 60% to 70% of normal sleep. For an 8-hour sleeper, that is 4.5 to 5.5 hours of sleep. A number of studies have shown that insomniacs actually perform as well on tests of cognitive performance as good sleepers.

3. If you are not sleepy during the day, you may be trying to get more sleep than you need. A number of studies have shown that insomniacs are **not** sleepier than good sleepers during the day.

4. The major effect of moderate sleep loss is irritability and fatigue, often due to stressful appraisals about sleep loss. Most individuals have experienced sleep loss due to socializing, recreational activities, travel, and so on, which was not appraised as stressful. However, tossing and turning during the night and then appraising sleep loss as stressful will adversely affect daytime mood. Thus, for moderate sleep loss, the **perception** of sleep is more important than the amount of sleep. The less you fear insomnia, the better you will sleep!

5. Insomniacs tend to overestimate time to fall asleep and underestimate total sleep time, probably due, in part, to their tendency to perceive light sleep (stage 2) as being "awake." The average good sleeper awakens, on average, 4 to 6 times per night. In other words, you are probably getting more sleep than you think!

6. Attributing mood and daytime functioning entirely to sleep exacerbates insomnia. It is important to realize that nutrition, exercise, stress, and many other factors also affect our daily functioning.

ESTABLISH A REGULAR BEDTIME AND AWAKENING TIME

A regular bedtime routine and stable in-bed time are very important to establish to overcome your sleep problem. It is even more critical that you get up the same time each day, even after nights when you slept very little or not at all. Therefore, I suggest that you set an alarm clock each evening, before you know how you will sleep that night. Get up at about the same time both during weekends and weekdays. Although this is very difficult in the beginning, over weeks and months, it will help establish a routine for your sleep/wake cycle.

AVOID THE BEDROOM CLOCK

It is very difficult to relax and fall asleep when you see how time is slipping by. When you go to bed, set the alarm for the next morning, but then turn the clock around or hide it in a dresser drawer. Similarly, put away your watch. If you need to be up by a certain time, make sure your alarm is set properly. Usually, one sleeps best away from all time pressures. This also applies to those who have long awakenings during the night.

AVOID TRYING TO SLEEP

The more you TRY to sleep, the more awake you will become. Lying in bed frustrated and unable to sleep needs to be avoided at all costs. As long as you lie in bed comfortable and relaxed, continue to do so. If you find yourself awake for more than "20 mental minutes," get out of bed and go to another room. Once out of bed, you can engage in reading or listening to music to help you relax and distract your mind from your worries. The reading material or music you select should not be very stimulating. Remember the goal is to relax and *allow* sleep to come. Once you begin to feel drowsy, return to the bedroom to sleep. Repeat this procedure as often as necessary until you fall asleep. This procedure to help you learn to sleep in your bedroom environment is called "stimulus control."

CUT DOWN ON YOUR TIME IN BED

The longer one stays in bed beyond the time that is actually required for sleeping, the more shallow and unsatisfactory sleep gets. It will be difficult in the beginning to cut down on your bed time to no more than 4 hours per 24-hour period because your body is used to getting more time in bed than that. However, if you can endure the shorter bedtime hours for a few weeks, I predict that your sleep will become considerably deeper and more refreshing. Obviously, the time out of bed has to be spent active and alert. If you simply substitute dozing somewhere else for time spent in bed, this will not help. Also, the time spent napping during the day is included in the above total. Do not take naps for longer than 1 hour, as longer naps can significantly affect sleep onset that night.

SCHEDULE "WORRY" TIME IN THE EARLY EVENING

Reserve about 30 minutes during the early evening to be alone. During that time, sit in a comfortable chair and simply let your mind wander. If you hit on unpleasant thoughts, worries, or something that needs to be worked through or planned, write each such thought on a separate piece of paper, for example, a 3 × 5 card. When you have collected most of the thoughts that are currently listed on these cards, sort the cards into different categories. Then take each card and, in turn, think about what needs to be done. Try to settle as many worries and thoughts as you can by planning the next step you can do in each case. Make lists. Write down your decisions about each worry or thought on the appropriate card in black and white. Then, if that thought strikes you later in the night, you can tell yourself that you have thought about it carefully, that you have a plan, and that tomorrow you will carry out that plan. However, the same worry occasionally comes back to you night after night. This usually indicates that your plan is not working. Try to come up with a different solution.

RELAXATION TRAINING

Typically, I expect the skill of relaxation to be developed in approximately 5 to 15 sessions, but occasionally it takes more time. The type of relaxation that you use is not important, but it is important that you practice your skill daily at home until you are proficient at it. Here are some basic instructions for relaxation training:

1. Use a quiet, nondistracting environment to practice your relaxation techniques.
2. Practice relaxation in a comfortable body position, preferably lying down.

3. Don't worry about whether you are "successful" in achieving a state of deep relaxation. Maintain a passive attitude and permit relaxation to occur at its own pace. If distracting thoughts occur, simply say "oh well" and return to focusing on relaxation techniques. This ability to let "relaxation happen" is termed "passive volition" and will eventually facilitate sleep onset.

4. During the first 2 weeks of relaxation training, practice the relaxation techniques once or twice daily, but not at bedtime. The afternoon is probably the best time to practice.

5. During the third week of training, use the relaxation techniques once or twice during the day and then at bedtime when you turn off the lights and close your eyes to go to sleep.

6. When practicing the relaxation techniques at bedtime, combine the relaxation techniques with sleep scheduling and stimulus control. If you don't fall asleep within 25 minutes, do not continue the relaxation techniques. Open your eyes, get out of bed and distract yourself by reading, listening to music, or by any other activity, until you feel drowsy. Then close your eyes and use the relaxation techniques again. Repeat this process until you fall asleep.

7. Regular daily use of relaxation techniques will have long-term stress-reducing effects, in addition to helping you fall asleep.

TRY TO EXERCISE IN THE LATE AFTERNOON OR EARLY EVENING

During the day, body temperature and metabolism increase; during the night, they decrease. In people who have problems with sleeping, metabolism and temperature do not drop as much during the night as they do in people who sleep well. Exercise, if done intensively for about 20 minutes, increases body metabolism and temperature. Five to six hours later, metabolism and temperature then decrease much more than if you had not exercised. This helps your sleep. Therefore, I recommend exercise about 5 to 6 hours before you want to fall asleep. If you exercise right before sleep it will delay sleep onset because it leads to increased arousal.

The kind of exercise you do is less important than the intensity of it. Intensity of exercise is typically evaluated by measuring your heart rate. Here is a simple formula that you can use to calculate your approximate "target zone," that is, the speed with which your heart should beat during the most intensive part of your exercise:

Simply subtract your age from 180, and then subtract 10 from this to get the low end of your range. For example, if you are 40 years old, your top rate is 140 (180 − 40) and your low end is 130 (140 − 10). Once you have obtained your target heart rate zone, apply it to your exercise session.

Obviously, this only applies to medically healthy people. If you have medical problems, check with your doctor.

Also, if you have exercised little up to now, check with your doctor before starting and follow his or her advice. Usually the ideal form of exercise consists of about 5 minutes of warm up, then about 20 minutes in the target zone, followed by about 5 minutes of slowing down. If you are out of condition, however, start by staying in the target zone only for a few minutes. Certainly, if you are out of breath or have difficulty talking, start the slow-down phase. Gradually increase the time in the target zone until you can stay there for 20 minutes. If your heart rate does not increase to the levels that are specified by the formula, you may need to exercise more intensively. If walking is your exercise, for example, you might have to walk faster, swing your arms more, or attach some weights to your arms.

Exercising three or four times per week is sufficient. You do not need to exercise every day.

TAKE A HOT BATH 2 TO 4 HOURS BEFORE GOING TO BED

The idea is to increase your body temperature before bedtime, which will lead to a drop in temperature about 2 or 3 hours later. If you have a spa or Jacuzzi, sit in it for about 20 minutes or until you break into a good sweat. If you sit in your bathtub, make the water slightly hotter than is comfortable and keep it at that temperature for about 20 minutes by occasionally letting some cool water out and adding some hot water.

Before you do the hot-bath routine, check with your doctor. For the first few times that you do it, have someone else around during that time and do it for less than 20 minutes. Some people get dizzy or faint from hot baths, and if that happens to you, discontinue taking a hot bath.

EAT A LIGHT SNACK BEFORE GOING TO BED

There is good research showing that foods that contain the substance tryptophan (a naturally occurring amino acid) may promote sleep. Foods that are high in tryptophan are turkey, milk, cheese, and bananas. If you find that you are hungry before bedtime or in the middle of the night, you may want to try a glass of milk (warm or cold), cheese and crackers, or something similar. This may help you to sleep better. Try it for a week or two and see whether it helps you.

AVOID TOBACCO AND CAFFEINE

Smoking clearly disturbs sleep. However, if you were a heavy smoker, you will find that you also sleep quite poorly during the process of withdrawing from nicotine. In a few weeks after withdrawal, you will sleep better.

Caffeine is a powerful stimulant and can disturb sleep even several hours after consuming a caffeinated product. Measurable harmful effects on sleep can be seen 16 hours after consuming 200 mg of caffeine (the equivalent of a strong cup of brewed coffee). The practice of consuming 1 to 2 cups of coffee in the morning may be tolerated by most people, but insomniacs may be sensitive even to small amounts of stimulants. Gradual withdrawal from caffeine should be considered (abrupt withdrawal may lead to headache), starting with the elimination of caffeine products after noon.

SLEEP MEDICATION

Taking a sleeping pill every night is not recommended because the body habituates to it. This means that after a few months of taking sleeping pills every night, these pills do not work any more. However, you then are "hooked." If you stop the medication, you will sleep much worse for a few weeks.

Although I rarely recommend that people be on chronic sleeping pills for the rest of their lives, I do think that such medications are occasionally helpful, as long as they are taken no more than once per week on average. Take them after you have had a few very poor nights or if there is a particular night when you just have to sleep well because the next day is very important. Make sure that you do not get into the habit of taking them more and more often.

Although the continued use of sleeping pills is not recommended, occasionally we have had success with very low doses of sedating antidepressant medications. These medications do not seem to cause physical dependency as readily as the sleeping pills and can be taken nightly without developing habituation.

PSYCHOTHERAPY

Although no one can change what happened in the past, many patients find that only by talking about things to a professional can they gradually come to terms with and get over what is causing the problem(s). If we do not discuss these things, they often will continue to nag at us from the inside. You may want to ask your own physician whether he/she can recommend someone or ask some friends who have been in therapy and have been helped who they would recommend.

BRIGHT-LIGHT THERAPY

Bright light activates the brain and stimulates alertness. It can move the sleep phase. Thus, if you get sleepy early in the evening but then cannot sleep early in the morning, you should have bright light in the evening (a few hours before going to bed). If you have difficulties falling asleep and then cannot get up the next morning, you should have bright light in the morning when you first awaken.

Bright light is defined as light bright enough to take a picture with a simple camera, simple film, and without flash. If you wonder whether a certain light is bright enough, simply take a simple camera and snap a picture of someone illuminated by it. If the flash went off, it is not bright enough. Most outdoor light is bright enough, even if the sky is overcast. Avoid being under shade trees or large overhangs. Indoor light is almost never bright enough to change your sleep/wake cycle.

During the summer, you will do best with outdoor light. It is usually bright enough from 30 minutes after sun up to 30 minutes before sun down. However, during the winter, you may need an artificial light source. Bright light boxes can be costly. They are not usually covered by insurance. If possible, I recommend that you first try outdoor, natural light before purchasing one of these boxes.

Start with about 15 minutes of bright-light therapy. If you feel no effects after a week, go to 30 minutes. Some people might even have to use the bright light for 1 or 2 hours before they feel the effect. We are interested in the amount of light that enters your eyes.[1] Do not wear sunglasses during exposure to the bright light. If you have sensitive skin and notice some redness of the face after using the bright light, you may need to apply some ultraviolet protection/sunscreen during bright-light use.

The bright-light unit should be set up on a desk, table, or countertop. You should be sitting directly facing the unit (about 1–1½ feet away) and have your eyes open. You should have a clear horizontal line of vision to the center of the light box. It is neither necessary nor recommended to look directly at the unit. Rather, you should focus on reading, writing, or eating in front of the unit.

If you have any type of eye problems (other than needing corrective glasses), check with your eye doctor first. Discontinue bright-light treatment if you have any unusual visual symptoms that last more than 2 or 3 minutes after the bright-light treatment. Cut down on your amount of bright-light exposure if you feel "hyper" or irritable later on in the day, or experience any discomfort consistently during or after using the lights.

RECOMMENDED READING

Because you will be undergoing treatment for your insomnia for the next several weeks, it is strongly recommended that you become educated on this topic. One book that we highly recommend is a paperback called *No More Sleepless Nights* by Dr. Peter Hauri. Dr. Hauri is a highly respected practitioner. The information provided in *No More Sleepless Nights* will help you identify aspects of your behavior that may be contributing to your sleep difficulty and will guide you in how to resolve some of these issues.

NOTE

1. It may be recommended during the summer months that you wear sunglasses at other times of the day.

References

A Profile of Older Americans. (2010). Administration on Aging U.S. Department of Health and Human Services, Washington DC. http://www.aoa.gov/aoaroot/aging_statistics/profile/2010/docs/2010profile.pdf

Acton, G. J., & Kang, J. (2001). Interventions to reduce the burden of caregiving for an adult with dementia: A meta-analysis. *Research in Nursing & Health, 24*(5), 349–360.

The ADVANCE Collaborative Group. (2008). Intensive blood glucose control and vascular outcomes in patients with type 2 diabetes. *New England Journal of Medicine, 358*, 2560–2572.

Agargün, M. Y., Kara, H., & Solmaz, M. (1997). Sleep disturbances and suicidal behavior in patients with major depression. *Journal of Clinical Psychiatry, 58*(6), 249–251.

Akincigil, A., Olfson, M., Walkup, J. T., Siegel, M. J., Kalay, E., Amin, S., … Crystal, S. (2011). Diagnosis and treatment of depression in older community-dwelling adults: 1992–2005. *Journal of the American Geriatrics Society, 59*, 1042–1051. doi: 10.1111/j.1532–5415.2011.03447.x

Akkerman, R. L., & Ostwald, S. K. (2004). Reducing anxiety in Alzheimer's disease family caregivers: The effectiveness of a nine-week cognitive-behavioral intervention. *American Journal of Alzheimer's Disease and other Dementias, 19*(2), 117–123.

Alberti, R. E., & Emmons, M.L. (2001). *Your perfect right: Assertiveness and equality in your life and relationships* (8th ed.). Atascadero, CA: Impact Publishers.

Alexopoulos, G. S. (2003). Role of executive function in late-life depression. *Journal of Clinical Psychiatry, 64*, 18–23.

Alexopoulos, G. S. (2005a). Depression in the elderly. *The Lancet, 365*(9475), 1961–1970.

Alexopoulos, G. S. (2005b). The role of medical comorbidity on outcomes of major depression in primary care: The PROSPECT Study. *American Journal of Geriatric Psychiatry: Official Journal of the American Association for Geriatric Psychiatry, 13*(10), 861.

Alexopoulos, G. (2008). Personalizing the care of geriatric depression. *American Journal of Psychiatry, 165*(7), 790–792.

Alexopoulos, G. S., Kiosses, D. N., Choi, S. J., Murphy, C. F., & Lim, K. O. (2002). Frontal white matter microstructure and treatment response of late-life depression: A preliminary study. *American Journal of Psychiatry, 159*(11), 1929–1932.

Alexopoulos, G. S., Kiosses, D. N., Heo, M., Murphy, C. F., Shanmugham, B., & Gunning-Dixon, F. (2005). Executive dysfunction and the course of geriatric depression. *Biological Psychiatry, 58*(3), 204–210.

Alexopoulos, G. S., Meyers, B. S., Young, R. C., Kalayam, B., Kakuma, T., Gabrielle, M., … Hull, J. (2000). Executive dysfunction and long-term outcomes of geriatric depression. *Archives of General Psychiatry, 57*(3), 285–290.

Alexopoulos, G. S., Meyers, B. S., Young, R. C., Campbell, S., Silbersweig, D., & Charlson, M. (1997). "Vascular depression" hypothesis. *Archives of General Psychiatry, 54*(10), 915.

Alexopoulos, G. S., Raue, P., & Areán, P. (2003). Problem-solving therapy versus supportive therapy in geriatric major depression with executive dysfunction. *American Journal of Geriatric Psychiatry, 11*, 46–52.

Alexopoulos, G. S., Reynolds, C. F., Bruce, M. L., Katz, I. R., Raue, P. J., Mulsant, B. H., … PROSPECT Group. (2009). Reducing suicidal ideation and depression in older primary care patients: 24-month outcomes of the PROSPECT study. *American Journal of Psychiatry, 166*, 882–890.

Alexopoulos, G. S., Vrontou, C., Kakuma, T., & Meyers, B. S. (1996, July). Disability in geriatric depression. *The American Journal of Psychiatry, 153*(7), 877–885.

Alloy, L. B., & Clements, C. M. (1992). Illusion of control: Invulnerability to negative affect and depressive symptoms after laboratory and natural stressors. *Journal of Abnormal Psychology, 101*(2), 234.

Alvarez, J. A., & Emory, E. (2006). Executive function and the frontal lobes: A meta-analytic review. *Neuropsychology Review, 16*(1), 17–42.

Alvidrez, J., Areán, P. A., & Stewart, A. L. (2005). Psychoeducation to increase psychotherapy entry for older African Americans. *American Journal of Geriatric Psychiatry, 13*(7), 554–561.

American Academy of Pediatrics, Council on Pediatric Practice. (1967). Pediatric records and a "medical home." In *Standards of child care* (pp. 77–79). Evanston, IL: Author.

American College of Family Physicians, & American Academy of Pediatrics, American College of Physicians, & American Osteopathic Association. (2007). *Joint principles of the patient-centered medical home.* http://www.aafp.org/online/en/home/media/releases/2007/20070305pressrelease0.html

American College of Medicine and the Association of American College of Nursing 2010. (2010). *Nursing: Scope, standards of practice.* Silver Spring Maryland, American Nurses Association.

American Geriatrics Society. (2002). AGS Panel on persistent pain in older persons. *Journal of the American Geriatrics Society, 50*(6 Suppl.), S205–S224.

American Geriatrics Society & Beers Criteria Update Expert Panel. (2012). American Geriatrics Society updated beers criteria for potentially inappropriate medication use in older adults. *Journal of the American Geriatrics Society,* 1–16.

American Psychiatric Association. (1980). *Diagnostic and statistical manual of mental disorders* (3rd ed.). Washington, DC: American Psychiatric Press.

American Psychiatric Association. (1987). *Diagnostic and statistical manual of mental disorders* (3rd ed., rev.). Washington, DC: American Psychiatric Press.

American Psychiatric Association. (1994). *Diagnostic and statistical manual of mental disorders* (4th ed.). Washington, DC: American Psychiatric Press.

American Psychiatric Association. (2000). *Diagnostic and statistical manual of mental disorders* (4th ed., text rev.). Washington, DC: American Psychiatric Press.

American Psychiatric Association. (2013). *Diagnostic and statistical manual of mental disorders* (5th ed.). Washington, DC: American Psychiatric Press.

American Psychological Association (APA). (2013). Guidelines for psychological practice in health care delivery systems. *American Psychologist, 68*(1), 1–6.

Ancoli-Israel, S., Klauber, M. R., Jones, D. W., Kripke, D. F., Martin, J., Mason, W., … Fell, R. (1997). Variations in circadian rhythms of activity, sleep, and light exposure related to dementia in nursing-home patients. *Sleep, 20*(1), 18.

Andel, R., Kåreholt, I., Parker, M. G., Thorslund, M., & Gatz, M. (2007). Complexity of primary lifetime occupation and cognition in advanced old age. *Journal of Aging and Health, 19*(3), 397–415.

Andreescu, C., Lenze, E. J., Dew, M. A., Begley, A. E., Mulsant, B. H., Dombrovski, A. Y., … Reynolds, C. F. (2007). Effect of comorbid anxiety on treatment response and relapse risk in late-life depression: Controlled study. *The British Journal of Psychiatry, 190*(4), 344–349.

Andreescu, C., Mulsant, B. H., Houck, P. R., Whyte, E. M., Mazumdar, S., Dombrovski, A. Y., ... Reynolds, C. F., III. (2008). Empirically derived decision trees for the treatment of late-life depression. *American Journal of Psychiatry, 165*(7), 855.

Aneshensel, C. S., Pearlin, L. I., Mullan, J. T., Zarit, S. H., & Whitlatch, C. J. (1995). *Profiles in caregiving: The unexpected career.* New York, NY: Academic Press.

Angell, B. (2006). Measuring strategies used by mental health providers to encourage medication adherence. *Journal of Behavioral Health Services and Research, 33*(1), 53–72.

Antony, M. M., & Barlow, D. H. (2002). *Handbook of assessment and treatment planning for psychological disorders.* New York, NY: Guilford Press.

Antony, M. M., & Swinson, R. P. (2000). *Phobic disorders and panic in adults: A guide to assessment and treatment.* Washington, DC: American Psychological Association.

Arch, J. J., & Craske, M. G. (2009). First-line treatment: A critical appraisal of cognitive behavioral therapy developments and alternatives. *Psychiatric Clinics of North America, 32*(3), 525.

Areán, P. A., & Cook, B. L. (2002). Psychotherapy and combined psychotherapy/pharmacotherapy for late life depression. *Biological Psychiatry, 52*(3), 293–303.

Areán, P. A., Gum, A., McCulloch, C. E., Bostrom, A., Gallagher-Thompson, D., & Thompson, L. (2005). Treatment of depression in low-income older adults. *Psychology and Aging, 20*(4), 601.

Areán, P., Hegel, M., Vannoy, S., Fan, M. Y., & Unuzter, J. (2008). Effectiveness of problem-solving therapy for older, primary care patients with depression: Results from the IMPACT project. *The Gerontologist, 48*(3), 311–323.

Areán, P. A., Perri, M. G., Nezu, A. M., Schein, R. L., Christopher, F., & Joseph, T. X. (1993). Comparative effectiveness of social problem-solving therapy and reminiscence therapy as treatments for depression in older adults. *Journal of Consulting and Clinical Psychology, 61*(6), 1003.

Areán, P. A., Raue, P., Mackin, R. S., Kanellopoulos, D., McCulloch, C., & Alexopoulos, G. S. (2010). Problem-solving therapy and supportive therapy in older adults with major depression and executive dysfunction. *American Journal of Psychiatry, 167*(11), 1391.

Ashford, J. W., & Borson, S. (2008). Primary care screening for dementia and mild cognitive impairment. *Journal of the American Medical Association, 299*(10), 1132–1133.

Ashford, W. (2008). Screening for memory disorders, dementia, and Alzheimer's disease. *Aging Health, 4*(4), 399–432.

Attix, D. K., & Welsh-Bohmer, K. A. (Eds.). (2006). *Geriatric neuropsychology: Assessment and Intervention.* New York, NY: Guilford Press.

Ayers, C. R., Sorrell, J. T., Thorp, S. R., & Wetherell, J. L. (2007). Evidence-based psychological treatments for late-life anxiety. *Psychology and Aging, 22*(1), 8.

Azocar, F., Cuffel, B., McCulloch, J., McCabe, J. F., Tani, S., & Brodey, B. B. (2011). Monitoring patient improvement and treatment outcomes in managed behavioral health. *Journal for Healthcare Quality, 29*(2), 4–12.

Bäckman, L., Jones, S., Berger, A. K., Laukka, E. J., & Small, B. J. (2005). Cognitive Impairment in preclinical Alzheimer's disease: A meta-analysis. *Neuropsychology, 19*(4), 520–531.

Bäckman, L., & Small, B. J. (2007). Cognitive deficits in preclinical Alzheimer's disease and vascular dementia: Patterns of findings from the Kungsholmen Project. *Physiology and Behavior, 92,* 80–86.

Baddeley, A. D. (2003). Working memory and language: An overview. *Journal of Communication Disorders, 36*(3), 189–208.

Baddeley, A. D., Bressi, S., Della Sala, S., Logie, R., & Spinnler, H. (1991). The decline of working memory in Alzheimer's disease. A longitudinal study. *Brain, 114,* 2521–2542.

Baddeley, A. D., & Hitch, G. J. (1974). Working memory. In G. H. Bower (Ed.), *The psychology of learning and motivation* (Vol. 8, pp. 47–89). London: Academic Press.

Baer, R. A. (2003). Mindfulness training as a clinical intervention: A conceptual and empirical review. *Clinical Psychology: Science and Practice, 10,* 125–143.

Baker, L. D., Frank, L. L., Foster-Schubert, K., Green, P. S., Wilkinson, C. W., McTiernan, … Craft, S. (2010). Effects of aerobic exercise on mild cognitive improvement: A controlled trial. *Archives of Neurology, 67*(1), 71–79.

Baldwin, R. C., Anderson, D., Black, S., Evans, S., Jones, R., & Wilson, K. (2003). Guideline for the management of late-life depression in primary care. *International Journal of Geriatric Psychiatry, 18*(9), 829–838.

Ball, K., Berch, D. B., Helmers, K. F., Jobe, J. B., Leveck, M. D., Marsiske, M., … Willis, S. L. (2002). Effects of CT interventions with older adults: A randomized controlled trial. *Journal of the American Medical Association, 288*(18), 2271–2281.

Baltes, M. M., & Carstensen, L. L. (1996). The process of successful ageing. *Ageing and Society, 16*(4), 397–422.

Barberger-Gateau, P., Fabrigoule, C., Helmer, C., Rouch, I., & Dartigues, J. F. (1999). Functional impairment in instrumental activities of daily living: An early clinical sign of dementia? *Journal of American Geriatrics Society, 47*, 456–462.

Barg, F. K., Huss-Ashmore, R., Wittink, M. N., Murray, G. F., Bogner, H. R., & Gallo, J. J. (2006). A mixed-methods approach to understanding loneliness and depression in older adults. *Journals of Gerontology Series B: Psychological Sciences and Social Sciences, 61*(6), S329–S339.

Barkley, R. A. (1997). Behavioral inhibition, sustained attention, and executive functions: Constructing a unifying theory of ADHD. *Psychological Bulletin, 121*(1), 65.

Barkley, R. A. (2012). *Executive functions: What they are, how they work, and why they evolved.* New York, NY: Guilford Press.

Barkley, R. A., & Murphy, K. R. (2010). Impairment in occupational functioning and adult ADHD: The predictive utility of executive function (EF) ratings versus EF tests. *Archives of Clinical Neuropsychology, 25*(3), 157–173.

Barlow, D. H. (2004). *Anxiety and its disorders: The nature and treatment of anxiety and panic* (2nd ed.). New York, NY: Guilford Press.

Barlow, D. H. (2007). *Clinical handbook of psychological disorders: A step-by-step treatment manual.* New York, NY: Guilford Press.

Barlow, D. (2010, August 18). *The transdiagostic model in psychotherapy. Workshop presented at APA's annual convention.* Boston, MA.

Bartholomew, J. B., Morrison, D., & Ciccolo, J. T. (2005). Effects of acute exercise on mood and well-being in patients with major depressive disorder. *Medicine and Science in Sports and Exercise, 37*(12), 2032.

Basak, C., Boot, W. R., Voss, M. W., & Kramer, A. F. (2008). Can training in a real-time strategy videogame attenuate cognitive decline in older adults? *Psychology and Aging, 23*, 765–777.

Bazaldua, O, Ables, A. Z., Dickerson, L. M., Hansen, L., Harris, I., Hoehns, J., & Saseen, J. J. (2005). Suggested guidelines for pharmacotherapy curricula in family medicine residency training: Recommendations from the Society of Teachers of Family Medicine Group on Pharmacotherapy. *Family Medicine, 37*, 99–104.

Beaudreau, S. A., & O'Hara, R. (2008). Late-life anxiety and cognitive impairment: A review. *American Journal of Geriatric Psychiatry, 16*(10), 790–803.

Beaudreau, S. A., & O'Hara, R. (2009). The association of anxiety and depressive symptoms with cognitive performance in community-dwelling older adults. *Psychology and Aging, 24*(2), 507.

Beck, A. T., Guth, D., Steer, R. A., & Ball, R. (1997). Screening for major depression disorders in medical inpatients with the Beck Depression Inventory for Primary Care. *Behaviour Research and Therapy, 35*, 785–791.

Beck, A. T., Steer, R. A., Ball, R., Ciervo, C. A., & Kabat, M. (1997). Use of the Beck Anxiety and Beck Depression Inventories for primary care with medical outpatients. *Assessment, 4*, 211–219.

Beck, J. G., & Stanley, M. A. (1998). Anxiety disorders in the elderly: The emerging role of behavior therapy. *Behavior Therapy, 28*(1), 83–100.

Beckett, N. S., Peters, R., Fletcher, A. E., Staessen, J. A., Liu, L., Dumitrascu, D., ... Bulpitt, C. J. (2008). Treatment of hypertension in patients 80 years of age or older. *New England Journal of Medicine, 358*(18), 1887–1898.

Beckman, A. G., Parker, M. G., & Thorslund, M. (2005). Can elderly people take their medicine? *Patient Education and Counseling, 59*(2), 186–191.

Beekman, A., van Schaik, A., van Marwijk, H., Adèr, H., van Dyck, R., de Haan, M., ... van Hout, H. (2006). Interpersonal psychotherapy for elderly patients in primary care. *American Journal of Geriatric Psychiatry, 14*(9), 777–786.

Beekman, A. T., de Beurs, E., van Balkom, A. J., Deeg, D. J., van Dyck, R., & van Tilburg, W. (2000). Anxiety and depression in later life: Co-occurrence and communality of risk factors. *American Journal of Psychiatry, 157*(1), 89–95.

Beekman, F. J., van der Have, F., Vastenhouw, B., van der Linden, A. J., van Rijk, P. P., Burbach, J. P. H., & Smidt, M. P. (2005). U-SPECT-I: A novel system for submillimeter-resolution tomography with radiolabeled molecules in mice. *Journal of Nuclear Medicine, 46*(7), 1194–1200.

Belar, C. D. (2011, October). *Psychology workforce development for primary care*. Paper presented at the Collaborative Family Heahlthcare Association annual conference, Philadelphia, PA.

Belleville, S., Chertkow, H., & Gauthier, S. (2007). Working memory and control of attention in persons with Alzheimer's disease and mild cognitive impairment. *Neuropsychology, 21*(4), 458–469.

Bendheim, P. (2009). *The brain training revolution: A proven workout for the healthy brain*. Naperville, IL: Sourcebooks.

Benek-Higgins, M., McReynolds, C. J., Hogan, E., & Savickas, S. (2008). Depression and the elder person: The enigma of misconceptions, stigma, and treatment. *Journal of Mental Health Counseling, 30*(4), 283–296.

Bernabei, R., Gambassi, G., Lapane, K., Sgadari, A., Landi, F., Gatsonis, C., ... Mor, V. (1999). Characteristics of the SAGE database: A new resource for research on outcomes in long-term care. *The Journals of Gerontology Series A: Biological Sciences and Medical Sciences, 54*(1), M25–M33.

Bhalla, R. K., Butters, M. A., Becker, J. T., Houck, P. R., Snitz, B. E., Lopez, O. L., ... Reynolds C. F., III. (2009). Patterns of mild cognitive impairment after treatment of depression in the elderly. *American Journal of Geriatric Psychiatry: Official Journal of the American Association for Geriatric Psychiatry, 17*(4), 308.

Bhandari, H., & Yasunobu, K. (2009). What is social capital? A comprehensive review of the concept. *Asian Journal of Social Science, 37*(3), 480–510.

Bherer, L., Kramer, A. F., Peterson, M. S., Colcombe, S., Erickson, K., & Becic, E. (2008). Transfer effects in task-set cost and dual-task cost after dual-task training in older and younger adults: Further evidence for cognitive plasticity in attentional control in late adulthood. *Experimental Aging Research, 34*(3), 188–219.

Bierman, E. J., Comijs, H. C., Rijmen, F., Jonker, C., & Beekman, A. T. (2008). Anxiety symptoms and cognitive performance in later life: Results from the longitudinal aging study Amsterdam. *Aging and Mental Health, 12*(4), 517–523.

Bissig, D., & Lustig, C. (2007). Who benefits from psychological training? *Psychological Science, 18*, 720–726.

Bjerrum, L., Søgaard, J., Hallas, J., & Kragstrup, J. (1998). Polypharmacy: Correlations with sex, age and drug regimen A prescription database study. *European Journal of Clinical Pharmacology, 54*(3), 197–202.

Black, W., & Almeida, O. P. (2004). A systematic review of the association between the behavioral and psychological symptoms of dementia and burden of care. *International Psychogeriatrics, 16*, 295–315. doi: 10.1017/S1041610204000468

Blackburn, I. M., Bishop, S., Glen, A. I., Whalley, L. J., & Christie, J. E. (1981). The efficacy of cognitive therapy in depression: A treatment trial using cognitive therapy and pharmacotherapy, each alone and in combination. *British Journal of Psychiatry, 139*(3), 181–189.

Blanchard, E. B., & Hickling, E. J. (2004). *Albany MVA project* (pp. xvii, 475). Washington, DC: American Psychological Association.

Blazer, D., George, L. K., & Hughes, D. (1991). The epidemiology of anxiety disorders: An age comparison. In C. Salzman & B. D. Lebowitz (Eds.), *Anxiety in the elderly: Treatment and research* (pp. 17–30). New York, NY: Springer.

Blazer, D. G., Celia, F., Hybels, C. F., Fillenbaum, G. G., & Pieper, C. F. (2005). Predictors of antidepressant use among older adults: Have they changed over time? *American Journal of Psychiatry, 162*, 705–710. 10.1176/appi.ajp.162.4.705

Blazer, D. G. (1997). Generalized anxiety disorder and panic disorder in the elderly: A review. *Harvard Review of Psychiatry, 5*(1), 18–27.

Blazer, D. G. (2003). Depression in late life: Review and commentary. *Journals of Gerontology Series A: Biological Sciences and Medical Sciences, 58*(3), M249–M265.

Blount, A. (1998). *Integrated primary care: The future of medical and mental health collaboration.* New York, NY: Norton.

Blount, A. (2008). *Training mental health clinicians to practice in primary care.* Paper presented to National Council for Community Behavioral Healthcare Conference, Boston, MA.

Blount, A., Schoenbaum, M., Kathol, R., Rollman, B. L., Thomas, M., O'Donohue, W., & Peek, C. J. (2007). The economics of behavioral health services in medical settings: A summary of the evidence. *Professional Psychology: Research and Practice, 38*(3), 290.

Bockting, C. L., Schene, A. H., Spinhoven, P., Koeter, M. W., Wouters, L. F., Huyser, J., & Kamphuis, J. H. (2005). Preventing relapse/recurrence in recurrent depression with cognitive therapy: A randomized controlled trial. *Journal of Consulting and Clinical Psychology, 73*(4), 647.

Boddice, G., Pachana, N. A., & Byrne, G. J. (2008). The clinical utility of the geriatric anxiety inventory in older adults with cognitive impairment. *Nursing Older People, 20*(8), 36–39.

Bodenheimer, T., Lorig, K., Holman, H., & Grumbach, K. (2002). Patient self-management of chronic disease in primary care. *Journal of the American Medical Association, 288*(19), 2469–2475.

Bogner, H. R., Cary, M. S., Bruce, M. L., Reynolds, C. F., III, Mulsant, B., Ten Have, T., Boman, I. L., Lindstedt, M., Hemmingsson, H., & Bartfai, A. (2004). Cognitive training in home environment. *Brain Injury, 18*(10), 985–995.

Books Received. (2011). *Gerontologist, 51*(5), 728–729.

Boone, K. B., Lesser, I. M., Miller, B. L., Wohl, M., Berman, N., Lee, A., ... Back, C. (1995). Cognitive functioning in older depressed outpatients: Relationship of presence and severity of depression to neuropsychological test scores. *Neuropsychology, 9*(3), 390.

Boron, J. B., Willis, S. L., & Schaie, K. W. (2007). Cognitive training gain as a predictor of mental status. *Journals of Gerontology Series B: Psychological Sciences and Social Sciences, 62*(1), P45–P52.

Borson, S., Scanlan, J., Brush, M., Vitallano, P., & Dokmak, A. (2000). The Mini-Cog: A cognitive 'vital signs' measure for dementia screening in multi-lingual elderly. *International Journal of Geriatric Psychiatry, 15*(11), 1021–1027.

Bothune, S. (2013). Health-care falls short on stress management. *Monitor on Psychology, 44*(4), 23–25.

Bouton, M. E., & King, D. A. (1983). Contextual control of the extinction of conditioned fear: Tests for the associative value of the context. *Journal of Experimental Psychology: Animal Behavior Processes, 9*(3), 248.

Boyd, C. M., Darer, J., Boult, C., Fried, L. P., Boult, L., & Wu, A. W. (2005). Clinical practice guidelines and quality of care for older patients with multiple comorbid diseases. *Journal of the American Medical Association, 294*(6), 716–724.

Boyle, P. A., Malloy, P. F., Salloway, S., Cahn-Weiner, D. A., Cohen, R., & Cummings, J. L. (2003). Executive dysfunction and apathy predict functional impairment in Alzheimer disease. *American Journal of Geriatric Psychiatry, 11*(2), 214–221.

Braak, H., & Braak, E. (1991). Neuropathological stageing of Alzheimer-related changes. *Acta Neuropathologica, 82*(4), 239–259.

Brandtstädter, J. (1999). The self in action and development: Cultural, biosocial, and onto-genetic bases of intentional self-development. In J. Brandtstädter & R. M. Lerner (Eds.), *Action and self-development: Theory and research through the life span* (pp. 37–66). Thousand Oaks, CA: Sage.

Braun, M., Mikulincer, M., Rydall, A., Walsh, A., & Rodin, G. (2007). Hidden morbidity in cancer: Spouse caregivers. *Journal of Clinical Oncology, 25*(30), 4829–4834.

Brenes, G. A., Guralnik, J. M., Williamson, J. D., Fried, L. P., Simpson, C., Simonsick, E. M., & Penninx, B. W. (2004). The influence of anxiety on the progression of disability. *Journal of the American Geriatrics Society, 53*(1), 34–39.

Britton, P. C., Duberstein, P. R., Conner, K. R., Heisel, M. J., Hirsch, J. K., & Conwell, Y. (2008). Reasons for living, hopelessness, and suicide ideation among depressed adults 50 years or older. *Am J Geriatr Psychiatry, 16*, 736–741.

Broadbent, D. E., Cooper, P. F., Fitzgerald, P., & Parkes, K. R. (1982). The Cognitive Failures Questionnaire (CFQ) and its correlates. *British Journal of Clinical Psychology, 21* (Pt. 1), 1–16.

Brodaty, H., Green, A., & Koschera, A. (2003). Meta-analysis of psychosocial interventions for caregivers of people with dementia. *Journal of the American Geriatrics Society, 51*(5), 657–664.

Brodaty, H., Griffin, D., & Hadzi-Pavlovic, D. (1990). A survey of dementia carers: Doctors' communications, problem behaviours and institutional care. *Australasian Psychiatry, 24*(3), 362–370.

Brodey, B. B., Cuffel, B., McCulloch, J., Tani, S., Maruish, M., Brodey, I., & Unützer, J. (2005). The acceptability and effectiveness of patient-reported assessments and feedback in a managed behavioral healthcare setting. *American Journal of Managed Care, 11*(12), 774–780.

Brommelhoff, J. A., Gatz, M., Johansson, B., McArdle, J. J., Fratiglioni, L., & Pedersen, N. L. (2009). Depression as a risk factor or prodromal feature for dementia? Findings in a population-based sample of Swedish twins. *Psychology and Aging, 24*(2), 373.

Brown, K., Streubert, G. E., & Burgess, A. W. (2004). Effectively detect and manage elder abuse. *Nurse Practitioner, 29*(8), 22.

Brown, T. A. (2007). Temporal course and structural relationships among dimensions of temperament and *DSM-IV* anxiety and mood disorder constructs. *Journal of Abnormal Psychology, 116*(2), 313.

Brown, T. A., Antony, M. M., & Barlow, D. H. (1995). Diagnostic comorbidity in panic disorder: Effect on treatment outcome and course of comorbid diagnoses following treatment. *Journal of Consulting and Clinical Psychology, 63*(3), 408.

Brown, T. A., Hertz, R. M., & Barlow, D. H. (1992). New developments in cognitive-behavioral treatment of anxiety disorders. *American Psychiatric Press Review of Psychiatry, 11*, 285–306.

Bruce, M. L., Ten Have, T. R., Reynolds, C. F., Katz, I. I., Schulberg, H. C., Mulsant, B. H., … Alexopoulos, G. S. (2004). Reducing suicidal ideation and depressive symptoms in depressed older primary care patients: A randomized controlled trial. *Journal of the American Medical Association, 291*(9), 1081–1091.

Bryan, C. J., Rudd, D. (2011). *Managing suicide risk in primary care.* New York, NY: Springer Publishing Company.

Burish, T. G., Carey, M. P., Wallston, K. A., Stein, M. J., Jamison, R. N., & Lyles, J. N. (1984). Health locus of control and chronic disease: An external orientation may be advantageous. *Journal of Social and Clinical Psychology, 2*(4), 326–332.

Burish, T. G., Snyder, S. L., & Jenkins, R. A. (1991). Preparing patients for cancer chemotherapy: Effect of coping preparation and relaxation interventions. *Journal of Consulting and Clinical Psychology, 59*(4), 518.

Buschkuehl, M., Jaeggi, S. M., Hutchison, S., Perrig-Chiello, P., Däpp, C., Müller, M., … Perrig, W. J. (2008). Impact of working memory training on memory performance in old-old adults. *Psychology and Aging, 23*(4), 743–753.

Bush, K., Kivlahan, D. R., McDonell, M. B., Fihn, S. D., & Bradley, K. A. (1998). The AUDIT Alcohol Consumption Questions (AUDIT-C): An effective brief screening test for problem drinking. *Archives of Internal Medicine, 158*(16), 1789–1795.

Butters, M. A., Becker, J. T., Nebes, R. D., Zmuda, M. D., Mulsant, B. H., Pollock, B. G., & Reynolds, C. F. (2000). Changes in cognitive functioning following treatment of late-life depression. *American Journal of Psychiatry, 157*(12), 1949–1954.

Buysse, D. J., Reynolds, C. F., Monk, T. H., Berman, S. R., & Kupfer, D. J. (1989). The Pittsburgh Sleep Quality Index (PSQI): A new instrument for psychiatric research and practice. *Psychiatry Research, 28*, 193–213.

Byers, A. L., Vittinghoff, E., Lui, L. Y., Hoang, T., Blazer, D. G., Covinsky, K. E., ... Yaffe, K. (2012). Twenty-year depressive trajectories among older women twenty-year depressive trajectories in older women. *Archives of General Psychiatry, 69*(10), 1073–1079.

Byers, A. L., Yaffe, K., Covinsky, K. E., Friedman, M. B., & Bruce, M. L. (2010). High occurrence of mood and anxiety disorders among older adults: The National Comorbidity Survey Replication. *Archives of General Psychiatry, 67*(5), 489.

Callahan, C. M. (2001). Quality improvement research on late life depression in primary care. *Medical Care, 39*(8), 772.

Callahan, C. M., Boustani, M. A., Unverzagt, F. W., Austrom, M. G., Damush, T. M., Perkins, A. J., ... Hendrie, H. C. (2006). Effectiveness of collaborative care for older adults with Alzheimer disease in primary care. *Journal of the American Medical Association, 295*(18), 2148–2157.

Callahan, D., & Nuland, S. (2011, May 19). The quagmire: How American medicine is destroying itself. *The New Republic.*

Campbell-Sills, L., Barlow, D. H., Brown, T. A., & Hofmann, S. G. (2006). Effects of suppression and acceptance on emotional responses of individuals with anxiety and mood disorders. *Behaviour Research and Therapy, 44*(9), 1251–1263.

Carey, M. P., & Burish, T. G. (1988). Etiology and treatment of the psychological side effects associated with cancer chemotherapy: A critical review and discussion. *Psychological Bulletin, 104*(3), 307.

Carnes, B., Olshansky, S., & Hayflcik, L. (2012). Can human biology allow most of us to become centenarians? *Journal of Gerontology: Biological Sciences, 68*(2), 136–142.

Carpenter, W. T., Jr., Gold, J. M., Lahti, A. C., Queern, C. A., Conley, R. R., Bartko, J. J., ... Appelbaum, P. S. (2000). Decisional capacity for informed consent in schizophrenia research. *Archives of General Psychiatry, 57*(6), 533.

Carr, A. J., Robertsson, O., Graves, S., Price, A. J., Arden, N. K., Judge, A., & Beard, D. J. (2012). Knee replacement. *The Lancet, 379*(9823), 1331–1340.

Carstensen, L. L. (1993, October). Motivation for social contact across the life span: A theory of socioemotional selectivity. In *Nebraska symposium on motivation* (Vol. 40, pp. 209–254). Lincoln, NE: University of Nebraska Press.

Carstensen, L. L., & Turk-Charles, S. (1994). The salience of emotion across the adult life span. *Psychology and Aging, 9*(2), 259.

Carstensen, L. L., Fung, H. H., & Charles, S. T. (2003). Socioemotional selectivity theory and the regulation of emotion in the second half of life. *Motivation and Emotion, 27*(2), 103–123.

Caselli, R. J., Chen, K., Lee, W., Alexander, G. E., & Reiman, E. M. (2008). Correlating cerebral hypometabolism with future memory decline in subsequent converters to amnestic pre-mild cognitive impairment. *Archives of Neurology, 65*(9), 1231.

Casper, R. C., Redmond, D. E., Jr., Katz, M. M., Schaffer, C. B., Davis, J. M., & Koslow, S. H. (1985). Somatic symptoms in primary affective disorder: Presence and relationship to the classification of depression. *Archives of General Psychiatry, 42*(11), 1098.

Cassidy, E. L., Baird, E., & Sheikh, J. I. (2001). Recruitment and retention of elderly patients in clinical trials: Issues and strategies. *American Journal of Geriatric Psychiatry, 9*(2), 136–140.

Cavallini, E., Pagnin, A., & Vecchi, T. (2003). Aging and everyday memory: The beneficial effect of memory training. *Archives of Gerontology and Geriatrics, 37*(3), 241–257.

Centers for Disease Control and Prevention. (2008). Self-reported falls and fall-related injuries among persons aged > 65—United States, 2006. *Morbidity and Mortality Weekly Reports, 57,* 225–229.

Centers for Disease Control and Prevention. (2011). 10 Leading causes of nonfatal injuries, United States among persons aged >65—United States, 2011. *CDC WISQARS Leading Causes of Nonfatal Injury Reports.* Retrieved from http://webappa.cdc.gov/sasweb/ncipc/nfilead2001.html#precompiled

Cernin, P. A., & Lichtenberg, P. A. (2009). Behavioral treatment for depressed mood: A pleasant events intervention for seniors residing in assisted living. *Clinical Gerontologist, 32*(3), 324–331.

Chadwick, P. D. J. (2006). *Person-based cognitive therapy for distressing psychosis.* New York, NY: Wiley.

Chamberlin, J. (2011). Protecting *your* aging brain. *Monitor on Psychology, 42*(9), 48–49.

Chambless, D. L., & Ollendick, T. H. (2001). Empirically supported psychological Interventions: Controversies and evidence. *Annual Review of Psychology, 52,* 685–716.

Charlson, M., & Peterson, J. C. (2002). Medical comorbidity and late life depression: What is known and what are the unmet needs? *Biological Psychiatry, 52*(3), 226–235.

Chein, J., & Morrison, A. (2010). Expanding the mind's workspace: Training and transfer effects with a complex working memory span task. *Psychonomic Bulletin & Review, 17,* 193–199.

Cheng, Y., Wu, W., Feng, W., Chen, Y., Shen, Y., Li, Q., ... Li, C. (2012). The effects of multi-domain versus single-domain CT in non-demented older people: A randomized controlled trial. *BMC Medicine, 10*(1), 30. doi: 10.1186/1741-7015-10-30

Chobanian, A. (2007). Isolated systolic hypertension in the elderly. *New England Journal of Medicine, 357,* 789–796.

Chopra, M. P., Zubritsky, C., Knott, K., Ten Have, T., Hadley, T., Coyne, J. C., & Oslin, D. W. (2005). Importance of subsyndromal symptoms of depression in elderly patients. *American Journal of Geriatric Psychiatry, 13*(7), 597–606.

Chorpita, B. F., Daleiden, E. L., & Weisz, J. R. (2005). Modularity in the design and application of therapeutic interventions. *Applied and Preventive Psychology, 11*(3), 141–156.

Chorpita, B. F., Rotheram-Borus, M. J., Daleiden, E. L., Bernstein, A., Cromley, T., Swendeman, D., & Regan, J. (2011). The old solutions are the new problem: How do we better use what we already know about reducing the burden of mental illness? *Perspectives on Psychological Science, 6*(5), 493–497.

Clark, L. A., & Watson, D. (1991). Tripartite model of anxiety and depression: Psychometric evidence and taxonomic implications. *Journal of Abnormal Psychology, 100*(3), 316.

Clark, L. A., Watson, D., & Mineka, S. (1994). Temperament, personality, and the mood and anxiety disorders. *Journal of Abnormal Psychology, 103*(1), 103.

Clarke, G., Hawkins, N., Murphy, M., Sheeber, L., Lewinson, P., & Seeley, J. (1995). Targeted prevention of unipolar depression disorder in an at risk sample of high school adolescents: A randomized trial of a group cognitive intervention. *Journal of the American Academy of Child and Adolescent Psychiatry, 34,* 312–321.

Clarke, D. A., & Beck, A. T. (1999). *Scientific foundations of cognitive theory and therapy of depression.* Wiley. com

Clay, R. (2013, May). Treating mind and body: Health-care reform is integrating physical and behavioral health care. *Monitor on Psychology, 40*(5), 55–56.

Clyburn, L. D., Stones, M. J., Hadjistavropoulos, T., & Tuokko, H. (2000). Predicting caregiver burden and depression in Alzheimer's disease. *Journals of Gerontology: Series B, 55*(1), 2–13.

Cobb-Clark, D., Kassenboehmer, S., & Schurer, S. (2012). Healthy habits: The connection between diet, exercise, and locus of control. IZA Discussion Paper No. 6789.

Coffey, C. E., Wilkinson, W. E., Parashos, L. A., Soady, S. A. R., Sullivan, R. J., & Patterson, L. J. (1992). Quantitative cerebral anatomy of the aging human brain: A cross-sectional study using magnetic resonance imaging. *Neurology, 42*(3), 527–536.

Cogbill, E., Dinson, K., & Duthie, E. (2010). Considerations in prescribing medication to the elderly. In V. Hirth, D. Wieland, & M. Dever-Bumba (Eds.), *Case-based geriatrics: A global approach*. New York, NY: McGraw-Hill.

Cole, M. G., & Yaffe, M. J. (1996) Pathway to psychiatric care of the elderly with depression. *International Journal of Geriatric Psychiatry, 11*, 157–161.

Collins, L. M., Murphy, S. A., & Strecher, V. (2007). The multiphase optimization strategy (MOST) and the sequential multiple assignment randomized trial (SMART): New methods for more potent eHealth interventions. *American Journal of Preventive Medicine, 32*(5), S112–S118.

Conwell, Y. (1994). Suicide in the elderly. In L. S. Schneider, C. F., Reynolds, B. D., Lebowitz, & A. J. Friedhoff (Eds.), *Diagnosis and treatment of depression in late life: Results of the NIH Consensus Development Conference* (pp. 397–418). Washington, DC: American Psychiatric Press.

Cook, I. A., Leuchter, A. F., Morgan, M. L., Dunkin, J. J., Witte, E., David, S., ... Rosenberg, S. (2004). Longitudinal progression of subclinical structural brain disease in normal aging. *American Journal of Geriatric Psychiatry, 12*(2), 190–200.

Cook, J. M., O'Donnell, C., Moltzen, J. O., Ruzek, J. I., & Sheikh, J. I. (2006). Clinical observations in the treatment of World War II and Korean War veterans with combat-related PTSD. *Clinical Gerontologist, 29*(2), 81–93.

Cook, J. M., Ruzek, J. I., & Cassidy, E. (2003). Practical geriatrics: Possible association of posttraumatic stress disorder with cognitive impairment among older adults. *Psychiatric Services, 54*(9), 1223–1225.

Coudin, G., & Alexopoulos, T. (2010). "Help me! I'm old!": How negative aging stereotypes create dependency among older adults. *Aging and Mental Health, 14*(5), 516–523.

Covinsky, K. E., Newcomer, R., Fox, P., Wood, J., Sands, L., Dane, K., & Yaffe, K. (2003). Patient and caregiver characteristics associated with depression in caregivers of patients with dementia. *Journal of General Internal Medicine, 18*(12), 1006–1014.

Cowan, N. (2005). Working-memory capacity limits in a theoretical context. In C. Izawa & N. Ohta (Eds.), Human learning and memory: Advances in theory and application: The *4th Tsukuba International Conference on Memory* (pp. 155–175). Mahwah, NJ: Erlbaum.

Cox, J., & Gray, A. (2009). Psychiatry of the person. *Current Opinions in Psychiatry, Psychiatry, 22*(6) 587–593.

Cozolino, L. (2010). *The neuroscience of psychotherapy: Healing the social brain*. New York, NY: W. W. Norton.

Craik, F. I., & Bialystok, E. (2006). Cognition through the lifespan: Mechanisms of change. *Trends in Cognitive Sciences, 10*(3), 131–138.

Craik, F. I., Winocur, G., Palmer, H., Binns, M. A., Edwards, M., Bridges, K., ... Stuss, D. T. (2007). Cognitive rehabilitation in the elderly: Effects on memory. *Journal of the International Neuropsychological Society, 13*(1), 132–142.

Creamer, M., & Parslow, R. (2008). Trauma exposure and posttraumatic stress disorder in the elderly: A community prevalence study. *American Journal of Geriatric Psychiatry, 16*(10), 853–856.

Crimmins, E. M., Kim, J. K., & Seeman, T. E. (2009). Poverty and biological risk: The earlier "aging" of the poor. *Journals of Gerontology Series A: Biological Sciences and Medical Sciences, 64*(2), 286.

Crowe, M., Clay, O., Martin, R., Howard, V., Wadley, V., Sawyer, P., & Allman, R. (2013). Indicators of childhood quality of education in relation to cognitive function in older adulthood. *Journal of Gerontology, 68*(2), 198–204.

Cuijpers, P., van Straten, A., & Smit, F. (2006). Psychological treatment of late-life depression: A meta-analysis of randomized controlled trials. *International Journal of Geriatric Psychiatry, 21*(12), 1139–1149.

Cuijpers, P., van Straten, A., Smit, F., Mihalopoulos, C., & Beekman, A. (2008). Preventing the onset of depressive disorders: A meta-analytic review of psychological interventions. *American Journal of Psychiatry, 165*(10), 1272–1280.

Cuijpers, P., van Straten, A., & Warmerdam, L. (2007). Behavioral activation treatments of depression: A meta-analysis. *Clinical Psychology Review, 27*(3), 318–326.

Cully, J. A., & Teten, A. L. (2008). *A therapist's guide to brief cognitive behavioral therapy.* Houston, TX: Department of Veterans Affairs South Central MIRECC.

Cummings, N. A., O'Donohue, W. T., & Ferguson, K. E. (2002). *The impact of medical cost offset on practice and research: Making it work for you: A report of the first Reno conference on medical cost offset.* Reno, NV: Context Press.

Dahlin, E., Neely, A. S., Larsson, A., Bäckman, L., & Nyberg, L. (2008). Transfer of learning after updating training mediated by the striatum. *Science, 320*(5882), 1510–1512.

Dakin, E., & Arean, P. (2013). Patient perspectives on the benefits of psychotherapy from late-life depression. *American Journal of Geriatric Psychiatry, 21*(2), 155–163.

Daneman, M., & Carpenter, P. (1980). Individual differences in working memory and reading. *Journal of Verbal Learning and Verbal Behavior, 19*(4), 450–466.

Dattilio, F. M., Edwards, D. J., & Fishman, D. B. (2010). Case studies within a mixed methods paradigm: Toward a resolution of the alienation between researcher and practitioner in psychotherapy research. *Psychotherapy: Theory, Research, Practice, Training, 47*(4), 427–441.

Davidson, J. R., Hughes, D., Blazer, D. G., & George, L. K. (1991). Post-traumatic stress disorder in the community: An epidemiological study. *Psychological Medicine, 21*(3), 713–721.

Davidson, R. J. (2004). What does the prefrontal cortex "do" in affect: perspectives on frontal EEG asymmetry research. *Biological Psychology, 67*(1), 219–234.

Daviglus, M. L., Bell, C. C., Berrettini, W., Bowen, P. E., Connolly, E. S., Cox, N. J., ... Trevisan, M. (2010). *NIH state-of-the-science conference statement: Preventing Alzheimer's disease and cognitive decline.* NIH consensus and state-of-the-science statements, 27(4), 1–30.

Davis, K., Schoen, C., & Stremikis, K. (2010). *Mirror, mirror on the wall: How the performance of the US health care system compares internationally: 2010 update.* New York, NY: Commonwealth Fund.

Davitt, J. K., & Kaye, L. W. (1996). Supporting patient autonomy: Decision making in home health care. *Social Work, 41*(1), 41–50.

Day, M., Demiris, G., Oliver, D. P., Courtney, K., & Hensel, B. (2007). Exploring underutilization of videophones in hospice settings. *Telemedicine and e-Health, 13*(1), 25–32.

De Vasconcelos Cunha, U. G., Ávila de Melo, R., de Souza Neto, J. J., Martins de Oliveira, F., da Costa Júnior, A. L., & Sakurai, E. (2007). A placebo-controlled double-blind randomized study of venlafaxine in the treatment of depression in dementia. *Dementia and Geriatric Cognitive Disorders, 24*(1), 36–41.

De Vasconcelos Cunha, U. G., Lopes Rocha, F., Ávila de Melo, R., Alves Valle, E., de Souza Nebes R, Pollock B, Houck P, et al. (2003). Persistence of cognitive impairment in geriatric patients following antidepressant treatment: A randomized, double-blind clinical trial with nortriptyline and paroxetine. *Journal of Psychiatric Research, 37*(2), 99–108.

Degenholtz, H. B., Rosen, J., Castle, N., Mittal, V., & Liu, D. (2008). The association between changes in health status and nursing home resident quality of life. *The Gerontologist, 48*(5), 584–592.

Delamater, A. R. (2004). Experimental extinction in Pavlovian conditioning: Behavioural and neuroscience perspectives. *Quarterly Journal of Experimental Psychology Section B, 57*(2), 97–132.

DeLuca, A. K., Lenze, E. J., Mulsant, B. H., Butters, M. A., Karp, J. F., Dew, M. A., ... Reynolds, C. F. (2005). Comorbid anxiety disorder in late life depression: Association with memory decline over four years. *International Journal of Geriatric Psychiatry, 20*(9), 848–854.

Depp, C. A., & Jeste, D. V. (2006). Definitions and predictors of successful aging: A comprehensive review of larger quantitative studies. *American Journal of Geriatric Psychiatry, 14*(1), 6–20.

Depp, C., Vahia, I., & Jeste, D. (2010). Successful aging: Focus on cognitive and emotional health. *Annual Review of Clinical Psychology, 6,* 527–550.

Deshields, T., Tibbs, T., Fan, M. Y., & Taylor, M. (2006). Differences in patterns of depression after treatment for breast cancer. *Psycho-Oncology, 15*(5), 398–406.

Devanand, D. P., Mikhno, A., Pelton, G. H., Cuasay, K., Pradhaban, G., Kumar, J. D., ... Parsey, R. V. (2010). Pittsburgh compound B (11C-PIB) and fluorodeoxyglucose (18 F-FDG) PET in patients with Alzheimer disease, mild cognitive impairment, and healthy controls. *Journal of Geriatric Psychiatry and Neurology, 23*(3), 185–198, 440.

deVol, R., & Bedrosian, A. (2007). *An unhealthy America: The economic burden of chronic disease—Charting a new course to save lives and increase productivity and economic growth.* Los Angeles, CA: The Milken Institute.

Diener, E., & Eunkook Suh, M. A. R. K. (1997). Subjective well-being and age: An international analysis. In K. Schaie & M. P. Lawton (Eds.), *Annual review of gerontology and geriatrics* (Vol. 17, pp. 304–324). New York, NY: Springer Publishing Company.

Dietrich, A. J., Oxman, T. E., Williams, J. W., Jr., Schulberg, H. C., Bruce, M. L., Lee, P. W., ... Nutting, P. A. (2004). Re-engineering systems for the treatment of depression in primary care: Cluster randomised controlled trial. *British Medical Journal, 329*(7466), 602. doi:10.1136/bmj.38219.481250.55

DiMatteo, M. R., Lepper, H. S., & Croghan, T. W. (2000). Depression is a risk factor for noncompliance with medical treatment meta-analysis of the effects of anxiety and depression on patient adherence. *Archives of Internal Medicine, 160*(14), 2101–2107.

Dimidjian, S., Hollon, S. D., Dobson, K. S., Schmaling, K. B., Kohlenberg, R. J., Addis, M. E., ... Jacobson, N. S. (2006). Randomized trial of behavioral activation, cognitive therapy, and antidepressant medication in the acute treatment of adults with major depression. *Journal of Consulting and Clinical Psychology, 74*(4), 658.

DiTomasso, R. A., Golden, B. A., & Morris, H. J. (Eds.). (2010). *Handbook of cognitive behavioral approaches in primary care.* New York, NY: Springer Publishing Company.

Dohrenwend, B. S., & Dohrenwend, B. P. (1981). Life stress and psychopathology. *Risk factor research in the major mental disorders.* DHHS Pub. No. (ADM), 81-1068. Washington, DC: National Institute of Mental Health.

Dombrovski, A. Y., Lenze, E. J., Dew, M. A., Mulsant, B. H., Pollock, B. G., Houck, P. R., & Reynolds, C. F., III. (2007). Maintenance treatment for old-age depression preserves health-related quality of life: A randomized, controlled trial of paroxetine and interpersonal psychotherapy. *Journal of the American Geriatrics Society, 55*(9), 1325–1332.

Dooley, N. R., & Hinojosa, J. (2004). Improving quality of life for persons with Alzheimer's disease and their family caregivers: Brief occupational therapy intervention. *American Journal of Occupational Therapy, 58*(5), 561–569.

Drayer, R. A., Mulsant, B. H., Lenze, E. J., Rollman, B. L., Dew, M. A., Kelleher, K., ... Reynolds, C. F. (2005). Somatic symptoms of depression in elderly patients with medical comorbidities. *International Journal of Geriatric Psychiatry, 20*(10), 973–982.

Dubois, B., Feldman, H. H., Jacova, C., Cummings, J. L., DeKosky, S. T., Barberger-Gateau, P., ... Scheltens, P. (2010). Revising the definition of Alzheimer's disease: A new lexicon. *The Lancet Neurology, 9*(11), 1118–1127.

Dubois, B., Feldman, H. H., Jacova, C., DeKosky, S. T., Barberger-Gateau, P., Cummings, J., ... Scheltens, P. (2007). Research criteria for the diagnosis of Alzheimer's disease: Revising the NINCDS–ADRDA criteria. *The Lancet Neurology, 6*(8), 734–746.

Duffy, J. D., & Coffey, C. E. (1996). Depression in Alzheimer's disease. *Psychiatric Annals, 26*(5), 269–273.

Dugas, M. J., Gagnon, F., Ladouceur, R., & Freeston, M. H. (1998). Generalized anxiety disorder: A preliminary test of a conceptual model. *Behaviour Research and Therapy, 36*(2), 215–226.

Dunn, L. B., Cooper, B. A., Neuhaus, J., West, C., Paul, S., Aouizerat, B., ... Miaskowski, C. (2011). Identification of distinct depressive symptom trajectories in women following surgery for breast cancer. *Health Psychology, 30*(6), 683.

Durso, S. (2006). Using clinical guidelines designed for older adults with diabetes mellitus and complex health status. *Journal of the American Medical Association, 295*, 1935–1940.

D'Zurilla, T. J., & Nezu, A. M. (2010). Problem-solving therapy. In K. Dobson (Ed.), *Handbook of cognitive-behavioral therapies* (3rd ed., pp. 197–225). New York, NY: Guilford Press.

Eaton, W. W., & Muntaner, C. (1999). Socioeconomic stratification and mental disorder. In A. V. Horowitz, & Scheid, T. L. (Eds.), *A handbook for the study of mental health: Social contexts, theories, and systems* (pp. 259–283). Cambridge, UK: Cambridge University Press.

Eaton, W. W., Smith, C., Ybarra, M., Muntaner, C., & Tien, A. (2004). Center for Epidemiologic Studies Depression Scale: Review and revision (CESD and CESD-R). In M. E. Maruish (Ed.), *The use of psychological testing for treatment planning and outcomes assessment* (3rd Ed.), Volume 3: *Instruments for adults* (pp. 363–377). Mahwah, NJ: Lawrence Erlbaum.

Edenfield, T. & Saeed, S., (2012). An update on mindfulness meditation as a self-help treatment for anxiety and depression. *Psychology Research and Behavior Management, 5*, 131–141.

Eisen, S. V., Wilcox, M., Leff, H. S., Schaefer, E., & Culhane, M. A. (1999). Assessing behavioral health outcomes in outpatient programs: Reliability and validity of the BASIS-32. *Journal of Behavioral Health Service Research, 26*, 5–17.

Elderkin-Thompson, V., Ballmaier, M., Hellemann, G., Pham, D., Lavretsky, H., & Kumar, A. (2008). Daily functioning and prefrontal brain morphology in healthy and depressed community-dwelling elderly. *American Journal of Geriatric Psychiatry, 16*(8), 633–642.

Elderkin-Thompson, V., Kumar, A., Bilker, W. B., Dunkin, J. J., Mintz, J., Moberg, P. J., ... Gur, R. E. (2003). Neuropsychological deficits among patients with late-onset minor and major depression. *Archives of Clinical Neuropsychology, 18*(5), 529–549.

Elhai, J. D., Grubaugh, A. L., Richardson, J. D., Egede, L. E., & Creamer, M. (2008). Outpatient medical and mental healthcare utilization models among military veterans: Results from the 2001 National Survey of Veterans. *Journal of Psychiatric Research, 42*(10), 858–867.

Ellard, K. K., Fairholme, C. P., Boisseau, C. L., Farchione, T. J., & Barlow, D. H. (2010). Unified protocol for the transdiagnostic treatment of emotional disorders: Protocol development and initial outcome data. *Cognitive and Behavioral Practice, 17*(1), 88–101.

Emerson, J., Johnson, A., Dawson, J., Anderson, S., & Rizzo, M. (2011). Predictors of driving outcomes in advancing age. *Psychology and Aging, 27*(3), 550–559.

Engels, G. I., & Vermey, M. (1997). Efficacy of nonmedical treatments of depression in elders: A quantitative analysis. *Journal of Clinical Geropsychology, 3*(1), 17–35.

Engle, R. W., Kane, M. J., & Tuholski, S. W. (1999). Individual differences in working memory capacity and what they tell us about controlled attention, general fluid intelligence and functions of the prefrontal cortex. In A. Miyake & P. Shah (Eds.), *Models of working memory: Mechanisms of active maintenance and executive control* (pp. 102–134). New York, NY: Cambridge University Press.

Ercoli, L., David, S., Siddarth, P., Miller, K., Dunkin, J., Kaplan, A., Dorsey, D., & Small, G. (2007). Memory enhancement training effects in healthy older adults compared to health education and wait list conditions. *Presented at the 12th Annual UCLA Research Conference on Aging Proceedings and Abstracts.*

Ercoli, L., Siddarth, P., Harrison, T., Jimenez, E., & Jarvik, L. F. (2005). Similar neurocognitive performance of adults with and without a history of parental Alzheimer's disease: A pilot study. *Journal of Geriatric Psychiatry and Neurology, 18*(4), 208–212.

Erickson, K. I., Voss, M. W., Prakash, R. S., Basak, C., Szabo, A., Chaddock, L., ... Kramer, A. F. (2011). Exercise training increases size of hippocampus and improves memory. *Proceedings of the National Academy of Sciences, 108*(7), 3017–3022.

Ernst, M., & Moser, M. (2009). Use of diuretics in patients with hypertension. *New England Journal of Medicine, 361*(22), 2153–2164.

Erskine, J. A., Kvavilashvili, L., Conway, M. A., & Myers, L. (2007). The effects of age on psychopathology, well-being and repressive coping. *Aging and Mental Health, 11*(4), 394–404.

Escobar, J. I., Golding, J. M., Hough, R. L., Karno, M., Burnam, M. A., & Wells, K. B. (1987). Somatization in the community: Relationship to disability and use of services. *American Journal of Public Health, 77*(7), 837–840.

Espie, C. A., Inglis, S. J., & Harvey, L. (2001). Predicting clinically significant response to cognitive behavior therapy for chronic insomnia in general medical practice: Analyses of outcome data at 12 months posttreatment. *Journal of Consulting and Clinical Psychology, 69*(1), 58.

Etkin, A., & Wager, T. D. (2007). Functional neuroimaging of anxiety: A meta-analysis of emotional processing in PTSD, social anxiety disorder, and specific phobia. *American Journal of Psychiatry, 164*(10), 1476.

Eustache, F. & Desgranges, B. (2008). MNESIS: Towards the integration of current multi-system models of memory. *Neuropsychological Review, 18*, 53–69.

Fabrigoule, C., Letenneur, L., Dartigues, J. F., Zarrouk, M., Commenges, D., & Barberger-Gateau, P. (1995). Social and leisure activities and risk of dementia: A prospective longitudinal study. *Journal of American Geriatric Society, 43*(5), 485–490.

Family Caregiver Alliance. (2012). *Selected caregiver assessment measures: A resource inventory for practitioners* (2nd ed.). [Electronic edition: http://caregiver.org/caregiver/jsp/content/pdfs/SelCGAssmtMeas_ResInv_FINAL_12.10.12.pdf]

Fava, G. A., Grandi, S., Zielezny, M., & Rafanelli, C. (1996). Four-year outcome for cognitive behavioral treatment of residual symptoms in major depression. *American Journal of Psychiatry, 153*(7), 945–947.

Fava, G. A., Rafanelli, C., Cazzaro, M., Conti, S., & Grandi, S. (1998). Well-being therapy. A novel psychotherapeutic approach for residual symptoms of affective disorders. *Psychological Medicine, 28*(2), 475–480.

Federal Interagency Forum on Aging-Related Statistics. (2010, July). *Older Americans 2010: Key indicators of well-being* (Federal Interagency Forum on Aging-Related Statistics). Washington, DC: U.S. Government Printing Office.

Feldman, M. D., Franks, P., & Duberstein, P. R. (2007). Let's not talk about it: Suicide inquiry in primary care. *Annals of Family Medicine, 5*, 412–418.

Feldner, M. T., Monson, C. M., & Friedman, M. J. (2007). A critical analysis of approaches to targeted PTSD prevention current status and theoretically derived future directions. *Behavior Modification, 31*(1), 80–116.

Fellous, J. M., Armony, J. L., & LeDoux, J. E. (2002). Emotional circuits and computational neuroscience. *The handbook of brain theory and neural networks* (2nd ed.). Cambridge, MA: The MIT Press.

Fennig, S., Craig, T. J., Tanenberg-Karant, M., & Bromet, E. J. (1994). Comparison of facility and research diagnoses in first-admission psychotic patients. *American Journal of Psychiatry, 151*, 1423–1429.

Ferris, S. H., Aisen, P. S., Cummings, J., Galasko, D., Salmon, D. P., Schneider, L., ... Thal, L. J. (2006). ADCS Prevention Instrument Project: Overview and initial results. *Alzheimer Disease and Associated Disorders, 20*, S109–S123.

File, S. E., Jarrett, N., Fluck, E., Duffy, R., Casey, K., & Wiseman, H. (2001). Eating soya improves human memory. *Psychopharmacology, 157*(4), 430–436.

Finn, S. E., & Butcher, J. N. (1991). The clinical psychology handbook. In M. Hersen, A. Kazdin & A. Bellack (Eds.), *Pergamon general psychology series* (2nd ed., Vol. 120, pp. 362–373). Elmsford, NY: Pergamon Press.

Finn, S. E., & Tonsager, M. E. (1997). Information-gathering and therapeutic models of assessment: Complementary paradigms. *Psychological Assessment, 9*(4), 374.

Finn, S. E., & Tonsager, M. E. (2002). How therapeutic assessment became humanistic. *Humanistic Psychologist, 30*(1–2), 10–22.

First, M. B., Gibbon, M., Spitzer, R. L., Williams, J. B., & Benjamin, L. (1997). *Structured clinical interview for DSM-IV personality disorders (SCID-II): Interview and questionnaire*. Arlington, TX: American Psychiatric Publishing.

First, M. B., & Gibbon, M. (2004). The Structured Clinical Interview for DSM-IV Axis I Disorders (SCID-I) and the Structured Clinical Interview for DSM-IV Axis II Disorders (SCID-II).

Fisher, P. A., & Gunnar, M. R. (2010). Early life stress as a risk factor for disease in adulthood. *The impact of early life trauma on health and disease* (pp. 133–141). Cambridge, UK: Cambridge University Press.

Fisk, J. E., & Sharp, C. A. (2004). Age-related impairment in executive functioning: Updating, inhibition, shifting, and access. *Journal of Clinical and Experimental Neuropsychology, 26*(7), 874–890.

Fixen, D., Naoom, S., Blasé, K., Freedman, R., & Wallace, F. (2005). *Implementation research: A synthesis of the literature.* Tampa, FL: University of South Florida, Department of Child and Family Studies.

Flaherty, J. H., Perry, H. M., Lynchard, G. S., & Morley, J. E. (2000). Polypharmacy and hospitalization among older home care patients. *Journals of Gerontology Series A: Biological Sciences and Medical Sciences, 55*(10), M554–M559.

Flint, A. J. (1994). Epidemiology and comorbidity of anxiety disorders in the elderly. *American Journal of Psychiatry, 15*(5), 640–649.

Floyd, M., & Scogin, F. (1997). Effects of memory training on the subjective memory functioning and mental health of older adults: A meta-analysis. *Psychology and Aging, 12*(1), 150–161.

Folstein, M., Folstein, S., & McHugh, P. P. (1975). Mini mental state: A practical method for grading the cognitive state of patients for the clinician. *Journal of Psychiatric Research, 12*, 189–198.

Ford, D. (2004, September). *Decision support/depression.* Paper presented to HRSA Health Disparities Collaboratives National Congress, Nashville, TN.

Fournier, J. C., DeRubeis, R. J., Hollon, S. D., Dimidjian, S., Amsterdam, J. D., Shelton, R. C., & Fawcett, J. (2010). Antidepressant drug effects and depression severity. *Journal of the American Medical Association, 303*(1), 47–53.

Frank, J. D. (1993). *Persuasion and healing: A comparative study of psychotherapy.* Baltimore MD: Johns Hopkins University Press.

Frank, E., Kupfer, D., Perel, J., Cornes, C., Jarrett, D., Mallinger, A., Thase, M., McEachran, A., Grochocinski, V. (1990). Three-year outcomes for maintenance therapies in recurrent depression. *Archives of General Psychiatry, 47*, 1093–1099.

Freedman, V. A., Grafova, I. B., Schoeni, R. F., & Rogowski, J. (2008). Neighborhoods and disability in later life. *Social Science and Medicine, 66*(11), 2253–2267.

Freedman, V. A., Martin, L. G., & Schoeni, R. F. (2002). Recent trends in disability and functioning among older adults in the United States. *Journal of the American Medical Association, 288*(24), 3137–3146.

Freilich, B., & Hyer, L. (2007). The relationship of the RBANS and measures of daily functioning in dementia. *Psychological Reports, 101*, 119–129.

Freud, S. (1905). *On psychotherapy.* Reprinted (1953–1974) in the Standard Edition of the Complete Works of Sigmund Freud (trans. & ed. J. Strachey), vol. 7. London, UK: Hogarth Press.

Fried, L. P., Bandeen-Roche, K., Chaves, P. H., & Johnson, B. A. (2000). Preclinical mobility disability predicts incident mobility disability in older women. *Journals of Gerontology- Biological Sciences and Medical Sciences, 55*(1), 43.

Friedman, H. S., & Martin, L. R. (2011). *The longevity project: Surprising discoveries for health and long life from the landmark eight-decade study.* New York, NY: Penguin.

Frisch, M. B. (1998). Quality of life therapy and assessment in health care. *Clinical Psychology: Science and Practice, 5*(1), 19–40.

Frisch, M. B., Clark, M. P., Rouse, S. V., Rudd, M. D., Paweleck, J. K., Greenstone, A., & Kopplin, D. A. (2005). Predictive and treatment validity of life satisfaction and the quality of life inventory. *Assessment, 12*, 66–78.

Fujikawa, T., Yamawaki, S., & Touhouda, Y. (1993). Incidence of silent cerebral infarction in patients with major depression. *Stroke, 24*(11), 1631–1634.

Fulmer, T., Hyer, K., & Flaherty, E. (2005). Geriatric interdisciplinary team training: Program results. *Journal of Aging Health, 17*, 443–470.

Fulton Picot, S. J., Youngblut, J., & Zeller, R. (1997). Development and testing of a measure of perceived caregiver rewards in adults. *Journal of Nursing Measurement, 5*(1), 33–52.

Gagnon, N., & Flint, J. (2003). Fear of falling in the elderly. *Geriatrics & Aging, 6,* 15–17.

Gallagher, D., Rose, J., Rivera, P., Lovett, S., & Thompson, L. W. (1989). Prevalence of depression in family caregivers. *The Gerontologist, 29*(4), 449–456.

Gallagher-Thompson, D., & Thompson, L. W. (1995). Psychotherapy with older adults in theory and practice. In B. Boner & L. Beutler (Eds.), *Comprehensive textbook of psychotherapy.* New York, NY: Oxford University Press.

Gallagher-Thompson, D., & Coon, D. W. (2007). Evidence-based psychological treatments for distress in family caregivers of older adults. *Psychology and Aging, 22*(1), 37–51.

Gareri, P., DeFazio, P., & Stilo, M. (2003). Conventional and atypical antipsychotics in the elderly. *Clinical Drug Investigations, 23,* 287–322.

Gatchel, R. J., & Oordt, M. S. (2003). *Clinical health psychology and primary care: Practical advice and clinical guidance for successful collaboration.* Washington, DC: American Psychological Association.

Gatz, M., Fiske, A., Fox, L. S., Kaskie, B., Kasl-Godley, J. E., McCallum, T. J., & Wetherell, J. L. (1998). Empirically validated psychological treatments for older adults. *Journal of Mental Health and Aging, 4,* 9–46.

Gaughler, J. (2010). *Doing the best we can: An overview of online and clinical resources for care providers of families struggling with dementia.* Presentation on line from University of Minnesota, Minneapolis MN.

Gaugler, J. E., Kane, R. L., & Newcomer, R. (2007). Resilience and transitions from dementia caregiving. *Journals of Gerontology, Series B: Psychological Sciences and Social Sciences, 62*(1), P38–P44.

Gawande, A. (2011). *Medical report: The hot spotters: Can we lower medical costs by giving the neediest patients better care?* [Electronic Version]. New York. Retrieved January 24, 2011.

Gaynes, B. N., Rush, A. J., Trivedi, M. H., Wisniewski, S. R., Spencer, D., & Fava, M. (2008). The STAR* D study: Treating depression in the real world. *Cleveland Clinic Journal of Medicine, 75*(1), 57–66.

George, L. K., Blazer, D. F., Winfield-Laird, I., Leaf, P. J., & Fischback, R. L. (1988). Psychiatric disorders and mental health service use in later life: Evidence from the Epidemiologic Catchment Area program. In J. Brody & G. Maddox (Eds.), *Epidemiology and aging,* (pp. 189–219). New York, NY: Springer.

Gerson, S., Belin, T. R., Kaufman, A., Mintz, J., & Jarvik, L. (1999). Pharmacological and psychological treatments for depressed older patients: A meta-analysis and overview of recent findings. *Harvard Review of Psychiatry, 7*(1), 1–28.

Gibson, S. J., Katz, B., Corran, T. M., Farrell, M. J., & Helme, R. D. (1994). Pain in older persons. *Disability & Rehabilitation, 16*(3), 127–139.

Gilbody, S., Bower, P., Fletcher, J., Richards, D., & Sutton, A. J. (2006). Collaborative care for depression: A cumulative meta-analysis and review of longer-term outcomes. *Archives of Internal Medicine, 166*(21), 2314.

Gilhooly, M. L., Sweeting, H. N., Whittick, J. E., & McKee, K. (1994). Family care of the dementing elderly. *International Review of Psychiatry, 6*(1), 29–40.

Gitlin, L. N., Roth, D. L., Burgio, L. D., Loewenstein, D. A., Winter, L., Nichols, L., Arguelles, S., … Martindale, J. (2005). Caregiver appraisal of functional dependence in individuals with dementia and associated caregiver upset: Psychometric properties of a new scale and response patterns by caregiver and care recipient characteristics. *Journal of Aging and Health, 17*(2), 148–171.

Gitlin, L. N., Reever, K., Dennis, M. P., Mathieu, E., & Hauck, W. W. (2006). Enhancing quality of life of families who use adult day services: Short-and long-term effects of the adult day services plus program. *The Gerontologist, 46*(5), 630–639.

Gliklich, R., & Dreyer, N. (2010). *Registries for evaluating patient outcomes.* NICE 2006: Tackling Health priorities, Annual conference and exhibition, 6–7 December 2006. Birmingham, AL.

Glueckauf, R. L., Jeffers, S. B., Sharma, D., Massey, A. J., Davis, W. S., Wesley, L. M., … Martin, C. (2007). Telephone-based cognitive-behavioral intervention for distressed rural dementia caregivers. *Clinical Gerontologist, 31*(1), 21–41.

Goldberg, D. P., Prisciandaro, J., & Williams, P. (2012). The primary health care version of ICD-11: The detection of common mental disorders in general medical settings. *General Hospital Psychiatry, 34*, 665–670.

Goldman, L. S., Nielsen, N. H., Champion, H. C. (1999). Awareness, diagnosis, and treatment of depression. *Journal of General Internal Medicine, 14*(9), 569–580.

Goldsilver, P. M., & Gruneir, M. R. (2001). Early stage dementia group: An innovative model of support for individuals in the early stages of dementia. *American Journal of Alzheimer's Disease and Other Dementias, 16*(2), 109–114.

Goldstein, M. G., Whitlock, E. P., & DePue, J. (2004). Multiple behavioral risk factor interventions in primary care: Summary of research evidence. *American Journal of Preventive Medicine, 27*(Suppl. 2), 61–69.

Goodheart, C., & Lansing, M. (1997). *Treating people with chronic disease: A psychological guide*. Washington, DC: American Psychological Press.

Goodwin, J. (2003). Embracing complexity. A consideration of hypertension in the very old. *Journal of Gerontology: Medical Science, 58*, 653–658.

Gopnik, A. (2013, May 4). The brain as a quick-change artist. *Wall Street Journal*.

Gould, C., Edelstein, B. A., & Ciliberti, C. (2010). Older adults. In D. L. Segal, M. Hersen (Eds.), *Diagnostic interviewing* (pp. 467–494). New York, NY: Springer Publishing.

Graham, E. K., & Lachman, M. E. (2012). Personality stability is associated with better cognitive performance in adulthood: Are the stable more able? *Journals of Gerontology, Series B: Psychological Sciences and Social Sciences, 67*(5), 545–554.

Green, C. S., & Bavelier, D. (2008). Exercising your brain: A review of human brain plasticity and training-induced learning. *Psychology and Aging, 23*(4), 692–701.

Greenaway, M. C., Hanna, S. M., Lepore, S. W., & Smith, G. E. (2008). A behavioral rehabilitation intervention for amnestic mild cognitive impairment. *American Journal of Alzheimer's Disease and Other Dementias, 23*(5), 451–461.

Greve, K. W., Love, J. M., Sherwin, E., Mathias, C. W., Ramzinski, P., & Levy, J. (2002). Wisconsin Card Sorting Test in chronic severe traumatic brain injury: Factor structure and performance subgroups. *Brain Injury, 16*(1), 29–40.

Grigsby, J., Kaye, K., & Robbins, L. (1992). Reliabilities, norms, and factor structure of the Behavioral Dyscontrol Scale. *Perceptual and Motor Skills, 74*, 883–892.

Gross, A, Rebok, G., Unverzagt, F., Willis, S., & Brandt, J. (2011). Cognitive predictors of everyday functioning in older adults: Results from the ACTIVE cognitive Intervention trial. *Journal of Gerontology, Series B: Psychological Sciences, 66*(5), 557–566.

Grossberg, S. (2009). Cortical and subcortical predictive dynamics and learning during perception, cognition, emotion and action. *Philosophical Transactions of the Royal Society B: Biological Sciences, 364*(1521), 1223–1234.

Gruenewald, T. L., Seeman, T. E., Karlamangla, A. S., & Sarkisian, C. A. (2009). Allostatic load and frailty in older adults. *Journal of American Geriatric Society, 57*, 1525–1531.

Gulpers, M. J., Bleijlevens, M. H., Ambergen, T., Capezuti, E., Rossum, E., & Hamers, J. P. (2013). Reduction of belt restraint use: Long-term effects of the EXBELT intervention. *Journal of American Geriatrics Society, 61*, 107–112.

Gum, A. M., Areán, P. A., Hunkeler, E., Tang, L., Katon, W., Hitchcock, P., ... Unützer, J. (2006). Depression treatment preferences in older primary care patients. *The Gerontologist, 46*(1), 14–22.

Haber, D. (2010). *Health promotion and aging: Practical applications for health professional* (5th ed.). New York, NY: Springer Publishing.

Haber, D., Logan, W., & Schumacher, S. (2011). Health promotion and disease prevention. In V. Hirth, D. Wieland, & M. Dever-Bumba, (Ed.), *Case-based geriatrics: A global approach*. New York, NY: McGraw-Hill.

Hachinski, V. (2008). Shifts in thinking about dementia. *The Journal of the American Medical Association, 300*(18), 2172–2173.

Hadjistavropoulos, T., Herr, K., Turk, D. C., Fine, P. G., Dworkin, R. H., Helme, R., ... Williams, J. (2007). An interdisciplinary expert consensus statement on assessment of pain in older persons. *Clinical Journal of Pain, 23*, S1–S43.

Hagberg, B., & Sameulson, G. (2008). Survival after 100 years of age: A multivariate model of exceptional survival in Swedish centenarians. *Journal of Gerontology, 63A*(11), 1219–1226.

Hagger-Johnson, G. E., Shickle, D. A., Deary, I. J., & Roberts, B. A. (2010). Direct and indirect pathways connecting cognitive ability with cardiovascular disease risk: Socioeconomic status and multiple health behaviors. *Psychosomatic Medicine, 72*(8), 777–785.

Haight, B. K. (1988). The therapeutic role of a structured life review process in homebound elderly subjects. *Journal of Gerontology, 43*(2), P40–P44.

Hall, R., Hall, R., & Chapman, M. (2009). Anticholinergic syndrome: Presentations, etiological agents, differential diagnosis, and treatment. *Clinical Geriatrics, 17*(11), 22–28.

Halliwell, J. F. (2003). How's life? Combining individual and national variables to explain subjective well-being. *Economic Modelling, 20,* 331–360.

Ham, R., Sloane, P., Warshaw, G., Bernard, M., & Flaherty, E. (2006). *Primary care geriatrics. A case-based approach* (5th ed.). St. Louis, Philadelphia: Mosby Elsevier.

Hamer, M., & Chida, Y. (2009). Physical activity and risk of neurodegenerative disease: A systematic review of prospective evidence. *Psychological Medicine, 39*(1), 3.

Hampstead, B. M., Sathian, K., Moore, A. B., Nalisnick, C., & Stringer, A. Y. (2008). Explicit memory training leads to improved memory for face-name pairs in patients with mild cognitive impairment: Results of a pilot investigation. *Journal of the International Neuropsychological Society, 14,* 883–889.

Hanley-Peterson, P., Futterman, A., Thompson, L., Zeiss, A. M., Gallagher, D., & Ironson, G. (1990). Endogenous depression and psychotherapy outcome in an elderly population. *The Gerontologist, 30,* 51A.

Harman, J. S., Brown, E. L., Have, T. T., Mulsant, B. H., Brown, G., & Bruce, M. L. (2002). Primary care physicians' attitude toward diagnosis and treatment of late-life depression. *CNS Spectrums, 7,* 784–790.

Harper, D. G., Volicer, L., Stopa, E. G., McKee, A. C., Nitta, M., & Satlin, A. (2005). Disturbance of endogenous circadian rhythm in aging and Alzheimer disease. *American Journal of Geriatric Psychiatry, 13*(5), 359–368.

Harper, S., & Lynch, J. (2007). Trends in socioeconomic inequalities in adult health behaviors among U.S. states, 1990–2004. *Public Health Reports, 112*(2).

Harrow, B. S., Mahoney, D. F., Mendelsohn, A. B., Ory, M. G., Coon, D. W., Belle, S. H., & Nichols, L. O. (2004). Variation in cost of informal caregiving and formal-service use for people with Alzheimer's desease. *American Journal of Alzheimer's Disease and Other Dementias, 19*(5), 299–308.

Hartman-Stein, P. E., & LaRue, A. (Eds.). (2011). *Enhancing cognitive fitness in adults: A guide to the use and development of community-based programs.* New York, NY: Springer Publishing.

Hawes, C., Morris, J. N., Phillips, C. D., Mor, V., Fries, B. E., & Nonemaker, S. (1995). Reliability estimates for the Minimum Data Set for nursing home resident assessment and care screening (MDS). *The Gerontologist, 35*(2), 172–178.

Hayes, S. C. (2004). Acceptance and commitment therapy and the new behavior therapies: Mindfulness, acceptance, and relationship. In S. C. Hayes, V. M. Follette & M. M. Linehan (Eds.), *Mindfulness and acceptance: Expanding the cognitive-behavioral tradition* (pp. 1–29). New York, NY: Guilford Press.

Hayward, R., & Krause, N. (2013). Changes in church-based social support relationships during adulthood. *Journals of Gerontology, Series B: Psychological Sciences and Social Sciences, 68,* 85–96.

Heckhausen, J., & Schulz, R. (1995). A life-span theory of control. *Psychological Review, 102*(2), 284.

Heisler, M., Cole, I., Weir, D., Kerr, E. A., & Hayward, R. A. (2007). Does physician communication influence older patients' diabetes self-management and glycemic control? Results from the Health and Retirement Study (HRS). *Journals of Gerontology, Series A: Biological Sciences and Medical Sciences, 62*(12), 1435–1442.

Heisler, M., Spencer, M., Forman, J., Robinson, C., Shultz, C., Palmisano, G., ... Kieffer, E. (2009). Participants' assessments of the effects of a community health worker intervention on their diabetes self-management and interactions with healthcare providers. *American Journal of Preventive Medicine, 37*(6), 270–279.

Henin, A., Otto, M. W., & Reilly-Harrington, N. A. (2001). Introducing flexibility in manualized treatments: Application of recommended strategies to the cognitive-behavioral treatment of bipolar disorder. *Cognitive and Behavioral Practice, 8*(4), 317–328.

Herring, M. P., O'Connor, P. J., & Dishman, R. K. (2010). The effect of exercise training on anxiety symptoms among patients: A systematic review. *Archives of Internal Medicine, 170*(4), 321.

Hertzog, C., Kramer, A. F., Wilson, R. S., & Linderberger, U. (2009). Enrichment effects on adult cognitive development: Can the functional capacity of older adults be preserved and enhanced? *Psychological Science in the Public Interest, 9*, 1–65.

Hicken, B. L., & Plowhead, A. (2010). A model for home-based psychology from the Veterans Health Administration. *Professional Psychology: Research and Practice, 41*(4), 340–346.

Hicks, J. A., & King, L. A. (2007). Meaning in life and seeing the big picture: Positive affect and global focus. *Cognition and Emotion, 21*(7), 1577–1584.

Hillman, C. H., Erickson, K. I., & Kramer, A. F. (2008). Be smart, exercise your heart: Exercise effects on brain and cognition. *Nature Reviews Neuroscience, 9*(1), 58–65.

Hinrichsen, G. A. (2008). Interpersonal psychotherapy as a treatment for depression in later life. *Professional Psychology: Research and Practice, 39*(3), 306.

Hinrichsen, G. A., & Clougherty, K. F. (2006). *Interpersonal psychotherapy for depressed older adults.* Washington, DC: American Psychological Association.

Hinrichsen, G. A., & Emery, E. E. (2005). Interpersonal factors and late-life depression. *Clinical Psychology: Science and Practice, 12*(3), 264–275.

Hoffman, C. C. (1996). Health promotion. *Journal of the American Medical Association, 276*, 1473–1479.

Holahan, C. J., Moos, R. H., Holahan, C. K., Brennan, P. L., & Schutte, K. K. (2005). Stress generation, avoidance coping, and depressive symptoms: A 10-year model. *Journal of Consulting and Clinical Psychology, 73*(4), 658.

Holley, C., Murrell, S. A., & Mast, B. T. (2006). Psychosocial and vascular risk factors for depression in the elderly. *American Journal of Geriatric Psychology, 14*(1), 84–90.

Hollon, S. D., Muñoz, R. F., Barlow, D. H., Beardslee, W. R., Bell, C. C., Bernal, G., ... Sommers, D. (2002). Psychosocial intervention development for the prevention and treatment of depression: Promoting innovation and increasing access. *Biological Psychiatry, 52*(6), 610–630.

Holsinger, T., Deveau, J., Boustani, M, Williams, J. (2007). Does this patient have dementia? *Journal of the American Medical Association, 297*, 2391–2404.

Hudson, J. I., Mangweth, B., Pope, H. G., Jr., De Col, C., Hausmann, A., Gutweniger, S., et al. (2003). Family study of affective spectrum disorder. *Archives of General Psychiatry, 60*(2), 170–177.

Huffman, K. (2012). The developing, aging neocortex: How genetics and epigenetics influence early developmental patterning and age-related change. *Frontiers in Genetics, 3*, 212. Published online 2012 October 17.

Hulette, C. M., Welsh-Bohmer, K. A., Murray, M. G., Saunders, A. M., Mash, D. C., & McIntyre, L. M. (1998). Neuropathological and neuropsychological changes in" normal" aging: Evidence for preclinical Alzheimer disease in cognitively normal individuals. *Journal of Neuropathology & Experimental Neurology, 57*(12), 1168–1174.

Hunter, C. L., Goodie, J. L., Oordt, M. S., Dobmeyer, A. C. (2009). *Integrated behavioral health in primary care: Step-by-step guidance for assessment and intervention.* Washington, DC: American Psychological Association.

Hunter, C. L., & Goodie, J. L. (2010). Operational and clinical components for integrated-collaborative behavioral healthcare in the patient-centered medical home. *Families, Systems, & Health, 28*, 308–321.

Hurwicz, M. L., & Tumosa, N. (2011). Cultural competence in geriatric care. In V. Hirth, D. Wieland, & M. Dever-Bumba (Eds.), *Case-based geriatrics: A global approach*. New York NY: McGraw-Hill.

Husain, M. M., Rush, A. J., Sackeim, H. A., Wisniewski, S. R., McClintock, S. M., Craven, N., ... Hauger, R. (2005). Age-related characteristics of depression: A preliminary STAR* D report. *American Journal of Geriatric Psychiatry, 13*(10), 852–860.

Hybels, C. F., Blazer, D. G., Pieper, C. F., Landerman, L. R., & Steffens, D. C. (2009). Profiles of depressive symptoms in older adults diagnosed with major depression: A latent cluster analysis. *American Journal of Geriatric Psychiatry: Official Journal of the American Association for Geriatric Psychiatry, 17*(5), 387.

Hyer, L. (2009, August). *Depression and anxiety at late life: Assessment and treatment. Workshop for the American Psychological Association's annual meeting "What Psychologists Should Know about Working with Older Adults."* Toronto, ON, Canada.

Hyer, L., & Intrieri, R. (Eds.). (2006). *Geropsychological interventions in long-term care*. New York, NY: Springer Publishing Company.

Hyer, L., Kramer, D., & Sohnle, S. (2004). CBT with older people: Alterations and the value of the therapeutic alliance. *Psychotherapy: Theory, Research, Practice, Training, 41*(3), 276.

Hyer, L., & Kushner, B. (2007). EMDR: A review. In P. Lehrer & R. Wolfolk (Eds.), *Handbook of stress* (2nd ed). New York, NY: Guilford Press.

Hyer, L., Damon, J., & Nizam, Z. (2008). Vascular cognitive impairment: Perspective and review. *Psychiatry and The Law, 35*, 520–548.

Hyer, L., Molinari, V., Mills, W., & Yeager, C. A. (2008). In T. Millon & C. Bloom (Eds.), *The Millon inventories: A practitioner's guide to personalized clinical assessment* (2nd ed., pp. 296–326). New York, NY: Guilford Press.

Hyer, L. A., & Ragan, A. M. (2003). Training in long-term care facilities. *Clinical Gerontologist, 25*(3–4), 197–237.

Hyer, L., Scott, C., & McKenzie, L. (2013). A randomized trial on the value of duloxitine for older spinal surgery patients. *American Journal of Geriatric Psychiatry*.

Hyer, L., Scott, C., Atkinson, M. M., Mullin, C., McKensie, L., Lee, A., & Johnson, A. (2013). Cognitive program to improve working memory in older adults with MCI. *Aging and Mental Health*.

Hyer, L., Scott, C., Lyles, J., Dhabliwala, J. & McKenzie, L. (2013). Memory intervention: The value of a clinical holistic program for older adults with memory impairments. *Aging and Mental Health*.

Hyer, L., & Stanger, E. (1997). Interaction of posttraumatic stress disorder and major depressive disorder among older combat veterans. *Psychological Reports, 80*(3), 785–786.

Hyer, L., Yeager, C. A., Hilton, N., & Sacks, A. (2009). Group, individual, and staff therapy: An efficient and effective cognitive behavioral therapy in long-term care. *American Journal of Alzheimer's Disease and Other Dementias, 23*(6), 528–539.

Hyer, L. A., Yeager, C. A., Hyer, R., & Scott, C. (2010). Psychotherapy with older adults: The importance of assessment. In P. A. Lichtenberg (Eds.), *Handbook of assessment in clinical gerontology* (2nd ed., pp. 61–100). London, UK: Academic Press.

Hyer, L., Yeager, C., Scott, C., & Hyer, R. (2010). Psychotherapy with older adults: Importance of assessment. In P. Lichtenberg (Eds.), *Handbook of assessment for older adults*. New York, NY: Guilford Press.

Institute of Medicine. (1996). *Primary care: America's health in a new era*. Washington, DC: National Academies Press.

Institute of Medicine. (2012). *The mental health and substance use workforce for older adults: In whose hands?* Washington, DC: National Academies Press.

Institute of Medicine. Committee on the Future Health Care Workforce for Older Americans. (2008). *Retooling for an aging America: Building the health care workforce*. Washington, DC: National Academies Press.

Institute of Medicine. Committee on Quality of Health Care in America. (2001). *Crossing the quality chasm: A new health system for the 21st century*. Washington, DC: National Academies Press.

Institute of Medicine (IOM). Food and Nutrition Board. (2001). Iodine. In *Dietary reference intakes for vitamin A, vitamin K, arsenic, boron, chromium, copper, iodine, iron, manganese, molybdenum, nickel, silicon, vanadium and zinc* (pp. 258–289). Washington, DC: National Academies Press.

Institute of Medicine; O'Connell, M. E., Boat, T., & Warner, E. (Eds.). (2009). *Preventing mental, emotional and behavioral disorders among young people: Progress and possibilities.* Washington, DC: National Academies Press.

Iovieno, N., van Nieuwenhuizen, A., Clain, A., Baer, L., & Nierenberg, A. A. (2011). Residual symptoms after remission of major depressive disorder with fluoxetine and risk of relapse. *Depression and Anxiety, 28*(2), 137–144.

Irwin, M., & Olmstead, R. (2012).Mitigating cellular inflammation in older adults: A randomized controlled trial of Tai Chi Chih. *American Journal of Geriatric Psychiatry, 20*(9), 764–772.

Jack, C. R., Albert, M. S., Knopman, D. S., McKhann, G. M., Sperling, R. A., Carrillo, M. C., ... Phelps, C. H. (2011). Introduction to the recommendations from the National Institute on Aging–Alzheimer's Association workgroups on diagnostic guidelines for Alzheimer's disease. *Alzheimer's and Dementia, 7*(3), 257–262.

Jacobson, N. S., Martell, C. R., & Dimidjian, S. (2001). Behavioral activation treatment for depression: Returning to contextual roots. *Clinical Psychology: Science and Practice, 8*(3), 255–270.

Jaeckles, N. (2009). Early DIAMOND adopters offer insights. *Minnesota Physician, 23*(1), 1–2.

Jaeggi, S. M., Buschkuehl, M., Jonides, J., & Perrig, W. J. (2008). Improving fluid intelligence with training on working memory. *Proceedings of the National Academy of Sciences of the United States of America, 105*(19), 6829–6833.

Jak, A. J., Bondi, M. W., Delano-Wood, L., Wierenga, C., Corey-Bloom, J., Salmon, D. P., & Delis, D. C. (2009). Quantification of five neuropsychological approaches to defining mild cognitive impairment. *American Journal of Geriatric Psychiatry: Official Journal of the American Association for Geriatric Psychiatry, 17*(5), 368.

Jamison, C., & Scogin, F. (1995). The outcome of cognitive bibliotherapy with depressed adults. *Journal of Consulting and Clinical Psychology; Journal of Consulting and Clinical Psychology, 63*(4), 644.

Janzing, J. G., Hooijer, C., van't Hof, M. A., & Zitman, F. G. (2002). Depression in subjects with and without dementia: A comparison using GMS-AGECAT. *International Journal of Geriatric Psychiatry, 17*(1), 1–5.

Jetten, J., Haslam, C., Haslam, S. A., & Branscombe, N. R. (2009). The social cure. *Scientific American Mind, 20*(5), 26–33.

Johns, M. W. (1994). Sleepiness in different situations measured by the Epworth Sleepiness Scale. *Sleep, 17*, 703–710.

Joling, K. J., van Hout, H. P., van't Veer-Tazelaar, P. J., van der Horst, H. E., Cuijpers, P., van de Ven, P. M., & van Marwijk, H. W. (2011). How effective is bibliotherapy for very old adults with subthreshold depression? A randomized controlled trial. *American Journal of Geriatric Psychiatry, 19*(3), 256.

Jorm, A. F. (2001). History of depression as a risk factor for dementia: An updated review. *Australian and New Zealand Journal of Psychiatry, 35*(6), 776–781.

Kabat-Zinn, J. (2005). *Full catastrophe living: using the wisdom of your body and mind to face stress, pain, and illness* (15th anniversary ed.). New York, NY: Delta Trade Paperback/Bantam Dell.

Kahana, E. (1982). A congruence model of person–environment interaction. In M. P. Lawton, P. G. Windley, & T. O. Byerts (Eds.), *Aging and the environment: Theoretical approaches* (pp. 97–121). New York, NY: Springer Publishing Company.

Kahn, J. R., & Pearlin, L. I. (2006). Financial strain over the life course and health among older adults. *Journal of Health and Social Behavior, 47*(1), 17–31.

Kalaria, R. N. (2000). The role of cerebral ischemia in Alzheimer's disease. *Neurobiology of Aging, 21*(2), 321–330.

Kalayam, B., & Alexopoulos, G. S. (1999). Prefrontal dysfunction and treatment response in geriatric depression. *Archives of General Psychiatry, 56*(8), 713.

Kane, R. A., Lum, T. Y., Cutler, L. J., Degenholtz, H. B., & Yu, T. C. (2007). Resident outcomes in small-house nursing homes: A longitudinal evaluation of the initial green house program. *Journal of the American Geriatrics Society, 55*(6), 832–839.

Kane, M. J., Brown, L. H., McVay, J. C., Silvia, P. J., Myin-Germeys, I., & Kwapil, T. R. (2007). For whom the mind wanders, and when an experience-sampling study of working memory and executive control in daily life. *Psychological Science, 18*(7), 614–621.

Kane, M., Hambrick, D., Tuholski, S., Wilhelm, O., Payne, T., & Engle, R. (2004). The generality of working memory capacity: A latent-variable approach to verbal and visuospatial memory span and reasoning. *Journal of Experimental Psychology: General, 133*(2), 189–217.

Kangas, M., Henry, J. L., & Bryant, R. A. (2002). Posttraumatic stress disorder following cancer: A conceptual and empirical review. *Clinical Psychology Review, 22*(4), 499–524.

Karel, M. J., & Hinrichsen, G. (2000). Treatment of depression in late life: Psychotherapeutic interventions. *Clinical Psychology Review, 20*(6), 707–729.

Karlin, B. E., & Duffy, M. (2004). Geriatric Mental Health Policy: Impact on Service Delivery and Directions for Effecting Change. *Professional Psychology: Research and Practice, 35*(5), 509.

Karlin, B. E., Duffy, M., & Gleaves, D. H. (2008). Patterns and predictors of mental health service use and mental illness among older and younger adults in the United States. *Psychological Services, 5*(3), 275.

Karp, A., Andel, R., Parker, M. G., Wang, H. X., Winblad, B., & Fratiglioni, L. (2009). Mentally stimulating activities at work during midlife and dementia risk after age 75: Follow-up study from the Kungsholmen project. *American Journal of Geriatric Psychiatry, 17*(3), 227–236.

Karp, J. F., Rudy, T., & Weiner, D. K. (2008). Persistent pain biases item response on the geriatric depression scale (GDS): Preliminary evidence for validity of the GDS-PAIN. *Pain Medicine, 9*(1), 33–43.

Kastorini, C. M., Milionis, H. J., Esposito, K., Giugliano, D., Goudevenos, J. A., & Panagiotakos, D. B. (2011). The effect of Mediterranean diet on metabolic syndrome and its components: A meta-analysis of 50 studies and 534,906 individuals. *Journal of the American College of Cardiology, 57*(11), 1299–1313.

Katsnelson, E., Motro, U., Feldman, M. W., & Lotem, A. (2011). Individual-learning ability predicts social-foraging strategy in house sparrows. *Proceedings of the Royal Society B: Biological Sciences, 278*(1705), 582–589.

Katz, S., Ford, A. B., Moskowitz, R. W., Jackson, B. A., & Jaffe, M. W. (1963). Studies of illness in the aged: The index of ADL: A standardized measure of biological and psychosocial function. *Journal of the American Medical Association, 185*, 914–919.

Katz, I. R., Parmelee, P. A., Beaston-Wimmer, P., & Smith, B. D. (1994). Association of antidepressants and other medications with mortality in the residential-care elderly. *Journal of Geriatric Psychiatry and Neurology, 7*(4), 221–226.

Katz, I. R., Reynolds, C. F., Alexopoulos, G. S., & Hackett, D. (2002). Venlafaxine ER as a treatment for generalized anxiety disorder in older adults: Pooled analysis of five randomized placebo-controlled clinical trials. *Journal of the American Geriatrics Society, 50*(1), 18–25.

Katzman, R., Terry, R., DeTeresa, R., Brown, T., Davies, P., Fuld, P., ... Peck, A. (1988). Clinical, pathological, and neurochemical changes in dementia: A subgroup with preserved mental status and numerous neocortical plaques. *Annals of Neurology, 23*(2), 138–144.

Kawachi, I., Sparrow, D., Vokonas, P. S., & Weiss, S. T. (1994). Symptoms of anxiety and risk of coronary heart disease. The normative aging study. *Circulation, 90*(5), 2225–2229.

Kayalam B., & Alexopoulos, G. S. (1999). Prefrontal dysfunction and treatment response in geriatric depression. *Archives of General Psychiatry, 56*, 713–718.

Keefe, F. J., Rumble, M. E., Scipio, C. D., Giordano, L. A., & Perri, L. M. (2004). Psychological aspects of persistent pain: Current state of the science. *The Journal of Pain, 5*(4), 195–211.

Keeler, E., Guralnik, J. M., Tian, H., Wallace, R. B., & Reuben, D. B. (2010). The impact of functional status on life expectancy in older persons. *Journals of Gerontology, Series A: Biological Sciences and Medical Sciences, 65*(7), 727–733.

Keller, M. B., McCullough, J. P., Klein, D. N., Arnow, B., Dunner, D. L., Gelenberg, A. J., ... Zajecka, J. (2000). A comparison of nefazodone, the cognitive behavioral-analysis system of psychotherapy, and their combination for the treatment of chronic depression. *New England Journal of Medicine, 342*(20), 1462–1470.

Kelly, J. F., & Coons, H. L. (2012). Integrated health care and professional psychology: I. The setting right for you? *Professional Psychology: Research and Practice, 43*, 586–595.

Kennedy, G. J., Martinez, M. M., & Garo, N. (2010). Sex and mental health in old age. *Primary Psychiatry, 17*(1), 22–30.

Kessler, D., Lloyd, K., Lewis, G., Gray, D. P., & Heath, I. (1999). General practice cross sectional study of symptom attribution and recognition of depression and anxiety in primary care commentary: There must be limits to the medicalisation of human distress. *British Medical Journal, 318*(7181), 436–440.

Kessler, R. C., Nelson, C. B., McGonagle, K. A., Liu, J., Swartz, M., & Blazer, D. G. (1996). Comorbidity of *DSM-III-R* major depressive disorder in the general population: Results from the US National Comorbidity Survey. *British Journal of Psychiatry, 168*(Suppl. 30), 17–30.

Kessler, R. C., Berglund, P., Demler, O., Jin, R., Merikangas, K. R., & Walters, E. E. (2005). Lifetime prevalence and age-of-onset distributions of *DSM-IV* disorders in the National Comorbidity Survey Replication. *Archives of General Psychiatry, 62*(6), 593.

Kessler, R. C., Demler, O., Frank, R. G., Olfson, M., Pincus, H. A., Walters, E. E., & Zaslavsky, A. M. (2005). Prevalence and treatment of mental disorders, 1990 to 2003. *New England Journal of Medicine, 352*, 2515–2523.

Kessler, R. C., Berglund, P., Demler, O., Jin, R., Koretz, D., Merikangas, K. R., ... Wang, P. S. (2003). The epidemiology of major depressive disorder. *Journal of the American Medical Association, 289*(23), 3095–3105.

Kessler, R. C., Heeringa, S., Lakoma, M. D., Petukhova, M., Rupp, A. E., Schoenbaum, M., ... Zaslavsky, A. M. (2008). The individual-level and societal-level effects of mental disorders on earnings in the United States: Results from the National Comorbidity Survey Replication. *American Journal of Psychiatry, 165*(6), 703.

Keyes, C. L., Shmotkin, D., & Ryff, C. D. (2002). Optimizing well-being: The empirical encounter of two traditions. *Journal of Personality and Social Psychology, 82*(6), 1007–1022.

Kim, E., & Rovner, B. (1995). Epidemiology of psychiatric disturbances in nursing homes: Nursing homes have evolved to subacute medical facilities. *Psychiatric Annals, 25*(7), 409–412.

Kim, E., & Rovner, B. W. (1994). Depression in dementia. *Psychiatric Annals, 24*(4), 173–177.

Kiosses, D. N., Arean, P. A., Teri, L., & Alexopoulos, G. S. (2010). Home-delivered Problem Adaptation Therapy (PATH) for depressed, cognitively impaired, disabled elders: A preliminary study. *American Journal of Geriatric Psychiatry: Official Journal of the American Association for Geriatric Psychiatry, 18*(11), 988.

Kiosses, D. N., Klimstra, S., Murphy, C., & Alexopoulos, G. S. (2001). Executive dysfunction and disability in elderly patients with major depression. *American Journal of Geriatric Psychiatry, 9*(3), 269–274.

Kiosses, D. N., Teri, L., Velligan, D. I., & Alexopoulos, G. S. (2011). A home-delivered intervention for depressed, cognitively impaired, disabled elders. *International Journal of Geriatric Psychiatry, 26*(3), 256–262.

Kirkman, S. M., Briscoe, V. J., Clark, N., Florez, H., Haas, L. B., Halter, J. B., ... Swift, C. S. (2012). Diabetes in older adults: A consensus report. *Journal of the American Geriatrics Society, 60*(12), 2342–2356.

Kirsch, I. (2000, April). Are drug and placebo effects in depression additive? In *Clinical trials in mood disorders: The use of placebo… past, present, and future*. Amsterdam, The Netherlands: Elsevier Science.

Klap, R., Unroe, K. T., & Unützer, J. (2003). Caring for mental illness in the United States: A focus on older adults. *American Journal of Geriatric Psychiatry, 11*(5), 517–524.

Klerman, G., DiMascio, A., & Weissman, M. (1974). Treatment of depression by drugs and psychotherapy. *American Journal of Psychiatry, 131*, 186–191.

Klingberg, T., Fernell, E., Olesen, P. J., Johnson, M., Gustafsson, P., Dahlström, K., ... Westerberg, H. (2005). Computerized training of working memory in children with ADHD—A randomized, controlled trial. *Journal of the American Academy of Child and Adolescent Psychiatry, 44*(2), 177–186.

Klingberg, T., Forssberg, H., & Westerberg, H. (2002). Training of working memory in children with ADHD. *Journal of Clinical and Experimental Neuropsychology, 24*(6), 781–791.

Köhler, S., Allardyce, J., Verhey, F., McKeith, I., Mathews, F., Brayne, C., & Sava, G. (2013) Cognitive decline and dementia risk in older adults with psychotic symptoms: A prospective cohort study. *American Journal of Geriatric Psychiatry, 21*, 2, 119–129.

Köhler, S., Thomas, A. J., Barnett, N. A., & O'Brien, J. T. (2010). The pattern and course of cognitive impairment in late-life depression. *Psychological Medicine, 40*(04), 591–602.

Krahn, D. D., Bartels, S. J., Coakley, E., Oslin, D. W., Chen, H., McIntyre, J., ... Levkoff, S. E. (2006). PRISM-E: Comparison of integrated care and enhanced specialty referral models in depression outcomes. *Psychiatric Services, 57*, 946–953.

Kramer, A. F., Colcombe, S. J., McAuley, E., Scalf, P. E., & Erickson, K. I. (2005). Fitness, aging and neurocognitive function. *Neurobiology of Aging, 26*(1), 124–127.

Kramer, A. F., Erickson, K. I., and Colcombe, J. (2006). Exercise, cognition, and the aging brain. *Journal of Applied Physiology, 101*, 1237–1242.

Kraus, C. A., Seignourel, P., Balasubramanyam, V., Snow, A. L., Wilson, N. L., Kunik, M. E. ... Stanley, M. A. (2008). Cognitive-behavioral treatment for anxiety in patients with dementia: Two case studies. *Journal of Psychiatric Practice, 14*(3), 186–192.

Krause, N. (1996). Neighborhood deterioration and self-rated health in later life. *Psychology and Aging, Psychology and Aging, 11*(2), 342.

Kremen, W., Lachman, M., Pruessner, J., Slowinski, M., & Wilson, R. (2012). Mechanisms of age-related cognitive change and targets of intervention: Social interactions and stress. *Journal of Gerontology A: Biological Medical Science, 67*(7), 760–765.

Krishnan, K. R. (2002). Biological risk factors in late life depression. *Biological Psychiatry, 52*(3), 185–192.

Krishnan, K. R., Taylor, W. D., McQuoid, D. R., MacFall, J. R., Payne, M. E., Provenzale, J. M., & Steffens, D. C. (2004). Clinical characteristics of magnetic resonance imaging-defined subcortical ischemic depression. *Biological Psychiatry, 55*(4), 390.

Kroenke, K., Spitzer, R. L., Williams, J. B., & Löwe, B. (2010). The patient health questionnaire somatic, anxiety, and depressive symptom scales: A systematic review. *General Hospital Psychiatry, 32*, 345–359.

Kroenke, K., Spitzer, R. L., Williams, J. B., Monahan, P. O., & Löwe, B. (2007). Anxiety disorders in primary care: Prevalence, impairment, comorbidity, and detection. *Annals of Internal Medicine, 146*(5), 317.

Kubzansky, L. D., Cole, S. R., Kawachi, I., Vokonas, P., & Sparrow, D. (2006). Shared and unique contributions of anger, anxiety, and depression to coronary heart disease: A prospective study in the normative aging study. *Annals of Behavioral Medicine, 31*(1), 21–29.

Kunik, M. E., Veazey, C., Cully, J. A., Souchek, J., Graham, D. P., Hopko, D., ... Stanley, M. A. (2008). COPD education and cognitive behavioral therapy group treatment for clinically significant symptoms of depression and anxiety in COPD patients: A randomized controlled trial. *Psychological Medicine, 38*(3), 385.

Lachman, M. E., Howland, J., & Tennstedt, S., (1998). Fear of falling and activity restriction: The Survey of Activities and Fear of Falling in the Elderly (SAFE). *Journal of Gerontology, 53B*, P43–P50.

Lachman, M. E., Weaver, S. L., Bandura, M., Elliott, E., & Lewkowicz, C. J. (1992). Improving memory and control beliefs through cognitive restructuring and self-generated strategies. *Journal of Gerontology: Psychological Sciences, 47*(5), 293–299.

Ladouceur, R., Léger, É., Dugos, M., & Freeston, M. H. (2004). Cognitive-behavioral treatment of generalized anxiety disorder (GAD) for older adults. *International Psychogeriatrics, 16*(2), 195–208.

Lahey, B. B. (2009). Public health significance of neuroticism. *American Psychologist, 64*(4), 241–256.

Lambert, M. J., & Bergin, A. E. (1994). The effectiveness of psychotherapy. Theory and practice. In B. Boner & L. Beutler (Eds.), *Comprehensive textbook of psychotherapy* (pp. 357–379). New York, NY: Oxford University Press.

Lambert, M. J., & Hill, C. E. (1994). Assessing psychotherapy outcomes and processes. In A. E. Bergin & S. L. Garfield (Eds.), *Handbook of psychotherapy and behavior change* (4th ed., pp. 72–113). New York, NY: Wiley.

Lambert, M. J., Harmon, C., Slade, K., Whipple, J. L., & Hawkins, E. J. (2005). Providing feedback to psychotherapists on their patients' progress: Clinical results and practice suggestions. *Journal of Clinical Psychology, 61*(2), 165–174.

Langan, R., & Zawistoski, K. (2011). Update on vitamin B_{12} deficiency. *American Family Physician, 83*, 1425–1430.

Lantz, P. M., House, J. S., Lepkowski, J. M., Williams, D. R., Mero, R. P., & Chen, J. M. (1998). Socioeconomic factors, health behaviors, and mortality: Results from a nationally representative study of US adults. *Journal of the American Medical Association, 279*(21) 1703–1708.

Latham, K., & Peek, C. (2013). Self-rated health and morbidity onset among late midlife U.S. adults. *Journals of Gerontology, Series B: Psychological Sciences and Social Sciences, 68*, 107–116.

Lavretsky, H., Siddarth, P., Kepe, V., Ercoli, L. M., Miller, K. J., Burggren, A. C., ... Small, G. W. (2009). Depression and anxiety symptoms are associated with cerebral FDDNP-PET binding in middle-aged and older non-demented adults. *American Journal of Geriatric Psychiatry: Official Journal of the American Association for Geriatric Psychiatry, 17*(6), 493–502.

Lawton, M. P., & Brody, E. M. (1969). Assessment of older people: Self-maintaining and instrumental activities of daily living. *The Gerontologist 9*, 179–186.

Lawton, M. P., & Nahemow, L. (1973). Ecology and the aging process. In C. Eisdorfer & M. P. Lawton (Eds.), *Psychology of adult development and aging.* Washington, DC: American Psychological Association.

Layard, R. (2006). *Happiness: Lessons from a new science.* New York, NY: Penguin.

Lebowitz, B. D., Pearson, J. L., Schneider, L. S., Reynolds, C. F., III, Alexopoulos, G. S., Bruce, M. L., ... Parmelee, P. (1997). Diagnosis and treatment of depression in late life. *Journal of the American Medical Association, 278*(14), 1186–1190.

Leckey, G. S., & Beatty, W. W. (2002). Predicting functional performance by patients with Alzheimer's disease using the Problems in Everyday Living (PEDL) Test: A preliminary study. *Journal of the International Neuropsychological Society, 8*(1), 48–57.

LeCouteur, D. G., & Sinclair, D. A. (2010). A blueprint for developing therapeutic approaches that increase healthspan and delay death. *Journal of Gerontology. Series A, Biological Sciences and Medical Sciences, 65*(7), 693–694.

Lehrer, P. (2012, December). *Heart rate variability.* Symposium presented at the DDEMC Invited Presentation, Augusta, GA.

Lehrer, P. M., & Vaschillo, E. (2008). The future of heart rate variability biofeedback. *Biofeedback, 36*, 11–14.

Lenze, E. J., Mulsant, B. H., Dew, M. A., Shear, M. K., Houck, P., Pollock, B. G., & Reynolds C. F., III. (2003). Good treatment outcomes in late-life depression with comorbid anxiety. *Journal of Affective Disorders, 77*, 247–254.

Lenze, E. J., Mulsant, B. H., Mohlman, J., Shear, M. K., Dew, M. A., Schulz, R., ... Reynolds, C. F., III. (2005). Generalized anxiety disorder in late life: Lifetime course and comorbidity with major depressive disorder. *American Journal of Geriatric Psychiatry, 13*(1), 77–80.

Lenze, E. J., Mulsant, B. H., Shear, M. K., Dew, M. A., Miller, M. D., Pollock, B. G., ... Reynolds, C. F. (2005). Efficacy and tolerability of citalopram in the treatment of late-life anxiety disorders: Results from an 8-week randomized, placebo-controlled trial. *American Journal of Psychiatry, 162*(1), 146–150.

Lenze, E. J., Rollman, B. L., Shear, M. K., Dew, M. A., Pollock, B. G., Ciliberti, C., ... Reynolds, C. F., III. (2009). Escitalopram for older adults with generalized anxiety disorder. *Journal of the American Medical Association, 301*(3), 295–303.

Lenze, E. J., Sheffrin, M., Driscoll, H. C., Mulsant, B. H., Pollock, B. G., Dew, M. A., ... Reynolds, C. F., III. (2008). Incomplete response in late-life depression: Getting to remission. *Dialogues in Clinical Neuroscience, 10*(4), 419.

Lesser, I. M., Boone, K. B., Mehringer, C. M., & Wohl, M. A. (1996). Cognition and white matter hyperintensities in older depressed patients. *American Journal of Psychiatry, 153*(10), 1280–1287.

Leveille, S. G., Bean, J., Bandeen-Roche, K., Jones, R., Hochberg, M., & Guralnik, J. M. (2002). Musculoskeletal pain and risk for falls in older disabled women living in the community. *Journal of the American Geriatrics Society, 50*(4), 671–678.

Levy, B. R., & Banaji, M. R. (2002). Implicit ageism. In T. Nelson (Ed.), *Ageism: Stereotyping and prejudice against older persons* (pp. 49–75). Cambridge, MA: MIT Press, Inc.

Levy, B. R., Hausdorff, J. M., Hencke, R., & Wei, J. Y. (2000). Reducing cardiovascular stress with positive self-stereotypes of aging. *Journals of Gerontology, Series B: Psychological Sciences and Social Sciences, 55*(4), P205–P213.

Levy, B. R., Slade, M. D., & Kasl, S. V. (2002). Longitudinal benefit of positive self-perceptions of aging on functional health. *Journals of Gerontology, Series B: Psychological Sciences and Social Sciences, 57*(5), P409–P417.

Lewinsohn, P. M., Muñoz, R. F., Youngren, M. A., & Zeiss, A. M. (1986). *Control your depression*. New York, NY: Prentice-Hall.

Lezak, M. D. (1983). *Neuropsychological assessment*. New York, NY: Oxford University Press.

Li, S. C., Schmiedek, F., Huxhold, O., Röcke, C., Smith, J., & Lindenberger, U. (2008). Working memory plasticity in old age: Practice gain, transfer, and maintenance. *Psychology and Aging, 23*(4), 731–742.

Lichstein, K. L., & Johnson, R. S. (1993). Relaxation for insomnia and hypnotic medication use in older women. *Psychology and Aging, 8*(1), 103.

Lichstein, K. L., Wilson, N. M., & Johnson, C. T. (2000). Psychological treatment of secondary insomnia. *Psychology and Aging, 15*(2), 232.

Lichtenberg, F. R. (2001). Are the benefits of newer drugs worth their cost? Evidence from the 1996 MEPS. *Health Affairs, 20*(5), 241–251.

Lichtenberg, P. A. (1999). *Handbook of assessment in clinical gerontology*. West Sussex, UK: Wiley.

Lim L., Mitchell, P., Seddon, J., Holz, F., & Wong, T. (2012). Age-related macular degeneration. *The Lancet, 379*, 1728–1738.

Lin, E. H., Katon, W., Von Korff, M., Rutter, C., Simon, G. E., Oliver, M., ... Young, B. (2004). Relationship of depression and diabetes self-care, medication adherence, and preventive care. *Diabetes Care, 27*(9), 2154–2160.

Lindberg, B. (2013, March). Transforming advanced care: Have we reached a tipping point? *Gerontology News*, 4–5.

Linehan M. M. (1993). *Skills training manual for treating borderline personality disorder*. New York, NY: Guilford.

Livesley, W. J. (2001). Commentary on reconceptualizing personality disorder categories using trait dimensions. *Journal of Personality, 69*(2), 253–276.

Lockwood, K. A., Alexopoulos, G. S., & van Gorp, W. G. (2002). Executive dysfunction in geriatric depression. *American Journal of Psychiatry, 159*(7), 1119–1126.

Loevinger, J., & Blasi, A. (1976). *Ego development: Conceptions and theories*. San Francisco, CA: Jossey-Bass.

Loewenstein, D. A., Acevedo, A., Czaja, S., & Duara, R. (2004). Cognitive rehabilitation of mildly impaired Alzheimer's disease patients on cholinesterase inhibitors. *American Journal of Geriatrics Psychiatry, 12*, 395–402.

Loewenstein, G., & Lerner, J. (2003). The role of emotion in decision making. In R. J. Davidson, H. H., Goldsmith, & K. R., Scherer (Eds.), *Handbook of affective science* (pp. 619–642). Oxford, UK: Oxford University Press.

Logie, R., Gilhooly, K., & Wynn, V. (1994). Counting on working memory in arithmetic problem solving. *Memory & Cognition, 22*(4), 395–410.

Logsdon, R. G., Pike, K. C., McCurry, S. M., Hunter, P., Maher, J., Snyder, L., & Teri, L. (2010). Early-stage memory loss support groups: outcomes from a randomized controlled clinical trial. *The Journals of Gerontology Series B: Psychological Sciences and Social Sciences, 65*(6), 691–697.

Longmore, R. J., & Worrell, M. (2007). Do we need to challenge thoughts in cognitive behavior therapy? *Clinical Psychology Review, 27*(2), 173–187.

Looper, K. J., & Kirmayer, L. J. (2002). Behavioral medicine approaches to somatoform disorders. *Journal of Consulting and Clinical Psychology, 70*(3), 810.

Lorant, V., Deliege, D., Eaton, W., Robert, A., Philippot, P., & Ansseau, M. (2003). Socioeconomic inequalities in depression: A meta-analysis. *American Journal of Epidemiology, 157*(2).

Lowenstein, D. (2011, November). *Mild cognitive impairment: Problems and directions.* Workshop at the National Association of Neuropsychologists, Marco Island.

Lu, B. Y., & Ahmed, I. (2010). The mind-body conundrum: The somatopsychic perspective in geriatric depression. *American Journal of Geriatric Psychiatry, 18*(5), 378–381.

Luis, C. A., Keegan, A. P., & Mullan, M. (2009). Cross validation of the Montreal Cognitive Assessment in community dwelling older adults residing in the Southeastern US. *International Journal of Geriatric Psychiatry, 24*, 197–201.

Lunde, L. H., Nordhus, I. H., & Pallesen, S. (2009). The effectiveness of cognitive and behavioural treatment of chronic pain in the elderly: A quantitative review. *Journal of Clinical Psychology in Medical Settings, 16*(3), 254–262.

Lyketsos, C. G., DelCampo, L., Steinberg, M., Miles, Q., Steele, C. D., Munro, C., ... Rabins, P. V. (2003). Treating depression in Alzheimer disease: Efficacy and safety of sertraline therapy, and the benefits of depression reduction: The DIADS. *Archives of General Psychiatry, 60*(7), 737.

Lyketsos, C. G., & Olin, J. (2002). Depression in Alzheimer's disease: Overview and treatment. *Biological Psychiatry, 52*(3), 243–252.

Lynch, T. R., Morse, J. Q., Mendelson, T., & Robins, C. J. (2003). Dialectical behavior therapy for depressed older adults: A randomized pilot study. *American Journal of Geriatric Psychiatry, 11*(1), 33–45.

Lyons, K. S., Zarit, S. H., Sayer, A. G., & Whitlatch, C. J. (2002). Caregiving as a dyadic process perspectives from caregiver and receiver. *Journals of Gerontology, Series B: Psychological Sciences and Social Sciences, 57*(3), P195–P204.

Mackin, R. S., & Arean, P. A. (2005). Evidence-based psychotherapeutic interventions for geriatric depression. *Psychiatric Clinics of North America, 28*(4), 805–820.

MacNeill, S. E., & Lichtenberg, P. A. (2000). The MacNeill–Lichtenberg decision tree: A unique method of triaging mental health problems in older medical rehabilitation patients. *Archives of Physical Medicine and Rehabilitation, 81*(5), 618–622.

Magruder, K. M., Frueh, B. C., Knapp, R. G., Johnson, M. R., Vaughan, J. A., III, Carson, T. C., ... Hebert, R. (2004). PTSD symptoms, demographic characteristics, and functional status among veterans treated in VA primary care clinics. *Journal of Traumatic Stress, 17*(4), 293–301.

Mahncke, H. W., Connor, B. B., Appelman, J., Ahsanuddin, O. N., Hardy, J. L., Wood, R. A., ... Merzenich, M. M. (2006). Memory enhancement in healthy older adults using a brain plasticity-based training program: A randomized, controlled study. *Proceedings of the National Academy of the Sciences of the United States of America, 103*(33), 12523–12528.

Makris, A. P., Rush, C. R., Frederich, R. C., Taylor, A. C., & Kelly, T. H. (2007). Behavioral and subjective effects of d-amphetamine and modafinil in healthy adults. *Experimental and Clinical Psychopharmacology, 15*(2), 123.

Mandavia, D., & Newton, K. (1998). Geriatric trauma. *Emergency Medicine Clinics of North America, 16*(1), 257–274.

Mantella, R. C., Butters, M. A., Dew, M. A., Mulsant, B. H., Begley, A. E., Tracey, B., ... Lenze, E. J. (2007). Cognitive impairment in late-life generalized anxiety disorder. *American Journal of Geriatric Psychiatry, 15*(8), 673–679.

Mark, T. L., Levit, K. R., & Buck, J. A. (2009). Datapoints: Psychotropic drug prescriptions by medical specialty. *Psychiatric Services, 60*(9), 1167.

Martell, C. R., Addis, M. E. & Jacobson, N. S. (2001). *Depression in context: Strategies for guided action.* New York, NY: Norton.

Martire, L. M., Schulz, R., Reynolds, C. F., III, Morse, J. Q., Butters, M. A., & Hinrichsen, G. A. (2008). Impact of close family members on older adults' early response to depression treatment. *Psychology and Aging, 23*(2), 447.

Mash, E. J., & Foster, S. L. (2001). Exporting analogue behavioral observation from research to clinical practice: Useful or cost-defective? *Psychological Assessment, 13*(1), 86–98.

Mash, E. J., & Hunsley, J. (1993). Assessment considerations in the identification of failing psychotherapy: Bringing the negatives out of the darkroom: Treatment implications of psychological assessment. *Psychological Assessment, 5*(3), 292–301.

Mast, B. (2011). *Whole person dementia assessment.* Baltimore, MD: Health Professions Press.

Mast, B. T. (2012). Methods for assessing the person with Alzheimer's disease: Integrating person-centered and diagnostic approaches to assessment. *Clinical Gerontologist, 35*(5), 360–375.

Mast, B. T., Yochim, B. P., Carmasin, J. S., & Rowe, S. V. (2011). Vascular depression: A neuropsychological perspective. *Neurobiology of Depression,* 445.

Mather, M., & Knight, M. (2005). Goal-directed memory: The role of cognitive control in older adults' emotional memory. *Psychology and Aging, 20*(4), 554.

Mauer, B. J., & Druss, B. G. (2010). Mind and body reunited: Improving care at the behavioral and primary care interface. *Journal of Behavioral Health Services and Research, 37,* 529–542.

Mausbach, B. T., Aschbacher, K., Patterson, T. L., Ancoli-Israel, S., von Känel, R., Mills, P. J., ... Grant, I. (2006). Avoidant coping partially mediates the relationship between patient problem behaviors and depressive symptoms in spousal Alzheimer caregivers. *American Journal of Geriatric Psychiatry, 14*(4), 299–306.

Mausbach, B. T., Patterson, T. L., von Känel, R., Mills, P. J., Ancoli-Israel, S., Dimsdale, J. E., & Grant, I. (2006). Personal mastery attenuates the effect of caregiving stress on psychiatric morbidity. *Journal of Nervous and Mental Disease, 194*(2), 132–134.

Maust, D. T., Mavandadi, S., Eakin, A., Streim, J. E., DiFillipo, S., Snedden, T., & Oslin, D. W. (2011). Telephone-based behavioral health assessment for older adults starting a new psychiatric medication. *American Journal of Geriatric Psychiatry, 19*(10), 851–858.

Max, W., Webber, P., & Fox, P. (1995). Alzheimer's disease: The unpaid burden of caring. *Journal of Aging and Health, 7*(2), 179–199.

Mayou, R., Bryant, B., & Duthie, R. (1993). Psychiatric consequences of road traffic accidents. *British Medical Journal, 307*(6905), 647.

Mayr, U. (2008). Introduction to the special section on cognitive plasticity in the aging mind. *Psychology and Aging, 23*(4), 681–683.

McCall, W. V., Reboussin, B. A., & Cohen, W. (2001). Subjective measurement of insomnia and quality of life in depressed inpatients. *Journal of Sleep Research, 9*(1), 43–48.

McCartney, J. R., & Severson, K. (1997). Sexual violence, post-traumatic stress disorder and dementia. *Journal of the American Geriatrics Society, 45*(1), 76.

McCullough, J. P., Jr. (2000). *Treatment for chronic depression: Cognitive behavioral analysis system of psychotherapy (CBASP).* New York, NY: Guilford Press.

McCullough, M. E., Root, L. M., & Cohen, A. D. (2006). Writing about the benefits of an interpersonal transgression facilitates forgiveness. *Journal of Consulting and Clinical Psychology, 74,* 887–897.

McDaniel, S. H., Fogarty, C. T. (2009). What primary care psychology has to offer the patient-centered medical home. *Professional Psychology: Research and Practice, 40,* 483–492.

McGrath, R. E., & Sammons, M. (2011). Prescribing and primary care psychology: Complementary paths for professional psychology. *Professional Psychology: Research and Practice, 42,* 113–120.

McKann, G., Frachman, D., Folstein, M., Katzman, R., Price, D., & Stadlan, E. (1984). Clinical diagnosis of Alzheimer's disease: Report of the NINCDS-ADRDA work group. *Neurology, 34,* 939–944.

McLaughlin, S. J., Connell, C. M., Heeringa, S. G., Li, L. W., & Roberts, J. S. (2010). Successful aging in the United States: Prevalence estimates from a national sample of older adults. *Journals of Gerontology, Series B: Psychological Sciences and Social Sciences, 65*(2), 216.

McNab, F., Varrone, A., Farde, L., Jucaite, A., Bystritsky, P., Forssberg, H., & Klingberg, T. (2009). Changes in cortical dopamine D1 receptor binding associated with cognitive training. *Science, 323*(5915), 800–802.

Mechanic, R., & Altman, S. (2010). Medicare's opportunity to encourage innovation in healthcare delivery. *New England Journal of Medicine, 362,* 772–774.

Meeks, S., & Looney, S. W. (2011). Depressed nursing home residents' activity participation and affect as a function of staff engagement. *Behavior Therapy, 42*(1), 22–29.

Meesters, P., Comijs, H., Droes, R., de Haan, L., Smit, J., Eikelenboom, P., Beekman, A., & Stek., (2013). The care needs of elderly patients with schizophrenia spectrum disorders. *American Journal of Geriatric Psychiatry, 21*(2), 129–137.

Meguro, M., Kasai, M., Akanuma, K., Ishii, H., Yamaguchi, S., & Meguro, K. (2008). Comprehensive approach of donepezil and psychosocial interventions on cognitive function and quality of life for Alzheimer's disease: The Osaki-Tajiri Project. *Age and Aging, 37*(4), 469–473.

Mennin, D. S. (2006). Emotion regulation therapy: An integrative approach to treatment-resistant anxiety disorders. *Journal of Contemporary Psychotherapy, 36*(2), 95–105.

Merikangas, K. R., Ames, M., Cui, L., Stang, P. E., Ustun, T. B., Von Korff, M., & Kessler, R. C. (2007). The impact of comorbidity of mental and physical conditions on role disability in the US adult household population. *Archives of General Psychiatry, 64*(10), 1180–1188.

Meuser, T. M., Marwit, S. J., & Sanders, S. (2004). Assessing grief in family caregivers. In K. Doka (Ed.), *Living with grief: Alzheimer's disease* (pp. 170–195). Washington, DC: Hospice Foundation of America.

Meyer, G. J., Finn, S. E., Eyde, L. D., Kay, G. G., Moreland, K. L., Dies, R. R., ... Reed, G. M. (2001). Psychological testing and psychological assessment: A review of evidence and issues. *American psychologist, 56*(2), 128–165.

Meyer, T. J., Miller, M. L., Metzger, R. L., & Borkovec, T. D. (1990). Development and validation of the Penn State Worry Questionnaire. *Behaviour Research and Therapy, 28,* 487–495.

Miller, B., Paschall, C. B., & Svendsen, D. (2006). Mortality and medical comorbidity among patients with serious mental illness. *Psychiatric Services, 57*(10), 1482–1487.

Miller, K., Siddarth, P., Gaines, J., Parrish, J., Ercoli, L., Marx, K., ... Small, G. W. (2012). The memory fitness program: Cognitive effects of a healthy aging population. *American Journal of Geriatric Psychiatry, 20*(6), 514–523.

Miller, M. D. (2008). Using interpersonal therapy (IPT) with older adults today and tomorrow: A review of the literature and new developments. *Current Psychiatry Reports, 10*(1), 16–22.

Miller, M. D., & Reynolds, C. F., III. (2007). Expanding the usefulness of Interpersonal Psychotherapy (IPT) for depressed elders with co-morbid cognitive impairment. *International Journal of Geriatric Psychiatry, 22*(2), 101–105.

Miller, M. D., Frank, E., Cornes, C., Houck, P. R., & Reynolds, C. F., III. (2003). The value of maintenance interpersonal psychotherapy (IPT) in older adults with different IPT foci. *American Journal of Geriatric Psychiatry, 11*(1), 97–102.

Miller, N. A. (1992). Medicaid 2176 home and community-based care waivers: The first ten years. *Health Affairs, 11*(4), 162–171.

Miller, S. D., Duncan, B. L., & Hubble, M. A. (1997). *Escape from Babel: Toward a unifying language for psychotherapy practice.* New York, NY: WW Norton.

Millon, T., & Bloom, C. (2008). *The Millon Inventories: A practitioner's guide to personalized assessment.* New York, NY: Guilford Press.

Millon, T., & Antoni, M. H. (2001). Test manual for the millon behavioral medicine diagnostic (MBMD). Minneapolis, MN, National Computer Services.

Milstein, G., Manierre, A., & Yali, A. M. (2010). Psychological care for persons of diverse religions: A collaborative continuum. *Professional Psychology: Research and Practice, 41*(5), 371.

Milton, J., Hill-Smith, I., & Jackson, S. (2008). Prescribing for older people. *British Medical Journal, 336,* 606–609.

Mineka, S., & Zinbarg, R. (2006). A contemporary learning theory perspective on the etiology of anxiety disorders: It's not what you thought it was. *American Psychologist, 61*(1), 10.

Mitchell, A. J., Vaze, A., & Rao, S. (2009). Clinical diagnosis of depression in primary care: A meta-analysis. *The Lancet, 374*(9690), 609–619.

Mitsonis, C. I., Potagas, C., Zervas, I., & Sfagos, K. (2009). The effects of stressful life events on the course of multiple sclerosis: A review. *International Journal of Neuroscience, 119*(3), 315–335.

Miyake, A., Friedman, N. P., Emerson, M. J., Witzki, A. H., Howerter, A., & Wager, T. D. (2000). The unity and diversity of executive functions and their contributions to complex "frontal lobe" tasks: A latent variable analysis. *Cognitive Psychology, 41*(1), 49–100.

Mizrahi, R., Starkstein, S. E., Jorge, R., & Robinson, R. G. (2006). Phenomenology and clinical correlates of delusions in Alzheimer disease. *American Journal of Geriatric Psychiatry, 14*(7), 573–581.

Mohlman, J., & Gorman, J. M. (2005). The role of executive functioning in CBT: A pilot study with anxious older adults. *Behaviour Research and Therapy, 43*(4), 447–465.

Mohlman, J., Carmin, C. N., & Price, R. B. (2007). Jumping to interpretations: Social anxiety disorder and the identification of emotional facial expressions. *Behaviour Research and Therapy, 45*(3), 591–599.

Mohlman, J., Gorenstein, E. E., Kleber, M., de Jesus, M., Gorman, J. M., & Papp, L. A. (2003). Standard and enhanced cognitive-behavior therapy for late-life generalized anxiety disorder: Two pilot investigations. *American Journal of Geriatric Psychiatry, 11*(1), 24–32.

Mohlman, J., Price, R. B., Eldreth, D. A., Chazin, D., Glover, D. M., & Wates, W. R. (2009). The relation of worry to prefrontal cortex volume in older adults with and without generalized anxiety disorder. *Psychiatry Research, 173*(2), 121–127.

Mohr, D. C., Hart, S. L., Julian, L., Catledge, C., Honos-Webb, L., Vella, L., & Tasch, E. T. (2005). Telephone-administered psychotherapy for depression. *Archives of General Psychiatry, 62*(9), 1007.

Mojtabai, R., & Olfson, M. (2004). Major depression in community-dwelling middle-aged and older adults: Prevalence and 2- and 4-year follow-up symptoms. *Psychological Medicine, 34*(4), 623–634.

Molinari, V., Chiriboga, D., Branch, L. G., Cho, S., Turner, K., Guo, J., & Hyer, K. (2010). Provision of psychopharmacological services in nursing homes. *Journals of Gerontology, Series B: Psychological Sciences and Social Sciences, 65*(1), 57.

Moncada, L. (2011). Management of falls in older persons: A prescription for prevention. *American Family Physician, 84,* 1267–1276.

Monin, J. K., & Schulz, R. (2009). Interpersonal effects of suffering in older adult caregiving relationships. *Psychology and Aging; Psychology and Aging, 24*(3), 681.

Monroe, N. E., Greco, M. C., & Weiner, D. K. (2008). Mindfulness meditation for the treatment of chronic low back pain in older adults: A randomized controlled pilot study. *Pain, 134,* 310–319.

Monson, C. M., Schnurr, P. P., Resick, P. A., Friedman, M. J., Young-Xu, Y., & Stevens, S. P. (2006). Cognitive processing therapy for veterans with military-related posttraumatic stress disorder. *Journal of Consulting and Clinical Psychology, 74*(5), 898.

Montgomery, P., & Dennis, J. (2004). A systematic review of non-pharmacological therapies for sleep problems in later life. *Sleep Medicine Reviews, 8*(1), 47–62.

Montorio, I., Nuevo, R., Márquez, M., Izal, M., & Losada, A. (2003). Characterization of worry according to severity of anxiety in elderly living in the community. *Aging & Mental Health, 7*(5), 334–341.

Moore, R. G., & Blackburn, I. M. (1997). Clinical section cognitive therapy in the treatment of non-responders to antidepressant medication: A controlled pilot study. *Behavioural and Cognitive Psychotherapy, 25*, 251–259.

Mori, D. L., Lambert, J. F., Niles, B. L., Orlander, J. D., Grace, M., & LoCastro, J. S. (2003). The BAI-PC as a screen for anxiety, depression, and PTSD in Primary Care. *Journal of Clinical Psychology in Medical Settings, 10*, 187–192.

Morin, C. M., Culbert, J. P., & Schwartz, S. M. (1994). Nonpharmacological interventions for insomnia. *American Journal of Psychiatry, 151*(8), 1172.

Morris, J. C., Storandt, M., Miller, J. P., McKeel, D. W., Price, J. L., Rubin, E. H., & Berg, L. (2001). Mild cognitive impairment represents early-stage Alzheimer disease. *Archives of Neurology, 58*(3), 397.

Morrison, A. B., & Chein, J. M. (2011). Does working memory training work? The promise and challenges of enhancing cognition by training working memory. *Psychonomic Bulletin and Review, 18*, 46–60.

Mortimer, J. A., Ebbitt, B., Jun, S. P., & Finch, M. D. (1992). Predictors of cognitive and functional progression in patients with probable Alzheimer's disease. *Neurology, 42*(9), 1689–1689.

Mosconi, L., Pupi, A., & De Leon, M. J. (2008). Brain glucose hypometabolism and oxidative stress in preclinical Alzheimer's disease. *Annals of the New York Academy of Sciences, 1147*(1), 180–195.

Mowszowski, L., Batcheltor, J., & Naismith, S. (2010). Early intervention for cognitive decline: Can CT be used as a selective prevention technique? *International Psychogeriatrics, 22*, 4, 537–548.

Moyer, C. A., Donnelly, M. P., Anderson, J. C., Valek, K. C., Huckaby, S. J., Wiederholt, D. A., ... Rice, B. L. (2011). Frontal electroencephalographic asymmetry associated with positive emotion is produced by very brief meditation training. *Psychological Science, 22*(10), 1277–1279.

Muñoz, R., Beardslee, W., & Leykin , Y. (2012). Major depression can be prevented. *American Psychologist, 67, 6*, 285–295.

Muñoz, R. F., Cuijpers, P., Smit, F., Barrera, A. Z., & Leykin, Y. (2010). Prevention of major depression. *Annual Review of Clinical Psychology, 6*, 181–212.

Muñoz, R. F. (2010). Using evidence-based internet interventions to reduce health disparities worldwide. *Journal of Medical Internet Research, 12*(5), e60.

Murphy, C. F., & Alexopoulos, G. S. (2004). Longitudinal association of initiation/perseveration and severity of geriatric depression. *American Journal of Geriatric Psychiatry, 12*(1), 50–56.

Murphy, C. F., & Alexopoulos, G. S. (2006). Attention network dysfunction and treatment response of geriatric depression. *Journal of clinical and experimental neuropsychology, 28*(1), 96–100.

Nasreddine, Z. S., Phillips, N. A., Bédirian, V., Charbonneau, S., Whitehead, V., Collin, I., ... Chertkow, H. (2005). The Montreal Cognitive Assessment, MoCA: A brief screening tool for mild cognitive impairment. *Journal of the American Geriatrics Society, 53*(4), 695–699.

National Committee for Quality Assurance. (2011). *2011 PCMH standards and guidelines.* Washington, DC: Author. Retrieved from https://inetshop01.pub.ncqa.org/publications/product.asp?dept_id=2&pf_id=30004-301-11

Naugler, C. T., Brymer, C., Stolee, P., Arcese, Z. A. (2000). Development and validation of an improving prescribing in the elderly tool. *Canadian Journal of Clinical Pharmacology, 7*(2), 103–107.

Nebes, R. D., Pollock, B. G., Houck, P. R., Butters, M. A., Mulsant, B. H., Zmuda, M. D., & Reynolds, C. F., III. (2003). Persistence of cognitive impairment in geriatric patients following antidepressant treatment: a randomized, double-blind clinical trial with nortriptyline and paroxetine. *Journal of Psychiatric Research, 37*(2), 99–108.

Nelson, J., & Papakostas, G. (2009). Atypical antipsychotic augmentation in major depressive disorder: A meta-analysis of placebo-controlled randomized trials. *American Journal of Psychiatry, 166*(9), 980–991.

Newman, M. G., Louis, G. C., Thomas D. B., Aaron J. F., & Samuel S. N. (2008). An open trial of integrative therapy for generalized anxiety disorder. *Psychotherapy: Theory, Research, Practice, Training, 45*(2), 135.

Newport, E. (2013, May). New hope for the damaged brain. *Monitor on Psychology, 44*(5), 40.

Newton, J. P. (2010). Elder abuse: An issue not to be ignored. *Gerodontology, 27*(2), 83–84.

Nezu, A. M., Nezu, C. M., Friedman, S. H., Faddis, S., Houts, P. S. (1998). Helping cancer patients cope: A problem-solving approach. *American Psychological Association,* xiii, 314. Washington, DC, US. doi: http://psycnet.apa.org/doi/10.1037/10283-000\t_blank 10.1037/10283-000

Nezu, A. M., Nezu, C. M., & Perri, M. G. (1989). *Problem-solving therapy for depression: Theory, research, and clinical guidelines.* New York, NY: John Wiley.

Noack, H., Lovden, M., Schmiedek, F., & Lindenberger, U. (2009). Cognitive plasticity in adulthood and old age: Gauging the generality of cognitive intervention effects. *Restorative Neurology and Neuroscience, 27,* 435–453.

Norcross, J. C. (2002). Empirically supported therapy relationships. In J. C. Norcross (Ed.), *Psychotherapy relationships that work: Therapist contributions and responsiveness to patient needs* (pp. 3–16). New York, NY: Oxford University Press.

Norcross, J. C. (2006). Integrating self-help into psychotherapy: 16 practical suggestions. *Professional Psychology: Research and Practice, 37*(6), 683.

Nordal, K. (2012). Healthcare reform: Implications for independent practice. *Professional Psychology: Research and Practice, 43*(6), 535–544.

Norman, S. B., Means-Christensen, A. J., Craske, M. G., Sherbourne, C. D., Roy-Byrne, P. P., & Stein, M. B. (2006). Associations between psychological trauma and physical illness in primary care. *Journal of Traumatic Stress, 19*(4), 461–470.

Norris, F. H. (1992). Epidemiology of trauma: Frequency and impact of different potentially traumatic events on different demographic groups. *Journal of Consulting and Clinical Psychology, 60*(3), 409.

Norton, P. J., & Philipp, L. M. (2008). Transdiagnostic approaches to the treatment of anxiety disorders: A quantitative review. *Psychotherapy: Theory, Research, Practice, Training, 45*(2), 214.

Norton, P. J., & Price, E. C. (2007). A meta-analytic review of adult cognitive-behavioral treatment outcome across the anxiety disorders. *Journal of Nervous and Mental Disease, 195*(6), 521–531.

Nussbaum, P. (2008). *Save your brain.* New York, NY: McGraw Hill.

Nutting, P. A., Gallagher, K., Riley, K., White, S., Dickinson, W. P., Korsen, N., & Dietrich, A. (2008). Care management for depression in primary care practice: Findings from the RESPECT-Depression trial. *The Annals of Family Medicine, 6*(1), 30–37.

Nyberg, L., Lövdén, M., Riklund, K., Lindenberger, U., & Bäckman, L. (2012). Memory aging and brain maintenance. *Trends in Cognitive Sciences,* 1–14.

O'Connor, D. W., Ames., D., Gardner, B., & King, M. (2009). Psychosocial treatments of behavior symptoms in dementia: A systematic review of reports meeting quality standards. *International Psychogeriatrics 21*(2), 225–240.

Odden, M., Peralta, C., Haan, M., & Covinsky, K. (2012). Rethinking the association of high blood pressure with mortality in older adults. The impact of frailty. *Archives of Internal Medicine, 172,* 1162–1168.

O'Donohue, W. T., Cummings, N. A., Cucciare, M. A., Runyan, C. N., & Cummings, J. L. (2006). *Integrated behavioral healthcare: A guide to effective intervention.* Amherst, NY: Humanities Books.

Ogles, B. M., Lambert, M. J., & Fields, S. A. (2002). *Essentials of outcome assessment.* New York, NY: John Wiley.

Ogles, B. M., Lambert, M. J., & Sawyer, J. D. (1995). Clinical signifi cance of the National Institute of Mental Health Treatment of Depression Collaborative Research Program data. *Journal of Consulting and Clinical Psychology, 63*(2), 321.

O'Hara, R., Schröder, C. M., Kraemer, H. C., Kryla, N., Cao, C., Miller, E., ... Murphy, G. M. (2005). Nocturnal sleep apnea/hypopnea is associated with lower memory performance in APOE ε4 carriers. *Neurology, 65*(4), 642–644.

Öhman, A., & Mineka, S. (2001). Fears, phobias, and preparedness: Toward an evolved module of fear and fear learning. *Psychological Review, 108*(3), 483.

Olesen, P. J., Westerberg, H., & Klingberg, T. (2004). Increased prefrontal and parietal activity after training of working memory. *Nature Neuroscience, 7*(1), 75–79.

Olfson, M., & Marcus, S. C. (2009). National patterns in antidepressant medication treatment. *Archives of General Psychiatry, 66*(8), 848.

Olfson, M., Marcus, S. C., Druss, B., Elinson, L., Tanielian, T., & Pincus, H. A. (2002). National trends in the outpatient treatment of depression. *Journal of the American Medical Association, 287*(2), 203–209.

Olin, J. T., Schneider, L. S., Katz, I. R., Meyers, B. S., Alexopoulos, G. S., Breitner, J. C., ... & Lebowitz, B. D. (2002). Provisional diagnostic criteria for depression of Alzheimer disease. *The American journal of geriatric psychiatry, 10*(2), 125–128.

Ong, J. C., Shapiro, S. L., & Manber, R. (2009). Mindfulness meditation and cognitive behavioral therapy for insomnia: A naturalistic 12-month follow-up. *Explore—Journal of Science and Healing, 5*(1), 30.

Orlinsky, D. E., Grawe, K., & Parks, B. K. (1994). Process and outcome in psychotherapy: Noch einmal. theory and practice. In B. Boner & L. Beutler (Eds.), *Comprehensive textbook of psychotherapy* (pp. 357–379). New York, NY: Oxford University Press.

Ortega, A. N., Feldman, J. M., Canino, G., Steinman, K., & Alegría, M. (2006). Co-occurrence of mental and physical illness in US Latinos. *Social Psychiatry and Psychiatric Epidemiology, 41*(12), 927–934.

Ostling, S., & Skoog, L. (2002). Psychotic symptoms and paranoid ideation in a nondemented population-based sample of the very old. *Arch Gen Psychiatry, 59,* 53–59.

Ostling, S., Borjesson-Hanson, A., & Skoog, I. (2007). Psychotic symptoms and paranoid ideation in a population-based sample of 95-year-olds. *American Journal of Geriatric Psychiatry, 15,* 999–1004.

Owen, A. M., Hampshire, A., Grahn, J. A., Stenton, R., Dajani, S., Burns, A. S., ... Ballard, C. G. (2010). Putting brain training to the test. *Nature, 465*(7299), 775–778.

Ownby, R. L., Crocco, E., Acevedo, A., John, V., & Loewenstein, D. (2006). Depression and risk for Alzheimer disease: Systematic review, meta-analysis, and metaregression analysis. *Archives of General Psychiatry, 63*(5), 530.

Pacala, J. (2010). *Geriatrics review syllabus (GRS7)* (7th ed.). American Geriatrics Society. New York, NY.

Pacala, J., & Yueh, B. (2012). Hearing deficits in the older patient. *Journal of the American Medical Association, 307,* 1185–1194.

Pachana, N., Byrne, G., Siddle, H., Koloski, N., Harley, E., & Arnold, E. (2007). Development and validation of the Geriatric Anxiety Inventory. *International Psychogeriatrics, 19,* 103–114. doi: 10.1017/S1041610206003504

Palmese, C. A., & Raskin, S. A. (2000). The rehabilitation of attention in individuals with mild traumatic brain injury, using the APT-II programme. *Brain Injury, 14*(6), 535–548.

Papageorgiou, C., & Wells, A. (2001). Metacognitive beliefs about rumination in recurrent major depression. *Cognitive and Behavioral Practice, 8*(2), 160–164.

Paris, J. (2004). Is hospitalization useful for suicidal patients with borderline personality disorder? *Journal of Personality Disorders, 18*(3: Special issue), 240–247.

Park, D. C., & Reuter-Lorenz, P. (2009). The adaptive brain: Aging and neurocognitive scaffolding. *Annual Review of Psychology, 60,* 173–196.

Parker, M. G., & Thorslund, M. (2007). Health trends in the elderly population: getting better and getting worse. *The Gerontologist, 47*(2), 150–158.

Parmelee, P. A., Katz, I. R., & Lawton, M. P. (1991). The relation of pain to depression among institutionalized aged. *Journal of Gerontology, 46*(1), P15–P21.

Paterniti, S., Dufouil, C., & Alpérovitch, A. (2002). Long-term benzodiazepine use and cognitive decline in the elderly: The Epidemiology of Vascular Aging Study. *Journal of Clinical Psychopharmacology, 22*(3), 285–293.

Patterson, T. L., Goldman, S., McKibbin, C. L., Hughs, T., & Jeste, D. V. (2001). UCSD Performance-Based Skills Assessment: Development of a new measure of everyday functioning for severely mentally ill adults. *Schizophrenia Bulletin, 27*(2), 235–245.

Paykel, E. S., Scott, J., Teasdale, J. D., Johnson, A. L., Garland, A., Moore, R., ... Pope, M. (1999). Prevention of relapse in residual depression by cognitive therapy: A controlled trial. *Archives of General Psychiatry, 56*(9), 829.

Peacock, S. C., & Forbes, D. A. (2003). Interventions for caregivers of persons with dementia: A systematic review. [interventions aupres des aidantes naturelles dispensant des soins aux personnes atteintes de demence: Une evaluation systematique]. *Canadian Journal of Nursing Research, 35*(4), 88–107.

Pearce, S., & Cheetham, T. (2010). Diagnosis and management of vitamin D deficiency. *British Medical Journal, 340*, 142–147.

Pearlin, L. I., Schieman, S., Fazio, E. M., & Meersman, S. C. (2005). Stress, health, and the life course: Some conceptual perspectives. *Journal of Health and Social Behavior, 46*(2), 205–219.

Pearson Assessments. (2012). *Cogmed working memory training.* San Antonio, TX: Author. Retrieved from http://www.cogmed.com

Pearson, J., Conwell, Y., & Lyness, J. (1997). Late-life suicide and depression in the primary care setting. *New Directions for Mental Health Services, 76*, 13–38.

Peck, B. M., Hurwicz, M. L., Ory, M., Yuma, P., & Cook, M. A. (2010). Race, gender, and lifestyle discussions in geriatric primary care medical visits. *Health, 2*(10), 1150–1155.

Peek, M. K., Howrey, B. T., Ternent, R. S., Ray, L. A., & Ottenbacher, K. J. (2012). Social support, stressors, and frailty among older mexican american adults. *The Journals of Gerontology Series B: Psychological Sciences and Social Sciences, 67*(6), 755–764.

Pennington, B. F., & Ozonoff, S. (1996). Executive functions and developmental psychopathology. *Journal of Child Psychology and Psychiatry, 37*(1), 51–87.

Penninx, B. W., Van Tilburg, T., Kriegsman, D. M., Boeke, A. J. P., Deeg, D. J., & van Eijk, J. T. M. (1999). Social network, social support, and loneliness in older persons with different chronic diseases. *Journal of Aging and Health, 11*(2), 151–168.

Perlis, M. L., Giles, D. E., Buysse, D. J., Tu, X., & Kupfer, D. J. (1997). Self-reported sleep disturbance as a prodromal symptom in recurrent depression. *Journal of Affective Disorders, 42*(2–3), 209–212.

Perneczky, R., Alexopoulos, P., Schmid, G., Sorg, C., Förstl, H., Diehl-Schmid, J., & Kurz, A. (2011). Cognitive reserve and its relevance for the prevention and diagnosis of dementia. *Nervenarzt, 82*(3), 325–330, 332–335.

Persons, J. (2005). Empiricism, mechanism, and the practice of cognitive behavioral therapy. *Behavior Therapy, 36*, 107–118.

Persons, J. B. (1989). *Cognitive therapy in practice: A case formulation approach.* New York, NY: WW Norton.

Persons, J. B., Burns, D. D., & Perloff, J. M. (1988). Predictors of dropout and outcome in cognitive therapy for depression in a private practice setting. *Cognitive Therapy and Research, 12*(6), 557–575.

Persson, J., & Reuter-Lorenz, P. (2008). Gaining control: Training executive function and far transfer of the ability to resolve interference. *Psychological Science, 19*(9), 881–888.

Petkus, A. J., Wetherell, J. L., Stein, M. B., Liu, L., & Barrett-Connor, E. (2012). History of sexual assault is associated with greater declines in executive functioning in older adults with APOE ε4. *The Journals of Gerontology Series B: Psychological Sciences and Social Sciences, 67*(6), 653–659.

Petrie, E. C., Cross, D. J., Galasko, D., Schellenberg, G. D., Raskind, M. A., Peskind, E. R., & Minoshima, S. (2009). Preclinical evidence of Alzheimer changes: Convergent cerebrospinal fluid biomarker and fluorodeoxyglucose positron emission tomography findings. *Archives of Neurology, 66*(5), 632.

Peyriere, H., Cassan, S., Floutard, E., Riviere, S., Blayac, J. P., Hillaire-Buys, D. A., ... Hansel, S. (2003). Adverse drug events associated with hospital admission. *Annals of Pharmacotherapy, 37*(1), 5–11.

Pfeffer, R. I., Kurosaki, T. T., Chance, J. M., Filos, S., & Bates, D. (1984). Use of the mental function index in older adults: Reliability, validity, and measurement of change over time. *American Journal of Epidemiology, 120*, 922–935.

Pfeffer, R. I., Kurosaki, T. T., Harrah, C. H., Chance, J. M., Filos, S. (1982). Measurement of functional activities in older adults in the community. *Journal of Gerontology, 37*, 323–329.

Pflieger, M., Winslow, B., Mills, K., & Dauber, I. (2011). Medical management of stable coronary artery disease. *American Family Physician, 83*, 819–826.

Pinquart, M., Duberstein, P., & Lyness, J. (2006). Treatments for later-life depressive conditions: A meta-analytic comparison of pharmacotherapy and psychotherapy. *American Journal of Psychiatry, 163*(9), 1493–1501.

Pinquart, M., Duberstein, P. R., & Lyness, J. M. (2007). Effects of psychotherapy and other behavioral interventions on clinically depressed older adults: A meta-analysis. *Aging & Mental Health, 11*(6), 645–657.

Pinquart, M., Silbereisen, R. K., & Körner, A. (2010). Coping with family demands under difficult economic conditions: Associations with depressive symptoms. *Swiss Journal of Psychology/SchweizerischeZeitschriftfürPsychologie/Revue Suisse de Psychologie, 69*(1), 53.

Pinquart, M., & Sörensen, S. (2003a). Associations of stressors and uplifts of caregiving with caregiver burden and depressive mood: A meta-analysis. *The Journals of Gerontology Series B: Psychological Sciences and Social Sciences, 58*(2), P112–P128.

Pinquart, M., & Sörensen, S. (2003b). Differences between caregivers and noncaregivers in psychological health and physical health: A meta-analysis. *Psychology and Aging, 18*(2), 250.

Pinquart, M., & Sörensen, S. (2005). Caregiving distress and psychological health of caregivers. In K.V. Oxington (Ed.), *Psychology of stress* (pp. 165–206). Hauppauge, NY: Nova Biomedical.

Pivec, R., Johnson, A., Mears, S., & Mont, M. (2012). Hiparthroplasty. *Lancet, 380*, 1768–1777.

Plassman, B. L., Williams, J. W., Jr., Burke, J. R., Holsinger, T., & Benjamin, S. (2010). Systematic review: Factors associated with risk for and possible prevention of cognitive decline in later life. *Annals of Internal Medicine, 153*(3), 182.

Pluijm, S. M., Smit, J. H., Tromp, E. A., Stel, V. S., Deeg, D. J., Bouter, L. M., & Lips, P. T. A. M. (2006). A risk profile for identifying community-dwelling elderly with a high risk of recurrent falling: results of a 3-year prospective study. *Osteoporosis International, 17*(3), 417–425.

Porensky, E. K., Dew, M. A., Karp, J. F., Skidmore, E., Rollman, B. L., Shear, M. K., & Lenze, E. J. (2009). The burden of late-life generalized anxiety disorder: effects on disability, health-related quality of life, and healthcare utilization. *The American Journal of Geriatric Psychiatry: Official Journal of the American Association for Geriatric Psychiatry, 17*(6), 473.

Potter, G. G., Kittinger, J. D., Wagner, H. R., Steffens, D. C., & Krishnan, K. R. (2004). Prefrontal neuropsychological predictors of treatment remission in late-life depression. *Neuropsychopharmacology: American College of Neuropsychopharmacology, 29*(12), 2266–2271.

Powlishta, K. K., Storandt, M., Mandernach, T. A., Hogan, E., Grant, E. A., & Morris, J. C. (2004). Absence of effect of depression on cognitive performance in early-stage Alzheimer disease. *Archives of Neurology, 61*(8), 1265.

Price, J. L., & Morris, J. C. (1999). Tangles and plaques in nondemented aging and" preclinical" Alzheimer's disease. *Annals of Neurology, 45*(3), 358–368.

Price, R. B., Siegle, G., & Mohlman, J. (2012). Emotional Stroop performance in older adults: Effects of habitual worry. *American Journal of Geriatric Psychiatry, 20*(9), 798–805.

Pruchno, R. A., Kleban, M. H., Michaels, J. E., & Dempsey, N. P. (1990). Mental and physical health of caregiving spouses: Development of a causal model. *Journal of Gerontology, 45*(5), 192–199.

Rajan, K., Herbert, L., Scherr, P., Mendes dee Leon, C, & Evans, D. (2013). Disability in basic and instrumental activities of daily living is associated with faster rate of decline in cognitive function of older adults. *Journal of Gerontology: A Biological Science of Medical Science, 68*(5), 624–630.

Rajji, T. K., Voineskos, A. N., Butters, M. A., Miranda, D., Arenovich, T., Menon, M., ... Mulsant, B. H. (2013). Cognitive performance of individuals with schizophrenia across seven decades: A study using the MATRICS consensus cognitive battery. *The American Journal of Geriatric Psychiatry, 21*(2), 108–118.

Randolph, C., Tierney, M. C., Mohr, E., & Chase, T. N. (1998). The Repeatable Battery for the Assessment of Neuropsychological Status (RBANS): Preliminary clinical validity. *Journal of Clinical and Experimental Neuropsychology, 20*, 310–319.

Rapoport, M., Judd, L., Schettler, P., Thase, M., Kupfer, D., Frank, E., ... Rush, J. (2002). A descriptive analysis of minor depression. *American Journal of Psychiatry, 159*, 637–643.

Rapoport, M., Mamdani, M., Shulman, K. I., Herrmann, N., & Rochon, P. A. (2005). Antipsychotic use in the elderly: Shifting trends and increasing costs. *International Journal of Geriatric Psychiatry, 20*(8), 749–753.

Rebok, G., Parisi, J., Gross, A., Spira, A., Ko, J., Saamus, Q., ... Holtzmn, R. (2012). Evidence-based psychological treatments for improving memory function among older adults (pp. 131–166). In F. Scogin and A. Shah (Eds), *Making evidence-based psychological treatments work with older adults*. Washington, DC: APA Press.

Rebok, G. W. (2008). CT: Influence on neuropsychological and brain function in later life. *State-of-Science Review*, SR-E22.

Rebok, G. W., & Balcerak, L. J. (1989). Memory self-efficacy and performance differences between younger and older adults: Effects of mnemonic training. *Developmental Psychology, 25*, 714–721.

Reichman, W., & Katz, P. (2008). *Psychiatry in long-term care*. New York: Oxford University Press.

Reichman, W. E., & Conn, D. K. (2010). Nursing home psychiatry: Is it time for a reappraisal? *American Journal of Geriatric Psychiatry, 18*(12), 1049.

Reid, K. J., Martinovich, Z., Finkel, S., Statsinger, J., Golden, R., Harter, K., & Zee, P. C. (2006). Sleep: A marker of physical and mental health in the elderly. *American Journal of Geriatric Psychiatry, 14*(10), 860–866.

Reiman, E., Brinton, R., Katz, R., Peterson, R., Negash, S., Mungas, D., & Aisen, P. (2012). Considerations in the design of clinical trials for cognitive aging. *Journal of Gerontology: Medical Sciences, 67*(7), 766–772.

Reuter-Lorenz, P. A., & Park, D. C. (2010). Human neuroscience and the aging mind: A new look at old problems. *Journal of Gerontology, Series B. Psychological Sciences and Social Sciences, 65*(4), 405–415.

Reynolds, C. F., III, Dew, M. A., Pollock, B. G., Mulsant, B. H., Frank, E., Miller, M. D., ... Kupfer, D. J. (2006). Maintenance treatment of major depression in old age. *New England Journal of Medicine, 354*(11), 1130–1138.

Richmond, L. L., Morrison, A. B., Chein, J. M., & Olson, I. R. (2011). Working memory training and transfer in older adults. *Psychology and Aging*, 1–11.

Richter, H., Ambrée, O., Lewejohann, L., Herring, A., Keyvani, K., Paulus, W., ... Sachser, N. (2008). Wheel-running in a transgenic mouse model of Alzheimer's disease: Protection or symptom? *Behavioural Brain Research, 190*(1), 74–84.

Richter, E., Hyer, L., Noorani, S., & Toole, M. (2009). To treat or not to treat: Ethical deliberation on epilepsy treatment. *Journal of Psychiatry and Law, 36*, 543–576.

Robins, L. N., & Regier, D. A. (1991). *Psychiatric disorders in America: the epidemiologic catchment area study*. New York, NY: Free Press.

Robinson, P. J., & Reiter, J. T. (2007). *Behavioral consultation and primary care: A guide to integrating services.* New York, NY: Springer Publishing Company.

Robinson, P. J., Gould, D. A., & Strosahl, K. D. (2011). *Real behavior change in primary care: Improving patient outcomes & increasing job satisfaction.* Oakland, CA: New Harbinger Publications Incorporated.

Rollnick, S., Miller, W. R., & Butler, C. C. (2007). *Motivational interviewing in health care: Helping patients change behavior.* New York, NY: Guilford Press.

Rollnick, S., Miller, W. R., & Butler, C. C. (2008). *Motivational interviewing in health care: Helping patients change behavior.* New York, NY: Guilford Press.

Rosen, C. (2011). Vitamin D insufficiency. *The New England Journal of Medicine, 364,* 248–254.

Rosenberg, P. B., Mielke, M. M., Xue, Q. L., & Carlson, M. C. (2010). Depressive symptoms predict incident cognitive impairment in cognitive healthy older women. *American Journal of Geriatric Psychiatry: Official Journal of the American Association for Geriatric Psychiatry, 18*(3), 204.

Rosengren, A., Hawken, S., Ôunpuu, S., Sliwa, K., Zubaid, M., Almahmeed, W. A., ... Yusuf, S. (2004). Association of psychosocial risk factors with risk of acute myocardial infarction in 11 119 cases and 13 648 controls from 52 countries (the INTERHEART study): Case-control study. *The Lancet, 364*(9438), 953–962.

Rosenkranz, M. A., Davidson, R. J., MacCoon, D. G., Kalin, J. F., Sheridan, N. H., & Lutz, A. (2013). A comparison of mindfulness-based stress reduction and an active control in modulation of neurogenic inflammation. *Brain, Behavior, and Immunity, 27,* 174–184.

Rotheram-Borus, M. J., Swendeman, D., & Chorpita, B. F. (2012). Disruptive innovations for designing and diffusing evidence-based interventions. *American Psychologist, 67*(6), 463.

Rothermund, K., & Brandstädter, J. (2003). Coping with deficits and losses in later life: From compensatory action to accommodation. *Psychology and Aging, 18*(4), 896.

Rothi, L. J., Fuller, R., Leon, S. A., Kendall, D., Moore, A., Wu, S. S., ... Nadeau, S. E. (2009). Errorless practice as a possible adjuvant to donepezil in Alzheimer's disease. *Journal of the International Neuropsychological Society, 15*(2), 311–322.

Rounsaville, B. J., Chevron, E. S., & Weissman, M. M. (1984). Specification of techniques in interpersonal psychotherapy. *Psychotherapy research: Where are we and where should we go,* 160–171.

Rowe, J. W., & Kahn, R. L. (1997). Successful aging. *The Gerontologist, 37*(4), 433–440.

Rowe, J. W., & Kahn, R. L. (1998). *Successful aging: The MacArthur foundation study.* New York, NY: Pantheon.

Royall, D., Lauterbach, E., Kaufer, D., Malloy, P., Coburn, K., & Black, K. (2007). The cognitive correlates of functional status: A review from the Committee on Research of the American Neuropsychiatric Association. *Journal of Neuropsychiatry and Clinical Neurosciences, 19*(3), 249–265.

Royall, D. R., Chiodo, L. K., & Polk, M. J. (2004). Misclassification is likely in the assessment of mild cognitive impairment. *Neuroepidemiology, 23*(4), 185–191.

Roy-Byrne, P., Post, R. M., Uhde, T. W., Porcu, T., & Davis, D. (2007). The longitudinal course of recurrent affective illness: Life chart data from research patients at the NIMH. *Acta Psychiatrica Scandinavica, 71*(s317), 1–33.

Roy-Byrne, P. P., Stein, M. B., Russo, J., Mercier, E., Thomas, R., McQuaid, J. R., ... Sherbourne, C. D. (1999). Panic disorder in the primary care setting: Comorbidity, disability, service utilization, and treatment. *J Clin Psychiatry, 60,* 492–499.

Ruscio, J., & Ruscio, A. M. (2000). Informing the continuity controversy: A taxometric analysis of depression. *Journal of Abnormal Psychology, 109*(3), 473.

Russo, J., & Vitaliano, P. P. (1995). Life events as correlates of burden in spouse caregivers of persons with Alzheimer's disease. *Experimental Aging Research, 21*(3), 273–294.

Russo, J., Vitaliano, P. P., Brewer, D. D., Katon, W., & Becker, J. (1995). Psychiatric disorders in spouse caregivers of care recipients with Alzheimer's disease and matched controls: A diathesis-stress model of psychopathology. *Journal of Abnormal Psychology, 104*(1), 197.

Rutjes, A. W., Jüni, P., da Costa, B. R., Trelle, S., Nüesch, E., & Reichenbach, S. (2012). Viscosupplementation for osteoarthritis of the knee: A systematic review and meta-analysis. *Annals of internal medicine, 157*(3), 180–191.

Rybarczyk, B., Lopez, M., Benson, R., Alsten, C., & Stepanski, E. (2002). Efficacy of two behavioral treatment programs for comorbid geriatric insomnia. *Psychology and Aging, 17*(2), 288.

Ryff, C. D. (1995). Psychological well-being in adult life. *Current Directions in Psychological Science, 4*(4), 99–104.

Rygh, J. L., & Sanderson, W. C. (2004). *Treating generalized anxiety disorder: Evidence-based strategies, tools, and techniques.* New York, NY: Guilford Press.

Sacks, F., & Campus H. (2010). Dietary therapy in hypertension. *New England Journal of Medicine 362,* 2012–2012.

Saczynski, J. S., Willis, S. L., & Schaie, K. W. (2002). Strategy use in reasoning training with older adults. *Aging, Neurology, and Cognition, 9,* 48–60.

Sadavoy, J. (Ed.). (1996). *Comprehensive review of geriatric psychiatry—II.* Washington, DC: American Psychiatric Press.

Sakashita, C., Slade, T., & Andrews, G. (2007). Empirical investigation of two assumptions in the diagnosis of *DSM-IV* major depressive episode. *Australian and New Zealand Journal of Psychiatry, 41*(1), 17–23.

Sale, A., Berardi, N., & Maffei, L. (2009). Enrich the environment to empower the brain. *Trends in Neurosciences, 32*(4), 233–239.

Salthouse, T. A. (2001). Structural models of the relations between age and measures of cognitive functioning. *Intelligence, 29*(2), 93–115.

Salthouse, T. A. (2012). Are individual differences in rates of aging greater at older ages? *Neurobiology of Aging, 33*(10), 2373–2381. doi:10.1016/j.neurobiolaging.2011.10.018

Salthouse, T. A., & Babcock, R. L. (1991). Decomposing adult age differences in working memory. *Developmental Psychology, 27*(5), 763–776.

Samuels, S. C., & Katz, I. B. (1995). Depression in the nursing home: Depression in the nursing home, elderly as a clinical problem, and the psychiatrist's role in screening, recognition, and treatment. *Psychiatric Annals, 25*(7), 419–424.

Sánchez Palacios, C., Torres, T., & Blanca Mena, M. J. (2009). Negative aging stereotypes and their relation with psychosocial variables in the elderly population. *Archives of Gerontology and Geriatrics, 48*(3), 385–390.

Sanders, K. M., Stuart, A. L., Williamson, E. J., Simpson, J. A., Kotowicz, M. A., Young, D., & Nicholson, G. C. (2010). Annual high-dose oral vitamin D and falls and fractures in older women. *JAMA: Journal of the American Medical Association, 303*(18), 1815–1822.

Sareen, J., Cox, B. J., Stein, M. B., Afifi, T. O., Fleet, C., & Asmundson, G. J. (2007). Physical and mental comorbidity, disability, and suicidal behavior associated with posttraumatic stress disorder in a large community sample. *Psychosomatic Medicine, 69*(3), 242–248.

Satre, D. D., Knight, B. G., & David, S. (2006). Cognitive-behavioral interventions with older adults: Integrating clinical and gerontological research. *Professional Psychology: Research and Practice, 37*(5), 489.

Scarmeas, N., Luchsinger, J. A., Schupf, N., Brickman, A. M., Cosentino, S., Tang, M. X., & Stern, Y. (2009). Physical activity, diet, and risk of Alzheimer disease. *Journal of the American Medical Association, 302*(6), 627–637.

Scarmeas, N., Stern, Y., Tang, M. X., Mayeux, R., & Luchsinger, J. A. (2006). Mediterrranean diet and risk for Alzheimer's disease. *Annals of Neurology, 59*(6), 912–921.

Schacter, D. L., & Addis, D. R. (2007). Constructive memory: The ghosts of past and future. *Nature, 445*(7123), 27–27.

Schiff, G. D., Galanter, W. L., Duhig, J., Lodolce, A. E., Koronkowski, M. J., & Lambert, B. L. (2011). Principles of conservative prescribing. *Archives of Internal Medicine, 171,* 1433–1440.

Schmand, B., Huizenga, H. M., & Van Gool, W. A. (2010). Meta-analysis of CSF and MRI biomarkers for detecting preclinical Alzheimer's disease. *Psychological Medicine, 40*(01), 135–145.

Schmiedek, F., Lovden, M., & Lindenberger, U. (2010). Hundred days of cognitive training enhance broad abilities in adulthood: Findings from the COGITO study. *Frontiers in Aging Neuroscience, 2*(27), 1–10.

Schnurr, P. P., Spiro, A., III, & Paris, A. H. (2000). Physician-diagnosed medical disorders in relation to PTSD symptoms in older male military veterans. *Health Psychology, 19*(1), 91.

Schoevers, R., Smit, F., Deeg, D. J., Cuijpers, P., Dekker, J., van Tilburg, W., & Beekman, A. T. (2006). Prevention of late-life depression in primary care: Do we know where to begin? *American Journal of Psychiatry, 163*(9), 1611–1621.

Schooler, C., Mulatu, M. S., & Oates, G. (1999). The continuing effects of substantively complex work on the intellectual functioning of older workers. *Psychology and Aging, 14*, 483–506.

Schultz, R., Beach, S. R., Lind, B., Martire, L. M., Hirsch, C., Jackson, S., & Burton, L. (2001). Involvement in caregiving and adjustment to death of a spouse. *Journal of the American Medical Association, 285*, 3123–3129.

Schultz, R., Burgio, L., Burns, R., Eisdorfer, C., Gallagher-Thompson, D., Gitlin, L. N., & Mahoney, D. F. (2003). Resources for Enhancing Alzheimer's Caregiver Health (REACH): Overview, site-specific outcomes, and future directions. *The Gerontologist, 43*(4), 514–520.

Schultz, W. (1998). Predictive reward signal of dopamine neurons. *Journal of Neurophysiology, 80*(1), 1–27.

Schuurmans, J., Comijs, H., Emmelkamp, P. M., Gundy, C. M., Weijnen, I., Van Den Hout, M., & Van Dyck, R. (2006). A randomized, controlled trial of the effectiveness of cognitive-behavioral therapy and sertraline versus a waitlist control group for anxiety disorders in older adults. *American Journal of Geriatric Psychiatry, 14*(3), 255–263.

Scogin, F., & McElreath, L. (1994). Efficacy of psychosocial treatments for geriatric depression: A quantitative review. *Journal of Consulting and Clinical Psychology, 62*(1), 69.

Scogin, F., Rickard, H. C., Keith, S., Wilson, J., & McElreath, L. (1992). Progressive and imaginal relaxation training for elderly persons with subjective anxiety. *Psychology and Aging, 7*(3), 419–424.

Scogin, F., Welsh, D., Hanson, A., Stump, J., & Coates, A. (2005). Evidence-based psychotherapies for depression in older adults. *Clinical Psychology: Science and Practice, 12*(3), 222–237.

Scogin, F., & Shah, A. (2012). Introduction to evidence-based psychological treatments for older adults. In F. Scogin & A. Shah (Eds.), *Making evidence-based psychological treatments work with older adults* (pp. 3–8). American Psychological Association.

Scott, R. D. (2009). II. The direct medical costs of healthcare-associated infections in US hospitals and the benefits of prevention. Division of Healthcare Quality Promotion National Center for Preparedness, Detection, and Control of Infectious Diseases Coordinating Center for Infectious Diseases Centers for Disease Control and Prevention March 2009.

Scott, S., Whitehead, B., Bergeman, C., & Pitzer, L. (2013). Combinations of stressors in midlife: Examining role and domain stressors using regression trees and random forests. *Journal of Gerontology, Series B: Psychological Sciences and Social Sciences, 68*(3), 464–475.

Scott, S. B., Jackson, B. R., & Bergeman, C. S. (2011). What contributes to perceived stress in later life? A recursive partitioning approach. *Psychology and Aging, 26*(4), 830–843.

Segal, D. L., Coolidge, F. L., & Hersen, M. (1998). Psychological testing of older people. In I. H. Nordhus, G. R. VandenBos, S. Berg, & P. Fromholt (Eds.), *Clinical geropsychology* (pp. 231–257). Washington, DC: American Psychological Association.

Segal, Z. V., Williams, J. M. G., & Teasdale, J. D. (2012). *Mindfulness-based cognitive therapy for depression*. New York, NY: Guilford Press.

Selbæk, G., Kirkevold, Ø., & Engedal, K. (2007). The prevalence of psychiatric symptoms and behavioural disturbances and the use of psychotropic drugs in Norwegian nursing homes. *International Journal of Geriatric Psychiatry, 22*(9), 843–849.

Seligman, M. E., Rashid, T., & Parks, A. C. (2006). Positive psychotherapy. *American Psychologist, 61*(8), 774.

Selwood, A., Johnston, K., Katona, C., Lyketsos, C., & Livingston, G. (2007). Systematic review of the effect of psychological interventions on family caregivers of people with dementia. *Journal of Affective Disorders, 101*(1–3), 75–89.

Serfaty, M. A., Haworth, D., Blanchard, M., Buszewicz, M., Murad, S., & King, M. (2009). Clinical effectiveness of individual cognitive behavioral therapy for depressed older people in primary care: A randomized controlled trial. *Archives of General Psychiatry, 66*(12), 1332.

Sexton, C. E., Mackay, C. E., & Ebmeier, K. P. (2013). A systematic review and meta-analysis of magnetic resonance imaging studies in late-life depression. *The American Journal of Geriatric Psychiatry, 21*(2), 184–195.

Shah, A., Scogin, F. & Floyd, M. (2012). Evidence-based psychological treatments for geriatric depression. In F. Scogin & A. Shah (Eds.), *Making evidence-based psychological treatments work with older adults* (pp. 131–160). Washington, DC: APA Press.

Shah, P., & Miyake, A. (1999). Toward unified theories of working memory: Emerging general consensus, unresolved theoretical issues, and future research directions. In A. Miyake & P. Shah (Eds.), *Models of working memory: Mechanisms of active maintenance and executive control* (pp. 442–482). New York, NY: Oxford University Press.

Sharp, E., & Gatz, M. (2011). Relationship between education and dementia: An updated systematic review. *Alzheimer's Disease and Associated Disorders, 25*(4), 289–304.

Shaw C., McNamara, R., Abrams K., Cannings-John, R., Hood, K., Longo, M., ... Williams, K. (2009). Systematic review of respite care in the frail elderly. *Health Technology Assessment 13*(20), 1–246.

Shedler, J. (2010). The efficacy of psychodynamic psychotherapy. *American Psychologist, 68*(2), 98–109.

Shega, J. W., Hougham, G. W., Stocking, C. B., Cox-Hayley, D., & Sachs, G. A. (2004). Pain in community-dwelling persons with dementia: Frequency, intensity, and congruence between patient and caregiver report. *Journal of Pain and Symptom Management, 28*(6), 585–592.

Shekleton, J. A., Rogers, N. L., & Rajaratnam, S. M. (2010). Searching for the daytime impairments of primary insomnia. *Sleep Medicine Reviews, 14*(1), 47.

Sheline, Y. I., Wang, P. W., Gado, M. H., Csernansky, J. G., & Vannier, M. W. (1996). Hippocampal atrophy in recurrent major depression. *Proceedings of the National Academy of Sciences, 93*(9), 3908–3913.

Sia, C., Tonniges, T. F., & Osterhus, E. (2004). History of the medical home concept. *Pediatrics, 113*, 1473–1478.

Sigström, R., Skoog, I., & Sacuiu, S. (2009). The prevalence of psychotic symptoms and paranoid ideation in nondemented population samples aged 70–82 years. *International Journal of Geriatric Psychiatry, 24*, 1413–1419.

Silverstein, M. (2013). Gerontology gone viral. *Journals of Gerontology, Series B: Psychological Sciences and Social Sciences, 68*, 71–72.

Simning, A., Richardson, T. M., & Friedman, B. (2010). Mental distress and service utilization among help-seeking, community-dwelling older adults. *International Psychogeriatrics, 22*, 739–749.

Simning A., van Wijngaarden, E., Fisher, S. G., Richardson, T. M., & Conwell, Y. (2012, May). Mental healthcare need and service utilization in older adults living in public housing. *The American Journal of Geriatric Psychiatry, 20*(5), 441–451. ISSN 1064–7481, http://dx.doi .org/10.1097/JGP.0b013e31822003a7

Simon, G. E., Ludman, E. J., Tutty, S., Operskalski, B., & Von Korff, M. (2004). Telephone psychotherapy and telephone care management for primary care patients starting anti-depressant treatment. *Journal of the American Medical Association, 292*(8), 935–942.

Simon, G. E., VonKorff, M., Rutter, C., & Wagner, E. (2000). Randomised trial of monitoring, feedback, and management of care by telephone to improve treatment of depression in primary care. *British Medical Journal, 320*(7234), 550–554.

Simon, S. S., Yokomizo, J. E., & Bottino, C. (2012). Cognitive intervention in amnestic mild cognitive impairment: A systematic review. *Neuroscience & Biobehavioral Reviews, 36*(4), 1163–1178.

Sink, K. M., Leng, X., Williamson, J., Kritchevsky, S., Yaffe, K., Psaty, B., ... Goff, D. (2007, April). Centrally active ACE inhibitors may slow cognitive decline: The cardiovascular health study. *Journal of the American Geriatrics Society, 55*(4), S14–S14.

Sinoff, G., & Werner, P. (2003). Anxiety disorder and accompanying subjective memory loss in the elderly as a predictor of future cognitive decline. *International Journal of Geriatric Psychiatry, 18*(10), 951–959.

Sinusas, K. (2012). Osteoarthritis: Diagnosis and treatment. *American Family Physician, 85*, 49–56.

Sitzer, D. I., Twamley, E. W., & Jeste, D. V. (2006). Cognitive training in Alzheimer's disease: A meta-analysis of the literature. *Acta Psychiatrica Scandinavica, 114*, 75–90.

Sitzer, D., I., Twamley, E. W., Patterson, T. L., & Jeste, D. V. (2008). Multivariate predictors of social skills performance in middle-aged and older outpatients with schizophrenia spectrum disorders. *Psychological Medicine, 38*(5), 755–763.

Slade, T., & Andrews, G. (2005). Latent structure of depression in a community sample: a taxometric analysis. *Psychological Medicine, 35*(4), 489–497.

Slade, T. I. M., & Watson, D. (2006). The structure of common DSM-IV and ICD-10 mental disorders in the Australian general population. *Psychological Medicine, 36*(11), 1593–1600.

Smith, G. E., Housen, P., Yaffe, K., Ruff, R., Kennison, R. F., Mahncke, H. W., & Zelinski, E. M. (2009). A cognitive training program based on principles of brain plasticity: Results from the improvement in memory with plasticity-based adaptive cognitive training (IMPACT) study. *Journal of the American Geriatrics Society, 57*(4), 594–603.

Smith, N. M., Floyd, M. R., Scogin, F., & Jamison, C. S. (1997). Three-year follow-up of bibliotherapy for depression. *Journal of Consulting and Clinical Psychology, 65*(2), 324.

Smith, T., Gildeh, N., & Holmes, C. (2007). The Montreal Cognitive Assessment: Validity and utility in a memory clinic setting. *Canadian Journal of Psychiatry, 52*, 329–332.

Smith, T. L., & Toseland, R. W. (2006). The effectiveness of a telephone support program for caregivers of frail older adults. *The Gerontologist, 46*(5), 620–629.

Sneed, J. R., Culang, M. E., Keilp, J. G., Rutherford, B. R., Devanand, D. P., & Roose, S. P. (2010). Antidepressant medication and executive dysfunction: A deleterious interaction in late-life depression. *American Journal of Geriatric Psychiatry, 18*(2), 128–135.

Sneed, J. R., Roose, S. P., Keilp, J. G., Krishnan, K. R. R., Alexopoulos, G. S., & Sackeim, H. A. (2007). Response inhibition predicts poor antidepressant treatment response in very old depressed patients. *American Journal of Geriatric Psychiatry, 15*(7), 553–563.

Sneed, J. R., Rutherford, B. R., Rindskopf, D., Lane, D. T., Sackeim, H. A., & Roose, S. P. (2008). Design makes a difference: A meta-analysis of antidepressant response rates in placebo-controlled versus comparator trials in late-life depression. *American Journal of Geriatric Psychiatry, 16*(1), 65–73.

Snow, A. L., Powers, D., & Liles, D. (2006). Cognitive-behavioral therapy for long-term care patients with dementia. *Geropsychological interventions in long-term care* (pp. 265–294). New York, NY: Springer Publishing Company.

Snow, K. (1999, November). *Cognitive behavioral therapy with compromised older adults.* Paper presented at the fifty-second annual scientific meeting of the Gerontological Society of America. San Francisco, CA, November 1999.

Snowden, M., Sato, K., & Roy-Byrne, P. (2003). Assessment and treatment of nursing home residents with depression or behavioral symptoms associated with dementia: A review of the literature. *Journal of the American Geriatrics Society, 51*(9), 1305–1317.

Snyder, L., Jenkins, C., & Joosten, L. (2007). Effectiveness of support groups for people with mild to moderate Alzheimer's disease: An evaluative survey. *American Journal of Alzheimer's Disease and Other Dementias, 22*(1), 14–19.

Snyder, L., Bower, D., Arneson, S., Shepherd, S, & Quayhagen, M. (1993). *Coping with Alzheimer's disease and related disorders: An educational support group for early-stage individuals and their families.* San Diego, CA: University of California, San Diego, Alzheimer's Disease Research Center.

Sokal, J., Messias, E., Dickerson, F. B., Kreyenbuhl, J., Brown, C. H., Goldberg, R. W., & Dixon, L. B. (2004). Comorbidity of medical illnesses among adults with serious mental illness who are receiving community psychiatric services. *Journal of Nervous and Mental Disease, 192*(6), 421–427.

Solomon, P. R., Hirschoff, A., Kelly, B., Relin, M., Brush, M., DeVeaux, R. D., Pendlebury, W. W. (1998). A 7-minute neurocognitive screening battery highly sensitive to Alzheimer's disease. *Archives of Neurology, 55*, 349–355.

Song, H. S., & Lehrer, P. M. (2003). The effects of specific respiratory rates on heart rate and heart rate variability. *Applied Psychophysiology and Biofeedback, 28*, 13–23.

Sörensen, S., Pinquart, M., & Duberstein, P. (2002). How effective are interventions with caregivers? An updated meta-analysis. *The Gerontologist, 42*(3), 356–372.

Souchay, C. (2007). Metamemory in Alzheimer's disease. *Cortex, 43*(7), 987–1003.

Spector, W. D., Mutter, R., Owens, P., & Limcangco, R. (2012). Thirty-day, all-cause readmissions for elderly patients who have an injury-related inpatient stay. *Medical Care, 50*(10), 863–869.

Sperling, R. A., Aisen, P. S., Beckett, L. A., Bennett, D. A., Craft, S., Fagan, A. M., ... Phelps, C. H. (2011). Toward defining the preclinical stages of Alzheimer's disease: Recommendations from the National Institute on Aging–Alzheimer's Association workgroups on diagnostic guidelines for Alzheimer's disease. *Alzheimer's and Dementia, 7*(3), 280–292.

Spijker, A., Verhey, F., Graff, M., Grol, R., Adang, E., Wollersheim, H., Vernooij-Dassen, M. (2009). Systematic care for caregivers of people with dementia in the ambulatory mental health service: Designing a multicentre, cluster, randomized, controlled trial. *BMC Geriatrics, 9*(1), 21.

Spira, A. P., Friedman, L., Aulakh, J. S., Lee, T., Sheikh, J. I., & Yesavage, J. A. (2008). Subclinical anxiety symptoms, sleep, and daytime dysfunction in older adults with primary insomnia. *Journal of Geriatric Psychiatry and Neurology, 21*(2), 149–153.

Spiro, A., Schnurr, P. P., & Aldwin, C. M. (1994). Combat-related posttraumatic stress disorder symptoms in older men. *Psychology and Aging, 9*(1), 17.

Spiro, R. J., & Sherif, C. W. (2011). Consistency and relativity in selective recall with differing ego-involvement. *British Journal of Social and Clinical Psychology, 14*(4), 351–361.

Staab, J. P., & Evans, D. L. (2000). Efficacy of venlafaxine in geriatric depression. *Depression and Anxiety, 12*(S1), 63–68.

Staff, R. T., Murray, A. D., Deary, I. J., & Whalley, L. J. (2004). What provides cerebral reserve? *Brain, 127*(5), 1191–1199.

Stanghellini, G. (2009). The meanings of psychopathology. *Clinical Opinion in Psychiatry, 22* (6), 557–562.

Stanley, M. A., Bush, A. L., Camp, M. E., Jameson, J. P., Phillips, L. L., Barber, C. R., ... Cully, J. A. (2011). Older adults' preferences for religion/spirituality in treatment for anxiety and depression. *Aging & Mental health, 15*(3), 334–343.

Stanley, M. A., Wilson, N. L., Novy, D. M., Rhoades, H. M., Wagener, P. D., Greisinger, A. J., ... Kunik, M. E. (2009). Cognitive behavior therapy for generalized anxiety disorder among older adults in primary care. *Journal of the American Medical Association, 301*(14), 1460–1467.

Steffen, A. M. (2000). Anger management for dementia caregivers: A preliminary study using video and telephone interventions. *Behavior Therapy, 31*(2), 281–299.

Steinman, M., & Hanlon, J. (2010). Managing medications in clinically complex elders. "There's got to be a happy medium." *Journal of the American Medical Association, 304*, 1592–1601.

Stessman, J., Hammerman-Rozenberg, R., Cohen, A., Ein-Mor, E., & Jacobs, J. M. (2009). Physical activity, function, and longevity among the very old. *Archives of Internal Medicine, 169*(16), 1476.

Stine-Morrow, E. A. L., Parisi, J. M., Morrow, D. G., & Park, D. C. (2008). The effects of an engaged lifestyle on cognitive vitality: A field experiment. *Psychology and Aging, 23*, 778–786.

Stone, M., Laughren, T., Jones, M. L., Levenson, M., Holland, P. C., Hughes, A., ... Rochester, G. (2009). Risk of suicidality in clinical trials of antidepressants in adults: Analysis of proprietary data submitted to U.S. Food and Drug Administration. *British Medical Journal, 339*.

Strack, S. (1991). Factor analysis of MCMI-II and PACL basic personality scales in a college sample. *Journal of Personality Assessment, 57*(2), 345–355.

Strandberg, T., Pitkala, K., Bergline, S., Nieminen, M., & Tilvis, R. (2006). Multifactorial intervention to prevent recurrent cardiovascular events in patients 75 years or older: The Drugs and Evidence-Based Medicine in the Elderly (DEBATE) study: A randomized, controlled trial. *American Heart Journal, 152*, 585–592.

Studenski, S., Carlson, M. C., Fillit, H., Greenough, W. T., Kramer, A., & Rebok, G. W. (2006). From bedside to bench: Does mental and physical activity promote cognitive vitality in late life? *Science of Aging Knowledge Environment 2006*(10), 21.

Styron, W. (1989). Darkness visible: A memoir of madness. *Vanity Fair*. New York, NY: Conde Nast.

Sudak, D., Roy, A., & Sudak, H. (2007). Deficiencies in suicide training in primary care specialties: A survey of training directors. *Academic Psychiatry, 31*, 345–349.

Suthers, K. (2008). *Evaluating the economic causes and consequences of racial and ethnic health disparities*. Washington, DC: American Public Health Association.

Szasz, T. S. (1997). *The manufacture of madness: A comparative study of the inquisition and the mental health movement*. Syracuse, NY: Syracuse University Press.

Tariot, P. N., & Ismail, M. S. (2002). Use of quetiapine in elderly patients. *Journal of Clinical Psychiatry, 63*, 21–26.

Tariot, P. N., Raman, R., Jakimovich, L., Schneider, L., Porsteinsson, A., Thomas, R., ... Thal, L. (2005). Divalproex sodium in nursing home residents with possible or probable Alzheimer disease complicated by agitation: A randomized, controlled trial. *American Journal of Geriatric Psych, 13*(11), 942–949.

Teachman, B. A., Siedlecki, K. L., & Magee, J. C. (2007). Aging and symptoms of anxiety and depression: Structural invariance of the tripartite model. *Psychology and Aging, 22*(1), 160.

Teasdale, J. D., Segal, Z. V., Williams, J. M. G., Ridgeway, V. A., Soulsby, J. M., & Lau, M. A. (2000). Prevention of relapse/recurrence in major depression by mindfulness-based cognitive therapy. *Journal of Consulting and Clinical Psychology, 68*, 615–623.

Teresi, J., Abrams, R., Holmes, D., Ramirez, M., & Eimicke, J. (2001). Prevalence of depression and depression recognition in nursing homes. *Social Psychiatry and Psychiatric Epidemiology, 36*(12), 613–620.

Teri, L., & Gallagher-Thompson, D. (1991). Cognitive-behavioral interventions for treatment of depression in Alzheimer's patients. *The Gerontologist, 31*(3), 413–416.

Teri, L., Curtis, J., Gallagher-Thompson, D. & Thompson L. (1994). Cognitive-behavioral therapy with depressed older adults. In L. S. Schneider, C. F. Reynolds, B. D. Lebowitz & A. J. Friedhoff (Eds.), *Diagnosis and treatment of depression in late life: Results of the NIH consensus development conference* (pp. 279–291). Washington, DC: American Psychiatric Press.

Teri, L., Logsdon, R. G., Uomoto, J., & McCurry, S. M. (1997). Behavioral treatment of depression in dementia patients: A controlled clinical trial. *Journals of Gerontology, Series B: Psychological Sciences and Social Sciences, 52*(4), P159.

Teri, L., McCurry, S. M., Logsdon, R., & Gibbons, L. E. (2005). Training community consultants to help family members improve dementia care: A randomized controlled trial. *The Gerontologist, 45*(6), 802–811.

Thapa, P. B., Gideon, P., Cost, T. W., Milam, A. B., & Ray, W. A. (1998). Antidepressants and the risk of falls among nursing home residents. *New England Journal of Medicine, 339*(13), 875–882.

Thase, M. E., Greenhouse, J. B., Frank, E., Reynolds, C. F., III, Pilkonis, P. A., Hurley, K., ... Kupfer, D. J. (1997). Treatment of major depression with psychotherapy or psychotherapy-pharmacotherapy combinations. *Archives of General Psychiatry, 54*(11), 1009.

Thielke, S., Vannoy, S., & Unützer, J. (2007). Integrating mental health and primary care. *Primary Care: Clinics in Office Practice, 34*(3), 571–592.

Thomas, A. (2012). Keep calm and carry on: Progress in understanding depression, neuro-cognitive impairments, and dementia. *The American Journal of Geriatric Psychiatry, 20*(8), 641–644.

Thompson, L. W., Coon, D. W., Gallagher-Thompson, D., Sommer, B. R., & Koin, D. (2001). Comparison of desipramine and cognitive/behavioral therapy in the treatment of elderly outpatients with mild-to-moderate depression. *American Journal of Geriatric Psychiatry, 9*(3), 225–240.

Thompson, L. W., Gallagher, D., & Breckenridge, J. S. (1987). Comparative effectiveness of psychotherapies for depressed elders. *Journal of Consulting and Clinical Psychology, 55*(3), 385.

Thompson, S., Herrmann, N., Rapoport, M. J., & Lanctot, K. L. (2007). Efficacy and safety of antidepressants for treatment of depression in Alzheimer's disease: A metaanalysis. *Canadian journal of psychiatry. Revue canadienne de psychiatrie, 52*(4), 248.

The TIME Investigators. (2001). Trial of invasive versus medical therapy in elderly patients with chronic symptomatic coronary-artery disease (TIME): A randomised trial. *Lancet, 358*, 951–957.

Tinetti, M., Baker, D., McAvay, G., Claus,E., et. al. (1994). A multifactorial intervention to reduce the risk of falling among elderly people living in the community. *New England Journal of Medicine, 331*, 821–827.

Tinetti, M. E., Bogardus, S. T., Jr., & Agostini, J. V. (2004). Potential pitfalls of disease-specific guidelines for patients with multiple conditions. *New England Journal of Medicine, 351*, 2870.

Tomlinson, B. E., Blessed, G., & Roth, M. (1968). Observations on the brains of non-demented old people. *Journal of the Neurological Sciences, 7*(2), 331–356.

Treiber, K. A., Carlson, M. C., Corcoran, C., Norton, M. C., Breitner, J. C., Piercy, K. W., ... Tschanz, J. T. (2011). Cognitive stimulation and cognitive and Functional decline in Alzheimer's disease: The Cache County Dementia Progression Study. *Journals of Gerontology, Series B: Psychological Sciences and Social Sciences, 66*(4), 416–425.

Troyer, A. K., Murphy, K. J., Anderson, N. D., Moscovitch, M., & Craik, F. I. (2008).Changing everyday memory behaviour in amnestic mild cognitive impairment: A randomized controlled trial. *Neuropsychological Rehabilitation, 18*(1), 65–88.

Uebelacker, L. A., Wang, P. S., Berglund, P., & Kessler, R. C. (2006). Clinical differences among patients treated for mental health problems in general medical and specialty mental health settings in the National Comorbidity Survey Replication (NCS-R). *General Hospital Psychiatry, 28*(5), 387.

Unützer, J., Patrick, D. L., & Simon, G. (1997). Depressive symptoms and cost of health services in HMO patients aged 65 years and older. *Journal of the American Medical Association, 277*(1618), 23.

Unützer, J., Schoenbaum, M., Katon, W., Fan, M., Pincus, H., Hogan, D., & Taylor, J. (2009). Health care costs associated with depression in medically ill fee-for-service Medicare participants. *Journal of the American Geriatric Society.* [E-pub ahead of print Jan. 16, 2009].

Unützer, J., Katon, W., Callahan, C. M., Williams, J. W., Jr., Hunkeler, E., Harpole, L., ... Langston, C. (2002). Collaborative care management of late-life depression in the primary care setting. *Journal of the American Medical Association, 288*(22), 2836–2845.

Unverzagt, F. W., Smith, D. M., Rebok, G. W., Marsiske, M., Morris, J. N., Jones, R., ... Tennstedt, S. (2009). The Indiana Alzheimer Disease Center's symposium on mild cognitive impairment. CT in older adults: Lessons from the ACTIVE study. *Current Alzheimer Research, 6*(4), 375–383.

U.S. Department of Health and Human Services. (1999). *Mental health: A report of the sur-geon general.* Rockville, MD: U.S. Department of Health and Human Services, National Institutes of Health.

U.S. Preventive Task Force. (2009). Screening for depression in adults. *Annals of Internal Medicine, 151*, 784–792.

Vaillant, G., & Sharp, T. (2002). Ageing well: Surprising guideposts to a happier life. *Sort,* *5*, 4.

Valentijn, S. A., van Hooren, S. A., Bosma, H., Touw, D. M., Jolles, J., van Boxtel, M. P., & Ponds, R. W. (2005). The effect of two types of memory training on subjective and objective memory performance in healthy individuals aged 55 years and older: A randomized controlled trial. *Patient Education and Counseling, 57*(1), 106–114.

Valenzuela, M., Brayne, C., Sachdev, P., Wilcock, G., Matthews, F., & Medical Research Council Cognitive Function and Ageing Study. (2011). Cognitive lifestyle and long-term risk of dementia and survival after diagnosis in a multicenter population-based cohort. *American Journal of Epidemiology, 173*(9), 1004–1012.

Valenzuela, M., & Sachdev, P. (2009). Can cognitive exercise prevent the most onset of dementia? Systematic review of randomized clinical trials with longitudinal follow-up. *American Journal of Geriatric Psychiatry, 17*(3), 179–187.

Vannoy, S. D., Duberstein, P., Cukrowicz, K., Lin, E., Fan, M. Y., & Unützer, J. (2007). The relationship between suicide ideation and late-life depression. *American Journal of Geriatric Psychiatry, 15*(12), 1024–1033.

van Ojen, R., Hooijer, C., Bezemer, D., Jonker, C., Lindeboom, J., & van Tilburg, W. (1995). Late-life depressive disorder in the community. I. The relationship between MMSE score and depression in subjects with and without psychiatric history. *British Journal of Psychiatry, 166*(3), 311–315.

van't Veer-Tazelaar, N., van Marwijk, H., van Oppen, P., Nijpels, G., van Hout, H., Cuijpers, P., ... Beekman, A. (2006). Prevention of anxiety and depression in the age group of 75 years and over: A randomised controlled trial testing the feasibility and effectiveness of a generic stepped care programme among elderly community residents at high risk of developing anxiety and depression versus usual care [ISRCTN26474556]. *BMC Public Health, 6*(1), 186.

van't Veer-Tazelaar, P., Smit, F., van Hout, H., van Oppen, P., van der Horst, H., Beekman, A., & van Marwijk, H. (2010). Cost-effectiveness of a stepped care intervention to prevent depression and anxiety in late life: Randomised trial. *The British Journal of Psychiatry, 196*(4), 319–325.

Vasterling, J., Jenkins, R. A., Tope, D. M., & Burish, T. G. (1993). Cognitive distraction and relaxation training for the control of side effects due to cancer chemotherapy. *Journal of Behavioral Medicine, 16*(1), 65–80.

Verhaeghen, P., & Marcoen, A. (1996). On the mechanisms of plasticity in young and Older adults after instruction in the method of loci: Evidence for an amplification model. *Psychology and Aging, 11*(1), 164–178.

Verhaeghen, P., Marcoen, A., & Goossens, L. (1992). Improving memory performance in the aged through mnemonic training: A meta-analytic study. *Psychology and Aging, 7*(2), 242–251.

de Villers-Sidani, E., Alzghoul, L., Zhou, X., Simpson, K. L., Lin, R. C., & Merzenich, M. M. (2010). Recovery of functional and structural age-related changes in the rat primary auditory cortex with operant training. *Proceedings of the National Academy of Sciences, 107*(31), 13900–13905.

Vincent, N., & Lewycky, S. (2009). Logging on for better sleep: RCT of the effectiveness of online treatment for insomnia. *Sleep, 32*(6), 807.

Vink, D., Aartsen, M. J., & Schoevers, R. A. (2008). Risk factors for anxiety and depression in the elderly: A review. *Journal of Affective Disorders, 106*(1–2), 29.

Vitaliano, P. P., Russo, J., Young, H. M., Teri, L., & Maiuro, R. D. (1991). Predictors of burden in spouse caregivers of individuals with Alzheimer's disease. *Psychology and Aging, 6*(3), 392.

Vitaliano, P. P., Zhang, J., Young, H. M., Caswell, L. W., Scanlan, J. M., & Echeverria, D. (2009). Depressed mood mediates decline in cognitive processing speed in caregivers. *The Gerontologist, 49*(1), 12–22.

Vogt Yuan, A. S. (2007). Perceived age discrimination and mental health. *Social Forces, 86*(1), 291–311.

Waldorff, F. B., Siersma, V., Vogel, A., Waldemar, G. (2012). Subjective memory complaints in general practice predicts future dementia: A 4-year follow-up study. *International Journal of Geriatric Psychiatry, 27*, 1180–1188.

Walker, J., & Wynne, H. (1994). Review: The frequency and severity of adverse drug reactions in elderly people. *Age and Ageing, 23*(3), 255–259.

Walling, A., & Dickson, G. (2012). Hearing loss in older adults. *American Family Physician, 85*, 1150–1156.

Wallston, K. A., Wallston, B. S., Smith, S., & Dobbins, C. J. (1987). Perceived control and health. *Current Psychology, 6*(1), 5–25.

Walsh, R. (2011). Lifestyle and mental health. *American Psychologist, 66*(7), 579.

Walters, G. (2010). Dementia: Continuum or distinct entity. *Psychology and Aging, 25*(3), 534–544.

Wampold, B. E. (2001). *The great psychotherapy debate: Models, methods, and findings.* Routledge.

Wang, H., Karp, A., Winblad, B., & Fratiglioni, L. (2002). Late-life engagement in social and leisure activities is associated with a decreased risk of dementia: A longitudinal study from the Kungsholmen project. *American Journal of Epidemiology, 155*, 1081–1087.

Wang, J-J. (2005). The effects of reminiscence on depressive symptoms and mood status of older institutionalized adults in Taiwan. *International Journal of Geriatric Psychiatry. 20*(1), 57–62.

Warburton, D. E., Nicol, C. W., & Bredin, S. S. (2006). Health benefits of physical activity: The evidence. *Canadian Medical Association Journal, 174*(6), 801–809.

Warner, M. L. (2000). *The complete guide to Alzheimer's proofing your home.* West Lafayette, IN: Purdue University Press

Wechsler, D. (2011). *Wechsler abbreviated scale of intelligence* (2nd ed.). San Antonio, TX: Pearson Education.

Weeks, S. K., McGann, P. E., Michaels, T. K., & Penninx, B. W. (2003). Comparing various short-form geriatric depression scales leads to the GDS-5/15. *Journal of Nursing Scholarship, 35*(2), 133–137.

Weintraub, D., Datto, C. J., Streim, J. E., & Katz, I. R. (2008). Second-generation issues in the management of depression in nursing homes. *Journal of the American Geriatrics Society, 50*(12), 2100–2101.

Weiss, J. H. (1974). The current state of the concept of a psychosomatic disorder. *International Journal of Psychiatry in Medicine, 5*(4), 473–482.

Weissman, M. M., Markowitz, J. C., & Klerman, G. (2008). *Comprehensive guide to interpersonal psychotherapy.* New York, NY: Basic Books.

Wells, A. (2002). *Emotional disorders and metacognition: Innovative cognitive therapy.* New York, NY: John Wiley.

Wells, A., & King, P. (2006). Metacognitive therapy for generalized anxiety disorder: An open trial. *Journal of Behavior Therapy and Experimental Psychiatry, 37*(3), 206–212.

West, R. L., Bagwell, D. K., & Dark-Freuderman, A. (2008). Self-efficacy and memory aging: The impact of a memory intervention based on self-efficacy. *Aging, Neuropsychology, and Cognition, 15*, 302–329.

West, R. L., Dark-Freudeman, A., & Bagwell, D. K. (2009). Goals-feedback conditions and episodic memory: Mechanisms for memory gains in older and younger adults. *Memory, 17*(2), 233–244.

West, R. L., & Hastings, E. C. (2011). Self-regulation and recall: Growth curve modeling of intervention outcomes for older adults. *Psychology and Aging, 26*(4), 803–812.

Westen, D., & Morrison, K. (2001). A multidimensional meta-analysis of treatments for depression, panic, and generalized anxiety disorder: An empirical examination of the status of empirically supported therapies. *Journal of Consulting and Clinical Psychology, 69*(6), 875.

Westerberg, H., Jacobaeus, H., Hirvikoski, T., Clevberger, P., Ostensson, M. L., Bartfai, A., & Klingberg, T. (2007). Computerized working memory training after stroke–A pilot study. *Brain Injury, 21*(1), 21–29.

Westra, H. (2012). *Movivational interviewing in the treatment of anxiety.* New York, NY: Guldford Press.

Wetherell, J. L. (1998). Treatment of anxiety in older adults. *Psychotherapy: Theory, Research, Practice, Training; Psychotherapy: Theory, Research, Practice, Training, 35*(4), 444.

Wetherell, J. L., Ayers, C. R., Sorrell, J. T., Thorp, S. R., Nuevo, R., Belding, W., ... Patterson, T. L. (2009). Modular psychotherapy for anxiety in older primary care patients. *American Journal of Geriatric Psychiatry: Official Journal of the American Association for Geriatric Psychiatry, 17*(6), 483.

Wetherell, J. L., & Gatz, M. (2001). Recruiting anxious older adults for a psychotherapy outcome study. *Journal of Clinical Geropsychology, 7*(1), 29–38.

Wetherell, J. L., Gatz, M., & Craske, M. G. (2003). Treatment of generalized anxiety disorder in older adults. *Journal of Consulting and Clinical Psychology, 71*(1), 31.

Wetherell, J. L., Kaplan, R. M., Kallenberg, G., Dresselhaus, T. R., Sieber, W. J., & Lang, A. J. (2004). Mental health treatment preferences of older and younger primary care patients. *International Journal of Psychiatry in Medicine, 34*(3), 219–233.

Wetherell, J. L., Lenze, E. J., & Stanley, M. A. (2005). Evidence-based treatment of geriatric anxiety disorders. *Psychiatric Clinics of North America, 28*(4), 871–896.

Wetherell, J. L., Liu, L., Patterson, T. L., Afari, N., Ayers, C. R., Thorp, S. R., ... Petkus, A. J. (2011). Acceptance and commitment therapy for generalized anxiety disorder in older adults: A preliminary report. *Behavior Therapy, 42*(1), 127–134.

Wetherell, J. L., Reynolds, C. A., Gatz, M., & Pedersen, N. L. (2002). Anxiety, cognitive performance, and cognitive decline in normal aging. *Journals of Gerontology, Series B: Psychological Sciences and Social Sciences, 57*(3), P246–P255.

Whitmer, R., Karter, A., Yaffe, K., Quesenberry, C., & Selby, J. (2009). Hypoglycemic episodes and risk of dementia in older patients with type 2 diabetes mellitus. *Journal of the American Medical Association, 301*, 1565–1572.

Wierzbicki, M., & Pekarik, G. (1993). A meta-analysis of psychotherapy dropout. *Professional Psychology: Research and Practice; Professional Psychology: Research and Practice, 24*(2), 190.

Wilamowska, Z. A., Thompson-Hollands, J., Fairholme, C. P., Ellard, K. K., Farchione, T. J., & Barlow, D. H. (2010). Conceptual background, development, and preliminary data from the unified protocol for transdiagnostic treatment of emotional disorders. *Depression and Anxiety, 27*(10), 882–890.

Wilkins, C. H., Wilkins, K. L., Meisel, M., Depke, M., Williams, J., & Edwards, D. F. (2007). Dementia undiagnosed in poor older adults with functional impairment. *Journal of the American Geriatrics Society, 55*, 1771–1776.

Williams, J. W. J., Gerrity, M., Holsinger, T., Dobscha, S., Gaynes, B., & Dietrich, A. (2007). Systematic review of multifaceted interventions to improve depression care. *General Hospital Psychiatry, 29*, 91–116.

Williams, J. W. J., Rost, K., Dietrich, A. J., Ciotti, M. C., Zyzanski, S. J., & Cornell, J. (1999). Primary care physicians' approach to depressive disorders. Effects of physician specialty and practice structure. *Archives of Family Medicine, 8*(1), 58–67.

Williamson, G. M., & Schulz, R. (1993). Coping with specific stressors in Alzheimer's disease caregiving. *The Gerontologist, 33*(6), 747–755.

Willis, S. L., Jay, G. M., Diehl, M., & Marsiske, M. (1992). Longitudinal change and prediction of everyday task competence in the elderly. *Research on Aging, 14*(1), 68–91.

Willis, S. L., Tennstedt, S. L., Marsiske, M., Ball, K., Elias, J., Koepke, K. M., ... Wright, E. (2006). Long-term effects of CT on everyday functional outcomes in older adults. *Journal of the American Medical Association, 296*(23), 2805–2814.

Wilson, R. S., Barnes, L. L., Krueger, K. R., Hoganson, G., Bienias, J. L., & Bennett, D. A. (2005). Early and late life cognitive activity and cognitive systems in old age. *Journal of International Neuropsychological Society, 11*(4), 400–407.

Wilson, R. S., Bennett, D. A., Beckett, L. A., Morris, M. C., Gilley, D. W., Bienias, J. L., … Evans, D. A. (1999). Cognitive activity in older persons from a geographically defined population. *Journal of Gerontology: Psychological Sciences, 54B*, 155–160.

Wilson, R. S., Krueger, K. R., Arnold, S. E., Schneider, J. A., Kelly, J. F., Barnes, L. L., … Bennett, D. (2007). Loneliness and risk of Alzheimer disease. *Archives of General Psychiatry, 64*, 234–240.

Wilson, R. S., Mendes de Leon, C. F., Barnes, L. L., Schneider, J. A., Beinias, J. L., Wilson, R. S., … Evans, D. A. (2003). Cognitive activity and cognitive decline in a biracial community population. *Neurology, 61*(6), 812–816.

Wilson, R. S., Segawa, E., Boyle, P. A., Anagnos, S. E., Hizel, L. P., & Bennett, D. A. (2012). The natural history of cognitive decline in Alzheimer's disease. *Psychology and Aging, 27*(4), 1008–1017.

Wittchen, H. U., Kessler, R. C., Beesdo, K., Krause, P., & Hoyer, J. (2002). Generalized anxiety and depression in primary care: Prevalence, recognition, and management. *Journal of Clinical Psychiatry, 63*(Suppl 8), 24–34.

Wium-Andersen, M. K., Ørsted, D. D., Nielsen, S. F., & Nordestgaard, B. G. (2012). Elevated C-reactive protein levels, psychological distress, and depression in 73,131 individuals. *Archives of General Psychiatry*, 1–9. [E-pub ahead of print, doi:10.1001/2013.jamapsychiatry.102]

Wolinsky, F. D., Mahncke, H. W., Vander Weg, M. W., Martin, R., Unverzagt, F. W., Ball, K. K., … Tennstedt, S. L. (2009). The ACTIVE Cognitive Training Interventions and the Onset of and Recovery from Suspected Clinical Depression. *Journal of Gerontology, Series B. Psychological Sciences and Social Sciences, 64B*(5), 577–585.

Wolinsky, F. D., Mahncke, H., Vander Weg, M. W., Martin, R., Unverzagt, F. W., Ball, K. K., … Tennstedt, S. L. (2010). Speed of processing training protects self-rated health in older adults: Enduring effects observed in the multi-site ACTIVE randomized controlled trial. *International Psychogeriatrics, 22*(3), 470.

Woods, B., Aguirre, E., Spector, A., Orrell, M. (2012). Can cognitive stimulation benefit people with dementia (review). *Cochrane Database System Revision*, E-pub ahead of print.

Wright, L. K., Clipp, E. C., & George, L. K. (1993). Health consequences of caregiver stress. *Medicine, Exercise, Nutrition, and Health, 2*(4), 181–195.

Xu, X., Zuo, X., Wang, X., & Han, S. (2009). Do you feel my pain? Racial group membership modulates empathic neural responses. *Journal of Neuroscience, 29*(26), 8525–8529.

Yaffe, K., Barnes, D., Nevitt, M., Lui, L. Y., & Covinsky, K. (2001). A prospective study of physical activity and cognitive decline in elderly women women who walk. *Archives of Internal Medicine, 161*(14), 1703–1708.

Yaffe, K., Haan, M., Blackwell, T., Cherkasova, E., Whitmer, R. A., & West, N. (2007). Metabolic syndrome and cognitive decline in elderly Latinos: Findings from the Sacramento Area Latino Study of Aging study. *Journal of the American Geriatrics Society, 55*(5), 758–762.

Yeager, C., Hyer, L., Hobbs, B., & Coyne, A., (2011). Alzheimer's disease and vascular dementia: The complex relationship between diagnosis and caregiver burden. *Issues in Mental Health Nursing.*

Yen, I. H., Michael, Y. L., & Perdue, L. (2009). Neighborhood environment in studies of health of older adults: A systematic review. *American Journal of Preventive Medicine, 37*(5), 455–463.

Yesavage, J. A., Brink, T. L., Rose, T. L., Lum, O., Huang, V., Adey, M., Leirer, V. O. (1982). Development and validation of a geriatric depression screening scale: A preliminary report. *Journal of Psychiatric Research, 17*(1), 37–49.

Yesavage, J. A., Friedman, L., Ashford, J. W., Kraemer, H. C., Mumenthaler, M. S., Noda, A., & Hoblyn, J. (2008). Acetylcholinesterase inhibitor in combination with CT in older adults. *Journals of Gerontology, Series B, Psychological Sciences and Social Sciences, 63*(5), 288–294.

Yochim, B. P., Lequerica, A., MacNeill, S. E., & Lichtenberg, P. A. (2008). Cognitive initiation and depression as predictors of future instrumental activities of daily living among older medical rehabilitation patients. *Journal of Clinical and Experimental Neuropsychology, 30*(2), 236–244.

Young, A. S., Klap, R., Sherbourne, C. D., & Wells, K. B. (2001). The quality of care for depressive and anxiety disorders in the United States. *Archives of General Psychiatry, 58*(1), 55–61.

Yuan, A., Farber, E. L., Rapoport, A. L., Tejada, D., Deniskin, R., Akhmedov, N. B., & Farber, D. B. (2009). Transfer of microRNAs by embryonic stem cell microvesicles. *PLoS One, 4*(3), e4722.

Yuhas, D. (2012). "A Dirty Trick." Review: The self illusion: How the social brain creates reality. *Scientific American Mind, 23,* 70–71.

Zarit, J. M. (2006). *Mental disorders in older adults: Fundamentals of assessment and treatment.* New York, NY: Guilford Publications.

Zarit, S. H., & Zarit, J. M. (1983). *The memory and behavior problems checklist and the burden interview.* University Park, PA: Penn State University Gerontology Center.

Zarit, S. H., Femia, E. E., Kim, K., & Whitlach, C. J. (2010). The structure of risk factors and outcomes for family caregivers: Implications for assessment and treatment. *Aging and Mental Health, 14,* 220–231.

Zarit, S. H., Reever, K. E., & Bach-Peterson, J. (1980). Relatives of the impaired elderly, correlates of feelings of burden. *The Gerontologist, 20,* 649–655.

Zatzick, D., Jurkovich, G., Russo, J., Roy-Byrne, P., Katon, W., Wagner, A., ... Rivara, F. (2004). Posttraumatic distress, alcohol disorders, and recurrent trauma across level 1 trauma centers. *Journal of Trauma, 57*(2), 360.

Zeiss, R. A., Delmonico, R. L., Zeiss, A. M., & Dornbrand, L. (1991). Psychologic disorder and sexual dysfunction in elders. *Clinics in Geriatric Medicine, 7*(1), 133.

Zhan, C., Correa-de-Araujo, R., Bierman, A. S., Sangl, J., Miller, M. R., Wickizer, S. W., & Stryer, D. (2005). Suboptimal prescribing in elderly outpatients: Potentially harmful drug–drug and drug–disease combinations. *Journal of the American Geriatrics Society, 53*(2), 262–267.

Zijlstra, G. A. R., Van Haastregt, J. C. M., Van Eijk, J. T. M., Van Rossum, E., Stalenhoef, P. A., & Kempen, G. I. J. M. (2007). Prevalence and correlates of fear of falling, and associated avoidance of activity in the general population of community-living older people. *Age and Ageing, 36*(3), 304–309.

Zweig, R. A., & Agronin, M. E. (2006). Personality disorders in late life. In M. E. Agronin, G. J. Maletta (Eds). *Principles and practice of geriatric psychiatry* (2011, pp. 523–543). Philadelphia, PA: Lippincott, Williams, and Wilkins.

Index

AAGP. *See* American Association of Geriatric Psychiatry
AAMI. *See* age-associated memory impairment
acceptance and commitment therapy (ACT), 59–60
anxiety, 132
ACT. *See* acceptance and commitment therapy
ACTIVE. *See* advanced cognitive training for independent and vital elderly
ADAS. *See* Alzheimer's Disease Assessment Scale
ADD. *See* attention-deficit disorder
advanced cognitive training for independent and vital elderly (ACTIVE) study, 180
age, mental health care model
challenges, 13
culture change, 11
health, 13–14
lifestyle problems, 11–12
mental health treatment, 12
risk and safety issues, 12
somatic problems, 12
variability, 11
age-associated memory impairment (AAMI), 154–156
Agency for Healthcare Research and Quality (AHRQ), 25
AGS. *See* American Geriatrics Society
AHRQ. *See* Agency for Healthcare Research and Quality
alliance, mental health therapy, 67–69
Alzheimer's disease (AD). *See also* dementia
AB amyloid pathology, 159
biomarkers for, 160
clinical findings, 148

diagnostic approach, 160
normal aging, 157
vascular problems, 162–163
Alzheimer's Disease Assessment Scale (ADAS), 321
American Association of Geriatric Psychiatry (AAGP), 7
American Geriatrics Society (AGS), 200
amygdala, 131
anxiety. *See also* generalized anxiety disorder (GAD)
acceptance and commitment therapy, 132
and brain, 130–131
case study, 139–141
and cognition, 129–130
cognitive behavioral therapy, 131–133
comorbidity phenomena, 128
and depression, 99–100
diagnostic distinction, 123
DSM distinctions, 127
exercise treatment, 136
falls phenomena, 128
fear learning, 126
late-life anxiety, 125–126
medications, 133–134
mental health care model, 16–17
modular intervention, 134–136
negative affectivity, 126
pharmacology, 133–134
physical complications, 128
PTSD, 143–146
stepped-care approach, 137
subthreshold disorders, 127
symptoms, 123
Watch and Wait therapy, 141–143
worry phenomena, 126–127

assertive communication, 271
attention-deficit disorder (ADD), 164

Barlow's unified protocol, 78
Barona Index of Intelligence, 320
BCRS. *See* Brief Cognitive Rating Scale
behavioral activation, 74
behavioral health interventions
    ABC model, 269
    assertive communication, 271
    behavior activation/pleasant events,
        265–266
    cognitive disputation, 267–268
    goal setting, 267
    mindfulness practice, 266–267
    motivational interviewing strategies,
        270–271
    problem-solving strategies, 268–269
    relaxation training, 266
    self-monitoring, 269–270
    stimulus control, 271
behavioral health professional, 252
behavioral health treatment
    patient-centered medical home
        (*See* patient-centered medical home
        [PCMH])
    primary care clinics, 249–250
brain and anxiety
    higher cognitive centers, 130–131
    limbic system, 130
    mood disorders, 131
    neurotransmitters, 131
    phobia, 131
brain and mental health care model
    age and dementia, 16
    cognition, 15
    depression, 14–15
brain reserve models, 158
Brief Cognitive Rating Scale (BCRS), 321
Brief Pain Inventory (BPI) scale, 220
brief psychodynamic therapy, 376
bright-light therapy, 391–392

caregiving
    anticipatory grief, 301
    caregiver burden, 297
    caregiver characteristics, 297
    caregiver's health status and therapy,
        336
    clinical interview and interventions,
        337–338
    dementia, 335
    depression, 296–297
    depression-specific burden, 299
    identified patient, 335

idiographic assessment, 336, 338
    lack of concordance, 336
    resilience, 299
    stress, 297
    treatment, 297–299
    values, 300–301
care management model, 253, 254
case-based approach, 71–72
case manager (CM), 80
CBT. *See* cognitive behavioral therapy
central nucleus of the amygdala (CeA), 130
Clock Drawing Test, 321
CM. *See* case manager
Cogmed
    demographic markers method, 191
    implications, 193–195
    intervention, 191–192
    measures, 191
    posttesting method, 191
    RBANS and MMSE methods, 190
    results, 192–193
Cogmed Satisfaction Scale, 193
Cognistat, 321
cognition
    aging, 146–147
    brain health, 149–150
    case study, 171–174
    episodic and semantic memory, 164–165
    executive functioning, 166–169
    factors affecting, 148
    neural plasticity, 149
    neuroanatomical changes, 149
    normal aging, 150–153
    voluntary exercises, 149
cognition testing
    cognitive screen tests (*See* cognitive
        screen tests)
    ecological validity, 318
    functional areas, 319
    Mini Mental State Examination, 320, 322
    poor memory and executive
        functioning, 324
    premorbid functioning measures, 320
    Schafer-Johnson study, 322–323
    sensitivity and specificity, 319
    test batteries and areas, 323
    test issues, 318
cognitive behavioral therapy (CBT)
    adaptations, 382
    anxiety, 131–133
    assertive communication, 370–371
    behavioral activation, 375
    case formulation, 361
    cognitive conceptualization, 374
    cognitive distortions, 363–364

dementia, 383
depression, 104–107, 371
executive functioning problems,
168–169
insomnia, 227–228
model, 362
modules, 370
stages, 365
structure of individual session, 364–365
cognitive disputation, 267–268
cognitive decline
age-associated memory impairment,
154–156
dementia (See dementia)
mild cognitive impairment, 156–158
cognitive screen tests
Alzheimer's Disease Assessment Scale
(ADAS), 321
Brief Cognitive Rating Scale (BCRS), 321
Clock Drawing Test, 321
Cognistat, 321
Dementia Rating Scale (DRS), 321–322
Mini-Cog, 320–321
Mini Mental State Examination, 320
7-Minute Screen, 322
Montreal Cognitive Assessment, 320
Saint Louis University Mental Status
examination, 321
Short Portable Mental Status
Questionnaire, 322
cognitive training (CT), 82–84.
See also memory training
brain training, 178–180
empirically supported treatments, 179
environmental enrichment tasks, 175
holistic programs, 180–181
"holistic" training, 175
memory strategies, 179
neurocognitive knowledge, 178
neurorehabilitation, 176
types of, 177
working memory (WM), 181–182
co-located behavioral health care, 254
community care
adjustment/functioning, 295–296
caregiving, 296–301
case study, 304–305
home care, 301–303
socioeconomic status factors, 293–294
Watch and Wait model, 306–307
compensation-related utilization of neural
circuits hypothesis (CRUNCH), 151
coronary artery disease, 238
age related, 236
aspirin, 236–237

CABG surgery, 237
medical management, 237
CRUNCH. See compensation-related
utilization of neural circuits hypothesis

dementia, 159. See also Alzheimer's disease
attention-deficit disorder (ADD), 164
DSM-5 workgroup categories, 161–162
functional markers, 160
medical treatment, 169–170
mild NCD, 161
patient-centered medical home, 279–281
risk factors, 159
Dementia Rating Scale (DRS), 321–322
depression
antidepressant drugs, 90
anxiety, 94, 99–100
bereavement, 92, 94
care algorithms, 98
clinical presentation, 113–114
clinical and psychosocial predictors,
110–111
cognitive functioning, 114
dementia, 95
electroconvusive therapy, 109–110
executive function, 100–104
expectancy-based strategy, 112
grief, 120–121
home care, 121–122
IMPACT study, 108
MDD diagnosis, 93
minor, 93
nested potential predictors, 112
patient-centered medical home, 274–275
poststroke, 95
prevalence and biology, 90–91
primary care, 109
subsyndromal, 92, 94
social genomics, 89
somatic complaints, 97
suicide, 98–99
symptoms, 89
Watch and Wait model, 115–119
depression, cognitive behavioral therapy
dialectical behavior therapy, 105–106
efficacy of, 104–105
health care policy restructuring, 105
interpersonal therapy, 106
meta-analysis, 105
mild dementia, 106
PST, 105, 107
vs. psychopharmacology, 105
sexual dysfunction, 106
depression without sadness, 94
depressive executive dysfunction, 94

depressive symptoms, 97–98
diabetes, 235–236
Diagnostic and Statistical Manual of Mental Disorders-III (DSM-III), 92, 324
Diagnostic and Statistical Manual of Mental Disorders-IV (DSM-IV), 161, 225
Diagnostic and Statistical Manual of Mental Disorders-5 (DSM-5), 18, 92–93, 124, 161, 225
dialectical behavior therapy, 105–106
DIP. *See* drug-induced Parkinsonism
DRS. *See* Dementia Rating Scale
drug-induced Parkinsonism (DIP), 244
DSM-III. See Diagnostic and Statistical Manual of Mental Disorders-III
DSM-IV. See Diagnostic and Statistical Manual of Mental Disorders-IV
DSM-5. See Diagnostic and Statistical Manual of Mental Disorders-5
DSM-5 workgroup categories
  asymptomatic phase, 161–162
  diagnostic phase, 162
  preclinical phase, 162

EBIs. *See* evidence-based interventions
ECT. *See* electroconvulsive therapy
electroconvulsive therapy (ECT), 100–110
embedded behavioral health care, 253
EMDR. *See* eye movement desensitization and retraining
episodic memory, 164–165
evidence-based interventions (EBIs), 289–290
executive functioning, 100–104
  cardiovascular risk factors, 167
  depression, 166, 167
  trauma, 167
  treatment, 168–169
exercise
  anxiety, 136
  lifestyle/prevention, 210
  sleep, 389–390
  voluntary, 149
eye movement desensitization and retraining (EMDR), 145

falls, geriatric health care, 242–243
financial strain, 214
functional competence, psychological assessment
  behavioral triggers, 325–326
  cognitive performance, 326–327
  DSM-5, 324–325
  MLDT test, 325
  neuroimaging techniques, 328
  performance-based scales, 327

functional markers, dementia, 160
functional specificity theory, 212

GAD. *See* generalized anxiety disorder
generalized anxiety disorder (GAD).
  See also anxiety
  brain, 131
  cognition, 129
  early-onset disorders, 125
  National Comorbidity Study, 124
  primary care clinics, 125
  treatment effects, 131, 132
  worry, 124
geriatric health care
  coronary artery disease, 236–238
  diabetes, 235–236
  falls, 242–243
  hearing impairment, 245–247
  hypertension, 233–235
  osteoarthritis, 240–242
  polypharmacy, 243–245
  visual impairment, 246–247
  vitamin B_{12} (cobalamin) deficiency, 238–239
  vitamin D deficiency, 239–240
group, individual, and family treatment/ group, individual, and staff therapy (GIFT/GIST) model
  behavioral activation, 379
  experience mapping, 380–381
  goal selection, 377–378
  group-session content, 378
  long-term care (LTC) setting, 377
  social support, 380

hearing impairment, 245–247
hippocampus, 131
home care, 301
  behavioral symptom, 303
  dementia, 302
  depression, 302
  PATH care model, 302
  primary care clinic, 303
  psychological symptom, 303
hypertension
  elevated blood pressure, 233–234
  lifestyle interventions, 233
  medications, 234
  multiple high-quality randomized trials, 233
  reduce systolic blood pressure, 234
  secondary, 233
  systolic and diastolic, 233
  treatment, 234–235

IC. *See* integrated care
insomnia
    cognitive behavioral therapy, 227–228
    complaints, 224
    depression, 226
    DSM-5, 225
    impairments, 226–227
    mood and anxiety disturbances, 225–226
    primary insomnia, 225
    relaxation techniques, 228–229
    self-help therapy, 229
    symptoms, 225
integrated care (IC), 199
intellectually and socially stimulating
    activity, 180
interpersonal psychotherapy (IPT), 75–76,
    106, 376

Jacobson's model, 74

laboratory-based training, 348
late-life depression (LLD), 90
late-life psychotherapy
    efficacy of, 58–59
    evidence based treatments, 57–58
lifestyle, 349
lifestyle/preventive care
    "can do" attitude, 212–213
    dementia, 209
    diet, 210–211
    exercise, 210
    functional specificity theory, 212
    meditation, 210
    mental health, 209–210
    physician/health care provider, 213
    religious practices, 212
    risk factors, 209
    socialization and religious coping, 211
limbic system, 131
LLD. *See* late-life depression

MacNeill-Lichtenberg Decision Tree
    (MLDT), 325
MBMD. *See* Millon Behavioral Medicine
    Diagnostic (MBMD)
MCI. *See* mild cognitive impairment
memory clinic model
    clinic sessions, 353
    Cogmed tests, 359–360
    diet, 358–359
    exercise, 184, 357–358
    GUP + Link method, 354
    holistic approach, 185
    intervention, 186
    lifestyle components, 184

low-risk subjects, 189
    Mediterranean-type diet, 183
    relaxation, 355
    social support, 356–357
    stress, 357
    working memory, 189
memory training. *See also* cognitive
    training
    holistic Memory Clinic, 188
    holistic programs, 180–181
    self-regulation, 195
    types, 177, 348
mental health care model
    adjustment, 21–22
    age, 11–14
    anxiety, 16–17
    brain issues, 14–16
    caregiving, 26–27
    case study, 2–4
    clinical presentation, 2
    depression, 18–19
    depressive symptoms, 6
    emotional assessment, 2–3
    health care providers, 9
    holistic approach, 27–28
    medical care, 5
    medical/somatic issues, 20–21
    pain and sleep, 3
    placebo effect, 9
    predictors, 8
    process of care, 6–8
    psychotherapy, 10, 23–24
    SOC model, 9
    stress moderators, 3
    test results, 2
    translational research, 10
    treatment prognostics, 3
    Watch and Wait model, 4, 10–11
    "whole person" approach, 9
metabolic syndrome, 208
MI. *See* motivational interviewing
mild cognitive impairment (MCI)
    Alzheimer's disease, 158
    biomarker profile, 157
    brain reserve models, 158
    Cogmed (*See* Cogmed)
    diagnosis, 158
    epidemiological studies, 156
    geropsychiatry, 182
    memory clinic, 184–189
    procedural memory, 182
    self-regulation, 195
Millon Behavioral Medicine Diagnostic
    (MBMD), 140, 172, 305, 334
mindfulness practice, 266–267

MINI. *See* mini-international neuropsychiatric interview
Mini-Cog, 320–321
mini-international neuropsychiatric interview (MINI), 172
MiniMental State Examination (MMSE), 320
7-Minute Screen (7MS), 322
MLDT. *See* MacNeill-Lichtenberg Decision Tree
Montreal Cognitive Assessment (MoCA), 320
motivational interviewing (MI), 71–73
  strategies, 270–271
7MS. *See* 7-Minute Screen
multi-approach system tackling memory, 178–179

NART. *See* National Adult Reading Test (NART)
National Adult Reading Test (NART), 320
National Committee for Quality Assurance (NCQA), 251–252
National Comorbidity Survey Replication (NCS-R), 20
National Health and Nutrition Examination Survey (NHANES), 93–94
NCD. *See* neurocognitive disorders
NCQA. *See* National Committee for Quality Assurance (NCQA)
NCS-R. *See* National Comorbidity Survey Replication
neurocognitive disorders (NCD), 161
neuropsychiatric inventory (NPI), 302
NH. *See* nursing home
NHANES. *See* National Health and Nutrition Examination Survey
normal aging, cognition
  brain dynamics, 151–153
  dementia risk, 153
  disability and cognitive decline, 153
  "life span developmental" perspective, 150–151
  MCI, 153
  memory problems, 150
  neuropsychiatric symptoms, 154
  synaptogenesis, 150–151
NPI. *See* neuropsychiatric inventory
nursing home (NH)
  ADL, 307–308
  depression, 308–309
  facts related to, 308
  long-term care, 308

OFC. *See* orbitofrontal cortex
Oklahoma Premorbid Intelligence Estimate-Verbal, 320
old-age perspectives, life issues
  activities of daily living, 286
  adverse drug reactions, 285
  blood pressure medication, 285–286
  functional limitations, 286
  health care costs, 285
  obesity and malnutrition, 286
  smoking and alcohol use, 286
  U.S. hospitals, 285
older adults, psychotherapy
  cognitive and behavioral strategies, 56
  CONSORT criteria, 55
  continuance and maintenance therapy phases, 55
  inclusion and exclusion criteria, 54
  psychological template, 55–56
  therapy outcomes, 56
orbitofrontal cortex (OFC), 131
osteoarthritis, 240–242

PACL. *See* Personality Adjective Check List
pain
  assessment, 218
  case study, 219–222
  classification, 217
  control, 218
  depression and anxiety, 217
  ethical issues, 216
  prevalence rates, 217
  subjective experience, 217–218
  treatments, 222–224
PATH. *See* problem adaptation therapy
patient-centered medical home [PCMH]
  behavioral health interventions, 265–271
  behavioral health professional, 252
  care management model, 253, 254
  dementia, 279–281
  depression, 274–275
  gold-standard model, 253–253
  IMPACT trial, 251
  intermediate model, 254
  NCQA, 251–252
  primary care psychologist, 254–265
  psychosis, 276–279
  suicide risk, 274–276
PCC. *See* primary care clinic
PCMH. *See* patient-centered medical home
Personality Adjective Check List (PACL), 334
personality assessment
  axis II indicators, 333
  differential diagnoses, 335

double think perspective, 334
multi assessment package, 334
personality disorder measures, 334
structured interviews, 333
PES. *See* Pleasant Events Schedule
pharmacology, anxiety
advantage, 133
benzodiazepine, 133
modules, 134
vs. psychotherapy, 134
somatic symptoms, 134
SSRI medications, 133
placebo effect, 9
Pleasant Events Schedule (PES), 328
point-of-care learning, 287
polypharmacy, 243–245, 350
posttraumatic stress disorder (PTSD)
age, 143–144
cardiac care, 144
comorbidities, 144
elder abuse, 144
hypothesis, 145
incidence, 144
treatment, 145–146
prefrontal frontal cortex (PFC), 130–131
Prevention of Suicide in Primary
Care Elderly Collaborative Trial
(PROSPECT), 80, 98, 99
preventive life ideas
evidence-based interventions, 289–290
flourishing, 290–292
happiness, 292–293
normal and clinical aging, 288–289
primary care clinic (PCC)
anxiety, 17
behavioral health care (*See* patient-
centered medical home [PCMH])
case management, 80
depression, 125
medical/somatic issues, 21
medications, 60
treatment alliance, 68
primary care psychologist
assessments, 259–263
behavioral health intervention, 255
core competencies, 255–257
guidelines, 254
psychopharmacology, 257–259
responsibilities, 254–255
Watch and Wait model, 263–265
problem adaptation therapy (PATH), 122
care model, 302
problem-solving strategies, 268–269
problem-solving therapy (PST), 52, 76, 376
depression, 107

procedural memory, 164
process of care, mental care model
algorithms, 7
psychosocial predictors, 7–8
psychotherapy, 7
signal detection theory, 6–7
STAR*D study, 6
PST. *See* problem-solving therapy
psychoeducation, 65–67, 345
psychological assessment
anxiety, 330–332
baseline functioning and outcomes,
314–316
caregiving, 335–338
clinical data collection, 313–314
cognition testing, 318–324
depression, 328–330
functional competence, 325–328
general adjustment, 338, 340
long-term care, 340–341
multimethod assessments, 313
participatory decision making, 341–342
personality assessment, 333–334
primary care setting, 340
psychometric information, 339
therapeutic process, 313
unstructured, single-method
approaches, 314
whole-person, 316–318
psychosis, patient-centered medical home
case study, 277–279
risk factors, 276
psychotherapy
acceptance and commitment therapy,
59–60
alliance, 53
antidepressants, 61
cognitive behavioral therapy, 52
empirically based treatments, 52–53
FDA data, 54
features, 65
health care providers, 63
late-life psychotherapy, 57–59
medications, 60–61
multiphase optimization strategy, 61
nonpharmacological intervention, 63
older adults, 54–56
primary care setting, 63–64
problem-solving therapy, 52
psychodynamic ingredients, 54
psychological and psychosocial
context, 53
psychological flexibility, 63
psychosocial intervention model, 62, 63
rubrics of, 56–57

psychotherapy (*cont.*)
  STAR*D study, 53–54
  step-care model, 63–64
  therapist effects, 53
  therapists, resultant feedback, 64
  variance of change, 53
  Watch and Wait therapy (*See* Watch and
    Wait therapy)
PTSD. *See* posttraumatic stress disorder

RBANS. *See* Repeatable Battery for the
    Assessment of Neuropsychological
    Status
REACH. *See* Resources for Enhancing
    Alzheimer's Caregivers Health
relaxation training, 266
  sleep, 388–389
reminiscence therapy, 375–376
Repeatable Battery for the Assessment of
    Neuropsychological Status (RBANS),
    172, 219
Resources for Enhancing Alzheimer's
    Caregivers Health (REACH), 336

Saint Louis University Mental Status
    examination (SLUMS), 321
scaffolding theory, 178
SCD. *See* self-control desensitization
SCID. *See* Structured Clinical Interview for
    DSM-IV Axis II Personality Disorders
selective optimization and compensation
    (SOC) model, 9
self-control desensitization (SCD), 142
self-rated health (SRH), 207
semantic memory, 164–165
Sequenced Treatment Alternatives to Relieve
    Depression (STAR*D) study, 53–54
serotonergic antidepressants, 61
Short Anxiety Screening Test (SAST), 219
Short Portable Mental Status
    Questionnaire (SPMSQ), 322
sleep
  bedroom clock avoidance, 387
  bright-light therapy, 391–392
  dementia, 229–230
  education/cognitive restructuring,
    386–387
  exercise, 389–390
  hot-bath and light snack, 390
  insomnia, 385 (*See* insomnia)
  medication, 391
  psychotherapy, 391
  recommended reading, 392–393
  regular bedtime and awakening
    time, 387

relaxation training, 388–389
  shorter bedtime, 388
  stages of, 385–386
  stimulus control, 387
  tobacco and caffeine, 390–391
  worry time, 388
SLUMS. *See* Saint Louis University Mental
    Status examination
SMI. *See* subject memory impairment
socioeconomic status factors
  mean cognition score decline, 294
  mental illness, 294
  NHANES data, 293–294
SOC model. *See* selective optimization and
    compensation
SPMSQ. *See* Short Portable Mental Status
    Questionnaire
SRH. *See* self-rated health
stress
  acute and chronic stressors, 213
  acute stress, 215
  ageism, 214
  Americans report stress level, 213–214
  financial strain, 214
  health care provider, 216
  life stress, 214
  lifestyle change, 216
  loneliness, 215
  neighborhood strain, 214
  physical and emotional health
    outcomes, 215
  psychiatric problems, 214
  social and cognitive factors, 215
Structured Clinical Interview for *DSM-IV*
    Axis II Personality Disorders
    (SCID-II), 334
subject memory impairment (SMI), 129–130
suicide, depression, 98–99
suicide risk, patient-centered medical
    home
  depressed mood, 274–275
  risk factors, 275
  standard operating procedure, 275–276
  suicidality degree, 276
  Watch and Wait approach, 275

therapist effects, psychotherapy, 53
transdiagnostic model, 76–78
translational research, mental health care
    model

VaD. *See* vascular dementia
vascular cognitive impairment (VCI), 163
vascular dementia (VaD), 162–163
VCI. *See* vascular cognitive impairment

visual impairment, 246–247
vitamin B$_{12}$ (cobalamin) deficiency, 238–239
vitamin D deficiency, 239–240
voluntary exercises, 149

Watch and Wait model
  anxiety, 347
  checklist, 344
  cognition, 348
  community care issues, 306–307
  depression, 115–119, 346–347
  health issues, 348–351
  health care costs, 343–344
  life issues, 351
  lifestyle, 348–349
  pain, 220–222
  psychoeducation, 345
  recommended treatment factors, 345
  treatment ideas, 345–346
Watch and Wait sessions, CBT
  beliefs and biases, 367–368
  core beliefs and assumptions, 369
  distortions and biases, 368
  evaluate and change beliefs, 368
  model introduction, 365–366
  pleasant events/behavioral activation
    strategies, 367
  relapse prevention/termination, 369–370
  self-monitoring, 366
Watch and Wait therapy
  alliance, 67–69
    anxiety, 141–143
    behavioral activation, 74
    booster sessions, 85–87
    case-based approach, 71–72
    case manager, 80
    cognition, 173–174
    cognitive training, 82–84
    exercise, 81
    interpersonal therapy, 75–76
    modular interventions, 81–82
    monitoring, 69–70
    motivational interviewing, 71–73
    prevention, 78–79
    problem-solving therapy, 76
    psychoeducation, 65–67
    psychosis, 278
    psychotherapist, 84
    suicide risk, 275
    transdiagnostic model, 76–78
Wechsler Test of Adult Reading (WTAR),
    320
Wisconsin Star method, 201
working memory (WM), 164
worry, 123, 124. *See also* anxiety
  behavioral changes, 127
  CBT, 135
  and cognition, 129
  stimulus control, 143
WTAR. *See* Wechsler Test of Adult Reading

Zarit Burden Scale, 338